THE EXTRAORDINARY FRANKS

Germany, France, Normandy, Scotland, Cleveland North Yorkshire & across the world

Douglas Frank Blackmore

Paperback edition first published in the United Kingdom in 2018 by
WuffWuffPublishing

eBook edition first published in the United Kingdomin 2018 by
WuffWuffPublishing

Copyright © Doug Blackmore 2018

Doug Blackmore has asserted his rights under the Copyright Designs and Patents Act 1988 to be identified as the author of this work.

All rights reserved

No part of this book may be reproduced or transmitted in any form or by any means, electronic, mechanical, photocopying, recording, or otherwise, without prior written permission from the author.

A CIP catalogue record for this book is available from the British Library.

ISBN: 978-1-9995954-0-1

WuffWuffPublishing 2018

Typeset in the United Kingdom by aSys Publishing 2018

THE EXTRAORDINARY FRANKS

Douglas Frank Blackmore

CONTENTS

Preface 1
The Author – Early recollections 2
   Rape, revenge, annihilation 2
Officers' Club, Phalsbourg Airbase, France 4
Reflection and Reconsiliation 5
Introduction 7

PART ONE – THE FRANKS

Emergence of the early Europeans and their evolvement 13
Religion relating to women and secular society today 16
The importance of being frank 19
   The female predicament 20
   The niqab complex 22
   The castration of tyranny 23
   Transition from Islamic feudalism to cohesion, modernity and enlightenment . 25
Emergence of the early Europeans part two & summary 29
Frank origins 31
Exempli gratia lex salica 32
   Preamble 32
The Robertians (links to forebear Robertus Francais Cum Fraunceys) 38
Interlude 49
Righteous belief 53
Historical context 57
The creation of Normandy 60
Frankish master builders 63

Normandy Franks from 1030, their names, data and location 64
    Post-invasion dates and events 65
Normandy summary, the Franks, the Monarchy and the de Brus 71
Domesday book entries 1086–1087 75
Robert de Brus and Robertus Francais, post-1066. 80
    Preamble 80
    The story..82
Robber Barons and the untouchable...86
Main story continued 87
Yorkshire, the Borders and Scotland from 1120..94
    Prenotation 108
Story continued..109
Frank law, the Annandale, Ayton, and award to the Franks of the additional Scottish seats of Sprustoun, Kelso, Thornydykes, Jedburgh and Frankysland, Peeblesshire by King Robert de Brus...115
    On the orders of the King for the restoration of Frauncey land....................121
A perilous climb 123
    Two interconnected events 127
Lairds of Thornydykes..129
    Thomas Franch 132
Returning to the Thornydykes, 1490...134
    Frankysland, Peebles as it relates to current times 135
    Returning to the main theme, translations and transcripts shown in date order. 137

PART TWO – THE YORKSHIRE–SCOTTISH FRANKS

Preamble 143
The story..144
    Use of nom de guerre and extended family interconnections 144
    De Percy, Baron Leconfield and the acquisition of village land 149
    The Franks in context 150

The King's highway 152

Norman conquerors 153

Orthodoxy 154

The Cleveland Franks family tree 155

Sir Robertus Francaise. 156

Pre-insight, William le Franceis 156

Sir Robert de Fraunceys, early Yorkist recumbent knight 158

Thomas, his son Sir John Fraunceys 160

Family intrigue 161

Sir Richard Francis/Fraunceys, the year 1286, Cumbria 162

Sir Robert and his arrival in Yorkshire: 163

Here the tree splits, the main Willielmus line is shown later. 164

Departing from the main tree, a confusion of Johns 166

Destruction of the ancient and handsome bridge over the River Tees, the King's highway and main trade route to Scotland 170

The King's highway 171

The main Willielmus line continued 174

The main Willielmus line 177

Famine 178

Pedigree of Willielmus le Franceis, 1199, and his son Johes, or John le Francéis 180

The Magna Carta 180

Stone walls 185

Main Willielmus line continued 189

Justice and the law of the strongest 191

Frank burials, Richmond Castle 192

Durham 196

The main Willielmus line continued 196

Arguments regarding land 197

The main Willielmus line continued 202

- The wool trade 203
- The broader picture 205

Robert de Brus's invasion of England 207
- The Forest of Pickering 212
- Men-at-arms were needed, and as ever North Yorkshire bore the brunt 213
- Adam French of Scotland family connection 214
- Whitby 214
- Durham 215

The main Willielmus line continued 215
- Roger Frank, Abbot of Fountains Abbey 1410–1415 216
- Robertus offshoot 218
- The main Willielmus line continued 220
- Enormous holdings and an interfamily mystery 221
- Sir John Frankland aka Fraunceys, his wife Isabell and daughter Alice 223
- The Auld Alliance 227

John Fraunceys, York and surrounds 228
- Inquisitions 228
- The bridges at York 231
- Deforciant actions in the fictitious acquisition of land and counterclaims ...232

The main Willielmus line continued 236
- The dissolution 237
- Libera terra; liberque animus 239
- The name Frank and Frankland in relation to Danby, Glaisdale and surrounds 242
- The manor of Ness, reinstatement of the Frankland arms, and purchase of Danby Forest 245

The main Willielmus line through Hugh Franckland and his son John, Pater de Familias, and Franke as a surname. 247
- Henry Frank, gentillman 248
- The Hutton pedigree 251
- The Thirsk pedigree 269

The heirs apparent relating to William 270

Sir Hugh Frankland, his line, Richard, William and John 271

Sir Richard Frankland, his line, Hugh, John and Ralph 273

Ralph Frankland 274

Sir Henry 274

Sir Thomas 275

Second Baron Sir Thomas Frankland, children 277

Third baron, Sir Thomas Frankland 1685–1747 279

Lady Dinah Frankland 279

Sir Charles Henry Frankland, fourth baronet 280

Fifth baron, Sir Thomas 280

Agnes 281

Aldwick 285

Immediate ancestry, Cleveland Franks 285

The main tree continued 287

The Reformation 289

Changes to the more Catholic name of Frankland for Frank and the family tree from 1606 293

Woodwark Frank 299

The Franks cum de Lacy ties 301

Methodists 303

Harland 303

Main tree continued 303

Robert Frank senior 308

Jacobite Rising of 1745, Charles Edward Stuart and the Egton Recusants, 1745 309

Interlude 318

Robert Frank continued 318

The Shanie story, see Aunt Shanie, Jane Frank above, family tree 320

Robert Hart-Frank 321

Tom Frank and Sarah, my true grandmother..327

Thomas Henry Frank..329

Thomas Henry Frank part two...330

A note on Mary...336

Dorothy Frank..336

Wiped out..337

The Dorothy Frank saga, World War Two, continued 338

Dad..339

Granddad Frank and the early expansion of modern Middlesbrough..........339

Of life and death..342

Summary..344

PART THREE – OFFSHOOT CLEVELAND FRANKS

Primitive Methodism 354

Miscellaneous Franks..354

Robert Frank...356

The mystery of Hannah Frank 356

Miscellaneous...357

Fom Egton Old Churchyard 359

PART FOUR – THE FRANKS ARMORIAL

Introduction...361

Prequel..363

Context..364

Index armorial, conclusions on names 371

Index armorial, lineage additions..373

Frank armorial bearings 1...383

    The Franks and early Frauncey coats of arms...................................383

    Returning to the earlier analysis of the Earls of Dunbar and the Franks or French's of Thornydykes 386

De Brus motto 'Fuimus' we have been...388
Frank amorial bearings 2 389
Court of the Lord Lyon, Edinburgh 390
    Summary..394
Francisca regius nos; franks royal us..395
A fitting epitaph 396
Non nobis nati 398

ADDENDUM...400

Take a name, one's mother's maiden name, my middle name and wrap a story around it.

Art, civilisation and the written word, crude markings upon a cave wall; architecture, music and dance, that from the advent of Eve began the civilising process of man, transformational rules and principles of new truth viewed as a guide for moral conduct, that every man, woman and child will be free to embrace the technological destine for social integration and human progress.

From the Levant evolved writing and later in Europe a word like no other, a name of great authority, both frank in nature and as a name, from which medieval meme has evolved a story of duty and moral purpose.

A past written into the landscape of today and all the tomorrows, a little bit more than just ordinary people …

THE EXTRAORDINARY FRANKS

PREFACE

In the Cotentin Peninsula, Normandy, young nobleman Robert Frank (a knight known as Robertus Francais), was too young to join Robertus de Brus and their kinsman William of Normandy (later known as William the Conqueror) in the initial 1066 invasion of England. Although aware that this was a momentous time in history, he had no knowledge of being alive at a midway point in the history of the Franks. He would have been aware of his royal antecedence and something of his heritage, but had no concept of even a fraction of the whole story. How could he?

Spirited back to the Rhine 900 years prior to his birth, Robertus might have seen his Frank predecessors repel the Roman Empire and in continuing the assault threaten the Mediterranean. In AD 258, having settled along the right bank of the Rhine, he might have seen his predecessors using this as a base from which to continue to infiltrate Gaul and Italy. Later he might have seen the Franks, together with the Saxons, ravage the coast of Britain. For the Romans, the Franks became the scourge of the Western Empire, blocking the spread of Roman control and effectively superseding continued Roman expansion, in itself quite a feat, but nothing compared to the later growth of Frank influence and enlightenment.

As the architects of France the Franks were the monarchy, but the early part of this story deals with the history leading up to the events surrounding one man, ascertaining his likely parentage and his generational relationship with the de Brus. It traces their journey to Yorkshire and north to Scotland, highlighting factual data concerning their lives on both sides of the border in what was the ancient Kingdom of Bernicia. Part two concentrates on the Frank family tree post-1066 through to the present day, part three concentrates on the Cleveland Franks and part four provides supportive lineage and armorial data.

The Franks of yesteryear and the Franks of today (my mother being the last of that long and wearisome trail). Delving into their past, like Pandora's box, its evils once revealed, asks pertinent questions for today, and using the authority of old age, throughout this work I speak my mind. But what really matters are those who follow, particularly as relates to women: their role and the heavy mixture of the good and the not so good that past generations have left behind. To lighten the tale and provide perspective, I have made use of my own thoughts and personal experience, interposing modern-day assertions of moral conduct.

Douglas Frank Blackmore

THE AUTHOR – EARLY RECOLLECTIONS

Prior to the main introduction, the next three sections provide insight as to one's formative experience as a young man thrust into a largely unprepared sink-or-swim situation.

Fast forward 900 years to 1961, I'm aged twenty-one still in England and having learnt something of the language have been recruited for a long-term assignment in Germany. And now a typical last minute volte-face by my superiors has found me with an almost total absence of French on a train heading for Toul-Rosieres in the Alsace region of France. It is pitch black and I'm having difficulty reading station names through steamy windows and poor station lighting; although not sure, I can just make out what appears to be my destination. Hastily lifting my bag and alighting from the train, I look across what seems an uninviting dark and empty platform – empty except for two very Algerian-looking men standing together in the gloom. Defying their looks they are anything but Algerian, and their car is a clapped-out old banger with a rope tied around its middle to keep the doors from dropping off. Twenty minutes later I am in my hotel room trying to make out what the strange looking toilet with two taps might be used for.

A few months before, Kennedy had warned we would not be driven out of Berlin. I am on quasi-military attachment, essentially a civilian component of the US Military, as well as working for the British. The episode speaks of a period during the Cold War following the Berlin Airlift and Bay of Pigs stand-off against the USSR. My passport reads Technical Adviser: my future destination unclear.

By circuitous transition between the Alsace and Germany, now in Bavaria, working between there and the East German border, I somehow found myself engaged to a girl from the Rhine district, whose surname originated in the beautiful medieval Bavarian city of the same name, Rothenberg – notorious as a centre for the Nazi movement. In the area of Bavaria and Austria where I initially worked the Nazi party still openly flourished and in Berlin's East Germany, its population under constant scrutiny, the Stasi had a reputation for state-induced thuggery, relishing the opportunity to kick some unfortunate senseless and much worse; the Stasi's headquarters in Normannen Strasse was viewed as a place of no return.

Rape, revenge, annihilation

Carrying the genes of their Russian conquerors, to me the facial appearance of many Berlin youths showed characteristic differences compared to their elders. Only seventeen years before, and as the Russian army advanced towards Berlin, A predominant number of East German pregnancies were the product of a hierarchical decree of the conquerors for the systematic and bestial multi-rape of females of all ages. This was in revenge for Stalingrad: a counter to Hitler's previous order for the carte blanche slaughter of anyone they didn't like the look of and Germany's barbaric treatment of Russian POWS. Russia's resultant Judeo-Bolshevism retribution was an orgy of pitiless barbarism.

Despite high levels of unsafe abortion, and way out of proportion to the male population, a huge increase in births betrayed Slavic origins. Added to this were births emanating from the occupation of West Berlin; the French, British and American soldiery also taking advantage of what was on offer, sex being a commodity for women's survival as opposed to starvation.

It is estimated that two million German women suffered multi-rape at the hands of the Russian occupiers, including girls as young as seven or eight. So intense was the gender targeting of females, used as an instrument of terror, that many women suffered the penes onslaught as much as sixty to seventy times over; the mass rape resulting in an unbelievable quarter of a million female deaths. For each bloodied body the rampant sword of male liberticidal annihilation became for them a tormentous prayed-for release into God's grace. For each pierced body the tears of heaven would never erase its sin.

So masterful and grotesque was Stalin's act of revenge, the Tartarean decree of terror and oppression was viewed as unprecedented, but in truth nothing compared to the intended extermination of all Jewry by a supposed advanced and enlightened European meme. But as this work shows, history is laden with human atrocities and remains so to this day.

Berlin was a shattered city. All around the Kothenerstrasse had been decimated by shellfire and incessant allied bombing leaving only rubble, known as trümmer. Skeletal remains of buildings poked skywards interspersed in every direction with tooth-gapped areas of clearance alive with construction. New masonry covered areas where gangs of raped and bloodied women and starving Berliners had chipped away old mortar so the bricks could be reused and the unwanted waste dumped in huge piles beyond the city confines. The very centre of Germany's cohesion, socially, culturally and economically, had been pulverised. Viewing this, one could but admire the Germanic resolve for the eventual reconstruction of a truly decimated city.

On the western side, and with a preference for dollars, in the clubs and upon the streets an abundance of skimpily dressed women, absent of underwear and deft in the performance of lewd acts, competed with each other for business. With the threat of oblivion raging, blind to race, colour or persuasion, the business and normality of vice had become so persuasive even those in the top echelon had become drawn to its allure. Until the 13th August 1961, even upon the eastern side, Berliners with an eye for business, Western music or just wanting to forget, joined in. Its heavily used asylum for women with advanced cases of venereal disease was overwhelmed.

Yet ignorant among such head-spinning madness, caught unawares, the overnight erection of a massive wire barrier had closed the west to residents from the eastern side: now caught on the wrong side their every move was under the constant gaze of informers. With the construction of border towers, to me, everything seemed to be overladen with a sense of foreboding – that omnipresent divide – the DDR constantly watchful over a strangulation of barbed wire, the bravery of those shot trying to escape left to bleed to death where they lay.

OFFICERS' CLUB, PHALSBOURG AIRBASE, FRANCE

Under Operation Tack Hammer, my accommodation in BOQ Phalsbourg was a continuous-flight American Air Base also used for soldiers in transit: the skies heavy to the constant flight and sound of take off and waves of returning aircraft, a counterbalance to all-out nuclear war. Of vital importance was the buzz of signal traffic, its vital data transmitted twenty-four hours a day via the huge network of radio relay stations scattered across a network of US bases and the more remote hills of Europe: operatives such as Charles Lee chosen as among the brightest and the best.

JFK had predicted a 'one-in-three to evens' prediction for all-out war, seconds ticking, right up to the minute the American military unremittingly pushed for a pre-emptive strike. Realistically, had Khrushchev not eased the situation this book would not have been written nor would there have been any readership. In terms of annihilation, it's a sad fact; the American military echelon would have preferred the sacrifice of Britain, parts of Europe and a portion of America, all turned to dust, rather than give way to protocol.

Despite taking his shoe off and striking it repeatedly on a plinth in order to make a point, it took a crude uneducated country yokel named Khrushchev to see the merits of co-existence with the West, yet less than ten years later he was dead. Vehemently anti-Stalinist, Nikita was both colourful and pragmatic, someone you might wrestle yet at the same time 'do business' with, the opposite to Putin's mastery of chess in the po-faced tactics of sacrificial pawns and the tally of putrefied dead, something sadly missing today.

At twelve-thirty or thereabouts on the 22nd November 1963, and with the easing of tension between East and West, I found myself standing amid a crowd of dazed American officers and their wives hearing the news of the death of an American President.

But such things would be a concept way beyond any form of understanding for the central character of this book, Robertus Francais. He might be a knight and born of royal antecedence but certainly he was un-bloodied and much too young, just entering his teens yet finding himself on the threshold of a great adventure, and riding with a man carrying in his veins the bloodline of a future king, Robert de Brus, father to the future King of Scotland.

Two very different wars 900 years apart, yet on the eve of their invasion of Britain, France in 1066 stood in stark contrast to one's observance of the undisguised panic upon the faces of one's compatriots on that day in 1963.

Bridging that time lapse, as sole English contingent I stood in line in close proximity to the airbase mascot, a dog of whose name escapes me, and also the base commander and ranking officers. For this special occasion all of them were suitably uniformed and be-medalled, their polished insignia glinting in recognition of the moment as a ray of sunlight broke through an untimely shower of rain.

It was as if nature itself was washing away the past signalling new hope, akin to the ticking of a clock keeping time with the military contingent as they marched and various salutes and tributes were made following the assassination of their commander-in-chief, President John Kennedy. The moment even then seared into memory with the timely recognition and growing wave of relief felt as the threat of oblivion through immediate all-out nuclear war with Russia slowly diminished.

Under de Gaulle, the American bases in France threatened with takeover by the French gave rise to a return to the ever-present thriving heart of Nazism in Bavaria and, several months on, a decision I'd had enough. Truly exhausted, aged only twenty-four, unable to properly function but still tied to the American military, I returned first to Yorkshire. Finding my lovely Ann, we married and settled in Scotland along with our dog, Sally, and with us was Ann's seven-year-old sister Yvonne. A previously somewhat pampered and sickly child, some weeks into her new school, Von was now seen playing barefoot with the local farm kids paddling in the trout stream running through our land, the vastness of the open countryside and fresh air bringing a bloom of colour to the young girl's cheeks.

REFLECTION AND RECONSILIATION

With the land came a row of ancient cottages and garaging big enough for several vehicles, with supporting iron beams ideal for hanging venison. A solid stone seven-foot high surround to the adjacent church hid ancient burials stacked twelve or more deep, so dense to the one side that the ground lay level with the top of the old wall. Sally often proudly arrived in our garden carrying the gift of a human shinbone or other recognisable skeletal remains; her tail wagging profusely.

John, the old gravedigger, told us tales of the Resurrectionists belonging to the early 1800s, and how hidden behind the thick stone walls of our house lay many a human skeletal remain. Used by medical schools for dissection, these had been dug up by the body snatchers of yore and held ready for collection for transport to Edinburgh. But nothing was said about the presence of woodworm that as we slept continued to munch its way through the ancient and crumbling beams of our house, nor the history of Burke and Hare who, being short of bodies, resorted to murder in order to feed the anxious needs of anatomists such as Robert Knox.

Kennedy ancestors had been widespread around this area of western Scotland, where a multitude of the clan lay buried one on top of the other not so far away from where Sally lay on guard quietly snoozing in her favourite sunny spot, her nose less than an inch away from her most recent acquisition, all the time her ears alert for any chance to play. And while standing there sharing the same blessed sun upon my face, on the other side of the stream, being spring, newborn lambs could be heard bleating, the wondrous sound of new life drifting quietly upon the air, its orchestrate melody washing away resonant memories. For me it had been a toll of slowly receding exhaustion, one's ears still attuned to the reverberating drone of wave after wave of American aircraft, cognisant how close had been annihilation from all-out nuclear war.

Thinking back one's memory intruding upon the balm of another sunny day, the difficulty of shaking off the imprint-grubbiness wrestling with the dirt and filth of residue Nazism, its mental apparition discordant to the sight of row upon row of hidden battalions of American tanks preparing to warm up in an instant upon the order to attack; the Russians equally prepared.

Recalling that time, one's mind playing tricks, once again standing there my feet upon the front line facing east, numerous coughs, start-up chokes and splutters intervene, the ear-piercing reverberation of two or more hundred engines in unison now a thunderous roar. Seconds later the impact of sudden silence, the mists clearing, another sound intruding, now peaceful in one's garden the balm of nature calming. And as I stood there, as if a passing dream the detritus memory of hells damnation confined to history. And as if responding to the sound of laughter and children at play, Sally coming from the trout stream fully refreshed from her doggy dreams, playfully slosh-shaking her dripping fur in my direction as if to remind who's boss.

As a youngster, through my grandfather Thomas Henry Frank, I had received an intimate working knowledge of architectural drawing, construction and farming, had taught myself to ride bareback up near-vertical rough terrain and was a decent shot. Now such combination of experience seems increasingly 'other person' and with its impossible array surely massively overstated or imagined. But in essence everything I've written about is absolutely true and simply a matter of how things were and how life panned out; one door closing meant another sure to open whether skill-based, labour intensive or academic, always on-the-go, eclectic and for the most part disparate and exciting, with a mind full of ideas set to challenge.

Following a lifetime wrestling with dyslexia, twenty years working in finance and twenty more indulging my own interests, Ann and I find great pleasure through our three married grown-up children and four grandchildren. I returned to academia in psychodynamics and a treatise on humanisation, that done, another volte-face and a return to my pre-twenties stuff, a distinction in computer design, making redundant an old post-grad degree superseded by a first honours degree in fine art, based on drawing, installation, sculpture and art history.

Now in my late seventies I largely focus on my great passion for design and art history, and while still writing, I dabble in painting and have a large and ever-growing library with a desire to compile a first-hand visual narrative history of art. But in taking time out to tell the story of one's Frank heritage, there is a strange kind of reverence in reawakening the account of the emergence of the Franks of Germania from the mists and swamps of their piratical birth through to their life in Britain.

Yet being the last of a long line of Franks, and speaking for a family name now dispersed across the globe, I feel an obligation to present their story. The central characters are ancestor Sir Robertus Francais and his successors, his Norman kinsman Robert de Brus and his successors, and my grandfather Thomas Henry Frank, his daughter Dorothy Frank and her son, as author of this work, the last Frank standing.

INTRODUCTION

This is a story of a little bit more than just ordinary people. Inspired by the life events of the author it is a story of the extraordinary Franks: a story of an historic family line ending with my mother Dorothy and her father Thomas Henry Frank. Its history illuminating the past, the work demonstrates the beginning and end of destiny and the interlude sandwiched between. And here the phrase 'in all respects true Franks' emerges, where the intervening period between the Franks origin in AD 210 and today has been painstakingly unwrapped, its reveal showing a name and disparate clan seen threading their way fleetingly through life and death towards man's common destination of eternal rest.

For the record, the ancient Kingdom of Bernicia ran from the River Tweed to the Tees, bordering Cleveland and Tom Frank's predecessor's homeland extending across Eskdale to Whitby, Pickering and its surrounds.

The purpose of this book is fourfold:

1. To trace the Frank line from its origin to the more recent North Yorkshire/Scottish line, proving its continuance and interconnection through to the present day.

2. To provide an historic narrative and context for one of the most understated but foremost peoples in European history.

3. To provide a storyline connecting past and present and the effects of Frank influence and their relationship with the most dominant figures in British history.

4. To emphasise issues of moral conduct with specific focus on the process of humanisation and enlightenment.

And with the latter in mind, early on I delve into female deity, feudalism, war, women's rights, subjugation, cohesion and the emergence of civil society. Being conscious from the start this work might be viewed as the very tome of male supremacy, in truth I want to dispel any thoughts I might espouse the exclusivity of male patriarchy. Having said that, the existence of male descendancy has provided the tools from which to weave a story predicated by an early investigation into the female epoch.

Anyone who has attempted research of this kind will know the pitfalls. It is not an exact science, and reliance on historians and ancient documents confounds even the best experts. Although drawn from evidential sources, the story pretends no absolutes in terms of academic accuracy. Hopefully the work is not too mired in detail, its light touch on history explaining something of the uniqueness of the Franks, inalienable in its use as a word, unassailable as a name and as a people.

History is strange; mostly it's mere words upon a page of schooltime dates and events instilled as somehow important. Sometimes we see vistas but little of the real personalities of ordinary folk or of a name. Looking back is like peering through the murk, like cloying fog, voiceless shapes moving through the gloom for thousands of years, and to what end – so much of the past having simply disappeared leaving silent victims and haunted souls with so much to say but with no escape or atonement for their sins, their god a figment of imagination confined to unheard prayers and fading ink.

During periods of turmoil, and in particular 1130–1190, data is sketchy and providing common descendant first names against relevant dates is not as I would have wished. Where data begins to reappear, balanced against probability, continuance has been evidenced by related events; the information gleaned, together with a unique name, for me seems to satisfy hierarchical continuance.

I will be looking into the origins of the Franks from AD 210, the Frank monarchy, the invention of Frank law, the creation of France and the defeat of Muslim rule over Europe. Mitigating sketchy data specific to the Franks, their well-documented cousins the Brus have been used as a means of smoothing the storyline and providing information, all the time carrying reference to their Frank cousins.

My initial focus has been on what I have come to recognise as the Frank homeland settlement of the Cotentin Peninsula of Normandy and its links with the de Brus. The origins of de Brus prior to Normandy are disparate and a source of fierce debate. The argument has so little bearing on what I wanted to achieve that I have settled on the known fact of the family de Brus as having lived contemporaneous with the more established Normandy Franks, where the Franks ancient lineage dating well beyond Clovis, originally began to coalesce out of earlier small Germanic groups in 210 CE around the Lippe and the Sieg, and along the lower and middle Rhine valley.

By 1066, the Franks and Robert de Brus were at the Battle of Hastings. It seems a further body of Normans may have entered Britain via the River Humber some time following 1066. Born in 1030, Robert de Brus would be in his mid to late thirties. Three knights feature in relevant charters and were together with de Brus in England, and I will explain more of the knight Robertus Francais later. I will also provide the Scottish link in relation to the Yorkshire settlers, as well as their family tree.

Knowing my limitations, in essence this work is as far removed from a beautifully scripted novel as might be possible. In recognising forebear R D Blackmore, of *Lorna Doone* fame, I offer no apology for occasionally wandering off-piste in purposely laying bare my thoughts, also in acknowledging my literary limitations in the pursuance of a honest-to-goodness warts and all account.

The work is littered with words and phrases as shown in their original interpretation. Appearing as grammatical oversights and misspellings ripe for correction and evidenced by ever-changing place and name spellings, I have purposely included such spellings as ordinary narrative so as to convey the inherent characteristics and fundamental nature of original source material distilled from a language and format foreign to our tongue, their inclusion aiding understanding of its evolvement. Normally these would have been shown in italics, however due to their frequency, especially where a passage of work becomes difficult or involved, such interruption would leave the work ragged and untidy. Therefore in order to aid the flow, these words have been shown mostly as normal text.

Stylised to retain interest, details relating to one's self are substantially factual. The mare I rode most nights and came to love, although referred to as mine, was just one of many animals belonging to the farm whose extensive farmland I was supposed to inherit. Daughter to a working horse, it was me who broke her in, yet being aged only fifteen, for in excess of a year I was mostly separate from the day-to-day bustle of human contact, the mare being my sole companion.

What I wasn't aware of was the source of my affiliation with animals, where, via the Franks and their rural ties, I have been able to trace approaching 1000 years of unbroken familial connection intersecting with Sir Robertus Francais and his contemporary Robert de Brus; and where used domestically or in battle, the horse has proven such a major part.

As opposed to an academic thesis, any poetic licence in the storytelling has been rigorously scrutinised, first to aid the storyline, and second to maintain flow for which I take sole responsibility. These judgement calls in no way alter the genuine intention of the work. During research it has been mostly impossible to apportion original authorship used as source material, especially where factual data has been variously repeated. The story being either original or interpretational, in terms of recognition I have cited as I have gone along, and apologise for any lapses as being wholly unintentional, having necessarily let my mind free-flow across a mass of data in order to find a consensus, making my own judgement backed by factual evidence.

I expect not everyone, not least the experts, to agree with the cogency of this work. It is after all a story, its telling emanating from my own jumbled start in life, the settled calm and heat of Africa swapped for the receiving end of bombing in England, and aged twelve my submission of drawings for large-scale house building duly rubber-stamped and approved for construction. The precise nature of architectural penmanship for hundreds of houses was later replaced, at aged fifteen, by moonlight ploughing and the early morning round of cattle and pigs, where the stillness of each grey dawn muffled the shuffle and stomp of stirring beasts, each awakening day resonant to the 6 a.m. pulse of an Alfa Laval milking machine.

Mine was a strange life sandwiched between birth and the age of sixteen, heightened by the knowledge of my being born in Jerusalem amid surrounding death and the Nazi's hugely militarised rounding up of Jews shipped from the Middle East to the death camps of Europe. And my own father, an ex REME (Royal Electrical and Mechanical Engineers) officer in later years stuck in the memory of a desert war, a once proud soldier resigned to innocuity and dreams.

As a Londoner plonked in Yorkshire amid cowpats and the downwind smell of pig manure, he was out of kilter with a world and country folk he had no understanding of. And with only a margin of remaining sight, Tom Blackmore became an old man resigned to having long conversations with three long-deceased brothers, where for him the world became a pseudo-imaginary existence only he understood and where survival became dependent on reliving old tales and chit-chatting with long-past brothers and comrades.

Whether art, life or mortality, as an artist I'm increasingly startled by creation, whether by God's hand or by man, the accident of everything around and the surge of wonder felt at seeing something visually wonderful emerge from the everyday mundane. Then there is the matter of that huge question mark hanging over the person of man – what is he about anyway; a vehicle through whose mortal existence the all-seeing eye enables us to express something of temporary existence, that cruelty, playing games with humanity's concept of eternity. And in a sense my attempt at being either frank or Frank is just that, a philosophical attempt to make amends relating to the birthright accident of a name, and of a heritage within the desperate ambition and desire of man and the concept of continuance.

I comment from time to time providing context or useful stories, some with comments relating to the present day. I start from the very beginning with the image of disparate Germanic tribes and pirates blindly negotiating the cloying mists of the Rhine who, after restless sleep, waken to the sound of stirring wildlife, suddenly alive as the sun breaks through on a fantastic new dawn, bringing with it a vision of the birth of new nations.

It is easy today to dismiss the idea of war and slaughter as the gradual means of nation building, yet we have only to bow our heads over our own war dead to try and make sense and pray. The people of this story are long dead yet, having lived, their very existence seems to echo the spirit of Frankcorum Rex and of times past. These are the words; the story is myriad.

PART ONE

THE FRANKS

EMERGENCE OF THE EARLY EUROPEANS AND THEIR EVOLVEMENT

Before commencing with the story proper, as a Frank I thought it would be useful to use my mother's DNA as a tool in tracing her matriarchal line from Yorkshire and her Scottish cousins to the early tribal Franks of Germany. Based on the certainty her J type DNA would emerge there, this would confirm my findings of early German ancestry. It would also provide the means of tracing type J back through time to the beginnings of modern humans, 150,000 years ago.

Through my mother, Dorothy Frank, my personal matrilineal DNA results show as J1B1A1. What I found amazing – all humans of every colour and persuasion in truth emanate from a single source. Set against this, my own petty argument for the Franks might appear somewhat fatuous and self-indulgent. For this I pray forgiveness, one's interest being drawn from the name itself and the name *Frank* used as a word, its very usefulness so distinct, representing so much within the English language and everyday use. And then there are the people I knew and grew up with, the remnants of that clan so recently dispersed around the world. Should I just let it all fade away and leave it to others, or none, to recall something of its people and its history?

It seems to me the moment is now or not at all, with the world shifting and moving at such a pace, leaving this tiny piece of the jigsaw unrecorded is something of which I'd be ashamed; heedless of honouring the grandfather I adored and what he and those before him represent. Also it seems to me that future generations will inevitably need something of typical family evolvement to find solace in an increasingly mad whirl of superfast technology. And what of language, the very tongue of human communication and its source, where for me, revealed in all its glory, this story is truly remarkable.

Venturing from the main thrust of this study, the following data provides weight to one's Frank origins. Through my mother, Dorothy Frank, our matrilineal DNA is an exact match to people currently living in such diverse regions as Stockholm in Sweden, Romania, Russia, Poland, Persia, Turkey and Estonia, also Iran and the Ukraine, with the greatest cluster being Braunschweig in Germany. Brunwick as it is now called, is located south of Hamburg in triangulation with Berlin to the east, much later Franks having been shown to have emerged not far from this region at the Lippe and Sieg, along the lower and middle Rhine valley.

It is this location in central Eastern Europe, type J of J1B1A1, that represents a modest 6.1% of current European DNA. Fortunately a stable measurement had been made prior to distortions caused by the huge influx of current migration. Type J is also very typical for the Near East, where the matrilineal J is said to have developed in a likely single woman descendant of the original out-of-Africa pioneers, type N being a mutation of L3a.

By way of explanation, the Eve origin for all current humans was designated L0, 130,000 years ago, followed by a string of African offshoots designated L0, 1, 1a, 2, 3, 3a and 3b, ranging between 40,000 and 80,000 years ago. It was type L3a that mutated into type N and type M, 40,000 to 60,000 years ago. Both type M and N populated East Asia running north and across the ocean forming the Indigenous First Generation North American. Both types also expanded along the coast of the Indian Ocean as far as Papua New Guinea, type N expanding to Australia and those who became known as the Aborigines, whose people retain a genetic similarity to their African forebears today.

Data from Dr Forster and his team show that Europeans derived entirely from N types, migrating across the narrow Red Sea Straits. The group must have been very small, as research has found a single female survivor who amazingly started the whole thing off.

Type L3a must have been a busy girl and somewhat productive, as this solitary young woman was to be the mother of all Europe. Her progeny became type R and type U, immediately following type M and N's own mutation 40,000–60,000 years ago. The spread across Europe continued to mutate, thus producing the string of types W, I, K, H/V, T, and X, together with one's own type J. The crucial point is that type L3a was a very small group where only a couple or so survived. It is utterly amazing that one unknowing but courageous early human woman should be the forebear of all Europe.

Evidence shows that this event was momentous as no significant further migration happened until modern times: mutation upon mutation resulting in clusters of red and blonde hair, and a light skin that would burn in the sun; a people so removed from their African origins and Asian and Arab cousins, that it makes one wonder at today's hate created on a wholly false precept, where the medieval justification for subjugation and murder of even members of one's own family flies in the face of scientific fact and the courage of these tiny few.

It is likely the original group were of the same gene, a close-knit tribe, ignorant and naked – their very human inclination to venture forth and face the challenge of crossing of the Red Sea was a massive leap for humanity, something never to be repeated until long after the advent of the slave trade. There is evidence that males either couldn't swim or had great difficulty in doing so, whereas females appeared more able. The greatest persuasion of evidence is that most of the original group perished leaving at least one male and half dozen or so females.

Supportive of much later female meme is the study of the teeth and bones belonging to burial sites, proving significant groups of women continued traversing great distances whereas the males remained in situ to their place of birth. The National Academy of Sciences found people buried south of Augsburg, Germany. The majority of women originated hundreds of miles from their final resting place in the Lech Valley, and it's here DNA tests by German scientists support evidence found in burial sites right across Europe.

Study of the earliest four age groups of much later Amazonian women emanates from an ancient female warrior deity situated around the area now known as Libya; a deity that lasted for a thousand years, predating the Trojan War (1250–1180 BCE) by many generations. Later burial sites reveal sizeable groups of women buried alongside their most prized possessions of bows and arrows together with a variety of quivers, daggers and spears. By comparison male burials were sparse and quite separate from those of female graves. Amazingly many a woman's final resting place was shared by the horse she had rode into battle, these horse and women said to be the forerunners of modern cavalry. Increasingly evidence is emerging of thousands of years of strong women, equal to men in battle and often superior to them in terms of ultimate survival, determination and sense of purpose.

Type J humans came to Central Europe around 10,000 years ago with the first farmers, emanating from the fertile crescent that stretched from the Euphrates and Tigris Rivers of Mesopotamia across Anatolia to Lebanon and Palestine. Subtype J1a is found mostly in Central and Northern Europe, i.e. the German speaking region, whereas the J1b part of one's makeup is lightly present elsewhere in Europe but more strongly in the Near East.

Returning to the first paragraph. The people of Braunschweig were the first European farmers, going by the name Linearbandkeramik. They were importers of agriculture, products and methods, moving the first domesticated animals and plants from the Near Far East and Central Asia into Europe. They fought against the Mesolithic hunter-gatherers where whole villages were regularly massacred and their bodies mutilated, even cannibalised. Evidence has unearthed quite extensive early fortifications, their sophistication becoming reminiscent of later Franks. They reached the Rhine and Neckar valleys of Germany about 5,500 years BC, where, in time, the Franks homeland evolved and it's here their journey began.

While currently upholding the aforesaid dates and data, and not wanting to get particularly mired on information pertaining new discoveries, I must add caution where recent finds of a human jawbone in Northern Israel is said to have been carbon dated 180,000 years ago. Reported to the BBC News 25th January 2018 by professor Israel Hershkovitz of Tel Aviv University, this news has sent shockwaves challenging previously held views.

If true, such revelation indicates modern humans having left Africa as much as 240,000 years ago. The supposition is what we consider as modern humans lived alongside other ancient species at varying stages of evolvement where we have to consider interbreeding having been the forerunner for many modern-day differences.

Adding to this research, German Neanderthal remains suggest a mixing of types and a team in the Altai region of Siberia claim evidence of the interbreeding of Neanderthals with pioneer groups from Africa 100,000 years ago. And in more recent history, in Britain the DNA discovery of Cheddar Man having dark skin and blue eyes, dated 10,000 years ago, whereas his eyes might have remained blue, the process of Cheddar Man's progedy to lighter skin would take as long as 8000 years to evolve.

RELIGION RELATING TO WOMEN AND SECULAR SOCIETY TODAY

Gravesites show the presence of polished adzes, particularly buried alongside males. The adze, shown as a status indicator, was tooled like an axe with an arched blade at right angles to the handle, used for adzing wood but useful as a weapon. In terms of the DNA chain, this later extends to the Paris basin of France, the Netherlands, Belgium and Poland, extending as far as Western Ukraine.

Study has shown the preference for men to hold onto their hard-won land. Women, however, continued to pioneer, carrying with them their own unique DNA, its progeny spread across new lands in a hierarchy led by women. Fertility and reverence for the womb led to Goddess worship for a good harvest and the fruitfulness of nature per se. In this, the female was predominant, and it's the reverse idea of male dominance and control through a subconscious fear of women and the birth of religion that seems to have triggered the need for males to subjugate their more resilient and pioneering opposite sex.

The Extraordinary Franks

My thesis on *Phallocentrism and the female epoch* and *The process of psychosymbolic symbolic humanisation 2003,* has shown that the Goddess matriarchal society castration of males led to the concept of eunuch or abstinent male Catholic priests, where once the priestess became pregnant, male lovers, their earthly task fulfilled, were strangled or ritualistically sacrificed, thus ensuring continuance of the female deity.

The escalation of high-ranking eunuch males cum the shorter life-span of postnatal females caused a shift of power where later high-level eunuchs became dominant. Having gained the upper-hand their mindset became the avoidance of any erosion of the male-myth of superior rein, now become imbedded and absolute.

This product was later to be indoctrinated into myth, the precursor of imagined gods and deity having religions demandant on obedience. As seen in the crusades, Christian and Islam alike, the ultimate of death a sword with which to smite any dissention. In time male dominance became so embedded that under the umbrella of modesty and protection and the heat of the sun, females of those climes became cowered into servitude.

The kind of subjugation and fear for women that lies deep within the psyche of Islam, early indications are such unworthy imbalance is losing its grip within the Catholic faith. We see signs its non-married or what I describe as its reign dominant eunuch priest ethic under strain, the world view of such misology an antiphrasis to reason within the modern world.

Change is happening. And as we see in Saudi Arabia at its centre financing discord and Jihad extremism across the globe, change appears to be coming with a slackening of rules for women, a move welcomed but heavily laden with suspicion. And as in Iran, its youth held under the yoke of medieval scholarship its pent up outrage ensuing an outburst scream for freedom.

Whereas the aforesaid has much to say in the process of evolved civilisation, history often shows lessons and points the way. Over 3000 years ago women in Britain had at least an equal role, as men and women unsurprisingly seem to have been in charge of proceedings during Stonehenge rituals. Examination of the remains of at least twenty-seven people show a predominance of women; tests revealing the more middle-aged and older females to be of high status at a time when most people died young. Today it seems important to keep this thought in mind when considering the intervention of the hate-filled bearded male, a neurotic paranoia to moral Islam, secular society and the European idee.

Yet in the not so distant past the blood-let and cruelty of our Christian forebears saw the painful and gradual emergence of the modern European, and with it the slow abandonment of the Bible as gospel. Indeed the less religion so the growth in moral conduct: freedom of thought and endeavour that has made Western society so appealing that everyone wants it. And where the word 'Christian' today means more 'doing the right thing' than going to church, and doing the right thing, men support the freedom for women and people of difference to decide for themselves without rancour or interference.

While seeming a departure from the main theme, the world events of today causing such a seismic religious and cultural shift, I make comment in support of Muslim women, the observation counterpoising a work otherwise dominated by male descent, and where the importance of women per se becomes increasingly vital to the self perception and ordinance of the most enlightened human species on earth, the broader aspect of being European, and furthermore the necessary inclusion of Muslims as part of secular society no matter how wearisome and difficult the journey.

I use the terminology European to include North America, Canada and the Australian antipodes et al. globally. And while one might wonder about Russia, roughly on a par with Europe, Russian advances are ideologically stymied within a dogma of intellectual superiority and self-pitying isolationist 'backs against the wall' persecution complex exacerbated by a propensity for brutality, as might a bully having nothing to vent their angst but brute strength. Whereas Russian advances in sexual equality have long been superior to Europe, transformative freedoms that should be on a par with Europe are decades behind, where the USSR must have the courage to shake off the perception that everyone is against them, stop their spoilt-child sabre-rattling and cheating and shake hands, both sides having more that unites them and more pressing needs, having an urgent need to work together.

The Muslim separation of women from men is one thing, but we should make no mistake, the misogynist cruelty and subjugation of women by men is led by fear. It is his psychological weakness and reluctance to let go and venture into the light that binds him to eternal hate, where within the misery of misogyny he is forever condemned to a self-fulfilling archaic prophecy of the damned.

As in France and Belgium, where it is illegal to wear the full veil, I agree it would be a huge leap of faith when the rest of European Muslim women abandon the burqa and other symbols of oppression. By a long way, American women would never stand for subjugation, their women a million miles ahead of the rest. And by far, Americans voice their opinion, whereas in Britain we remain sotto voce, constrained and overwhelmed by influxes that seek to subjugate, racist if we resist.

As if to provoke and ridicule the wearing of the hijab, an American filmmaker uses porn to make a cultural point concerning liberalisation where, but for face covering, a stark-naked Islamic woman is portrayed leading a Muslim male, fastened with a chain around his neck, ascending a treacherously rocky incline. In a reversal of the sexes, the production is seen as a symbol for human rights against violations such as rape and domestic violence, his so-called *property* now unwrapped for all to see, as she walks, the swaying dip and fall of her fulsome breasts her naked sex and buttocks arouse, the pertness of her dark areola and erect nipples a poke in the eye for generation upon generation of hateful male misogyny. Led by his captor and eternally fettered, the man stumble, helpless in millennia of self-prophesising deep-seated hatred, bound in a misogynistic malevolence of anything that fails the intractable mindset of revenge.

But what has all this to do with the Europeanising of Britain and the Franks per se? Well, everything. Humankind having come so far, the hospitality shown by Europeans has allowed too rapid an influx of Islam, many Muslims coming to Britain from Pakistan with terrorism as a neighbour. Add to this a dash of North African slaughter and counter-slaughter combined with Russia's counter to western expansionism, and we have mass immigration throwing Europe into turmoil.

No longer do we have the comfort of known boundaries and the norms of nine-to-five as a certainty. As in a blink of an eye, everything we have sleepwalked into thinking of as assured has been thrown into question. This work is as much about Britain's evolvement and duration as an entity born of a secular past founded in much let of blood, and with law and religion seen once again in a tussle for man's salvation, as it was for the de Brus and the Franks in their time.

THE IMPORTANCE OF BEING FRANK

While this work is mostly concerned with the Franks and the influence of Norman culture on Britain, it seems necessary to put into context some of the seismic events that have shaped and formed where we are placed today.

I start off around 1016 with the Danes and Canute, immediately followed by the Norman invasion. Throughout this work I touch on subjects such as the Magna Carta, the Hundred Years War, and the Black Death between 1348 and 1350, culminating in the death of 50% of the population – skipping over the War of the Roses and Henry's Dissolution of the Monasteries, and in 1588 Queen Elizabeth's principles so angering the Spanish determinate on restoring Catholic rule over England. Thus thwarted came two civil wars and the return of the Black Death in 1665 wiping out 15% of the population.

At this point it's relatively easy to visualise a country beset by turmoil yet midway in the formulation of civil society with its institutions, law and Christian idee, so much so we can hear the bells ring in affirmation, not of a country in isolation, but underlining its success at the Battle of Waterloo in 1815 and that of empire. Britain had conquered the world bringing with it civilisation, being blunt, England's idea of civilisation: brutal, beset by flag flying and all conquering, clothing the native in uniform; perceived as necessary body fodder in case of uprising or threat against its imperial domain. Britain was on top of the world, unrecognisable. It being amazing how a mere a 150 years had transformed it into a modern marshal enterprise, in all ways victorious, bringing with it a new kind of social conscience in the banning of slavery in 1833 and a female monarch in Victoria.

So much for the struggle to rise above the mundane, education for all, schools displaying atlases, motor vehicles, a mighty navy and approaching full employment, albeit many had to do without shoes and the working class were miles separate from those in top hats. But war would sort that out: plenty of employment, sixteen million dead upon the battlefields post-1914, and a war to end all wars. Here, if you didn't fight, you were summarily executed as a coward.

I talk about Europeanisation and the process of civilisation – what was that all for, so much death and destruction? Yet with it came that great leap in terms of enlightenment, as if born from grief, the pools of blood not deep enough, inadequate, the sacrifice insufficient, so how many more lives? A Second World War and fifty-five million more; the overpowering stink of twisted and bundled corpses now bound within one glorious heap of lost and forgotten faces, a dollop of faded sepia memory carved into stone. Yet out of that purge came a world we can now get a sense of and recognise, a world where we can fly, even to the moon. But is this world we fought for and gave our very souls, the free world we in Britain envisaged?

Some may consider the following few paragraphs a diversion and may not agree with the arguments presented; yet given the nature of this work and the historic parallels and influences affecting modern-day society, it would be difficult to escape comment on the influence of Islam in Britain, rising from a population of 50,000 in 1961 to over three million today, 50% having been born outside the UK. And here I speak as much for Muslim society as for the greater population and being cognisant the majority of Muslims feel depressed and distinctly alienated, they themselves stymied by the intransigent and all pervasive Mullah, omnipresence, having strict limitations and defined lines pertaining interrelations.

For me the compulsion to write about sufferance is a matter of conscience, whether man, woman or child, those invisible multitudes on the receiving end, terrified of each waking day; a seeming never-ending torment of workplace bullying, a brutal landlord, debt, terrifying neighbours, thugs upon the streets, those on the receiving end of beatings or molestation and where selecting just one aspect of injustice and writing about it remains a plea for all.

The female predicament

Women having come so far, the very nature of 1000 years of history formed through male antecedence viewed from the perspective of that gender is to my mind just wrong. But given the structure of inheritance, this work is driven by the diktats of male descendancy, and one has to work with that presented. Offsetting this I feel bound to raise the female predicament exacerbated by the parade of voiceless women living in our midst, yet living in this most sexually liberated society. Therein lies a predicament, where Muslim girls are knowingly forced into marriage sometimes to men so old as to be their parent or older. On arrival in Britain many become condemned to drudgery, isolated and enslaved, forbidden to integrate or learn English, becoming a huge stumbling block in the wilful subversion of female emancipation, repudiating the principles of free and liberal society.

I expressly use the expression 'forced' whereas the word's compulsion or coercion ranges between outright violence to psychological abuse, as exampled by a man from Bangladesh, one of a great number of males forbidding their wives to speak or use an interpreter even though she might be desperately ill – dragged slave-like to a surgery, tyrannically, her ward speaking exclusively for her. Unable to examine her, the doctor stymied by the husband's ignorance as to her true condition, yet in the purest sense not husband, she a voiceless prisoner subjugated even until death. Yet silent upon one's ears, at a time her sisterhood might rise in anger, where is today's female opprobrium?

Throughout this work I have tried to strike a balance in referencing the parts played by women, sometimes heroic, sometimes mundane, in true part whatever sex playing its role conscientiously and to its full potential. Yet the age-old meme of physical strength is beset by the testosterone dominant mindset of men – he carries the sword, her the sheath. In an exploration of frankness, or what it is to be forthright, the following remains a blunt appraisal.

Today two main issues stand out: those of Islam and the rights of women. I use the latter on the principle that acceleration for woman's emancipation will counter if not conquer many of the ills that stand in the way of continued progress towards full civilisation. As things stand, the macho chess-play by Putin and the blood of innocent people is in one sense not so different from the cruel stamp of extremism exercised by thousands of Muslims today, viewed as valid terms for their aims and successors. On 11th March 2015, Lebanese presenter Rima Karaki abruptly cut off an interview with Sheikh Hani Al Sibal when he contemptuously scorned: 'Shut up so I can talk. It is beneath me to be interviewed by you, you are a woman.' Her retort: 'Either there is mutual respect or the conversation is over.' Sheikh Sibai was reported of having been convicted in-absentia as a terrorist related Islamist in Egypt, and of having skipped to England in 1999.

Akin to another battle for Britain, the courage of these remarkable Muslim women shedding their garb in defiance is critical, the fight for integration lying in their hands, especially where the majority of white and black British women remain complacent and so confined as to be silent, while at the same time sotto voce on the matter of Islam as a no-go area. We once again see suffrage, but this time without the privilege of wealth to support them, we might applaud the stance of these brave and intelligent trailblazers, for the future for Britain, Europeanism and indeed the world, remains with them.

While the main concern of this work is the Franks and the inevitable mundane of wills and succession, the underlying theme is of conflict turned society. The democracy people have slaved so hard and died for now put under threat, one's obligation to raise comment especially as relates the latest onslaught wrecked upon an otherwise stable meme and more so concerning women held in punitive durance. Two world wars, peace across Europe, stability and the development of education, healthcare and welfare, the ordinary everyday lives of men, women and children interrupted, now set asunder by daily reports from all quarters of new kinds of lawlessness, greed and vengeful menace, where defiance of the statute rules of cultured society has no belonging.

The niqab complex

Now seems to be a balance where the greater good for young women, particular those who choose to wear the full burqa or niqab as a statement for themselves, or where they are made to comply, should think of womankind's continued struggle and those who have been put to death or put themselves in danger in the drive for equality, and where the more simplistic reasoning for face covering seems more one of youthful defiance even within families not given to coverage. There is no excuse for Imams and teachers who exhort male spite in terms of subjugation, surely sufficient reason to defy such malevolence.

Often in dismay at the subjugation fostered on Muslim women, recent surveys show that a large majority of British men vocalise for increased legitimacy and empowerment for women at large, whereas Western women appear largely complacent. It is a scandal that feminists are so muted about the appalling things done to women in Islamic theocracies, and shocking that western feminists are so pusillanimous about condemning misogyny in Islam

Women as a whole should think of the Suffrage Movement that in the UK in 1903 was a mostly upper and middle class institution that struggled against resistance for equality even from its own sex. Those resistant were hidebound in terms of their vows and ties of love and family affection where fifteen years later women could only vote if they held property. In Britain it was 1928 before full voting rights were granted, and in France 1944. It is a sad reflection that fraternity, equality and liberty, first voiced in France in 1790, should have taken 150 years to concede giving women the vote, yet having won the vote, subjugation and face covering was made illegal in that country.

So today the greater good should be understood and acted upon, where women of all persuasion should question the conventions that bind them, where through un-wanton action or inaction, those sisters who continue the fight see such small advances continue to be held in check. It is one thing to say it's my choice, but it's quite another seen in the light of women's plight across the globe that must be addressed, where being Muslim in particular, the female imperative should be to open one's face to the world that they might voice the shining light of determination and hope for mankind through the interjection of women's prerogative as equals.

But is it true that Muslim women are not standing up for themselves? In 2016 female Muslim candidates wanting to represent their party at council elections in Britain claim to have been blocked from standing by male Muslims in Peterborough and Birmingham, one woman in particular being the subject of an unwarranted smear campaign, people turning up at her parents' home intimidating her mother with the trumped-up charge she was having an illicit affair with another councillor.

This shameful act is all the more alarming set against all I have said, the excuse given that as a young woman, being a possession of her father, and not having his consent, she had to step down. Such atrocious misogyny is an affront to all that has been achieved in terms of democratic cohesion and equality. And as I have tried to express, the era we now live becomes inclusive of gay or transgender society, applauding equally the masculine and feminine in all their attributes.

The castration of tyranny

Out of fear of subversion of his masculine authority, the existence of any form of challenge to his meme produces psychological absolutes in terms of defiance. Having no way to turn other than hate of his enemy festers a hardening of oppression and tyranny, a bulwark against the infidel. Calling on Muslims to shed blood for Allah, half of British mosques are said to be controlled by hard-line Islamists, where unbelievably the Gladstone Institute's report of 16th June 2014 speaks of an army of Deobandi militant preachers, paid by the state, calling on prisoners convicted of terror related offences to hate the more and act upon it. Being systemic, and ours being a secular society, to my mind such activity should be challenged head-on and rigorously rooted out, the rights of all, the common man, woman and child standing superior to the human rights of a deranged few and those who stand in the way of cohesion.

Being both frank and continuing the feminist theme, a system that allows duplicitous cowardly bullies to lie and intimidate women too scared to show their emails for fear of recrimination, such unworthy acts can only be countered by enforced equal representation for women wanting to be as much European as Muslim. Again, it is a mystery how such male misogyny can be justified under Islam, balanced with equality and cohesion in the European idee.

Not commonly worn in most Muslim countries, and because of security fears, Morocco has banned the production and sale of burqas, so why not in Britain? In a country where radicalisation has undoubtedly flourished, Muslim defiance is regularly practised by one or another bearded male trailing eye slots for women draped in black often in the most unlikely of places, sometimes in the full heat of summer, and blatantly staged to provoke and antagonise the great majority in the hope of provoking confrontation.

Conjured to cock a snoop, its misogyny is a shocking affront to the Western male, on the streets its purposeful aspect played out before a succession of female shoppers and their male companions. And here the masculine instinct to protest becomes stymied, his psych paralysed before a barrier of alienation within the very country his parents fought for, rendered impotent, the disparaging effect of defiant eyes staring through a veil of closed communication, each rebuttal the price of social conscientiousness, not wanting to cause upset nor caught in-flagrante between the police and a frenzy of media publicity.

The frightening aspect of the bearded male, confused, dominant and defiant, raging war within our midst, is something not easily countered. What is puzzling is how a proportionately large number, wanting all that the West can offer, can engage in a range of vile activities apropos that reported against young white females as trash for sex, yet remain close to their faith as if being able to justify separating the two, the infidel fair game, and thus to be despised and, when challenged, the western world vilified.

Countering this is a Pakistani activist who needs no introduction, teenage Nobel Prize laureate Malala Yousafzai, who exemplifies much that I speak of in her fight for young women's rights against huge opposition and in the knowledge of a death warrant upon her head. In the light of such overwhelming argument how can any sensible Muslim continue to support the concept of face covering, forced marriage, genital mutilation and unequal representation, where compliance becomes nothing short of a stab to the heart of human emancipation and cohesion.

For those whose history has been defined as male dominant and to strict confines, morals, rituals and belief, now under scrutiny and challenged, non-belief is no longer confined to Christianity, where despite retribution, humanism has become the fastest demographic in Islamic countries, and where many Shia Muslim, in particular in Britain, don't believe a word of the Koran, and where rationalism and materialism stands in stark opposition to rampant bigotry and fanaticism within a growing trend for many Muslims to shy away from its teachings.

And it's here I applaud a young Muslim, born in Chelsea and raised in Edinburgh, Tasmina Ahmed Sheikh OBE WS NP MP, who exemplifies all I have spoken. Here is a woman her face made up, bright lipstick, intelligent, forthright, and her face lit upon the world. Her mother an actress, half Welsh, half Czech and although I am unaware of how she views her faith, if Tasmina is representative of how new Britain should look and behave, then this sceptred Isle might remain in safe hands.

Transition from Islamic feudalism to cohesion, modernity and enlightenment

Why don't we teach migrants that we are a Christian country? It's hard to accept that the Middle East, the region that gave birth to our faith, could soon see the virtual extinction of Christianity. Overheard, this might be the message of a cleric expressing heartfelt distress as to the faith's downfall and anguish over the terror felt of the few remaining Christians in that region. Overwrought as to their fate and fateful as to a huge reduction in churchgoers, the cleric might have good reason to worry.

But we have to take this in context with the evolutionary process, way beyond the concept of an earth-born divinity, our intellect telling us otherwise, the universe and that great beyond, endless and uncomprehending, so boundless we leave our earthly domain to fate. And when we pray, it is more personal and considered, and the Church should not be afraid that each person's view on Christianity, particularly as a precept for good, remains strong within the heart of man, and whereas for the many the idea of being preached to becomes an enigma.

Relating to man's evolvement and the evolutionary process, we have to examine both the here and now and the past. Crudely put, now lies a state where the battle for enlightenment is at a crucial point. Yet in terms of Islam what we are witnessing are the desperate death throes of a foreign meme born of Mecca and Medina's tribal mores, where historic differences having succumbed to violence turned barbaric; a homicidal conflict embraced by the inflamed passions of armies of Muslims today, and in the West where a stalemate exists in the conflict between the doctrine of old truths and new truth beliefs.

Old truth is beset by the doctrine of fundamentalism and a demand for the return to pure Islam. Fixed in a narrow interpretation of old readings and absent of prodigal concepts of freedom and enlightenment, it remains a dead in the water precept having nowhere to advance. Born of new truths, Christianity embraced the concept of enlightenment quickly transcending to modernity, each person's interpretation different from the other with no preserved absolutes, open to progress and new understanding, soft in the interpretation of Christianity as good a way to live as opposed to going to church or pray.

Mans intelligence and curiosity is so compelling the principles of endeavour, new frontiers, and the overriding spirit and goodness of man will inevitably rule over evil intent and that which seeks to crush all that is creative, bright and inventive. It is therefore a paradox that those who aim to impede and repudiate, by their very actions, defeat themselves. And just as life itself evolved crawling belly like out of the slime of creation, so human evolvement will cause those fixed in the abyss of medievalism or suspended somewhere between the sloth of archaism and new truth, irrespective their maker, will inevitably play catch-up and join the rest of the human race.

Through the concept of Adam and Eve, the awareness of nakedness brought shame and the need for covering. And from its shelter evolved the man-cave concept of female incarceration, put forward as protection and God worship attributed to praying for fruitful births and the overriding need for food. With cognitive development came bizarre ideas of religious belief that for the primitive mind ensued holy writ. Once gospel, its diktats were codified as real and not shaman collusion developed as a way of instilling absolute authority and control over the tribe.

I mention Mesopotamia as the historic centre of Islam and ironically Iraq being the cradle of civilisation, now turned upon itself in acts of barbarism and destruction: the very soul of civilisation it first created and cradled into notions of modernity now reviled and denigrated into wasteland. Not a notion; the crazy irony of art belonging to the ancient cities of Nineveh and Babylon mentioned in the Bible, which became a major canon of Western art and Western culture, and its writing, commencing 3100 BC, without which the process of enlightenment and progress in the West would have been severely impeded.

And now comes the litany of tribalism and sectarianism, the 'new truth' values of Christianity put under assault 600 years after Christ, and now involved in the split between the warring factions of Sunni and a 15% minority of Shia, spilling over with such devastating effect. The cradle of Levant, its agriculture and the proto-urban forebear canon of art and modernity, once gifted to Europe now beset and held ransom by the perversity of Medievalist dogma and disassociation.

Thus comes the process of liberation, sometimes short, other times long and painful, and common to various religions. The ritual of head covering etc., for women going to church or in Islam, seems to me akin to carrying an umbrella, a just-in-case ritual determined from the sentiment of Adam and Eve's nudity, its shame become a requirement to cover one's nakedness. Now seen through enlightenment as sheer nonsense, in secular parlance: the individual might wear what they will with a modicum of decency, or absent themselves from spiritual attendance entirely, it being their choice.

For Muslims the process of liberalisation is oft observed in the pursuance of extreme acts of endeavour, most prominent is scholarship and the everyday things of makeup, bright clothing and jewellery for women, where as a counter to repression, intimate thoughts such as parading nude upon lush green meadows become real. Freed from restraint, such liberating notions accentuate becoming part and parcel of the pursuit of individualism, its journey invoked by ideas and free expression. Whereas the Islamic idiom of old truth was stymied into an almost total absence of development, new truth encouraged rapid advancement in technology, science, and industry, preceded by a compulsion towards the arts and the development of economics and weaponry from which to conquer and do trade.

Now enveloped in the transition towards modernity, Islam is happy to utilise Western inventions such as transport, iPhones and modern housing, and while pursuant on advancement favouring education and occupations such as medicine, others of faith wilfully pursue destruction and carnage in the hateful pursuit of a hell's damnation, tearing down man's endeavour, the fertile crescent of Mesopotamia now a veritable waste devoid of all that was good within that domain, in its carnage thousands slain: women and children, Muslim against Muslim. Through failed cohesion and enforced isolation we find among our midst the Islamic doctrine of Ummah insistent upon the conversion of all to an Islamic community of one, and for the fundamentalists a return to the narrowest interpretation of pure Islam, such fate a majority of Muslims might justifiably be horrified at, let alone terrified.

Set against this we have the issue of pornography, sexting and cyber attacks, the price of rapid advance, pushing ahead of our ability to properly control events as they happen, and where *Ann Summers* and *Forty Shades of Grey* is considered mainstream, causing affront for some and a shrug of the shoulders for the young that might be described as a degradation of moral consciousness. Yet Darwin's natural order, conclusions on evolution, the inventiveness and curiosity of man will inevitably prevail.

From the above one can see how complicated the dilemma, whereas Muslim compulsion is towards separatism and separate laws, we need to remind that this is a Christian-based society, its institutions and all that has been developed having been determined by new truth, and having with it with the principles of openness. Given an invitation to enter and enjoin the European idee, now within its fold, it's somewhat rude of Islam not to cojoin the tenants of Europe's embrace, thus enjoining the cultivation of modernity and civilisation to which it first gave birth. Europe, a child of the ancients of Levant, setting up some sort of medieval fortification in our midst with the intention of breaking down and attacking the very principles of new truth is not something that can be tolerated nor condoned.

This whole work has been produced on the principle of truth and the journey of advancement at its core. Now under attack, those British values must be protected and in some way brought under contract. A proposition already put forward is that of an oath sworn of all public office holders, councillors, school governors, civil servants *et omnia*, that should include democracy, equality, tolerance, freedom of speech and respect for the institution of common law.

And here we have a dilemma: firstly no one of right mind would be under any illusion 'the taking of oaths' had been introduced specifically as a result of Muslim intransigence, dismissing the fact of Islam representing a basic third of immigration and a miniscule 4.5% of total population; and second, a faith stirring such disproportionate discontent upon the rest, no one should be under any illusion the presence of an oath would stir resentment, especially within the 95% of mixed population, black, white, Jew, Hindu, Sikh, Chinese, Jamaican, Filipino etc., not causing problems, getting on with life, yet obliged to swear allegiance due to a defiant meme beset by disassociation, turning on itself, out of kilter and disorientated.

With the threat of a minority causing havoc, division and disunion, having as its aim the overthrow of a democracy harmonised by associated laws and assembly, it is not fair placing unnecessary obligations set against a law-abiding majority. By way of an answer, it seems nonsense to allow private education, Muslim, parental or otherwise, absent of Ofsted inspection, such education being in urgent need of more rigorous scrutiny along with a resurgent effort to educate those women unable to speak English. If issues of incarceration and indoctrination were located outside the doctrine of Islam, these would be swiftly investigated and dealt with. But having areas of no-go like Islam, the ingrain hesitancy in Britain in dealing with like issues, is like facing a brick wall of paralysis.

How to deal? Existing laws relating to those of democracy, equality, tolerance and freedoms, including those of prevention of association, should be revisited, made stringent within existing law or the introduction of more severe legislation. Nobody in their right mind would think the swearing of an oath would cause those avowed to Islam having British law override the divine and unassailable beliefs of Sharia law and its associated beliefs. Oath taking by obligation, such utterances would be immediately repudiated and change nothing. Only the rigorous enforcement of legislation and policing will have any impact specific to the values of Britishness, where carefully managed it would minimise the subversion of deeply held beliefs, affecting only a minority bent on mischief.

As if echoing one's concerns, the European Court of Human Rights has legislated that integration precedes rights to freedom of thought, conscience and religion, especially concerning children of foreign origin. In Germany, in areas of integration such as swimming, Muslim girls must take part in mixed lessons. The judge's decision for the integration of society outstripping religious rights and constraints was the protection of children from any sort of social exclusion, particularly where it impacted on the presence of boys for such as swimming. While not binding on Britain the ruling paves the way for the UK to make a stance against religious fundamentalism and claims their human rights are being abused.

Pursuant on the transitional process of humanisation and enlightenment, here we are talking about hundreds of years of evolved democratisation set against an ancient belief system, so deeply held it cannot be so easily transformed let alone overridden. Change can be encouraged or tickled along by legislation, but in the end full integration cannot be achieved by coercion but by the long road of patience, perseverance and the Darwinism process of evolution. Unfortunately beset by such malevolent medieval psyche becomes a journey widely out of step with the rest of humanity where our hopes and aspirations alight upon the generation emerging.

EMERGENCE OF THE EARLY EUROPEANS PART TWO & SUMMARY

Having shown its face in mutilation, cruelty, hate and death, for all those sins and more, Islam is not alone. Christianity has shown all this and more, and by having taken a brief look at the challenges that face us in Britain today we can better contextualise, peer into our own past and shed new light. Robert de Brus is hailed a hero by the Scots, perhaps the greatest of them all, what with the myth of him watching a spider weave its web and of him showing the patience to overcome adversity. But was he as patient, calm and assured as suggested, after all he was a prayerful man and believed in God.

Victim to a very real stab to the heart, in 1305 Robert de Brus's great rival was John Comyn, each man vying for the Scottish throne. De Brus having set Comyn up, stabbed him in the heart before the altar of Greyfriars Church in Dumfries, whereupon six weeks after the murder de Brus seized the Scottish throne. Although a divided country, de Brus ruled until his death in 1329, but in essence under the governance of the King of England. By 1306 Scotland had became a conquered land where for the next 400 years Scotland remained a self-conscious European nation-state.

De Brus was Catholic, but moving back in time, we arrive at the thirteenth century BC and the time of Moses. I mentioned the Linearbandkeramik, and having left the matter of Jewishness until now, I'd like to point out that that the Jewish heritage is most prevalent where the predominant feature is shown in the current Ashkenazi and their ancient Levantine origins. The name Ashkenazi derives from the biblical figure of Ashkenza, first son of Gomer, identified with the Cimmerians. Prominent Ashkenazi recently identified are Moses, Heinrich Heine, Sigmund Fraud, Albert Einstein, Golda Meir, Leonard Bernstein and many others.

Being non-Jewish, personally difficult to comprehend but true, my own matriarchal DNA matches members of the Ashkenazi Jewish faith, whereas one's more recent paternity is indicative of Arab Moroccan. Such determinates show that an Arab today might well have been something else yesterday, where current faiths even within a common belief outrageously maim and kill on the precept of some difficult to comprehend man-made religious divide.

Through a half-cousin I have a direct connection with the Franks journey to America via Britain. Alluding to the Jewish faith, successful American writer and critic Michael Frank's story is brilliantly portrayed in his bitter-sweet amusing Hollywood memoir *The Mighty Franks*, a story drawn from his own family background as Jewish émigrés from Europe. Within one shared antecedent DNA we have Catholic, Protestant and Jew and through each marital union, offspring of a myriad persuasions.

At the beginning I made it clear the DNA investigation focused on the mother, or matrilineal, branch known as mtDNA, daughter of Eve or the Haplogroup. As regards my mother's DNA, as a Frank, J1b1a1 was a 100% match to a number of current living people across eighteen regions whose DNA has been recorded. Within these, most prominent were the Ashkenazi Jews of Romania, Russia, Poland and the Ukraine. These were followed by Western Europe, the strongest being situated in Braunschweig, now Brunswick, Germany, also London, Northern England and Stockholm. Third in line are the tribes of the Fars, Kerman, Lorestani and the Gilaki of Iran. Before getting to hung up on this revelation, one has to put in context the human world emanating from a single source where evolution has seen the change of skin pigmentation etc., thousands of years before the advent of religion split into designated tribes and states.

I would like to thank Dr P. Forster of Genetic Ancestors Ltd in providing the DNA data, June 2014, together with a section on genetic dating and the prehistory of one's Motherline. These include mtDNA Branches of the World, copyright 2003–2006. Drawn from separate research is data relating to hunter-gatherers, the compunction towards massacre and mutilation, information relating to the adze, biblical related issues and so on. The critical fact remains that all humans are bound by our Motherland African beginnings marked by the reference L0, becoming L3a, mutating into Eurasian M and N, founder types that populated the world.

With the end of the glacial age, it became possible to raise crops and cattle where a mere 8000 years ago farming arrived in Europe from what is New Turkey into Greece, and thus via the Mediterranean into Central Europe. Genetic work on skeletons of the first European farmers show their predominant matrilineal line N1a survives in less than 1% of Europeans today. From a distance of a mere 8000 years, nothing of the future tribes that made up the Franks of Frankia would be known, for this the human race would have to patiently wait. What has now been established is a clear link between today's Franks and that arduous path back 130,000 years to Eve. Today everyone has the opportunity to apply a simple and painless DNA test that is sure to surprise.

FRANK ORIGINS

Here I draw from *Liber Historiae Francorum*, an anonymous work of 727 CE indicated around the late Bronze Age. Following the fall of Troy 12,000 Trojans led by Priam and Antenor, moving along the River Don, settled around Pannonia, known as the Sea of Azov. It was here that Priam and his son Marcomer founded the city of Sicambria, which early Franks believed to be their tribal origin. From an early work of 660 CE, *Fredegar Histores book II* states the existence of a king named Francio, from where the name emerged.

Modern-day scholars agree that the Franks emerged out of various smaller Germanic groups of the Salii, Sicambri, Chamavi, Bructeri, Chatti, Chattuarii, Ampsivarii, Tencteri, Ubii, Batavi and the Tungri. They inhabited the lower and middle Rhine valley between the Zuyder Zee and the River Lahn, extending eastward to the Weser, the densest settlement being around the Ijssel, between the Lippe and the Sieg. This ties in nicely with the previously mentioned DNA findings for German Braunschweig as being conclusive.

The period 50 CE shows the Franks invading the Roman Empire across the Rhine. *Tabula Peutingeriana* mentions 'Chamavi qui-est Pranci', Pranci meaning Franci. The invaders were of the tribe Chamavi, and in 357 CE, a Frankish King of the Salian tribe is recorded as entering Roman soil, where he stayed.

German archaeologists recently unearthed evidence of a lost Roman camp that formed a vital part of the frontier, protecting the empire against the German hordes. The camp was said to be home to around 1000 or more legionaries. Located on the River Lippe, near Olfen, it seems to have served as a base for General Drusus in the Roman general's long and bloody war against tribes such as the Salii, the Chamavi, and the Franci: tribes that once inhabited what is now Western Germany.

One hundred years ago, the discovery of a bronze Roman helmet near Olfen indicated the presence of ancient remains, and it is only now the last missing link in the chain of Roman defences in Westphalia has been found. The camp was occupied between 11 and 7 BCE, and was probably used to control crossing points on the Lippe, acting as a supply depot for outlying posts.

History has shown that in time such empires seem to exhaust themselves, this work demonstrating how dynasties come and in their storytelling, fade vane glorious.

Douglas Frank Blackmore

EXEMPLI GRATIA LEX SALICA

Preamble

The Frank dynasty dates back to 210 CE and beyond. Emanating from warlike Germanic Salian tribes, the Franks were pirates, but pirates with their own rules and laws. Evolving into pre-eminence, rapid coalescence saw Frank dominance and the quick formation of monarchy. Resultant Frankish law, derived from their Salian heritage, became exempli gratia, more properly Lex Salica in today's common law, early Frank legislation being the direct basis of most legal systems throughout the world today.

Referring to the Early European, systematic with the evolvement of the Early European people was the short-lived Britannic Empire. The Roman Carausius was tasked with clearing the Channel between Britain and the Continent of Frankish and Saxon raiders, but upon being found in cahoots with the pirates was condemned to death. As a way of survival Carausius declared himself emperor of Britain in 286 CE, and with his immense army seized for himself all of Gaul. Along with most of Britain, the empire encompassed modern-day France, Luxembourg, Belgium, part of the Netherlands, most of Switzerland, part of northern Italy, and in Germany the western banks of the Rhine, its ancient meme having similarities with the EU, but Britannic as opposed to today's Franco-Germanic conglomerate.

As I say, for a short-lived ten years Carausius reigned as emperor between 286 and 293 CE and Allectus for the following three years, Constantinus regaining for Rome Britain in 296 CE, Gaul itself falling to the Franks in 486 CE. And this in a sense, with the demise of Britannica as an empire, as seen within these pages, is when the story for the Franks properly took off.

As previously stated, yesterday's Franks were the factual creators of modern-day law, where out of piracy and basic weapons of war was born a new dawn of Lex Salica governing agnatic succession and statute law. These included codified inheritance, crime, murder, theft and insult, not forgetting damage and recompense for injury to person, property and goods and, above all, the introduction of a jury of peers. It is no small wonder that the surname Frank, Old English for javelin or spear, equivalent to the modern-day sword of justice, should become a word synonymous with today's meaning of openness and of being avowed. For the Franks this became a symbolic legacy akin to one's hand on the Bible, swearing by Almighty God the affirmation of truth.

The Frank dynasty was fundamental in the creation and evolution of statehood, where following the decline of the Carolingian period in Normandy the use of Lex Salica and the establishment of legislation ensuring law and order was paramount.

The Extraordinary Franks

For the Franks, their name became synonymous with statute, justice and truth, the name Frank or of being frank, rapidly becoming part of everyday language used both by the state and the Church.

The word 'frank' became the most used adjective shown extensively in charters and other legal documents, derivatives of the word meaning 'avowed' used in many hundreds of thousands of records and later an ink-stamp, hence 'franked letter' and so on. In terms of medieval history Francus meant 'free' as only the Franks had full freedom in Gaul. Today, Frank is used severally as a name for a country, a word, a currency, an official ink-stamp, a first name and a surname; all derived from former Franks and that sovereign-reign.

From the University Library of California, A D Weld French writes: 'In regard to the early use of these names, from the Latin word Francus, with the addition of suffixes, we have the following compound words Franc-ensis, Franc-iscus and Franci-gena and that by reducing the ns to s we have Francesis in the seventh century, by reducing the s, Franceis in the tenth century, and Francais in the twelfth century. From Francus or Free, derives the French surnames of Le Franc and Le Franceis; and later, owing to changes to language orthography, Le Francois and finally Francais.'

The connotation of a surname meaning 'free' is important in the recognition of it becoming synonymous with words associated with honesty, quietude, diligence and strength of character, characteristics seemingly in conflict with the warlike might, destiny and strength of purpose wielded by the earlier German tribal warlords. One such warlord, the first prominent Frank, was Chlodio le Chevelu, son of Theudemeres, Chlodio being the first warlord to be named Rex Francorum, King of the Salian Franks in 428–448 CE.

While the Merovingian dynasty started with Chlodio, France itself only came into existence with another Frank, Clovis I in 481 CE. Although the Franks converted to Christianity under Clovis, they continued to bury their dead with their possessions, where excavation of graves in what was north-east Gaul, has revealed the wealth and great status of their owners reflected in their weapons and jewellery.

A vast collection of artefacts can be viewed at the British Museum and from donations of one's family namesake, the late Sir Augustus Franks, among whose jewellery is a replica of Chileric's gold signet ring, taken from the original at the Ashmolean Museum at Oxford. I mention elsewhere the battleaxe as an invention of the Franks, a highly decorated example of which might also be found at the British Museum whose online site is also worth a visit.

In all, there were nineteen true Merovingian monarchs who ruled until 737 CE. Born in 466 CE, Clovis united the disparate Frankish kingdoms as well as most of Roman Gaul under one rule. Conquering Soissons, held by the Roman general Syagrius, he also took the Visigothic Kingdom of Toulouse. Taking his seat in Paris, his main residences included Soissons, Reims, Metz and Orleans. Clovis reign until his death on the 27th November 511 CE, the kingdom being split among his four sons.

These were: Chlothar I having Soisssons; Childebert I, Paris; Chlodomer, Orleans and Theuderic I, Reims and Austrasia. Theuderic reigned from 511 to 534, thence passing to his son Theudebert I from 534 to 548, and his son Theudebald from 548 to 555, when Reims and Austrasia passed to Soissons, Orleans passing to Soissons in 524, and Paris in 558, when Chlothar inherited all of the Frankish kingdoms, the kingdom only to be split again among Chlothar's four sons upon his death in 561.

The sons were: Chilperic I having Soissons (becoming Neustria); Charibert I, Paris; Guntram, Orleans (becoming Burgundy), and Sigebert I, Reims and Metz (becoming Austrasia). Chilperic reigned from 561 to 584, his son Chlothar II reigning from 584 to 629. Charibert reigned from 561 to 567 when Paris was partitioned, the city eventually passing to Soissons. Guntram reigned from 561, his kingdom passing to Reims and Metz in 592. Sigebert reigning from 561 died in 575, his kingdom passing to his son Childebert II in 575, thence to Guntram's son Theuderic II, who ruled until Reims and Metz passed to Orleans in 612, all three of Reims, Metz and Orleans passing back to Soissons in 613.

War was ever-present, and Chlothar II in defeating Brunhilda and her grandson, reunified the kingdom. Yet in 623, in order to appease the quarrelsome factions and secure borders, he gave the Austrasians his young son Dagobert to serve as their king. Dagobert I emulated this clever move by reuniting the kingdoms under one rule, appointing a sub-king for Aquitane. Dagobert ruled from 629 to 634, Charibert ll, son of King Clotaire ll ruling Aquitaine as an appointee from 629 until April 632 when he died aged only 14, the kingdom becoming autonomous until 634.

In 634, Dagobert I still had Neustria and Burgundy, Sigebert III, of Sigebert pedigree, having Austrasia until 656. Clovis II had Neustria and Burgundy from 639 until 655, his son Chlothar III ruling until 673. Childebert the Adopted had Austrasia from 656 to 661, Austrasia again being inherited by Chlothar III, but being passed on by him to Childeric II in 662.

Childeric unified rule and had Neustria and Burgundy in 673, and Austrasia until 675, but was displaced in Neustria and Burgundy by Theuderic III until Childeric's death in 675. Austrasia was ruled by Clovis III from 675 until 676, and by Dagobert II until 679, when Austrasia was once again reunited under Theuderic III.

Theuderic ruled Neustria and Burgundy from 675, ruling a united kingdom from 679 until 691. And now having emulated Clovis l in bringing his kingdom under proper rule, he became undoubted king of all the Franks.

But for a brief period of civil turmoil there was a unity that continued to flourish. Instead of arguing, the two sides were brought together as a single entity, the inventiveness of the Franks opening the way to a period of great advancement.

The Extraordinary Franks

Son of Theuderic, Clovis IV reigned from 691 until 695, his brother Childebert III from 695 until 711, and his brother Dagobert III, ruling from 711, aged eight, until his death 31st December 715, aged sixteen. His cousin, once removed, Chilperic II, reigned until 720, when Dagobert III's son, Theuderic IV, also aged eight, took reign, his father having died five years previously.

From this it's clear that life was short-lived, the paramount need for heirs being the reason for boys to marry a chosen girl prior to or immediately upon reaching puberty. Theuderic died around March or April of 737 aged twenty-five when an interregnum of six years took place. Absence of a living heir caused Childeric III to accede in 743 until his death in 752. Although blood related, Childeric, not being of descent, was at best a stand in, and it was becoming clear the Merovingian line had run its course, the way being set for a new dynasty, a dynasty that had been forming from 623 through Pippin of Landen, Mayor of Austrasia from 623 to 629 and from 639 to 640.

Starting with Pippin I in 623, the succession of mayors loyal to the Merovingian monarchy was followed by Grimoald I, then Pippin II of Heristal, who following the conquest of Neustria at the Battle of Tertry in 687, took for himself the title dux et princeps Francorum. Pippin II, Duke and Prince of the Franks, was followed by Drogo of Burgundy whose rule passed to Grimoald ll. Theudoald ruled from 714 to 716 and Charles Martel until 741. Rule passed to Carloman from 741 until 747, then to Pippin the Short who in March 752 was proclaimed King of the Franks

But before this, around AD 711, at a pre-eminent point in history, the Franks were to exert their strength against the rapid and powerful advance of North African Arabs. The enemy was a Muslim horde of invaders, who having been seen moving rapidly northward through Spain, had advanced beyond the Pyrenees and having taken Narbonne, had propelled inexorably forward into Burgundy, also conquering Bordeaux.

The France and Europe we know today owes a huge debt to the Frank of yesteryear. In AD 732, having destroyed a church near Poitiers, it was at Tours that the victorious Muslim army confronted the Franks. It was on this spot, under the command of the illegitimate son of Pepin, Charles Martel, that battle ensued and where the relentless Muslim advance was halted, reversed and pushed back into Spain. The Muslims were never again able to regain prominence, and following an uprising of Berber tribes, soon began their retreat. Yet, having been so enriched, it is fitting to commend the heritage of Moorish-Islamic culture, art and language bestowed upon Spain by their uninvited Islamic guests.

Frank intervention had prevailed, Charles the Hammer was a brilliant general and was seminal in the creation of feudalism and the formation of knighthood. Grandfather to Charlemagne, it was through the descendants of Charles Martel, using

Martel's first name Carolus, the Carolingian monarchy was formed. And hereafter, named after the great man, Frank succession seemed assured.

Effectively, the office of mayor had disappeared; Pippin III had ascended the throne as monarch, and through the proclamation the Carolingians had displaced the Merovingians as the ruling dynasty. Pepin the Short ruled from 752 to 768, and until 771 Carloman I ruled, followed by Charlemagne himself.

Charles I, Charlemagne, Emperor of the Holy Roman Empire, ruling at first Neustria and Aquitaine, being northern Austrasia, between 768 and 814, became King of the Lombards in 774 and Emperor in 800, until 814. Louis I, called the Pious, ruled alongside Charlemagne between 813 and 814, and as Emperor and King of the Franks until 840, many divisions having been made to the empire during his tenure.

Between times a series of mass baptisms forced upon swathes of reluctant Saxons culminated in the treaty signing of 777. Immediately the Saxons rebelled Charlemagne unleashed the mass execution of close to 5000 of their kind, succeeding in bending all of the Germanic tribes to his will. Details better described elsewhere than this snapshot, in his actions Charlemagne succeeded in defeating the Bavarians, the Frisians, the Alemanni and the Thuringians.

German practice was to divide the father's holdings among his sons, and it was through Charlemagne's only son's progeny of four boys that the empire was divided in two: the French half, consisting of most of modern-day France, was Romanised, speaking dialectic Latin; the German half speaking a form of German not too dissimilar to today. In 842, the oath of Strasbourg was written in both German and French in recognition of their division. While the French portion remained united, the German half broke into a muddle of independent states that remained discordant, amazingly, not being reunited until as late as 1870.

It was during the ninth and tenth centuries the Franks devised an overlord form of localised government. Called the manor system, it was by this method the long string of French kings held the unity of the Frankish Kingdom, and it was through the loyalty of a majority of lords of the manor that the Frankish Kingdom evolved, becoming France; the Hundred Years War merely completing the process.

The feudalistic manorial system was basically a town or group of villages owned and completely controlled by a noble who might be a knight or of higher rank. The noble ruled and supplied justice, controlling the milling of grain and iron smelting, as well as the production of food and fodder. While the system favoured the unification of France, the earliest manor system evolved in Germany, where by the eighth century the heavily armed and increasingly insurmountable Frankish warrior had evolved.

The Extraordinary Franks

The Franks had taken the concept of armed horsemen to a new level. Having bred larger horses, and by reducing the weight of their armour and honing their weaponry to the needs of the horseman, they had demonstrated superiority over any infantry force in Europe, including the Romans who by now had lost much of their earlier discipline. It would be five centuries before any effective infantry would be created that could take on and beat the man on horseback.

By the ninth century, the Franks had gone further: their kings, in combining their invention of the manor system and with the system of knights providing trained soldiers for the Crown who could be called upon to raise an army in local positions of authority; an army that by 1066, combined with the skill and knowledge of combative Norsemen, could wield such mortal effect upon England.

It was through the inventiveness of the Franks that the Normans had perfected the close-quarter infantryman, and the methods of 'shield and pike' wall defences that were sufficiently mobile as to handle hilly terrain and manoeuvre and remerge, making it difficult for horsemen to charge uphill. Used to great effect, in England the Normans' combination of Yorkshire yeomen, bowmen and Swiss pike-men, supported by the ruthlessness of knights on horseback, were later to prove insurmountable. It wasn't until 1340 during the Hundred Years War against the French, during the battle of Sluts and later at Agincourt in 1415, that the English longbowmen had at long last perfected their supremacy.

I mentioned the empiric split between Germany and France, yet during the ninth century the split had also caused the creation of a Middle Kingdom ruled by Lothair from 843 until his death in 855, a realm further divided between his three sons. Louis II succeeded as emperor, receiving Italy, ending his reign in 875. Lothair II, having the northern-half of Middle Francia, becoming Lorraine, ruled until 869. And Charles, being the youngest, received Burgundy, ruling as king until 863.

To the east was the Eastern Kingdom, later to become known as Germany. It was ruled by Louis II as emperor from 843 until 876, when it was divided between his three sons. Carloman took Bavaria, ruling until his death in 880, in addition becoming King of Italy in 877. Louis III, called the Younger, became King of Saxony, and of Franconia and Thuringia until 882, inheriting Bavaria from his brother Carloman in 880. Having become emperor in 881, Charles the Fat became King of Swabia, Alemannia, and Rhaetia, until 887, inheriting the remainder of East Francia from his brother Louis in 882.

Charles II's deposition saw East Francia going to his nephew Arnulf, who between 887 and 899 became King of Italy, becoming emperor in 896. A further split saw Ratold becoming King of Italy in 896, and Zwentibold as King of Lotharingia between 895 and 900. Louis the Child succeeded in 899, ruling until 911. Louis was the last East Frankish ruler, and effectively the last of the Carolingians, being succeeded by Conrad of Franconia and the Saxon Ottonian dynasty.

THE ROBERTIANS (LINKS TO FOREBEAR ROBERTUS FRANCAIS CUM FRAUNCEYS)

The Robertians were the original Frankish predecessors to the ruling houses of France, their members being the forefathers of the Capetian dynasty. In owing fealty to the Carolingians holding power of West Francia, they were later succeeded by their own Robertian lineage, the house of Capet itself. The family frequently named its sons Robert, and it's from this pedigree that a forgotten son, Robert of Frankrike briefly emerged, only to be immediately lost to history, yet unbeknown even to himself, Robert became likely father to a future Frank heritage whose unlikely author may have become its storyteller today.

In only being able to source scant information on Robert Frankrike, his very existence seems to have been the linchpin between that great dynasty and all that follows in demonstrating continuance of both the names Robert and Frank throughout history, from its very earliest beginnings through to the present day. The reader will later appreciate the significance of the name Robert in relation to both the Franks and de Brus as a joint family name.

But what of the Western Kingdom and the name France, its name taken from the Franks: it is from France that the Normandy story evolved and the invasion of Britain took place. Charles ll 'the Bald' of France, King of Italy, was Emperor of the Roman Empire from 875 until 877. Preceding him, Louis ll the German ruled from 858 to 875 upon his father Lothair I's death. Lothair had led his brothers Pippin l and Louis ll in several revolts against their father Louis l in an attempt to make their half-brother Charles ll co-heir to the Frankish Empire. On the death of Louis l, Charles ll and Louis ll joined forces against their brother Lothair which conflict led to the break-up of the Frankish Empire. This break-up laid the ground for the development of modern-day France and Germany.

Louis lll, son of Louis ll, ruled the Western Kingdom jointly with his brother Carloman ll 879–882, Carlman succeeding Louis upon his death and ruling until 884. Charles lll, the Fat, who reigned until 888 was succeeded by Odo of France who reigned for ten years until his succession by Charles IV, the Simple, in 898, Robert I reigning for a single year from 922 until 923.

Being a crutial time for the appearance of names, Odo was of the House of Robertians, his father being Robert the Strong, Duke of the Franks, Marquis of Neustria and Count of Anjon, hence come the prominence of the name Robert. It was for his skill in resisting a Viking attack upon Paris between 885 and 886 that Odo was chosen by the western Frankish nobles to be made their king. Overthrowing Charles the Fat, Odo was crowned in February 888.

Hugh Capet was the first true King of France. Son of Robert ll he was born in 972 and died in 1031, his son being Henry I of France.

The significance of first names in relation to continuance and ancestry is worthy of attention. Across the royal family, second, third, or even fourth marriages were not uncommon and dalliances such as taking a mistress, together with a plethora of illegitimate births, was rife. Christian names such as Robert, used each side of the blanket, were used generationally within a recognised family pedigree, where illegitimacy didn't necessarily stand in the way of advancement.

Born in 866, Robert I was the posthumous son of Robert the Strong, Count of Anjou, and brother to King Odo. They were powerful landowners at a time when West Francia was in a state of evolution, over time becoming France.

So where did the name Robert spring from, and what was its source? Count Robert and Odo's family were a prominent Frankish predecessor family who ruled the Frankish Kingdom, through whom Hugh Capet founded the Capetians and thence the Bourbon dynasty, becoming founders of the Second French Republic, 1848–1852, and until this day still rule Spain and Luxembourg.

Hugh Capet was the first true King of France. Son of Robert ll he was born in 972 and died in 1031, his son being Henry I of France.

The Robertians, or Robertines, originated in the county of Hesbaye around Tongeron, Belgium, the succession being Robert of Hesbaye whose son married Ermengarde, daughter of Ingram and her husband Louis the Pious; not a nice man. Robert of Hesbaye's son, also Robert, sired Robert of Worms who in turn sired Robert the Strong, Count of Paris, who sired Robert and Odo, both of whom became kings.

Prior to succession, Robert I had secured the office of dux Francorum, a military dignity of high importance. He later defended northern Francia from the attacks of Norsemen, defeating a large band in the Loire Valley in 921. Not content at his victory, Robert saw the defeated invaders kneeling before the cross. Being converted to Christianity, they and their families eventually settling near Nantes. From this it is easy to see how the modern-day version of the name Robert Frank came into being and the strong indication of a link via Robertus Francais of the Cotentin and the family predecessor spelling of Robertus having been derived from the Robertians.

But Charles the Simple was king, and this was too much to bear for Robert. Taking up arms, and supported by the clerics and powerful Frankish nobles, he drove Charles into Lorraine, taking the crown for himself as King of the Franks, Rex Francorum, at Rheims 29th June 922.

These were turbulent times; Robert's elevation angered the Viking Rollo, who was allied to and loyal to Charles. Brought together near Soissons, battle ensued and, leading his men, Robert was killed, but his army won the battle and captured Charles. Charles remained in captivity until his death in 929. The question remains, what of the deceased Robert, his kin and successors? And from what source did the Roberts of Cotentin and their lands evolve that gave such prominence? For answers we have to bear in mind the intertwined estates of the Franks and Bruce who shared their forebears name and were later to perpetuate the interfamily Christian name into modern parlance.

It is significant that the blood ties belonging to both Robert's families were carried forward generationally, the prequel of a highly unusual bond of mutual affection perpetuated over centuries, where seemingly both families emanated from a single source. Records repeatedly refer to both the Franks and de Bruce being indicated as brothers or kin. How this bond succeeded generationally is probably not as puzzling as one might think.

As stated elsewhere in this work, coming from their Norman roots, and in observing the aloof bearing of current-day Franks, the ease and demeanour each of the Franks and de Brus enjoyed in each other's company seems to imply a kinship beyond that of routine friendship.

In the Cotentin, the name Frank being of such elevated provenance, its antecedence appears to be through Eudes, or Odo, Count of Paris, 882–888, King of Western France, the conduit being his youngest son Robert. Odo was born in 852 and died 898. A son of Robert the Strong of Margrove of Neustria, Neustria being north-west France, Count or King Odo had five sons, Raoul, who became King of Aquitaine, Prince Leopold and his brothers Arnulf and Guy, both Princes of Frankrike equivalent to Frankland.

Appendix 6 shows a map of early Frankland indicating Neustria and the Cherbourg Peninsular, and as indicated in Appendix 3, is where one's ancestor Robert Francais, Robertus de Bruce and their generational predecessor Robert the Strong originated. The map showing Neustria, situated between the Seine and the Loire, is where Robert the Strong held most power. Further south is Aquitaine, which was held by Odo's son Raoul.

Robert of Frankrike was the fifth and youngest son of King Odo or Eudes, and despite the name Robert being used abundantly thereafter within the ruling class, specific information as to his marriage and children escape me. Living around the area of what became the Cotentin, Robert de Frankrike, was born somewhere either side of 891, the name Robert having links with the name Franceis, as in Robertus le Franceis d' Abrincis of the Avranches, Normandy. And whereas it can't be ruled out, the Abrincis great pedigree of today has no proven connection with one's own line of succession.

The Extraordinary Franks

However, derivatives of the name Frank are shown to have perpetuated in the same location of Normandy forward to its modern equivalent in Yorkshire and Frankisland in Scotland. William Longsword having been murdered in 942, his illegitimate son Richard I succeeded. Known as 'the Fearless', he reigned until 996. In previously mentioning Scotland, coins bearing the Duke's name have been found in just that location and as far away as Russia.

Then there is the Germanic Frankrike meaning France and France itself with *rike* meaning empire or realm, a name at once synonymous with that country. Being the youngest of five sons, it is easy to see how Robert de Frankrike had been happy to settle in the Cotentin and raise a family distant from the conflict that prevailed, while still bearing the distinction of that royal name and heritage. But was he father of all that followed?

Taking a snapshot of the Cotentin from 911 to 1309, it is remarkable to see how the individual name-spelling of the original name Frank, taken from Frankrike, has been individualised in terms of identification. Assuming Robert Frankrike had lived to fifty-five, would take us to 933 with a son aged thirty-seven named Robert.

Suggestive of today's family having a royal connection is the period in which Robert's son was growing up; their relation Charles the Simple, King of the Franks, having created the Dukedom of Normandy in Falaise in 911. Falaise being the first city of the new Duchy, it was conveniently situated in the middle of the wide spread of Frank and de Bruce estates, and where William the Conqueror was born in 1027 not far from Bayeux. In terms of ancestry, indications are strongly in favour of a close family connection; the aforementioned showing one possible scenario how the name Robert Francais/Fraunceys originated, where shown as a knight, given the cost of training, such a boy would likely been of wealthy parentage.

By now the name Robert had been used extensively for male heirs across an ever-expanding ruling class. Spelling of the name Fraunceys pre-1066 would have shown as Franceis or similar, which for Robert would likely be a place name or assumed. The proliferation of the name Robert verses the rarity of Franceis has made the task of deciphering likely candidates from the scant records of ruling families near impossible. The families were massively interrelated and naturally accepting of a couple or so concubines, while turning a blind eye to other dalliances as if on a whim.

Whether unrecorded or recognised, given the level of illegitimate births such as William the Conqueror, the more probable outcome for Sir Robertus Fraunceys is that of bastard. While William was fully recognised and taken into the family, others were not so lucky, finding themselves on the periphery, on the one hand of high-ranking paternity but subject to the sub-level rank of knight as opposed to count, duke, etc.

The double whammy of questionable birth, while foisting the popularly used family name of Robert together with the distinctive but more rarely used Franceis, for a time rendered the puzzle of placing Robert definitively hazardous. Added to this is the scant survival of Norman documentation; where, next to the loss of official records, is the appalling loss of archive data of the bishoprics and cathedrals such as L' Abbey Saint-Vigor de Cerisy near Bayeux, many having lost practically everything from this period.

Part surviving are the ducal charters of Cerisy and Montivillers ascribed to Robert, Duke of Normandy, succeeded by William the Conqueror in 1042. Among these are those of Saint Amand, Rouen (1030), and Cerisy (1032), on the coast west of Rouen; Cerisy-la-Foret being established as a convent in the diocese of Bayeux. Witnesses commence with the clergy, where working down the list are the household officers and others less defined. Such personages are Osbern (seneschal), Turold (constable) and Robert (*pinerna,* akin to a butler). I mention Robert; as the probable discomposed product of many a duke's extramarital dalliance, Robert would be held close within the household, where the chance of assassination ensured only the most trusted, such as a son, held positions of trust. Pure conjecture determining a direct line with our Robert Frauceys, but I make the point.

I variably mention Rosel, especially in connection with Robert Frauceys's fellow knight Rogrus de Rosel, both of whom were present with de Brus in Yorkshire, and Hugh de Rosel with William the Conqueror around 1066. Rozel is situated towards the west coast of the Cotentin Peninsular, its placement tying in nicely with the Robert de Rosel who granted land to Saint-Sauveur-le-Vicomte, which the Brus family of Brix also patronised, the lords of Saint-Sauveur being hereditary viscounts of the Cotentin, of which Robert or latin *Rotbertus comes* or count, Duke of Normandy was also a patron.

Among many possibilities for Robert Frauceys, being a connection through Viscount Erchembald and his brother Franco who were related to Gunnora, wife of Richard I, as liegemen, we find Erchembaldus Vicecomes (sheriff) donated 'prata de Salhus etin Sarlosville jure hereditario' to the Abbey of Sainte-Trinite de Rouen by charter dated 1030–1035, signed Roberti comitis (earl), Osberni dapiferi (steward), eiusdem Erchenbaldi, Franconis fratriseius (brother) Gisleberti senescalli, and Normanni de Herolcurt. Then there is the charter of Croco, son of Archamband of the family Gunnora, being witnessed by Osmundi de Francaville in 1058, having a possible connection with Robertus Francaville.

Gisleberti was positively the son of Viscount Erchembald. The term 'Normanni' above applies to the duke's household officers, whereby Normanni de Herolcurt, possible son of Erchenbald, held the region south of Saint Pol, an early caput of the later Earls of Derby, where Erchenbald aka Achard II is credited with the founding of Framecourt, a Frank domain. From a series of rough notes in progress; Frame Family Origins, Michael Stanhope 2009, 2010: the Frames, the Umfrevilles, some Fresney, Frenches and positively the Hamiltons (aka Frauceys in Yorkshire) were part of a conglomeration of early Frank settlers of Framecourt, Freschnes and Fresquienne, where DNA matches are consistent with Franco, Franconis (above), Franz, Franklin, French, Franc, and Franceis, becoming Frauceys and Frank.

Looking to Robert Frauncey's post-invasion companions for affirmation as to parentage, and pinning down one or more of his brother knights to a specific Normandy location, among the Brus tenants making gifts to the monks of Guisborough were Alvred and Roger de Rosel of the Cotentin Peninsular together with Theobald and Wydo de Lofthus, Lofthus being today's Loftus in Cleveland. A Hughe de Roussel (Rosel) was with William the Conqueror during the invasion as was William de Feugeres, Feugeres being situated some forty miles from Brix, Normandy.

This same William de Feugeres held descendant 'chief' of the manors of Castle Leavington, Cleveland and neighbouring Brierton in Hartness, held of de Brus, which feudal ancestry of Hart was added to my great-grandfather's name of Frank in the twentieth century. To these names should be added the above Rogrus de Rose, also known as *Roger de Franceis* and Rogrus de Rosel together with brothers *Willielmus le Franceis and Osmo La Franceis*, found in Yorkshire having the lordship of Rosell in the Cotentin, Normandy.

From the *Index Armorial*, Willielmus and Osmo la Franceise are located in later dates in the nearby bailiwick of Bessin, and also Mathew le Franc and Hubert de la Franche together with Ricardus, Willielmus and Arnoldus-le-Franc. Also of later date, found in the bailiwick of Oximin, are Robertus and Johannes Le Franc and Willielmus cum Franceis or Francus and Walter in Pont-Audemer, to the east of Caen towards Rouen, Rouen being immediately adjacent the settlement of Freschenes, John Le Franc being at adjacent Pont Arche, and Osbern de Fresch at nearby Pavilly.

Generationally these distant relatives were located in Normandy some 130 years following the invasion. We might add to that another twenty years plus for possible insights into Sir Robert's parentage, the generational repeat of familiar names returning to their family fiefs in Normandy, while retaining their Yorkshire ties, provide insights and likely clues.

The following shows how spellings of the name Frank were individualised over a period of around 400 years:

Robert de Frankrike	900 (about mid twenties in age)
Charles the Simple de Frankrike, King,	911
Franconis	1030 (Rouen)
Franco	1058
William the Conqueror	1066
Robertus Francaise	1066
Robertus de Brose or Bruise	1066
William Francise, the Shambles, Falaise	1124 (living next door to Gervase Cornet)
De Franca	1136
Franco	1136
Francus	1147–1153
Franco & de Franca	1155
Franc	1252–1334
Le Francois	1272
Franceis	1298
Le Franc	1309

To add confusion, somewhere within these derivative spellings are de Fresch and Freschenes, belonging to a cluster group to the north-east around Pavilly and Fresquienne. But we are talking about seven or so generations between that of the first Robert de Frankrike and the invasion of Britain in 1066, and, from that, the emergence of Robertus de Bayeux cum Francaise aka Frauncey, knight to the first Robert de Bruce.

But returning to Robert's namesake Robert I, dux Francorum, who now deceased, gave way to the new monarch Rudolph, who ruled between 923 and 936. Robert's wife Beatrice of Vermandois, daughter of Emma of France, had a son, Hugh, who grew in stature emerging as Hugh the Great, dux Francorum, father of Hugh Capet, being crowned King of the Franks, Rex Francorum at Noyon in Picardy, 3rd July 987.

And while historians agree the coronation of Hugh Capet as the beginning of modern France, the royal bloodline of Rex Francorum had effectively broken up. Superceded by the Capetians in 987, the Carolingians dispersed in small numbers, where a couple or so families settled in Normandy, making sense of the idea of Robert Frankrike as a possible pater among the earlier, more scattered, Franks and the cluster formed in the later settlement of Fresquienne.

However what later emerges is that Robertus Fraunceys, as he later became known, might have been a likely son of Roger de Bayeux, descendant of Richard I, Viscount de Cotentin; the future Robert Fraunceys having been trained from the age of seven or eight for knighthood, having substituted the family place name of de Bayeux for a derivative combination of Fresquienne, de Fresch or Frankrike, Robert now being of that place. To add to the confusion, come the invasion, it is probable a number of knights may have altered their names representing coming from France, hence de Franc, le Franceis and similar, the invaders becoming known as Frenchies or Frani.

Of Roger de Bayeux (954–1074) and his son Robert's late birth around 1048, being one among a number of Roger's illegitimate children may have been akin to drawing the short straw, son of a lord but insignificant in terms of age or rank, to be raised other than a mere knight. Robert's two companion knights 'et tres suis militibus Rogerus de Rosel, Wydo de Lofthous et Roberus Faunceys' Roger and William I later ascertain as brothers, seem likely to have been raised together from early childhood and trained inseparably in the manner of brother knights. Of Sir Robert's two companions, Rogrus de Rosel, namesake of Roger de Bayeux, could hardly be other than a near relative; here I have made the decision to accept the existence of all three knights as true brothers in service to the Brus. For the purpose of this work it hardly matters whether all three knights were father-related, especially seeing the confusion of bastard births prevalent within the Bayeux family at large and those connected with them.

The position of Fresquienne, immediately north of Rouen, lies central to the broader scattering of Frank settlement, its very name a derivative of the people who settled and their rulers. Originally thick woods surrounding Rouen, north of Rouen the territory was dense and full of game, handy for huntsmen and those bent on claiming it as their fiefdom. Research into Fresquienne finds its origin in the archaic settlement of Rouen by the Viking Rothomagus, from whom the place was named. And while Charles the Simple de Frankrike of the Carolingian dynasty ruled, he lost Western France to Raoul d'Ivry, brother of Rollo the Viking, whereby Rollo was made Duke of Normandy, who under his baptism assumed the Robertian Frankish name of Robert, the Frankrike name thus conveniently utilised.

Throughout this research, facts kept returning to Richard I de Saint Sauveur, Viscount de Cotentin, that domain and the area north of Rouen, where a story began to emerge assisted in no small part from details gleaned of Sir Francis Palgrave's work found under 'Historia de Fresquienne' from *A History of the Normans of England Volume Two*, which provides great insight. Foresta de Roumare surrounding Rouen provided Rollo and his descendants constant sport, recreation and great hunting, extending to its city walls.

Now considered to be the palace park, adjacent Chevilly provided less dense cover and shady glens, more calming than the awe inspiring Foresta de Leonibus, Nemus de Leonibus and Sylva Leonum. Among these the Foresta de Leonibus was so dense it offered natural fortification and defence from hostilities, the area being traversed by a single narrow road where deer and boar constituted a huntsman's paradise for Rollo and his son Guillaume, it being here that Guillaume de Fresquiennes built a hut near the Morte-Mer, tilled the ground and peacefully cropped its produce.

By degrees, among a mix of mainly Frank settlers, a small *bourgade* was founded where forest courts ensued, aided by the construction of a church, the lodge itself being replaced by a castle. Although himself a mix of Viking and Frankish blood, among his chieftains and liegemen, Guillaume's contingent contained three princes of France; while being welcomed, they were content to be under the protective auspice of such fearsome Viking rulers within the forest chamber.

Chief among these guests were Hugh-le-Grand and Herbert de Vermandois, who between them asserted unchallenged precedence over the company, burning with inward rivalry, each contriving to further his own power. My hope here is to explain the confusion of more than one Capet; Hugues 'le Grand' (Hugh 'The Great' 'Magnus' Capet) de Paris copte de Paris, Duke of the Franks 898–956, was son to Robert I of France. Hugh le Great, sometime Grand of Paris, married Hedwig when he was forty, their son being Hugues 'capet' Roi Des France, 941–996.

Herbert, Count of Vermandois, Meaux and Soissons, was also a direct descendant of Charlemagne but of a lower order. Indignant of his lower standing and bursting with a false sense of pride he contrived marriage to a daughter of King Robert I and it was through this union he obtain the county of Meaux.

Despite having an intermix of matriarchal Frank blood, among such company and as the son of a Viking, Duke Guillaume grieved not being entirely of Frank nobility, his bloodline viewed as that of a buccaneer, insufficient and less refined. While through his mother's line this was untrue, the male line reigning paramount, such disparity caused him to seek female company other than the several more esteemed marriages on offer.

Doting on Espriota, quote, 'a damsel of low degree, *a mean hustrue*', Espriota was actually a Breton captive-cum-concubine and, although most probably well-versed in the sexual arts, could never be considered an equal or of sufficient rank to be at Guillaume's side in marriage. Yet besotted via a heady mix of desire, sex and the birth of two children, he remained reluctant to cast her off despite the gnawing disutility of not being a Frank tearing at his conscience.

Yet the offer of marriage to Liutgarda, Countess of Vermandois, her mother Adele being the daughter of Robert I of France, was too much: he would deal with Espriota as his father Rollo had dealt with Guillaume's mother in accepting the proposal of marriage. Hence in continuance of the grand alliance of Normandy, the espousal conducted in the Palace of Rouen, took no worth of Espriota's existence.

The following an excerpt from Sir Francis Palgrave, 'Historia de Fresquienne': 'Now Guillaume could feel accepted, and had the noble science of blazonry then existed, it would have displayed the golden leopards of Normandy quartering Vermandois, check or and azure a chief of the second, three fleur-de-lys of the first, and no pursuivant.' Pursuivant meaning follower or a rank below, *absentia pousivre* showed the holder as being second to none. I mention the significance of the fleur-de-lys, *symbolus inventio le Franc,* elsewhere in this work *emblematique de Franc..*

While accepted as a concubine, Espriota aka Sprota must have felt bereft, unable to be endured at the palace, her child was removed out of sight and far away. Yet despite the snub, her firstborn, the illegitimate Richard the Fearless de Espriota, born 28th August 933 became first Duke of Normandy. Twelve years later, his mother living in her own household in Bayeux, Sprota gave birth to Raoul around 945. The events of history moving quickly, as second ruler of Normandy, William Longsword as he had become, in pledging loyalty to King Louis IV, had confirmed lands previously belonging his father restored. Almost three years later he was ambushed and killed by Arnulf while at a peace conference to settle differences.

Now in danger following the death of her lover and the capture of her son, Richard, Count Esperleng removed Sprota from her situation. Having taken Sprota for his own, Esperleng de Vaudreuil, son of Richard I de Saint Sauveur, Count of Cotentin, while born in the Cotentin, died in England in 975 leaving two sons, one stepson, one daughter and a stepdaughter, where generationally I purposely allude to the existence of many additional illegitimate offspring on the precept of several known concubines.

Raoul, Seigneur, Compte d'Ivry et de Bayeux, more truly king of West France was born around 945 at Canville, Canville lying a few miles towards the coast from Rouen, married to Aubree Alberede Eremburge de Canville. Their son Hughes d'Ivry, Bishop of Bayeux, born around 1005, had several illegitimate children to at least two unknown mistresses, one of them giving birth to Roger de Bayeux (approximate date 1025). Data is vague, but Roger is recorded as fathering at least two sons, namely Osbert and Robertus de Bayeux. Robertus, after the popular baptismal name of Robert, born around 1025–1028, is thought to have continued succession through his son Sir Robertus de Bayeux le Francais, aka Fraunceys, born 1047–1049.

Suggestive of this Robert Frank (de Bayeux) being a likely predecessor later located in Yorkshire, further research finds a priest named Osbert, of known Norman descent, shown as the father of Thomas de Bayeux, Archbishop of York 1070–1100, who died in 1100. A later connection is the name Bayeux found in Yorkshire where Robert de Bayeux with Mascy de Curcy and William de Plaiz confirmed a gift made by

John de Plaiz in the City of York 1160–1175. The proposition of Sir Robert and his brother Osbert found in close proximity around York seems conclusive as to this Robert Frank, undoubtedly one and the same.

As family related Bayeux, the de Brus having the fiefdom of York, the connection between the Bayeux found both in Yorkshire and Normandy related to that of Robertus, recorded knight of Robert de Brus, seems irrefutable. Robert de Brus maintained strong connections with the families of Folgeriis de Feugeres to the west of Bayeux and Robert de Vipont de Calvados de Isigny, Bayeux, whose family has present-day northern ties. Around 1066, the name Robert seems to have been shared between the Brus, de Frauncey and de Vipont families, coming from the same area of Bayeux, their appearance in Yorkshire at this exact moment in history argues demonstrably in terms of historical significance.

While all history might be seen contentious, the aforesaid continuum between the current Cleveland Franks and Normandy has proven irrefutable. But relating Robertus de Bayeux-Frauncey; proven his father was Roger de Bayeux, his mother Sprota, his grandfather Hugh d'Ivry and great-grandfather Raoul, king of West France, doubt lies as to the murderous Raoul's real father. Of the two contenders, first is Guillaume whose father was Rollo, second, Count Esperleng de Vaudreuil, son of Richard I, the latter of the two being correct.

Thus we have Robertus Frauncey, found as the third great-grandson of Richard I de Saint Sauveur, Viscount de Cotentin: the Cotentin coming to the fore time and again throughout this work. It should be mentioned that Richard was born in 870 in Maer, Norway, his wife, mother of Esperleng, was actually Richard's niece, Niece de Normandy being of maternal Frank origin, as was Sprota proven by her name-spelling and female DNA indicators.

Returning to the Viking Rollo, he was born around 846 on the Atlantic side of Scandinavia, being known to have traversed Scotland and Ireland prior to the Viking landings in northern France. Although recorded as having several concubines he married Poppa of Bayeux, the daughter of Berenger, Count of Bayeux. Poppa was born in 872, her recorded death in Rouen around 925. Poppa's father died in 896 having previously married a daughter of Gurvand, Duke of Brittany; Gurvand's wife being the daughter of Erispoe, Duke of Brittany, who had battled against the same Franks his erstwhile father Nominoe had battled, his father being Despoyni, King of the Franks, direct descendant of Jesus.

As an aside, Raoul, Comte d'Ivry de Bayeux's wife Aubree Alberede Eremburge de Canville, built the castle of Ivry. What is not clear is where she accumulated sufficient funds, her father Canville de Craux's parentage being a mystery, as are details of his wife. Born in 960, in an attempt to expel her husband from the castle, Aubree was murdered by Raoul in 1010. Having gained a castle, titles and land, as if the absence of Aubree were a mere detail, wonderful Raoul continued life and the business of producing children for another five years prior to his death in 1015 aged seventy.

Research is littered with corrupt data, mistaken antecedence and the like, where absolutes are truly impossible. I have demonstrated possible scenarios concerning a warrior of sufficient status having the name Robert homed with Fraunceys, carrying the distinction of knight alongside one of William the Conqueror's most trusted leaders, Robert de Brus.

This work is adamant on the preposition of Robertus and his line being of wholly Frank descent, yet research shows that to be only partly true, from the female side his bloodline certainly so. Alliances were dependent on intermarriage, whether Viking, Norman, Frank, Germanic or any other combination, then there's the historic propensity for childbirth outside of wedlock. Nonetheless DNA testing is clear regarding Frank antecedence, showing the bloodline to have survived both the test of years and infusion of disparate blood types. My own dear deceased mother Dorothy Frank carried the same washed-out pale grey-blue eyes of the early Normandy Franks, and as frequently said, the family being quite distinctive in both their carriage and manner representative of a class above.

On assumption of the aforesaid family link with Richard I, Saint Sauveur de Cotentin, its heritage is so entwined as to become mind-boggling. Shown on a number of websites, one www.davidkfaux.org/files/deTosnyReport.pdf has proven useful in supporting findings. Hugh de Cavalcamp de Tosny (ancestor de Tosny) a brother of Richard I (ancestor de Beaufou in the female line), the de Beaufou and Tosny male lineage finds a common ancestor in the Viking Chief Eystein, the Tosny in direct line, Richard and Hugh's father Malahuc Eysteinsson being a brother of Ragnavald, whose son Hrolf, namely Rollo Ragnavaldsson, is found ancestor of William the Conqueror.' So intermarriage seems to have graduated towards a common heritage found through the histrionic convolution of maternal filiation and illegitimate births consistent with DNA findings and the effects of bastardisation on judgement calls relating to antecedence.

For me such reveal as the aforementioned, the Franks of today having maternal links with the aforesaid wanton and productive Breton concubine Sprota, seen as directly related seems as good an outcome as any. The idea of such a scurrilous and disreputable past, heaven-sent.

INTERLUDE

But history must be seen in context set against the great players, our past often stroked with maleficence, its aftermath touching centuries. The period under discussion considered death something they had little or no control over, or through constant rage and lust for power a kill or be killed malevolence prevailed in the expediential removal of an enemy, turbulent brother, father, wife, cousin or best friend. And then there is genocide, where familiar names are often plainly writ when the pain of war is present and blood is spilt.

Partly influenced by changing times, Hugh Capet is attributed as having established a class of dynasty set against the pretention of electoral power on the part of the aristocracy. While apparently worthy, it is difficult to reconcile this idea with Hugh Capet's massive personal wealth, him possessing towns and estates amounting to 400 square miles. Hugh died in Paris 24th October 996, his son Robert II continuing the reign.

Whichever way one cuts it, Robert was a vicious cut-throat, mad with power, an outright murderous thug. Too difficult to describe, his marriages were a disaster, but entangled with ever-present Roman Catholic teaching he couldn't rid himself of his current wife. Later, having at last found a way of untangling himself from his latest acquisition, in the process of divorce he was excommunicated. After an interval, having regained approval from Rome, he married Constance of Arles, daughter of William I, which despite his renowned thuggery and bestial appetites, was a long-lasting marriage.

Imbued with an insane sense of religious fervour, Robert II, known intimately as 'The Wise', more widely as 'The Pious', set out to destroy all that stood in the way of his idea of Christ and the Cross. His stance on religion caused him to reinstate the Roman imperial custom of burning heretics at the stake. Such was his fervour; he was in conflict with anything or anyone who failed to succumb to his rule, including his sons, Hugh, Henry and Robert. Hugh having died in battle, it was in the middle of war against his own sons Henry and Robert, their mad father died on the 20th July 1031.

Referring to Robert's idea of warfare and retribution and the Norman propensity for wilful bloodshed and slaughter; a mere thirty-five years later, William the Conqueror, including such cohorts as the de Bruce and the Franks, was party to the same kind of butchery that was to befall England. These were not nice times, and let's not forget, the Franks were past masters of brutal warfare, how else could they have kept their realm than by instilling fear upon those who opposed them causing head-on death and destruction.

Looking at William in context, like so many others of the time, he was the product of his father, Robert, Duke of Normandy's liaison with the beautiful concubine Herleva, and from birth was sufficiently schooled as to be educated and highly intelligent, knowing several languages. Eight-year-old William became duke upon his father's death in 1035 on his way back from a pilgrimage to the Holy Land. But something of his ascendance infused an indomitable manic streak when during a siege at Alencon in 1052, aged twenty-five and faced with some taunters as to his birth, he had their hands and feet chopped off. But like most tyrants this was just the beginning, much worse was to follow.

Prior to this, in 1047, using heavy cavalry and superior skill, supported by the King and letting no quarter against his own clan, he massacred a large bunch of rebel Norman lords at Val-es-Dunes, the bloodlust wetting his appetite for more. I go into more detail as to the cavalry, the Franks in general and more profoundly the genocidal Harrying of the North elsewhere in this work, where William's brute force and physicality shows no quarter in the bestial acts of rape, murder and waste. Even in later years, managing his dual realm from his beloved Normandy, the now corpulent William died in battle while setting fire to Mantes, the chronicler William de Malmesbury stating William's intestines having ruptured when jumping his horse over a ditch. One saving grace was William's Domesday survey of England in 1086, details used in this work.

Relating to modern history, in 1943 one such Frank was notorious Nazi governor-general of occupied Poland, Hans Frank, responsible for the shooting of 17,000 Poles. He boasted if he had to post a sign for every person he had ordered killed, he would have to fell a whole forest. Like most Germans of his ilk, he was also a recipient of the looting of paintings and art treasures across Europe. The book *Monuments Men*, by Robert Edsel (2009), provides a full account of the German people caught up in this blight on humanity. From one's personal experience seventeen years following World War Two, around Munich and into Austria, the Nazi movement remained openly defiant.

Using history as argument, we tend to forget the Teutonic mindset demonstrated when Germany crushed their French neighbours in the war of 1870. Then the consequence of the German occupation of Alsace and Lorraine rendering such a seismic shock to the European balance of power it became the precursor to two world wars. The question is, were these armies the same bloodline as the Germanic tribes who first created France; we hasten to think not, but reality tells us otherwise. Thinking they were invincible, it was the French who first initiated military action, their innate Gallic pride soon knocked on the head as typical French fluff and bluster, their enemy, Germany, succeeding in the unification of a powerful nation-state previously consisting of a cluster of independent entities.

This crushing defeat caused France a mere 140,000 casualties; neighbourhoods having been blown to pieces, the survivors were offered a choice between staying in the conquered territory and becoming German or giving up everything and moving to France. Most of the Jewish population decided to become German, an irony to become iniquitous beyond redemption, within a single child's lifetime, their new-found country become a debauched one-nation factory bent on the genocidal extermination of a race of human beings.

I mention Alsace-Lorraine because of my posting there in 1963, and the extermination of millions of Jews less than twenty years earlier, a race of people that included a semblance of Franks, not forgetting Ann Frank who was herself a Jew. There is no point in denying the past or the involvement of many thousands, even millions, of people across Europe who were complicit or turned a blind eye to this blot upon the heart of mankind. It was in 1870 that the French were making overtures with Russia, seventy years later Russia and Britain were allies, Russia's very survival dependent on supplies sent by Britain via the Artic. Yet it was only seventeen years later, around 1961, when the Cold War with Russia was at its zenith I found myself slouching around BOQ. Wiesbaden awaiting orders.

War is war and Europe seems to have been forever in turmoil. We see France's unsure relationship juxtaposed against their well-ordered German neighbours, strident with their shrill overtones, arrogance and bark of martial command. This assumes a view where France's fluctuating and wavering alliances with the Fatherland might be seen as occasional mistress, prostitute or vengeful grand-madam. Worse, even under German occupation, many were quite happy to collaborate as pimps and whores to a despotic idiom with the Jews a handy outlet for man's own self-loathing, the extinction of the Jews a means by which Nazi cohorts might somehow wash away the filth of their own abomination, their paradise become the bottomless pit of writhing hell and damnation briefly glimpsed in the raving madness of Hitler's last days.

Back in 1031, the dead Robert the Pious's son, Robert, Duke of Burgundy, became known as Robert the Old. Born in 1011, he lived to the relative old age of sixty-five, dying 21st March 1076, some ten years after the Battle of Hastings. Brother to Henry I of France, three times married Robert had rebelled against his father and his brother Hugh Magnus, which following the award of Burgundy in 1032, being little more than a robber baron, and having no control over his own vassals, separately they ravaged the countryside including those of his own estates which he often plundered, especially targeting those of the Church. His venom was such that he assassinated his wife's brother and murdered her father by his own hand. Probably suffering from syphilis, it is said Robert's mind became tormented by visions of the dead visiting him in hell.

In summary, looking back, there had been thirty-five true Frank monarchs, most notable of these being Charlemagne who as the ultimate recognised King of the Franks was also ruler of the Holy Roman Empire. With the abrupt end of monarchic rule, the Franks who survived had mostly exhausted their bloodlust leaving a handful still imbued with a sense of power and authority. Armed with that hauteur, they had no option but to adapt to their current state, bound by a code born of Norman knights and new leaders.

The key turning point in history had come with the dissolution of the Carolingian monarchy, and come 954, Normandy was in the throes of massive turmoil. In pace with the demise of the Frank monarchy, the Northmen Viking invaders' grip on Normandy had now firmly taken over. The Norsemen were powerful and eager to fight and cut to pieces anyone willing to take them on.

Caught betwixt these Northmen and a fading monarchy were those of doubtful royal descent and a somewhat scurrilous and promiscuous king-some-like heritage going by the name Francais, Franco and the like; these extremely literate and capable few, linked by a common heritage of duty, state and Church, fought, held property, farmed and got on with life.

Interspersed with their more established cousins were those of more recent royal descent, fallout from a recent dynasty who, like their cousins, had a fearsome past and a restless need to avenge. Previously shown is the interrelation between the Norsemen and the indigenous population, the causation of new blood feeding the need to face new challenges with sharpened swords and their eyes now firmly set upon Britain.

Flotsam from a past era, the heritage of all held a common past, a past awash with one of the most amazingly violent, blood-let empire-spread the world had witnessed. The spread saw Frankish domination of such diverse regions and titles as Kings of Jerusalem and Cyprus, Counts of Edessa, Princes of Antioch, Counts of Tripoli, Kings of Thessalonica, Dukes of Athens, Princes of Achaea and Grand Masters of various military monastic orders. In addition, rule was placed over Serbia, Bulgaria and New Rome, with Franks serving as Latin Emperors and Patriarchs of Constantinople reaching across the dominion of what was Romania.

These Franks were the offspring of a prolific dynasty, yet with a common sense of purpose and heritage. One can only wonder at their downfall from grace and how quickly they assimilated, the dissolution only confirming their individual self-sufficiency, self-belief and status. As natural providers they were highly capable and as prominent liegemen had a wealth of knowledge that, together with their Norman spirit, infused with Norseman seed, created a hugely intelligent revitalised warrior entity that was supremely ruthless, set upon terrifying merciless war, subjugation and rule.

RIGHTEOUS BELIEF

It seems to me to be a natural consequence that people and the birth of nations can only really develop and learn through collective purges and devastating blood-let, seen in violence, slaughter, torture and war. History's mindset is littered, and we see hate-filled neighbours kill and maim before their conversion as born-again heroes of peace. Countries once purged about-turn in their determination to apply reason from the experience of death and mass destruction. Or do they?

One such example is Louis VII, King of the Franks. He was a zealous man, so vigorous in his prerogatives that his misplaced piety limited his ability as an effective statesman. Yet he had little in the way to bother him and few disturbances other than minor issues brought to attention by the burgesses of Orleans and Poitiers who wished to organise communes.

So pious was Louis, he became inflamed and torn with anger towards Pope Innocent II over the vacant archbishopric appointment for Bourges. The Pope, in turn, imposed an interdict upon Louis, and violent conflict ensued. This was exacerbated by Louis's war with Theobald II of Champagne, the matter merely relating to a marriage suit whereby Champagne sided with the Pope over his choice for the new appointment of Archbishop at Bourges.

In this world, does anything really change; so easily wars of words can quickly escalate into the kind of fundamentalist God and Country bloodshed and wholesale slaughter so quickly evoked today. By example, President Bush of America was such a modern-day fanatic that vainglorious Blair was blind-sided into a blood-soaked holy and prayerful alliance, whose consequences have unleashed modern-day fundamentalist alliances of medieval retribution, whereby, worrying though it may seem, a survey polled by ComRes of 1,000 Muslims in Britain in February 2015, 27% had sympathy for the motives behind the attack upon the Paris cartoonists who portayed their prophet.

While grossly misrepresented and overstated, the continued focus on race and religion is akin to turning the clock back 1000 years, seen through the eye of subjugation, an abomination in direct conflict with free society values enhanced through equality, creativity and invention, aided by ambition, liberal thought and endeavour.

The gap between an increasingly secular Britain and the cloaked dark-age mindset of bearded male domination is a million miles separate from the rest of society as to cause increasing disquiet, alarm and disgust among the bulk of society; a people who are obliged to witness execution upon execution and the wholesale annihilation of innocents, and here the destruction of ancient civilisations in the name of Allah goes beyond redemption.

Who are these people who believe it is them who are under attack when the rest of the world wants to be left alone with their own beliefs and their own ideas of a god, or the concept of none, without interference, where within the certain belief of Islamic dogmatic domination lies a quandary as to whether the Muslim faith can truly release ancient shackles and adapt to a secular world society, and whether the

West can find a way of allowing space and time for different and opposing cultures to evolve without having resort to kinds of wholesale slaughter that inevitably maims and kills innocents.

Without resolution we are as 1000 years before, both East and West bound within an ancient concept of death and religion, as in America's 'God and country' anthem, an excuse as age-old as man himself, placing the idea of God on the side of the righteous whether right or, as so often, darned wrong; as if a despairing god might choose to be on one side or the other during conflict. As with sword raised, it seems a perpetual self-fulfilling prophecy that a combination of indignation and revenge should rule over sense in the instinct of man to strike out child-like in an attempt to draw first blood, thence to ram to the hilt its lethal blow.

But we are not knights, and Louis's war lasted three years from 1141 to 1144, ending with his occupation of Champagne, where he was personally involved in the burning of the town of Vitry le Francois, ordering the burning of a church wherein more than 1000 people had sought refuse and died in the flames, whereas each of Blair and Bush's narcissistic guiles were able to mentally justify their actions in Iraq, the screams of burning humanity being so intense as to drive any man with an ounce of humanity insane. Louis's conscience rendered him overcome with guilt: humiliated by the contempt of all he came into contact with and resolving to atone for his sins, he removed his armies from Champagne declaring his intention to go on a crusade to the Holy Land.

The issue had started with a bunch of people wanting to form a localised form of democracy; the Catholic Church, as ever, had meddled over an appointment they should have kept their nose out of. But in the end, wishing for redemption, during Louis's march towards the Holy Land good relations between the various kingdoms continued to flourish. In the twenty-first century, akin to Louis, Tony Blair's atonement for Iraq started with his conversion to the Catholic faith, kneeling in prayer before the Pope with the idea of conversion fixing things with his maker. Whereas different from Blair, Louis didn't dip into the dosh, but on the whole continued the path of true righteousness.

As for Iraq and now across the Middle East, the determinate pages of history will be the final arbitrator. Condemned, the ink-stained litany assumes an egotistic megalomania, a genocidal madness once released turned upon itself, and once again the age-old story of innocents turned victim. Where through Islam and its aims, and for some its and hate and loathing, every place is seen as the domain of Allah, the genie once released, how swift comes the shadow of retribution.

But pre-1066, peace was far from the minds of the Norman invader – young men across the region stirred in preparation, kneeling before God in prayer, their dreams of glory mixed with dread thoughts of battle, for wasn't God on their side; the side of righteousness.

I have plotted a limited number of Frank families across Normandy and added the de Brus. The map (Appendix 3) demonstrates the widespread settlement of Franks in relation to the manorial landholdings of de Brus. The Brus were of distinguished Northmen decent, had well-proven fighting qualities, were confident and intelligent, and without question natural liege lords held in high regard by their kinsmen. Robert de Brus, as a child and a confidant of the Bayeux/Francais family, restlessly flexing both brain and sinew, must have been straining on the leash, anxious for adventure.

One can imagine how infectious a character de Brus must have been, and for a neighbouring boy, in his imagination being a liege-knight riding alongside such a person, for Robertus Francais the times must have been head-spinning. Pre the invasion of Britain in 1066, if young Robertus had been any older than fourteen or maybe younger, due to the date him first appearing in later documents in England, he would have by then been a very old man, hardly a knight trotting around on a horse in Yorkshire.

Historically it's not unusual to find young boys and girls either betrothed or, as boys, enjoining in battle. But records show that Robertus was a knight and as such would have needed to complete his training. There is no question, in order to join the company of knights, Robertus would have had to reach the necessary standard, it being shown that Robertus joined de Brus later than 1066 seemingly with two other fledgling knights fresh from training.

However, records show at least one member of the family located south immediately following the invasion. This was another William, namesake and kin of William the Conqueror, both finishing knight's training around the same time, both sharing the same tutor. Following the invasion, William de Franceis's wife, Aelizea, gave birth to Alfred, in London in 1070. This dynasty followed the line moving north towards Derby concluding with Sir Robert de Fraunceys of Foremark, Sheriff of Nottinghamshire and Derbyshire. Born in 1357, he died 4th January 1404.

As to the North York Franks; Robert sired two sons, the first, Thomas, born 1382, and Robert born 1386, whose progeny ties with Sir Robert de Fraunceys of Foremark, a Yorkist recumbent knight who died in 1420. Thomas, born of Robert in 1409, sired John in 1425. Now a Sir, John married Isabell Plessington, a wealthy heiress, possessing many estates of her own. John having retired in 1434, records show part of the Franceys/Plessington northern estates passing to their Frankland cousins, and thence down the line, linking with one's immediate family and the post-1066 fledgling knights who joined de Brus north of York, related, one and the same.

HISTORICAL CONTEXT

In order to show the background of events and Frank influence and power, I have taken a step back in history to 925. Prior to being proclaimed king, aged two and due to his father being deposed, Louis IV of Western Francia was taken to England by his mother for safety. Another Frank, Rudolph, Duke of Burgundy, took reign. Following Rudolph's early death, the nobles wishing to prevent Herbert II or Hugh the Black from taking the throne, aged just thirteen in 936, Louis was summoned back to France and eventually crowned. Louis's father was Charles the Simple, his mother becoming Eadgifu of England.

Such was the Frank's power, that to be received as king, Louis first had to take oaths of the legate Franks. Louis was sent to the Frankish Kingdom together with Frank bishops and other followers. Hugh the Great and other Frank nobles met Louis, kneeling in commitment before him, Louis having first been crowned king by Lord Archbishop Artold.

Louis's sovereignty was limited to Laon and some northern areas wholly dependent upon Frank support, it's there that he displayed amazing courage and foresight in obtaining recognition and authority over the various feuding nobles. Louis was aged just thirty-one when he fell from his horse and was killed 10th September 954.

Of Louis IV's offspring there were eight legitimate children. Fifth born, Louis V in 948, following the interim reign of elder brother Lothair, was the last of the true Carolingian monarchy signalling the end of Frank reign. Married aged fifteen to Adelaide, she on her third marriage aged thirty-three, Louis V only reigned for a year leaving no heir. Coupled with the influx of the Vikings, the end of this period was a defining point, seeing the beginning-of-the-end for major Frank influence and rule.

Norman raids on the north-west coast of France during the late ninth century continued to grow in scale, and by 900 the Vikings had secured a permanent foothold on the lower Seine. Rollo, a leader of previous raids on Scotland and Ireland, was ceded land around the mouth of the Seine, what is now Rouen, and within a generation had extended rule westward across Lower Normandy.

Until the mid eleventh century, forceful up-and-coming rulers vied for position in Normandy. Calling themselves counts or dukes, they struggled to establish political hegemony over the indigenous Frankish population. During the hiatus of rapidly shifting alliances and power, these self-professed ruthless and conniving so-called nobles were in a sense little different from the dynastic nobles they supplanted or married in order to take advantage for the purpose of advancement and status.

The first private individual to style themselves as count in Normandy was Rodulf of Ivry, half-brother of the first Duke Richard, predecessor of Robertus de Bayeux de Frauncyes, who assumed the title around 1006. Thereafter, several sons of the duke were similarly designated. One such example is was Viscompte de Argues whose title was identified well before such a position was officially set over the district of Argues. The regions of Normandy, namely the Cotentin, Auranchin and Bessin, produced the greatest number of families of viscompte never possessing a previous countship of their own. Between 1015 and 1035, no less than twenty viscomptes were identified, with the number of trumped-up titles rapidly increasing.

While not always the case, it is true that many a future lord, duke or count's noble house was created on the back of very doubtful bloodlines. The trick of gaining lands, property, fiefs, and great station was by brute force and allegiance, supported by somewhat dubious cobbled-together heraldic duplicity. Many a great house of today has a somewhat creative heritage, whereas, a truly great dynastic line such as the Franks, due to durational diminished self-interest, declining birth rate and clan dispersal, has faded with the whirligig of time. The same being said of their de Brus cousins, who despite their monarchic heritage, the Brus name too has faded.

If the fantastic, historic, genetic heritage of blood-let and bloodline seemed to have diluted or exhausted itself, the surname Frank, its derivative, meaning avowed, must have taken some living up to. What is true, the Frank settlers in Britain, in their quietude, appeared happy enough to take on a more ministerial role. Despite their military heritage, with instinctive ties to the land and Church, they became administrators, monks, fiefmen, yeomen and the like. Exception is found in a small number of breakaway North Yorkshire Franks. Being kinsmen to de Brus, the knight-militaire tenure of 200,000 acres of Scottish land was taken by the sword, aided by a Scottish king and a Yorkshire army. But this was later.

In Normandy, with Norman influence and power on the assent, together with intermarriage and the importance of religion as a means of buying favour with God, the Church held great sway. This was especially true of the mortally ill, elderly or infirm. Being able to purchase blessings through prayer, once sweetened by the amount they paid, or by gifts of land or property, they could have their sins erased through absolution, opening the door to everlasting grace. Based on fear and man-made myths of such magnitude, there is no wonder the wealth of the churches culminated in great feats of architecture.

With skirmishes raging, engendering a kind of stalemate, liaising between Charles the Simple, King of France, and Rollo, first Duke of Normandy, was a relatively little known Frank: a Frank soon to become crucial in the annals of history – Archbishop Franco of Rouen, 910–919. It was Franco who converted the fearsome Viking Rollo to Christianity, and was the amazing man who caused such a powerful murderous and fearful warlord to kneel before him in supplication. Put simply, the conversion was basically a deal whereby Rollo gave allegiance to Charles the Simple in exchange

The Extraordinary Franks

for recognition, also the return of lands recaptured by Charles. However he managed to pull it off, Franco earned his place in history obtaining such a welcome alliance.

There is evidence that Archbishop Franco was a brother of Viscount Erkenbald, both of whom, in relative old age, prior to monastic retirement, were liegemen to young Duke Robert. After a short gap, Duke Robert I of Normandy, himself, became Archbishop of Rouen, Count of Evreux and an unknowing future ancestor of the Franks of Cleveland, North Yorks.

Born 22nd June 1000, Robert Duke of Normandy died 3rd June 1035. During his lifetime and against a background of repeated sexual impropriety and many births he spawned yet another child, the illegitimate William, future conqueror of England. And while it is difficult to legitimise exactly who spawned whom, contemporaneous with William the Conqueror, Robertus Francais was of most certain illegitimate descent, and through Sprota circuitously related to Rollo. Although different in age, William the Conqueror and the young knight were so closely associated they must have known each other. And whereas Robert Fraunceys aka de Bayeux accompanied Robert de Brus, William the Conqueror, founder of the House of Normandy, became King of England.

The family name of Erkenbald, mentioned previously, dates back to Erchembaldus, 590–661, who was Major Domus to King Clovis II of the Franks. The list of interconnecting Franks, interspersed with a myriad of royals and so on is confusing, vastly complex and impossible to provide any meaningful conclusion. First, second and third marriages, mistresses, cousins, children born outside of wedlock or births conveniently assigned, among a mass of documentation consists a listed précis outlining the bare bones of the Franks dating from Capet 987 back to Chlodio, Rex Francorum, first King of the Franks, 428.

Following the time of Archbishop Franco, around 919, was a period during which the population of Normandy had time to get used to their invaders, The Northmen however, were not fully settled, and more than restless, having set their sights on England. Meanwhile, for the dominant classes, normal life in Normandy continued, while post-1066, those in England with possessions to protect in Normandy had an increasingly difficult time keeping what they had before it all came crashing down.

Putting this in context, one has to appreciate the influence and genius of the Frank dynasty being way beyond that of mere monarchy. These were people who were the literal architects of a new world of law and order and the formation of democratic persuasion. It's true that counter to this was a sideshow of ruling class misbehaviour and much worse. Yet dynastic influence extended way beyond the confines of monarchy into the realms of art and invention. And while those modest family groups in Normandy continued the struggle of everyday existence, there was another France, a France built upon true knowledge and of skill born of great minds.

Douglas Frank Blackmore

THE CREATION OF NORMANDY

For this section I have taken inspiration from R Allen Brown's *The Romans,* published in 1984 by Boydell Press. Academically incisive, I would recommend it as not too difficult a read and very useful.

The creation of Normandy as a state grew from the first grant of territory to the Viking Rollo by Charles the Simple around 1060. The date is amazing put in context with the date of 1066, six years later, when Normandy became the strongest feudal principality born out of the divided kingdom of the West Franks.

Although of the same extraction, the Norse were seen as traders whereas Rollo was an all-out Viking warrior, his settlements concentrated along the coast towards the Northern Cotentin imposing a different kind of warrior ruling class. Far more ruthless and skilled in close quarter combat than the French, they established overlordship over the neighbouring areas of seigneurial Main and Ponthieu together with most of Brittany and Boulogne, forming a combined entity of Norse, German and French identity. Utilising the much more advanced militaristic and construction skills of the Franks, they adopted the concept of manorial governance.

From C H Hastings *The Normans in European History*, first printed in New York in 1915, reading as shown: 'After Christianity itself, feudalism is the most important adoption by the Normans from the neighbouring Franks forming the bonds of secular society, holding the whole together in a hierarchy culminating in the prince that includes the abbots and bishops as vassals of the duke by 1066, owing knights to his service from their lands where the oath of fealty was sacrosanct'.

And thus it came to be, the society of the Viking settlers being an open one, they liberally recruited Frankish neighbours and immigrants from far afield, and due largely to a shortage of Scandinavian women Viking men were given to marrying Frankish women in particular. The result was a blood-mix of two or more separate but powerful combinations of DNA, so powerful a mix as would change the world forever.

The Northmen of Normandy became so Gallicised as to become distinctively Norman, more Frankish than the original Franks, culminating in a whole new identity. And as Normans with their dukes in the lead they turned their backs on Scandinavia, their faces, hearts and minds distinctively Frankia. Yet imbued with the lethal combination of Viking spirit and French élan they became increasingly restless, fuelling an overwhelming prepotency towards daring and lust for battle, their pre-invasion land-hunger seen as a quest, becoming a prequel for lethal bloodlust and slaughter.

Whereas most people know of 1066, it is little realised that the Danes invaded Northern England three years later in the autumn of 1069, thus in combination with the English, pushing the Norman invaders south. In retaliation William ordered the complete destruction of land to the west and north of York as far as the River Tees. Known today as the 'Harrying of the North', these were a series of campaigns carried out during the winter of 1069 and well into the early part of 1070. Having set the scene, I deal with this subject in more detail later.

The spirit of Normanitas defined, the original Viking craft of shipbuilding was brought to the fore. Yet for the Franks, the heavy military tactics of war depended on the warhorse or *destrier,* necessitating two horses and heavy armour for every knight, together with the paraphernalia of war requiring heavy ships. The military elite of knights were also the social upper class, the warhorse being specially bred and trained to do a particular job, no movie version of a knight galloping hither and thither gallantly saving young maidens, no, the destrier and its rider were the equivalent of a modern-day tank comprising of a whole battalion of well-trained knights, lethal beyond anything seen before.

The warhorse was led by the right hand and not ridden to the place of battle. The *haukerk* was a long coat of mail and very expensive, as was a good sword. A good sword was not easily obtained due to a shortage of ore and the particular skill needed to fold and refold the red-hot metal over and over again in order to give the finished article a combination of thinness and great strength so as to be able to slice through any opponent and not break. A good sword was everything, being as much a weapon as a symbol of what a knight became, beyond mere mortality, within himself a symbol of righteousness, a chevalier.

But for a child, that aspiration was a long way off, and much like the sword he carried, and being especially chosen, the pre-pubescent boy had to be honed into this other entity, a killing machine. The early skills of horsemanship and arms could only be attained from the tender age of around nine or ten as it is well-recorded that good horsemanship must have been attained well before the age of twelve, as too the fundamentals of weaponry, else the young man would only be fit to serve as a priest.

Such training included the ability to fight in concert with peers, as in the Battle of Britain concept of gentlemen only being suitable as officers. With the Norman knight we're dealing with the ruling class and the spirit of Normanitas that came to conquer and dominate. From this we see the Normans develop from the Frankish lords and militaire together with Latin Christianity and the influx of German, Norse and Viking, combined to form a love of warfare for which the knight was born and bred. It was young men like Robertus Francaise who with his shield and lance became an extremely heavy cavalryman whose ultimate weapon and purpose was the charge, a heady full-on race towards a specifically targeted enemy in unison where no quarter was given and from which there was no escape.

It follows therefore that Robertus Francais must have been born to a particular role in life and trained from an early age. The huge cost of training and weaponry was no mean undertaking, especially with brothers and others of the family also in training. The very name of Bayeux-Francaise confirming their status, this was a special family, and while one can find no evidence of Robertus enjoining the main battle, members of the family were most certainly present, which in the case of the Battle of Hastings brought 2000 knights. Elsewhere and at other times it's certain that 100 knights would be a lot. Often skirmishes would see a handful of knights, and battles fought with fifty or less depending on what number could be mustered for a particular cause.

All the major campaigns were undertaken with the blessing of the Pope, and with Italy as allies it was the Normans who came up with the idea of Holy Wars and eventually the Crusades as a solution to the burning question for the justification of war. War became seen as a battle for Christendom emanating in the birth of Norman ecclesiastical revival as sacrosanct, and the construction of Norman churches with their dioceses, synods, chapter and archdeacons, ruled by the Archbishop of Rouen, the Archbishop in turn being under the close scrutiny and control of the all powerful Duke of Normandy.

The Duke now had his armies, the people, the Church and God on his side in one cohesive entity, where even scholars of the greatness of Lanfranc were attracted to Normandy. This was a time of true revival, where churches and monasteries and the great houses of worship were under construction and where the great beasts of warfare were being fed and groomed and trained individually and in battle array. The destrier were no lightweight animals, these were big handsome brutes, strong in leg and heavy-hoofed, having their own attendants to watch over and hone their temperament for battle.

This was a time of clerics, great writers and architects and monks and musicians, culminating in immense prosperity caused by an ever-expanding population, and out of it an endless supply of sons of all ages ripe for training, many as foot soldiers; the younger ones who would follow on having had longer training would bolster and enforce the occupation. What was coming was no idle skirmish, England was a prize ready for the taking, and once taken would remain under Norman rule no matter how bloody the fighting and regardless the opposition. Born out of Normandy, these were a new type of Frank, a warrior elite led by a revered conqueror named William.

Taken in context, we have to consider that 1066 was only the precursor. This was superseded in 1096 when a large portion of the chivalry of Latin Christendom and of the Franks especially, were riding east to assemble at Constantinople and thence to the Holy Land, their righteous cause Christ and the Crusades, with moral rectitude seen as a virtue in freeing the Holy Land from the infidel. The Franks had rid France and most of Spain of the Muslim horde, their beliefs only intensified by their reawakened invincibility and prayerful absolution, their buildings rising ever higher to the glory of God and righteousness beyond mere mortality.

FRANKISH MASTER BUILDERS

The influence of the Franks in construction is shown through what has today become known as Norman architecture. A builder of some repute, Tom Frank, my grandfather's ancient predecessor influenced the arrival of the Romanesque style of construction. The Franks seemed to have an unparalleled capacity for forms of art and invention, whether through warfare, the state, religion or a combination of all three. These skills, infused with a combination of drive and determination, were pivotal in shaping the modern world through the influence of European architecture. Built in a distinctive Norman style this new form of construction combined borrowed influences such as the Romanesque, identified across Europe today.

Layered stone by stone and brick by brick, it was through the Franks in Western Europe that the Roman architectural tradition survived the collapse of that mighty empire, and where their Merovingian dynasty continued to employ and refine the masonry skills necessary for the large-scale construction of monasteries, churches and palaces. The unification of the Franks under Clovis I and his successors corresponded with the urgent need for more and more churches; the monasteries that controlled them being used as power-houses in the persuasion of the Merovingian Christian ethic.

By 911, the Franks were the masters of horse warfare, refining their battle skills aided by the construction of castles from which they might hold and control lands won. Over the next century, the population of land ceded by the Franks to the Vikings had themselves merged and become Norman, quickly adopting the skills of the Franks, their customs, religion and language d'oil.

The Norman barons first built timber castles on earth mounds, quickly replaced by solid motte and bailey forms of construction and the building of great stone churches, all built in the Romanesque style derived of the Franks.

It is a myth that the influence of the Normans only arrived in England post-1066, the Frankish influence having already affected much late Anglo-Saxon architecture. In 1042, Edward the Confessor, having been brought up in Normandy, brought masons from across the Channel to work on Westminster Abbey, the Abbey being the first Romanesque- or Frank-styled building in England.

Edward was so concerned about the Welsh that in 1051 he brought in Norman knights who built motte castles as a defence. Following the Norman invasion in

1066, the Frankish style was used in the rapid construction of motte and bailey castles supported by a burst of activity in the building of churches and abbeys, and within their castles, the Norman keep.

In Britain, what is called Norman architecture owes itself to profuse development evolved from the Frankish style of Romanesque. Across the land, as well as their fortifications, the Normans built their cathedrals, abbeys, and churches and in the north, massively proportioned monasteries. North Yorkshire was pivotal, and it was here 'come what may' the Normans would hold their ground, using York as a base from which to advance and rule the northern territories.

Their bulwark would be the group of monasteries and abbeys to be built north of York, from Whitby on the coast working inland. In plain view, their monasteries and castles would be seen dotted strategically across that magical landscape, beautiful buildings that made a statement, where beyond the River Tees was still uncertain territory. Rievaulx, Rosedale, Lastingham, Kirkham, Kirkdale, Byland, Malton – in excess of an amazing 100 priories, abbeys and monasteries were constructed, Fountains Abbey being built in 1132, and Skelton Castle in 1140 by the second Robert de Brus. Whitby Abbey itself was built on the site of Saint Hilda's (657) in 1078, a mere twelve years following the Conquest.

NORMANDY FRANKS FROM 1030, THEIR NAMES, DATA AND LOCATION

The main purpose of this story has been in tracing the Franks and their migration, names and background, following them north into Yorkshire and beyond. However, I have recorded some of the activity of the Franks who remained in Normandy showing who these people were in relation to their future cross-Channel cousins. Appendix 3, maps individual's names and their various locations.

A note on the multifarious spellings of the name Frank. Having used various French-Latin spellings of the name Frank, the Anglo-Saxon form of Frank changed as if on a whim, sometimes misspelt or the name added to to add flair, sound posh or differentiate between many of an extended family bearing the same name.

At the time of Robert de Brus's birth in 1030 at Bruis Castle, Brix, Franconis was witness to two charters donating Prata de Salhus (a meadow) et Sarlosville to the Abbey-Sainte-Trinite-de-Rouen, also in 1030. The donation came from the family of Guanora, together with prayers for the life of a son. Guanora was mistress to the Compte de Normandy, whom she later married. Coincidentally Robert de Brus later married a different Guanora of uncertain origin.

Further to the above is a charter of Osmund-de-Franca of 1058, witnessed by Croco son of Archamband of the family Guanora. Note: Gunnora was of noble Danish origin, mistress of Richard I, Compt-de-Normandy.

Being a widow, the first extract indicates an historical association of Francais coming from Bayeux. The second extract shows William Frank aka Francheville de Rouen as a high-ranking witness to the monarchy, *originem familia Franceis de Rouen et Bayeux:*

> 'Concerning Agnes wife of Michel-le-Franceis, of the town of Bayeux, 1068, wherein she gives to the Abbey of Troarn, Bayeux, all that she possesses.'

> 'Whereas there is the tithe of Amfreville-de-Mivoye given to Holy-Trinity-de-Rouen with the assent of King William I, witnessed by William Francheville 1091.'

Here is clear evidence for the origin of Francais, coming from Francheville, the spelling of Francheville de Rouen changed from the original Fresquienne, this being the forest area previously frequented by Rollo and his son Guillaume, the name Francheville/Francaise cum Frank having been used pre-invasion, discerned in Robertus Francaise and others.

In 1098, Chevalier Francon distinguished himself in the First Crusade. He was among a company of crusaders belonging the army Lorraine. Francon came from Mechel on the River Meuse. Encountering the Turks, and in a brave rescue in defending his kinsmen, the Turks were annihilated leaving Francon mortally wounded.

Post-invasion dates and events

Through to the early 1400's the following shows running through to the early 1400s, the following shows a series of post-invasion dates and events located mostly in northern France:

Witnessed by Hugo Francus a charter of Guido, Lord of Lavelle to Gaudinus Rahier between 1113 and 1151 regarding confirmation that Juhellus de Crapon, knight, granted land in perpetual alms to the monks of Savigny, for which they must pay yearly eleven shillings.

In 1124, William Francise had a house on the chief street, near the shambles in Falaise that Henry I, King of England, Duke of Normandy, confirmed the next door house previously held by Gervase Cornet to the Abbot and Monks of Sainte-Evroul.

Ten acres of land is granted in 1136 to Abbey-Saint-Sauveur-le-Vicomte of the Ville of Radulfus (Rauville-le-Bigot, Valognes area) witnessed by Ricardo Franco.

A confirmation charter of the Abbey of Saint-Sauveur-le-Vicomte concerning Rannulfus Francus was made between 1146 and 1154. In it, Rannulfus, with the consent of his sons, grants Gaufridus Britonus (conditional he gives his daughter as a marriage portion) the land Rannulfus previously held of the abbey, whereby said Gaufridus should hold it peacefully and freely without other service other than returning all the harvested grain to Rannulfus. Not a bad deal, good old Rannulfus gains a wife for one of his sons, and gets Gaufridus to do the hard work of producing grain he's obliged to return to Rannulfus, a deal approved of and sealed by Abbot Huge Franc.

Dated 1147, mainly consisting of the Abbey-Saint-Sauveur-le-Vicomte, Ranulphus Francus is shown holding land and possessions directly from King Stephen of England.

Charters of 1147–1153 show Ranulphus and Ricardus Francus being feudally related to Robert de Brus.

Witnessed by Hugone Franco around 1150:

> 'Juhellus de Crepon, knight, grants to God and the monks of Savigny the land of Gaudinus Rahier as will always remain.'

Witnessed by the same Ricardo Francesio, shown feudally related to Robert de Brus, dated 1150:

> 'Amaury son of Raoul grants to canons of Notre-Dame-du-Voeu all the land of Guenestorp and house and rents due from his possessions in the parishes of Guenestorp, Arreville and Gatteville for the souls of Empress Matilde, her father, mother and ancestors, that they keep a Canon of his family to serve God.'

Richardo Franceso, as to his testament to all the lands and house of Amauri, son of Ralf, given to the Canons of Cherbourg 1154.

William de Vauville gives to Saint-Sauveur the Church of Saint-Jean-des-Chenes (Island of Jersey) all tithes and rents as well as all possessions of the Church of Saint-Pierre-de-Fontenio near the ford, such tithes and rents having been given with the consent of William's wife and sons Richard and Leone. Witnessed by Ricardo Franco, Presbyter of Vanville and Petro, who was Presbyter of Saint-Savuveur in 1155.

The Mill of Brencia and the adjoining house is granted to the Abbey of the Holy Trinity, Savigny, March 1157, attested by Richardo Franceso.

The *Magui Rotuli Scaccarii Normanniae* shows Willielmus Franceis and Rogerus Franceis, in the Cotentin district of Normandy, dated 1180.

The Extraordinary Franks

Ricardo Franco's testament of around 1185, in respect of a charter giving the Abbey of Saint Saauveur, together with the Church of Saint-John-de-Caisnibus on the Island of Gersoi (Jersey), with all its tithes and revenue as well as all the rights of the Church of Saint-Peter-de-Fontenaio (Fortenay), together with its tithes and revenue, passing to the Canons of Cherbourg.

Document showing the de Brus and Frank alliance in the Cotentin of Normandy:

'Magni Rotuli Scaccarii 1195,

Rogerus et Willielmus de Franceis.'

Evidence of unbroken family ties with the monarchy is found in Franco and Franconi's contribution towards a ransom payment of Richard-Coeur-de-Lion in 1195. Richard the Lion Heart, Duke of Normandy, 1157–1199, reigned as King of England, 1189–1199.

In 1198, Willelmus-le-Fraceis and Osmo-la-Francease, husband and wife are indicated in Caen.

In the bailiwark of Caen, also in 1198, are shown Matthew-le-Franc, Hub't-de-la-Franche, Ricardus-le-Franc, Willielmus-le-Franc (again) and Arnoldus-le-Franc.

Also in 1198, appearing among the Crown debtors, Robertus-le-Franc and Johannes le Franc.

The Exchequer Roll of the bailiwark of Pont-Audemer in 1198 and 1203 has Willielmus and Walter le Franceis.

On 27th January 1203 at Sees, due to Walter's opposition to the King, King John issued a writ to the Seneschal of Normandy commanding him to cause Walter le Franceis Francigena to give up his lands, tenancies and chattels at Hudimersnil. Note: Francigena meaning royal bloodline or genus relating to that dynasty.

In a Yorkshire charter of Robert de Brus dated 1218, we find William Franceis in relation to the Abbey of Montebourg in Manche, Normandy; providing clear indications of ongoing family ties between the Franks and the Brus, having interconnected links with their Normandy kin.

Also in 1218, William Franceis is shown with Michiel Le Franc indicated as a grantee.

Around 1200, Robert-de-France and his wife Alix, daughter of Onfroy-le-Chat, grant the ruins and mansion close to Abbey-de-Saint-Jean-de-Falaise, founded in 1127.

Relating to the confiscation of Normandy by King Phillipe II of France in 1204, charters numbers 6–11 in the records of the Abbeys of Caesarisburgus and Montebourg, as well as the archives of the Abbey of Cerisy, continue to show the names of

Willielmus and Rogerus Franceis appearing well after the confiscation, with family members shown thereafter.

Gautier-le-Francais witnesses a charter of 1206 concerning the church of Saint-Evroult.

Under King Phillip II, in 1210, Galterous Franceis held 'one-third of a knights fee' at Cleville.

An act passed in 1227 agreeing a yearly rent to the Abbey of Sainte-Trinite-de-Caen for land at Falsted was witnessed by Guillaume-le-Francois.

Richard-des-Moutiers assigns to the Abbot and Convent of Cherbourg land in the parish of Saint-Petrus-de-Alumna and Mill of Ketefri, measured in the presence of Prior Ricardus-de-Kerqueville of La-Taille and his companion Canon Willelmo Francesio, 1234.

A further charter in favour of Cherbourg dated 1234, witness, Canon Willelmo Francesio of Cherbourg.

Two further charter witnesses identified with the Viscounty of Valognes:

1. A charter in favour of Mathieu le Franceis and his wife Rose.

2. A charter relating to Johannes le Franc of Cherbourg and his wife Juliane.

Then there is the 'Evech'e-et-Chapitre-de-Bayeux,' where in 1243 the Chaplain Richard-le-Francois and his son, William, grant land at Bayeux for the service of homage.

Another Frank, Henricus Francois was present at the assizes of Caen in 1245.

Roger-le-Francois gives to the Abbey of Berberie the land of Vieux-Frene, Bayeux in 1250.

William Franceis, son of Richard, gives a yearly rent to the alms of Saint-Pierre-sur-Dives, dated 1251.

Also in 1251, Beatrix-la-Francaise makes a donation to the Abbey of Falaise.

Again in 1251, the son of the Burgess of Falaise grants to the abbey all the privileges that Mathilda-la-Francaise held of him.

The following year Mathilde Francaise gives a yearly rental to be taken from the parish of Fay to the Abbaye-de-Ardennes, Bayeux, dated 1252.

From the official charter of the Archdeacon of Paris 1252, the Archdeacon makes known Richard-de-Cherbourg (Ricardus de Caroburgo) aka Richard-le-Franc, son of the 'late' Oden-le-Franc:

'Has given to the Abbey of Cherbourg all that he received as successor to his father and mother, being all his inheritance, lands and title in perpetuity.'

1257, William-le-Francheis aka le-Francois, gives a yearly rent for the repose of the souls of Robert-le-Gamp, Prebendary of Bayeux.

Alongside a meadow belonging to himself at Sotevillam, John le Franc is witness to a charter of King Louis dated 1257, granting the rights of adjoining land to one Beate-Marie-de-Bonupartu.

In 1258, Raoul-le-Francois grants to the Abbey of Sainte-Marie-de-Villers the land and rent of Lessart.

Nicholas-le-Francois, son of William, in 1270, grants a yearly rental for the repose of the soul of Richard-de-Clermont, former Prebendary of Bayeux.

A charter of around 1270, shows Johan-le-Franc and his wife Juliane belonging to Cherbourg.

Dated around 1270, the Viscount of Valognes grants a charter in favour of Mathieu le Franceis and his wife Rose.

Petronville-la-Francaise, daughter of Faoulques, grants a rental to the Abbayea Ardennes, Bayeux in 1271.

Dated 1272, Alain le Francois of Tessy, with the consent of his wife Thomasse, assigned to the lords, abbot and Convent of Cerisy one sextier of barley measure every year from his fief.

In 1277 at Caen, John le Franc provides gifts to the Monastery of Saveigneio.

Also in 1277, Richard-le-Francoise gives a rental for the services of the Priory of Sainte-Barbe in prayer.

In 1278 in Paris, King Philip III gives the land of William-le-Fracheis of Baiocas and Caen to the Chapter of Bayeux.

Richard-le-Franc, in 1283, resigns to the abbey his rights to the fields of Perche.

Charter dated 1290, William-le-Francois is granted homage in exchange for a house at Mathieu.

Also in 1290, his wife Troe confirms the rental given by Raoul-le-France at Ouville.

To Mathieu le Franceis and his wife Rose and heirs, a letter from the Viscount of Valognes dated 1298, states that Henri Godel is ordered to pay yearly homage of a loaf of bread and a hen at Christmas, and that said Godel sells to Mathieu Franceis:

> '*Dis sous de tornois* … two pieces of land, the first in the parish of Sainte-Genevieve adjoining the Manor of Nicole Durdenier, the second, Cavees-de-Hotot on the road to Barfleu.'

A charter of Johan-le-Franc and his wife Juliane, both of Cherbourg 1309, states: of their free will they will deliver to the Abbot a Convent of Notre-Dame-du-Voeu, a piece of their land in the parish of Esqueud Reville near Le Machon. Also, that they will deliver at St Miichiel a loaf of bread and a hen at Christmas. The aforementioned being confirmed by a letter of Robert de Conflans, Keeper of the Seal of the Viscountcy of Valognes.

Richard-de-la-Laude of Montebourg and his wife Pennonele, in their charter of 1316, confirm the sale of the land of Micheal-le-Franc, pertaining to the parish of Saint Floissel near the bridge of Colin-du-Marest, sealed by the Viscount of Valognes. The translated document reads:

> 'To all who see or hear this letter, I Johan de Bandiancourt, Keeper of the Seal of the Viscounty of Valognes, greetings. Know that before Vincent Surel, sworn clerk of the said Viscounty, were present one Richard de La Lande of the parish of Montebourg, and Perronele, his wife, to whom he gave authority as hereafter stated, they freely and without being constrained, having sold, quit, and transferred to Michiel Le Franc all their right to lands of the parish of Saint Floissel. This letter sealed with the seal of the Viscounty in the year of our Lord 1316.'

Among the archives of the Abbey of Montebourg, in charter number 10, in 1316, is found Michiel Le Franc as the grantee of landholdings in the parish of Saint Floissel; charter number 11 showing Alain le Francois of Tessy in favour of the Abbey of Cerisy along with his wife Thomasse.

A 1334 document records the sale of the above rent to the Monks of the Abbey of Montebourg by Thomas Le Franc for the price of 'trente sous de tournois'.

Document dated 1371 relating to a house: a mistake is found in the accounts of William-de-France with the Abbey of Falaise.

Richard-le-Francois acknowledges he owes a yearly rent for land at Boissey, dated 1381.

In respect of Pierre-de-France an Act regarding fiefs in Falaise, 1410–1417.

In 1418, the King gives Lord Thomas Andrew the Villa of Harefleu adjoining the Hospicium of Radulphus-de-France for his lifetime.

Mahiet-le-Francheys is conferred Sergeantry-of-the-Wood in the forest of Yang, such appointment having become vacant upon the death of William-le-Francheys in 1419.

In the parish of Canon, jurisdiction of the Castle of Falaise is placed under the protection of Galfidus-le-Franceys esquire by order of the King at the Royal Castle of Dalenson, 28th October, 1417–1422.

The last of these entries:

> 'King Henry the fifth to all his people, know that we have given and granted to our diligent Lord William (Guillaume) Fraunceys Esquire for his faithful service, the Castle and Houses of Clinchamp, in the Earldom of Perche which lately belonged to Baldevini-de-Tuny, Knight, together with all his land and possessions, rents, profit, forfeiture and all other advantages belonging to said Castle, and 'after him' the said Castle and Houses, together with all said advantages are granted to the male heirs of his body. For this, he shall annually give a 'sword' at the Feast of Saint George at the Castle of Caen, and the said William and his heirs must always, at their own cost, be ready for service in the time of war and keep sufficient provisions in the Castle for the soldiers. Given at Villa-de-Bernay, June 1418, by the King himself.'

Extracted from a conflation of mass data, itemising everything would overwhelm the work's objective. Nonetheless, the information paints a picture showing the Franks post-invasion activity, where there is evidence they regularly visited their possessions both sides of the English Channel.

NORMANDY SUMMARY, THE FRANKS, THE MONARCHY AND THE DE BRUS

The above entries demonstrate the Franks being right at the heart of events, intimately entwined between the Church and state. Approximately 500 years before the last entry, a largish settlement of Franks of recent royal descent was established around Frequiennes, a previously heavily wooded forest area, Pavilly and adjacent locations nearby. The Franks held various prominent positions within the Church, and as nobles having strong links to the monarchy the spread of landholdings and property throughout Normandy reflects their highborn status.

Notwithstanding Robertus Bayeux de Fraunceys's parentage, the Franks I am most interested in, are those scattered westward and northward from Falaise in the east, where Robertus's elder relative, William the Conqueror, was born in 1027, and where in 1124 William Franc can be pin-pointed to a certain house in a particular road where the family lived for many years as immediate neighbours. At what point

Robertus's use of Bayeux was exchanged for Francais or Fraunceys, or whether indeed he had always used the Frank diminutive, is not clear. It is probable the change from Francais to Fraunceys came by association with those he was influenced by as he trained for knighthood.

Through their lineage the Franks were related to Charles III, who created the Dukedom of Normandy. It should be noted, Falaise became the first city of the new Duchy in 911, and Appendix 3 shows the distribution of a number of Brus and Franc holdings where 100 years previous, Charles III had created the Dukedom of Falaise. William the Conqueror was born there in 1027 when three years later, in 1030, Franconis was a witness to two charters regarding a meadow of the family Gunnora, where in 1058 Croco was a witness to Osmundi de Franca. Gunnora was married to Richard l of Normandy, King of the Franks, and it's reasonable to assume their connection with Osmundi de Franca and Franconis, is indicative of an interfamily relationship influencing Robertus's use of Franc. Incidentally Gunnora was Duchess of Normandy and her husband Rollo's grandson.

A hundred years later, in 1147–1153, Ranulphus Francus was recorded holding land and possessions directly of King Stephen of England. The name Francus in close proximity to a monarch of the same pedigree makes it impossible to place Ranulphus other than of Royal descent. A grandson of William the Conqueror, King Stephen or Stephen of Blois was derived of Frankish nobility, his wife Matilda was a German queen and in her own right Queen of the Franks

The Franks mapped from around Mortain to the tip of the peninsular at Cherbourg exclude extended family members scattered across Normandy. Those shown show property transactions and land donations, as well as rents and grants to various abbeys. Many were either Frank donations or transactions witnessed by them. The records show well-acquainted familiarity and a fraternity between them; of Franks totally at ease in their common heritage, working quietly and diligently between Church and state.

In terms of lineage, due to his youth, Robertus Fraunceys/Francais's arrival in England is consistent with the rank of knight, his parentage being ascribed to the Franks and the monarchy around Falaise. The first Duchy City was established in 911 where the family were established patrons of the monarchy, and where his direct relative, William the Conqueror, was born. William succeeded the Dukedom of Normandy aged eight, and as described elsewhere, such laudatory children were schooled around this age, beginning with mounted horsemanship to determine the most able cadency among the younger males. Among other martial youths of the family, his father's steward Osbern Herfasston personally mentored William's tutorship, training later pursuant upon the young Robertus Fraunceys.

The Extraordinary Franks

As well as the mundane of literature, numeration and several languages, was the mastery of swordsmanship and even castle building, Osbern schooling each successive generation as knights-to-be, each novice becoming first page so as to learn the manners and protocol of court, then squire where their skills were polished for pronouncement as knight.

Of Robert Fraunceys, there is a dated translation depictive of a Robert designated equivalent to page that for a while threw me, at the time my being unaware of the rigid process to knight then used, and my looking for a Robert of suitable status other than mere page and the right date. I mention elsewhere Robert being too young to join the 1066 invasion, and it follows he and his cohorts would have to complete the procedure from mere child to that of fully fledged warrior, the three protagonists' softer arrival upon British soil under the guidance of their kin Robert de Brus in stark contrast to their warrior overlord and William the Bastard's totally ruthless and bloody meme.

As regards William, his biographer, William of Poitiers, described him as a fearsome master of the saddle, sword and lance. Aged fifteen and knighted by King Henry I, he first honed his skills proving himself to be a fearsome warrior and a leader, having victories in Brittany, Maine and Ponthieu.

On the issue of knighthood, the start of this socially elite brotherhood was derived of the original freemen cum wealthy landowners that set them apart, who fought for the Frankish kings whereby the grant of a knighthood became a reward for bravery proven worthy of the accolade. Useful in gaining more and more land, such territory was passed down generationally, the idea developing that the qualities required of a knight could only be passed on through inheritance, hence the concept 'no man can be knighted lest he be the son of a knight' and hence the development of huge estates bringing with it further ennoblement.

Due to knighthoods handed down, being set in stone lest in special consequences by direct consent of the King, Robert de Bayeux cum Frauncays and his brother knights are seen historically as having no recourse but that of direct descent, and thus wise Robert directly related to William the Conqueror. Incidentally the term freeman equates to the name Frank as freemen and territories belonging the name such as Fresney sur Sarthe, Normandie-Maine, Fresnes north of Amiens, Falaise and other domain.

Regarding interbreeding, although a bastard, William was of Norse descent yet also French, using that language as his mother tongue. His mother was Herleva, the daughter of a tanner of Falaise, whereas his father's mother was Judith of Brittany. Ancestry indicates Gunnora as a forester's daughter of Pays de Caux; daughter of Sprota, who was a Breton captive, thence back in time to the marriage of Rollo to Poppa de Bayeux. Guillaume or William I, Duke of Normandy, took Sprota as his concubine; where through her Breton origins, the spelling of her name shows she was undoubtedly a Frank, and by marriage to Count Esperleng de Vaudreuil, son of Richard I, maternal predecessor of Robertus de Francais.

The Franks of Falaise had close ties with the Rouen Franks to the immediate east and interfamily ties with the de Brus lying to the west. Significantly, given their rank as first witnesses, the Franks links with Gunnora and that family is indicative of an immediate family connection going straight to the heart of the ruling monarchy, the names William, Robert, Charles and Richard being royal names, together with Robertus's father's name William; these names used in such close proximity, affirming mutual ancestry.

Around 1103–1106, nine years following the death of the first Robert de Brus in Cleveland, the de Brus were still recorded as tenants in Mortain, Normandy, holding eight manors 'Terra Regis' in 1086. Closely related to the Franks, the first Robert de Bruse built the Castle de Bruise also known as Brix or Brux, his first wife the daughter of the Count of Brittany, descended from Charlemagne. Incidentally the de Bruise feudal home of Castle Brix abuts the coastal town of Rozel, place of origin for Rogrus de Rosel, one of the three Yorkshire de Brus knights.

Accompanying William on his invasion, the first Robert de Brus, born in 1030, set off for England in 1066, a few of his family being left behind to run things, the rest to follow on. Born of Gunnora, who died before 1050, he was aged around eighteen or nineteen. Remaining in Normandy, de Brus's first son, Alan, Lord of Brix, succeeded to the de Bruise Normandy dynasty.

Regarding 1066, the invasion dateline seems unsure for the arrival in England of young knights, Robertus Francais, Roger de Rosel and Guy de Lofthus. Although all three were related, Roger was a son of the Lord of Rosel. Whereas Guy de Francais, a very close associate of de Brus, later took his name from the hamlet of Loftus that lay within the de Brus estates in Cleveland, North Yorks.

Adam, son of Robert de Brus, was born in 1050 at Bruis Castle, Brix de Manche, Normandy, being the son of Robert's second wife Emma-de-Bretagne, born in Rennes in 1035. Adam came over from Normandy with his father Robert, where a son was born to Adam in Cleveland Yorkshire in 1071 or 1078. Christened Robert like his grandfather, his mother Emma-de-Ramsey, wife of Adam, was born in Penthievre, Normandy around 1052. All three young knights, Francais, Rosel and Lofthus appear in the Whitby charter of 1131 together with the second Robert de Brus. This would place the then age of the second Robert de Brus around fifty-three to sixty. A second son, born to the elder Robert's first wife, was William de Braose, born 1049, dying some time after 1089.

In terms of age, it would be wholly impossible for the younger knights and retinue to have been old enough to have engaged in the 1066 invasion and turn up in

The Extraordinary Franks

Yorkshire in 1131. I'm of the opinion that a follow-up retinue of de Brus and the young knights entered England as liege-lord occupiers, probably via the Humber, almost certainly bringing with them a contingent of Franks and de Brus family members who, once established, settled in Yorkshire. There would be need for a sizeable number of de Brus and loyal followers sufficient to provide occupation on the scale recorded.

As to Franks evidenced around Hastings and the south, they must have been associated family. Also, Domesday records a fair number of Franks scattered inland and running north from the Humber, and some south from there, which seems to support my theory of the Humber as a subsequent and well-used port of entry.

On Robert de Brus's arrival following the Battle of Hastings he was charged with the job of subduing Northern England. On his success, as a reward he was bestowed an amazing forty-three lordships in the East and West Ridings and fifty-one in the North Riding of Yorkshire. Already one of the largest landowners in the north, Robert, Count of Mortain, half-brother of William the Conqueror, around the time of the harrying, gave his friend Robert de Brus the additional lands of Guisborough, coming with it the lordship of Skelton.

The Count of Mortain's mother was Herleva of Falaise, also the mother of William the Conqueror. Herleva and the location of Falaise was of great significance, being indicative of a closely interrelated Norman group contemporaneous with the Franks, and where the family name of Robert was used repeatedly and again in the person of the Count of Mortain.

In preparation of William's invasion, Count de Mortain offered 120 ships, and for his endeavours was granted 797 manors. He appears seated with his brothers Odo and William in the Bayeux Tapestry on the day of their successful landings in England.

DOMESDAY BOOK ENTRIES 1086–1087

These entries are some twenty years following the Battle of Hastings, and should be taken in the context of established settlements in the form of fiefs, land that was farmed ad hoc in shared or allocated strips, a practice that continued for many decades. The practice of administration, doctrine and law, was well advanced, laid down many years previous. It seems the influx of families from northern France came mostly on the heels of the initial invasion, the Humber being one of the more strategic rivers from which to land.

On the basis of settled families and the evidence of father, mother, son and daughter succession, the main contingent of Franks seem to have arrived immediately following 1066. I have purposely chosen the Humber as an entry point due to its position relative to Yorkshire and the task of bringing in heavy weapons, as well as horses and goods with which to subdue and rule over the northern population. Shortened land routes were also necessary in order to bring in the necessary expertise to build churches and arrange fortification. It was one thing to win a war, quite another to fully conquer.

And it must be remembered the Norwegian King Harald Hardrada had invaded via the Humber into York with 500 ships, landing there 20th September, being defeated by the English 25th September. The enemy was allowed to depart with only thirty ships a mere seven days prior to William's own invasion in the south, departing from Saint Valery 27th September 1066. Thus distracted and faced with an invasion from the south caused the English to respond, thus weakening protection of the more northern entry point, allowing subsequent heavy material, troops and craftsmen to be off-landed there, the Normans fully intent on remaining forever.

Informed by the Franks, knowledge of the military system of motte and bailey castles was vital, and with the Humber giving immediate access to the North Sea and to inlets further up the coast, the river's position, with the added bonus of access to York, would be seen as a strategic imperative. Once established, Whitby too became vital, many charters showing Whitby as being a useful additional outreach of York.

Domesday evidence of early Frank settlement on the Humber is recorded with both Franco and Franci mentioned in relation to Drogo, Knut and the King:

> Drogo, was a noble Fleming who attended William Duke of Normandy and on becoming Earl of Holdeness, held a castle and vast estates, marrying a niece of the Conqueror.
>
> Knut, ruler of Norway and Denmark was slain by rebels in 1086 around the time of the Domesday Book.

For an explanation of Knut, one needs to take a step back to the Vikings and in particular Bluetooth. Bluetooth was a pretty fearsome character who, despite his reputation, brought Christianity to Denmark. To put in context, the Vikings were masters of the sea and apt at raiding as far as Greenland and the Black Sea and deep inland on navigable rivers such as the Thames, Trent, Ouse, Shannon, Loire, Seine, Rhine and Dnieper, raiding Muslim held Seville in 844.

The Viking ships were huge, ninety-four of which attacked London in 994. On display at the British Museum is a warship known as the Roskilde: built around 1020, this giant military transport vessel is thought to have belonged to Knut the Great, who for a short period united England, Denmark and Norway within a brief North Sea empire. The connection with Bluetooth follows a temporary unification that, although brief, marked the transition of a collection of provincial warlords

The Extraordinary Franks

into one cohesive international Christian kingship. So already, Christianity was not merely a province of the invading Norman coming with banners raised resounding to Catholic tribulations and retribution. As it was, the concept of prayer and the Almighty had long since shown its face and was about to vent something of its fury.

It has always been that York attracted invaders. The Vale of York hoard consists of items from as far apart as Ireland and Samarkand, the second largest city in Uzbekistan, its contents being contained in a single plundered Frankish chalice buried in 927. But we have to imagine the vast distances travelled, Samarkand situated 7000 miles away midway between the Caspian Sea and China and that of York. The Vikings used the Dnieper River, navigating all the way from Finland through Russia to the north shore of the Crimea and, once there, met the Tashkent and Samarkand traders, as well as the people of Turkey and Constantinople, who themselves were trading betwixt there and China.

Strange as it might seem, far away Samarkand was a melting pot of the world's cultures, the York hoard being shown to embody three faiths: Christianity, Islam and the worship of Thor, the name Thor being brought into our everyday language as Thursday or Thors day. It seems remarkable that a simple bowl of Frankish origin should contain the whole of the Viking world buried at York, including that of Islam, symbolic of all of that great religion. The date of 927 is significant too as the same date the Wessex King Athelstan took over Viking York to create, for the very first time, a unified England.

The chalice? Well I like to think of it as emblematic of what the Frankish warriors became, their swords struck deep into the ground of Yorkshire from whence they prayed and ploughed and lay at rest.

But time is not set in stone. The period now is post-1066, and set against a system of overlords. Drogo de Bevrere was a particularly trusted overlord and held La Beuvriere in the arrondissement of Bethune near Aumale, Normandy and was a trusted confidant of King William. Taken from the Domesday Book, Franco held sizeable lands north of Hull as tenant 'in capite' under Drogo in the Wapentake of Gerlestre. As a senior figure indentured to Drogo, Franco too seems to have ranked as a knight.

Seemingly lost to history, the following incident must have seemed disastrous, particularly for those in the north: around that time Swein, King of Demark, disputing the rule of England, invaded with 250 ships sailing up the Ouse taking York and in the process slew 3000 Normans. Two months later, through a sea of turmoil and terrible slaughter, William and his Normans recaptured York.

I have translated information taken from the Domesday Book, settling for places and names relating to the Franks. Working from the Humber, I have been able to establish a pattern of settlement specific to this family name. Frank incursion appears to have divided roughly north and south of the entry point of the Humber, *Franco* movement surmised as south and *Frani* and some additional *Franco* inland towards York and northward. Settlement should be evaluated against a backdrop of immense conflict. Appendix 4 illustrates west to north migration.

At that time, the territory of Yorkshire, north of the Humber, became known as 'north of the Humber land', hence Northumberland, running originally as far as Edinburgh; Edinburgh and its territory north of the River Tweed being captured in 954 by the Scottish King Indulf, and Northumberland losing its Yorkshire shires, became sandwiched between the Tweed and Tees, pre-invasion, in 1065. The territory of Northumberland now became a gruesome field, its tumultuous past and terrible future becoming the site of the greatest number of battles in history, it beautiful hills and valleys, fords and streams awash with blood. Today sees its glorious landscape home to the greatest number of castles than any other county, and just as the quietude found in an ancient graveyard, becomes a sacrosanct province of wondrous peace and tranquillity.

Yet actually, the territory south of the River Tweed in Scotland formed the ancient Kingdom of Bernicia encompassing the southern reaches of the Scottish Borders and the whole of Durham to the River Tees, edging south of the river and its border with Cleveland. And once immense Northumberland, its southern province now in the grip of the Norman invader, and with York as its stronghold had made its presence felt as that of North Yorkshire and a new breed of Englishman.

Frani, French ascertained as Franks, dated 1086 working north from landings close to current-day Hull:

> Frani at Southcoats, Sproatley, closest settlement, Hull.
>
> Frani located off an inlet north of the Humber, west of Hull, Umlouebi or Unlouebi, Anlaby (Drogo).
>
> Frani and another Frani, Preston, near Hedon (see Drogo).
>
> Frani, Roos. Just north of Withernsea, on the coast.
>
> Franco at Bilton, immediately north of Hull (see Drogo).
>
> Frani found at Gagenestad, Ganstead.
>
> Frani at Old Ellerby, north of Hull moving towards the coast.
>
> Franco situated at South Skirlaugh (see Drogo).
>
> Frani, Widfornewic or Widfornewinc cum Withfornewinc hence Withernwick.

Franco at Marton, south of Hornsea, just north of Withernwick (see Drogo).

Franklin, Rise, immediately south of Hornsea (see Knut and Drogo).

Frani, Wadsande, Wathsand (or wasteland) becomes Wasssand, Hornsea Marshes (Drogo).

Franklin, Catfoss, triangle point York, Hornsea, Malton, moving north (see Knut and Drogo).

Frani at Wilsthorpe, further north, close to Bridlington.

Frani at Nortone or Norton near Malton, Pickering, one of the initial Franks of Cleveland, Yorkshire.

Settlement stretching north from Hull to Pickering is significant historically both in terms of Rise and the Abbey of Meaux to the south and in relation to the many present-day Franks located around Pickering and its ancient connection with Frani-de-Nortone or Frank of Norton, Malton, North Yorks.

Further settlements of Franks were established around York and to the north of York, occupation that remains today, lightly scattered northward linking the locations of Fountains Abbey and the Abbeys of Jervaulx, Rievaulx and Bylands, also lapping Guisborough and the de Brus lands of Cleveland abutting the Franks north of York, along what is now the A19. These are the Frank estates of Thirkleby abutting Byland Abbey and Newburg Priory, with Ampleforth, also associated with the Franks close by leading to Ness, the linchpin of one's own family tree, my late mother Dorothy Frank.

These are a quick snapshot for 1086:

Frani, Riplingham, north-west of Hull, working towards York.

The trans-location of another Frani, located Bricstune, Briston, Bristone or Bristun, Breighton being strategically situated midway between Hull and York, just off the River Ouse.

Franco at Thornton, Pocklington, east of York.

Frani at Wressle and Spaldington, off the Ouse towards York.

Frani located at Melbourne, south-east of York.

Located north of York at Mitun or Mitune now Myton, between Ripon and Malton, is a Frani.

Set in 1086, around a time of massive upheaval, the great works of the Domesday Book are a remarkably detailed record and weight of evidence for the various surname spellings of Frank, Franc, Francais, Frani, Franco, ad-infinitum, directly linked to York and further north to Whitby, Cleveland, Greater Yorkshire and Scotland.

On the question of name-spelling variations. Literacy was confounded by the use of a combination of various languages suddenly coming together with alien or misheard sounding of names, nicknames being a common occurrence. How a name might be used, heard, wrongly spelt or applied, as I will show, differed for the same person repeatedly within various documents and among people of different background.

Put simply, the origins of Frank have been altered variously from Frenchy, French, Fraunc, Frauncey, etc. These and other Franc, Frani and so on, have the same antecedence and bloodline, rooted in their dynastic heritage and forebears, being one and the same.

The first entry in England that includes a Christian name is Robert Francais, who appears in the published records of York in 1097 and again later in 1100. A combination of Christian name and surname in England had not really occurred until introduced by the Normans, and it was Normans such as Robert Francais who first introduced the practice of surnames that took time to take hold across Britain.

Records demonstrate the connection between the Franks in England as high-ranking Normans, together with their associated interrelated Normandy family. York records confirm Robert Francais's status as a Norman knight having a particularly close relationship with Robert de Brus. The web of interconnected family names in England and their ties with Normandy are numerous and complex.

ROBERT DE BRUS AND ROBERTUS FRANCAIS, POST-1066.

In the history that unfolds, I have tried to provide a storyline based on real events and fact. In this type of research, difficulty can occur due to the frequent and contentious nature of non-family take up of a given surname. Also, for much of the early period, persons' second names were of the place they lived, not that of a given bloodline, and the lower the family ranking, the less available information.

Preamble

The tree commences in Yorkshire with Sir Robertus Francaise, an intimate closely allied to Robert de Brus of Skelton and Scotland fame. For the purpose of this story, the tree then branches north to Scotland with Robertus and his son William, and later his grandson Roger. The Cleveland branch appears to consist of Sir Robertus' son Robertus, and soon after, Bernardo, Sir Robert's grandson and an initial small group of family members. The Cleveland contingent, now enfeoffed to the de Brus, appears to be engaged in the business of settlement, fortification and farming, its knights supporting and funding the institutions of Church and their de Brus liege lord. In this arena the Franks at first seem very much junior partners in the arrangement, the de Brus seemingly much more robust, undisputed masters in their universe and the wider stage.

Though the Franks gained holdings of their own, records are scarce. By contrast, the de Brus were prominent among several overlords and widely recorded. Following 1066, the early Franks appear to have spread thinly across Yorkshire, exacerbating the problem of finding data. But it is with the North Yorkshire settlers of Cleveland across to Pickering, Whitby and York I am most concerned. Incidentally, there is a cross-legged effigy of Sir William de Brus in Pickering Church.

However, through intermarriage and population spread, prominent familial Franks in Scotland and south of York began to vie for status and land, extending and maintaining essential allegiances, ensuring the protection and expansion of their property and rising influence. One such Frank was William, son of Sir Robertus Francaise – he wasn't about to stand on his laurels. William remained a prominent and personal confidant of the de Brus with his eye, too, firmly fixed on Scotland.

With an eventual eye to the Scottish throne, the six feet, one inch tall and powerful Robert de Brus seemed consumed with advancing his position. Come the invasion of Scotland, whereas the de Brus were awarded 200,000 acres of Scottish land, the small contingent of Franks who tagged along left behind a larger remnant of Yorkshire Franks, seemingly more closely tied to the land and the general routine of rural existence, taking up the sword only when called upon. With exceptions, it is this line through to Thomas Henry Frank of modern times, a family who mostly continued a tradition of hard work, farming and moral duty, I later focus on and whose own family this work owes allegence.

More prominent Franks were active in the hierarchy and engaged in political and marital interrelation, demonstrating a class of person determined to take advantage of their place within the system, whereas many of their North Yorkshire counterparts subsided within a more lowly existence. Today, for many of the families, the job of gleaning data has been hampered by the scarcity of information and damaged records.

Despite their status, the rural Franks were to all intent tenants and therefore indentured. It was simply the system of governance that ruled. Coming from noble Norman stock and knights feudally related to the de Brus, it seems that, regardless of their rural existence, their Norman status prevailed. In terms of exempli gratia, Lex Salica, or Frank law, scattered remnants of the Cleveland Franks appear to have settled as leaders bound to a destiny of prayerful quietude, where fixed by certainty of belief and determination they might seem less inclined than the de Brus to engage in the ruthless slaughter of innocents. But was this true?

The story

The use of historical corroboration linking the de Brus to the Franks in Yorkshire and Scotland has proven invaluable. And in reconciling their commonality, as kin, the de Brus were matchless and totally without mercy, theirs being a reign of terror and all-out war on a scale unprecedented in England. Instigated in Yorkshire by William the Conqueror and skills brought over from Europe, the resultant slaughter brought a stain upon the character of the Norman foe and what must have been complicity on the part of the Franks in their involvement and support.

The Harrowing of the North was an act of genocide. These were a series of campaigns waged by William the Conqueror during the winter of 1069–1070 while he celebrated Christmas in York. The Harrowing effectively ended the quasi-independence of the region through the large-scale destruction and pacification of Anglo-Danish lords replaced with Normans.

Having traced an apparent route from the Humber to the Tees as an entry point for a contingent of Franks, this same route must have seemed littered with the corpses of those who had been slaughtered and the ground lay bare. The emancipated souls who survived resorted to eating the same flesh of those needing to be buried. From today's perspective, being devoid of any kind of feeling, it is difficult to think of those who took the land as being anything approaching human. Yet among the many names of the Domesday records it's impossible to judge who belonged to the good and who belonged to the bad.

Whole villages were burnt to the ground, the inhabitants slaughtered, their food stores and livestock destroyed. One hundred thousand bodies lay strewn from the Humber to the Tees, the land laid to waste by salting in order to destroy its productivity for decades. Succumbed to starvation, any who survived were either reduced to cannibalism or died in the worst act of genocide known to Britain, an act later to be surpassed by the Nazis in the Second World War.

Two decades later, the Wastes, as it became known and as recorded in the Domesday Book, would be easy to be thought of as mere uncultivated land. Untrue: this was land necessary for farming and survival whoever occupied the land, land that had been destroyed along with the skills needed for production, land that would remain unproductive for years to come. The Harrowing was an act of genocide that would come to haunt the few survivors and their masters for generations.

Yet despite his ruthlessness, it was necessary for William to make alliances. One such alliance was Copsi. Copsi was of Danish origin, administering Northumberland under Earl Tostig at the time of a revolt in 1065. Upon losing office at the deposition of his master, Copsi would have shared Tostig's banishment, but by taking advantage of the situation, and having made a submission to the newly crowned king, he was granted the earldom of Northumberland, an area known to many as the ancient Kingdom of Bernicia. William unaware the grant involved the deposition of Oswulf, a descendant of ancient earls, and in his haste to appoint as his lieutenant a man he considered to be a native, hoped to accelerate subjugation of the yet unconquered north.

Copsi, full of self-aggrandisement by his appointment, gathered together an army and marched north. Coming across their enemy, Oswulf was dispossessed during the affray and forced to hide among the forests and mountains. But the banished Oswulf was of old stock, the family having a loyal following scattered across the region. Being of broken fortune, most men decided it would be no bad thing to band together, and irrespective of the Normans to the south and their intended incursion, what had they to lose.

Feasting upon his success at Newburn on 12th March 1067, Copsi was oblivious of the danger he was to befall. Coming upon him unawares, the earl took fright at Oswulf's men and fled to the nearest church for sanctuary. But like Copsi, Oswulf was of Viking stock, the burning of churches was nothing new, and having set fire to the building, Oswulf stood ready, sword raised, and when the door swung back, Copsi emerged choking through smoke-filled lungs whereupon his head fell to the ground, sliced off with a single blow of Oswulf's blade.

That might have been the end of the tale, only the Normans, unhappy at the situation, decided to make a hero of Copsi, speaking of the nobility of his birth and of his fidelity to the King and that his death was the consequence of his faithfulness. The deceased earl's stock made good by the Conqueror's gift of lands to the Church and other promises, William brought to his side a sufficiency of additional armed men to finally quell the population.

Put into context, having fought and won many major battles, in their journey the Normans had suffered huge losses, and while their exhausted army welcomed the pillage and slaughter of unarmed villagers as easy prey, not being stupid, they knew it was one thing causing unwelcome skirmishes and quite another benefiting from battles that could be won by other means.

Henry I, fourth son of William the Conqueror, schooled in Latin and the liberal arts, was an educated man. On William's death in 1087, Henry's older brothers, William and Robert, inherited England and Normandy respectively. Left landless, Henry purchased the Cotentin in Normandy from Robert, but soon after, in 1091, was deposed his brothers. Preoccupied with other matters, Robert was unaware that Henry had cleverly allied himself with William and was being supported by the

Franks of the Normandy peninsular. These were the same Franks as those of Yorkshire, where Henry had gradually rebuilt his power-base in the Cotentin heartland, an area belonging the old Frank monarchy.

It seems not inconsequential that in 1100, when out hunting, Henry was present when William just happened to accidentally die. Whereupon, whether or not he had killed his brother, Henry seized the English throne.

Having married Matilda of Scotland, true to form generationally, Henry continued to have a large number of mistresses by whom he had many illegitimate children. And as regards the name Robert, both in the Cotentin and England, the propensity for illegitimate offspring supports the idea of Frank progeny emanating from the fructification of earlier royal dalliances.

Henry's brother Robert was not a happy man, and in disputing Henry's control invaded England in 1101, the campaign ending in a negotiated settlement. But Henry was unsettled and having the other waspish brother at his back he invaded Normandy. Having finally defeated Robert in 1106, Henry imprisoned his brother for the remainder of his life.

Ruthless and educated though Henry was, he was also clever and skilfully manipulated the barons of both Normandy and England. Drawing upon the Frankish manor system of justice evolved by the Anglo-Saxons, local governance was strengthened by an exchequer, together with a system of taxation. Loyalty was rewarded to those followers and families of ranking Norman settlers, and it was through these families administrators were created and through whose sons ecclesiastical reform ensued. And this aspect of the Franks is later evidenced in relation to the Church and the justices, typical of the type of reward given by Henry to his most loyal trustees.

The northern lands beyond the Tees had long been conquered: de Brus was in control, and Henry, by playing a personal and major role in the selection of the senior clergy in England and Normandy, granted the monks of Whitby and the church of Middlesbrough lands in Newham. The grant was conditional on certain Whitby monks serving in the town of Middlesbrough, the grant being confirmed by Pope Eugenius III to Abbot Benedict by gift of Robert de Brus on behalf of the King.

The same records show the confirmation by Alan de Percy to the monks of Whitby in Fylingdales-Fylinghall, Normanby and Hawsker, for their use of forest, pasture and woodland.

Stephen, the first abbot of Whitby gives good account, relating that when he first took habit in 1078, living like a hermit with his brethren, they sought to restore the monastery that had previously been reduced to nothing following recurring invasions of pagans and rovers. When he commenced restoration of the main buildings and started the cultivation of the surrounding land given by William de Percy, Stephen's reward was his election, made with the full approval of the King and Archbishop Lanfranc of Canterbury.

Seeing how the monks had improved what had previously been desert, de Percy and his men, aided by pirates and robbers, harried the monastery by land and sea, their mission to cause so much injury as to drive the monks away. Following the initial attempt, so aggrieved was Stephen, that he followed the King and William de Percy all the way to Normandy, personally laying his complaint before the King.

De Percy, infuriated because of the slight, on his return to Yorkshire, was so enraged he forced home his attack driving the monks from Whitby to Lastingham. Suffering great depredation and debauchery, the monks sought out and received the patronage and refuse of Count Alan of Brittany at his church of St Olave, close to the city of York. Stephen was subsequently recorded as abbot of the monastery of St Mary, York, around the same year as the Domesday Book in 1086.

I mention Whitby, Lastingham and Normandy, for that which connects them. Also the importance of Lanfranc, coming from Normandy, his principles, teachings and support, crucial to the foundation of Church and state throughout the country. Lastingham, adjacent to Rosedale and Hutton-le-Hole was a Frank stronghold.

Records show the volatile nature of the Normans, often found in dispute with each other, this time involving lords William de Percy, Count Alan and the de Brus. The following are three snippets of useful data:

> Adam de Brus was born around 1051, Bruis Castle, Brix, in Manche, Normandy. Later, in Yorkshire, aged thirty, he married Emma Ramsey. Emma was also born around 1052, in Carrick, Argyllshire.
>
> Robert de Brus was found named in a charter of the Earl of Chester in 1094 granting the church of Flamborough to the church of Whitby.
>
> Robert de Brus died around 1094, his son Adam succeeding.

The one and only child of Adam de Brus, was named Robert after his grandfather. Baby Robert was born either 1071 or 1078, Robert in turn marrying Agnes Paynel, who in 1095 bore a child named Adam after his father. A second child, Agatha was born 1105.

A Whitby endowment, immediately preceding 1096, provides a detailed list of all the de Brus lands, possessions, forests, churches, tithes, hamlets, towns and manors then existing. These included Fylingdales, Whitby Flowergate and Eskdale, together with adjacent forest. With the exception of Whitby itself, all of the places lie to the south of the river Esk. A later confirmation states that Ernald de Percy as the founding lord of Kildale, was a feudatory of de Brus. Besides other lands, Acklam in Cleveland remained under Robert de Brus.

The Percy were a powerful family descended from William de Perci, and took what appears to be the coward's way out in crossing to England over a year after the invasion. For his trouble, de Perci was created first baron of Topcliffe in Yorkshire. Derived from the manor of Percy-en-Auge in Normandy, I have to concede, being cousin-related, the family's claim to indirect ties with the Frankish royal house is probably right.

While others were fighting, putting self-interest first, the Percys instead employed tradesmen in the rebuilding of York Castle in 1070. Grand and aloof in their new abode, the house of Percy somehow managed to get hold of the titles of Earl and Duke of Northumberland. And through to modern times, true to form, whereas the tumbled houses of Frank and the de Bruce quietly faded into obscurity, due to the lack of a male heir the Percy surname also died, only to remerge like a phoenix from the ashes, a magical conjuring trick born of the marriage of an opportunist to an heiress. History shows how the Percys and titles such as Duke of Northumberland today, absent of true genetic male descent, remain extraneous at best.

The de Percy was hugely powerful, and there's no doubt, tricky and conniving. And I mention them and the house of Neville proving the argument for the uncertain pedigree of much of today's aristocracy, privileges often gained on very shaky ground in relation to the true nature of said bloodline. Brought to question are the true bloodlines of male births camouflaging the truthfulness of inheritance. The problem of insisting upon and producing suitable male heirs was a real problem exacerbated by the common presence of impotency rife in the twelfth century.

The Percy line was revived, whereby the son of Agnes de Louvain, through her marriage to Joscelin of Louvain, dumped his name for that of the surname Percy. More recently, in the eighteenth century, Hugh Smithson, upon his marriage to Elizabeth Seymour and having dropped the name son-of-Smith, took for himself the surname Percy and by so doing gained the title Duke of Northumberland.

Most old titles today assume their ownership, wealth and privilege founded on some exceedingly dodgy historic premise exacerbated by the practices of a large section of today's elite in their many wilful acts of self-interest, thus denying the circulation of vast amounts of untold wealth within a needful economy and detriment of the country at large.

ROBBER BARONS AND THE UNTOUCHABLE

In our modern world we seem fixated in clinging to the concept of inherited supremacy at the top level of society, where privilege can be bought irrespective of intelligence or ability, the nation's nagging resentment of autocracy being a major cause of disillusionment and apathy due to all of the strings being pulled by a few at the top.

Short of the French guillotine, to many, it seems that revolution may be the only resort. One's own belief in evolutionary change may have suddenly skidded to a juddering halt as the 'nose in the trough' brigade bring to light how wide is the spider's web of corruption, cover-ups, self-interest and self-preservation. We see, once in power, how politics is used covertly to divert millions into the clutch of one's fellow elite and how cleverly the art of magic is used to conceal such activity, its deception masked by superficial gestures of largely useless action set against a hidden plutocrat. Such undisclosed wealth denied the underclass; its lack of circulation within the economy remains hugely damaging and an affront to the majority where the confluence of immense world wealth remains married within a superclass.

Referring to Janice Turner's article in *The Times* 19th December 2013, what rankles is one such amply padded baron waddling into the Lords, claiming his £300 per diem for the few minutes it takes for him to squeeze his bulk through the corridors of power and, as if of right, immediately turn and exit, clutching to his wheezing breast arms full of dirty dosh without any work being done. She writes, 'In what other career could you defraud your employer, receive a nine-month prison sentence and still keep your job'. Certainly for the privileged elite, their public schools and the Bullington Club seem to offer a special kind of anonymity, and with it an exclusive ticket to dance. And all the while, ragged two-penny proletariats watch unelected lords and their heirs hop-skipping with glee, carrying bulging wallets of public money, waltzing all the way to the bank.

At the heart of both hidden worlds remains an unspoken politeness and undeclared fellowship; guardian to an elite fraternity, a fraternity it might be possible to join, given you're of the right sort. Blind to a world spinning in indignation, nothing changes, in theirs remains the power; in theirs remains the authority, in theirs remains the wealth, untouchable except for the saving grace of the internet and press media.

But in times past, there was no such luxury as reporters, and it largely fell to the monks to record. It is amazing such detailed records were kept, their transcripts being a source of pride in both their making and documentation, much as a computer may possess information today.

MAIN STORY CONTINUED

A transcript of the *Cartularum Abbathiae de Whiteby* (1097–1101) at the British Museum, positively identifies the Franks Yorkshire–Normandy family having a connection with the Valognes district of the Cotentin, with exactly the same names of Willielmus Franceis and Rogerus Franceis, now found in Scotland. The transcript is conclusive as to the Franks route into Scotland, as well as them maintaining the Normans well-used route and ongoing connection between Yorkshire and Normandy.

The Commune de Valognes lies immediately inland of the Cherbourg peninsula, Le Rozel close by. My thoughts are of a recent conflation of younger and less experienced knights containing members of this family under possible late stages of training. This would explain the knight names of de Rosels together with Fraunceys and their brother William Franceis cum Lofthus, the area being an assembly point, the peninsular ideal for a post-invasion force.

Records of Robertus Fraunceys, knight, appear soon after the death of his friend, the first Robert de Brus, in 1100. He appears as a witness to a charter of the neighbouring Abbey of Whitby.

Records of Whitby Abbey 1101: Hugh Lupus d'Avranches, Earl of Chester, Viscount of Avraches in Normandy, nephew of King Wilham I, became Lord of Whitby soon after the Conquest. He died 27th July 1101, granting Whitby to William de Percy. William was father to Alan de Percy, his charter being held in the British Museum.

William de Percy, of the Cotentin of Normandy, contemporary of Robertus Francais and the de Brus, his conveyance to include:

> 'The monks, lands, forests, pastures and woods.'

The grants were made for:

> 'The safety of the souls of his lords the King of England and his heirs, Hugo Earl of Chester, etc.'

Above said witnessed by:

> 'Willelmus, Walterus, Ricardus de Percy and Robertus de Brus, together with tres de suis militibus Robertus Fraunceys, Rogrus de Rosels and Willelmus de Lofthus.'

This entry positively connects Robertus Francais with the de Brus. As a knight, Robertus Fraunceys and his two brothers, shown together, along with Robert de Brus and the three Percy, united at a pivotal point in history.

Research had long shown strong knowledge of localised changes of surname to that of a place or occupation as a means of identification. And it was only after further research into the Normandy Franks did the penny drop that all three of *'tres de suis militibus knights'*, accompanying de Brus, appeared to be related. It answers questions concerning the Christian names of all three appearing together in Normandy indicated as Franks, and as was the custom, Willielmus for a time taking the surname Lofthus, and his brother Rogerus, the surname de Rosels, for instance, later reverting back to Francais or sometimes Frounceys, depending on how the name was transcribed.

Many Norman families used both their Norman name and names derived from their newly acquired lands in England. Research has shown the Franks as Franceys freely used the names Hameldon, Osgodby and Armyn, as well as marrying into the family, and taking the name of Vesy. There is also an account of Walter Fitz-Gilber's ancestry, as a Francey, holding fiefs called Hameldon or Emeldon, the Francey family being closely connected to the Hansards, as joint and consecutive witnesses in charters.

Shown in 1103–1106, de Brus attests a charter of Count of Mortain the Abbey of Marmoutier.

Portions of Cleveland are enfeoffed to de Brus in Lofthouse, Ingleby Barwick and other places by the Earl of Chester in 1100–1104.

Side note:

Among land and property scattered across Cleveland, up until around 1990, were several adjacent and largely substantial farms grouped along the upper reaches of the River Tees, namely Ingleby, Barwick, Quarry Farm and White House. These were owned by my 100-year-old mother Dorothy Frank's cousins, her father Tom Frank being born there. On entering the twenty-first century, the whole district was sold up and built upon, becoming the township of Ingleby Barwick. Charters showing Ingleby and Barwick previously belonging the de Brus, together with the de Brus fiefdoms of Acklam and Linthorpe later belonging to Tom Frank, such coincidences defy explanation other than having strong historic associations.

Whitby from around 1100:

> 'Ville de Whiteby a tenit cum Frankburgh et Fraunches leis dreitours et aquitance'

Translated it reads:

> 'Grant of the burgers of Whitby and the town of Whitby has hold when Frankburgh and frenchies quietly bear and aquitance agree.'

This shows a friendly but nervous welcome, when translated reads, '… but Franks, please don't trash the place or bully the populous', and:

'Littera directa abbati de Whiteby quod admittat Francs cum de killum common achum de Whiteby apostatum.'

Translated, it reads, 'Letter plain from Whitby Abbey, to admit the Franks when about killing (when war for us), but to impress upon them when about Whitby (normal times), to renounce their previous belief'.

Each clearly addresses the Franks directly and the Frenchies, referring to the Normans, and their reputation for being thuggish, arrogant and quick-tempered, and represents a plea to the Franks to save their bloodlust for the common enemy and not the populous. Just one problem, where once fired up and glorifying in slaughter, what's a man to do with no one left to kill?

Relating to names and name spellings there is a later undated reference to Christance Franke, *viduse,* widow of Baxtergate, thought to be between 1087–1130.

Prior to becoming King, as Prince of the Cumbrians, David I, King of Scotland, first gained control of Cumberland and Northumberland, and later as King, founded the English-speaking Monasteries of Kelso, Dryburgh, Melrose and Holyrood. Of his tenants-in-chief were a clutch of Anglo-Normans derived from the region of Normandy and Brittany, among these were the Morevilles, the Soulises, the PitzAlans and most important, de Brus and his knights. De Brus's retinue included Franks from which royal ancestry the feudal system originated, a methodology de Brus drew inspiration from in the creation of military fiefs.

Following the Battle of Tinchebrai 28th September 1106, King Henry awarded Robert de Brus his Yorkshire fee. In 1107, the second Robert de Brus, together with other Normans, attempted to oblige King Alexander to yield part of the Scottish Kingdom to his brother David. The appeal was in vain causing de Brus and his young son Adam to renounce their allegiance to David, throwing the weight of their feudal power against the Scots.

Borrowed from *Sweet Civility and Barbarous Rudeness*, William M Aird, Cardiff University, page 62: 'David's political and cultural education in England made him aware of the advantages to be gained from subscribing to the values of the Norman elite. When he succeeded his brother Alexander I as King of the Scots in 1124, David modelled his kingship on practices learned at Henry's court. Even before his accession, David had made use of the barons of Northern England in securing Scottish Cumbria and the lands in eastern Scotland as an appendage. As king, David began to reward his Norman and French allies by creating lordships for them.'

The above extract mentions rewards given to David's supposed Norman and French allies, the argument being those with vested interests siding with the Scottish king on receiving their reward might be doubly satisfied. The second observation is the mention of *French allies* where in parlance, mention of *the French* as opposed *the Franks* might be mistaken as little different from one and the same. I touch on this later, nonetheless; the Franks too were direct recipients of the King's largesse.

At a council of all England in 1109, de Brus attests a charter of Henry I, confirming to the church of Durham possessions that certain men of Northumberland had previously claimed.

Of Yorkshire, from 1109 on, de Brus possessed the lands of Orm, Turbern, Ulchil, Chetel and Ravenchil together with thegns in Borgescire wapentake, and as Chief Lord, consents to gifts made to the monks of Marmoutier by one of his tenants. Later, he attests King Henry's confirmation of said gift.

Information from around 1113–1114 shows what drove the Cleveland Franks, through marriage and allegiances, to expand across England and Scotland, and like their overlords the de Brus, retain their Yorkshire family ties. They consistently maintained contact travelling across what had been the Kingdom of Bernicia, the land between the Tweed and the River Tees, and those Frank settlements and holdings found around Middlesbrough and their Cleveland heartland.

Regarding the above, I am grateful for information drawn from the County Records of A D Weld French, author of the *Index Armorial: Franks, Francus, Franceis, French, Fraunceys, in England and Scotland*.

The surname French taken from the slang, as in Johan Fraunceys 'the Frenchman', became 'Frenchman' aka French, all of the variously spelt Franks in Scotland and England stemming from one main source. Emanating from Normandy, a few settled south, a number from Yorkshire migrating north via Durham into Scotland. Evidenced by subtle unexplained name changes, some of the clan branched into separate identifiable families along the River Tweed. Established family took positions in Edinburgh and Glasgow, frequent travel taking them south to Yorkshire, their kin there and south again to York and London.

The more complicit of the Franks who moved north with de Brus quickly took for themselves the rank of Count or equivalent title. Their pre-eminence seemed to work as they very quickly moved into positions of honour with handsome endowments, some into the Church and some into the law.

Around the time of 1115–1118, de Brus was in possession of the manors of Horncastle and Alford, when it is presumed that King Henry had given Robert his Yorkshire fee soon after the Battle of Tinchebrai 28th September 1106.

Elderly Sir Robert Fraunceys, one of three recorded knights of the second Robert de Brus, witnessed a document of Adam de Brus's son Robert founding Guisborough Priory, near Skelton, around 1119.

Also around 1119–1124, religion playing such an important part of life, litigation taken by the canons of Guisborough regarding an informal deed of Adam's grandfather fell into dispute. And although Lord of Skelton, it was deeds concerning Skelton church that continued to haunt Adam. Thinking his soul was in mortal danger for standing his ground, he gave up all claims.

Then we find a grant of Robert de Brus and his wife Agnes and son Adam dated 1120:

> 'Given for the health of King Henry the first, and to the monks of Whitby and of Midlesburc'.

This important grant, confirmed by Pope Eugenius III, corroborates the gift made by Robert de Brus of land and his interests south of Middlesbrough, about Cleveland, which included the church of St Hilda.

I mention Middlesbrough in relation to twentieth century T H Frank, builder.

Robert de Brus and elderly Robertus Francais attest a confirmation of Alan de Percy to the monks of Whitby, also around 1120.

Approximately 1120, most likely at the court of Henry I, de Brus's friendship with David, King of Scots flourished, causing him to derive the Annandale and 200,000 acres of land in 1124. Putting the event in context historically, Henry purchased the Cotentin from Robert Curthose, one of two older brothers of Henry in 1087.

Henry, fourth son of William the Conqueror, William himself, the de Brus, the Franks and others, all of the Cotentin peninsular and all historically interrelated. And it must be remembered it was a Frank who made peace with King Henry over disputes over Normandy in 1120, namely King Louis VI, King of the Franks.

Now is a grant of 1120 testified by 'Robertus de Brus et tres de suis militibus', knights Robertus Francais and his brother knights Rogerus de Rosel et Wydo de Lofthus, the latter two men using assumed names in place of Francais.

The largesse and many gifts granted by de Brus at his time of life, is consistent with the practice of ensuring a place with God. It shows differences in character between some warlords and de Brus's need to be seen as righteous and beneficent. The document is also important in reaffirming the whereabouts and status of Robert Francais and his affiliation with de Brus, as knights bound by a common bond.

Reaffirming their Frank held origins, Robert de Rosel aka Francais granted land in the nearby parish of Pieux in Normandy to the Abbey of Saint Sauveur where the Franks held the viscountcy, being the same abbey the de Brus of Brix patronised.

In relation to names, Lofthus was used by Wydo Francais and by Theobold, coming from the local place known as Loftus, its origin the old Norse words of 'lopt hus', or loft house. Rogerus, however, had used the name Rosel, previously taken from Rozel on the west coast of the Cotentin, Normandy. As regards Robertus Francais, Rogerus stayed by his brother's side, whereas his other brother Alvred de Rosel, or Alfred, taken from old Breton, went on to hold lands in Yorkshire that were part of the Chester honour.

The Extraordinary Franks

In affirmation of that connection, Alfred coming from old Breton, I would remind readers that Robertus Francais's mother Sprota, who died 21st May 940 was a Breton captive. I've mentioned the propensity for the reuse of family names such as William, and remind that Rollo's son was Guillaume, affirming the use of William as a family name.

Alvred was described in 1130 as 'the man of Robert de Brus', his descendants continuing to support the abbey of Whitby. This bore the toponym of Acclum, consisting of the church of Acklam that in 1086 had been held by Earl Hugh and of him by Hugh, son of Norman. The word toponym meaning a name derived from a place or region; the Rosel descendants took their name as being derived of their founder and his associations with Acklam. And it's Acklam and the nearby enclave of Linthorpe that the Franks were previously recorded as having derived the enfeoffment of land, the same acquired by my grandfather in the twentieth century.

In 1121, de Brus was present at the great gathering of magnates at Durham. The gathering came about due to great unsettlement on the part of the northern barons when the claims of St Cuthbert's to Tynemouth became vocal.

And within a couple of years history highlights the presence of a large army of Yorkshiremen and knights advancing towards Scotland, Robertus and the Franks being with the de Brus. Named after his grandfather, Robert was made first Lord of Annandale by King David of Scotland in 1124. Having acquired the manor of Fulco Paynell at Carlton via his first wife Agnes Paynell, true or otherwise, his second marriage to Agnes Annard is said to have been instrumental in causing him to be granted the Lordship of Annandale.

When David I of Scotland invaded England in 1130, the elder Robert de Brus renounced his fealty. However, Robert's son, also Robert, remained loyal to David and took over his father's lands and property in Scotland. The English territory, including that of Cleveland, remained with the older man prior to it being passed to his oldest son, Adam.

Turning the clock back to the early part of the twelfth century, during Alexander's reign there was a desire to separate the Scots Church from the English, thereby increasing the sense of political nationhood. Breakdown of royal authority by King Stephen of England allowed King David to re-affirm Scottish territorial ambitions in north-east England; David I's campaigns in Northumbria being seen as manifestations of his support for Empress Matilda's claim to the English throne. The period 1135–1157 saw an attempt by David to add to his realm from the Tweed to the Tees in what might be termed 'regnum Scottorum'.

To put in context, David I had a half-baked claim to Northumbria viewed through his wife Matilda, daughter of the Earl Waltheof and his wife Judith, niece of William the Conqueror. King David's ambitions and continued invasions brought problems for the northern lords and baronial families who had been encouraged to settle in Scotland and the neighbouring environs.

The leading protagonist was Robert de Brus: exultant over his triumph over the Scots, and encouraged by David's grant of the lordship of the Annandale, he sided with the King. But in a twist of circumstance, in 1138, the elder Robert was forced to renounce his allegiance to David and opposed him in the Battle of the Standard, but his headstrong younger son Robert joined the Scots, father and son now being on opposing sides.

The younger Robert, le Meschin aka the Cadet, as Robert II, was captured by his father following the Battle of the Standard in 1138, and given over to King Stephen of England. Robert de Brus's second marriage produced William, and a daughter, Agatha, who married Ralph, son of Ribald, being Ribald Lord of Middleham. The third Robert, released by his father, produced the fourth Robert de Brus in 1189, and a second child, William who produced yet another Robert.

YORKSHIRE, THE BORDERS AND SCOTLAND FROM 1120

Concerning Robertus Francais, his sons William and Robert, and grandchildren. Due to Robertus's apparent good health and ability to take sword and fight, he seems somewhat robust and likely to have fathered more children than appear on record. Following their settlement in Scotland, some family members from Yorkshire seem to have moved north and joined their brethren there, and through subsequent marriage and childbirth reformed, splitting into cousin-related families.

Through being closely grouped in the Borders area, the Scots Franks looked for means of separate identification, using variations of spelling of the original name. Despite this, the Franks of Northern England and the Scottish Borders continued to maintain contact, despite the spelling variations much favoured by the Scottish Franks, including some of York, as to become a class apart.

Robert de Brus, Companion-in-Arms to King David of Scotland, married twice: firstly to Agnes, daughter of Geoffrey Bainard, Sheriff of York and second to Agnes, daughter and heiress of Fulk de Bagnell, Lord of Carleton, North Yorks. Other than his friendship with David, little is known of Robert's early life, although, as far back as 1120, he was often seen at King David's side, yet finding time to visit his estates in Scotland, North Yorkshire and Normandy.

Demonstrating the comings and goings, the complexity of intermarriage and the ongoing relationship with the Frank dynasty, I refer to the above Fulk de Bagnell, a descendant of the Fulk dynasty. Bertrade de Montfort, Queen Consort of the Franks, one-time Queen of the Franks and France, who lived between 1070 and 1117, being a rarefied beauty, married Fulk IV, Count of Anjoui, long enough to have family. Being so enamoured of her, Phillip I, King of France stole her away from Fulk, marrying her despite both already having a spouse. For his efforts, Phillip was excommunicated in 1095.

So anxious was Bertrade for one of her sons to succeed Phillip, she sent King Henry a letter asking him to arrest her stepson, Louis. Records indicate she tried to kill Louis, first by sorcery and then through poison. Both failing, Louis survived sufficient to succeed Phillip as King in 1108.

And hence evidence of the dynastic interrelation affecting descendants of the Franks via its very Queen culminating in the esteemed Fulk de Bagnell, Lord of Carlton, his estates abutting the de Brus North Yorks Skelton fee and one's more modest family domain. And then there's the lovely Agnes, heiress to the Fulk estates, whose lands were cosily situated close to those of the de Brus.

Robertus Francais, knight, enjoined with his son William and grandson Roger and Robert de Brus in taking the Annandale, Scotland, granted to de Brus by King David in 1124, tenure being assisted by Yorkshire knights and able Yorkshire yeomen. Records of respectable families in Dumfriesshire reveal many of their origins in Yorkshire. A number of sources including www.archive.org/stream/notes on the surnames of Francus, quote: 'According to the Scotch records circa 1218, wherein it states that:

> Roger, son of William Franciscus quit-claims to Sir Robert de Brus, Lord of Annandale, lands which the grantee held of him in the territory of Annan for the excambion of land in the territory of Moffatt, which William Franciscus, the grantees's father formally held of Sir Robert de Brus.'

Note: excambion in Scotland is the exchange of one piece of land for another. William is indicated as a son of Robertus, Roger a grandson.

Seen as coming from North Yorks, an increase in the number of Franks was evidenced close to Annandale and its surrounds. And it was during the same period 1124–1130 de Brus was known to be with King Henry at his hunting lodge of Brampton.

Of the Frank family left behind in Yorkshire, great religious houses like Guisborough were essential not only for people of high rank, but also the class below. In 1124–1129, the Franks are indicated as Franklins, a collective group, recorded along with yeomen who occur as donors to the priory, whose squires could only afford to give a few acres or sometimes rods. These gifts continue to the middle of the thirteenth century. Enfeoffed to overlords, the entry is significant as it specifically denotes and typifies the Franks or Franklins as a settled group of French or Norman freeholders, their rank indicated alongside knights and squires.

The location of Kildale and Danby, close to Guisborough, is significant in that the above information positively fixes both the location and the lineage of the Franks as benefactors alongside the de Brus having their roots in the Cotentin Peninsular of Normandy.

Skelton Castle and its surrounds being de Brus, deeds purporting to be foundation documents, one in 1119–1124 and another dated 1129, relate to Skelton church. In disputing the documents, Robert de Brus's grandson Adam became embroiled in litigation with the canons of Guisborough to whom the de Brus were huge benefactors.

The largesse of Robert gifted twenty-nine carucates, ten churches and other gifts. The de Brus family, the Franks and their descendants, having been shown to be munificent benefactors to the canons of Guisborough, for the canons to become so argumentative against the de Brus family, shows the elevated status of the Church and the necessity of maintaining observance with God's representatives on earth. Regardless of rank, the purchase of prayer ensured one's place in heaven, where, before his death, Adam relinquished all claims against the Guisborough canons.

East of York, Walter Fraunces appears as a witness testifying a 1130–1135 charter gifting land of Robert de Meinil the Second at Sutton Ougate by Stamford Bridge.

Dated Whitby, 1135–1139, the latter part of the document is obscured. Translated it reads 'Good greet, and Franks we wish see our …' seen in its original form:

'Bon greet Franche volunte ses soubtmistrrerent en nostre …'

In 1136, upon the death of King Henry I, King David of Scotland commences his invasion of Northern England. It is against the background of Church, Norman settlement, war and massive bloodshed that events unfold.

The Battle of the Standard on Cowton Moor in 1138 is well-documented; suffice to say Robert de Brus and his son, also Robert, were on different sides.

In 1141, the now elderly, de Brus endeavoured to gain consent of the prior of Durham and Archdeacon Ranulf to the election of William Cumin, Chancellor to King David of Scotland, to the See of Durham.

Robert de Brus died in late 1141–1142, apparently between the great age of seventy-one and seventy-eight. I have been unable to locate a date for the death of Robertus Francais, however he seems to have lived to some great age, and was survived by at least three sons and several grandchildren.

Adam son and heir of Robert de Brus survived his father for only twelve months and died in 1143. Before his death, Adam and his wife gave to the Archbishop of

York the church of Thorpe-Arch towards the endowment of the chapel of St Mary and the Angels that Archbishop Roger subsequently erected over the gateway near York Minster.

On his father's death in 1143, Adam de Brus's son, also Adam, having not obtained his majority, his inheritance was held by the Earl of Albemarle, who in the interim obtained Danby, Egton and Lythe. Following the Earl's death in 1179, Henry II failed to restore Adam's inheritance, but in 1184 gave other lands in lieu. Around 1200, all of Adam senior's lands were eventually restored to his son.

Revising the Frank's Normandy connection, Mr Dolbet, in his addition to the *Index Armorial* published in 1893, fixes the date of a vital charter of Rannulfus Francus of between 1147 and 1153. The charter observes the Francus family as having sons as well as a daughter of marriageable age, and it's his daughter to whom Rannulfus gives the land of the Abbey-Saint-Sauveur-le-Viscomte. In the charter, Ricardus Francus appeared as a witness on behalf of the monks, and the reference to viscompte shows Rannulfus holding the rank of viscount. While having sons to consider, due to such an important dowry being bestowed upon a daughter, Mr Dolbet's investigation assumes Viscount Francus having possessions far in excess of those his abbey fee were overlords of, having been shown as being of royal descent with direct links to Scotland and North Yorks.

This link is vital in showing that Rannulfus held his possessions directly from King Stephen of England, Dolbet seems to infer that the Frank family's primary status remained in the Cotentin of Normandy, their post-invasion youth sent to Britain, holding more minor ranks such as knight. Referred to as kin, the Franks in Britain became a mixed bunch, many seen as subservient to an overlord, a handful rising to and being referred to as lord, count or viscount, such titles being seen on a larger scale in Scotland where the de Brus held monarchy. Nonetheless, such an esteemed name, prevalent in Normandy, held great quarter, reflecting personal acclaim and respect for French royal antecedence in Britain.

Ricardus Francus, mentioned as a witness above, has been shown to be one of Rannulfus's sons, both sons having been shown to giving their blessings to the above marriage transaction. Also, possible brother of Rannulfus was Abbot Hugo Francus. A charter of Guido de Lavalle, 1113–1151, translated records:

> 'To all the sons of Holy Mother Church, Guido, Lord of Lavalle (Guy de Laval), Greetings. All of you know that Juhellus de Crapon, knight, granted to God and the monks of Savigny the land that Gaudinus Rahier had given them in perpetual alms, freely and quietly.'

The charter finishes:

> 'Given in our presence, and in order that this charter may always remain irrefutable, we have amended our seals.'

The aforesaid being witnessed by Abbot Hugone Francus, Francus reappears in Yorkshire in a confirmation of around the same date, this time connecting Lord Adam de Brus with Willelmus Francus as a witness. Despite such distance, the name Francus appears appended to important and historical documents relating to the Church and the certainty of faith shown by a commonality of name and persuasion.

Rosedale Abbey, North Yorks, was a Cistercian Nunnery founded in 1158 by William de Rosedale aka Francus. Consisting of nine nuns and a prioress, it survived for four centuries before being dissolved in 1535. The stone was used during the subsequent mining boom and today only one tower remains outside of the current nineteenth century St Mary and St Laurence Parish Church. Nonetheless for the Franks scattered across the landscape, Rosedale and its difficult terrain became their heartland, the very name Rose born of the Frank diminutive of Ros aka Rosel de Normandy.

Confirmation of King Henry II 1152:

> 'Be it known, I Walterus Ingerram give perpetual alms to the Church of St Mary Gyseburne, and to the canons the churches of my lands, this donation is made for myself, my wife, sons, and for my lord Adam de Brus the second, and for the souls of my father, mother and paternal uncle, also for the souls of Robertus de Brus and Adam, his son.'

The testimus includes Willelmus Francus. See also dates 1180 and 1195.

While Robert de Brus's cantonment, wife and children are a matter of record, piecing together Robertus Francais family has been tricky. William Franke-layn, given to Nostell, lands in Bramham 1160–1175. That Robertus took a wife and had at least two boys is affirmed. It appears fairly certain that William inherited the Scottish line and had a son, Roger. The de Brus embarkation to Scotland took with it a contingent of Yorkshiremen together with Frank nobles. These have proven to include the knight, Sir Robertus Francais the elder, and William Francais.

There appears to have been another son, also called Robertus, who was involved in the release of knights' service having connections with the de Stuteville, de Mowbray and Fossard. In 1170 Robertus shows as a witness to a charter relating to Egton, also, Bernardi and Roberto show as likely grandsons of Robertus the elder as they appear in records as sons of Robertus some time after Sir Robertus senior's death. For a proper analysis, see part two, which deals with the family tree in Yorkshire.

The Extraordinary Franks

Taken from extracts:

> In 1161 Adam de Brus junior obtained land in Carlisle through a complicated family settlement.
>
> In 1165 Adam de Brus contributes to the expenses of the Welsh war in respect of his knight's fees.
>
> Prefato Roberto F … (taken as Frank) cleric of the church of Gyseburna (Guisborough) canons, concerning an annual pension, dated 1165–1180.

Sometime after 1165, son of Robertus, William Franceis, is a witness to Grim, son of Guido of the Abbey of Melrose, who grants to God, the Church and monks the whole toft of Berwick for the welfare of Willielmus de Sumervilla and his heirs.
Note:
The above took place during the reign of King William the Lyon, the longest reigning Scottish monarch. I mention this due to the King's long list of legitimate and even longer list of illegitimate children. Of his illegitimate offspring, his daughter Isabella, born 1170, married the third Robert de Brus in 1183. Promiscuous interrelations being the status quo, she was aged just thirteen, and later married Robert de Ros, first Baron de Helmsley of Cleveland, Ros as in Rosel and by any other means a related Frank. Also, the foregoing perfectly illustrates the close Scottish-Cleveland interrelationship.

In a charter, of around 1165, land was conveyed to the church of St Mary of Melrose, witnessed by William le Franceis. The transcript:

> 'Prefato Roberto Francus clerico, church of Gyseburna …'

Dated 1165–1180, relating to the canon's pension, this and other references to a Roberto Francus twenty or so years after Roberto Francais death at Guisborough is more than mere coincidence. As well as William and his grandson Roger, it seems Robertus had a second son who either enjoined his father as a brother knight on his sojourn to the Annandale, subsequently returning to Yorkshire either with his father or alone, or, as seems possible, he never left preferring to remain in Yorkshire with his family.

1166, Robert de Brus III holds the lands of Pickering previously gifted by the Crown.

Between 1166 and 1180, Robertus Francus, the younger, is witness to the restoration of tithes wrongly withheld and now given to the monks of Whitby.

Franks, with their Christian names spelt Robertus, Roberto or Roberti, each with varying clerical titles, witness numerous documents. These are two examples:

> 'Roberti canonici. Canonicis molendina in Gyseburna (Guisborough) cum soca et molta, sicut ea habuit avus meus Robertus ... concssu ... ecclesiam de Danby ... habuit Robertus ... Testibus Roger de Rosel, Roberto fratre ejus, Ricardo de Normandy.'

> 'Willelmus de Rusmar, omnibus ministris suis fidelibus et amicis tarn Franci quam Anglis salutem.'

The second example reads, 'William of Rusmar records himself to serve faithfully, loyal and true his friendship with Franci ...', the name-spelling being unclear.

Roger de Rosel aka Francaise, a brother knight and others, appearing in documents relating to Robertus, gives credence to a son called Robertus after his father and hence the possibility of Bernardi, being a grandson, indicated as a son of Robertus. See pedigree.

Robertus Frauncetys is mentioned concerning tithes wrongly given to Whitby of Danby, dated 1166–1180. Also in 1166, there's record of William Francaise, elder brother to Roberto, being in Yorkshire from Scotland accompanying a retinue of de Brus. The document relates to a charter of 1166 concerning redress for forest trespass by Robert, son of Engelram, as well as a matter of knight's fees in the area of Pickering. Robertus thereafter returns to Scotland, periodically visiting Yorkshire.

It seems that although William's future mostly lay in Scotland, as titular head of the Franks, both in Scotland and Yorkshire, he too visited both locations, this time coming to Yorkshire because of some difficulty concerning his knights fees:

> 'Adam de Brus et pro anima patris mei et matris mee et patrui mei Willelmi Ingerram et pro anima Roberti de Brus et Adam filii ejus. Hii sunt testes Willelmus Francus.'

In 1168, Adam de Brus and Roberto Francaise pay fees in respect of lands in Yorkshire.

Bernardi, son of Roberto, sees a charter of 1170, relating to Egton in Cleveland.

Incidentally, There is evidence of a brother Robert to Bernardo Frauncetys where Roberto aka Robertus appears at a time when the older father was in Scotland. Unlike Bernardo, there appears to be no clear evidence of a father-son connection, but entries showing Roberto and the more formal spelling of Robertus Frauncetys. With the father deceased, it seems to clinch the prospect of the two brothers Bernardo and Robertus having spent time together. Bernardo Franke was witness to a charter whereby William de Stuteville gave assert, or clearing, to John de Ryton 'cleared in

The Extraordinary Franks

Hogtweit'. The land was situated to the south end of Westfield, Hutton-le-Hole, Lastingham, North Yorkshire; a Frank stronghold.

The above entry has links back to Normandy and the family Estouteville aka de Stuteville of Etoutteville-sur-Mer, being contemporaneous with the Brus and Franks of the Cotentin, Normandy. Robert de Stuteville like the Brus was granted several holdings for service following the Conquest.

Several prominent Norman families were interconnected by liege ties, marriage or both. While the Franks were prominent across France, following the Conquest the de Stuteville emerged pre-eminent, the de Stuteville's high status showing no impediment to the marital arrangement between the two families. Interrelated, the Franks were variously employed as advocates and clergy, having strong associations with York.

The succession goes: Robert de Stuteville from Estouteville, married Beatrix; their son Robert married Erneburga. Their son, Robert III, became Justice Itinerant of the Counties of Cumberland and Northumberland High Sheriff of Yorkshire, who in 1170–1175 married Helewise aka Hawise Murdac, their sons being William and Nicholas. Bernardo Franke being a witness to William in 1190.

When High Sheriff of Yorkshire, their daughter, also Hawise, married Hugh, son of Hugh de Morville, Constable of Scotland … his wife being Beatrice de Beauchamp. Hugh senior's daughter, Maude de Morville, married William de Veteriponte. Their son, Ivo de Veteriponte, married Isabel de Lancaster, their daughter Isabel, marrying Hugh Franceys around 1230–1238.

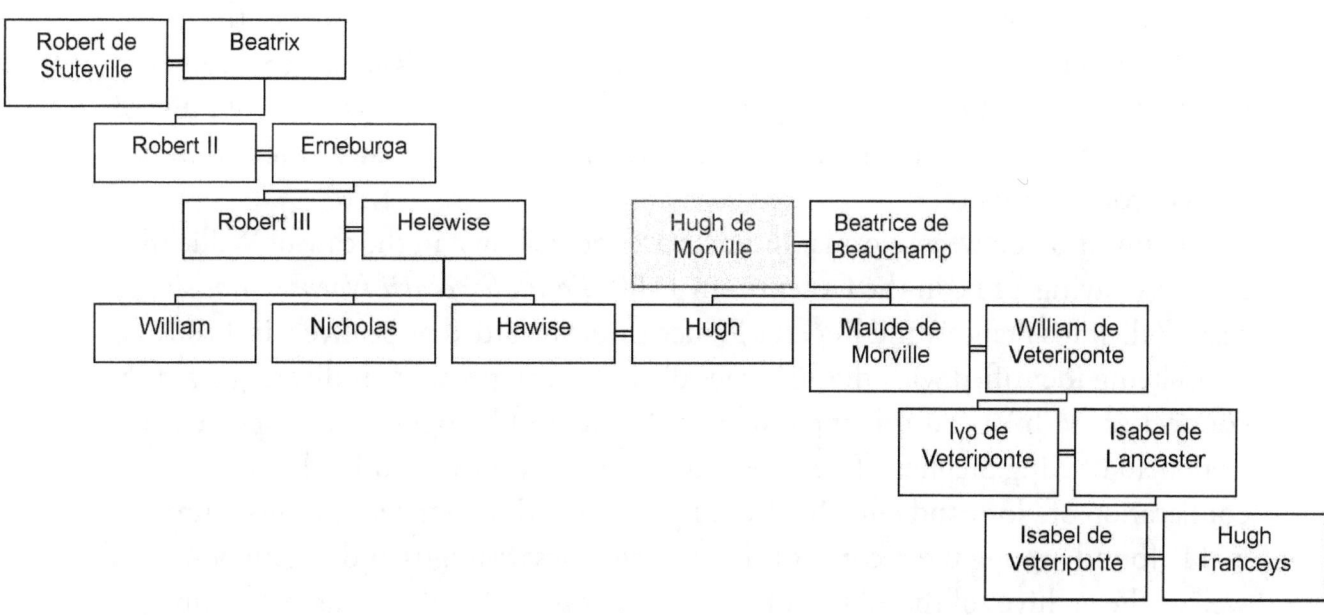

Going back to Robert de Stuteville: in 1177, while he was High Sheriff of Yorkshire, Robert de Stuteville's brother Roger received charge of Edinburgh Castle. Before his death in 1186, Robert de Stuteville claimed the barony from Roger de Mowbray, which was previously forfeited by his grandfather. By way of recompense, de Stuteville gave Mowbray the area of Kirkby Moorside, North Yorks. Robert de Stuteville aka Franceys was seen as a probable founder of the nunneries of Keldholme and Rosedale. A side note: Kirkby Moorside was recently a strong Frank domain.

The above brings together several significant threads: the specific location of Cleveland, North Yorkshire, the Franks association with York, the marital interrelation between known families, the status of individuals and clear Scottish connections via Hugh de Morville, as Constable of Scotland, himself a Frank, and Roger de Stuteville in relation to Edinburgh Castle, and somewhere in the background, Adam and Robert de Brus.

Franco clerico, 1170–1185, of unknown Christian name, is found providing a testament 'testibus' to a mill and land transaction 'Acklam from Bridlington', Acklam a later area of development by T H Frank.

In 1173, the land of Tibthorpe was given to Robert, forfeited by Hugh de Morevill. A Roger de Stuteville is mentioned in relation to various fees in connection with each of Adam and Robert de Brus.

By Adam, son of Richer, a grant to the hospital of St Peters at York for two bovates of land at Skelton, near the de Brus seat of Skelton Castle, 1175–1185. This is a testament witnessed by Robertus where Bernardi is referred to as son of Roberto Fraunceys.

Adam and Robert de Brus were amerced in 1176 for forest trespass around Eskdale. This reads as assumed deforestation and cultivation within the confines of the forest.

A Norwegian vessel found wrecked upon the rocks of Redcar in 1180 comes as too much of a temptation and is pillaged by the men of Cleveland. A long list of suspects from every town and hamlet were listed as implicated and amerced by the justices for the offence.

A connection between Normandy and Scotland is shown in the case of Willielmus Franceis paying a fine in the Cotentin in 1180. *Rotuli Scaccarii Normanniae* shows that Willielmus Franceis and Rogerus Franceis were recorded respectively in 1180 and 1195 being identified with the Valognes district, earlier records indicating a family connection with Viscount Francus of Saint Sauveur of Valognes, whose possessions were held of King Stephen. The same names later appear in Scotland following the confiscation of Normandy in 1204 by King Philippe II of France. Charters, numbers 6–11, found among the records of the Abbeys Caesarisbugus and Montebourg, as well as the archives of the Abbey of Cerisy, show these Frank surnames continuing in the Cotentin well after the confiscation.

The following extracts are incomplete, and try as I may, I can't make proper sense of the scramble of data:

'Odard, Vicecomes de Bebbanburgh, witnessed the foundation charter of Selkirk granted by Earl David. In 1181, William, son of the first Odard had Recognition of Right to three ... (something or other). John le Fraunceys, guardian of both the heir and the estates, admitted her ... (who, unknown), title to a widows portion of thirteen or fourteen years.'

1181 continued. John Frank had a significant legal role around this time in Scotland, his name showing in Soureby, Thirsk, in 1251 and York and Westmorland in 1254. Besides travel, the name also appears in connection with extensive landholdings.

Also in 1181, Robert de Brus attested a charter of William Count of Mortain, Marmoutier.

William Esturmi had issue, Henry, who was still a minor in the ward of John le Fraunceys when his father was amerced in water in 1193 for default as surety relating to Langbargh Wapentake, North Yorks. This and previous references to 1181 confirm John le Fraunceys having a legal role of some standing in Scotland and York, yet retaining ties of some kind with Langbargh. For Langbargh see Cleveland encompassing the de Brus Skelton estates.

Ayton in Scotland was an early Frank seat being positioned around twenty miles east of the Frank seat of Thornydykes and nineteen miles from the castle of Dunbar, where the Fraunceys had connections with the Earls of Dunbar.

The shire of Coldingham, with its priory, shows many of the donations and charters between 1188 and 1235 having as their witnesses David, Baron of Quixwood and Adam Francey; the same Fraunceys held possessions in Herwickshire and Linlithgow.

A charter of 1182, having the confirmation of King Henry II, shows Walterus Ingerram aka Francaise, giving to the church of St Mary of Gyseburne, being Guisborough, the church of Erncelive, Arncliffe and two bovates of land, a mansion, as well as the church of Haslintune with half an acre of land and a mansion, together with the chapel of Haslintune. The donation was made for himself, his wife and sons and for his lord Adam de Brus II, also for the souls of his mother and father and uncle, together with the souls of Robert de Brus, his son Adam and Willelmus Francus. The charter is significant in portraying unequivocally the ties between elderly Walterus, Willelmus Francus aka Franceis et-omnis, and the de Brus both in Scotland and Cleveland.

The above record is significant in confirming the Franks having holdings adjacent to Skelton Castle under their lord Adam de Brus. The other point is the difficulty in providing an absolute and complete synopsis given the Franks propensity for the use of pseudonym. Not being a full-time researcher, the wealth of archive material and diversity of names puts such commitment of research well beyond my reach or ability to dissemble. What I've tried to achieve is a light touch across a wide spectrum providing easy reading without becoming too bogged down in minutia.

Irrespective his status, in 1185, Adam de Brus himself is amerced. This relates to his unlawful cultivation of 135 acres of land sown with bread-corn; land previously within the confines of protected forest. See 1176 above. We have to take heed of the previous 100 year's toil in the recuperation of land made waste by salting, ordered by William the Conqueror. Carried out by his cohorts, this was presumed to include de Brus predecessor Robert de Brus.

During the period stated, forest didn't necessarily mean densely planted woodland, as we know it. It could include mildly covered terrain, copse and grazing, and ideal open land for hunting game. Whereas today we would have taken it as a given to produce bread-corn, the laws of the time restricted unauthorised cultivation.

Now follows a string of extracts:

Adam Franceys is found witness to a charter favouring the church of Coldingham. This was a North Yorkshire entry relating to land dated 1189–1190.

'Roberto de mara et multis aliis.'

1195, Ralph, the Archdeacon of York, recovers a debt from Adam, and also in 1195, Roger Franceis pays a fine in the Cotentin, Normandy.

Grant by Walter Ingram for the welfare of Adam de Brus, his Lord, for the soul of William Ingram and the canons of Guisborough. For Ingram see Frank.

Following a court summons relating to Adam de Brus in 1197, an agreement was made between the canons of Guisborough concerning a vicarage in Kildale, North Yorks.

In 1198, the third Adam died, his son and heir Peter de Brus inheriting.

The lands of Arnaldus Francigena at Berwick are shown lying adjacent to the son of Peter de Kelso's land, which was gifted to the church of St Mary's, Kelso, in 1200.

Also in 1200, William Francigena witnesses a charter in favour of St Mary's, and Adam Franceis stands witness to a charter conveying land at Stirling.

Three other charters of around the same date are also witnessed by William, but spelt Wilelmus Francigea.

King John restores the lands of Danby and all the forest, previously withheld in 1179, to Peter de Brus in 1200. Peter de Brus l, of Skelton Castle, gave up his interest in the Lordship of Berdesey, Coldingham and Risington, and paid King John £1,000 for the lordship and forest of Danby, later shown acquired by the Franks.

At the time, Peter de Brus was guardian of an area around Hartlepool for his cousin. The name Hart is shown as the middle part of my great-great-grandfathers surname. During this time Peter claimed some wrecks off the coast that had been taken by

The Extraordinary Franks

the Bishop of Durham's servants. For this he was fined 50 shillings. In retaliation Peter took captive of one of the Bishop's men imprisoning him in Skelton Castle.

Norman in origin, French pottery has recently been found at Danby.

Ecclesiastical history shows grants made by the de Brus family to the priory in the twelfth century. This was in respect of half a carucate of land to be added to existing landholdings, parts of which were to be made available adjoining the site of the prior's country house.

Peter de Brus was excommunicated by Bishop Poor and fined £20 by the justices. Peter's father-in-law, William, Earl of Albemarle, intervened and had the sentences quashed on condition the Bishop had total rights to sea-wrecks.

A busy period, a charter also of 1200 shows a transaction made by Arnaldus son of Peter de Kelso benefiting the church of Saint Mary of Kelso. Described as a gift in the Ville of Berwick, the land was situated between the property of Arnaldus Francigena and William de Bernahme. Dated the same period, the document also affirms a Frank holding in Berwick-upon-Tweed.

Also in 1200, Adam Franceis appears as a witness to a charter of Herbert of Chalmers conveying land at Donipace to the church of Saint Mary of Cambuskenneth, Clackmannanshire.

William le Franceis is found in a charter in favour of Saint Mary, Melrose, circa 1200, by Hugh de Normanville aka Francaise.

Such was the liberal interpretation of surnames, in the Coldingham Charters Norman Roll of 1203 historians show Walterus Francigena being that of Walter le Franceis. In the early part of the thirteenth century, Roger French is indicated as an early English translation of Rogerus Francigena and so on.

Yorkshire records conclude the likelihood that prior to 1204, when King Phillip Auguste reunited the province of Normandy to the Crown of France, like the Bruces, the Franceis held possessions both in the Cotentin, and England. This is proven by listings of British spellings of Frank shown active in Normandy continuing well after the date of the Conquest.

In Whitby:

> 'Post hec pers exit Robertus prior cum fratre Roberto de resons ad quandm,' reads:

> 'After this to cut through Robertus, my priority, when brother Roberto about to respond to it.'

In modern parlance 'excuse me, it's my priority to talk'.

On a visit from Scotland in 1207, William Franceis, grandson of William, attests an agreement by Walter de Chanci concerning land between Waitecroft and Bugthorpe

(South of Malton on the York–Pickering road) to the monks of Byland Abbey by exchange.

The above account observes the Franceis having feudal relations with the Brus as they appear in the Annandale. These show William Francais as the father of Roger Franceis and thereafter the name William Fraunceis perpetuating in the Scottish archives.

An Alan Franco appears between 1214 and 1249 whereto shown as a witness to a grant of John de Crawfurd. Said grant was given to the church of Newbottle in respect of:

> 'Land given for the soul of my sovereign lord Alexander, King of Scots and William, Malcolm and David, his predecessors.'

It is notable that with few exceptions e.g. Glasgow, Passelet and Newbottle, these Scottish charters are located close to the River Tweed, ten miles to the south of the Frank seat of Thornydykes.

Robert Fraunceys, son William, was an original settler with de Bruce in the Annandale where, according to Scottish records circa 1218, a feudality whereby I repeat the statement:

> 'Roger, son of William Franciscus, quit-claims to Sir Robert de Brus, Lord of Annandale, land which the grantee held of him in the territory of The Annan for the excambion of land in the territory of Moffat which William Franciscus, the guarantee's father formerly held of Robert de Brus.'

In Scots law he word excambion means an exchange of land.

In the same epoch, Roger Francisco is witness to a grant of Robert de Brus, Lord of Annandale:

> 'To William de Heneville concerning thirty-five acres of the grantors demesne in Moffet lying between the land of Sir Patrick, Earl of Dunbar, on the one side and the meadow of Sir Humphry de Kirkepatric to the other.'

This recalls an agreement on the 11th November 1218, between three parties. These were Patrick Earl of Dunbar, the Countess Christina and Sir Robert de Brus, son of William de Brus, where William Franceis appears as a notable witness. William Franceis also witnessed a grant of Robert de Brus to Humphrey, son of Simon. This transaction shows the confidence seen in young Roger Frank, whose great-great-grandfather, quote:

'I have admiration seen in a young man able to deal with men of considerable power and influence.'

These papers clearly show a familial relationship between the Franks, the Earls of Dunbar and the de Brus. This is despite a document, also of 1218, describing George Dunbar, as the incumbent Lord of Annandale conflicting with the certain knowledge of the Annandale belonging Robert de Brus.

Importantly the document reaffirms a charter given to Robert French, aka Franceis, by George Dunbar, Earl of March, aka Lord of Annandale, accepting Robert French's resignation in Robert having received a new enfiefment for himself and his wife Elizabeth and his sons Adam and Robert:

> 'In conjunct fie and the heirs of their bodie, which failyeing to Adame French sone to Robert, and his heirs male, which failyeing to airs what-some-ever …'

In which charter, the earl designates the said Robert French, aka Franceys:

> 'That he be pronounced Laird de Thornydykes, clarissimus consanguineous noster.'

In it the document translates as:

> 'Lord of Thornydykes, deep hearted, loud and clear, Robert Frank, our relation.'

In the charter, the Earl designates as follows:

> 'Designatus his lord Robertus Franceis the most famous of our cousins.'

These and other known documents confirm the interfamilial marriage between the Franks and the Dunbars. It seems in their quietude and loyalty to the de Brus and other nobility, recognition is shown to the Franks as a name in their own right.

Among the more regular transitions from Franceys/Franceis to Frenche and so on, the following is an example of regular changes involving such names as Fitzgilbert and Hameldone. Such changes seem to support the theory of individuals wanting to dispel name associations being French in origin, where early use of Frani etc. was often used as a euphemism for Frenchman. As can be imagined, the difficulty in tracking individuals and their relationship one to another has been frustrated to the point of exhaustion.

Prenotation

Walter Fitzgilbert, a Frank, was resident in Scotland as early as 1294. On the 10th January, with other barons, he witnessed a charter of James Steward of Scotland to the monks of Paisley granted at Blackwell in Renfrewshire. A few years later, about 1300, along with John Maxwell, Sir Alan of Glasford and others, Walter witnessed a charter to the same monks given by Herbert Maxwell.

On the 28th August 1296, Walter, together with other barons whose lands lay in the counties of Lanark and Renfrew, paid homage to King Edward I at Berwick. In the Ragman Rolls, Walter is described as 'Walter fiz Gilbert de Hameldone', Hameldon being a pseudonym for Franceys. In 1306, he is mentioned as having a grant from the English King of the lands of Crawford Priory in Fife, lands that were claimed by Sir Thomas de Grey.

In succession there's Sir John de Maxwell, who beget Robert, who beget John. Sir John Maxwell married Elizabeth de Lindsey, daughter of David and Egida née Stewart. Elizabeth's third marriage was to Sir James Douglas of Dalkeith. Her brother was Sir James de Lindsey, 'Jacobus de Lyndesay, filius David de Lyndesay, militis', grandfather of Lady Jane Lindsey, who espoused John de Franceys. Here, Lady Jane and John were shown as the parents of Robert Frenche, aka Franceys, first Laird of Thornydykes.

George, Earl of Dunbar and March, married Christiana de Seton, daughter of Sir William Seton, alias Gordon. George was a close friend and ally of the Percy family of England, their daughter, Lady Elizabeth Dunbar, married Robert Frenche, alias Francey, Laird of Thornydykes. Elizabeth's sister, Lady Janet Dunbar, married Sir John de Seton de Gordon, their daughter Janet being espoused to John Halyburton.

For the Franks, Thornidicke, Thornedykes or Thorndie Castle, was less a castle and more of a tower with walls, a place of defence. With it came a manor house, gardens, orchards, dovecots and estates in tenancy, good freeholders, mills, mill lands and mill fees. It was located in the Merse, near the foot of the Lammermoor Hills, now called Westruther. The manor of old was near the religious houses of Wedderlie and Bassendean.

A later charter of 1368 affirms Sir Robert de Brus shall pay money to the Earl of Dunbar and his mother, the countess. Around this time, William Franceis witnessed a resignation made to Robert de Brus, these two transactions typical of the ongoing relationship between them.

The above-mentioned Walter fiz Gilbert de Hameldon aka Sir Franceys, in 1306, had grant of the lands of Crawford Priory, Fife, claimed by Sir Thomas de Grey. Reference to the Greys is useful in tying together various strands, as well as painting in some of the background. The barony Gray is a title of the peerage of Scotland, descended from the Greys of Chillingham in Northumberland. French in origin, the surname was first borne by Fulbert, great Chamberlain to Robert, Duke of Normandy, from whom he gained the castle and lands of Croy, known as Gray, in Picardy.

What is significant is the birth of Fulbert's son, John, and a daughter, Arlotta, who, while unmarried, gave birth to William, her son being the illegitimate William the Conqueror. Fulbert was at Falaise, and a neighbour of William Francaise the elder before being elevated to the great office of Chamberlain. Grey was the first and foremost of William the Conqueror's closest companions. Stated as the Conqueror's kinsman, who, following the invasion obtained from the King several lordships, he was the progenitor of several families, all of who spelt their name Grey. Being raised to high rank in the peerage, he obtained such titles as dukes of Suffolk and Kent, earls of Stamford, barons of Codnor, Ruthyn, Wilton, Rolleston, Wark, and Chillingham and many others.

The accomplished Lady Jane Grey of 1554 fame belonged to the Suffolk family. Also, most readers will be familiar with the story of Eliza Courtney, born 20th February 1792 and who died 2nd May 1859, being the illegitimate daughter of Prime Minister Charles Grey and his lover, society beauty Georgiana, Duchess of Devonshire.

Charles Grey was the second surviving son of General Sir Charles Grey KB, and his wife Elizabeth, daughter of George Grey of Southwick, Co. Durham, connections with the north reaffirmed by Prime Minister Grey's former education at Richmond School, Yorkshire, prior to finishing at Eton and Trinity College, Cambridge.

Later, commencing around 1297 through to around 1331, I talk about an earlier General Sir Thomas Grey who during the Anglo-Scottish wars had connection with both Robert de Brus and the Franks. The usefulness of this information lies in the placement of the Franks repeatedly alongside the most prominent figures in history, and with such a name and pedigree it baffles belief that until now their story has remained untold.

STORY CONTINUED

Also, around 1218, a grant of de Brus to Sir Humphry, son of Sir Simon, is likewise witnessed by William Franceis.

Referring to The Franks of Rosedale, and Glaisdale specifically. At exactly the same time the de Brus and Franks were embroiled in Scotland, the Franks of Cleveland were also busy. The Rosedale Common and Glaisdale inhabitants were gifted their landholdings by the priory, confirmed by Peter de Brus II in 1223. In 1228, the priory surrendered all rights of the pasture land of Glaisdale, not including Danby and in 1234 surrendered all claims to the surrounding moorland; land that in turn was given over exclusively for sheep rearing.

The above was conditional on the priory retaining three shelters twenty feet by twelve feet on Glaisdale Moor for the use of shepherds, the carpenters and charcoal burners given access to woodland. Relative to the later Danby Franks estate, my five times great-grandfather's holdings contained several farms around Glaisdale and Danby where today many Franks remain scattered across the surrounding landscape, including those descendants of Robert Hart-Frank. Also historically, the Franks had spread from Guisborough to Ripon and York, with links to Ayton or Aytoun in Scotland.

Incidentally I hold Sir Robertus Francaise's descendant and namesake Robert Hart-Frank's beautifully written original will, passed to me by my grandad, Tom Frank. It is remarkable the name Robert, coined from the Robertians, should have continued generationally within the Franks for over 2000 years. The Robertians were the original predecessors of the ruling house of France under Odo, Count of Paris: being chosen as king in 888 he reined until 898. The Frankish Empire emerged from the ancient kingdom of Austrasia as early as the eighth century, the family generationally naming their sons Robert. And it's from this one draws attention to the names Robert and Frank, and hence the basis for this story.

No later than 1227, the beginning of the reign of King Alexander II, Adam Francigena was witness to a charter of David Olyfarde and his wife. This was the conveyance of a mill and land at Caders to the Church and Bishop of Glasgow. Founded in 1145, its canons came from Artois in France, close to Rouen, a nearby Frank domain and where those many years previous Rollo and his son Guillaume hunted among the woodland, and the spurned Espriota and her new husband Count Esperleng, son of Richard I emerged as unknowing predecessors to one's own family line and all that followed.

Inmates at the Hospital for the Sick Men of St Leonard, Guisborough, 1230–1250, were of both sexes, the healthy as well as the sick, including lepers, them also having a church there. The hospital was eventually merged with the priory under the master, John de Wyrke Frank. Translated, Wyrke meaning work.

Also dated 1230–1250, Willelmus Forestarius and Gundreda, his wife:

> 'Grant free perpetual etc., for the fabric fund of the church of St Mary's Gyseburne (Guisborough) and the land that lies next to

Holdebec. Testibus Roger, Canonico de Rypum, Willelmus, Clerico de Beverlaco and Petro Fraunces et multis aliis.'

Much of what has been shown shows how confusion can reign when dealing with inconstant names and how individual prevarication and spellings vacillate as if on a whim.

In York, Chancellor Sir William de Hamilton, aka Franceys, Dean of York, was closely connected with the Fresnel, themselves in the guise of Franceys. On Sir William's death, his executor was John le Franceys, Canon of York, dated 1231–1233. Related to John Franceys, Sir Richard de Osgodby, aka Richard of the place of Osgodby, was in truth Richard Franceys of Brampton-en-le-Morthen, Vicar of Bubwith.

Sir Richard was a son to Franceys from Robert de Osgodby, before that, John Franceys de Osgodby, son of Dame Clemencia Franceys, spouse of Roger de Vescy, before that, Sir Adam de Osgodby, Keeper of the Rolls of Chancery – son of Adam de Osgodby, alias Adam de Armyn.

A Yorkshire–Scottish connection:

Bubwith in Yorkshire was a Tison manor shown in Domesday. It was presented to Richard Franceys, being a benefice confirmed by Clemencia, daughter-in-law to Dame Isabel de Periton, whose husband was William de Vescy, Lord of Alnwick:

'Ricardi avus meus et Johannes pater menus.'

Roger de Vescy's wife Clemencia Franceys was a daughter of John Franceys, son of Richard Franceys of Bubwith, great-grandson of Reyner Franceys of Brampton, a contemporary of Adam Franceys of Aytoun, Scotland.

Cleveland, December 1231, on which date John Francigena paid the King 20 marks and half a mark annually to have for life the 'clostera of Warnel' plus ten acres of wood which the King grants: 'To give him seizin.'

As regards the names of Francigena and Franceis being synonymous, we have the record of the parson of Colderbec, in Cumberland, who is mentioned in 1231–1233 as John Francigena, and again in this same period as John le Franceis, both versions of the name shown by the historian M Stapleton of the University of California, as one and the same person.

Early vestiges of the Frank surname are found in the records of old monasteries and ancient charters where prototypes can be found under variants of Francus, Franciscus, Francigena, Franceis and Franke. These ancient surnames may also be seen in the Scottish Chartularies of Coldingham, Coldstream, Cambuskeneth,

Kelso, Melrose and Newbottle, such names also seen within the charters of de Brus, Normanville and others.

In 1232, Willielmus Francus, named both as Francus and Franco, witnessed a charter of John Normanville, of all lands, common, pasturage, and other easements within the manor of Mackestoun of John's father Hugh to St Mary's Melrose, in Scotland and the monastery. And again concerning a charter in favour of said Melrose monastery given by a grant of John de Normanville, witnessed by Willielmus Francus, the name Normanville too synonymous with the Franks.

Emanating from Normandy, the name Normanville is found in Scotland, as well as variations of the name Franceis, Valoines, de Brus and Morville, all of which surnames continue to appear in the records of the Cotentin in the early twelfth century. While the de Brus held the Annandale, the Morvilles held most of Lauderdale and parts of Teviotdale.

Together with the Valoines, these families were early benefactors of the Abbey of Melrose, Richard de Morville being the original founder of Dryburgh Abbey, who on becoming Lord High Constable in 1140 founded the celebrated abbey of Kilwinning. As the Anglo-French Lord of Cunningham, de Morville was the great territorial magnate of the district, upon whose death, around 1189, King David I gave the lordship of Cunningham to Richard's son Hugh.

Saint Winin being the founder of Sagtoun or Saint's Town in AD 715, the town became known as Kilwinning. A place I have the privilege of being Master Mason. Preceding Edinburgh, number one, Kilwinning was subsequently proven as the first and original Mother Lodge, being subsequently allocated the number nought.

I've mentioned Hamilton in relation to Yorkshire and the interrelation of various names having Frank antecedence. Two of Kilwinning's abbots were Hamilton-Franks respectively between 1527–1545 and 1550–1571. Originally Catholic, during the sixteenth century the abbey had become secularised and fully Protestant by the time of its last abbot, Archbishop Gavin Hamilton. A remarkable man, caught between two conflicting forces, Gavin was slain defending Christendom in a skirmish outside Edinburgh in 1571.

Swords drawn, in the ensuing scuffle Gavin was killed trying to make peace between supporters of the Catholic Queen and opposing Protestants. While championing reformation, caught between both sides Gavin also supported Mary Queen of Scots, defending to the death the ideals of Christendom. As a mediator his demise was unfortunate, and whereas the Franks had largely learned to take the middle ground, Gavin's death illustrates the downside of trying to appease everybody, all and at the same time.

Notes on Hugh de Morville: Hugh de Morville, aka Richard, is said to have come over with William the Conqueror. Professor G W S Barrow claims Hugh's name was

The Extraordinary Franks

not that of Hugh but Richard, the family being of knightly rank taking their name from the village of Morville in the canton of Briequebec. Like many individuals of the period, Richard's true parentage cannot be located. But what is known, sharing a common ancestry, the family belonged to the same class of gentry or petty nobility as the de Brus and closely associated Franks. Like many others, failing to have legitimate sons, within a couple of generations the Morville name also soon faded.

Similar to Robertus Francaise, the location of antecedent families has been fraught with difficulty, however, we come again to Le Rozel, Normandy and the previously mentioned adjacent Valognes, proven locations of the early three knights de Fraunceys. It just happens that the village of Morville de Canton, Bricquebec is located immediately between both locations in the Cotentin; further indicative of provenance, and the interrelated Franks a common thread between the various names, the above Ros being a Frank derivative.

Being lesser known, the following paragraphs provide insight principally as to the Franks and their influence ranging between Scotland, Yorkshire and the northern counties.

Robertus Fraiiuccys of York, and his donation of a parcel of land, Melsa (Meaux) Monastery, was witnessed in a charter to the chaplain and prior of St Mary of Coldingham in 1235. Occasioned by Robert Fraunceys of York, Coldingham was in the Frank's heartland of Berwickshire, on the Scottish border's south-east coastland north of Eyemouth.

In Scotland, 1235, the prior of Durham received services rendered by Adam le Fraunceys and his heirs from their land in Ayton. Durham appears strategically invaluable, positioned running north; York, Whitby, Durham, all three running north of the Humber to the Scottish Borders, Durham being a staging post between the Frank's holdings in Scotland and their counterparts in Yorkshire.

Dated 1235–1249:

> 'Unum toftum et Roberto Fraunceys aliam portionem.'

This is in relation to Fishergate, Whitby. According to subsequent statements, these tithes of Nafferton were specified among other gifts to Whitby seen in the charters of the founder and his successors and elsewhere. The surname spelling 'Fraunceys' in Yorkshire is the same as the initial Scots spelling of the name.

In Whitby 1235–1249, a translation talks about Fishergate and the monastic surrounds of Whitby, which extract proclaims:

> 'A certain person should solve their difference, cease harassment and
> pay one toft to Robert Fraunceys together with another portion.'

Alluding to this, a later family last will and testament refers to Frank ownership of property in Fishergate being the likely object of said dispute.

Concluding this section I finish with a selection of amended transcripts and again show Adam, this time concerning land given to the monks of Coldingham together with a quitclaim involving additional land. Benefiting the church of St Mary's, the donation was witnessed by Lord Anketino prior of Coldingham in 1239.

In Scotland, further charters where the orthography of Franceys, Fraunceys, Fraunceis and Frances appear, the last of these is dated 1245.

Around 1246, Adam Franciscus and his son Thomas witness a charter of land in Coldingham granted by Mabilia, daughter of Constantinus.

In another charter of Mabilia, widow, further land was given to the monks, the charter being witnessed by both Adam Fraunceys and his son Thomas. By 1247, assumed deceased, the name Adam drops away leaving the names Thomas and Richard Franceys.

Also in 1247, Thomas Franco witnesses Manumission, in the freedom from bondage of Reginuldus, praepositus of Adam de Prentirgest.

In Calderbeck Cumberland 1249, Johaiincs le Fraunceys or Francigena, parson of Caldebeck:

> 'Pope Innocent the fourth grants on the solicitation of King Henry the third, a dispensation to Johannes dictus Francigena, clericus Regis, to receive benefice, if granted in England.'

The following year 1250, Pope Innocent addressed a mandate to the Archbishop of York in favour of Johannes Francigena, clericus of the illustrious King of England, in which he commands:

> 'Notwithstanding his impaired sight ... no hindrance be given to his promotion to superior orders.'

In 1253, Johannes Francigena is granted the rectories of Lithum and Roney in the diocese of York.

John Fraunceis, son of Hugh le Fraunceis, held land in some of the northern English counties, including a manor under Robert de Veteripont. Records dated 1253–1258.

1254. A Papal mandate is given to Johannes Fraunceys clericus Regis for him to grant a dispensation to Henricus de Galdington, his kinsman and rector of Grossemer in Westmorland, to hold an additional benefice for the cure of souls.

On 2nd April 1255, a division of possessions shows that Robert le Franceys held of Isabella de Forde possessions in Wooler, Northumberland, situated south of Berwick-upon-Tweed and north of Newcastle and Durham.

Robert Frauceys is a witness to a charter of liberation of a mill to the Abbey of Whitby in 1256.

Johannes le Frauceys died in 1257, and was lamented 'siccis lacrimis' (to dry up tears) by the monks of St Mary of York and of Selby. His influence stretched from York to Cumberland and Westmorland and the huge de Brus holdings in the Scottish Borders around the Tweed.

In 1261–1262, an inquisition held in the forty-sixth year of King Henry III, shows Willelmus Franceys held one bovate and one toft in Aslakeby near Pickering.

FRANK LAW, THE ANNANDALE, AYTON, AND AWARD TO THE FRANKS OF THE ADDITIONAL SCOTTISH SEATS OF SPRUSTOUN, KELSO, THORNYDYKES, JEDBURGH AND FRANKYSLAND, PEEBLESHIRE BY KING ROBERT DE BRUS.

Ayton, in the shire of Coldingham, nineteen miles from the castle of Dunbar, became a Frank seat. Used as a court, exempli gratia or Frank law became pre-eminent, defined as Lex Salica now exemplified in practice by force majeure, and was assigned into Scottish Law. Scottish Law then different to English Law remains thus today.

Whereas the Franks were able to influence English Law, in Scotland it was the law as defined by the Franks that embodied future legislation. That said, up until the time of King John, authoritative rule and governance was imposed largely by the sword; 'vis et voluntas'.

Superseding the use of force and individual will, in England we have to give credence to the Magna Carta of 15th June 1213, the King acceding fitfully to the demands of the barons in ratification of the charter in the gradual codification of Frank law.

Frank law first started as a putative recension in the sixth century in Frankia, Germany. The concept of Lex Salica quickly became French legal statute, and in Britain became embodied as a prescript of unwavering quietude and persuasive religious doctrine codified into formulary law. Today, there is talk of discarding use of the Bible.

Having myself sworn-in many thousands of documents, I believe the concept of declaration 'in telling the truth' is fundamental and should be upheld within a composite religious framework. This should comprise of pages from each main religion that refer to the truth as an absolute 'whether a believer or not' and should be upheld on the principle of 'being sacrosanct', hence a suggestion for 'swearing in' to be renamed lex-novus-fas, or 'new law divine' replacing the Bible.

Born of the Franks, Salic law originally prohibited female succession, however this changed and a female such as a single female child could be permitted to inherit land. Pragmatism shows many instances where forms of female succession were permitted, usually as a result of calamity where the strict embodiment of law could be moulded to fit the circumstances.

Changes in society become secular demands, where pragmatism just as equalisation between the sexes was fought over and largely won. For the purpose of swearing-in within the changes and growth of secular society, and based on the argument for evolving advocacy, for court cases I see the premise for 'new law divine' paramount, and the pages of a wider more inclusive doctrine a substitute for one's hand upon the Bible written into twenty-first century statute.

The following: apologies for any repeated data:

1270, Richard Frauceys of Ayton grants messuage for his maintenance of Coldingham.

In the Medieval Seals in the Durham Cathedral Muniments, Richard Frauceys is indicated in the Rentale Antiquum of the Priors of Coldingham, holding six bovates of land in Upper Ayton valued at 40s per annum. His seal is shown as

> 'A lion rampant, with a quatrefoil, inscribed S' Ricardi Fraysoys (Franceys), de Aito.'

1271, Thomas Frances is followed in name by his son Thomas, and Richard Franceys of Ayton, both seen as witnesses to charters in favour of the monastery of Coldingham.

Holding court at Ayton, Magister Thomas Frances, 1271.

Around the same date, on the Scottish border, around the Eyemouth area, are found Thomas and Richard Franceys.

As recordings of the charters of Adam begin to wain, so the transactions of Richard and Thomas take over:

1272, Ricardo de Francisco of Ayton is shown as a witness concerning a tithe dispute over a fishery in Berwyc Stream.

De Brus, sixth Lord of Annandale, fathers Robert 11th July 1274. On becoming King, Robert the Brus reigns from 1306, dying aged fifty-four, 7th June 1329.

In 1275, in a charter of Henricus de Prendergest concerning an exchange of land with the prior of Coldingham the name Fraunc, as in Frank, first appears. Conducted at the Ayton court 7th March 'anno gregoriense 1275', it is witnessed by Richard Fraunc and Thomas Fraunc, both of Ayton.

Various spelling of Frank, 1275:

Thomas Franceys, a witness at Ayton, concerning land given to the church.

Thomas Francys of Ayton, concerning a toft and croft.

Thomas Franceis, witness to a quitclaim transaction, giving to God and the church all land and possessions.

Seen before the court of Ayton in 1276, a grant concerning land that Alice received in a dowry. Witnessed by Ricardus Franc, this is when the name Franc first appears in Scotland, his name changing again in 1278, to Franceys.

Between 1276 and 1296, Ricardus Fraunches is shown as a witness alongside Lord Henry de Horncastle, prior of Coldingham.

Dated 1279, another charter of the same period is found with the name-spelling Ricardus Fraunceys.

In 1278, Emma gifts to her family a croft and land next to the monastery. Witnessed by Ricardus Franceys of Ayton, pertaining gender, the realisation of female names in relation to property and land in Scotland, although gradual, demonstrates the pragmatic approach of Scottish Law compared to parity in English Law.

Ricardus witnessed the land and toft, given in Ayton court in 1279 to the prior and convent.

Adam Fraunceys, concerning a quitclaim of Ayton dated 12th March 1280.

In Scotland, the name Thomas Francys, Franceis, Franceys, appears followed by Thomas Franc in 1281.

Thomas Franc, 1281: this is a charter whereby Johannes, son of Bertramus, quitclaims the ville of Esteriston to the prior of Coldingham.

Another quitclaim, involving a lordship, witness by Thomas Franc of Ayton dated 1281.

The following two entries are part connected:

Prior to the earliest existing Thornydykes records, evidenced by an intermarital connection between the Earls of Dunbar and the Franks, records of William Franke in 1284–1289 appear consistent with a family member of the Dunbar tree receiving especially loyal treatment.

Prior to 1289, a charter of the Dunbar family witnessed by William Franke de Petcokyr, translates as:

> 'Mariota, Lady of Hume, formerly spouse of Sir Patrick Edeger in her lawful widowhood, grants and quitclaims all her rights ... to God and the blessed Mary of Caldestrem and the nuns there serving God in return for money paid to her in her urgent necessity.'

The then prior of Coldingham, Lord Henry de Horncastle, and Ricardus Fraunches witnessed land given to the sexton of Coldingham for the sustenance of the chapel of St Ebbe on the mountain, dated no later than 1276–1296.

Most of the above charters relate to abbeys, churches and monasteries located on the River Tweed, ten miles south of the Frank fiefdom of Thornydykes.

On 3rd June 1291, Henricus Franceys took an oath of allegiance to King Edward I. From the Ragman Rolls Oath of Fealty to Edward I family listing of 1291:

> Johan Franceis aka Fraunceys de Benefton, del Counte de Edeneburgh.
>
> Johan Franceis aka Fraunceys de Longaneuton, del Counte de Rokefburgh.
>
> Aleyn Franceis aka Fraunceys del Counte de Rokefburgh.
>
> Symund Franceis aka Fraunceys del Counte de Rokefburgh.
>
> Dominus Willelmus Miles aka William Fraunceys Chivalier.
>
> William Fraunceys del Counte de Fyf.
>
> William Fraunceys de Counte de Edeneburgh.

Extracts from a separate Rolls listing for the same family in 1291:

> Henricus Fraunceys, Burgenfis de Berewico, Burger of Berwick-upon-Tweed.
>
> Dominus Symon Frefch de ... aka Fraunceys.

Note:

The last surname from the list, Frefch, was taken from the slang Frenchman. For instance Richard Francis of Ayton, commonly known as The Frenchman, was Ricardo Fraunceys. So we have Francis, Frenchman, French and Fraunceys, all belonging Richard of Ayton, not forgetting the aliases of Symon, Count of Edinburgh.

Regardless the various name-spelling the protagonists were of the same immediate family. This applied too for other breakaway Franks, where the slang term 'French' became regular parlance; the listing shows different forms of spelling current in 1291.

As regards the use of the title of count, hesitating to describe it as real, it seems a number of the clan had achieved a level of status they felt the need to vaunt their superiority by a show of pomposity. How much they were truly counts is difficult to say, yet being close to the monarchy, on balance it seems the title, being a gift of the King, was valid evidence of royal antecedence.

The Extraordinary Franks

In 1294, Andrew Frances was witness to James, High Steward of Scotland, for the Abbey of Paisley, the transaction relating to a quarry.

From the List of Protection Roll, 1295, Robert de Brus, Earl of Carrick, together with William de Brus:

'Were about defending Carlisle Castle.'

Sir William Fraunceys, Knight, swore fealty in 1296 and is found named a number of times around this period.

Also in 1296, Sir William Fraunceys appears on the roll of the 4th July when John de Balliol, King of Scotland, together with King Edward I of England, renounce their league with the King of France.

The very next month, 28th August (immensely significant) at Berwick-upon-Tweed, the same nobles, prelates and knights, again renounce their league with France doing homage to King Edward. Present among the Franks were 'del Counte's':

John Fraunceys of Long Newton, Roxburgh.

John Fraunceys of Benestun, Edinburgh.

William de Fraunceys, Edinburgh.

Symon Fraunceys, Roxburgh.

William Franceys, Fife.

Aleyn Fraunceys, Roxburgh, heart of Scottish Borders Frank territory.

This information shows a family cluster, its spread seemingly around the Borders and north of Edinburgh and west towards Glasgow.

The 'esteemed heartland of Berwick' is significant as the place chosen for the meeting. Also listed together in the Ragman Rolls of 1296, were Fraunceys:

Johan de Ayton del Counte de Berewyk.

Henry de Ayton de Burgois de Hadington.

In both cases their given names of Fraunceys were substituted, Ayton given in preference to their surname. Proclaiming their status as count or burger rather than professing a surname seems to have been an age-old practice. Here again, the job of identifying individual Franks has been hampered, this time by the use of titles in preference to surnames.

Ragman Rolls extract for 1296, the name Coldingham substituted for Fraunceys:

> Henry, Prior de Coldingham aka Fraunceys, et Counte de Mefme-le-eu.
>
> Richard de Coldingham aka Fraunceys, del Counte de Berewyk.

At risk of being lost in perpetuity, names given under the guise of another have caused immense frustration concerning:

1. The identification of Franks using a moniker or patronymic.

2. Pinning down lines of succession from families assuming repeat name changes.

From the List of Protections Roll, 10th April 1296 and present at the Scottish Wars, quote:
 'Sir William Fraunceys, Knight, being with the King.'
 This annotation appears in the Roll of Submission and Fealty when John de Balliol, King of Scotland, together with the clergy, nobles and community of Scotland, present themselves to their liege lord King Edward I of England, whence they renounced their league with the King of France.
 Named together in the Parliament of Nobles and Prelates of both realms, held at Berwick-upon-Tweed, 28th August 1296, having made homage, were:

> John Fraunceys, Counte de Long Neuton, Roxburgh & Benestun, Edinburgh.
>
> William le Fraunceys, being Counte de Edinburgh and the county of Fife.
>
> Symon Fraunceys, de Roxburgh
>
> Aleyn Fraunceys, de Roxburgh.
>
> Richard Fraunceys

Also present for the Scottish Wars, the following shows a more diverse interconnected family relationship:

> William Fraunk of Grimsby.
>
> John Fraunk of Grimsby.
>
> John Fraunk, parson of Barnoldby Church, Lincolnshire.

On the orders of the King for the restoration of Frauncey land

An order for restoration was made by King Edward I, 3rd September 1296, to the former King of Scotland, their lords and under-tenants, caused under a writ issued to the sheriff of Roxburgh, for him to restore all the lands of Counte's Alan le Frauncéys and John le Frauncéys of Long Neuton.

Also in 1296, Counte Symon de Frauncéys had his lands in Roxburgh restored.

In terms of place and history, fresh from his victory at Stirling Bridge, William Wallace's invasion of Northern England commenced 1297, the following paragraphs providing insight and historic links with the Franks.

I previously mentioned Baron Fulbert Grey and his daughter being the mother of William the Conqueror. Fulbert was the progenitor of several families who rose to prominence, one such family descendant was the second surviving son of General Sir Thomas Grey, Prime Minister Charles Grey. Sir Thomas Grey was an eminent soldier in the Anglo-Scottish wars in the reigns of Edward I and Edward II.

In May 1297, General Grey was left for dead on the field when William Wallace attacked Lanark, killing the English Sheriff, William de Heselrigg. But Grey recovered and in the ensuing years was active in various campaigns. In May 1303 the Scots at Melrose Abbey captured Grey, and that spring, following his release, he was found at the siege of Stirling Castle where he affected a dramatic rescue of one Henry de Beaumont, with whom he was closely associated.

Later at Bannockburn, on 23rd June 1314, the day before the main battle, Grey was captured in a skirmish only to survive, becoming Constable of Norham Castle, 1319–1331. Having resisted two lengthy Scottish sieges, he appears to have died shortly before 12th March 1344. His son, Sir Thomas Grey, had been knighted prior to his father's death, and is said to have served alongside him in the 1330s. He became known for being the author of the *Scalacronica*, a five-part historical account from 'the earliest times to around 1362.' It refers to the reigns of all three Edwards from Edward I to Edward III, drawing on his and his father's experience as soldiers in the Anglo-Scottish and French wars.

Details of another branch of the Grey family are shown dated 1312, this time in relation to the taking of Edinburgh Castle, led by William Francis, together with a nephew of King Robert de Brus.

While the invasion of England took place, in the Frank seat of Ayton in Scotland, 1298, del Counte Thomas Frauncéys, apparently not shown in the restoration list, seems to have had his lands restored, which were previously forfeited and found to be in the hands of the prior of Coldingham.

In the rental of possessions records of the monastery of Coldingham dated 1298, Ricardus Frauncéys is shown, held of the prior, six oxgangs of land.

Richard appears in his own charter as Lord Ricardus Frauncays de Ayton Superior, concerning a toft and croft for 'pro sustentacione sua' in the house of the monastery of Coldingham. Executed the latter part of the thirteenth century, this is confirmed by documents from around 1298 showing that same land being held by Richard de Ayton Superior alias Fraunceys.

Immediately after 1298, Ayton Superior Thomas Fraunceys held land for assessment found in possession of the monastery.

Lord Richard Franceys appears as a witness to a charter of Nicholas de Renington in which he grants to Sir Henricus de Prendergest, knight, all the land Nicholas possessed in the ville of Renington.

Around the same period, I located a charter of Lord Ricardus Frauncays of Ayton, wherein he too grants messuages.

28th August 1300, William Fraunceys was recorded as valet to Lord Patrick, eighth Earl of March. Three weeks later, on the 18th September 1300, Lord William le Fraunceys was recorded as knight to the son of the Earl of Dunbar.

An agreement in 1302, between several knights and Sir William Fraunceys, affirms that Sir William would defend the castle of Kirkintilloch until Christmas. Among twenty-eight men-at-arms, he had three knights, together with Sir Henry de Pinckeney, Sir Thomas de Rameseye and Sir Gilbert de Manetethe. In addition, he had sixty trained foot soldiers, a chaplain, petty officers, and sufficient artificers to repair the gate, drawbridge and other defences. Also in attendance were the services of the tenants of the barony of Kirkintilloch. Records show that Sir William had his pay advanced until Christmas, and when war commenced, he was to provide the castle with all necessaries.

From the List of Protections Roll 9th April 1303, Walter Fraunceys and Robert de Brus Senior, are shown with the King, dated 28th May 1303.

Sir William Fraunceys is still recorded warden of the castle, and constable in 1304 and 1305, and is shown again between 1306 and 1307.

Symon Francey is shown 1306–1307, among four esquires of Lord Gerund of the barony of Complained, Cumberland, who was part of an expedition to Glenbrook in search of Robert de Brus. The terrain was around an extremely remote and wild mountain lake in south-west Scotland.

An extract from the Protections Roll of 15th April 1307 shows Walter Fraunceys present at the Scottish Wars.

Lord Flemington confirms a charter given to the Burgess of Berwick-upon-Tweed, the document being witnessed by Johannes Fraunceys in 1307.

In 1311, Richard Fraunceys and David Frauncis are mentioned as shield bearers to fellow knight, Lord William de Kautone. In it he is seen coming from Ireland on a mandate from the King to the Scottish wars with twenty-five men-at-arms.

A PERILOUS CLIMB

Annotated from archives.org – notes on surnames. Few periods in our nation's history are better known than the closing years of the thirteenth century, when, under Wallace and de Brus, Scotland battled for her independence. The fiercest and most decisive fights in that long, stubborn struggle were fought elsewhere than Edinburgh, but there is no single event in the whole campaign which better merits remembrance than the scene at Edinburgh Castle dated 14th March 1312.

The fortunes of King Robert de Brus had taken a favourable turn. The English had been driven back across the border, but these Scots were not yet masters of their own country. Three important strongholds were still held by English garrisons, the Castles of Edinburgh, Roxburgh, and Stirling and until these were captured Scotland was not free. Roxburgh fell first, being captured through the clever stratagem and bravery of Black Douglas. Stirling Castle, the strongest and most important stronghold, held out the longest and it wasn't until Bannockburn had been fought that the garrison of Stirling finally surrendered. But as a prize Edinburgh seemed insurmountable and needed some extraordinary brave thinking in order to breach its impregnable mass and clever inner defences.

Boasting a pedigree that can be traced back to William the Conqueror, General Gray of Scotland, spelt with an 'a', should not be confused with previously mentioned General Grey, the two men happening to live in close proximity. In the reign of Alexander III, John Gray (of Scottish spelling) was a steward to the earls of March and a witness to many donations to the monastery of Coldstream. Being deceased, his youngest son Hugh having also died, he left three sons, his eldest, also Hugh, died around 1300 leaving the next eldest, Andrew, as next in line.

By this circuitous route, Sir Andrew Gray rose to prominence. Being faithfully adhered to Robert de Bruce, in 1307 he enjoined in battle in command of a detachment of Scots sent against the Lord of Lorn. The English having recaptured Edinburgh Castle, like their comrades at Stirling, they were determined to hold on until their armies could regroup.

But Roxburgh had surrendered to the Scots and tidings of their success were carried to Edinburgh. Sir Thomas Randolph of Strathdon, first Earl of Moray, a relative of de Bruce, besieged the Castle time and again, but was always driven back, causing him to adopt the slower method of blockade. Fretting at the delay, the idea of a surprise assault seemed impossible; the castle was impregnable on three sides protected by a ring of precipices. But on the 14th March 1312, Sir Andrew Gray was at the forefront during a successful assault, the Castle being retaken.

The question remains how was the assault made successful? The answer lay in a combination of great bravery, luck and the local knowledge of a little known Frank.

It transpired, when in the company of thirty men, William Fraunceys (spelt Francis) took the lead in scaling the ramparts at midnight before descending the precipitous rock on the south side. Following him and immediately behind was Sir Andrew Gray, followed by Sir Thomas Randolph, nephew of Robert de Bruce. Although successful, much blood was spilt. Before the whole party could reach the summit, an alarm was given, the garrison ran to arms, whereupon desperate combat ensued; but their governor having been slain, the English gave quarter, once more yielding to the Scots.

A son of Sir William Fraunceys, William had spent all his life in the castle and knew every corner intimately. For his leading role in the taking of Edinburgh Castle, the family received the personal thanks of their kin Robert de Brus, gaining them great prestige. For his services Gray received from de Brus a grant of several lands and the barony of Longforgan in Perthshire previously belonging Edmund de Hastings.

Records state William Francis's father had once been Keeper of the Fortress, and having been brought up there, William knew the walls sufficiently well, and having conceived a surprise plan of attack, presented his ideas to a much frustrated Sir Randolph. Hearing the project with delight, Sir Thomas, together Sir Andrew Gray, selected thirty reliable men; and in the pitch darkness of that fateful night, headed by William Francis, they started the climb.

There's a fourteenth century poem by Barbour, called 'The Bruce', it reads:

> 'Methinks, sir, said William Francis to Sir Thomas,
>
> that you would be blithe if some one would
>
> but show you how to get over the castle walls.'
>
> 'I shall undertake to show you a way
>
> by which, with a short ladder of twelve foot,
>
> it may be done, and I shall be foremost of all.'

Brave William went on to tell how in his younger days, when living in the castle, he had fallen in love with a comely maiden who dwelt in the Grassmarket. Despite being forbidden to leave the castle he had found a way by which he could scale the rampart wall, descend the precipitous rock on the south side, visit his ladylove and return again without anyone being the wiser. So often had he done this, he could travel the route on the darkest of nights.

Looking at the rock face today, the climb seems madness to attempt even in broad daylight. What it must have been like, thirty men, all heavily clad in cumbersome armour, each man's perilous foothold carefully noted and followed by the next man, step by step, man by man, hauling their massive bulk and heavy weapons toehold by tortuous toehold up the cliff. The pain, hanging by torn fingers, sharp rock cutting through the thin layers of leather-soled feet. We have to visualise doing this laden with cumbersome armour, burdened by pitch darkness, blind to the drips of blood and abrasive cuts of the person above, all within earshot of an alert enemy. At the time, the assault was rightly reported:

'The clymbing richt perilous.'

The story goes, that halfway up they found a narrow ledge where they halted to recover their breath and prepare for the further climb. It was an anxious few minutes, for they were now in earshot of the soldiers above. And, as they steeled themselves for the remaining climb, they heard the officer of the watch going his rounds directly overhead, and said Barbour:

'Did a sound but reach his ear, or a glint

of armour catch his eye, for they were doomed men.'

'Now help them God, that all things may!

For in full gret peril are they.

For micht they see them there suld nane

Escape out of that place unslain:

To death with stanes they suld them ding

That they micht help themselves neathing.'

Suddenly there came a shout, 'Away with you! I see you well,' and a stone hurtled from the rampart above. With great presence of mind, all thirty men kept still as death, melting into the craggy rock face as the thud, thud, thud, of a boulder crashed and rebounded off the rocks continuing its journey to the bottom of the cliff. The sound of the boulder smashing as it passed was so deafening, the men barely heard the laugh of the miscreant, who, as a joke, had been trying to startle his own comrades.

Borrowing from Barbour's original work, under section 'The prophecy of Queen Margaret 1314':

Bot for Francois hattyn wes he,

That swa clam up in prevate,

> Scho wrat that as in prophesy:
>
> And it fell eftirward suthly
>
> Richt as scho said; for tane it was,
>
> And Francois led thame up that place.

The summit was reached, when nothing remained but the outer rampart wall not twelve feet in height, with the help of a rope ladder, the last obstacle was surmounted. Leading the gallant band to firm ground; William neatly disposed of a nearby guard. Hearing a disturbance, the alarmed men of the garrison came forth being roused unwillingly from their midnight sleep only to find themselves face to face with thirty determined men.

Alert, brave, and capable, and in spite of far greater odds, victory was complete: the Scots had won, the assault leaving many dead. The defence of the castle was led by the immense bravery of the English Governor. But although lauded by his victors, he had been among the first to fall, his dying blood mingling with that of many brave souls, the stain dark-red upon the stone they had so resolutely defended.

There are not many who would argue with old chronicler Barbour when he wrote:

> 'I heard never in nae time gane
>
> What castell was sae stoutly tane.'

Sir William Fraunceys, likely father of William Francis, was the same William who defended Kirkintilloch around 1302, becoming constable from 1304–1307. Descendant John Fraunceys was later stationed at the castle garrison of Edinburgh, shown in 1336.

At York, 1312, among the plenipotentiaries appointed by King Edward II of England to an unsuccessful treaty of peace with King Robert de Brus, were bishops, quote:

> 'Our dear clerks Meistre Robert de Pykeryng and Meistre
>
> Johan Franceys, Canons of St Peter of York.'

Among those present were Earl Patrick de Dunbar, Conte de la March, David, Conte d' Asceles and William, Bishop of Saint Andrews. The presence of the canons and their attendants, in this case Pykeryng and Franceys, as representatives of the clergy, was normal, the records of such events meticulously recorded by able clerics. The direct York family connection with Scotland and their fealty with de Brus reaffirms the Yorkshire Franks unassailably at one with their Scottish kin, and the Franks not only present at the heat of battle but as trusted mediators centre stage at many a critical point in history.

Among the assembly at Pickering were a Frank, a Dunbar and King Robert de Brus; though peace was not accomplished, the warm words of the King demonstrates certainty of respect and confidence in the very presence of said Frank as mediator. Being related to both de Brus and Dunbar the intriguing interconnection sees the northern Franks as kinsmen born of a common progeny.

Found recorded at regular intervals, presented as Lord William, in a Royal mandate dated at Westminster 18th March 1313, authorised the navy to be engaged in the war with Scotland. Leading the navy, Lord William Fraunceys was appointed by the King as Chief of the Royal Vessel *La Rodecogg*.

As an aside to the story I located, nearly fifty years later, between 1360 and 1361, the recently retired John King recorded as the last master and owner of the ex-naval ship *La Rodecogg* then registered at Dartmouth.

From the List of Protections Roll, Scottish Wars, Lord William Fraunceys, 1st April 1314: following the Battle of Bannockburn and the taking of Stirling Castle of the same year, King Edward II took shelter in the castle of Dunbar, its lord still on the side of England. It was here that William Fraunceys, having rendered good service, was rewarded an annuity by King Edward, recorded 24th April 1315.

In the reign of King Edward II, the earliest recorded charters of Scotland show Willielmus Franceis as witness to the Grim of Melrose Abbey. Around this same time, Jocelin Bishop of Glasgow presents charters in favour of the churches of Saint Mirini de Passelet and Saint Jacobus de Passelet, witnessed by Wilelmus Francigena, Capellanns (Chaplain) Glasguensis.

On the 20th January 1315, an order was made for Lord Ricardus Fraunce, Ayton Superior, to deliver to Eleanor, late of Henry de Percy, Tenant-in-Chief, the fees assigned to her, which Ricardus Fraunce seemingly held.

In 1317, Mario ta Fraunceys had her right of dower of all the lands of Paxton, Berwick-upon-Tweed, confiscated.

Between 1306 and 1329, in the reign of King Robert Brus I, James Fraunces held the feudatory rights of the barony of Cunynghame and the Shire of Ayr, which the incumbent Baron Fraunces, said title had previously been granted to Roger Blair.

Two interconnected events

Held by the King's hand by forfeiture, King Robert Bruce granted a charter concerning the land of Sproustoun, which Bruce granted to his son Robert, the barony of said land.

In 1321, King Robert Bruce's son Robert died. It was while mourning his son's death, King Bruce granted all of the same lands to his kin and loyal friend Baron William Francis, these being:

Sproustoun.

Kelso-on-Tweed.

Thornydykes.

Jedburgh.

Frankysland, Peebleshire.

A lovely hilltop property adjacent Frankysland shows later as the home of my late uncle, Surgeon Colonel, John Frank, M.D. Appendix 5 shows the close proximity of John Frank's home of Innerleithland, adjacent the River Tweed, to that of Frankislandis Nuncupates, situated midway between Thornydykes (Glasgow) and Coldingham cum Ayton lying on the coast, just north of Berwick-upon-Tweed. By now the spread of Franks across the width of Scotland is indicated well south of the Highlands and close to Northumberland on the Jedburgh route to England via the King's Road to Yarm and their Yorkshire cousins there.

Adam Frances, at an inquest for the right of the Abbey of Newbottle dated 1321, received an annual rent of 20s from the tenants of Berwick.

An agreement with the monks of Coldingham was witnessed in 1327 by Johannes Frankes, whereupon, Master Francisco received a donation for his expenses from the King.

Adam Frensh is among Scots patriots pardoned by King Edward III at Berwick on the 10th October 1335.

Also among the Scots men-at-arms pardoned, was Johannes Frances.

Records of John de Stryvelyn, Viscount of Edinburgh, show an early rental coming from the land of William le Frenche of Crawmond in the Viscountcy of Edinburgh, in 1335.

Also in 1335, the prior of Durham receives services rendered by Adam le Fraunceys and his heirs from their land in Ayton.

John Fraunceys was stationed at the garrison of Edinburgh in 1336.

Both Richard and John Fraunceys contributed to the construction of a bridge at Berwick, mostly from money received from their tenants, also of Berwick, dated 1337.

The Black Death of 1340 ravaged the country causing a drastic shortage of labour and monumental disruption to the old order. It is no wonder that records appear hard to come by. Black Death survivors realising their value, became restless and rebellious. Many of the lords gave up all attempts to hold onto their land, and instead leased it to a new class of yeoman farmer.

Name-ties to Yorkshire and the location of Scarborough between York, Pickering and Whitby, are seen in Adam le Fraunceys. Here he is found holding land under William de Scaresburgh aka Fraunceys, prior of Coldingham. His widow, Margaret, later donating four and a half acres of land in Flores to the alms-house of the priory, dated 1350.

Recorded in Scotland 22nd September 1359, are the names Richard Fraunceys de Ayton, William de Ayton aka Fraunceys, and Gilbert de Lumsden.

LAIRDS OF THORNYDYKES.

As previously stated, the name French came from the slang Frenchman when describing Franceis or Fraunceys, as in Johan de Franceis the Frenchman, and were among slang terms in common use in the 1200s. What happened was the French and Franc parts of the name were purposely merged into French in order to distinguish between different branches of the family, whereupon further derivative names emerged.

A charter of George Dunbar records that upon the resignation of Patrick, the ninth earl, the earldom of March was subsequently conferred upon Robert French aka Fraunceys, Robert becoming first Laird of Thornydykes. Of the previous earl:

> 'Where upon his resignation in the earle's hands for a new infeftment to himself and his wife Elizabeth in conjunct fie and the heirs of their bodie, which failyeing give to Adame French sone to Robert Franch aka Franck and his heirs male, which failyeing to airs what-some-ever …'

At which, the earl designates Robert French:

> 'Clarissimus onsanguineus Noster of Thornydyke.'

The designation was confirmed by King David II, 25th July 1368.

Note: Thornydykes was a place of defence, which besides a manor house, gardens, estates in tenancy, mills and mill lands, fees, etc., was located in Merse, now Westruther, midway between Berwick on the coast and inland Peebles, Galashiels. Under the spelling French with variations, Thornydykes became a Frank seat in 1368.

Showing an ancient but still close familial relationship between the Fraunceys and de Brus: on the 19th April 1390 to 4th April 1406, sometime in the reign of Robert III, the great-grandson of King Robert Brus, beneficiary Robert French aka Fraunceys, died. George, the current Earl of Dunbar kicks up and contests the previous charter with a view to claiming Thornydykes for himself. However Adam French succeeds in his claim, becoming the legitimate second Laird of Thornydykes.

In 1398, at a meeting of border chieftains and commissioners of the Scottish and English marches appointed to sort out border difficulties, prisoners, etc., the Scots Commissioners, for their part, gave heavy bonds in the name of their king. This was to render certain the chieftains' appearance before the ensuing meeting of both realms.

At the meeting, conspicuous among border chieftains, an exception was made for the release of Adam Gordon, William Baird and Adam French. It was not unusual for fights and open duels to break out, and on this occasion, like many times before, open warfare ensued. King Robert, wanting to preserve peaceful relations with his more formidable neighbour King Richard II of England, in a supposed fit of desperation, kowtowed to the monarch, and selected his kin Adam French as an example forfeiting his estates and titles.

After the forfeiture of his estates, Adam French or Franche, abandoned King Robert and together with the old earl, George of Dunbar, his feudal lord and his son Gaweyn, all three turned, becoming liegemen to King Henry IV of England; all three receiving considerable annuities directly from their new King.

The above Sir Adam Gordon, Lord of Gordon and Huntly, was killed at the battle of Homildone Hill, Berwickshire, 14th September 1402.

On the seventh of April 1402, Adam French was in England in the service of King Henry IV, having been granted an annuity, quote:

'Adam French receiving a prest of said annuity for his good service,
17th July 1403.'

Around this date, Adam's son Robert received a charter from King Robert III, relating to Thornydykes and Pitcoks, the seat apparently having been reinstated to the family, the previous forfeit supposed a foil concocted to appease King Richard.

Sir Adam Gordon now dead, in 1403, Adam Gordon's cousin, Adam Franche, having decided to secede from England, journeyed to Scotland and to the open arms of his son Robert. He returned in the full knowledge his allegiance had been restored with the Scottish throne, and aware his son Robert had received confirmation of the restoration of Thornydykes and Pitcoks.

On the 17th August 1403, King Henry IV grants Alexander Franche the tolls of Berwick.

Robert French prematurely appeared using the title Lord of Thornydykes, seen as a charter witness at the church of Cavers, Roxburgh 29th July 1406. There also appears to have been a younger brother, James.

The Extraordinary Franks

In 1407, Alexander Franc and his retainer Herteramus were recorded as being under the auspice of George, Earl of Dunbar, while they were together in England.

The 18th February 1426, King James I refers to Alexander Franche as the grandfather of James Franche. In his charter, the King grants James the land of Ayton and the Barony of Coldingham in Berwick, which his grandfather had previously forfeited.

Between 1429 and 1431, safe conduct was granted by Henry VI to Johannes de Fraunce, and in another document John Fraunc is found on his way to England to see Lord Andrew Keith of Inverugie. Sir Keith was one of a number of hostages being held for King James I of Scotland.

On the matter of Thornydykes and Pitcoks (entry 1403 above): on his return to Scotland, not content with his son holding his estates, Adam himself repossessed his inheritance; this was confirmed by a charter of 6th January 1433 conveniently signed by the new monarch, King James I of Scotland. A few days following the signing Adam died, with his son Robert succeeding as third Laird of Thornydykes.

The above illustrates the interconnection of the various Franks, also the familial relationship of the Aytons and Thornydykes being related both to the de Brus and the Gordons. Later in 1502, it will be shown Adam's brother William Frank has sasine of the new estates of Frankysland in Scotland, Frank-his-land, the modern version of the name Frank now emerging.

The emergence of Frankysland in Scotland coincided with the Frankland purchase of Danby Forest, near Whitby, Yorks.

Johannes (John above) Fraunce was fined for being absent from court, given at Perth, 10th July 1459, being fined:

'All the income and expenses of his bailiwick, etc.'

A previously unknown Highland occupation crops up in records dated 10th February 1474. These show George Frensch with holdings in Aberdeen.

An entry for the 22nd October 1478 shows Robert French indicated as fourth laird. Robert's father, Lord Robert of Thornydykes, seems to have died shortly before.

Dated 1478, Robert, fourth laird and James Fransche, among others, are held:

'For the contempcioune done to the Kings Hienes in taking horses and striking the canon, entir thair persnis in ward in the castell of Blacknes and remayne thair quhill (until) thai be fred be the king.'

Robert, the fourth laird, is later succeeded by his son Robert, and shows up as fifth laird in 1490.

Lord Johannes Franche appears in several charters, having the confirmation of King James III. As Johannes Franche, chaplain, he is among witnesses, having another two appearances in Edinburgh on the 25th June 1479.

Note: there being three family branches running together, to alleviate confusion, I have moved the 1490 Thornydykes entry forward, it now follows the highlighted John Franche 1592 entry, the fifth laird details commencing there.

By order of King James IV, in favour of Lord Nicholas Franche:

> 'Lord Nicholas Franche, chaplain and his successors, shall serve God at the altar of St Michael the Archangel in the parochial church of St Cross, Stirling, 1st April 1471.'

Sir Nicholas Franch solemnised a marriage at Strivelin as curate of Stirling in 1475, and his name appears in a number of records in the Royal Borough of Stirling, March 1476 to May 1477.

A William Franche appears June 1480.

An action taken and won against the offender by Sir John Franche, chaplain, on the 27th (month unreadable) 1484, this was due to:

> 'The spoliation (plunder or pillage) of half of the lands of Ballioffra.'

Sir John appears again on the 22nd June 1492. One assumes that Sir John, as chaplain, was a son of Sir Nicholas, curate, of the same surname Franch or Franche, above.

Thomas Franch

Around 1487, according to *Redditus Altarium Olim situat infra Parochiam de Linlythgow*, Johannes Franch held the office of burgess. From an inscription, formerly in the north aisle of the church of Linlithgow, Johannes Franch died in 1489. His son, Thomas, became Master Mason to the Crown of Scotland, appointed under the Privy Seal given by King James V at Kelso, 13th April 1535. The inscription reads:

> 'Hei lyes Ihon Franch, fadder to Tomas, Master Mason of Brig of Dee. Oblit anno Domini MCCCCLXXXIX.'

Coincidentally my grandfather, Thomas Henry Frank (mentioned elsewhere as a builder), shared the familial Christian name of Thomas with counterpart Tomas Franche of the Brig of Dee (see 1487 entry). As previously indicated, Granddad's son, my deceased uncle, Professor Surgeon Colonel John Frank, lived adjacent the same historic Frank fief-land area of the River Tweed.

The Extraordinary Franks

For many years prior to his death, John Frank was on the medical board at Edinburgh. As fiduciary laird he loved the countryside. Standing proud upon high ground with its view of the River Tweed, his rambling house boasted meandering paths climbing ever-steeply among shrubbery, where to the rear a huge stone-walled garden held a mysterious green-painted side gate opening to a meandering uphill path: a child's paradise. As I remember, the path lead through steep sloping woodland abruptly stopping at a wooden stile, its fence bordering open heath. Here the ground rose rapidly towering towards the right where an outcrop of rock poked majestically through the gorse and closely cropped grass. Close by an inviting knoll sat convenient for walkers to rest prior to their proper ascent of Lee Pen.

I previously mentioned my being a Master Mason of the Mother Lodge of Kilwinning in Scotland, but in Johannes and his son Thomas, we find the true worth of working stonemasons, working complex geometric shapes into immense buildings and fine bridges. Here we find the name Franch, the name taken from a combination of Franc and French of common Norman origin.

On the 13th April 1535, Thomas receives the appointment Master Mason. The office was proclaimed for Thomas Franch:

> 'Ane letter given to Thomas Franche mak-and him Maister Masown to oure souverane lord for all the dais of his lif wyth power to the said Thomas to use and exercise the siad office in all and by all thing is as ony vtheris vsit or exercit the samin in ony times bigane. And therefor to haue yeirlie in during his liftyme of our said souerane lord the soume of £40 to be pait yeirlie be our souerane lordis treasrer now present and being for the tyme.'

Thomas Franche appears to have had three sons, the first, Thomas, who died 1530 and whose body lies buried in Aberdeen Cathedral where his epitaph can be found. Brothers John and Robert (the third brother), were also masons. They appear in accounts of 1538–1539 under the heading 'Falkland a royal residence' where a George Frensh is also mentioned.

Following the death of his first son, Thomas Franche began work for the King on the palace of Linlithgow in 1535. Gratuities given to Thomas were bestowed over and again such was the King's appreciation.

There is a record of a warrant issued 22nd April 1535, by the King:

> 'For payment of a gratuity in overflowing thanks to Thomas Franc, for completing the work of the Palace, signed at Linlithquhow, James R.'

In 1537, Thomas joined his sons in recommencing work on the palace of Falkland.

By the King's command, 1538–1539, work undertaken on the garden dyke.

Thomas appears to have died after the 31st July, probably late 1551, being survived by his two sons.

John Franche is identified with the Royal Residence of Falkland, recognised in a gift for services done to the King in 1592.

Also rewarded, George Frensch, who appears to be the same George who held land near Aberdeen, recorded 1474–1475.

RETURNING TO THE THORNYDYKES, 1490.

Extract of a plea by Robert French, fifth Laird of Thornydykes, 8th March 1490:

'That the date of the inquest is changed to another day.'

This item is a court case where George Franche, a relative of Robert, is recorded in Lanark as a witness. This was confirmed by the King the 13th September 1486, and again in 1508–1509.

Robert the fifth laird appears to have died. Records confirm Adam French, sixth laird, had sasine (seizure) of Thornydykes and Pitcox, dated 1494.

Records confirm that William Frank, brother of Adam French, has sasine of Frankysland, Peebles, becoming viscount in 1502.

Dated 16th December 1503, an action on behalf of the King against Adam Franch, fifth laird and others, regarding land in Merton, Berwick and said to be:

> 'Unjustly held in blenchferme and therefore held as of no avail, force
> or effect in time to come.'

The above, with another recorded action concerning the Sheriff Depute of Berwick and Adam Franch, the two of them relating to land called Edmondis field (Edmond his field) Berwick, the action was dated 19th December 1505.

On the 23rd December 1506, Chaplain Thomas Franche received a gift from King James IV.

Thomas Franche is shown as Magister Thomas Frank, found a witness in August 1508.

There is a record of Thomas Frank shown as Chaplain and Magister to the high school of Edinburgh in the vennel of the Church of Saint Mary in the Fields August 1508; the same also dated 23rd October 1512.

There is an entry showing Chaplain Thomas Frank as having been succeeded in the estates of Thornydykes, dated 24th January 1516. As Adam succeeded as sixth laird, I assume that when Adam;'s father Robert died (seen pre-1494 above), his brother Thomas held the estate until Adam was of age, as intended, sufficient for Adam to resume continuance as sixth laird.

The following appeared at first confusing and took some working out, but as shown is correct: the sequence is, Robert, as fifth laird died, his son Adam, as sixth laird, succeeded. Adam had three male children, Robert, who succeeded his father as seventh laird, John in the middle and Adam, who inherited his father's estate.

In 1511, a Mergote Franche (female) is recorded in a charter holding property in Dumblane.

Sir William Franche is recorded as deceased, 12th June 1521. He is previously recorded, in 1502, as Viscount William Frank of Frankysland, Peebles, in Dumfriesshire.

Frankysland, Peebles as it relates to current times

During the Second World War, my uncle, Colonel John Frank, served out East as a surgeon. After a short interlude, he lived the remainder of his life around Frankysland, Peebles. Although not laird in the true sense, partially due to his occupation and standing in the community, deference was given to him as such, especially living in the big house on the hill. His apparent status was accentuated due to his demeanour and form of dress, having the countrified habit of wearing plus fours, his gun dogs and a love of shooting. He became Professor of Medicine at Edinburgh, and died suddenly one day in the middle of playing golf.

It seems strange how often coincidence brings things round in circles. What was he doing, living the life of squire around Frankysland? What brought him there? His attitude was a mix of gentlemanly kindness, yet with a demeanour aloof and distinctly superior. I was mildly aware of his fragile health but not of his immense courage resultant of the war out East while treating the sick and dying and others in desperate need, and I'm saddened like so many of his kind, their lives so drastically cut short.

My memories are of the hours John spent shut away in his study prior to undertaking a major operation. Like me he suffered from dyslexia, and often would arrive at hospital wearing different shoes, one black, the other brown. For a skilled surgeon, care had to be taken to ensure him knowing his left from his right – so total was his focus on what he had to do.

Once in open countryside, he would delight in showing off the skills of his gun dogs, sniffing the air as they tracked hidden objects no matter how difficult the terrain and the distance walked: all snapshots of a man impossible to really get to know and understand.

But that was normal for the Franks, once raised to twelve, you were considered old enough to take on full adult responsibility. At fifteen, this was the cut off point, you were on your own, the consequence of birth being yours alone to shoulder. With the absence of backing, it was beholden of you to make life-changing decisions and get on with it, always with the added responsibility of providing and looking out for others. Typically Ann and I are immensely proud of our three children's resolute foresight, firm resolve and sense of fair play and responsibility.

I can only guess this as being engendered generationally, just as my mother charged off to Canada as a teenager, and later in North Africa found herself pregnant, smack in the middle of a desert war. Certainly that kind of stoicism was never spoken about, it was just something assumed. It was the same as our own boys; each, upon becoming teenagers, separately bummed rides and hitched around Europe, being a shortcut towards adulthood. They had the skills, knew how to handle themselves and got on with it. Incidentally, before her death aged 100 and a bit, Mum received recognition for past services from the current Governor of Nova Scotia.

Overlooking the River Tweed, as neighbours to the Ballantine tweed manufacturing family, I spent some time at my uncle's house, once when his wife, Doreen, was giving tea, hosting the bishop of somewhere or other. Cultured and well-spoken, of impeccable manners, and admired for his work, John Frank left no issue. For me as the elder of two brothers and my mother a Yorkshire countrywoman, her brother John Frank's apparent parody and observance to a bygone era seems now to have been an unconscious attempt to cling to a superiority that compared to my brother and I, we must have seemed uncouth.

Having no progeny of his own must have been immensely hurtful to John, shown in often-sudden bursts of anger, most always vented in my direction as if lashing out. Having a ragtail nephew heir apparent must have been a great disappointment. Sorry, John, and all that, but …

As the eldest next in line, I could feel the weight of expectation and frustration as to one's apparent slowness in taking up the cudgel. And perhaps with the recent death of Dorothy is why belatedly, as if to make amends, I have felt it incumbent to record the passing of such an historic a saga. At aged 100-plus, my mother Dorothy Frank, last successor, unaware of her own heritage, had only her maiden name Frank to mark the end of a remarkable line. And as we've only now begun to realise, living her later life apropos Lady Dorothy, and still driving aged ninety-four.

As if to illustrate, Dorothy's one and only car crash involved Lady Guisborough at the gates of that esteemed estate (*Gisborough ut prius dictum de Brus*) of the Domesday spelling *Gighesbore*. Of the altercation: one of the two ladies involved was rumoured to enjoy more than just the odd tipple or two. One can just imagine the two of them, each railing to accuse the other, but far too polite to say or do anything but splutter a few indecisive words, nod, and each drive indignantly in the opposite direction, one a lady and the other in her own way a lady too.

Returning to the main theme, translations and transcripts shown in date order

A quitclaim of two oxgangs of land in 1520, relate to the grantor Thomas, son of the late Robert, Steward of Coldingham Priory, benefiting the monks there. The previous landholder was Godric, son of William Cook, the transaction having been witnessed by Richard Francis of Ayton.

Not being sure where this fits in, Elspeth French appears as a legatee in 1524.

See entries above for Thomas Frank 1508–1512. Uncle Thomas now appears as Thomas Frank, chaplain, performing as a witness at High School, Edinburgh 25th September 1526.

Shown 12th April 1526, Sir Adam Frenche appears to have entered the Church and was witness to an act of the chapter of the Holy Trinity Collegiate.

1526, Robert French, son of Sir Adam, succeeds as seventh laird, being related by marriage to Patrick: see next:

Patrick, was styled Sir Patrick French by Robert in his later will. Sir Patrick, married to Elizabeth, had two sons, George and James. Patrick, however was already fifth baron of Polwarth. See 1546 below.

Sir Adam, witness, appears 1st May 1531, a Katrina Franche, nun, appearing 3rd February 1537–1538.

Robert French, seventh laird, appears again, 20th May 1538.

Offspring of the sixth laird generation, Alexander Frenche is shown as a witness 20th February 1539, George Franche appearing, probable fourth son of Adam, 8th January 1540.

Alexander appears again as Franche, also George Franche, both as witnesses to a charter confirming Falkland by the King, dated 14th August 1541.

In a charter to King James V, Sir Adam Frenche is shown as chaplain in 1543. Sir Adam Frenche signs a grant in favour of the Church of the Holy Trinity Collegiate, dated 29th November 1544.

On 10th April 1546, Robert French, seventh laird, is on assizes. Around this date, he marries Anne Hume. About Anne Hume: her aunt, Margaret Hume, was Lady Abbess of North Berwick; Anne's brother Patrick being the fifth baron of Polwarth. A second brother, Adam, was a very early Protestant rector. Anne's third brother Alexander was an author of religious hymns.

Seventh laird Robert goes on to have two daughters, Margaret and Janet, and seven sons, two of whom, Henry and Hugh, perish many years prior to their father.

A milestone entry is shown at Edinburgh 4th September 1546. Queen Mary grants to James Frank, third son of Robert seventh laird, at Edinburgh the following:

> 'To his heirs and assigns, terras Frank is landis Nuncupatas, the Viscounty of Peblis (Peebles) Frankysland.'

The same estate had previously been enfeoffed to Sir William Frank, but deprived due to troubled times. See entries 1502 and 1521.

Daughter of Robert, Janet French, a later beneficiary of her brothers, Henry and Hugh, married Robert Watson of Yiflie, Westruther. Robert Watson died before 1546, leaving a son, also Robert; Janet marrying a second time to Robert Cranstoun of Broxmouth, Dunbar.

Janet's ninth child, Margaret French, in marrying George Nesbit, had two sons, John and George. Janet, appearing to have married again, seems to have married another George.

George appears again, 3rd December 1549, designed of (son of) Thornydykes around the same time Alexander Franche is indicated as a witness dated 18th May 1549.

On the 17th March 1549 Sir Adam Franche is shown witnessing a charter, later the same day shown witnessing a marriage contract.

A month later, in April 1549, Sir Adam succeeds, becoming eighth Laird of Thornydykes. This is despite his father still being alive and in good health. Sir Robert died some time before January 1588.

25th September 1550, Janet renounces her rights to a third part of Iverlie in favour of her son, Robert Watson.

On 13th November 1552, Queen Mary pardons Adam, Peter and James, for attacking and killing William Halyburton of Gogar.

Roberts's third son, James, witnesses a gift of barony in the name of the Queen dated 4th September 1556.

Queen Mary grants a charter to Sir Adam, eighth laird, and his wife Margaret Hopprigiel, of lands, a manor, mills and so on, dated 8th February 1556.

Indicated in sequence are Sir Adam, eighth laird's children Robert, James, John, Alexander, Thomas, Margaret, Christiane, Janet and Euthan, a William Franche being mentioned 8th April 1556.

A Christall Franche is a witness regarding lands of Dryburgh Abbey, 10th April 1567.

Sir Adam Fransche, 17th July 1567, takes an action for the removal of pretended occupiers of his land. A counter-action takes place 4th February 1575.

19th December 1567, Hugh is belatedly recorded as a fifth son of Sir Robert. Following service to Lord Erskine, and despite his relative young age, Hugh is shown as a pensioner dated 1573 at Dryburgh Abbey. The pension seems to relate to ill health,

The Extraordinary Franks

the incumbent having died in October 1574. In his will he lists his sister Janet and half-brother David.

Interestingly, Sir Robert's second son, Henry, went to Orkney and was there in 1544 indicated as a King's witness in 1536, having died January 1569.

So beside his daughters, Margaret and Janet, of Sir Robert's seven sons, in sequence were: Adam, Henry, James, Peter, Hugh, Alexander and Robert. Two of them, Henry and Hugh, having died, the seventh laird Robert, with quite a number of years still before him, died prior to January 1588.

Sir Robert's sixth son, Alexander French, was a witness dated 2nd July 1567, and again in 1573.

On the 23rd April 1573, Robert French was conferred vicar of Greenlaw by King James.

Sir Roberts's daughter Janet is shown recorded in 1574.

The 1st April 1576, Sir Adam, eighth laird, preceded his father and died soon after this date. Adam's first son, also Robert after his grandfather, becomes ninth laird.

A document of February 1578 shows Margaret, relict of Adam, together with her son and heir Robert.

Margaret, daughter of the Laird of Blindlie, wife of Sir Adam, eighth Laird of Thornydykes of Berwick, died 23rd February 1582.

Referring to the contested action relating to trespass dated July 1567, action was found against the pretenders for the violent spoliation of lands in the Sheriffdom of Berwick, dated 23rd February 1583.

Something of Sir Adam's children:

Robert	Having no clear date of birth, Robert became heir and ninth laird on the death of his mother, Margaret, Lady Thornydykis, in 1583.
James	Born 1569, was executor to his mother's will in 1582, and in 1583 institutes proceedings against Andrew Holm, Abbot of Jedburgh.
John	Became controller of horse for King James VI.
Alexander	Was lawless and was killed 13th March 1612.
Thomas	Was a favourite of the King, and was appointed 'only keeper of his majesty's outer door chamber'. Thomas was still in service 18th April 1604.

Margaret

Christiane

Janet

Euphan

Adam

The ninth laird Robert who died in 1603, his second wife Margaret Holm who outlived him, their children:

Adam	Adam's second son, Adam succeeds as heir, tenth lord of the manor.
Jean	Married John Cranston, brother of Lord William Cranston.
Alison	Married first Thomas Cranston, second, William Marjori Banks.
Margaret	Married Robert Brownfield.

Adam, tenth laird, second son of Adam, born 1599, was baptised 12th November 1601. He was a minor and became a ward of the Crown by no less a person than the King himself, King James VI together with Sir John Home of Berwick.

Adam was secretly married off as a young sixteen-year-old on the 16th November 1615 to Jean, daughter of Sir Patrick Chirnesyde. Adam died in February 1617 aged just eighteen. As there was no issue and only married sisters, effectively there was no successor.

This being the end of the line, a combination of monarchy and a cluster of lords made arrangements to honour such an esteemed name and family: whereas the Frank estates were ceded by charter dated 26th January 1619 to Viscount Adam Frenche of Frankysland, the period marked the death throes of a dynasty and 500 years of history for the Franks in Scotland.

With a little bit of research it seems the new laird was a distant kinsman of Jean, Alice and Margaret French. The pedigree of the family showing Adam as a descendant of Robert French, as third laird, he has been found to be of the same congeneric bloodline to the King Robert de Brus, hence both strands of de Brus and the Franks, through an arduous 500 years, still kin.

As if somehow attempting to revive a heritage of ancient heroes, the Franks came swords raised and for a time held sway then quietly faded, not quite making the throne nor even close. Yet, for their part, they left a legacy of democratic process and the gift of a name brought into everyday common use. Such a simple name as Frank, indispensable to the English language, its meaning candid, outspoken and free, a name absorbed within the magnitude of a million of other words, a surname ceded in the Viscountcy of Peebles and of Frank-his-land:

> And nature's way is ever thus
>
> Glimpsed with wondrous eyes
>
> that fade to dust.

DFB 2016.

In 1633, Viscount Adam Frenche, Franislandis Nuncupates, conveyed the whole estate to Mr George Brown, in terms of heritage, nought but history.

PART TWO

THE YORKSHIRE SCOTTISH FRANKS

PREAMBLE

Set in 1086, around a time of massive upheaval, the great works of the Domesday Book are a remarkably detailed record of the various spellings of Frank, Franc, Francais, Frani, Franco, ad-infinitum. It links the Franks with York, later, north to Whitby, Cleveland, Greater Yorkshire and Scotland. Wider spread continued with family settlement to the north-west in Cumbria and Westmorland and north via Durham to the Border Country and beyond. Other settlement worked its way along the east side of the country eventually connecting with Franks coming to England who had resisted the temptation to venture north.

Settlement in Ireland saw later interrelated activity mostly confined to Scotland and the north. Previous familial intermarriage seen in the Cotentin prior to 1066 continued unabated between Normandy and Britain. The continued blood mix, although maintaining vigour among the Norman population, created a complex antecedence through the adoption of supposedly unrelated surnames as if on a whim.

Today's interest in compiling a family tree is mostly found through the complex backtracking of paternal and maternal names. Now and again an expert may find a surname with links to well-known personalities or royalty, ultimately leading to Jesus Christ, that kind of thing. But this work is not about making any such dubious claim, its observations being more about a name having a distinct pathway of antecedence supported by DNA. Ultimately it would be untrue to say the individuals named in this work were undiluted descendants, yet in the spirit of the name, aided in no small part through DNA and the facts presented, it's reasonable to assume a bloodline through to the original Franks.

Often great play is made over a well-known person shown to have a connection with an historically famous name, its disclosure bringing instant surprise, pride and delight. Well good luck, all I will say is 'shown' is not proof-positive of an unbroken link however the connection was established, and anyway, most of these supposed glorious figures in history were scheming tyrants, despots and murderers, where being top of the tree, their class was seen as being ordained by God.

Well we can forget that, and if occasionally my authorship echoes pride in one's namesake Frank, I'm sorry to have been caught up in the moment. But the fact is the top 10% of the population of those times saw in their genes a superior being, born to rule within an elite class. Within that class was a strict hierarchy, a firm wall of solidarity founded on duty and chivalry, where the glory of war ennobled the brave upon the battlefield with a heaven-sent propensity for acrimony and brutality.

Outside of that was the politics of constantly shifting alliances and survival. Of the 10%, approximately 5% were the monks and priors of the clergy, the other 5%, knights and nobles that included the monarchy. The rest were peasants, although between a local lord and the lower peasantry might be found elders acting as go-betweens, and a range of positions such as vassal or squire, bailiff, that kind of thing. The position of knight did not preclude him working the land; land mostly enfeoffed to an overlord to whom the knight was indentured.

Particularly hated were the foresters who mostly worked for the King hunting down, under savage forest laws, anyone found poaching; often knights and nobles took it upon themselves to hunt, and when caught, they too were punished.

While this record is mainly concerned with tracing one's Yorkshire ancestry it necessarily researches the intricacies of interwoven marriage patterns. Emanating originally from Germany, as the name suggests, the Franks were the architects of France subsequently becoming Norman. Between 1245 and 1347, the Norman population in England had risen to over a third of the total population, whereas in the north, as their names suggest, the lowland Scots were of largely Danish origin. Prior to 1066, Scandinavian settlement had reached as far south as Derby, its influence being felt on the very banks of the River Thames in London.

THE STORY

Use of nom de guerre and extended family interconnections

As this work shows, the upheaval along the east side of the country was palpable, as was the confusion of names exacerbated by the embroil clash of war and turmoil, thrusting swathes of people and their allegiances to and fro creating a huge melting pot of names, name-spellings, given names and names taken from a place or borrowed from another family. A family clan was not always limited to bloodline descent, founding name or ancestor, but might encompass another extended family or cognate lineage prepared to embrace a particular agnatic leadership. In taking

The Extraordinary Franks

another's name, kindred fraternity or allied individuals were positively adopted without genealogical origin. In terms of research, the sudden persuasion to adopt another's name clearly has strangely been both a help and hindrance concerning the ongoing twists and turns of research.

Including the Franceys, many Norman families used both their Norman name and the names derived from their newly acquired lands in England, such as Hameldon, Osgodby and Armyn, and by marriage marrying into such as the Vesy family and taking their name. Walter Fitz-Gilbert, a Frank, held various fiefs called Hameldon or Emeldon, these Francey being connected to the Hansards, shown in their kinship as joint and consecutive witnesses to charters, at the time a clear indicator of the immediacy of relationship.

Unlike many borrowed names, the name Paynel is original and ancient, emanating from the Roman word 'pagan' meaning rustic or heathen. For pagan see paien from the Latin paganus. In Normandy, the Franks and Paynels intermarried, the name Paynel often being used by Franks marrying Paynels with the purpose of distinguishing themselves from the larger cluster of Franks and use of Franc, within the country of France and of the same origin.

Coming to England, and of the same branch as the Franks, the Paynels held land in Durham and in Hameldon and Osgodby near Selby. The nom de guerre of de Hameldon and Osgodby, as too the Norman names of Paynel, Stuteville, and Mowbray, are exampled by Mowbray emanating from the village of Montbray in La Manche. These were all closely related to the Franks, a small branch of the Franceys having taken the name Mowbray through marriage; those having kept the original Franceys were seen as vassals of Roger de Mowbray. Yet, being of Norman origin, all various branches of Franceys, including those of those place names, remained closely related to the Paynels.

Of the Stuteville: Estouteville in Normandy was one of the great Norman houses, Robert de Stuteville arriving in England around 1066. Pre-1170 we find Robertus de Stuteville who, post-1170, becomes Robert de Normandy. Later I show an example of the interrelation of the Franceys and Stuteville, also the de Brus as overlords to the Fraunceys.

Confusion grows when we see descendants of the Hameldons of Durham marrying descendants of Roger de Mowbray, aka Franceys, who, while retaining their Frank persona, used the more distinctive Mowbray pedigree. The confusion of name changes continued for decades, and is the cause of disagreement between current-day historians faced with the task of dissembling a plethora of conflicting data.

For example, in 1166 Jordan de Paynel de Hamildon of Yorkshire held a Durham fee. In 1204, the manor of Osgodby, North Yorks, was held by Jordon de Paynel de Hameldon, otherwise known as Jordan de Osgodby also known as Jordan de Franceys.

Shortly after we see Richard de Osgodby, also known as Richard de Franceys, son of John Franceys. Similarly, Dame Clemencia Franceys is actually the wife of Roger de Vesy. The name Vesey originated from the town of Vassy in Normandy, becoming the baronial name de Vesci. Various spellings of the name show the earliest recording in England in Domesday, Robertus Invesiatus Lascivus de Vesci being another version of the name.

The pedigree and interconnection of names is intriguing.

Robert de Stuteville, born 1010, is followed by a succession of Roberts, born 1040, 1075 and 1100, who are followed by Burga de Stuteville, female, born 1135, who married William de Vesci. Their son Eustace de Vesci, born 1171, married Margaret, daughter of David of Scotland, claimant to the Scottish throne – their son William, born 1205, married Agnes Ferrers, whose daughter, Julianna, married Richard de Vernon alias Franceys.

Adam was born 1178, son of John le Franceys, born 1153. Adam's son was Gilbert le Franceys, born 1203, who married Hawise de Vernon, born 1213. Hawise was daughter to Robert, born 1188, who was son to Richard, born 1155, who was a son of Warin, born 1135, son of Hugh, born 1113, who was a son of William de Vernon, Earl of Devon.

Gilbert le Franceys and Hawise de Vernon, had a son, Richard de Vernon de Franceys, born 1232, who retained the maiden name of de Vernon. Richard married Margaret de Vipont, born 1232, their son being Richard de Vernon-Franceys, born 1255, who married the previously mentioned Juliana de Vesci. The above shows how the dilution of surnames could take place, which through marriage, might be absorbed into a more distinguished or preferred family name, a causation of their disappearance.

An example of Scottish migration and the interconnection of names such as Dunbar, de Vescy and Franceys, is shown as follows: borrowing data gleaned from *Frame family origins*, the Aytoun family sprung from the Norman family of de Vescy, now in England possessing the great barony of Sprouston in Northumberland. From information found in Sir William Dugdale's *Baronage of England*, of great antiquity and now extinct, the baronage was a signatory that compelled King John to grant the Magna Charta. At around the same time, Gilbert de Vescy, upon his arrival in Scotland, received the lands of Aytoun from King Robert I, and being the custom of the period, by royal authority changed his name to that of the estate, Ayton becoming part of the Frank fee as shown in the Scottish account.

Coincidentally, Ayton lay about twenty miles from Thornydykes, and nineteen miles from the castle of Dunbar. It is in the shire of Coldingham and its priory, that many charters were witnessed by Adam Franceys, whose possessions were at that place.

The Extraordinary Franks

Despite having a perfectly good Norman name, many Norman families adopted the name of places of common settlement. De Hameldon was adopted from the Yorkshire parish of that name, so too Osgodby, taken from the Wapentake of Osgold-Cross, North Yorks.

Another great name, Fossart, descending from Nigel de Fossart, Baron of Doncaster, finds its origins in Fossard near Fontainebleau. In 1165, William de Fossard held eighty-three knight's fees in barony, while at the same time holding knight's fees of the Bishop of Durham and the de Stuteville.

On the matter of origin, prior to the name Cleveland, the district of Langbaurgh found its origin in the Vikings. It was first a tiny hamlet half a mile north of Great Ayton, eight miles from Roseberry Topping, which is a sort of volcanic peak sticking out of the Cleveland Hills. The nearby stiff, upward climb or long hill, termed langbaurgh, became the early settlement of Langbaurgh. In turn, the massive spread of the North York Moors and Cleveland became known geographically as Langbaurgh. The Crown retained the warpentake until 1207 when King John granted it to the first Peter de Brus.

Within Langbaurgh, the manor of Danby descended under de Brus until 1272, at which time the lands were divided between the four sisters of Peter de Brus III, later descending through various lines to Christopher, Lord Conyers, around 1509.

Returning to the origin of names: the name Franceys, and its many derivatives, seems to be the most altered surname spelling in history. Most of the great names of Western European history stem from Frank origins, a key pointer being the fleur-de-lys. The fleur-de-lys was brought over by the Franks from the image of flowers along the Rhine and incorporated for that dynasty and for France. Through intermarriage and association with the Franks many Norman families were privileged in using variations of the fleur-de-lys, where for Scotland today and many other great arms and royal houses, they owe their fleur-de-lys allegiance to the Franks of yesteryear.

The Lords de Franey and Barons French and Frame bear forms of the name Franck, Frank, Francis and Franc from Fresnay, Normandy, with a breakaway branch of the mainstream Franceys becoming enfeoffed to the de Brus. Names of Fresney found in Normandy were Roger de Fresney, 1180, and Robert and Roger de Fraisnio, 1198.

For Francus read Frank; Frankisli being an early English form of le Franceys, and Frankisland a form of Frank or Franklin. Whether a knight, its equivalent, or higher rank, Franchilanus or Fraunclein meant 'a free tenant holding military service'. The name Freeman corresponds to Franklin, also Forman and Robinson, whose names are affiliated to the original Frank/Franceys. This corresponds to all families bearing the fleur-de-lys, including names derived from de Fremond or Fremont, e.g. Radulfus de Frigido, its origin in Normandy derived from Franklein, as too Freemantle and Vreman for Freemaan and Franklin Vrenoli, an English translation of le Franceys.

Laid waste by the Danes in 867–870, the old name for Whitby was Streoneshalh. Having remained desolate for 200 years without a living soul, Domesday records a Presteb, the habitation of a priest or revival of religious life however slight. Presteb became known as Prest-ebi, otherwise spelt Hwit-ebi, hence Whitby or White Settlement. Reinfrid, a soldier of William the Conqueror, upon asking to be relieved to become a monk, was told to confer with William de Percy. Having been gifted the ruined monastery of Saint Peter, Reinfrid commenced restoration of the abbey in 1078. Joining him shortly after, and running the abbey under Benedictine rule, Stephen was recorded as first abbot.

Robertus Fraunceys, knight, appears in 1100 following the death of his friend, the first Robert de Brus, in 1094. Robertus appears as a witness to a charter of the neighbouring abbey of Whitby. De Brus's son Adam succeeded, marrying Emma Ramsey in Yorkshire.

A transcript of the *Cartularum Abbathiae de Whiteby* (1097–1101) at the British Museum, positively identifies the Yorkshire–Normandy families connection with the Valognes district of the Cotentin, and the same known name of Willielmus Franceis and Rogerus Franceis, now found in Scotland, is conclusive as to the Frank's route into Scotland and their ongoing familial connection with Yorkshire and Normandy. See the Cotentin de Normandy for details of the ongoing Frank names there. Following the Battle of Tinhebrai 28th September 1106, Robert de Brus was awarded his Yorkshire fee from King Henry I.

At Whitby Abbey, soon after the Conquest in 1101, Hugh Lupus d'Avranches, Earl of Chester, Viscount of Avraches in Normandy, nephew of King Wilham I, became Lord of Whitby. He died 27th July 1101, granting Whitby to William de Percy. William was father to Alan de Percy, his charter being found in the British Museum. The de Percy family being of Danish origin (William, born of a Danish chief and last of the de Percy), went from Normandy to England founding the house of Persey.

Extracts from documents relate to William de Percy, Norman contemporary of Robertus Francais and the de Brus:

> 'conveys … etc., to include the monks, lands, forests, being pastures, woods and …'

Grants were made for:

> 'the safety of the souls of his lords the King of England and his heirs, Hugo Earl of Chester, and …'

Witnessed by:

> 'Willelmus, Walterus and Ricardus de Percy, Robertus de Brus together with tres de suis militibus Robertus Fraunceys, Rogerus de Rosels and Willelmus de Lofthus ...'

The Frank surname spelt Fraunceys; this entry together with previous evidence positively identifies Sir Robertus and his brothers Rogerus and Willelmus as de Brus kinsmen, Robertus Fraunceys being centre stage at a pivotal point in history. Incidentally the name William is a family one emanating from the original Guillaume, son of Rollo and carried through to farmer, William Frank of Ingleby Barwick, recently deceased cousin of my mother Dorothy Frank, the Frank seats of Ingleby and Barwick shown previously as feoffs of de Brus.

De Percy, Baron Leconfield and the acquisition of village land

One of the manors held by the de Percy was that of Seamer Manor in the County of York, being held by the de Percy until 1555 when de Leconfield acquired the manor. By a quirk of fate, 400 years later, on the 7th September 1959, my grandfather, T H Frank, acquired many acres of that manor, running from one end of the village of Newby, North Yorkshire to the most southern aspect. Today, Tom Frank lies buried in Seamer Churchyard a few acres from his Newby abode; half of my mother's ashes lie scattered among her favourite Cleveland hills, the rest of her ashes placed beneath the grass belonging her father's resting place.

Visitors to Tom Frank and my mother's grave in the grounds of the Church of Saint Martin have only to turn about, walk uphill, climb the style and walk over a grassy knoll to see their home. Father and daughter, same grave, same love and devotion, a daughter returned to her beloved father, a great surname now confined to typeface and a son desperate to do justice to their paradigm.

Title belonging to the Right Honourable Charles Henry Wyndham, Third Baron Leconfield, of the manor of Seamer, said land being conveyed to my grandfather by Baron Leconfield, Lord Lieutenant of Sussex in person. Following its purchase, whereas the good baron trotted off into the sunset clutching his dosh, Tom Frank set about donating the aforesaid parcels of pasture and village green, gifted to the hamlet of Newby in perpetuity: a graceful legacy. There is something about this tale that talks about goodness and the vast chasm that exists between the elite and the sons of toil, a physical and psychological divide we know so well and recognise today between those who hold the wealth and power and the proletariat.

Hundreds of years of history, so much of it slipping into obscurity, yet just for a moment the recollection of a meeting of two separate worlds: Tom Frank having no concept of his heritage his rough hands barely capable of holding a pen, his counterpart the baron, the immense divide, each awkward in the company of the other. And now the transfer of money, the deal done, a handshake and scratch of ink on paper.

Tom Frank, his intentions a benifice of one who might be termed a true Christian, Granddad's immensely powerful shoulders providing lessons for life and how a man should truly live.

Then there is the other, a baron cum Lord Lieutenant, in many ways most likely a truly decent man, seen here cashing in on his gains while retaining the rights to any future underground mineral activity, letting nothing slip from his grasp: two men, each with a different perspective, one deeply grounded and the other given to a superior mien born of privilege.

Granddad's shoulders were indeed powerful, he had used saws all his life and relished the use of a tree saw, cutting logs from fallen trees dragged from the surrounding countryside. To be at the other end of that massive saw, being thrust to and fro to the rhythmic sound of sharp teeth cutting through wood and the gentle rosy-cheeked banter shared between man and boy resounded like no other.

The author as a child, right shoulder and muscles aching with pain, yet refusing to yield and lose grip, anxious to hold onto every precious word and every precious moment. Driven by an unexplained sense of urgency, the lesson an unspoken precept passed by one rapidly ageing Frank to a grandson.

The desperation of an old man forced to skip a generation, his words, his hope, the dilution of a barrage of ancient heritage belonging to 1000 or more souls, all passed to a boy with barely a smidgen of Frank in his veins, and with it the half-promised glimmer of a story waiting a lifetime to be told, come real.

The Franks in context

Sir Robert Fraunceys witnessed a document of 1119, around which time Adam de Brus's son Robert, who was named after his grandfather, founded Guisborough Priory near Skelton Castle. It was this Robert de Brus who was made first Lord of Annandale by King David of Scotland in 1124. Four years earlier, around 1120, Robert de Brus and elderly Robertus Francais, were located attesting a confirmation of Alan de Percy to the monks of Whitby.

Robertus Francais, knight, enjoined with his son William and grandson Roger and Robert de Brus in taking the Annandale. Granted to de Brus by King David in 1124, it is significant the tenure was established by sword, assisted by Yorkshire knights and able Yorkshire yeomen, where records of respectable families in Dumfriesshire today reveal many of their origins in Yorkshire. In particular, the Scottish records of 1218 state categorically that Roger, son of William Franiscus, quitclaimed to Sir Robert de Brus, Lord of Annandale, lands which the grantee held of him in the territory of Annan for the excambion of land in the territory of Moffat.

It's necessary at this point to provide names of known Franks, including some already shown. Indicated in Normandy, and by 1189 all having turned up in records in England, are William le Franceys, Roger, Richard, Azo, Robertus, Umfirev and Walter. Records show that by 1165, William le Franceys and several others of the name held knight's fees in England. It bears repeating the Lords de Freyne and Barons French and Frame share commonality with those of Franck, Frank, Francis and Franc: a branch emanating from Fresney, Normandy.

It is possible to formulate antecedence for the Robertus, Willielmus, Rogerus, Normandy, Langbaurgh and Scotland relationship. Robertus is known to have entered England around 1066, and fathered at least three sons. William appears to have been the eldest, himself fathering Richard and Walter. Both sons inherited lands in Normandy where they continued to pay fines in 1180 and 1195 respectively. The transcript of 1097–1101 showing William and Roger already in Scotland and with links to Cleveland has allowed the rest of the information to formulate around it.

The interconnection being so complex, it became necessary to create a chronometrical chart of individual names set against the date each person was found. It was ascertained that all three of Robertus, Rogerus and Richard were together in Guisborough 1166–1180, Robertus in Whitby in 1100 and Guisborough in 1119, whereas Willielmus was found in Guisborough in 1152, at the same date as Waterus, with Bernardi, son of Robertus, born around 1144, in Egton. In the background we find Hugone and Ranulphus, and in 1181 what seems to be the first appearance of a Johanne in Scotland, born prior to 1118 in Langbaurgh.

An Osmo in Scotland seems to disappear, there is also a Matthew, Hub't, Arnoldus and Walterus, with a William and Roger appearing both in Scotland and Yorkshire. Because of the timescale, the elder William appears to have gone to Scotland with a younger Robertus, probably a grandson, while William's two sons chose to remain in Yorkshire. While younger men may have gone to Scotland, whichever way the division was played out, the decision once made, succession was secured for Robertus, Willelmus and Rogerus in perpetuity both in Scotland and England.

The names Robertus, Rogerus and Richard are also found in Ireland following King Henry II's Norman-led landing in Waterford in 1171. Between 1210 and 1338 these separate Frauceys held positions as canons and bishops having amassed considerable land and possessions in that territory. To avoid confusion, I have purposely set aside further reference to Ireland.

The most recorded Franks are those found around Derby, directly related and immensely influential, who, by comparison, the York–Cleveland Franks appear more workaday and rurally grounded. The Cleveland Franks appear to have spread widely across the landscape, moving north from York with small groups appearing further inland having associations with Fountains Abbey as York Franks and their kinsmen, the nearby Thirsk Frankland.

The spread encroached south in isolated family pockets, gradually connecting with earlier Franks who settled inland towards York and north of the Humber towards Whitby. Completing the circle, continuous resettlement caused the Frankland to acquire land and integrate with descendants of the original Frankish knights who accompanied de Brus in 1066, settling briefly around Skelton Castle in Cleveland prior to their advance on Scotland. Many of their dependants settled across Cleveland and the North York Moors, some later joining their families in Scotland as evidenced in Scottish family records.

As Normans, the wider community of Franks, far from sticking in one place, travelled vast distances holding property and assets scattered far and wide; their travel encompassed the Cotentin and far away Jerusalem. Those who settled set their sights on property and the acquisition of land in order to provide for expanding family needs.

Suitable marriage ties, alliances and use of the law were employed in order to confirm hierarchical levels of ownership. Many inherited acquisitions, passed from father to son, were within striking distance of up to one day's travel, not too close but far enough away. These were occasioned by breakaway family migration to more appealing parts of the country. The process of law was integral to the Norman mind, as too the Church, the immediacy of impending death comforted by absolution and prayers as a precept.

The King's highway

The King's highway formed a vital part in the movement of people and goods. It ran north to south, cutting through the middle of two main areas of Frank settlement, with twenty miles or so separating them. Yarm was the crossing point for the River Tees, and the Dales people were spread across this vast area as far as Whitby and the surrounding area of Pickering, where around 1290 a single family of Franks moved inland settling around Marske, an area lying immediately west of Richmond, also Gilling, south of Darlington.

For purposes of trade, settlement was deliberately positioned close to the King's highway. The spread continued around Northallerton and Thirsk, clashing with settlement coming from Pickering, Malton and Norton, migrating towards York itself and Frank settlements there. The highway approximately followed the route of the A19 south to York, and from York to London.

The area of the Wapentake of Langbaurgh, Cleveland and Pickering, touching Whitby, Filey and the territory running west to the Hambleton Hills is huge, the sparsely populated North York Moors being typical Frank territory, where to the north, Skelton Castle and Guisborough remained a de Brus stronghold, the de Brus heirs claiming the wapentake as a liberty in 1276.

What is irrefutable, the de Brus and Frank familial bloodline from Normandy to Yorkshire were of the same blood as those who invaded Scotland and whose family joined them, and consanguineous with those who stayed to look after their North Yorkshire possessions, often in conflict yet steadfastly maintaining cross-border relationship through the generations.

I previously mentioned King John, where to add insight, it's well-known the King travelled extensively clocking up approaching 3000 miles a year around the country. One route well-favoured by the King was from York to Durham, where he took the coastal path to Scarborough entering Brus terrain, visiting Skelton Castle, Guisborough and Stockton, re-joining the King's Road at Yarm. Bernard, son of the second Robert de Brus, was in service to King John in 1212, a nephew being one of a group of Scottish hostages held by the King, released on custody to Peter de Brus at Skelton in 1213. It is amazing the distances covered; the de Brus and their Frank counterparts seen both as Scots and Northern English, as were many of the northern barons.

Norman conquerors

The conquerors often strained their right of jurisdiction over their tenants; their brutal hold, God-given and venal, their superiority, first as Normans, second as conquerors and masters. In summary, they were masterly, physically powerful and intelligent. Their playful humour often overshadowed by barbarous bouts of cruelty and short temper, often quick to judge, thoughtless in meting retribution. They were the lords, they were the masters and there was little to separate them from savagery.

Punishment was harsh, yet surprisingly, shortly after the grant of the wapentake to Peter de Brus in 1207, the knights and free tenants of Cleveland obtained from him a charter whereby:

> 'They were not to be impeded in the Warpentake Court except by judgement of that court. And in case of any forfeiture, they were to be fairly amerced.'

Amercement was a case of one's head being submerged in a barrel of water and being taken close to drowning; this was repeated over and again, depending on the number of amercements ordered by the court. It appears that Peter de Brus in an act of contrition for his own deeds tried to apply lesser acumen than other courts.

Interrupting the normal grind of life, conflict upon conflict came and went leaving behind the blood-let of battle. Yet it's true that great changes come out of war, necessitating the need for increased production, and for that period, whether it be for wood or for food, more importantly for battle one needed weaponry, and whereas for swords one needed iron, for shot one needed lead.

In 1300, across the Dales, landowners, whether lay or monastic, exploited minerals on their estates, producing both iron and lead. In Cleveland, smelting became an important industry, while across the Dales, at Northallerton, Ripon, Selby, Whitby and Yarm, cloth manufacturing became a major source of coinage for the barons and the abbots alike, whereas the King and the Exchequer wanted their share. While the pace of migration appears to have mimicked the pattern of industry spread across the region, for the most part, whether as tenants or landowners, the Franks seemed content to farm and acquire land.

On the matter of fiefdom pursuant to knights in service; this was a feudal arrangement whereby knights were permitted to hold territory on the basis of serving as a mounted *chevalier* to his *suzerain* or whoever the land belonged, usually for forty days a year. Now and again reference is made to say 'half a knight's service', as the most that can be afforded in terms of land etc. Conversely a knight may agree to increase service as might apply a higher authority, or indeed divide the single forty-day term among two or more suzerains.

Orthodoxy

Sir Robert Fraunceys, severally spelt Robertus Francaise, Francey etc., was pivotal in the founding of Skelton Castle in 1119 as well as a witness to a charter of the neighbouring abbey of Whitby. As they journeyed north to Scotland, affirmation as to the authenticity of Robertus Francaise's family left behind in North Yorkshire and the kinship between the Franks and de Bruce was inseparable.

Recognition is given to A D Weld French, author of the *Index Armorial*, Fellow of the Society of Antiquaries of Scotland, Member of the Scottish Historical Society, and of the Committee on Heraldry of the New England Historic Genealogical Society, for his work in confirming the authenticity of Robertus Francaise aka Sir Franceys of the Cotentin Normandy, his relationship with the de Brus and their Yorkshire familial connection with Scotland. The *Index Armorial* shows how Robert's grandsons and heirs, Roger and William, continue the line through to the Lairds of Thornydykes and Viscount William Franceys, 'ad unem omens'.

A D Weld French's research on the surnames of Francus, Franceis, French in Scotland, the Thornydykes, and Frank origins relating to the Frame family is extensive and should be applauded for its insight and historical content, which carries compelling authority, confirming beyond doubt North Yorks Franks ties with Scotland.

Many early dates are approximate, evidenced by recorded events and found names. Cluster groups of familiar names have proven useful in showing a pattern where known names having disappeared, reappear or in relation to historic events, new names have come to the fore. Individuals shown as related, e.g. uncle, son, etc., the presence of counterpart familial and well-known surnames interspersed with clear-dated events has been a tremendous help in compiling a fair assessment of the facts.

Name-spellings, as I have said before, are notorious in their continued interchange ability, dependent on the accuracy of recordings, misspelling and what name a person might currently be using.

Where gaps exist, I have done my best to provide collusive data in order to demonstrate reasonable antecedence. Where the argument for family succession appears contentious, due to possible erroneous identification between same-named individuals of the same bloodline, I take the view, unintentional identification of one Frank mistaken for another should be forgiven when faced with an interrelated same-name cluster that nonetheless remains compelling.

This is not an exact science; it cannot be, due to the frequent and contentious nature of family member and non-family member take up of particular surnames. Also, for much of the early period, person's second names were of the place they lived, and not necessarily that of a given bloodline, and the lower one's ranking, the less available information. Fortunately, the surname Frank not being of a place but an ancient family, gives credence as to a specific identifiable family entity.

The main thrust of argument is for a proven interrelated Yorkshire family with ties to one's Scottish cousins and the Cotentin offshoot having links with the French monarchy. That said, this remains a story, something about family origins, something of history, and something about morality and how one family, through perseverance, toil, disappointment and hardship, helped shape the country in which we live.

THE CLEVELAND FRANKS FAMILY TREE

The family tree is shown through an uninterrupted continuous link from Sir Robert Frank to the present day. To aid identification, each linking family member is shown in bold forming a continuous family tree.

As stated, the Frank dynasty runs from King Chlodio le Chevelu, Rex Francorum, 428 CE, its succession passing via the Carolingian monarchy to Normandy: Rollo, his son William and the Breton concubine Sprota. Having followed the trail of Sir

Robertus Francaise, via Robert de Brus to Scotland, Frank succession in Yorkshire continues thus:

SIR ROBERTUS FRANCAISE.

Robertus Francaise, knight,	born 1041, contemporary of Lord Robert de Brus of Skelton, of the Annandale, and Normandy, Robertus, surname sometimes spelt Fraunceys or Franceis, was shown recorded with the first Robert de Brus at Whitby in 1100 and 1120.
William le Franceis, knight,	born 1043, brother to Robertus, William is often mistakenly confused with Robert'sson, William or Willielmus as the name was then spelt.
Alfred le Francaise, knight,	'supposed' brother born 1050 who married Aelizea of unknown date.

Pre-insight, William le Franceis

Prior to continuing the main line through Robert, some insight into his brother William:

William le Franceis and his line went on to be hugely successful, and it is fortunate that records are reasonably intact. It is thought whereas Robert's son William, born around 1068, took the Annandale with de Brus in 1118 and remained associated with Scotland, William le Franceis Senior, instead, retraced his steps southward, the family settling first around York and Hull, migrating inland around Derby.

William was born in the Cotentin, Normandy, coming over with his brother and fellow knights, together with their liege lord de Brus. William le Franceis had a son Wm born around 1070, his son Robert, born in 1098, died around 1179 leaving three sons. Two of Robert's sons were Thomas known as Thomas le Francis born 1124 and William born around 1128. Thomas married Agnes daughter of Robert de Hurst. I have no knowledge when Agnes and her husband died.

Thomas and Agnes had a son Robert, giving his name as Robert de Franceis. Born in 1152 he married Isabela de Bretton, daughter of Roger de Bretton. Their children were Roger (bn. 1177), who died, Robert (bn. 1179), known as Robert de

Osmundeston alias le Frauceys who died in 1211, John (bn. 1182) and William, born in Shropshire 1183.

Born around 1183 William married Sibil de Segged she being born around 1185. Whereas William died in Guilford Surrey in 1234, date of wife's death unknown. Their children were John born 1205 and William born 1208. William married Agnes de Bradleye she being born in 1208, William died in 1242 and Agnes prior to 1256. Born in 1224, their son John married Margaret Scolice of Cambridge, their son William being born in 1246, he died in 1287 but not before siring John in 1266, he in turn siring Sir Robert le Fraceys knt of Eccleston born in 1286. Succession was followed by John born 1304, his son Henry born 1322, Robert born 1342 and his son Sir Robert Francis aka Frauceys born 1364 and his wife Isabel Pershale.

John le Franceis married Margery Beaufoy, daughter of William de Beaufoy, and their children were David, born 1285, Richard (bn. 1288), Robert (bn. 1290) and Agnes (bn. 1291). Third son, Robert, died in Drayton, Oxfordshire, but not before his marriage to Cecily de Formark of Formark, and having a son, John of Engleby, born 1304, who subsequently married Matildis, who in turn had Henry le Franceys, born in 1322. Henry's father died in 1391. Henry married, having a son, William, born 1341, who married Alice de Lacy, daughter of Richard de Lacy, the Lacy family being interconnected with the Franks. Sir William and Alice, in turn, had Robert, born 1360.

Sir Robert Frauceys, of Formark, married Isabel Pershale, daughter of Adam de Pershale and Elizabeth Reese. Isabel bore eight daughters and a son, Robert the Younger. The daughters were Cicely who married Thomas Charlton, Joan who married Sir Thomas Harcourt and died in 1420, and Isabel, who died in 1457, having married Sir John Clifton, who himself died in 1453. Then there's Alice, who married Richard Peyton of Chesterton, Joyce, who married Thomas Giffard and Anne, who in 1405, married William Greville, son of Lodowick Greville and Margaret Arden.

Of the last two daughters, only Elizabeth Francis can be accounted for, she died March 1488, having married Sir John Brecknock, who in 1440 was High Sheriff of the County of Buckinghamshire. Elizabeth's husband later became Treasurer to King Henry VI, and died 1st September 1475. Sir Robert Frauceys himself passed away in 1420.

As indicated, Sir Robert was born in 1360, and his kinsman John Frauceys, Canon of Wells, remembered him in his will of 23rd October 1411:

> 'I John Frauceys, Canon of Wells, Papal writer of the Papal Household, going to the Court of Rome in the 13th year of King Henry the fourth. To be buried where Almighty God shall dispose. I leave to … and to the Carmelite Friars 20s to pray for me. To the Friars

minors 20s, the Augustine Friars 20s. To the Lord Archbishop of Canterbury, a tabula of gold to have me in memory. To Sir John Bath a silver gilt box with gilt cover. To John Macchesfeld a box silver gilt with cover. To Robert Frauncey Knight my kinsman a silver Gilt box with cover gilt … All my goods not bequeathed to be sold and the money distributed between the poor and chaplains to pray and celebrate my soul, my father and mother and all faithful departed. Executors Sir Robert Fraunceys, Knight and John Macclesfeld preceptor of the House of St. Anthony … '

The bequests were extensive and interspersed with lengthy Latin phrases. The will goes a long way in demonstrating the interrelation between a diverse spread of Franks.

Sir Robert's son, Robert the Younger, born around 1385, married twice, firstly Anne, heiress of Sir Thomas Clinton de Amington, Knight, of the county of Warwick, and secondly Elizabeth, relict of John Fitzherbert de Somersail. Anne's father was the second son of John, Third Baron of Clinton's seat of Maxtoke Castle. Baron Clinton's wife Idonea was the daughter of Geoffrey, Lord Say and his wife Maud, daughter of Guy Beauchamp, Earl of Warwick. Having gained the title in 1420, Sir Robert the Younger died in 1463.

Sir Robert the Younger's first marriage to Anne produced Margareta who married Nicholas Fitzerbert of Tisssington, next was Cecily, who married Nicholas's brother William, then Joan and Elizabeth who both became nuns, and finally a son, Thomas, born around 1409, and died in 1482. Sir Robert's second marriage produced a second son, Ralph le Franceis, whose line descended through his daughter Jane, her estate passing to her husband Thomas Burdett de Bramcott.

Excluding Ralph, three knights of interest emerge, these were: Sir Robert Fraunceys, his son and heir Robert, and Sir Robert's grandson, Thomas, there being two stories to tell, the first Sir Robert, the second, Thomas:

Sir Robert de Fraunceys, early Yorkist recumbent knight

Near Derby, lies the body of Sir Robert de Fraunceys. Lying cold and alone upon an ancient alabaster monument, an effigy of a recumbent knight in armour stares with sightless eyes towards heaven, a Yorkist Pendant of the Lion of March hanging from a Suns and Roses Collar. The tomb of Sir Robert can be seen in Saint Wystan's Church, Repton, asleep in a place of worship, a place a Frankish knight might lay his head.

Born in 1364 (some have this as 1360), Sir Robert settled in Foremark at the end of the fourteenth century and died 1420. His children were Isabel born in 1382, become Clifton, who died 13th June 1457, Sir Robert born 1385, and Joan born 1386, become Harcourt, died 1450. Joan was followed by Joyce born in 1390 and Cecily born in 1400, become Knightly. Two others, Anne and Elizabeth, unfortunately I have no birth or death records. Their father Sir Robert, clothed in a style of armour being of an older period, points to a much earlier connection with Yorkshire.

The Lion of March Pendant together with the Suns and Roses Collar being of the House of York, it at first seemed to be present during the War of the Roses period, the war being fought sporadically across the country between 1455 and 1485. But as records suggest, this typifies Sir Robert having died in 1420 although his regalia vastly pre-dates the War of the Roses version.

It transpires the design of the pendant and collar is significantly rare that only three are known to have existed, the items predating the War of the Roses version by at least sixty years. The differences in design are slight, but enough to show the Sun and Roses version most definitely copied from the earlier, very rare, version.

Separate research has found that around 1411, Sir Robert had earlier service with Richard Duke of York. It transpires that one or two high-ranking associates of the Duke of York had the privilege of wearing an early Yorkist award, an award so admired as to be later copied, the regalia becoming known as the Lion of March Pendant and Suns and Roses Collar. The more recent version of the pendant is of King Edward IV who reigned 1461–1470, and therefore proves the Sun and Roses version must have been adapted from the original much rarer version and worn by Sir Robert de Frauncuys on his death in 1420.

Although related to the Yorkshire Franks, Sir Robert was a knight of Derby and Stafford, as well as being Sheriff of Nottingham and Derby. Research shows an ongoing association with York where he attended parliament and he also appears in many Yorkshire witness statements rubbing shoulders with contemporaries comfortable in the company of northern kinsmen, a knight in deed, immortalised in death.

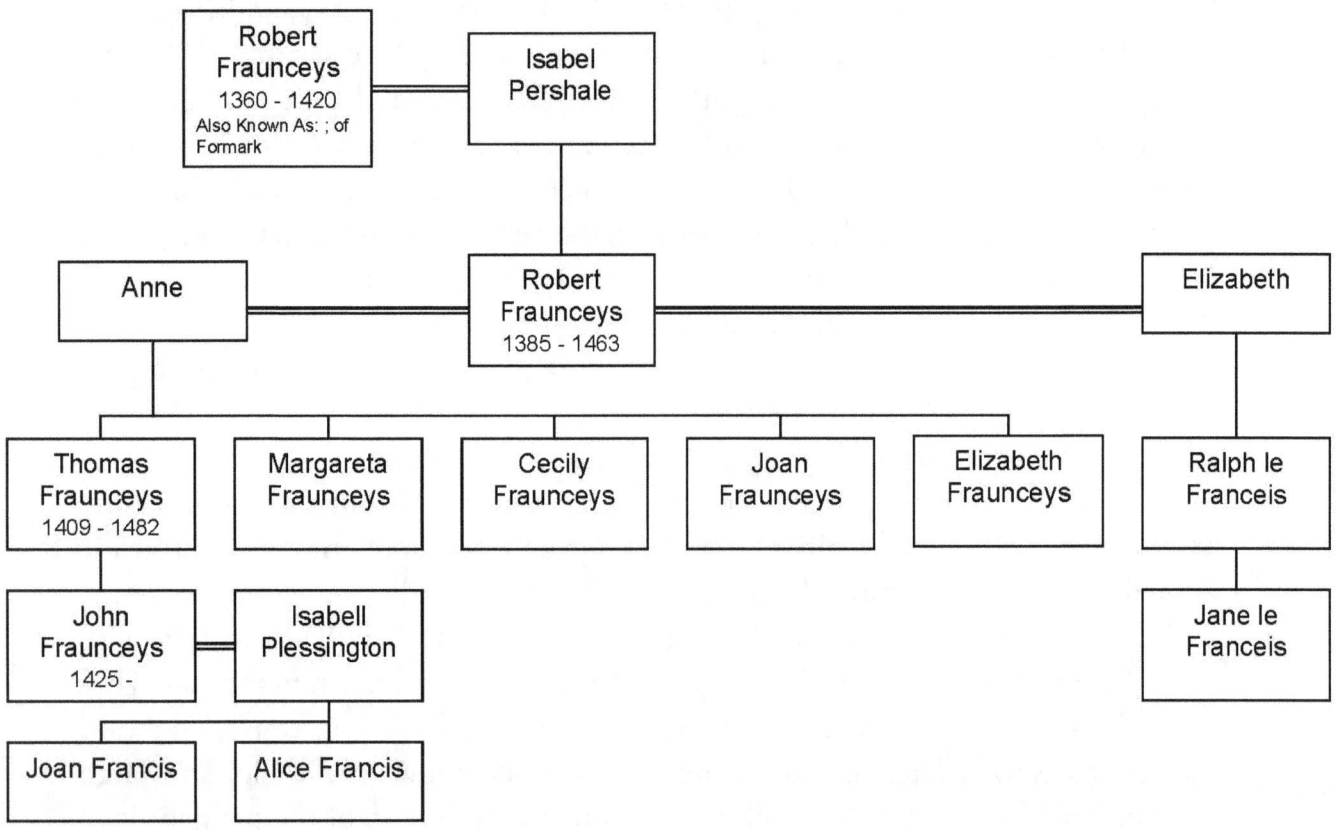

Thomas, his son Sir John Fraunceys

Born in 1409, Thomas Fraunceys sired John at the tender age of sixteen through an unrecorded alliance. Born in 1425, Sir John Fraunceys married Isabell Plessington, who had many estates of her own inherited from her cousin John de Plessington who died without issue in 1457. Over time an accumulation of vast estates had arisen, whereby having only daughters, the perennial problem of an heir arose; their daughters being Joan and Alice Francis.

As well as the city of Derby and elsewhere, their holdings stretched north towards Hull, westwards and inland across the southern reaches of York, swinging north again north-west of York where there were two estates, and further north to Thirkleby where they had interests bordering the Cleveland Franks. By any standards, this was an immense scattering of estates stretching across two counties, each overlapping the other with shared ancestry.

Later entries, dated 1434, show Sir John and Isabel Fraunceys facing retirement and downsizing by passing some of their holdings to Frankland cousins. Both metaphorically and in practice, the world of the Yorkshire and Derby Franks had come full circle; individually they had come so far and had achieved so much, but now were as one:

> Relieved of the burdensome mantle of wealth,
>
> privilege and esteem
>
> their mortality laid bare,
>
> where love and prayers console.

DFB 2016

The prayer paints a romanticised picture, viewed as an artist might seem okay, but should be measured against the times that held sway. Acquisition and the spoils of a ruthless Norman mien were at the centre of the acquisition of such massive Frauncey holdings. And these were Franks, and let there be no mistake, as Normans they were ruthless, quick-tempered and impetuous and above all fearsome and land-hungry, not people to be on the wrong side of. The Yorkshire armies fought over centuries, and despite heavy losses, continued to produce warriors born of Norman stock, imbued with a certainty of purpose and birthright absolute.

Family intrigue

Gilbert was born in 1220, probable son of Richard, one of five brothers (shown above) born between 1177–1185, the brothers being Richard, Roger, Robert, John and William. Gilbert le Francis of Foremark married Hawise de Vernon who was born in 1230. Their son Richard, possibly named after his grandfather, was born 26th May 1263 and died in June 1329 at Haddon Hall, Derbyshire. He is well-recorded due to having changed his name from Richard le Francis aka Frauncey to de Vernon, his son Sir Richard, being inspirational in that dynasty's rise to fame and fortune, the name Vernon being chronicled in history.

Richard married Isabel de Harcla, born 1255, her brother, Baron Andrew de Harcla, died in Carlisle. Their father was Michael de Harcla, who, born in 1235, died in 1311 at Hartley Castle, Kirby Stephen, in Westmoreland. Richard's mother was Joan le Fitzjohn, daughter of William Fitzjohn of York. Having taken the name de Vernon, Richard's son, Sir Richard de Vernon, born in 1280, continued the Vernon dynasty.

Relating to the de Harcla, created Earl of Carlisle by Edward II, the castles of Appleby, Brougham and Pendragon were held by one Andrew de Harcla (1270–1323), but as a result of political skulduggery, Sir Andrew was accused of colluding with

Robert de Bruce for a truce against the King's wishes, and was degraded from his knighthood by ungirding his sword, hacking off his spurs and being hung drawn and quartered at Carlisle Castle.

Sir Andrew's head ended up spiked high on London Bridge and his quarters disposed, one on the keep of Carlisle Castle, one on the keep at Newcastle, the third quarter on York Bridge, and the fourth part of his body at Shrewsbury. His brother John was also executed. The bones from the quarter hung at Carlisle were returned to Andrew's sister Sarah in 1328, and were buried at Kirby Stephen's Church in Cumbria.

This is a place I am familiar with; the one-quarter of John's bones resting in a Musgrave family tomb. Today the church is guarded by the monumental figure of a knight in armour, a symbol of honour and protection, a harbinger against a fearsome future, and a metaphor for good over evil. Thus might be found a crumbling relic in a hinterland church, an ancient knight holding lessons for a frightened land.

Yet in the Cathedral of the Dales, a recumbent knight lays mindfully on guard, serene ancient and old, an edifice in stone. Now benign, its image reminds us of our own period of religious fervour, a symbol of an inglorious past having survived the storm finds its mellowed form destined to crumble into nature's grace.

Sir Richard Francis/Fraunceys, the year 1286, Cumbria

This is a story relating to an area close to that of Sir Richard Musgrave, it relates to Crosby Ravesworth, east of Shap in Cumbria. What they were doing in the area is not clear, other than it was near the house of Thomas de Hastings, and the date was 1286. As previously stated, Sir Richard Francis also known as Fraunceys de Vernon was born in 1263, and aged twenty-three was well bloodied and in a somewhat vengeful mood. On the Whit Sunday of that year, being at nearby Mauld's Meaburn, he sent William de Harcla, John le Francis, Robert de Appleby and others to Crosby Ravensworth, where they found Nicholas de Hastings leaning on his bow, and immediately attacked him.

John le Francis struck Nicholas de Hastings with a staff and pushed him in the breast, and by pressing upon him with his horse, thrust him into a ditch. William de Harcla enjoined, leaping upon Sir Nicholas with his sword intending to run him through, but the sword fell from his hand, whereupon John le Francis bade Robert de Appleby shoot Nicholas in the breast with an arrow, whence Nicholas quickly died.

In returning the body to the manor the enraged villagers followed, intent on arrest of the felon Robert. In the ensuing affray John le Francis, William de Harcia and others drove the villagers back and by force of weapons rescued Robert de Appleby, taking him to the manor house of Richard de Francis whereupon the gate was shut letting no one in. The slain man's wife, Alice, climbed a wall to raise hue and cry, but to no avail, the perpetrators were too powerful a match, all that was left was a bereft family and villagers mouring a murderous loss.

While the above might seem a distraction, it's telling paints a picture of that early period and how those with power could get away with murder.

These insights complete, I return to the Franks' direct line of descent, commencing with the principal character Sir Robert of Normandy. Believed to have been born around 1049–1050, he must have been aged around seventeen when siring his first child. A note of caution concerning dates of birth and so on where ongoing reseach produces revisions.

SIR ROBERT AND HIS ARRIVAL IN YORKSHIRE:

Sir Robert's children:

Sir Robert born around 1067

William 1068

Roger 1070

In 1106 all three brothers, then aged in their forties, are seen recorded as *'tres militibus'* the latter two brothers having different takes on their name being: Robertus Frounceys, Willielmus Frounceis aka de Loftus, and Rogerus Frauceys aka de Rosel.

Sir William (1068) children:

Richardus b around 1095

Walterus 1094. Seen as a witness to Sutton Ouate charter 1130–1135.

Richardus (1095) children:

Richardus b around 1124

Walterus 1119, Also known as Francaise aka Ingram.

Walterus (1119) children:

Walterus b around 1144

Azo b around 1145

Umfire b around 1147 All three found together with related Franks e.g. Robertus, Richard, Roger and William dated 1189.

Sir Robert (1067) children:

Willielmus b around 1094 d 1182
Lamented, his soul prayed for at Guisborough in 1182.

Robertus b around 1092

Here the tree splits, the main Willielmus line is shown later.

Robertus (1092) children:

Johes b around 1118
Contemporous with the de Brus Johes went with them to the Annandale, Scotland, that line through Robert de Brus leading to the Scottish throne.

Hugone b around 1149

Hugone (1149) children:

Hugone born around 1175

Johanne 1176, was a Master of Work.

Gilbertus 1178

Johanne (1176) children:

Johanne born around 1201, Johan de Morsum, Moors-holme, found north of Danby towards Guisborough. Between 1230–1250 worked with his father.

The Extraordinary Franks

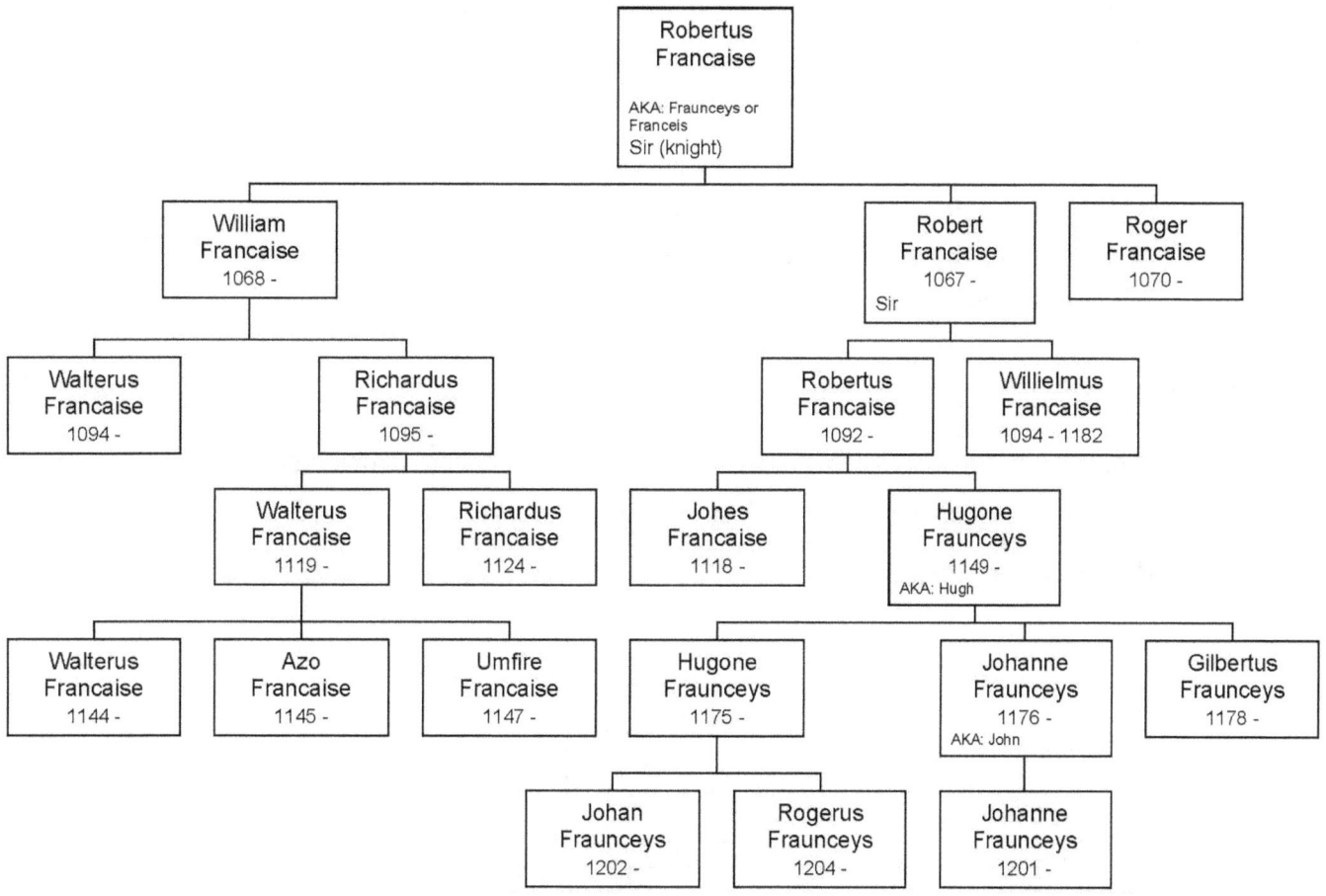

John Frounceys is mentioned in the assizes of the County of York 1251, for the homage and service of said John for the moiety of the manor of Soureby, Thirsk. In records dated 1253–1258, John, son of Hugh le Frounceis, is recorded holding land in the northern counties, including a manor under Robert de Vereripont. Due to the dates, John is a likely grandson of Hugh as opposed to his son.

Master de Wyrke John Frank oversaw the Hospital for the Sick Men of St Leonard, Guisborough (including leprosy) merging with Guisborough Priory. William Forestarius and Gundreda funded work for the fabric of the church of St Mary Guisborough and for the work to the highway to Holdebea, testimus Roger de Rypum, Willelmus Franceis, clerico de Beverl, also there, Petro Frances, Stephanus, Robertus and Rogerus, et multis alies.

Johanne (1201) children:

> Johanne born around 1225, found at Pickering with Juliane 1301, and in 1303 pays a toll for eleven acres of land at Fyveley. Filey being in arm's-reach of Pickering.

Henrico 1227, found at Neuton-under-Crakemor, being Little Newton, Kirkby Misperton, close to current-day Flamingo Park, Malton, Henry Franceys in a deal relating to a toft and one bovate of land dated 3rd Dec 1304.

Robertus 1229, also at Filey, Robertus and Henrico Frauceys, pertaining to the aforesaid eleven acres of their brother John, dated 20th April 1306.

Hugone (1175) children:

Johan born around 1202. Rogerus aka John Frauceys witnessed a charter, along with Thoraldo Francigena in 1250.

Rogerus born around 1204.

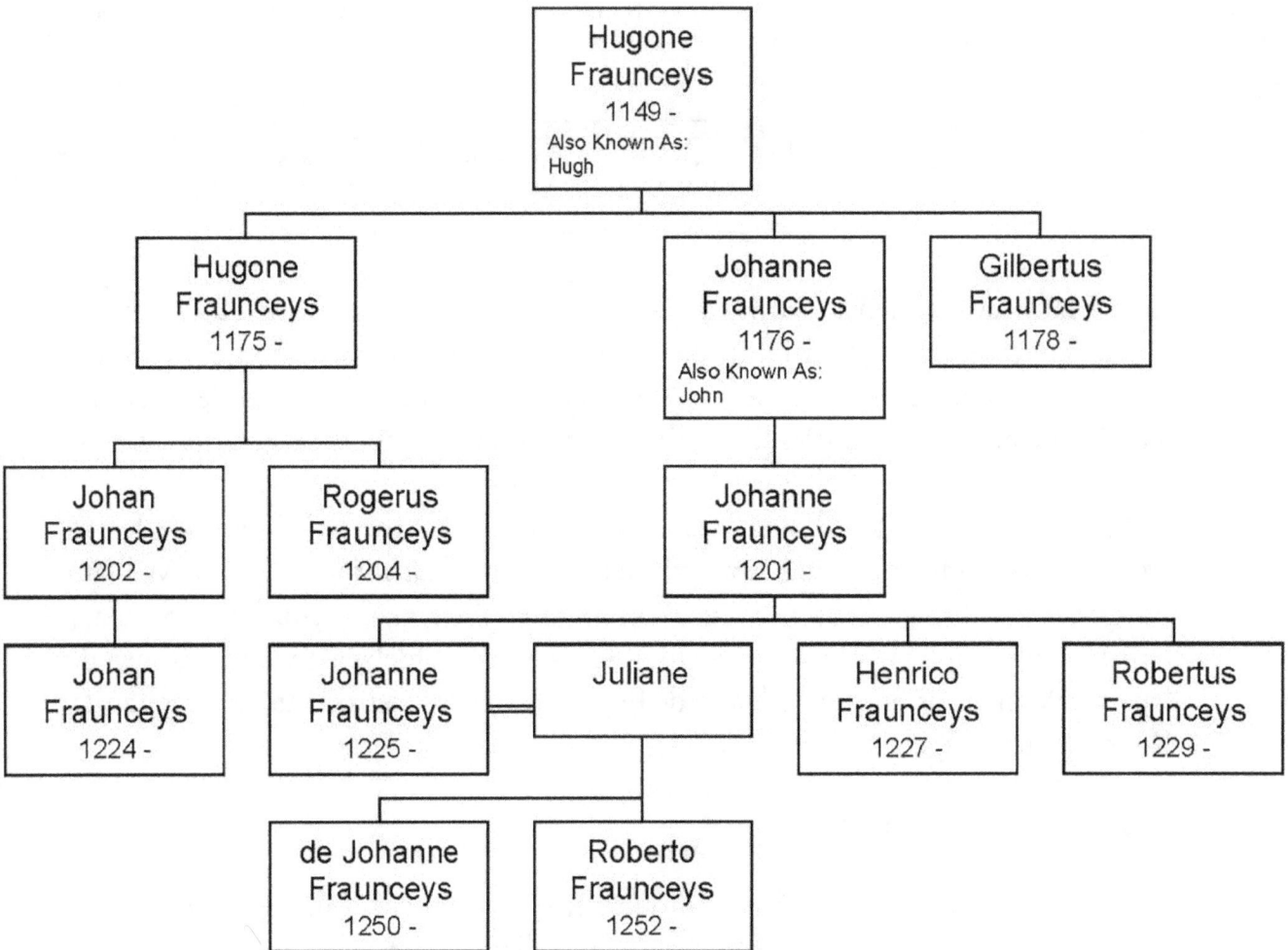

Departing from the main tree, a confusion of Johns

The Extraordinary Franks

One such is Johanne (1225), son of Johanne above, having sons to his wife Juliane, the firstborn, de Johanne Franceys, was born around 1250, being found at Ravensthorpe in the Wapentake of Birdforth in 1301 along with his brother Roberto, who was born approximately 1252. Roberto's sons were Robertus, born around 1275 and Thoma born around 1277. Robertus was located around Pickering 1303–1304, and Thoma, at Ness Rydale, 1301. Henry also appears at Pickering around 1303–1304, and Grimbald, born around 1278, shown on the Rydale List of 1301 together with Isabella de Frauceys.

De Johanne Franceys (1250) above, had a son, also Johanne, married to Ada, found located at Farndale, later found near Neasham Abbey, located on the western edge of the North York Moors adjacent Ravensthorpe. Their son William was born around 1299, also found at Neasham Abbey, later found located at Pickering around 1303–1304. Johanne (1250), his other sons, Walter, Thomas and Maurice, appear at Ness, Rydale, also around 1301.

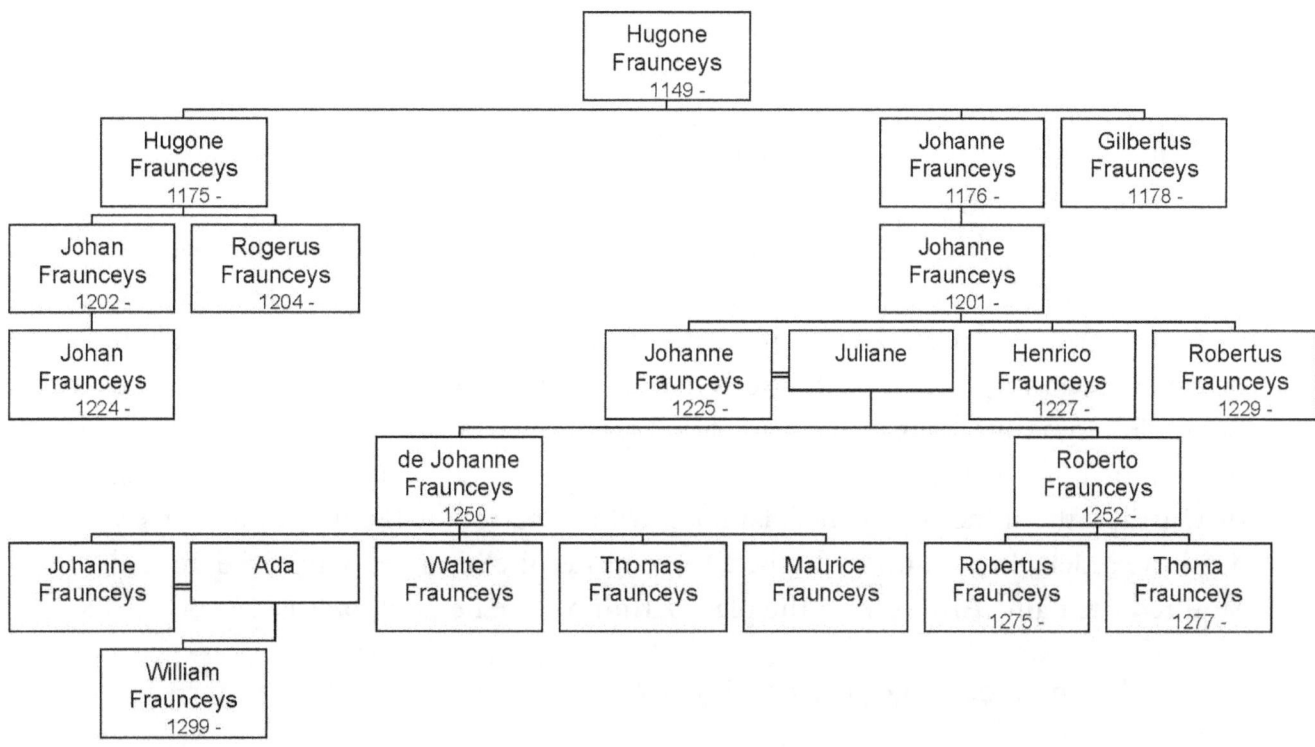

Once held by the Franks, the Ville of Ravensthorpe has disappeared, but the moat, which once surrounded its ancient manor house, may still be traced in a field near to Ravensthorpe Mill, lying one mile south of Boltby, North Yorks. Although faded into history, a quote made of the then monarch is telling:

> 'The King love et faithful Rex dilectis et filelibus suis Roberto Franceys et Thoma, Robert and Thoma.'

It is unclear what the double reference to Thomas relates to, however, the above clearly places this family juxtaposition Cleveland and Rydale on the one hand, and on the other Thirkleby with Osgodby, set in the Hambleton Hills adjacent Thirsk, in the liberty of Ripon, with clear indications of links with the Franklands of Thirkleby and the Franks of Ness and Pickering being one and the same extended family. I mention Hambleton and Osgodby due to their link with York and the mysterious use of the name Osgodby by the esteemed Sir Richard Franceys and Roger, Keeper of the Rolls of Chancery. Due to the practice of taking the name of a place of settlement, it follows that these Franceys were of the same pedigree as their cousin Franceys of Neasham Abbey, and therefore interrelated.

The following provides insight as to the difficulty with names and succession. Stepping back seventy years to 1204, the surname Hamelton is shown as Osgodby in the manor of the same name, Osgodby being six miles from Hambleton, Selby, North Yorks. Jordan de Hamelton, otherwise known as Jordan de Osgodby aka Franceys. See marital connection with the Franks and the Osgodby as Franks.

Around 1231, Jordan de Hamelton's daughter married a Chevreville from Sourdeval, Normandy, who took the name Adam de Hamelton. Their son, William de Hamelton, became Chancellor, Dean of York, with family related to Robert de Osgodby who, in 1284, held Osgodby. (William de Hamelton's executor was his great-nephew, the lawyer John Franceys).

Robert de Osgodby (Franceys) was succeeded by his two sons', Robert de Osgodby (Franceys) and Sir Richard de Osgodby alias Richard le Franceys, resident vicar of Bubwith. Now, Richard Franceys, in turn, fathered two sons, John Franceys and Sir Adam de Osgodby, Keeper of the Rolls of Chancery, who in turn was the father of Adam de Osgodby (Franceys), parson of Gargrave. Adam, having being noted in a petition of 1325 by the Abbot of Sawley, was defended by his uncle John Franceys. In a further suit of the same year, Adam (de Armin), parson of Gargrave, was actively pursuing a debt from John de Ryther. It seems despite his given name, Adam had acquired the name Armin from the place Armin where he had holdings.

'Johannes de Francigena domini clericus regis.'

John Franceys, baron, known as Johannes de Francigena was an attorney who represented William de Lindsey against the sisters of Peter de Brus III. He was also a witness in a dispute between the King and St. Mary's, York regarding the advowson of the church of St. Michael in Appleby, signing as John Frauncis of Cliburn. He was also known as John Fraunceys, Baron of the Exchequer, who held Meburn Matildae, the domain of Matilda de Morville and her husband William de Vereriponte. John Fraunceys was the son of Hugo Fraunceys, shown in 1243, where he appears in a charter of Rogerus de Veri Ponte, which confirms to John Franceys, son of Hugo Franceys:

> 'For his homage and services, the whole of the manor of Meburn Matildae.'

At the same period, he pleaded for the return of the custody of William de Pinkeny's son and lands. He died in 1267, and was the same person who held the manor of Rocliffe in Cumberland, and was there succeeded by Gilbertus Frauceys, 'a kinsman of this baron'.

Lady Jane de Lindsey, spouse of John Franceys:

> 'Dominus de Crawford, filius et lucres quondam Domini Alexandri de Lyndessay,'

Sir James de Lindsey,

> 'Jacobus de Lyndesay, filius David de Lyndesay, militis,'

Thomas de Lyndsey,

> 'Filio meo … Jaobo de Lindsey, Lady Jane Lyndesay.'

Spouse to John de Franceys; Lady Jane Franceys's cousin, Euphemia de Lyndsey, was married to Sir John Herries de Terregles, descendant of one William Heriz.

Robert Frauceys is found witness to a charter of liberation of a mill to the Abbey of Whitby in 1256.

Johannes le Frauceys who died in 1257, was lamented 'siccis lacrimis' (to dry up tears) by the monks of St Mary of York and of Selby. His influence stretched from York to Cumberland and Westmorland and to the huge de Brus holdings in the Scottish Borders around the Tweed.

John Franceys (Canon of York 1231–1233), was found at York alongside Sir Richard de Osgodby (aka Franceys, Vicar of Bubwith), grandson of Clemencia Franceys, who was wife of Roger de Osgodby aka Franceys, Keeper of the Rolls of Chancery, and in 1250, a mandate was granted to the Bishop of York for a dispensation for John Francigena, the King's clerk, notwithstanding the blemish to one of his eyes, he may be promoted to higher orders.

John Francigena provided money for ten acres of land for the Clostera of Warnel, plus ten acres of woodland, and in 1253 a supplication was granted to Johannes Frauceys dictus Francigena, clericus of the illustrious King of England, (see 1249–1250) for him to hold the rectories of Lithum and Ronay in the diocese of York.

Significantly, Lithum or Lythum in old records is four miles north of Guisborough, the Church-of-Leatham becoming Kirk-leatham. In the same year, as rector of Athelingfleet, York, John destroyed the bridge over the River Tees at Yarm. A Papal mandate was given of Johannes Frauncys Clericus in 1254; he died three years later in 1257, being lamented by the monks of St Mary of York and Selby.

It seems John's influence stretched further south around Selby. In January 1253, a mandate of the Cardinal of St Lauience's in Lucina assigned John Francigena rector of Athelingflete in the diocese of York the proceeds of all the men and towns of Usefleth, Witegift, Redenes, Swineflet, Esktoft, and thirteen bovates of land of the fee of the Abbot of York in Haldanebi, and other matters arisen in the suit between said John and the Abbots of St Mary's York and of Selby, relating to the chapel of Whitegift. John's plea-of-suit was won, having been awarded by the Archbishop, Dean and Precentor of York. This left the Abbots of St Mary being adjudged the adverse party.

In 1254, a Papal mandate was given to Johannes dictus Francigena Clericus Regis; this was for John to grant dispensation to one Henry de Galington.

1254, A Papal mandate is given to Johannes Frauncys Clericus Regis for him to grant a dispensation to Henricus de Galdington, kinsman and rector of Grossemer in Westmorland, for him to hold an additional benefice for the cure of souls.

Destruction of the ancient and handsome bridge over the River Tees, the King's highway and main trade route to Scotland

A stone bridge was built over the River Tees at Yarm near Stockton around 1200. Records show the 'handsome bridge' had been destroyed in 1253 by John le Frauncys, 'rector of y church de athelingflet', Athelingfleet, in the diocese of York, forty-four miles south of Yarm-on-Tees.

We have to imagine a road running from London to Scotland, it had to cross the River Tees somewhere; the narrowest and most trafficked route was via Yarm, which also had a busy inland port for shallow craft navigating up river from the North Sea. What our dear vicar was thinking about, smashing up the bridge, records don't say. A temporary fix must have occurred as the bridge wasn't rebuilt until around 1325, maybe later following the death of Edward II in 1327, who gave reconstruction of the bridge his approval. Records indicate work on the bridge wasn't completed until 1400, but that would conflict with the dates shown in relation to the monarch's death.

It seems John wasn't satisfied smashing up bridges. Around 1256, he appears to have got it into his head to destroy the Chapel of Whitgift, removing the stones to Athelingflet in order to build for himself a grand house. He died early 1257, being succeeded by Alan.

The King's highway

Rewritten from records of the North Riding Records Society. Right of Toll was called *Brudthall*, meaning Bridge Toll, or more commonly *Pontagium*. Where property was concerned, the grantee, or person to whom tax was granted, in turn, bound himself to make all necessary repairs. Sometimes the King accorded the right as a favour during certain periods of need for himself:

'To our Lord the King prays his vassal William de Latymer Lord of Yarm, that he will grant him pontage for five years at the bridge at Yarm which is broken down, where y men were wont to pass with carts and with horses on the Kings Highway between the waters of the Tees to Scotland.'

The King granted William Fraunceys pontage whereby reconstruction could proceed.

The road was crucial, not only as a route from London to Scotland, but, as one can visualise, necessary to the whole of North Yorkshire, skirting its cluster of closely grouped monasteries intertwining the de Brus fee and the thin spread of Franks from York to Whitby and inland to Yarm along the Tees.

The road was a vital trade route running from Yarm to Thirsk, edging the North York Moors, the Hamilton Hills, Mount Grace Priory, Rievaulx Abbey, Byland Abbey, thence to York. For the de Brus, Scotland had been a prize worth the taking, and the route via Yarm to and fro the Annandale critical.

It is difficult to understand why such a miserable cleric should want to interrupt an important and necessary route, which, upon reaching London, eventually crossed the Channel to Flanders. The route carried coal, timber, wine, beer, horses, sheep, butter, cheese, fish, millstones and even silk. Running south, the modern-day route would be Yarm, A135 and the A67 joining A19 into York.

Johan (1202) children:

Johan born around 1224. Johan, Parson of Calderbeck, Carlisle.

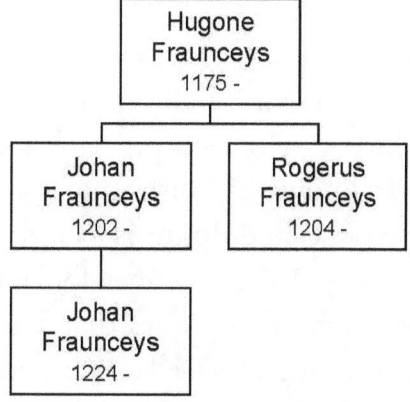

In 1243, an early record was found in a dispensation to John le Franceys, rector of Calderbeck in the diocese of Carlisle, for him to hold an additional benifice.

Around June 1247, an indult was given at the King's request, that his clerk John Francigena hold a benefice in Scotland, holding an additional benefice for the cure of souls in England.

In September 1247, another indult was issued: that John Francigena, rector of Calderbeck, hold an additional benefice for the cure of souls in Scotland.

In 1249, parson of Calderbeck, Johannes le Fraunceys also spelt Francigena, is located at Kirkleatham four miles north of Guisborough, not far from his cousin John at Moorsholm. This seems to confirm known family ties consistent with North Yorks.

York, 1312, among the plenipotentiaries appointed by King Edward II of England, to an unsuccessful treaty of peace with King Robert de Brus, were bishops and quote 'our dear clerks Meistre Robert de Pykeryng (Franceys) and Meistre Johan Franceys, canons of St Peter of York'.

Among those present were Earl Patrick de Dunbar (relative of the Franks in Scotland), Conte de la Marsh, David, Conte d'Asceles and William, Bishop of Saint Andrews.

Though peace was not accomplished, the significance of the event and warm words of the King shows the Franks as trusted mediators between an English Monarch and a Scottish King and the Franks having irrevocable ties with both entities. Robert de Brus reined 1306–1329.

Johes (1118) children:

> Johis born around 1143, was in Scotland 1181 and in Langbaurgh in 1193, John takes ward of Henry, son of William, whose father was Robert Esturmi.

> Radulphus 1145. Radulphus le Franceys found at Guisborough 1250–1270.

Succession shows:

1299, 'Radulphus Frauncey to make fealty on Monday next before the feast of St Dunstan to the lord of the priory of Guisborough for one toft and one croft in the Ville of Levingthorp' now known as Linthorpe.

The same Radulphus The same Radulphus is found paying is found paying the same amount of 2d at Guisborough 14th September, for land at Lythum (Kirkleatham), four miles north of Guisborough. This shows that Radulphus held land at both Linthorpe adjacent to Middlesbrough, as well as Kirkleatham, inland from Redcar.

The Extraordinary Franks

A similar rent call is made for the priory of Guisborough in 1300: there being two entries for Rogerus le Franceys relating to Levingthorp; the first states he must pay x amount for three bovates of land, second, he pay 6d for a further two bovates. Radulphus or Radulpho le Frauncey, of Guisborough, is also recorded in 1300.

Johis (1143) children:

> Johan born around 1168, became a lawyer in Soureby, found flourishing in 1198.

Johan (1168) children:

> Johan born around 1194. John Franceys, lawyer, is found at Soureby, Thirsk 1251, and at York 1254. He died around 1267 (see earlier entry for 1231).

Johan (1194) children:

> Johan born around 1279. In 1325, Adam de Osgodby aka Franceys, parson of Gargrave, was noted in a petition of the Abbot of Sawley, and defended by his uncle, John Franceys (see entry for 1231).

Note previous reference to Hamelton as Osgodby, and Osgodby as le Franceys.

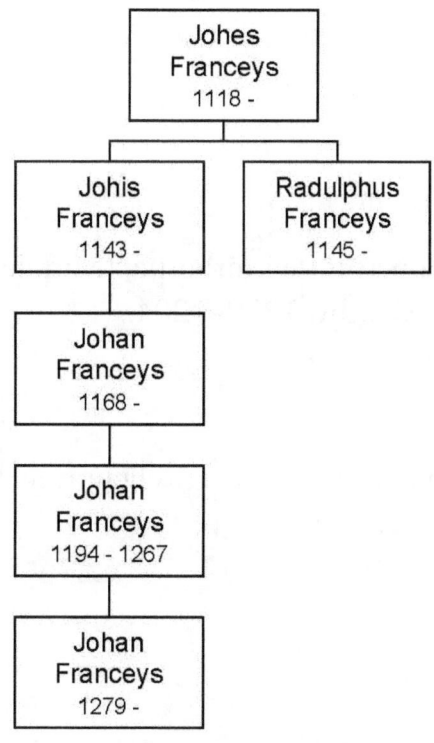

The main Willielmus line continued

Willielmus (1094) children:

> **Willielmus** born around 1118, retained lands in the Cotentin Normandy and Langbaurgh.

The above together with land in Aslakeby of the Prior of Malton, held of Sir Hugh le Bygot, 11th Feb 1161.

> Robertus 1120, had dealings with Adam de Brus regarding fees in 1168.

> Rogerus 1122. Rogerus Fraunke, Fylingdales, 15th Jul 1141, concerning marriage and land of Henry de Ormesby.

Robertus (1120) children:

> Bernardi born around 1144, of Egton.

> Robertus 1146, of Guisborough.

Brothers Bernardi and Robertus are recorded being witnesses at St Peters York regarding land at Skelton, and refer to their father Roberto, his father being found at Guisborough 1200 with his brother Willielmus. Robertus is found again at Whitby, and Willelmus le Franceys at Malton, also in 1120.

Robertus (1146) children:

> Stephanus born around 1173.

> Robertus 1171. Robertus de Linthorpe, (Middlesbrough) found at Guisborough and Whitby, 1200–1204.

Robertus (1171) children:

> Robertus born around 1196. Robertus Francey shown at Fishergate Whitby 1231– 1249.

Robertus (1196) children:

The Extraordinary Franks

Roberto born around 1221. Robertus de York donates land to Meaux Monastery.

In 1235–1249, Roberto Frauncey is found at Fishergate Whitby, relating to tithes at Nafferton and gifts to Whitby. Also Robertus regarding land at Whitby, 1249 and in 1256, relating to the liberation of a mill to the monks and Abbey of Whitby.

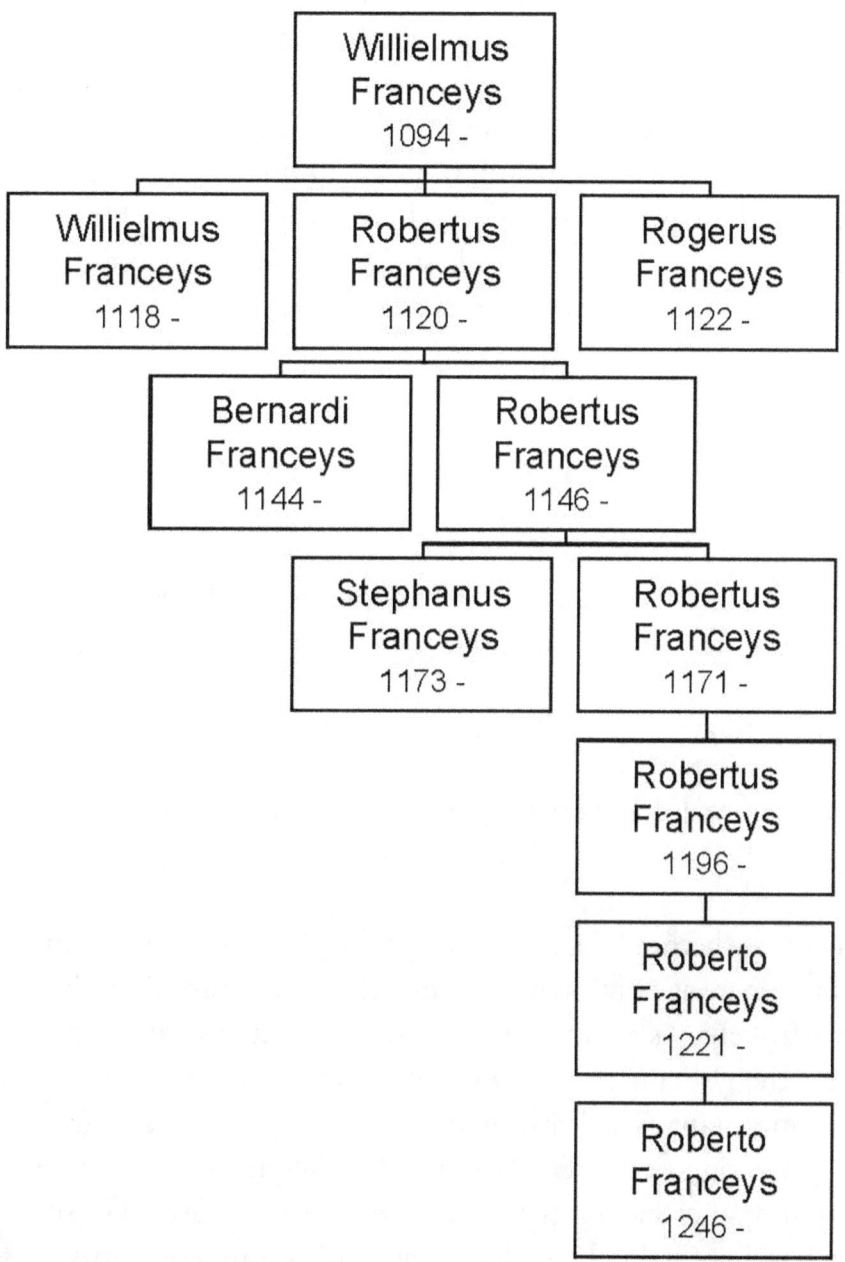

A charter of 1182, having the confirmation of King Henry II, shows Walterus Ingerram giving to the church of St Mary of Gyseburne (Guisborough) the church of Erncelive (Arncliffe) and two bovates of land, a mansion, the church of Haslintune, with half an acre of land and a mansion, together with the chapel of Haslintune. The donation was made for himself, his wife and sons and for his lord Adam de Brus II, also for the souls of his mother and father and uncle, together for the souls of Robert de Brus, his son Adam and Willelmus Francus. The charter is significant in portraying unequivocally the ties between Willelmus Francus, Franceis etc., and the de Brus both in Scotland and Cleveland.

Peter de Brus the first, having purchased the lordship and forest of Danby from King John for £1,000, gave moorland and woodland between Guisborough and Danby to Guisborough Priory, retaining the right of common pasture and hunting. Danby Forest and its surrounds later became free and unencumbered Frank land, my twice great-grandfather later owning the area around Glaisdale Head.

Peter also donated Glaisdale Moor, Swineheved and Rosedale Head, for pasture and timber supplies. He later donated his smithy at Glaisdale, retaining the right of taking iron ore anywhere within the Glaisdale area.

Roberto (1221) children:

> Roberto born around 1246. Note the historic military ties with the de Brus.

The strong military connection appears to have perpetuated through Roberto's son, Roberti, born around 1271, as about 1300, Roberti is indicated as having a daughter,

> 'Johannam filiam domini Roberti Fraunceys milittis.'

The entry clearly shows Johannam as the daughter of a senior rank, Roberti Fraunceys. An entry of 1301 shows de Johanne Fraunceys at Applegarth in the parish of Marske.

What is unsure is whether Johanne became a daughter as a result of marriage, and why at the approximate age of thirty, she should feature so prominently. In 1301, de Johanne, now Frankelyn, is shown having moved inland towards Richmond. She is now living at Skytheby, being Skeeby, now Easby, situated north-west of Richmond.

This entry is important as it clearly demonstrates migration at a critical time. The name change too is significant, Fraunceys to Frankelyn, yet little is known about Johanne, the grandfather having significant ties to the de Brus, Guisborough and one's own heartland of Glaisdale. Unless they be of prominent status, it is unusual for females to feature this early. Clearly Johannam, as her name was spelt, stood out as a person in her own right.

It is well-known, through its industry, the wool trade played a big part, and that Hutton-le-Hole and Lastingham were staging posts in the quasi-monastic trade in wool and cloth. It appears that one or more of the Cleveland Franks had decided to better themselves by joining their kin further inland, the event being marked by celebratory toast,

> 'Noveritis mepro salute animal meae et antecessorum et Fraunceys.'

The above refers to a toast given during a celebratory meal.

The main Willielmus line:

Willielmus (1118) children:

> **Willielmus** born around 1143, makes payment at Cotentin Normandy 1180, and 1182 at Malton.

Willielmus (1143) children:

> **Roald** 1169, gives land of Dalton to Warrin de Travers in 1190.
>
> Willielmus 1172. Wm of Malton, regarding a charter of Wm and Robert at Guisborough, 1200.

Willielmus relating to the land of Waitecroft and Bugthorpe, south of Malton, dated 1207. This is an agreement of Walter de Chanci to the Monks of Byland Abbey by exchange. The location is around the York–Pickering road, and William attests in 1223 that:

> 'Rosedale Abbey Priory surrender landholdings to the Franks and others.'
>
> 'All pasture be surrendered.'
>
> 'All claims to moorland be given over for sheep rearing.'

The above actions of procurement were significant as they led eventually to the amass of great wealth and titles obtained through Willielmus le Francis's son Willielmus, born around 1172.

Willielmus (1172) children:

> Walterus born around 1194. Was a witness for his brother Wm in 1250.

Willielmus 1199, Wm relating to a land transaction near Selby.

Rogerus born around 1200. Roger de Rypum.

In 1230–1250, Willielmus and his brother Rogerus had land in Aslakeby (Aislaby by Pickering). Among the many donations to the Abbey of St Mary, York, was a grant given by Willielmus Fraunceis in 1250. Also in the same year was a subsequent grant by Willielmus witnessed by his brother Walterus. Among my findings has been a finding of the marriage of Willielmus le Franceis to Sibil de Seggedon, thought to be around 1225.

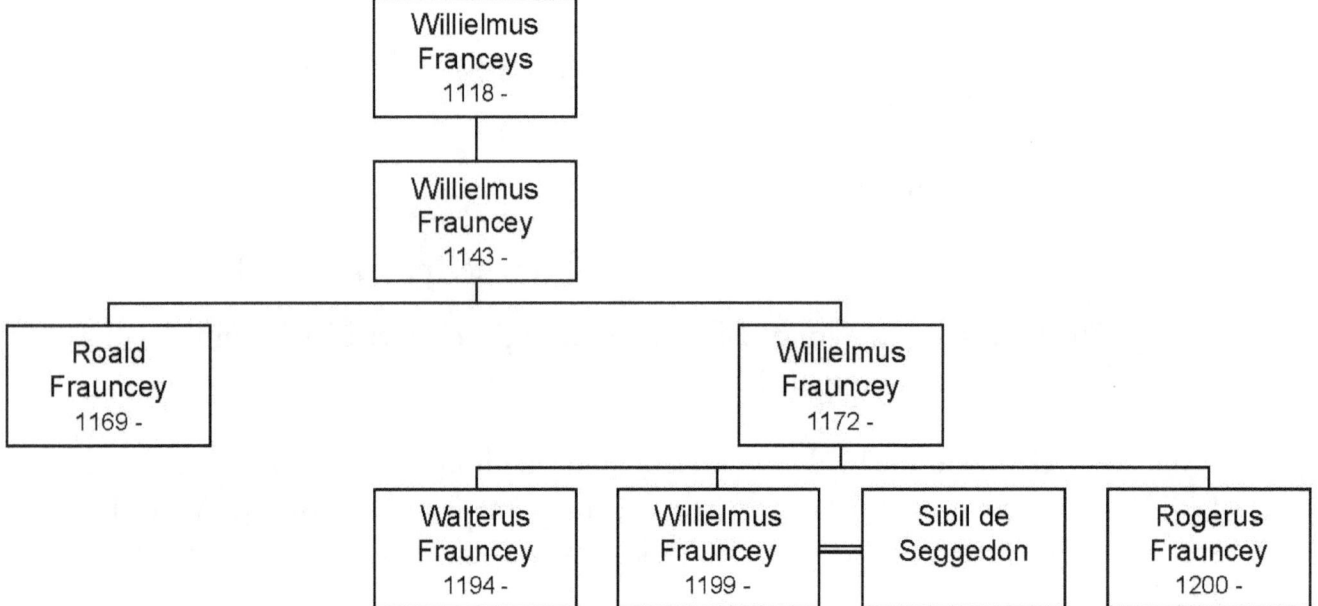

Famine

The winter of 1204–1205 was one of the most severe winters of history, and many rivers were completely frozen. The iron-solid ground was impossible to plough, and all work was suspended from 14th January to 22nd March. The winter seed was destroyed and there was widespread famine.

In 1207, Peter de Brus acquired the Liberty of the Wapentake of Langbaurgh. Becoming its Lord and Chief Bailiff, said Crown rights allowed him to levy fees and tolls, the control of weights and measures, and to hold certain courts.

The northern lords and barons had largely given up much of their land interests in France: declaring they were not bound to give service to King John in his war, Peter de Brus was defeated in the battle of Bouvines, now Belgium, losing all his French possessions.

The Extraordinary Franks

Willielmus (1199) children:

> Uctred born around 1225, Uctred le Franceys of Aslakeby.
>
> Ricardus 1227, Ricardus de Aslakeby alias Franceys.
>
> Alanus 1223. Alanus le Fraunceys of Selby, having been well provided, died in 1255, leaving a son and heir Henricus.
>
> Johes 1228. Johes Franceis married Agnes de Bradlege by 1256, and was third in line to what was to become the Foremark pedigree.
>
> Willielmus born around 1224, went on to purchase many holdings of his own.

Around 1250, Willielmus Fraunkelayn was one of several overseers of over 600 acres of land around Topcliffe, between Ripon and Thirsk. Ownership extended to other holdings reaching as far as Wilton and Carlton Edge, adjacent the North York Moors near Stokesley, and as far as Fountains Abbey to the west. He was one of four bondsmen handling ownership. In 1261, he is found owning lands is Aslakeby Pickering close to Ness in Rydale.

In 1261–1262, an inquisition held in the forty-sixth year of King Henry III, shows Willelmus Franceys held one bovate and one toft in Aslakeby near Pickering. This is the same Willelmo, Clerico seen around the dates 1230–1250. Also found in 1250, Rogerus aka Rogero, Canon de Rypum, as well as Willelmo Fraunceys, Clerico de Beverlace.

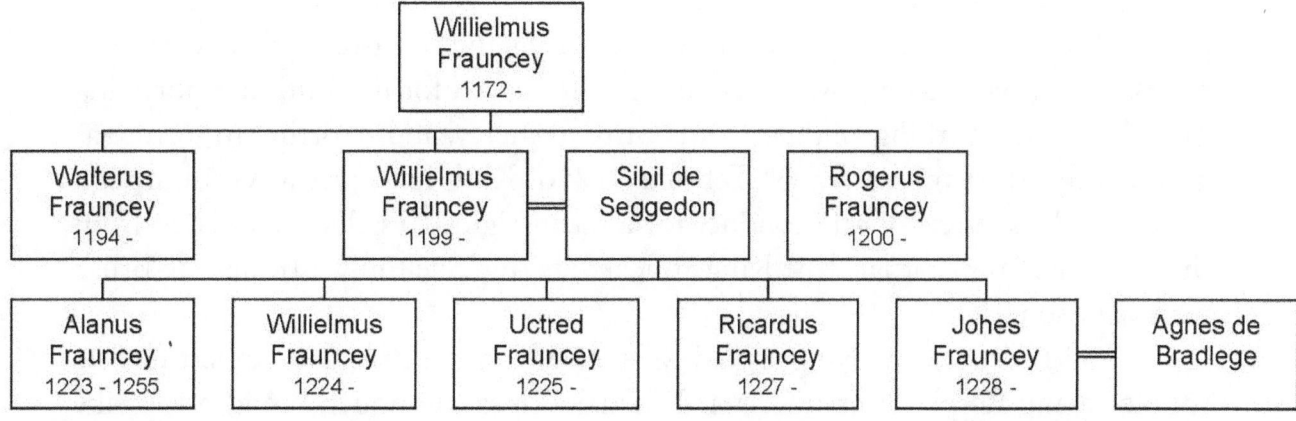

Pedigree of Willielmus le Franceis, 1199, and his son Johes, or John le Franceis

Using the modernised version of names, William le Francis was born around 1195 and his son John around 1224. John married Margaret Solice, their son William named after his grandfather, was born around 1246 and died around 1281. He married Agnes Tyckenhall in 1265 she being born in 1248, by this time William had the grand title Sir William, Baron of Osmondeston. Thought to have had two children, the only certain child was John Francis born around 1266. Known as Sir John of Derbyshire de Francis, he died in 1333. He married Margery Margaret Beaufoy become Lady of Burton Upon Trent

Through the John line was born Sir Robert le Franceys born 1286, Lady Agnes de Franceys and two others unknown. Robert had a son, Sir John Francis born 1304 who died in 1391. His son Sir Adam sired two known sons, not thought as twins both birth dates given as around 1322. John, who died around 1386, left two known children, William and Margaret. Henry Franceys' son Robert of Formark MP went on to form the dynasty pertaining Robert Francis of Formark. Born in 1342 he died around 1370.

The Magna Carta

Runnymede 1215 is the historic date Peter de Brus, together with northern barons, forced King John to sign the Magna Carta. In retaliation, and operating from Knaresborough Castle in 1216, John acquired a mercenary force from France waging war on the northern barons. Today, Knaresborough Castle remains Crown property.

Negotiations with the French finalised the King began to lay waste the northern parts of England, destroying the castles of the barons and compelling them to submit to his orders. Not content with retaliation John settled for retribution: oppressing the inhabitants, burning all their towns without mercy, and resorting to torture as a means to extort money. By 6th February 1216, King John was at Guisborough giving de Brus letters of safe conduct for a mean eight days. Two days later, from the 8th to the 10th February, the King attacked, taking Skelton Castle and de Brus's men as prisoners.

On 15th February, the King agreed to receive Peter de Brus and Robert de Ros (de Ros being Rosel aka Fraunceis de Rosedale) in safe conduct, the idea to make peace and win them over. Robert's negotiations received safekeeping for all of the prisoners, and by 1219 de Brus had recovered Carlton and all his manors in Cleveland. Succeeded by his son, de Brus died a year later in 1222 and was buried at

Guisborough Priory safe in the knowledge his son Peter would have a kinsman to guide him.

The background for the times was the localised effect of famine followed by war. Exacerbated by the savage looting and burning of villages and occasioned by oppression, torture and extortion, this was a time of continued barbarity set at the hands of an unhappy King and, as was the monarch's want, it reflected badly upon his subjects. And for those charged with carrying out his orders their actions were viewed as sport metered against an easy prey and those unable to defend themselves. And has been determined time and again, when times were bad the Franks seemed to have a knack of appearing invisible against the most belligerent of tyrants, only to appear again as trusted arbiters.

Peter de Brus II married Helwise, the daughter and co-heiress of William de Lancaster, Baron of Kendal. They had a son, also Peter, and five daughters. De Brus immediately quarrelled with the Prior of Guisborough over the agreements made by his father and destroyed the property belonging the priory at Glaisdale. However, he was forced to recompense the priory with gifts near Driffield retaining manors such as Glaisdale and Rosedale Head subsequentially gifted to the Franks

Evidenced by one's immediate family connection with the de Brus, the manors of Glaisdale and Rosedale Head were owned by one's Frank forebears, my grandfather being born there. The association is further evidenced by the antecedent ownership of Ingleby, Acklam, Barwick, Linthorpe, Yarm, Pickering, Middlesbrough, Whitby, Danby and Hart, all previously de Brus, identified as Frank through to modern times.

But this was still the thirteenth century and tempers continued to fester. Lasting from 1223 to 1246, the period ended with de Brus paying many fines. Yet money didn't seem to be much of a problem for de Brus, records of 1227 showing him taking tolls from markets in Skelton, Redcar, Marske, Brotton and Girrick. In addition he had his own fishing fleets at Redcar and Skinningrove, and in Danby his men were smelting iron for the production of tools and weapons. In controlling food production, he owned five local corn mills, using his immense power and tremendous wealth, adding yet more to overflowing coffers used as a means of paying for a personal standing army and many retainers. There is no doubt the de Brus was a force any foe would be better settling terms with rather than do battle.

This was exampled in 1230, Peter de Brus now being responsible under King Henry III for dispensing justice throughout Northumberland. The law was something the de Brus learned from the Franks, but was once again turned to his personal advantage, using his liegemen and kin as administrators to buy favour with the clergy.

In 1230–1250, William and Roger de Franceys are recorded having additional land in Aslakeby, being Aislaby by Pickering. Names also located are Willelmo, alias Clerico de Beverlace, and Rogero as Canonico de Rypum. In order to distinguish between shared names within a family, within 100 years and for the following 200 years, the practice of taking one's location as a surname grew, records of the name Fraunceys disappearing so fast as to be thin on the ground.

The problem for the people of the time was how to distinguish one family from another having shared names within close proximity. For the Franks, the problem of identification was solved using name-spelling variations. Exacerbated by such changes, misspellings and population decline, records confirm the gradual dispersal of Franks northward. Yet among the turmoil of continuous combat, death and migration, among those who stayed were a sparse scattering of Dales folk hanging on by a thread. Yet almost as if belonging to a separate class there were counterpart Franks who fared much better, a dynasty that remained largely untouched.

In 1231, related to the Chevrevilles of Sourdeval, Normandy, and contemporaneous with the Franks and William de Hamelton's executor was his great-nephew, the lawyer John Franceys. See earlier reference to the years 1231 and 1243, showing details of de Osgodby alias Richard le Franceys, vicar of Bubwith and his two sons, John Franceys and Sir Adam de Osgodby alias Franceys, the name Osgodby taken from the place Osgodby.

There is late mention:

'Unum toftum et aliam portionem.'

Dated 1235–1249, the above was in relation to Fishergate, Whitby and Roberto Fraunceys. Seen in his will, my four times great-grandfather held property in Fishergate. According to subsequent statements, the tithes of Nafferton, dated 1235–1249, are specified among several gifts to Whitby. These are found in the charters of the founder and his successors as well as elsewhere. Incidentally, the spelling 'Fraunceys' in Yorkshire is the same as the previous Scots spelling of the name.

The Franks rapid exodus north, destination Northumberland, and into Scotland exacerbated the devastation brought upon the remaining ordinary population. Around that time there seems to have been a corresponding growth of Franks in Scotland indicative of more than a localised birth rate. This is evidenced by a previous high birth rate in Yorkshire answering the question of the sudden lack of Cleveland data. Their youth were on the move, heading north in order to join their namesakes in Scotland, a safer bet than staying in Yorkshire.

Yet the continued importance of Cleveland as a Brus seat and York and Whitby as ports, and the terrain moving inland past Pickering, north to the Esk and across to Guisborough, remained vital. The fertile land and rich deposits of iron ore located at Glaisdale, together with the surrounding forest woodland, made the area perfect for induced settlement and the production of war material such as swords and armour.

The Extraordinary Franks

Early evidence is shown in the construction of a wooden castle at Guisborough using techniques prescribed by remaining Frank overseers and masons, rebuilt using quarried stone.

Not all Franks were necessarily well off. Records confirm the high rate of felling and quarrying used in the construction of castles and local monasteries. Subsequent tests of iron ore have shown the Glaisdale ore to be of extremely high quality. The very fact of the de Brus being able to raise troops locally and equip an army of Yorkshiremen seems irrefutable. Hard evidence shows a body of Franks, or Franklins, subsidising their income by part-time mining alongside their smallholder activity. Shown a route out, their youth were often drawn to the military or migrated north to Scotland, these being heady times and for the fit and strong, and with decisions to be made, what to do?

Yet history seems to show that a majority of Franks bore the bruising callouses of hard work, carrying in their minds a code of stoic single-mindedness and headstrong determination, their Bible serving both as a source of prayer as well as education through the written word. Schooling was often orchestrated by a more learned female relative and chapel conducted by a local lay preacher, where records show the Franks fully immersed at the centre of this activity.

In 1240, Peter de Brus II went on a pilgrimage to Palestine with the King's brother, Richard, Earl of Cornwall. He either died fighting in the Holy Land or at Marseilles on the way home. His son, Peter III, succeeded, marrying Hillaria, the eldest daughter of Peter de Mauley, Lord of Mulgrave. There were no children.

Such was the de Brus. Of the higher ranking Frank family tree:

Alanus (1223) children:

> Alanus 1248.
>
> Henricus born around 1249. Becomes son and heir.

From the survey of the County of York, Sir John de Kirby, 1277:

> 'Willelmus de Holtby tenet et idem Alaiius tenet de Alano le Franiiceys de Fencotes, Hamilton.'

The entry shows Holtby to be a tenant of Alan Frank, although by 1286, Holtby appears to hold a third share. In 1286–1287, an attempted land-grab by Holtby seems to have been thwarted. Kirby is a village in Hamilton, although Sir John Kirby is unlikely to have originated there.

Alanus de Fencotes, aka Alanus le Fraunceys, gives land to the monks of the Church of Germanus, Selby, York, 1269–1280. In 1269, the King grants Alanus the charter of land at Fencoats, located midway between Catterick and Northallerton, adjacent Kikby Fleetham. In the County of York survey of 1275, by charter of King Henry III, confirmation shows Alanus has free warren of Fencotes and its surrounds. In 1277, Alan is found in the district of Hamilton.

In 1286, Alanus le Fraunceys de Fencotes is seen holding a knight's fee, of which Willelmus de Holtby holds a third share. Besides this, Alanus le Fraunceys holds five caracutes of Hugo filius (his son) Henrici, who holds of Henricus, also filius (his son) Conani, who holds of the Earl, who holds of the King. This reference appears to be one of succession whereby Alanus's sons Hugo and Henricus held the estate on behalf of one or both of their sons Henrici and Conani, who must have been babies. Shortly after, around the same date, 1287–1287, Alanus is found at Stokesely:

> 'Robertus fihus Willelmi de Hoton (Holtby) tenet in eadem villa de rege i.e. di. f. de eodem honore et Willelmus de Holtby tenet iij. Car. et. Di Alano le Fraunceys; et idem … inquisicio capta apud Stokesley infra Wappentagium de Langbargh.'

The above refers to an Inquisitions Assessment relating to the feudal aids of 1286–1287, interpreted as:

> 'Robertus finds Willelmi of Hoton wrongfully occupying Eadlem Ville. I Robertus previously ruled about Eadlem and the official dignity of Willelmus of Holtby to occupy same ville, and Alano le Fraunceys also. Inquisitor Capta according to Stokesely in the Warpentake of Langbargh.'

The reference to William seems to be that of Alan's uncle, William (1224), who appears to have looked after Alan's interests subsequent to William's brother's death in 1255, as a surrogate in probate.

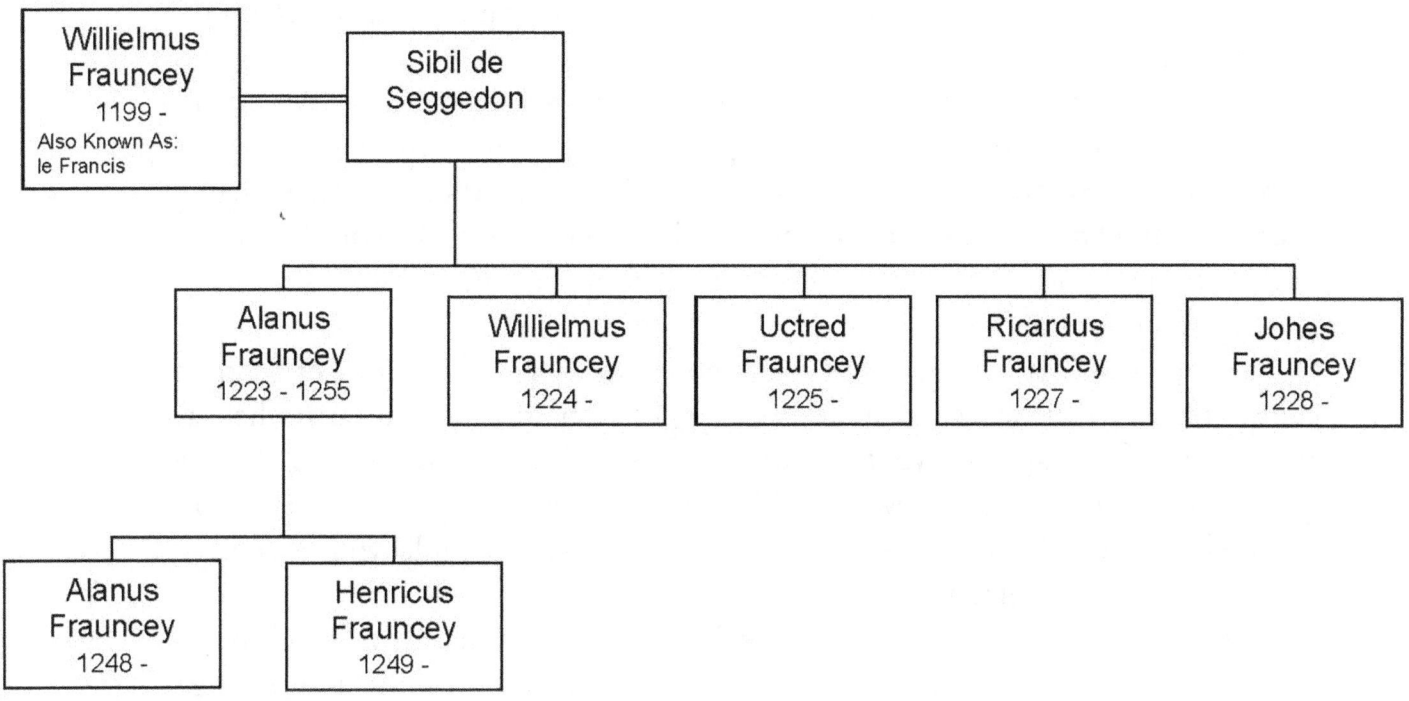

Stone walls

The *Oxford Dictionary* describes stoicism 'as a product member of the ancient Greek school of philosophy founded at Athens by Zeno circa 308 BC.' It sought virtue as the greatest good and taught control of one's feelings and passions or showing great self-control in adversity, hence:

In North Yorkshire, snowdrifts on high ground were a curse; sheep naturally sought shelter against the leeside of stone built walling. Bringing us forward to the late 1960s – for one Dales sheep farmer, high upon the Fells, this fateful winter's snowstorm was unprecedented; as opposed to losing a couple or more sheep, overnight the whole flock became immersed in high drifts of snow, where despite rescue attempts the whole flock was smothered and perished.

Among other things, my grandfather was a lay preacher and practising Christian, for him a parishioner in need and the business of setting things right was a blessing, whereby Tom Frank gifted the unfortunate Dales family a lowland farm. For him the gesture was just another day, never talked about and life went on. Years later there was occasion for my wife, Ann, and I to call upon the same farmer on some matter, whereupon the door was shut in our face. That doesn't matter: at first perplexed, yet fully cognisant Granddad's earlier actions had been unconditional, I suppose stupidity, our approach had touched a nerve, something so overwhelming and difficult to face the farmer had reacted through hurt pride, the festering notion of receiving largesse from another, coming face to face with his benefactor's grandson was to much to bear.

Many years before, as a youngster coming from the blistering heat of Africa and seeing the UK for the first time, I was immediately conscious of the odd behaviour of some of the country folk and became aware of the incidence of same surname marriages, and I'm reminded of that not-talked-about closed familial brother, sister, cousin, coupling. Manifest through a strange aberrant slowness, born successively, generationally and of things being not quite right.

Even today one has only to visit some remote pub, Cornwall enclave, or Scottish hideaway or as I experienced on more than one occasion, some remote farm where as many a five burly scary-eyed young men would descend, all together, with over-wide grins, where you instantly knew something was not right. Caught on the hop and unsure how to handle things would return a complementary smile while executing the calmest possible retreat.

As Dales folk it seems fortunate the widespread seed of successive Frank progeny employed a wiser approach towards marriage, its liaison having a knowledge of breeding, a barrier to such latent aberrations. The reader will be amazed at the territory they covered and the distance successive generations travelled, mostly with the idea of expansion, and with a network of family to support them along the way.

Willielmus (1224) children:

> Pertri born around 1246. Petri Franceis de Helmsley, is found at York as a joint benefactor to the Abbey of Rievaulx, his father having dealings at Fountains Abbey much around the same date.

> Thomas 1251, he is found at Aldfield, close to Fountains Abbey, disputing land bounding that previously held by his father Williemus. He is found 22nd December 1277 at Alder Felde Ripon.

> Ralphus 1255. In 1272, Ralph le Franceis is found at Little Stainton, situated between Stockton and Darlington, possibly connected with the Acclum (Acklam) Franks.

> Maurice 1256, is found together with brothers Walter and Thomas at Ness, Rydale in 1301.

> Walterus 1249. Walter and Willielmus make donations to the Abbey of St Mary's York.

> Ricardus 1253. A novel disseign is arranged by Richard de Fraunceys in Barforth, 1275–1276.

One Ricardus de Fraunceys is located at Barforth, south-west of Darlington in 1295–1296, and again on the Tax Roll in 1297.

Barforth is interesting as it is close to the early Frank settlement of Acklam, Linthorpe and Thornaby, yet slightly inland. Eight miles south-west of Darlington, Barforth is located in the parish of Forcett adjacent the River Tees. The connection between these early Frank settlements appears conclusive as to migratory drift. The growth of cluster groups of Franks around this area and towards Richmond, together with settlements north of York, Thirsk, Yarm and beyond, seemed to form a conflate unity of purpose.

> Willielmus born around 1248, takes ownership of land of Aslakeby Pickering, near Ness.

In 1261–1262, there was an inquisition involving William senior (1224), holding one bovate and one toft at Aslakeby. Willelmus le Frauceis also had a grant from King Henry III, seen in an inquisition held at York 26th July 1269, also present at the second inquisition was William's son Uctred le Franceys. In naming his son, the name Uctred had been used frequently in Northumberland before and after the Conquest

An inquisition at York, 31st October 1272, shows the witnesses as Peter Franceis de Helmsley, with Hugh de Thorneton, Simon de Carleton, Roger de Kirkeby, and Thomas son of Thomes de Ravensthorpe testifying that Nicholas de Bolteby held no land of the King. Yet, members of the Bolteby family occur as leading benefactors to the Abbey of Rievaulx near Helmsley, indicating wealth. Peter Franceis de Helmsley appears to be related to the Ness Frankland; Ness being within touching distance of Helmsley. Thorneton, Ravensthorpe and Bolteby, as then spelt, were also nearby.

Uctred le Franceys of Aslakeby near Pickering of Ricardus de Aslakeb alias Franceys of Yorkshire was required for an inquisition dated 1st December 1272, where Petinis Fraiiccis aka Francais was on the jury.

Willielmus is found regarding tenements at Langbaurgh and Mildeburg aka Middlesbrough, seen in the return for Langbargh 1277:

> 'Die Sabbati tenet iiij car. et. Di., Robertus filius Galfridi ij bov., Willielmus Frauceys.'

The reference to Galfridi suggests a son Robert being a son of Galfridi of Willielmus. If this is true, Galfridi would be a son of William's father (1224), the dates seem to support this.

In 1281, William de Lascell gave and confirmed to Alan Langdale:

'Land of this place and his heirs and assigns, seven acres and a half of territory, also arable in this meadow and pasture.'

As was commonplace, being situated in Langdale Forest, Alan exchanged his name for the place name Langdale. Situated in the triangle made up of Whitby, Pickering and Scarborough, the settlement was attested by Willielmus de Francais.

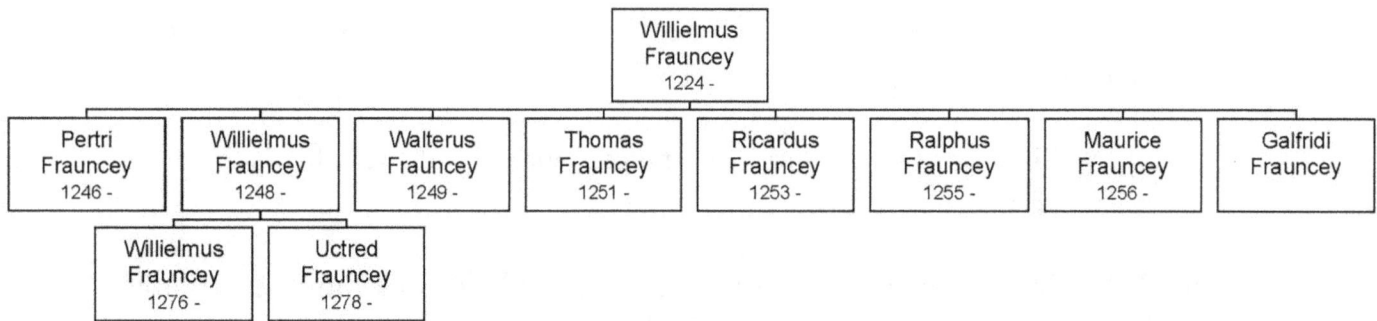

A rent call was located at Langbaurgh in 1300 for Willelmo Fraunceys, also located at Merske and Egton in the 1301 Langbaugh subsidy for Eggerton and Westingby, Charter Roll 5, Edward ll, No 22:

'De Willelmo Fraunceys xxdo of freewarren in all his demesne lands of xxio also Merske cum Redekerre, Castellevyngton, Tamton, Newby and Kildale.'

Also shown at Kildale, Willelmo Franceys at Wariaghby, being Warlaby, Ainderby Steeple, again in 1301.

Willielmus (1248) children:

Willielmus born around 1276, in 1304, was awarded land given for Foreign Service:

'Given by John de Sutton in 1304, for the great homage and Foreign Service of William Fraunk, one bovate of land and five acres of meadow at Gunnerside.'

Gunnerside is a remote and exposed territory positioned way west of Richmond and Reeth in what is now the Yorkshire Dales National Park.

Uctred born around 1278, son of Willielmus.

The Extraordinary Franks

Also, shown on the Rydale List for 1301, de Isabella Fraunceys, at Slengesby, now Slingsby, near Malton, Rydale and Ada de Fraunceys, of Kirby Misperton on the River Rye, the Rye running through Ness, Rydale.

Main Willielmus line continued:

Roald (1169) children:

Robertus born around 1196, makes a grant with Robert Travers.

Petrus 1202.

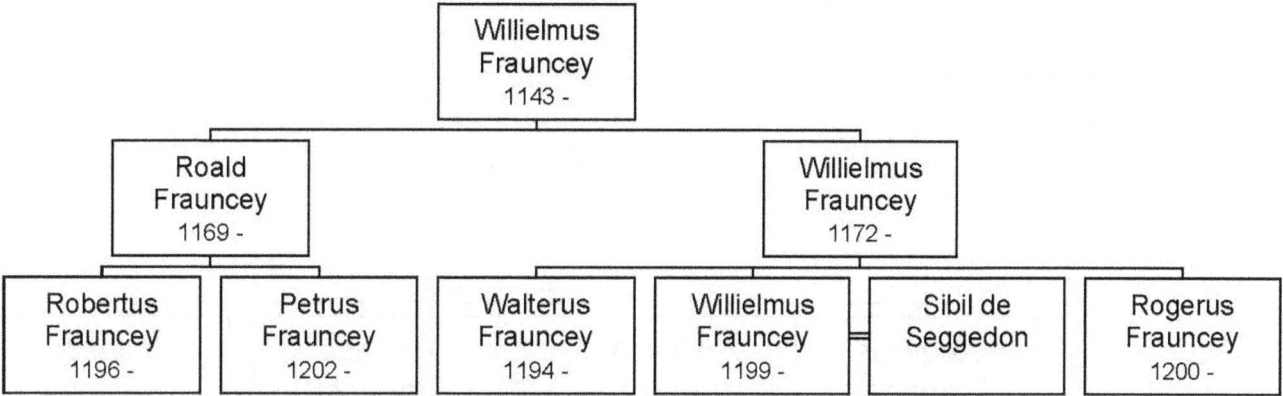

Robertus (1196) children:

Rogerus born around 1222, becoming Sir Roger de Mowbray aka Roger Franceys. Roger de Mowbray, is found at Levyngthorpe (Linthorpe, Middlesbrough) as a free tenant of the Priory of Gysburne (Guisborough).

Nicholas 1225.

Henrico 1228.

Johan 1230. John found at Danby 1250–1270.

In 1301, de Johan Fraunkleyn is found at Craythorne next to Borrowby, adjacent to the Yarm–York highway. And on 18th May 1304, he is party to an inquisition relating to land belonging Alice de Lund at Topcliffe, situated between Ripon and Thirsk.

A prior acquisition in 1286, relates to three carucates of land amounting to a quarter of a knight's fee held by John Frankes, and Henry Frankes, his son, one bovate.

A carucate is the amount of land a team of oxen could plough and reap in a year, and a bovate or oxgangs, the amount of land a yoke of oxen could plough in a season. This might vary depending on the type of land and how difficult or easy it was to cultivate, ranging from as little as eight to as much as twenty-four acres.

Rogerus (1222) children:

Christian born around 1250, found at Linthorpe 1300.

Johanus 1252. Applegarth is important being situated in Langbaurgh, west of Guisborough at Coulby Newham. Its location is a juxtaposition to the North York Dales cluster, the Richmond–Darlington settlement, and Cleveland– Richmond migratory route west. It is here in 1301–1312, that John Frounceys paid a subsidy.

Rogerus 1247.

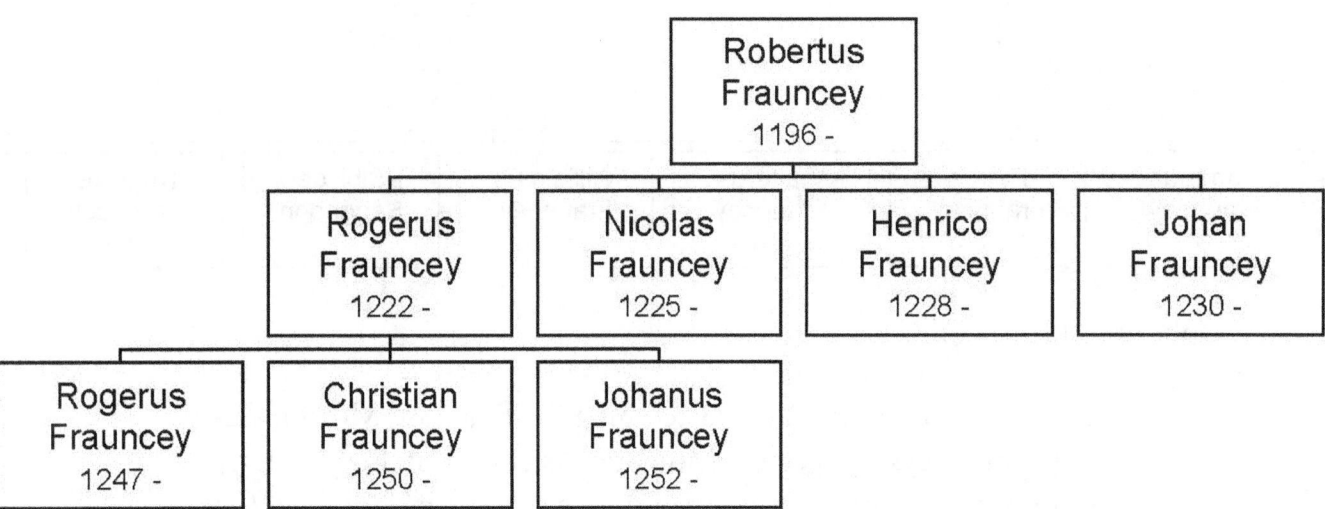

Rogerus Franceys senior was at Linthorpe, known as Levyngthorpe in 1262, around the same date as Gilberto, and his brothers Nicholas and Henrico, and as a free tenant of the priory of Gysburne, made suit to the court of Ralph, the prior, at Thornaby 1262–1280. As Sir Roger, he is found at both Danby and Levyngthorpe in 1270.

He appears again in an assizes in the fourth year of the reign of King Edward I in 1275. This related to a matter concerning the appointment of two justices to take assize of a novel disseisin arranged by Osanna, daughter of Humphrey of Leningethorp against said Roger Frounceis, touching a tenement in Levyngthorpe. Linthorpe in the twentieth century, becoming Thomas Henry Frank land, owned along with Acklam, most of Stokesley and a portion of Great Ayton.

Roger is located at Levyngthorpe in 1275, Middlesbrough in 1276, Egton in 1279, at Levyngthorpe in 1300 relating to land and the Manor of Acklam. Sir Roger died

20th May 1304, his brother John, above, became heir to an estate in Masham lying west of Northallerton and Bedale.

Around 1300, found in Christian Fraunceys records of Levingthorp in the Domesday survey, Roger Franceis is shown belonging to the manor of Aclum; a manor given to the first Robert de Brus by William the Conqueror. Later, the priors of Guisborough became overlords of Levingthorp just as Roger Francais, of that place, made suit to the Priors Court at Thornaby, a place close to neighbouring Acklam, Middlesbrough and the Franks twentieth century domain.

The following are listed in the Yorkshire lay subsidy of 1301 in the Wapentake of Langbaurgh. Skallinge is Scaling, adjacent Easington and Boulby, which was a mining area:

> Willelmo de Fraunceys, Merske cumm Redekerre, (Marske, Redcar).
>
> Willelmo de Fraunceys, Eggeton cum Lecerigge et Westingby et Cokewalde.
>
> Nicholao de Fraunceys, Buskeby, (Busby adjacent Stokesley, Middlesbrough).
>
> Gilberto de Fraunceys, Leventhorpe, (Linthorpe, Middlesbrough).
>
> Radulpho de Fraunceys, Leventhorpe, (Linthorpe, Middlesbrough).
>
> Henrico de Fraunceys, Skalinge (Esington cum Bolleby et Shalinge) Boulby.

Justice and the law of the strongest

Peter de Brus III made an agreement in 1241 with the priory of Guisborough that their men would cease disturbing Peter's wild beasts in Westworth Farm, an area behind Guisborough. Tenants had unfenced strips of land to feed their families, but had to work the lord's demesne on certain days. Villagers had to pay a fine in order to marry, and on a peasant's death, the lord had a right to take the family's best beast for himself. All hunting was the preserve of the Lord; the people lived in crude wooden sheds with an earthen floor, a cow or pig living alongside.

In order to survive, villagers resorted to poaching rabbits and any kind of bird, hoping to not get caught. Torture was rife, including the lesser punishment endured by both men and women, that of being whipped or branded for life with a red-hot iron. Punishment was metered out for offences such as begging or being a rogue or vagabond. Religious zeal manifest in the form of retribution carried out in the process of torture for the purpose of confession. Public hangings were rife, sometime accompanied by disembowelment in order to create a spectacle or induce fear among the populace, and assuaged as a means of letting them know who held the power. Justice was often a two-edged sword favouring the rich and powerful, especially that of the Church as perpetrators in cohorts with the barons.

Peter de Brus III died in 1272 and the estates were broken up and divided between his four sisters where, through marriage, the various estates were dispersed.

For many, owning land meant more than the land itself, it was a mark of respect and standing in the community and the world at large. Land ownership denoted status, where given a Norman name such as Frankys, Frаunceys or Frankland, held sufficient esteem as to set them apart. Put together with land possession, the term Frankland had become recognised as a mark of mid-rank and status, in this case denoting a position equivalent to knight or above and not people to cross swords with and to always be wary of.

Frank burials, Richmond Castle

Lying next to a wall, at the back of Frenchgate or Frankgate, Richmond Castle, in what was the Monastery of the Grey Friars, are buried several families of Frank. The monastery, founded in 1258, was surrendered in 1538. What included a walled meadow, house, garden and orchard, now consists of a solitary steeple to mark the residence and sanctuary of the Order of Mendicants, called after the Franciscans, the name Franciscan derived from the monastic Franks who originally settled the land.

Migration was a necessity and those families moving to Yorkshire from the surrounding counties of Northumberland, Durham, Cumberland, Westmorland, and Lancashire, having no settled place to stay within the county, had to settle for what ever came their way. Due to conflict, most survivors being women and children, and with male progeny scarce, what male population existed was constantly busy apropos the fairer sex. Intercourse with a succession of women and a succession of marriages due to early female demise was rife as too were births out of wedlock. The opposite might be said as to happiness or satisfaction for men, worn out, tired and hungry, the business of rutting an over-and-done-with necessary persuasion.

Christian (1250) children:

> Simon born around 1277, trading wool to London, owed money at Stokesley in 1347.

The Extraordinary Franks

The Close Rolls of 1347, in Stokesley, 'Robert de Bradenham acknowledges that he owes Simon Fraunceys citizen of London … x amount of money.'

Johanus (1252) children:

Johan born around 1278, found at Danby 1327 and 1347.

In Danby, Langbargh district, Yorkshire, 1327–1347, John Fraunceys of Lepynton, gives half a mark for a licence of concord with John de Melton.

A locally recorded Yorkshire lay subsidy tax of 10d was paid for the Scottish Wars by Roger Frank in 1327, a subsequent entry shows Margaret Frank, apparently a widow, her husband assumed killed fighting for king and country.

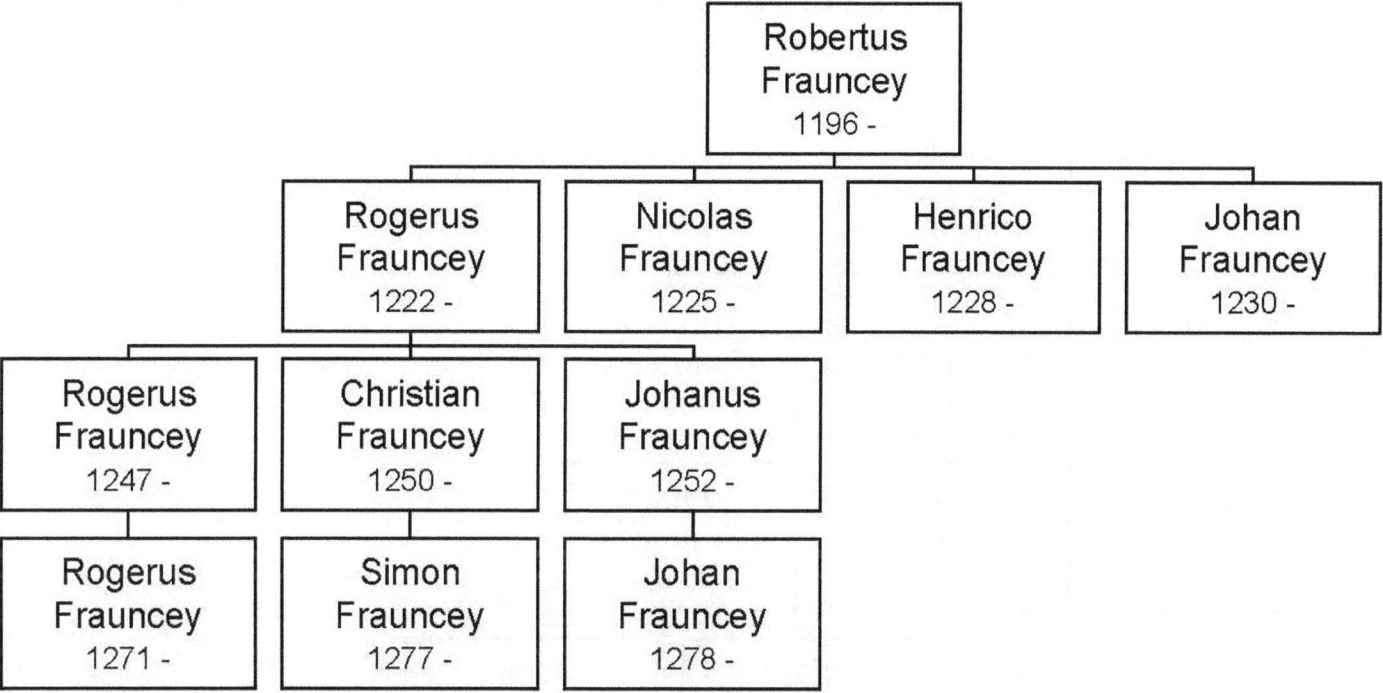

In London, matters discussed in parliament dated Wednesday 9th September 1332, relating to news received from Scotland, required that a lay subsidy grant of 'the fifteenth penny levied from the community at large' be awarded the King. It transpired the coffers were empty, and so the notice was addressed to all earls, barons and knights of the Shires; the monarch himself would journey north.

The notice highlighted dangers that might befall the Kingdom of England and her people by the absence of the King quote:

'Out of the king, it is best for the king to stay within England and to journey towards the North, having with him wise people and sufficient a strong force to defend the monarch.'

The King is known to have journeyed only as far as Yorkshire. Further north being too much of a risk, after a couple of nights he curtailed his stay, returning to London.

Having survived the Scottish Wars, and back home in Yorkshire, Roger Frank appears to have survived only to return to his family owing debts amounting to 12/6d worth of movable goods.

Of Johan's children found at Ness in Rydale, Adam was recorded born 1290, Johis around 1301, his son Johes born around 1325. Generationally, Walter was born of Johes approximately 1348, Thomas 1350 and Maurice 1352. There are no firm records for Adam's children, although the Yorkshire Poll Tax of 1379 shows an Adam Frauncey, possibly son of Adam, and an entry at Farndale (see Farndale Beck) shows 'Ada fillio et Johannes Frounceys'.

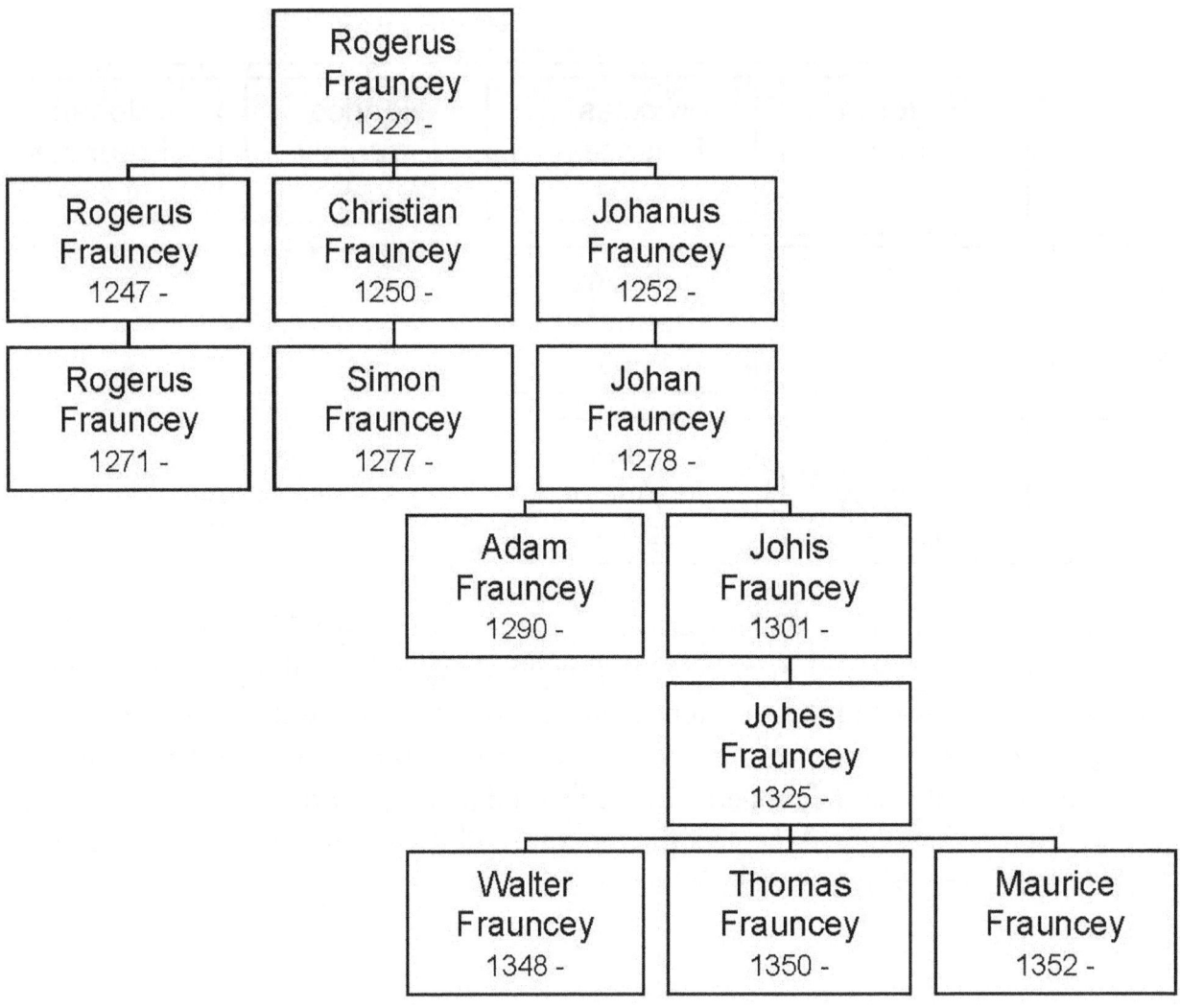

War might explain the scarcity of information between the birth dates 1325–1348, there being the possibility of unrecorded children and the necessity of second marriages.

Rogerus (1247) children:

> Rogerus born around 1271, had holdings abutting those of Baron de Roos, Lord of Helmsley, who in 1307 was in the process of disposing of land and meadow.

Extract of findings:

> 'Symon son of Symon de Denton to Dom. Robert de Roos, first Baron Roos, Lord of Wyville, concerning one rood of meadow in the meadows called Holdings against Denton near the meadow of said Dom, Robert on the east, and abutting the lands and property of Roger Frankeleyn on the south, 19th Jan 1307.'

Rogerus (1271) children:

> Willielmus born around 1296, continues neighbour relations with the first Baron Roos.

Willielmus (1296) children:

> Willielmus born around 1318, in 1358, aged forty Wm was in service to the 3rd Lord Roos.

Having first-hand knowledge of the family passed down through the generations, records of Willielmus confirm the correct pedigree of the previously uncertain Roos family tree. The first baron, born 3rd Jan 1290, died at Kirkam in 1326.

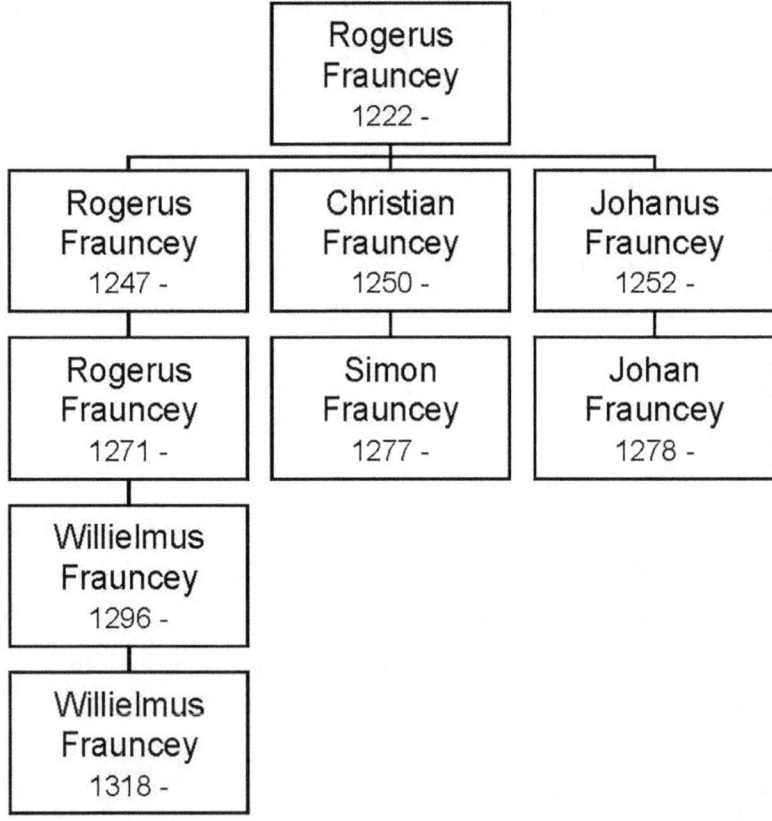

Durham

A lot of de Brus border land business was conducted around Durham en route to the King's highway, midway between their Scottish holdings and Skelton Castle in Cleveland. Located at Yarm, due to the amount of heavy two-way traffic, and made of wood, the River Tees crossing point was constantly in need of repair.

On 2nd April 1255, a division of possessions shows that Robert le Franceys held of Isabella de Forde possessions in Wooler, Northumberland. Wooler is situated south of Berwick-upon-Tweed, triangulating north of Newcastle and Durham.

Simon Frauncey was found guilty of an unknown infringement and amerced in 1296 at Merrington, a place situated midway between Darlington and Durham,

Also found in Bowes, near Barnard Castle, 1298–1299, a claim against Adam Franceys and others.

The main Willielmus line continued:

Petrus (1202) children:

> Johan born around 1227, of Dalton, Darlington, is found holding land in 1253.

The Extraordinary Franks

In 1267, John is located doing jury service in Melsonby, north of Richmond and is also found in Danby in 1270. In 1289, he is found holding the freehold of Gayles as well as being a freeholder of Kirkby Ravensworth Richmond. In 1290, aged sixty-three, John appeared at the assizes at York to ascertain if he had unjustly assized 100 acres of woodland, plus 20 acres of farm and moorland from the Abbot of Jorevalle at Feldom Darlington. Even into relative old age, he was recorded acquiring considerable tracts of land.

> Ralphus born around 1229, Ralph le Franceis is found at Little Stainton, between Stockton and Darlington, and in 1299 is found with land at Levyngthorpe.

In 1299, Ralph Fraunceys paid fealty to the prior for one toft and one croft in Linthorpe.

> **Gilbertus** 1225, Gilbertus Fraunceys had a plea-of-suit touching land at Dalton, being surety for Roger, son of Robert de Merske aka Fraunceys, in 1245–1246.

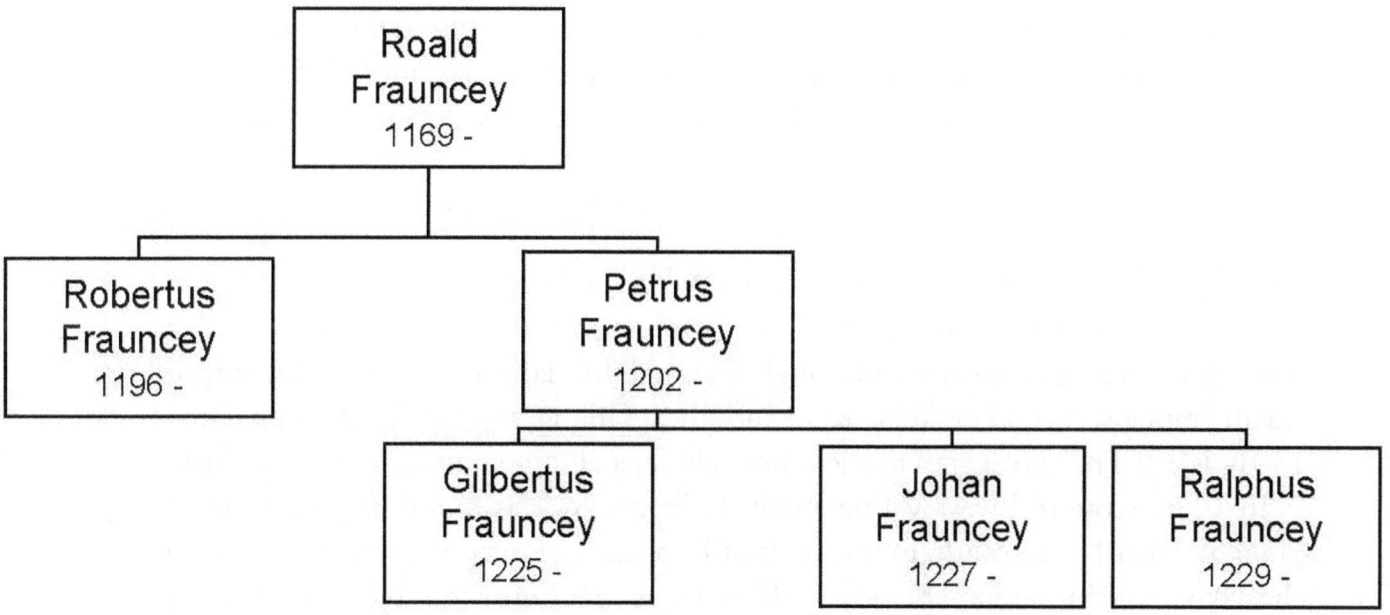

Arguments regarding land

Relating to the place now called Dalton Travers near Darlington; Roald le Fraunceys, who died in 1240, was claimed to have given land in Dalton Travers to one Warin de Travers of that place. In 1245, John Fraunceys acting on Robert Fraunceys' behalf, claiming the land was that of his brother Robert, counter-sued the current landholder Robert Travers for possession. Upholding John Fraunceys' claim, Warin de Travers (full title Robert Fitz-Waren of Dalton Travers, Richmond) confirmed to John le Fraunceys the previous grant subsequently made in Robert Travers favour be passed over to Robert le Fraunceys

Made by John le Fraunceys around 1245, John, son of Peter le Fraunceys, served a writ against Robert Travers concerning the diversion of a watercourse in the place of Dalton Travers to the injury of the plaintiff's freehold. Later in the period 1245–1256, 'Robert Travers conceded that the land was owned by John le Fraunceys and had been gifted by Robert's father, Warren Travers.

There is a plea-of-suit by Gilbert le Frauncis touching land in Dalton, north-west of Richmond, in 1245–1246, where le Fraunceys stood as surety for Roger, son of Robert de Mersk; the family Mersk apparently also Fraunceys.

Johan (1227) children:

> Robertus born around 1252 seems to have inherited from his father Johan at Richmond.

1316, John de Hertford, a claim versus Robert Fraunceys, son of John Fraunceys, concerning one messuage, ten tofts, forty acres of land and six and a half acres of meadow, pus half of a mill adjacent Barton and Newton, located Richmond area.

> Adam 1254, in 1278, found recorded as a son of John.

Relating to his journey to Jerusalem, a plea whether Adam Frauneis, son of Johan le Frauncey was unjustly disseised of land while on his journey to Jerusalem, this was defended as a false claim. Although it seems the claim was upheld, the son of Adam Frauneis, Adam Frankays, paid a subsidy at Gilling, south of Darlington dated 1301–1312. The above goes to show how name-spellings confound at every turn.

In 1290, close to Elyes, Master Adam le Fraunceys was found in possession of ploughland at Neatonwath, in the fields of Ryppeley, next to land belonging to the church of the same name. This was on the north *aquilonem* or aquiline, consisting of:

> 'Two-and-a-half acres with meadow adjoining, to hold of the Chief Lord, paying 2d at Christmas,and four pipes of wine at the date of St John the Baptist, being located at Ripley, north of Harrogate towards Ripon.'

Henricus 1253, Henry Fraunceys de Merston, York, was recorded 30th Apr 1281, regarding business at Moor-Monkton.

Johis 1251, aka Fraunkeleyn, in 1286, found at Kirby, Stokesley, holding land and a full knight's fee.

Close to Darlington, Dalton 1289, John Fraunkeleyn aka le Fraunceys, is ascertained holding the freehold of Gayles, owning three oxgangs of land. The story goes:

> 'John was considered to be wild and without religious moral conduct in his peremptory denial of worship, refusing to attend church. One Sunday, when out walking the moors, he found himself high up upon the aptly named Frankinshaw, the sparse terrain bespeaking John's tempestuous and mountainous solitude. Having not returned, a couple of anxious parishioners went searching, whereupon being found he was seen to be full of the powers of the air and being cured of his sins was said to have found peace within.'

It seems doubtful John had found God and peace, as in 1290 he's recorded at the assizes in York to ascertain if he and five others had unjustly asseized the Abbot of Jorvalle of 100 acres of woodland, twenty acres of farm and half an acre of moor in Feldom, south of Darlington.

In 1301, he is found at Craythorne and Pickering. The same year, he and his wife Ada are recorded on the Rydale List at Farndale.

On 18th May 1304, he is found at Topcliffe, yet again trying to obtain land, being located along with his son Henry at Skipton in 1307.

John is finally located at Neasham Abbey on the west edge of the North York Moors at Ravenscroft, dated 1311–1312.

Consistent with his nature, John was no shrinking violet, and seemed bent on securing land by any means, whether by deceit or force of temper, seemingly evident in a ruthless Norman throwback compulsion towards violence.

Johis children:

> Ricardus born around 1277. On the Pickering road to Scarborough, at Irton, 20th January 1315, Ricadus holds a one-sixteenth knight's fee. This was part of a dowry delivered to Eleanor, widow of Tenant-in-Chief, Henry de Percy.

> Johes 1279.

Henry 1281. Henry, being the youngest, seems to have been cajoled to stay with his father around Ravenscroft, south of Darlington.

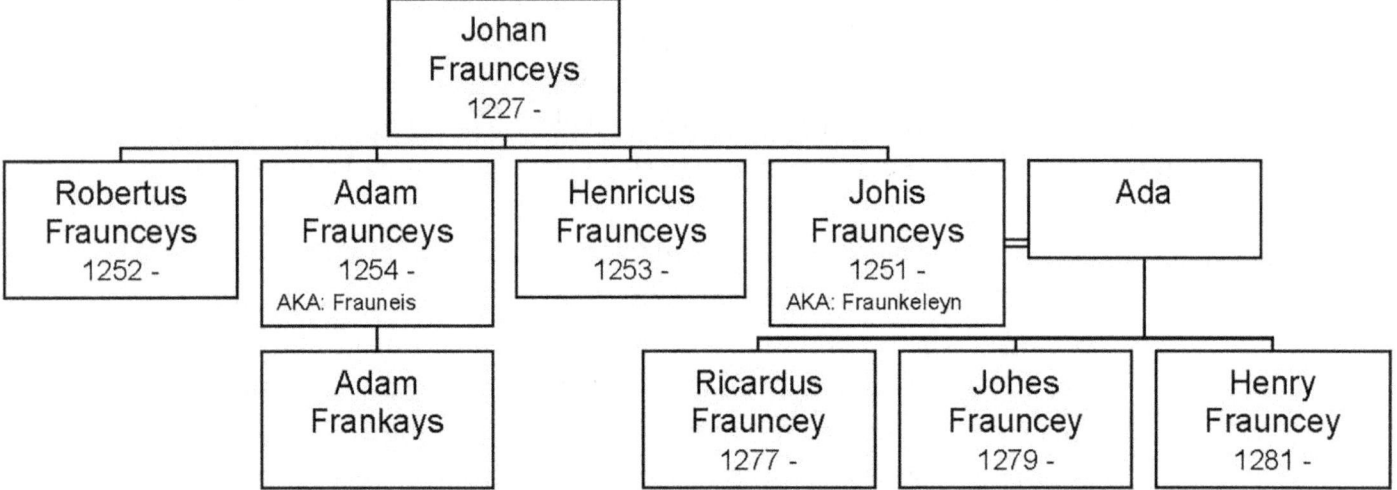

Gilbertus (1225) children:

Roberti (no data) Around this time is found belonging Gilbertus:

'Johannam filiam domini Roberti Fraunceys militis and Johannam, daughter of Master Roberti Fraunceys, soldier. Also de Johanne Fraunceys, Applegarth, Parish of Marske 1301.'

Grimbaldus born around 1255. At Barton Melsonby, 1300, Grimbald de Fraunceys sues Richard, third son of Gilbertus for 160 acres of land, plus a meadow and half a mill.

Grimbald was called John Grimbald or Grumbald alias Grimbald Fraunceys. In 1315–1316, Grimbald's heirs were also tenants of Barton. The list for Rythe Bank, Pickering, in 1301, shows Johanne de Fraunceys of Apyigarthe (now Applegarth) being shown alongside Grimbaldo de Fraunceys of Barton, where John appears to be a close relative. Barton consists of Barton St Mary and Barton St Cuthbert.

Richus 1257, Richus aka Richard de Vernun, aka Fraunceys, is shown in the Tax Roll of Yorkshire dated 1297.

Willielmus 1252. Son of Gilbertus, Willielmus appears as a witness in 1290 at Stainburne.

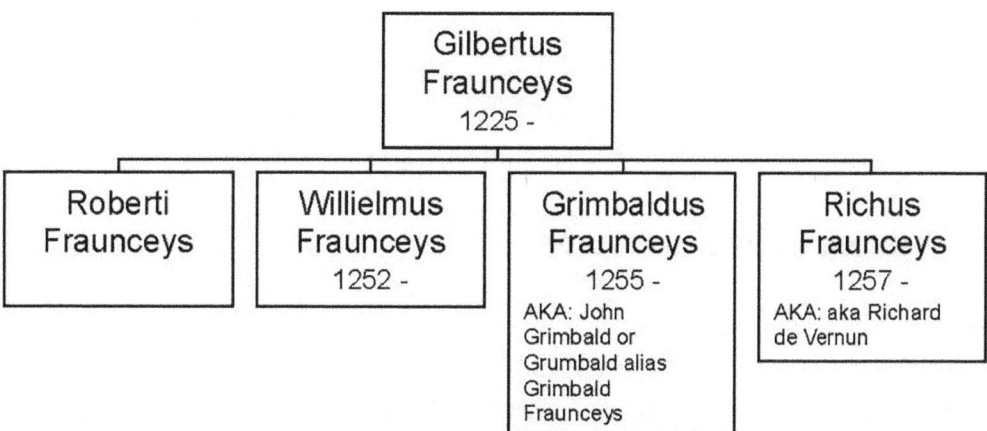

Concerning Richus and his succession: located at Sedbergh, farthest west on the Yorkshire Dales National Park, Robert Lang stood surety for John, son of Richard Fraunceys who in 1292 was fined 40s for contempt.

A legal action at Barton near Melsonby, dated 1300, finds John son of Ivo de Hertford in a case versus Grimbaldus de Fraunceys in a plea of land. In it, Grimbaldus de Fraunceys sued Richus de Vernun aka Fraunceys, third son of Gilbertus le Fraunceys in a plea that he should warrant to him a messuage, plus 160 acres of land, six acres of meadow and half a mill, which John de Hertford claimed against him. See also earlier entry relating to the berewick of Barton and Newton.

An example of the immense spread of these Norman holdings across North Yorkshire is seen approximately twenty miles due west, inland from Danby in the North Yorks Moors, near Whitby. In 1086, immediately following the 1066 invasion, within the soke of Barton and the berewick of Newton Richmond, was a parcel of land held by Count Alan under the honour of Richmond. The fee passed to Peter de Brus, Lord of Skelton, Whitby, within the soke of Cleveland in 1281. Today's distance Whitby to Richmond being sixty miles, adding to this the encumberance of travel by horseback via winding tracks would increase the mileage considerably. Put in context with the times, these were huge fiefdoms

Within Barton soke, Ingleby Manor consisted of a grant held by William de Lancaster consisting of one messuage and 160 acres of land, together with half a share of Barton Mill. These in turn were enfeoffed to John le Franceys, whose grandson and heir Richard de Franceys Vernun granted these same tenements to Grimbald le Franceys, who was the tenant in 1286–1287. Robert de Franceys, son of John le Franceys, succeeded in 1319, granting his lands to the Mowbrays prior to 1330. This is the date when Thomas, son of William de Mowbray was enfeoffed.

The above shows the interrelation between the various the names of Vernon, Mowbray, and de Brus, including the Lacys. Also, a charter of liberation of the Abbey of Whitby shows Roger de Mowbray aka Frauncey, being a nephew of William de Abencio, where Thoraldo Francigena of York is shown as a witness.

Previously around 1249–1250, Thoraldo Francigena appeared as a witness in a charter of liberation to the abbey of Whitby by Roger de Mowbray aka Fraunceys.

The main Willielmus line continued:

Willielmus (1252) children:

> **Willielmus** 1276, is found 27th May 1304 trying to extract land at Gisburn, Ainderby Steeple, Warlaby, near Northallerton. On 17th October 1302, is located nearby at Neasham Abbey.
>
> Ermna 1277. Ermna Frankys paid a subsidy in Feldom, Marske, close to Dalton, south of Darlington in 1301.
>
> Roberto 1279, titled De Roberto Fraunkeleyn, Roberto is found at Berygby.

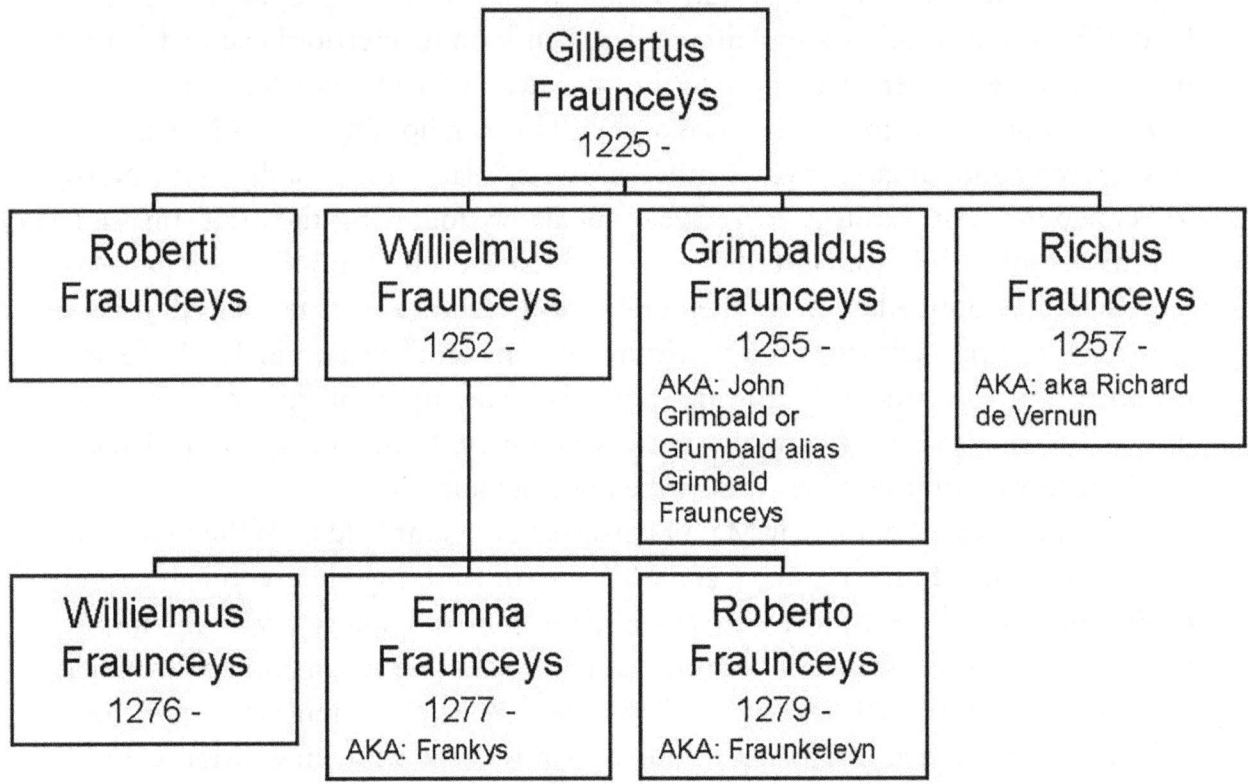

The wool trade

Berygby, being today's Borrowby, is located midway between Northallerton and Thirsk, handily placed for the wool trade just off the King's highway to York en route to London, where there was always a continental demand for English wool, the bulk of wool being destined for Flanders. Wool from the North York Moors was greatly prized, where just east of Borrowby in places like Hutton-le-Hole, adjacent to the monasteries, the looms were always busy; the area being a major centre for top-quality wool, spinning and weaving.

The Franks were prominent in wool production, being involved in weaving at Hutton-le Hole and its surrounds. Commercially, and through their religious connection with the monasteries, the Franks were known to have traded as far as London. In the absence of a stock market, English wool in particular became a vital commodity and highly valued as a form of currency, where one such Frank saw great opportunity.

Around 1267–1379, Venice had a form of stock market based on citizen forced-loans. But the war between Venice and Genoa, coupled with the Hundred Years War and the Black Death, caused the monarchs of France and England to default on their debts to the Italian banks and during the 1380s caused the suspension of all interest payments.

So it can be seen how a lowly occupation such as raising sheep had a vital role in the country's survival, its survival aided by a hitherto mild-mannered Frank, held in such high personal regard by the King as to be knighted. Granted arms in 1569, from a farming background, Sir William Frankland of Fewston, Bubberhouses, later purchaser of the manor of Great Thirkleby near Thirsk in Yorkshire. The significance of mentioning William of Ryes as he became known, was him being founder of the Guild of Clothworkers in London.

As well as his family connections in Yorkshire, William had estates in Ryes, Hertfordshire, hence in that pretext William of Ryes. It was through his work that cloth production modernised and moved rapidly from wool production and localised weaving to full-scale cloth manufacturing finding favour by the monarch.

I go into more detail later but wanted to illustrate how just one line of the family could spread across the landscape and that by dint of family succession the crying need to find new land to till or fresh pasture was ever-present.

By now, the Frank estates were considerable, their acquisitions spread among family members across the Dales and further afield, where due to conflict and the high death rate among recruit soldiery, smaller holdings might be absent of a male heir. This brought opportunities for those Franks whose males had avoided conflict, acquiring as much land as they were able, in a sense becoming minor nobles and people to look up to and from who to seek work.

Strip-land, made up as farms, was allocated according to each person's needs. On the topic of sheep, and farming in general, the Franks knew how to open up the fields and properly farm, producing fodder for the winter and more importantly producing food to alleviate shortages This was achieved by being able to attract necessary labour and working the separate holdings as a single entity.

As to food and alluding to the concept of providing for others, it seems to have had its origins in the acquisition of land: the Franks also branched out generationally. Imbued with an attitude of prayer, while usurping their Norman status, seems to have placed thems in an envious position apropos their neighbours, taking advantage of endless wars that needed to be paid for and the demand for wool a paramount commodity.

A letter of King Edward I issued by the English Crown deals with the preparations and actions of King Edward and his forces regarding the ongoing war with Scotland. Dated December 1302, the letter deals with the names of men-at-arms staying in the garrisons of Scottish Castles. The list must have been worrying for the great number of 'not come' leaders, with their army of men not being there.

Among those listed were Sir William le Fraunceys, Count de Edinburgh and the County of Fife, being shown to be with King Edward I during his invasion of Scotland in 1296. The King must have been amused knowing the very different life of Willielmus Fraunceys of Yorkshire to that of his statelier Scottish cousin, Count William, both sharing the same Christian name.

While Willielmus was tending sheep and enlarging his estates, Sir William Fraunceys, together with a three covered horse contingent, is shown defending Kirkintilloch in battle. Twenty archers, especially chosen by Sir William Fraunceys at Linlithgow, were there when the palace defences were shattered during the time of Edward's invasion of Scotland. Sir William is also mentioned in relation to his stand at Edinburgh, later taking command of the Royal Navy, a very different path from that of distant cousin and family forebear, Willielmus Fraunceys.

Willielmus (1276) children:

> Rogerus 1296, approximate. Roger Frank is shown in the lay subsidy returns in 1327 recorded as paying tax of 10d in Hutton-le-Hole.

Willielmus 1300, the name Willielmus Vernun aka Fraunceys is perpetuated, being linked with Neasham Abbey.

Willielmus (1300) children:

Willielmus 1327, a warrant for underage Willielmus, grandson of Willielmus (1276) relating to entitlement.

Johan 1329. A grant dated 31st March 1358, shows John Fraunceys relating to half an acre of arable in le Bothum, St Mary's York and a gordelas of meadow. Witness Roger Travers.

Robertus 1332. Robertus Franke shown in the Yorkshire Poll Tax of 1379.

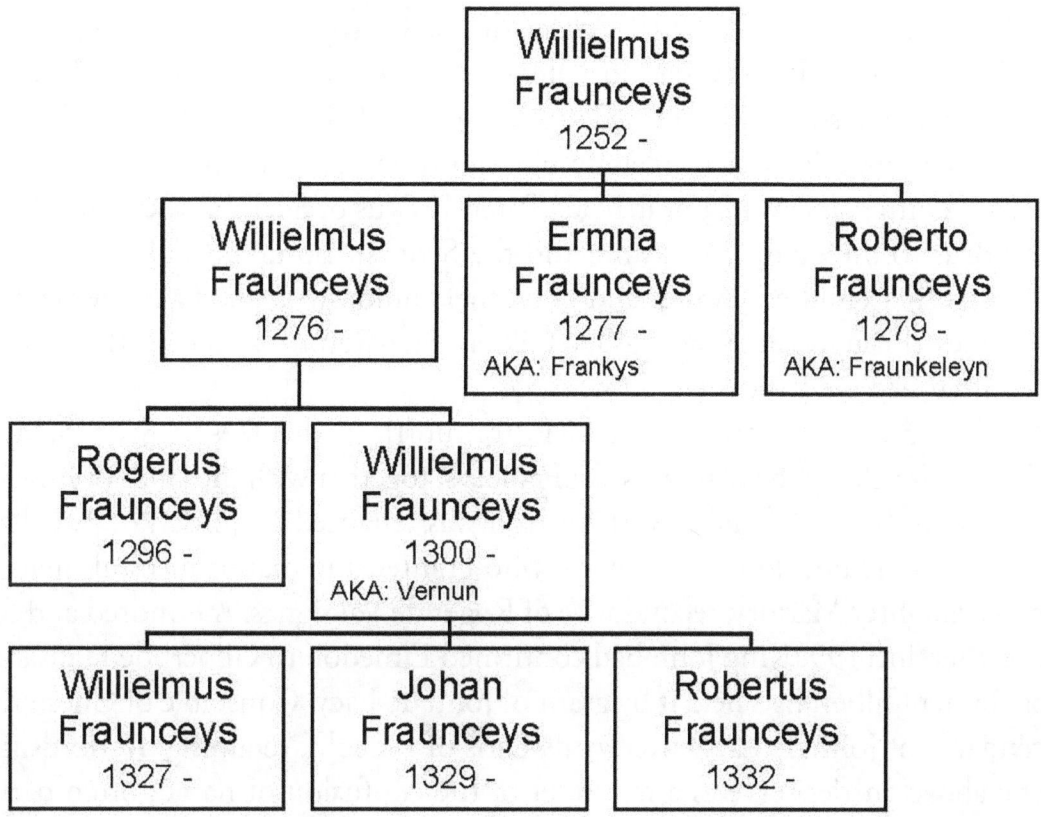

The broader picture

Hawise de Estoutville was the spouse of William de Lancaster, son of William de Lancaster, fifth Baron of Kendall. The title of Lancaster is said to have been granted by Roger de Mowbray, son of Nigel de Albini, and came into his hands after Nigel's decease having male heirs of Ivo de Tailbois. The Tailboys family was present in

Cliburn, Westmorland during the twelfth century, these being likely relatives of William de Lancaster.

Gilbert Fancey, aka Franceys, was an ancestor of de Cliburn. A grant of 1298 by Richard de Vernon shows the arms:

'Sealed fretty, a canton.'

Richard was paternally le Franceys:

From F W Ragg of the publication *Maud's Meaburn and Newby*, 'The Cliburn's being derived paternally from le Franceys, notes the similarity of the medieval arms of the de Cliburn family to them …

'Argent, fretty with a chief sable.'

William de Lancaster's daughter, Avicia, married firstly William de Peverel, and as second husband, Sir Richard de Morville. Their daughter, Elena, espoused Roland, Lord of Galloway, son of Sir Uchtred of Galloway and Gunnild of Dunbar. William de Lancaster's granddaughter, Heloise Fitz-Reinfred, daughter of Alice de Lydesay née Fitz-Reinfred and William, married Peter de Brus of Skelton, a kinship linking the de Brus to the Franks, Yorkshire and the Scottish Borders. William and Alice had three other children, Walter and two others unknown. The Lancaster connection comes through Alice, her father Gilbert Fitz-Reinfred, her mother Heloise Fitz-Reifred née De Lancaster.

Prior to 1339, the manor of East Morton north of the Tees in Sedgefield, Co Durham, was held by the Hansards aka Franceys, together with the lands of Emeldon belonging to the Lacy family. West Morton was tenanted by Jordan de Escolland, aka Jordan de Hameldon aka Francey, who granted the manor in frank marriage with his daughter Marjory, second wife of Roger de Valoignes. A hundred and forty years earlier, in 1199, King John had confirmed Elmedon to Gilbert de Hansard II, whose father Gilbert had held it by grant of John de Lacy, Constable of Chester, the descendants of John de Lacy, afterwards Earls of Lincoln, retaining overlordship.

The above entries serve as a reminder of the confusion of names often derived of places, whereas through their Norman origin, as with Francey above, the French monarchy were linked through marriage to the de Lacy (Normandy) and Hameldon (North Yorks) – a place name used by the Franks. The Francey were paternally related to the Hansards, Vernon and Cliburn, also the Dunbars, having links to Peter de Brus, Skelton Castle and Glaisdale, heartland of the Dales Franks.

ROBERT DE BRUS'S INVASION OF ENGLAND

The following is a tale of death and destruction, land grants and invasion.

Scotland 1321–1322: King Robert de Brus grants to his son, Robert, the land of Sprustoun. Following the death of his son, Robert de Brus grants the land of Sprustoun to his friend William Francis in recognition of his personal loyalty and the support given by him.

In Scotland, being near relatives and close allies, William Francis's loyalty to the king appears to have been handsomely rewarded, whereas in Yorkshire, things were not looking so good. In the early fourteenth century Yorkshire suffered from a series of poor harvests, cattle disease and plunder by the Scottish armies, Robert de Brus of Scotland's invasion of England in 1322 and 1326 adding to the woes inflicted upon a ravaged population.

The year 1322 highlights the date of a forgotten victory for Robert de Brus in the Frank's heartland of Byland in North Yorks, the area itself a de Brus fee. Whereas Robert's victory at Bannockburn in 1314 had emboldened him, the taking of Stirling was a total embarrassment for Edward II, being routed by an army a third the size of his own troops. On top of that, Edward had his own troubles in a divided England threatened by civil war.

Taking advantage, de Brus launched a series of sporadic raids: James Douglas 'The Black' harrying Hartlepool, belonging to the Earl of Moray, Thomas Randolph attacking Darlington, and Walter Stewart unleashing his army upon Richmond. A mightily harassed King Edward, having succeeded in suffocating the English rebellion, turned his attention on the Scots where on the 16th March 1322 at the Battle of Boroughbridge he successfully routed the invaders who turned tail and headed north followed in their wake by the English.

But the battle weary English needed to rest and replenish before heading north for a second sortie. Constant war had taken its toll upon the military, as too the surrounding population. On the one hand, Edward had a kingdom to defend, on the other de Brus was more than ready, where upon his retreat his scorched earth policy left bare the vacated terrain with neither food nor means of sustenance for those who followed. It was a classical tactic to bring an enemy towards you on your own terms. His troops hungry and exhausted, Edward's advance upon Edinburgh, being absent of tactical manoeuvre, bade a dispirited retreat.

In reverse order, the Scots followed the English destination south accruing men along the way. By the time they crossed the River Tees at Yarm, the English were finished and ready to be taken. And so battle ensued: the date 14th October 1322, the battleground Old Byland or Bylands Abbey as it's known today, the very heartland of the farming community of the Franks. John de Bretagne's troops far outnumbered the Scots but the ferocity of attack was too much; if Bannockburn secured Scotland for a single day, the Battle of Old Byland sent a clear message that in this first war of independence, Robert de Bruce could strike England a massive blow.

But what of the families of de Brus in Yorkshire and those of the Franks? The Franks who had previously gone north with de Brus mostly settled along the Borders while keeping contact with their immediate families in Yorkshire, evidence showing that a significant number of Yorkshire Franks joined their counterparts in Scotland. Come the war, there being reservations about taking up arms against one's kin on the opposing side, how many followers of de Brus actually enjoined with the Scots against the English Crown is not known.

Especially for the Franks a dilemma arose in the overlap of shared names in Scotland leading to fanciful surname variations, distinguishing one from the other, whereas in Yorkshire the Franks had already commenced migration north or inland, leaving behind a scattering of identifiable kin, stoic and independent, thinly spread across Cleveland and the much wider environ.

The date of 1322 is significant in that not wanting to waste time de Brus was consumed with winning battles. On the other hand, putting de Brus in his place, the King took his time in proclaiming William Francis his closest brother, the monarch awarding William the lands of Sprustoun previously belonging de Brus's son Robert.

Although proclaimed King of the Scots 27th March 1306, it wasn't until 1324 the Pope recognised Robert as monarch of an independent Scotland, whereupon the Franco–Scottish alliance was renewed and sealed in the treaty of Corbeil in 1326. In 1327, Edward III renounced all claims of superiority over Scotland, also of its King, Robert de Brus. The sickly King Robert de Brus died soon after, 7th June 1329.

Following Robert de Brus's death there were many rumours as to a likely illness, such as *la grosse maladie*, the probable cause being some form of sexual disease like syphilis. The King had an enormous sexual appetite, his many and varied liaisons producing a large number of illegitimate births in addition to a single child to his first wife, Isabella, and four to Elizabeth. Among the many undisclosed births were six that were acknowledged, these and quite a number of stillbirths were the result of de Brus slaking his lust wherever and whenever he felt the need of female company. On his death, Robert appointed his five-year-old son David heir to the throne and, although crowned the 24th November 1331, sadly David II died the following year.

Adding to the burden of war, nature itself brought its own problems. Changing weather pressure patterns bringing cold, moist air from the Artic clashed with dry air coming from Eastern Europe and Asia creating a combination of unhealthy atmosphere and drought, notably during the years 1343–1345 and 1353–1354. The years on either side almost as bad, the upshot was a decline in food production leaving people hungry. Occasioned by famine, the cool wet conditions favoured the development of malady, fungi and bacteria where the average life expectancy in England fell from age forty-eight to thirty-eight, partly due to hunger but mostly from disease.

Entire villages succumbed to ergotism caused by the ergot fungus (*claviceps pururea*). Ergot grows in grains of rye turning them dark purple, yet despite the change in colour being an identifier, perhaps through a lack of understanding, it was easy for infected grain to contaminate the food supply on which the community depended. Ergot produces toxins that survive milling; the toxin poisons the flour, which when consumed causes convulsions and hallucinations quickly followed by burning sensations and gangrene, primarily to the fingers and toes, in those days being often fatal. The disease was known as St Anthony's Fire. Even more serious was the bubonic plague that by 1349 had travelled up country to Yorkshire and the north-west infecting Scotland in 1350, whence throughout Europe up to one-third of the total population died.

Accepting the reasoning for the sudden shortage of Cleveland data, we see North Yorkshire plagued by repeated incursion, the populace suffering from malnutrition and poor health. Sensibly, the fittest and more able had left, and now, by the spring of 1349, the scourge of Black Death, working its way north, had reached their beloved Dales: whatever population remained was suddenly and drastically depleted.

Of the Franks who had moved to the more remote areas, a couple of families are recorded as having lost one or more children, but not anything on the scale seen elsewhere. Knowledge of the plague's ferocity caused a majority of Franks to survive, mostly by cutting themselves off and living healthily from their own produce, supplemented by eggs, the odd rabbit or two, berries and wild fruits, and also luck in being so remote as to avoid contact.

The above takes cognisance of other small-time isolated farmers who had managed to survive, albeit with news of relative's deaths and sadness with which to contend. The great sprawl of land ownership and massive estates were in a state of collapse: Black Death survivors realising their value became restless and rebellious. Many of the lords gave up all attempts to hold onto their land, providing opportunity for those yeomen wishing to expand. The plague was followed by a rise among established farmers purchasing available cheap land, themselves becoming minor gentlemen, through which succession developed the farms and landscape we recognise today.

I won't dwell on the effects of the Black Death other than to say the disease indiscriminately culled children, and the old and infirm without mercy. Depleted birth rates were immediately followed by incest, rape and all manner of debauchery. Irrespective of any marriage ties, survivors of both sexes, seemingly without regard to childhood innocence or propriety, in their madness openly took their pleasures.

A kind of depraved death throe had descended, where it is impossible today to make sense of it and formulate any meaningful conclusion other than nature's desperate call for continuance. The aftermath left land and fields abandoned or left to rot. The spadework of burying the dead was exacerbated by the burial of cattle, where wild flocks of sheep roamed unattended; however rebellious, the few remaining able survivors looking for leadership had no recourse other than to bow to dependency on their new-found masters. Bringing order, the Dales farmers provided work and sustenance. Already pillars of the church and having localised authority these devout farmers held sway.

The destitute were content to receive so much as a roof and the most basic of food in return for hard graft. Lowly, below the animals they tended, wholly subordinate, respectful and obedient, yokels gave deference by a simultaneous nod of the head while doffing their hats intoning the word 'master' or 'Sir'. By the middle of the twentieth century in rural Yorkshire one found the words 'now-n' used extensively as a greeting accompanied by a touch of the hat and 'Sir' for a superior.

In my time farm workers settled for a servile touch of a cap or a nod, a dour hangover from those early times, part in recognition or more probably disdain as to the others self-assuredness or accent. It is remarkable how such institutions carried on until the mid twentieth century and even later, with quite low pay and often a small scratch of land coming with a modest dwelling, barely sufficient to keep a single cow or some chickens to supplement their lives. Yet over time and with work becoming available elsewhere this was an era auguring change and the vision of something better, if not for them, perhaps their children.

In North Yorkshire and the Borders, this form of subservience evolved as a farm hind, farm hinds from around the 1600s often supplying a female to take on such menial tasks as milking, and supplying more of the family for fieldwork during harvest. Workers usually gathered at market each year hoping to be chosen for yet another year's work, the fittest and most able getting the pick of jobs and a token of pay, the rest just grateful for anything. Sunday was for prayer, all obliged to attend and give thanks – kept separate from their betters who paid for superior family pews.

The churches and monasteries too had suffered. The job of restoring a sense of law and order through the strict ordinance of faith was largely founded through a sense of duty and respectability born out of local worship and the mutual recognition and respect given to the new land owners and leading families. Churchgoing and respectability went hand in hand, those of superior standing forming the establishment, holding positions of office and authority, often seen preaching sermons on morality and the spirit of good over evil.

In North Yorkshire, affected by war and the destruction of property, records concerning the population remain scarce. The few records that were made were often written on scraps of paper, the few bits I've seen, having survived, were severely damaged and only partly legible, the bulk lost forever.

Yet literature was held in the highest regard, Robert de Brus spoke five or six languages with ease. Amid a sea of changing landscape and novitas, there is found a clash of culture set against ignorance and the stamp of law and order, where it seems apt to show a passage taken from Chaucer's 'The Franklin's Tale':

> 'He shewed him, er wente to sopeer,
>
> Forests, parks ful of wild deer;
>
> Ther saugh he hertes with hir hornes hye,
>
> The gretteste that evere were seyn with ye.
>
> He saugh of hem an hondred slain with houndes,
>
> And somme with arwes blede of bittre woundes.
>
> He saugh, whan voided were thise wilde deer,
>
> Thise fauconers upon a fair river,
>
> That with hir haukes han the heron slain.
>
> Tho saugh he knightes justing in a plain;
>
> And after this he dide him swich plesaunce
>
> That he him shewed his lady on a daunce,
>
> On which himself he daunced, as him thought.'

Given the date of 1343–1400, the above is a shrewd observation of a squire at play, and as Professor Hodgson puts it, the scene might have been reminiscent of a young squire among a group of peers, letting rip. Referenced in the Athlone Press, London, 1961, Emeritus Professor Phyllis Hodgson held her doctorate at Oxford University where she was a Medievalist and translator of Medieval texts.

But in Pickering, far from a bunch of knights out hunting and hawking, things had got out of control, innate arrogance and brutality had shown its hand again, the protagonists were no longer at play:

> Individually they had often witnessed deaths mortal grip,
>
> where their want upon the field of battle
>
> assuaged amidst the morn-day sunlight dapple and quietude of woodland
>
> now inseparable to the sight and sound of deaths mortal coil and the smell of blood.

DFB

The scene above envisages both a replay of past lives and a forecast of death and destruction to come. Thus for me as a latent Frank, the Franklin's Tale speaks of dead and bleeding harts where together the dead heron and the jousting knights form an implicit comment on the nature of passion. Its head-spinning call for revenge and destruction becomes a self-prophetic spiritual urge, replayed; it's a call upon the ancients in a race towards death not life. The vision of the harts is particularly effective, for they are bleeding with *bittre woundes* from arrows.

And this might especially apply where the penalty for extreme wealth and power befalls a sudden realisation of mortality, the envisaged loss of everything, its mighty fall feeding a desperate need and clinging desire for more. That being one version, conversely the heart of the Hart deer a metaphor of love, pierced by a death-dealing arrowhead, more likely demonstrates mortality and willingness to die in mortal combat for what one holds dear.

My great-grandfather's surname was Hart-Frank having connections with nearby Hart Hall and the Hart family.

The Forest of Pickering

The following is a list of a few historic and prominent names; surnames that appear littered throughout history. The names are a random sample of a much larger list, its significance, all of them appearing at the same place at the same time in the Forest of Pickering, the date 1335.

The jolt for me, seen through modern-day eyes, is the insight into their behaviour given their apparent status. All of them had been before the court and fined for a range of offences. Significantly, well-known Scottish names were found together with their Yorkshire contemporaries.

Pickering was a de Brus seat, and is where an effigy of William de Brus still stands today. Sir William died in 1346, being one son of many children sired by Robert de Brus. Born of a King of Scotland, here he is found alongside his companions at play at Pickering, and as was their want, breaking the law and causing havoc. Ten years later William was dead:

> Sir William Bruys, bailed by Robert Bruys aka de Brus, being at court for letting greyhounds escape.
>
> Sir William de Persay, aka Percy.
>
> John de Pickering, for illegal hare hunting.
>
> Sir Ralph de Hastynges, Keeper of the Castle, at court for taking twelve sheep.
>
> Hugh de Neville.

William de Creppyng.

Ralph de Morton.

The Prioress of Rosedale, for taking wood.

Nicholas de Repyngale bailed by Sir William de Bruys.

Richard de Dalby (see Dalby Forest), at court for taking pledges when not sworn.

Michael de Bulmere of Ayton.

John de Malton, associated with nearby Malton.

John de Lastingham, for taking cattle and other charges such as taking oak, pigs, etc.

Robert de Pikering, Bailiff of Rydale, brother to above John, done for poaching.

John Giliot, Chaplain.

The Prior of Melton, for falsely claiming a fishery.

Henry de Percy, knight, for falsely enlarging a claim.

Taken together, these names are astounding, supposed leaders, knights, a chaplain, a prioress, a bailiff and the Prior of Melton, each bailing the other, unashamedly visceral, dishonest and in it for themselves.

Men-at-arms were needed, and as ever North Yorkshire bore the brunt

Enduring a seeming endless toll. John of Gaunt, First Duke of Lancaster needed men: good Yorkshire stock had proven themselves as soldiers over and again in battle. The Duke had influence over many of his contemporaries in Northern England, and the menfolk of Yorkshire would fight under his command, there would be no argument, and on they came.

This was the beginning of what was to become the Hundred Years War. Fought over three phases, little did the combatants know what was to befall them, this was 1337 and the war wasn't to end until 1453.

Due to constantly changing loyalties, which side was who was not always as it might appear, and they had cause to change sides even during battle. The Nevilles of Middleham, Scropes of Bolton, Latimers of Danby and Snape, and Mowbrays of Thirsk, supported the House of York. The Percys and Cliiffords of Skipton, Ros of Helmsley and others from Holderness and Sheffield, fought for the Lancastrians.

Due to their association with nobles of divided loyalties, families like the Franks were suddenly caught in an impossible impasse: who to support. Henry VII suffered periods of insanity and his wife Margaret de Anjon, having assumed control, faced those same nobles. In opposition, on the death of Richard of York, (referenced Wakefield 30th December 1460), his titles and claim to the throne passed to his eldest son Edward. Stalwart Edward, finding enough backing to denounce Henry, declared himself King, the Battle of Towton affirming through force of arms the victor's right to rule.

The ensuing battle left the Yorkists, under Edward, to rule uninterrupted for nine years. Henry had fled the country; many powerful followers were either dead or exiled. The House of Lancaster being severely reduced, large landowners not proven to have given outright Yorkist support were viewed as suspect and were obliged to give up their holdings.

Adam French of Scotland family connection

In Scotland, Adam French aka Adam le Fraunceys, held land under William de Scaresburgh, prior of Coldingham, his widow, Margaret, in 1350, giving four and a half acres of land in Flores to the Priory Alms-house. Significant name-ties relate to Scaresburgh, otherwise Scarborough abounding Cleveland, where Adam Fraunceys, down from Scotland, is recorded visiting family in Cleveland in 1379.

In 1399, by preserving peace with King Richard II of England, King Robert III of Scotland, aka John Stewart, Earl of Carrick, selected Adam French for punishment, shown in the forfeiture of his lands, including the estates of Thornydykes and Pitcoks.

In response, Adam's kinsman George, the current and ever loyal Earl of March, being related to Adam and feudal lord, renounced his allegiance to King Robert. Adam too abandoned the Scottish King, both men, Earl George and Adam, then swore allegiance becoming liegemen to King Henry IV of England, Richard's successor. Having received the protection of the English monarch, with a retinue of eighty men, George and Adam French went to England. See Scottish text for full details.

Whitby

A document of 1396 roughly translates:

> 'About slaughter, having inherited in Coquine, I Franke to receive, perquisita, about nine stottes per cow pelt animal sale. Sunt qui shillings and pence about ovium pelt sale the pork about pigletts de stawro. [*Sunt qui*] shillings and pence for salty fish about these herrings about Fyschows indeed sale. Franke to sell according to the mortuary of Johannis Godland.'

Unable to translate the amount of shillings, I have substituted *sunt qui*.

Durham

A scattering of Franks had settled around Bishop Middleham vicarage in the Deanery of Stockton, situated along the King's highway to Scotland north of the Yarm crossing of the River Tees, bordering the county of Durham. William Fraunceys, vicar, is recorded there 27th April 1375 at a time when vicars were entitled to small tithes as a means of augmenting their income.

In the Hartlepool debacle of 1391, the justices were determiners of a complaint of Ralph de Lomley, knight, against Thomas Franche and 111 others of Hartlepool, Durham and two of Hart, being ill-doers for taking a boat, also of ejecting and assaulting his tenants.

THE MAIN WILLIELMUS LINE CONTINUED

In 1340, there is mention of a warrant given to underage William de Vernun aka Fraunceys concerning entitlement. William de Vernun was kinsman and heir to the great-grandson of Gilbert le Fraunceys. The suit was to remain until full age but was contested and allowed to proceed on the basis of William proclaimed to be of suitable age.

Willielmus (1327) children:

> **Willielmus** 1349, found at Helmsley, later in Poppleton in 1400.
>
> Edmundo 1352, located at Otley, 1402.
>
> Nicholas 1354, found at York Castle 1405.

The brothers appear to have moved around the same time, settling south around York. As in Guillaume son of Rollo, the name Willielmus seems to have perpetuated within the family for hundreds of years. The following are an example showing the involvement of this family in the centre of events:

> 'An inquisition at York, Richard Malbys regarding property at Scawton near Helmsley, conducted in the presence of William Fraunkeleyn, 12th Jul 1402.'

> 'The trial of Sir Robert de Plesyngton, knight, who hath seized of the moiety of the manor of Swaledale and the free chase thereof, conducted in the presence of Edmund Franke.'

'The trial of Sir John Dencourt, knight, 17th May 1406, at York Castle before Thomas Pickering, Escheator, in the presence of Nicholas Fraunklayn.'

Note too the variance in spellings of Frank.

Willielmus (1349) children:

Rogerus born around 1369, Roger de Hutton-le-Hole aka **Abbot of Fountains Abbey.**

Ralphus 1371. Ralph's son, named after his father, born around 1397

Johes 1376, found at York Castle 1420. Had a son, also John, b. 1400.

Robertus 1374, found at Poppleton, York, 1420.

Oliver 1373.

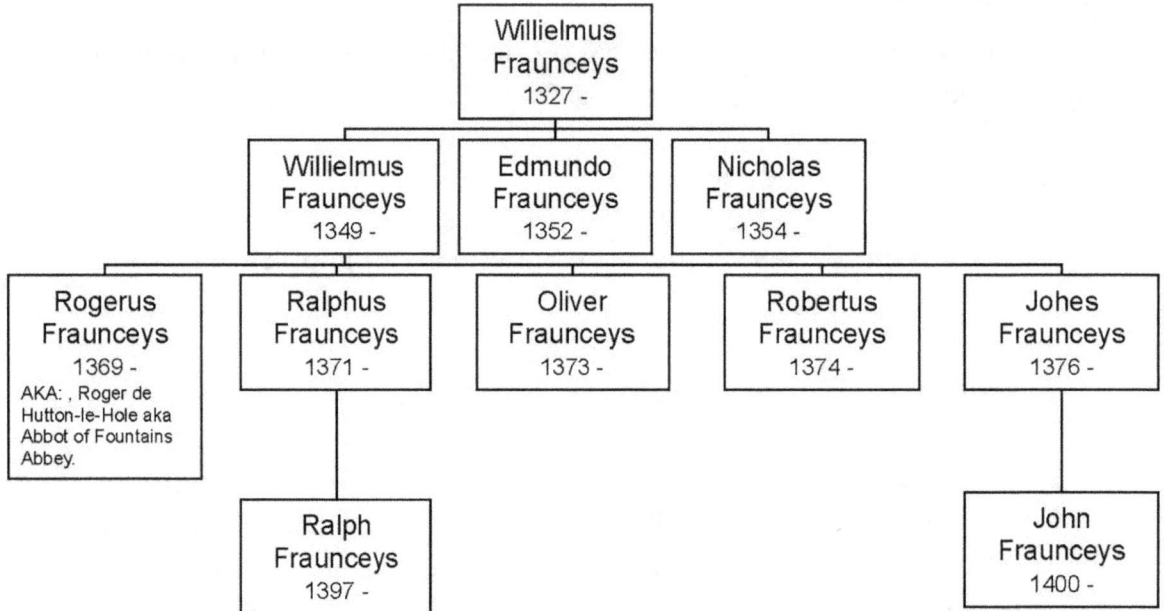

Roger Frank, Abbot of Fountains Abbey 1410–1415

Around 1410, predecessor Roger, born 1369, his brothers Ralph and Oliver, and his kin Robert together with more than forty armed men, attacked Fountains Abbey wounding John Rypon with arrows, Roger Frank imposing himself as abbot. The episode should be seen in the light of the times against the backdrop of the Black Death (1349–1409), and the desperation of the era. Yet, an examination of the history of the Franks shows they were adept at acquiring land, though taking an abbey by force does seem a somewhat bizarre and extreme action born out of delirium and the horrors rent upon desperate men.

Dated 1414, an extract from the National Archives Kew reads:

> 'John Rypon states that, on Sunday 6 May last as he was coming to the king to sue for restitution of various church ornaments and other goods taken from the abbey by Roger Frank, who had lately intruded into the office of the abbot and his inherents, thus to appear before the King's Bench in answer to a writ, Oliver Frank, Roger's brother and Robert his kinsman at the command of Roger and his brother Ralph, laid in wait for him at Welbeck Park with more than forty armed men in order to kill him, and wounded him and his servants with arrows.'

Rypon asked the commons to ask the King to ordain a remedy. In response, the King found Rypon had sufficient remedy through common law, as a result, de facto and through support of the King, Roger held the office of Abbot of Fountains Abbey for five years, between 1410–1415.

Not satisfied by the King's argument, John Rypon, contender for the post of abbot, complained of Roger's appointment directly to Rome. The complaint was damaging to the Order of monks, as Rypon's decision to undermine the orthodoxy of Roger Frank's appointment was an indictment on the commissioner's decision.

Each of Roger Frank and Rypon continued to cast aspersions as to the other's character and capability, Roger Frank denouncing Rypon for wandering around armed, semi-clothed and in public without his habit. For his part, Rypon, needing to convince parliament and the General Chapter of his legitimacy, caused a mass of petitions, interviews, litigation and paperwork to ensue.

Fountains Abbey was in a state of turmoil, and although Roger Frank had eventually been driven from the abbacy he continued to exercise authority: retaining the common seal he freely dispensed the communities' resources, his men being accused of attacking Rypon and plotting his murder. Taking sides in the conflict, the tenants caused property to be damaged and the granges to be looted and destroyed.

Over a number of years, the long drawn out conflict was brought to the Council of Constance in October 1415, eventually being resolved in Rypon's favour, with Roger Frank instructed by the Pope to restore certain properties of great value he was alleged to have appropriated, including the abbot's ring and seal.

Having been superseded as abbot by Rypon in 1415, Roger would have been aged around forty-six. Fountains Abbey was integral to the Franks, its position and status being adjacent to the King's highway to York, thence, south to London. Yet

Roger's involvement seems more localised, having originated around Hutton-le-Hole and nearby Rosedale, his interest drawn by religious fervour and the many monastic houses scattered nearby, including that of Lastingham where wool as a commodity brought *'sine qua non'* in terms of vital coinage to the Exchequer.

The aftermath of the Black Death, however, had left its mark. Although having taken place twenty years before his birth, Roger had other matters to keep him busy, and these issues lay closer to home, ministering to those who had lost everything and were desperate. It would take five generations, to around 1525, following the birth of William of Rye, before the trade in wool would fully occupy the mind. Roger's death around 1446 is consistent with his apparent departure from Fountains, and despite personal excesses, he was apparently aged around seventy-five to eighty on his death, a rarity for the time. But having retained the common seal, what came of it?

A solid gold ring of the form of those sometimes found in the tombs of bishops or abbots, was found near the remains of the old abbey of Rosedale in the parish of Middleton. Known as the Rosedale ring, is in fact a seal, the apex a crown, not soldered, but of the same mass as the ring, the whole weighing in at roughly half an ounce. The question is how and when did the seal come to be lost at that place, and by whom?

It seems illogical for so rarefied an abbot's ring to have been lost in the abbey of Rosedale and the Franks so prominent there: the ring must have belonged Roger Frank.

From early records it is apparent that the Franks were viewed as religious, often seen holding positions within the Church or involved with legal issues relating to religious institutions. This observation appears to support the idea of Roger, on the one hand, having no qualms whatsoever in exploiting the situation by satisfying the population's desperate need for food, and at the same time vying for wool, tools and weaponry and the money they could produce.

The question is, were Roger's actions self-seeking, or were they acts of desperation providing help for those left destitute? There was a huge void between the clergy and relative wealth of the Church and the common man, and Roger driven to draw his sword in order to take a share of the plunder withheld by the monastery, I will leave it to the reader to decide as to his intentions being self-serving, for the parish or maybe both.

Robertus offshoot

Prior to continuing the main tree via Rogerus, it is worth showing Willielmus's son Robertus of Poppleton progeny.

The Extraordinary Franks

Robertus (1374) children:

> Willelmus born around 1402, shown as le Frankelein.
>
> Ellen 1403.
>
> Richard 1405.
>
> John 1406.
>
> John Frank (1406) children:
>
> John born around 1430, aka John Frank.
>
> Thomas 1432.
>
> Margery 1433.
>
> Henry 1435.
>
> Isabel 1436.
>
> Margaret 1438.
>
> Ralph 1440.

The children's uncle, Willelmus le Frankelein, shown above, was recorded as coming from Richmond, and on 10th Jan 1464, was embroiled in an argument relating to an enfeoffment of John Frankeleyn, thought to be William's brother. In the ensuing legal tussle, it seems the bad blood and temper of William's father might have rubbed off on William junior. To distinguish himself from his kin, not surprisingly, John seemed to have favoured the use of Frank as opposed to Frankeleyn as a surname.

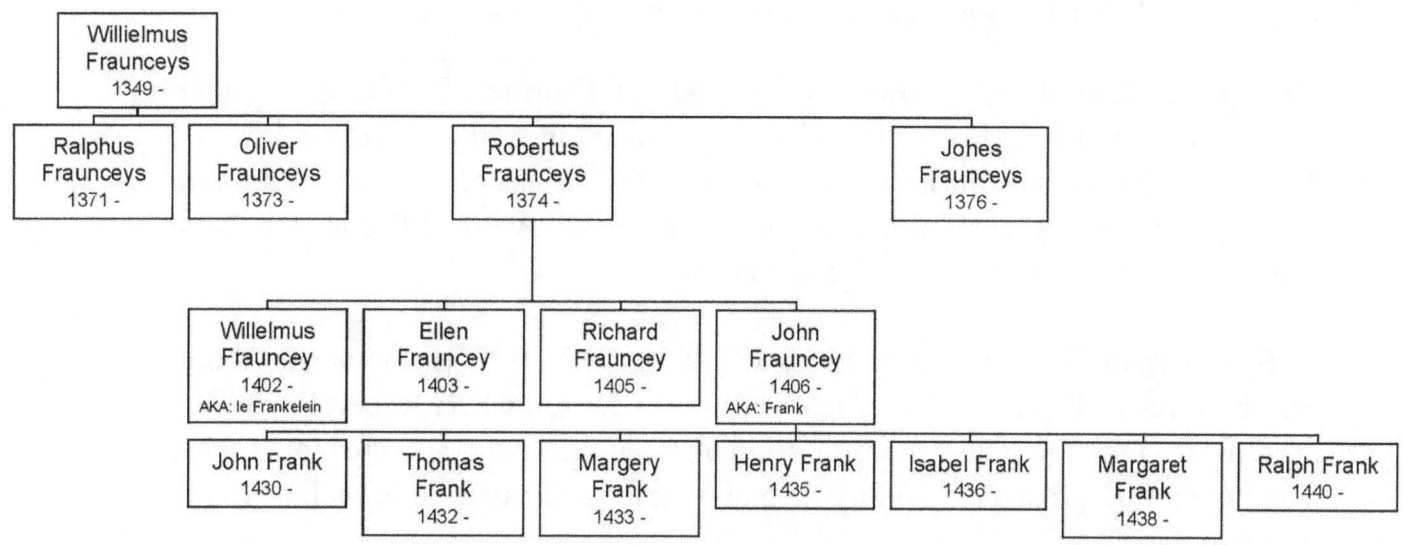

The main Willielmus line continued:

As has been explained, Rogerus aka Roger Frank de Hutton became Abbot of Fountains Abbey and through his sons Thomas and Henry, retained links with Hutton-le-Hole and the area around the Esk and that domain. Information is patchy due the huge death rate that sometimes decimated whole villages. It seems, despite his travels, Thomas somehow survived and on returning home was able to take over the reins looking after the Frank family Cleveland holdings. What is not clear is that of Henry's role.

Rogerus (1369) children:

> **Roger** born around 1410, Roger de Thornton Bishopside.
>
> Thomas Thomas Frauceys appears in the Close Rolls of Henry VI, 1435– 1436, given 'by virtue he be overseas, likewise concerning his other lands in Cleveland.'
>
> Henry In the Rolls of 1437, around the Esk, an item referring to 'the Court Expenses of Henry Frauceys', I'm unable to unscramble the rest.
>
> Daughter
>
> Daughter Three daughters born between 1416–1421.
>
> Daughter
>
> John born around 1423, died 1425.
>
> Robert 1429. Robert Franklan de Lynton-in-Craven, died 1504, and had a son, John, born around 1436.

The subsidy Roll of 1475 shows Roger Frankln of Thornton Bishopside together with John, and in 1504 Robert Frankland is found at Linton-in-Craven. In his will, he directed his body be buried in the Church of St Michael on the north side, and gave bequests for the fabric of Bolton Abbey and for kirk-work at Ripon. The John referred to I've assumed as Roger's son John born 1434.

By the Valor-Ecclesiasticus twenty-sixth of Henry VIII, it is shown the Abbot and Brethren of Fountains Abbey had property at Linton where Robert Frankland held the tenancy. From this, the association between the Franks and the monasteries relating to the land and its produce thereof is clearly indicated. In his will of 1544,

The Extraordinary Franks

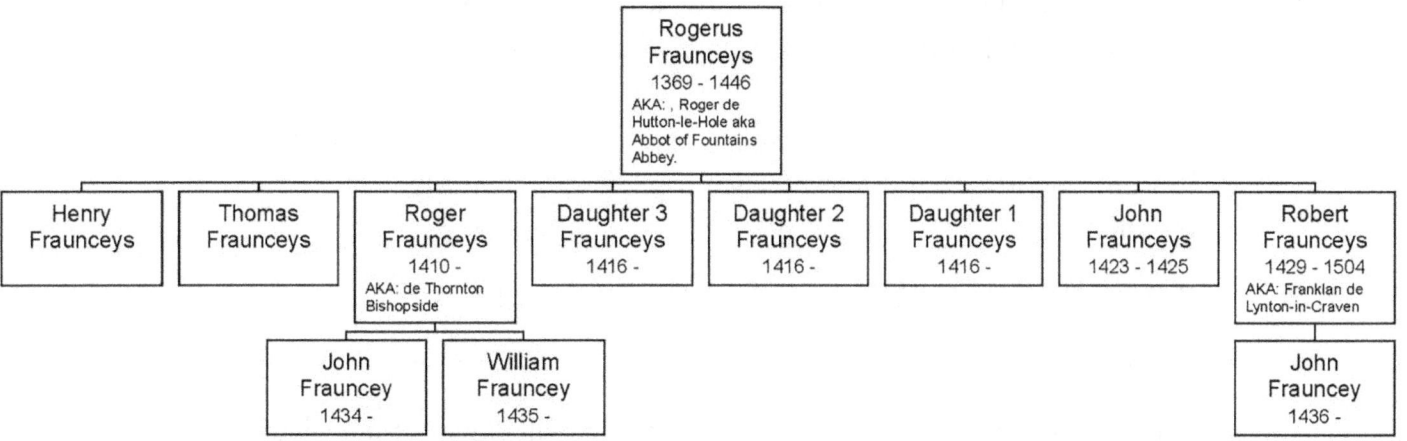

John Frankland, grandson of Robert, describes himself coming from Grassington, describing his lands and properties there. He also mentions Thomas Frankland, son of his brother Richard, and that of his own daughter Elizabeth, being the wife of John Pearte, and his sister Jennet being the wife of Christopher Oldfield. He left money for the vestures and ornaments 'about the altar' in the Church at Lynton, and typical of the Franks, money for the repair and maintenance of yet another bridge: the bridge at Lynton. I draw a parallel here to the reconstruction of the bridges at York and other restorations such as Fountains Abbey, these being part financed by the community and the Franks also supplying building material and occasional labour.

Enormous holdings and an interfamily mystery

The family having vastly different interests to occupy them, the continued acquisition of land caused the Frankland's to take stock. Rogerus of Fountains Abbey had other axes to grind; his brothers Ralphus and Oliver seemed inclined to be led by Rogerus, and to an extent Robertus, it apparently being left to Johes and his son John to manage the accumulation of land and property. About this time John Frankland's namesake John Fraunceys, having many estates, one abutting that of John Frankland, his sudden appearance in their lives, changed things forever.

During investigation a mystery appeared relating to John Fraunceys (1425) and his daughter Alice, of Formark Derbyshire having prior ownership of Thirkleby dated 1463, later shown as Frankland.

The question arises, what were the Formark Fraunceys aka Franceis, doing with such vast accumulation of estates situated so far north of their Derbyshire heartland, ownership stretching past York to an estate sat alongside the Frankland around Thirsk? The answer lies post-1066:

1. Concerning the arrival of three young knights around the Humber, all three being Franks and all sworn to the de Brus.

2. My previous mention of the Sheriff of Nottinghamshire and Derbyshire, Sir Robert Franceys's ancestor William landing with the invasion.

3. Whence come upon London, William sired Alfred in 1070.

4. Successive generations producing Thomas, born in 1409.

5. Then to Sir John who upon marriage to Isabell Plessington, who being an extremely wealthy heiress, he shared her wealth and the rest follows.

The Formark estates became so vast they did indeed extend right across, well south of York; a number of individual holdings swinging west of the city venturing north of York and further again to rest against those of the North Yorkshire Franklands. In setting the scene one should take account of the Franks in and around York and the swathe of Franks farming in isolation, scattered across the Dales, each and all of them interrelated – a family belonging to the three knights loyal to de Brus who first settled along the coastline north-east of York and those around Hull whose family maintained an ongoing connection with one's own family.

Casting back, it comes to mind how far-reaching was the extent of the Francis/Frauceys holdings, certainly as far as Cumbria and the manor house of Richard Francis at Mauld's Meaburn. In mentioning Cumbria, I have purposely avoided getting embroiled referencing the north-west and Northumberland. That, including the aforementioned Formark, would clutter and detract from the main theme and purpose of this work. That being said, it is necessary to visualise the reach and extent of the Franks and their progeny having vast influence right across the whole of the north, and as has been explained, their spread emulating partly out of luck in largely avoiding the plague, but also in their business acumen and skill as farmers in acquiring land, and as true pioneers each in his way not being afraid to venture forth and seek new ground.

Returning to the business of the Formark Franks and the Frankland, it is known that both families communicated and enjoyed roughly equal status and peer recognition. Continuing across the ages, family records clearly show the Cleveland Franks corresponding with the Hull Franks and by extension those south of York, and it's not too far a stretch to see York as the hub of a huge circle of interfamily activity. It is also possible to see how breakaway Franks might lose contact, forming new relationships unaware of the broader picture and what might be going on elsewhere.

This thought is amplified by no modern-day Frank having an iota, neither as to their origins of their name nor of their glorious past.

In 1434, ownership of the Hull/Yorkshire estates clearly lay with the Frauncey, but having no male heir, John and his wife Isabel had already released most of their holdings and retired. As the Frankland were still in the business of acquiring land, seeing both families were related anyway, it seems logical, that Thirkleby was transferred to the Frankland for use as a convenient family seat. Which Frankland member received Thirkleby is not certain, though it's likely to have been Roger of Thornton Bishopside born in 1410, the transfer of ownership occurring sometime after 1434, and with Roger's son William de Lynton inheriting, the rest falling into place.

Having been there several times I know Thirkleby Manor reasonably well, although Thirkleby Hall itself was demolished in 1927. Yes, it has a portal gateway adjacent to the main road and a long uphill road leading to it, but the current dwelling is more in the style of a manor house, its extensive farmland now taken over hosting fishing and a caravan park. The more recent family didn't have much in the way of pretentions, mostly still sticking to their farming roots, although they did have land, apparently lots of it and many tenants.

Situated on the A19 a couple of miles from Thirsk, where Dorothy Frank lived her final days, it's easy to see how Thirkleby fits in with adjacent Osgodby, the Osgodby Franks mentioned elsewhere in this work, as are the Hambleton, whose names were taken from local hill terrain. These along with Rievaulx and Ampleforth, Hutton-le-Hole, Ness and Pickering, all part of one conflation of names tied to the Franks with the Thirkleby seat placed on the A19 leading to nearby York.

Sir John Frankland aka Frauncesy, his wife Isabell and daughter Alice

In researching the Franklands, it is easy to forget the Cleveland Franks. In their comparative isolation, one shouldn't exclude the relevance of the widespread estates of John Frauncesy bordering the Franks of Hamilton, Cleveland and the Wapentake of Langbaurgh. John's estates were enormous, stretching from Derby cross-country south of York towards Leeds and north towards Richmond, and east to Hamilton touching the North York Moors and Cleveland immediately south of Kirkbymoorside, working west in the direction of Thirkleby adjacent Thirsk. Adding to the story, there's Hugh Frankland's aborted attempt to secure the purchase of Ness and, in its stead, a decision to finance the settlement and clearance of Danby Forest.

It is to these isolated farms that I feel most drawn, as too the scattering of holdings around Pickering. The picture is one of the Danby holdings and the confluence of the larger two, almost rival, Frauncesys and Frankland; the Derby estates sweeping north, south of York, to two holdings around Ilkley thence to Thirsk, abutting the Frankland estates around Pickering.

These related families had grown wealthy in their own right and prospered, and as previously indicated the early Cleveland–Pickering settlements being in the front line of repeated conflict remained short of male progeny, the more astute quickly buying into the idea of acquiring land away from the main areas of conflict and military recruitment. It's those Franks who formed the initial Richmond settlements, the fulcrum for all this, Thirsk.

Many Franks had already given their lives in battle, and in the Battle of Towton, regardless which side, huge numbers were lost: slain bodies found strewn one upon the other, arm and legs awkwardly sculptured in rigor mortis, where among the carnage a single hand might be seen raised, its finger pointing towards the heavens.

Many were veterans, and with an average age of thirty, their male progeny had been rapaciously put away for eternity. For their loved ones, this was a bitter pill to swallow. And for all the many knights and noblemen who fought, there was no hiding place, three-quarters of all the peers of England were also embroiled in battle. So bitter was the conflict, no quarter was given by either side, and following capture and being taken prisoner, forty-two Lancastrian knights were slain in cold blood, and those who fled were hunted down and murdered.

The Lancastrian power at court, namely Northumberland, Clifford, Roos and Dacre had died or fled. Edward named fourteen Lancastrian peers as traitors, and each noble controlling 100 of the rank of knight below, known in chivalric orders as *knights bacheor,* were retained in addition to knights retained by 40 days per annum military tenure or fief duty. In addition were those *knights banneret* fighting under their own banner. The balance of authority now firmly within his domain, Edward preferred to win over the remaining knights and land owners. Those who failed to submit or failed to satisfy his demands: such estates were unceremoniously confiscated by the Crown. Others were either reduced in size or left untouched, and by 1464 the Yorkists had demonstratively wiped out all effective resistance.

But the wounds and scars of conflict had taken their toll. Infirmity and old age, together with an absence of male heirs, made the business of running estates and farming an onerous burden. Successive generations had helped build the estates; inheritor John Fraunceys owned a huge succession of estates having a number of knights, their tenure providing loyalty, protection and service. He held several estates north of Hull and around the Humber, Bilton, Helperthorp, Tharlesthorpe, Beaume, Hedon and the Manors of Holderness and Fauconberge in Bilton.

Moving inland, the Manor of Nunappleton just south of York, and the Manor of Thirkylby near Thirsk, were part of a cluster of ten manors and land owned by John, and also locally related Franks. Moving closer to Cleveland, he owned the

Manor of Catwyk, not far from Helmsley, situated midway between the Yorkshire Dales and the North York Moors. The whole of the aforesaid formed a single lot, the lot itself being the latter of four huge estates now being relinquished.

John Fraunceys and his wife Isabell released the manors and land 20th May 1463. Perhaps due to their age and wanting to live out their remaining lives in peace, they retained the pre-existing advowson of the Prioress of the Monastery of the Nuns of Nunapplylton together with the park in the Manor of Nunapplylton and several fisheries, the bulk of the estate having been sold to John Warde and his son Thomas and their heirs forever. A sum of money was exchanged and a covenant was raised relating to the remaining property that on the decease of John, the Monastery, Nunapplylton and the fisheries, should pass to John Worsley and his wife Alice, daughter of John Fraunceys.

The following shows the extent of just a tiny part of John Frank's holdings:

Previously, 25th November 1461, John Fraunceys and Isabell provide a covenant of the Manor of Ilkley near Skipton. The manor and lands consisted of 20 messuages, 400 acres of ploughland, and 60 acres of meadow, 4000 acres of moor, 400 acres of woodland, money and a sparrow hawk.

In the covenant, John and Isabell also acknowledged the manor, its tenements and rent, together with all homages and all the services bound by Henry Vavasour (knight), and William Plumpton (knight), Abbot John and William Middleton esquire and all their heirs. The estate included the lands around Laxton, Addingham near Skipton and the surrounds of Fountains Abbey.

On the same date, 25th November 1461, Thomas Slater (chaplain), Richard Pudsey (querant), John Fraunceys esquire and his wife Isabell, appear as deforcients to the tiny parcel of nine messuages, nine bovates, six acres of land, and sixteen acres of meadow at Stretton, Broughton and Thurlby, east of Thirsk in Hamilton adjacent the North York Moors. This was a fictitious action whereby John and Isabell were being kept out of the possession of their rightful ownership of the estate. The truth being they were being dispossessed as part of a strategy invoked by King Edward.

The plea of covenant action was an agreement whereby John and Isabell acknowledged the aforesaid tenements, quote:

> 'To be the right of Richard, as those which Richard and Thomas have of their gift, and have remised and quit claimed them from themselves and the heirs of Isabel to Thomas and Richard'.

A release, indicated 8th September 1487, shows Ralph Fraunceys esquire, tenantry to his brother John Fraunceys as to the rent from the Manor of Tottley in Skaresdale.

The manor was situated between Leeds and Harrogate, the reversion of the manor having previously come to John on the death of John Barlowe.

John Frauncey's estates, indicated for 1463, included the Manor of Thirkylby* near Thirsk, also Catwyk, close to Helmsley, exactly midway between the Yorkshire Dales to the west and the North York Moors to the east. An entry of 1461 shows Thirlby in Felixkirk, which lies east of Thirsk towards Helmsley, and Ravensthorpe, Boltby and Mount St John, within the auspice of Hamilton District Council. This included Birdforth, twelve miles from Kirkbymoorside, as well as land in Broughton, Cleveland, I once farmed.

The break-up of a once immense scattering of separate estates left little in the way of property. Thirkleby itself having subsequently passed to the Frankland, such was the demise of the Francis, albeit they were of the same line, offspring of Rollo and via the Bayeux Franks, Henry II, King of England.

To a lesser extent, history repeated 300 years later. Recently married Betty Frankland, daughter and heir to Sir Thomas Frankland, died in 1742 aged twenty-five, the estate passing to her husband John Trevor. The entry shows how the absence of a single male heir could hasten the disappearance of a once prominent family; the holdings once transferred to Trevor, the Franks became confined to history.

As previously indicated, Thirkleby Manor now lay in the hands of the Franklands.

Roger (1410) children:

> John born around 1434, in 1457–1458, had layman connections with Rievaulx and Fountains Abbey. He also had Thirkleby which passed through William of Thurley down the family line.

William 1435, took the name William de Lynton.

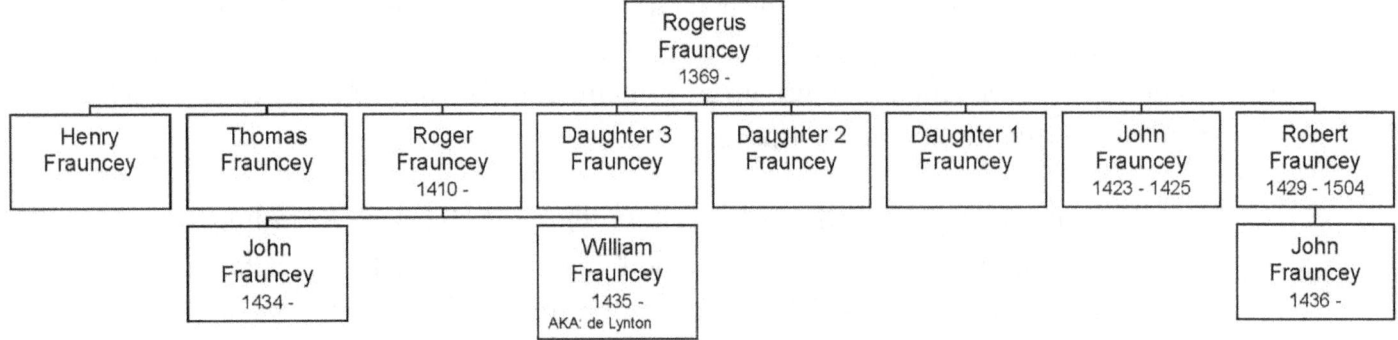

The Auld Alliance

As has been explained, plague, war and famine caused many thousands to be displaced or made destitute. The upshot being many records of trials, land transactions, births, marriages and deaths were not kept, or were otherwise damaged or lost. Hasty burials made the task of recording mass bodies wholly impossible.

Adding to their woes, due to personal ties to their feudal and titular peers, a significant clutch of Richmond and North Yorkshire Franks and their contemporaries were singled out having significant connections with Scotland and France. Their obligation related to the 'Auld Alliance' formed 350 years previously. These emanated from the old local ties of Balliol, Bruce and Stewart, being monarchs of Scotland, and lands that included the Scottish Royal Fiefdom of Northumberland. So, as if they hadn't already had trouble enough, the Old Alliance and Scotland, which the Franks were so much a part of, had come back to bite them.

War was a major headache, the War of the Roses (1455–1485), took place mostly in Yorkshire. But, to add to their troubles, in the North Riding, affecting Cleveland and the surrounding territory, loyalty was divided. This was not surprising given the history of the area and its constant supply of men needed for battle by those of different historic alliances.

Repeating previous evidence, due to constantly changing loyalties, who was on which side was not clear, loyalties often subject to frequent change depending on the perceived outcome of battle. The Nevilles of Middleham, Scropes of Bolton, Latimers of Danby and Snape, and Mowbrays of Thirsk, supported the House of York. The Percys and Cliiffords of Skipton, Ros of Helmsley and others from Holderness and Sheffield, fought for the Lancastrians.

Due to their association with nobles of divided loyalties, families like the Franks were suddenly caught in an impossible impasse: who to support. Repeating a previous transcript, Henry VII suffered periods of insanity, and his wife Margaret de Anjon having assumed control, faced those same nobles, and on the death of Richard of York at Wakefield 30th December 1460, his titles and claim to the throne passed to his eldest son, Edward. Edward found enough backing to denounce Henry and declare himself king; the Battle of Towton was fought in order to affirm, through force of arms, the victors right to rule.

The ensuing battle left the Yorkists, under Edward, to rule uninterrupted for nine years. Henry had fled the country; many powerful followers were either dead or exiled. The House of Lancaster being severely reduced, large landowners not proven as having provided outright Yorkist support were viewed as suspect and were obliged to relinquish their holdings.

JOHN FRAUNCEYS, YORK AND SURROUNDS.

On a lighter note, taking cognisance of the Domesday records (working inland towards York and north of the Humber towards Whitby), much later Frank migratory settlement, adjacent Thirsk, had worked its way west and inland from Whitby and Cleveland and then south: in a sense forming a huge circle abutting Frank settlements of 100 years previous around York. Around Selby, south-east of York, Franks are shown carrying identical father-to-son antecedence, indicators that more than match their northern counterparts.

The position of York itself, its roads like the spokes of a wheel fanning out within arm's-reach of the surrounding ground, is significant. York held the power and was the city-state for commerce, law and religion: good reason for keeping a toehold there. Family members holding positions within the Church had connections and through those contacts, influence, such alliances being necessary historically and important in fashioning Norman relationships: a power the Normans relished and wielded with élan and unparalleled physical power. The passing of 300 years had not diminished the Franks basic character. Tamed, yes, shaped and formed culturally, yes, but their unremitting determination and single-minded force of nature remained intact.

Inquisitions

> 'Poppleton York, 12th Feb 1400, inquisition of Miles de Stapulton in the presence of John and William Fraunkeleyn.'

> 'York Castle, 5th July 1420, trial of John Hothan, Chivaler, in the presence of John Frankeleyn.'

> 'Monescroft, Poppleton, 20th Nov 1420, trial of Sir John Goddard, Chivaler, in the presence of Robert Fraunkeleyn. Sir John subsequently died aged nineteen.'

Notes on the above:

Poppleton, a Frank settlement still today, and Otley, had earlier connections with the Forestarious family having previously held the moiety of the manor and archbishops of Otley and Little Timble.

Surname spelling: the family dropped the latter part of the surname, settled for Frank, Fraunk, Franke and Fraunke, although Fraunklay, Fraunkeleyn, Fraunklayne and Frankelein appeared around the Poppleton district of York towards Richmond.

The Extraordinary Franks

Those loyal to Robert Frank's distinctive leadership were engaged in the process of gaining tracts of farming land around York, whatever they could amass, which included female acquisitions within the group. This has been well-recorded, together with the actual dates and detailed payment made for the repair and maintenance of the two main bridges in York together with work paid for and carried out to Fountains Abbey.

Around York itself, the tendency was towards the more modernised use of Frank as a surname, whereas, irrespective of wealth, variations on Fraunkeleyn had more fanciful connotations at odds with the no-nonsense use of Frank or Franks increasingly in favour.

The following are a random sample of the surname Frank taken from records made in York between 1444 and 1486:

> A farm demised to William and Ellen Frank.
>
> Rent for farm demised to William and another farm to Ellen Frank.
>
> Payment for tenement maintenance to house of Ellen Frank where the Holtby family are neighbours.
>
> Received from Ellen Frank, payment for farm of the second tenement.
>
> Farm of fourth tenement of William Franke and his farm of the twenty-second and the twentieth.
>
> Farm of Richard Fraunkeleyn.
>
> Farm demised to John Frank.
>
> Farm of twelfth, John Franke.
>
> Repairs for John Fraunke.
>
> Farm of seventh to John Frank, and tenth to Richard Frank.
>
> Farm of eighth to Richard Fraunk.
>
> John Franke, the fifth tenement, Isabel Franke the twenty-first and Thomas the twenty-third.
>
> John Franke for his farm of the ninth.
>
> John Franke and the Earl of Northumberland provide urgent payment to the monks, necessary for the decay and depreciation of Fountains Abbey.

Seeming to be living in two parallel but different worlds, nonetheless, John Franke's friendship with the Earl of Northumberland seemed close. And while John was a workaday farmer, by comparison the earl was a gentleman. While each man carried the same Christian name, John Neville's title included that of First Marquess of

Montague. Having been a Yorkist leader in the War of the Roses, John Neville was knighted by Henry VI in 1469. Notwithstanding their comparative status, the two were apparent friends, both contributing to the repair of Fountains Abbey.

Continuing his long-standing feud with the Lancastrian Percy family, John Neville was based at nearby Middleham Castle. Following his capture and subsequent release, he led and defeated the Lancastrians at Hedgeley Moor and again at Hexham in 1464. As a reward, he was invested as a Knight of the Garter and Warden of the East March, being created Earl of Northumberland in 1464, a title previously confiscated from his enemy, the Percy family.

In a sad and ironic turn, due to reduced circumstances having changed his allegiance, and being unable to support his dignity, Sir John Neville aka Montague went into battle and was killed alongside his brother Richard, Earl of Warwick, both men fighting against previous loyal Yorkists in the Battle of Barnet in 1471.

The life of a farmer seems to have been much safer, and while John Franke had land and was the in the business of accumulating more, it was the Earl of Northumberland's lack of estates and income that contributed to his downfall, that and a desperate need for status and recognition. Meanwhile the Franks were quietly getting on with the workaday job of accumulating land and the creation of sustained methods of farming.

Continuing the list of names:

> Ellen Frank, a second tenement and John Frank the other tenement there.
>
> Farm and tenure of Thomas Frank.
>
> The thirteenth tenure, Richard Franke.
>
> Farm of the sixth tenure, Margaret Fraunk.
>
> Relating to prayer at Fountains Abbey, payment to Richard Fraunk for chapel bell-ringing at Saint Anne's, Fosse Bridge.
>
> Payment to William Parr and William Fox for work done for the Abbot and Convent of Fountains.
>
> Same payment for work done on the tenements of Thomas Fraunke.
>
> William Fraunke for the first tenement.
>
> 12s paid to William Fraunke for his various legal summonses, arrests and distraints.
>
> William, a further payment of 4s 4d.
>
> Further too, William Fraunke 20s for labour relating to arrests and summonses.

An entry at St Martin's York, 10th June 1550, shows Anthony Frankys; 'he Gentleman, as executor, having messuages in Stalybridge, Skipton and Ripon'.

The bridges at York

It is not known when the bridges at York were originally built, but they would have been of wooden construction and terribly unstable. Crossing the Ouse and Foss and found in the Cartulary of Whitby's Chartularium Sithiense and the Cartulary of Fountains around 1217–1235, the Ouse crossing was first mentioned in charters around 1189–1200, and the Foss around 1145–1148. First proper construction commenced in 1393, the bridges eventually being rebuilt in stone after the repeated collapse of the repaired wooden structures they replaced.

Payment was required both for construction and for the maintenance that followed. This coincided with changes taking place relating to strip farming and the advent of fields formed by those with the foresight to acquire several strips in order to create acreage Meanwhile, ahead of the game, yeomen such as the Franks were busy acquiring as many farm lots as became available.

The period around 1470 going forward was fortuitous for those prepared to take advantage. The more productive the cultivation of newly allocated land, the more payment it drew, much of the resultant revenue being set aside specifically for construction of the York bridges and their maintenance. And whereas the term 'farm' had already been assimilated into common parlance, John Frank and the family at large took the opportunity to extend their previous land tenant agreements subsequent to purchase and outright ownership.

What is interesting is the Frank's involvement with Fountains Abbey and its maintenance. In 1486, payments were made to Sir James Danby, knight and to the monks of Fountains Abbey. These were for:

> 'Decays and depreciation and for allowances made to the aforesaid individuals accounts…'

Persons making payment included John Franke and the Earl of Northumberland, and went towards the purchase of things like:

> 'Two wagon loads of burnt lime, a quantity of nails, 1,000 skotchym, twenty-four loads of lute with carriage, mydel spiking, sabulum, saplaths and playstre.'

Sir James Danby is significant having a namesake connection with Danby, it's forest, and the later Frankland purchase of said estate via Geoffrey Frank. Taken from the place Danby, the Sir John Conyers family used the name Danby prior to its demise through the lack of male heirs. The name Conyers is derived from Roger de Coigneries of Coigneries France, where he was born in 1010. Joining the invasion aged fifty-six, Roger later died from injuries sustained during the fighting: the incursion north finishing him off, he passed away peacefully in Durham that same year. Following his death the family remained local to Darlington, assuaging loyalty to the de Brus. Incidentally details as to the Conyers family are largely complete and available online.

Deforciant actions in the fictitious acquisition of land and counterclaims

The following is of considerable interest as it portrays and confirms the prosperity and influence of the Franks and their interests across a huge swathe of territory west of Masham abutting Thirkleby, and across a distance of fifty-five miles to Danby near Whitby, and again from Masham twenty miles north to Darlington and onward penetrating Durham. Also shown is Stainton. In recent memory abutting the Yarm crossing of the River Tees, Stainton and neighbouring Ingleby and Barwick were retained by recent Frank relatives. Also from the list, some of the placenames shown have associations southwest of York around Poppleton, well-known Frank territory.

From the list of Yorkshire Deeds of Henry Vll, dated 9th April 1493, an indenture of the aforementioned Sir James Danby, knight, quote:

> 'Doth grant to Ralph Evers, Geoffrey Frank, et al., all his lands, tenements, rents and services with appurtenances in Kirkby Massam, Swynton, Wardermarsk, Sutton, Ellyngton, Heiley, Thornbargh, Firthby, Exilby, Scabbednewton, Little Lemyng, Scruton, Warlainthby, Thrintofte, Yafforth, Newbiging, two closes at Little Danby called Marshaw and Execlose, Overwhitwell and Nethewhitwell in County York, and also all his lands etc. in Great Langton which lately belonged Thomas Langton there; also all his lands etc. in Derlington (Darlington), Little Staynton (Stainton), Sudbury, Bicheburn, Mawemedowe, Brafferton, Shynkley, Olduressam in the bishopric of Durham; to hold all the aforesaid lands to the grantees, their heirs and assigns in perpetuity.'

The Extraordinary Franks

What is not known is the exact division of lands and property between five recipients. Sir James was born in 1450 and died in 1499, six years following the indenture. Originally from Danby, and despite a quite extensive loss of land, the Danby family retained many titles and possessions. Incidentally Danby was named after the Danes from which the name Danvers derives.

Born June 1573, Henry Danvers took part in the siege of Rouen in 1591 being created first earl of Danby in 1626. Made late 1630's is a Knight of the Garter in 1633, Henry's image painted by Van Dyke in the late 1630 is part of a large collection on view at Houghton Hall, Norfolk. Having never married, the barony of Danby became extinct upon his death in January 1644.

Born of William Frank (Frauncey b. 1435), Geoffrey Frank (b. 1462) was listed as the second ranking beneficiary to the aforementioned indent, he became the lawful recipient of a large part of the estate consisting of land, tenements, rents and services, adding to an already bustling family estate mostly relating to farming and property.

And as the following paragraphs reveal, one can see how things panned out and where in 1534, sometime prior to Geoffrey's mysterious disappearance, we see Peter Frankland having messuages in Danby, his brother John being in possession of adjoining Glaisdale where my grandfather was born and whose ancestry and holdings have been meticulously recorded. These records together with details of associated families have been handed down generationally linking the Danby and Glaisdale Franks to Ingleby Barwick and the present day.

The largely complete record of births, deaths and marriages surrounding Danby show the interwoven fabric of both Frank and Frankland, its farming community being difficult to separate one from the other. And with later Frankland numbers reduced to one family, I'd already decided to omit the Frankland altogether, concentrating solely on the Franks. That both families were entwined is not difficult to visualise, their surnames appearing on adjacent gravestones, their names often overlapping one and the same: the spirited Frankland so soon to fade from view.

Returning to the mystery of Geoffrey himself, appearing from nowhere he just as soon disappeared. It transpires, being considered a threat he had to vanish, but where or if he had been disposed of remains wholly speculative. Yet from the point of view of the Franks, quite simply, Geoffrey had been acting on behalf of the family at large, as wealthy farmers the acquisition and accumulation of substantial holdings being normal fare. This goes a long way to explain the origin of one's family inheritances. And although passed down generationally, by dint of dubious means its extensive estate had been severely savaged by peers determined to restore territory previously lost. Shared out generationally, what remained of the residue accumulation of lands, property and estate eventually passed to my great-grandparents. And here I will explain:

Whereas, and as I have shown, from the very beginning the Franks had built up their estates largely on the basis of intellect and good farming practice, the Dales folk in particular remained true to the soil, steadily advancing their holdings across the terrain, linking with more affluent kin to become a 5000 square mile spread of different sized estates surrounded by a multitude of smaller holdings. Others spread coast to coast I have purposely left unrecorded. Historically its significance is quite amazing, and remains largely unrecorded.

Following the loss of many a lord's estate and with it its authority, the continued success of the Frank and their like became too much to bear for those wielding a greater authority. And it's due to the Frank's more grounded ethic and sense of moral purpose, as usurpers, the presumptive nature of their land-grab became both an insult and a threat posed against their lord's own grandiose hereditament and had to be stopped.

Just as now with the hereditary ruling elite, we need to understand the possession of huge estates going hand in hand relating to status. Underwritten by honours, which then as today, remains an accolade: title meaning everything. That a bunch of yeomen farmers had the better of them couldn't be tolerated.

For example: an earlier action dated 27th January 1480, was against deforciant Thomas Frank and his wife Mabel. This fictitious action was brought by Sir William Gascoygne, knight, the querent acquiring twenty-four acres of pasture in Werdley by Harewode, whereby Thomas and his wife were obliged to acknowledge the pasture to be the right of William Gascoygne, quote:

> 'That which he has of their gift, quitclaimed from themselves and their heirs forever'.

As for said gift, Sir William giving them a paltry forty marks of silver. The Thomas mentioned was a son of Rogerus, previous Abbot of Fountains Abbey. Born around 1412, Thomas Fraunceys or Frank as he became known, was recorded as:

> 'Having other lands in Cleveland'.

Thomas would have been aged approximately sixty-eight around the time of the action and would have been disappointed at the acquisition taken of his son, albeit it relating to only twenty-four acres.

And it's here the desperate battle for land, titles and influence became rife and much of it bloody. Against such powerful odds the Franks seemed to have little chance of regaining land subsequently taken by such ruthless and determined opponents. Yet while he remained alive Geoffrey would fight on, a later lawsuit enabling him to counterclaim.

As an aside I need to stress the barony of the aforesaid Thirkleby: the barony established in 1660 was passed down generationally, leading to Sir James Assheton Frankland, dated 1965 come Baron Zouche. Once again is the situation where a Breton nobleman, Alain Ceoche cum Zouche, come his arrival on English soil in the late 1100s, his bravery and that of his descendants leads to a barony. And here once again the repeated absence of male progeny caused the Zouche peerage time and again to be set aside, only to find itself conveniently remerging, favours bestowed and so on.

A twist to the original tale comes when the Duke of Gloucester and Richard Danby, under a plea of covenant on the 9th February 1482, 'enforced a fictitious action' for the reacquisition of land from Geoffrey Fraunk esquire and his wife Margaret under the terms of a deforciant. This was a huge stitch-up, formulating an arrangement whereby one may keep out of possession the rightful owner of an estate, against whom a fictitious action of fine was brought to enable the original acquisition. As pure gobbledegook the accusation proved a clever sleight of hand, an eventual counterclaim by Geoffrey retrieving at least some of that lost under the claim.

As a land-grab the Duke of Gloucester's favour must have really been in the ascent, as the enormous list of law suits in his name bear testimony, and we are talking about the enforcement of thousands upon thousands of acres of land, including the Frank's; countless holdings that couldn't be allowed to slip from the Duke and his cohort's grasp – the aforementioned Sir William and now the Duke of Gloucester, two of a number of peers and their well-paid lawyers against whom one had no real chance. This was a time of restoration and the big divide separating the ruling class from the ordinary.

Yet how clever was Geoffrey? While sensibly avoiding taking on the Duke (whose wanton influence he couldn't possibly win), when the Duke's attention was elsewhere, he eventually turned the tables on Danby, when in a return lawsuit of 1493 he gained part retrieval of lands lost. As for the bulk of the Danby family fortune, them being on the side of Gloucester, their connivance did manage to retain a large portion of those estates duplicitously gained, thus reaffirming their status as earls: the title passed to the Osborne's in 1631.

The property obtained by the querent Richard Danby were the manors of Eskerig, Ellerton and Derwent, plus 47 messuages, 500 acres of land, 54 acres of meadow, 200 acres of pasture, 200 acres of wood, and 50s 8d of rent coming from Eskerig, Ellerton, Derwent, Naburn and Scorouton. Added to that the advowsons of the churches of Eskerig and Kirkeby Underknoll in the County of York, and the manor of Barbron plus 20 messuages, 300 acres of land, 20 acres of meadow, 200 acres of pasture, and 200 acres of wood in Barbron and Middilton in the county of Westmoreland.

By comparison to these huge losses, while the property retrieved was miniscule measured against the purge set against them, Geoffrey's patience at least secured part retrieval of the families losses. And now so suddenly and mysteriously absent from the fray, Geoffrey wasn't around to cause trouble; he and other obstacles now swept aside, the path was clear for their lords and their cohorts, the robber barons, as was their want, to usurp the law for their own ends.

THE MAIN WILLIELMUS LINE CONTINUED

William (1435) children:

>**William** born around 1461. William de Thurley farmed at Nelsing, Giggleswick, founded in 1507, and later seen as the family ancestral home.
>
>Geoffrey 1462 (see acquisition of land from Sir James Danby 1493).
>
>John 1463, being John de Lynton, whose daughter was Elizabeth.
>
>Richard 1465.
>
>Jennet 1466, married Christopher Oldfield.

William (1461) children:

>**Richard** born around 1484, Richard de Nelsing, farmer, died 10th April 1532.
>
>Thomas 1485.
>
>John 1487.
>
>William 1490, became Rector of Houghton-le-Spring in 1522.

Elevated as Chancellor to Bishop Ruthal, Wolsey, Tunstall and the Dean of Windsor in 1538, he died in 1557 as rector of Chalfont in Buckinghamshire. Throughout his life William was known as a prominent and remarkable man, surviving the stirring times in which he lived.

The Extraordinary Franks

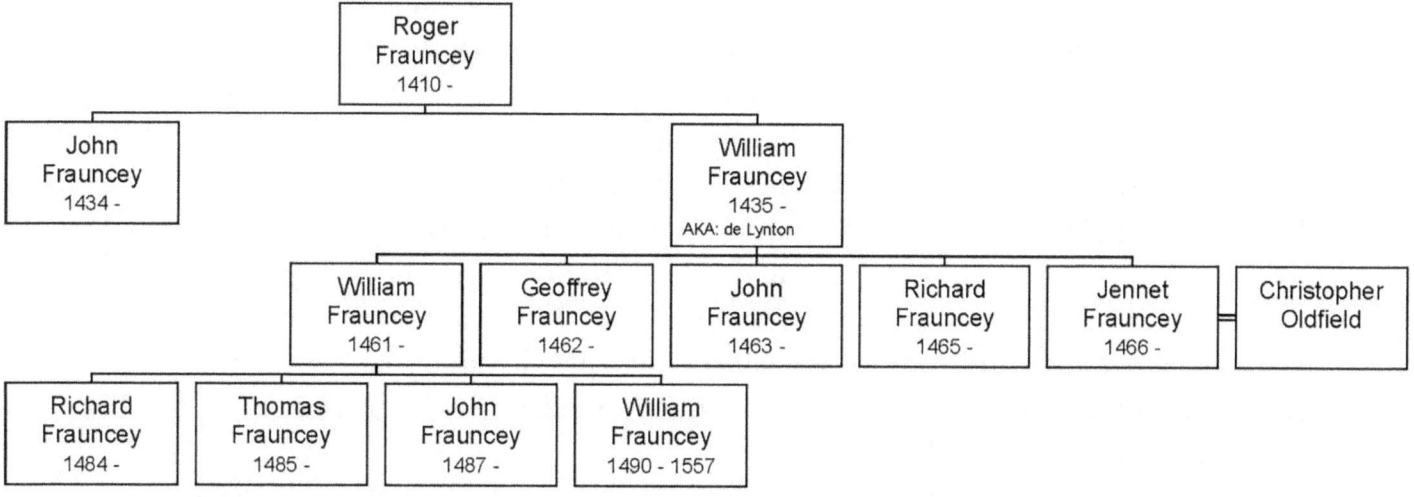

The dissolution

In 1485 the Earl of Richmond became King of England and the Yorkshire rebellion commenced in 1489. The people of Northumberland and Yorkshire refused to pay additional taxes to defend Brittany, which was allied to England against France. These folk were first and foremost Northern English, not Cornish or Londoners. They had given their all, and wasn't the very soil they worked soaked in their kinsmen's blood, the few remaining men appearing ragged, tired and exhausted by battle or weary and cripple-bent through manhandling the land they worked.

Often, there were no men whatsoever, the only males perhaps those impaired, seriously injured or young boys, the land mostly worked by bereaved and emancipated half-starved womenfolk. They had no more to give, God's gift of existence a luxury given over to exhaustion, sleep given over to quiet oblivion and burial. For the Franks, they had their heritage and a kind of pride from which to find courage against a sea of relentless persecution and adversity. But even among former Normans, hope was merely a concept to be realised, with ever-present thoughts of what may befall them constant to the sound of a knock on the door.

Henry VIII's ruthless dynasty was to destroy local resistance to his rule by confiscating people's religious rights, and in the face of resistance, confiscation of their economic livelihood, with torture and death the preserve for acts of rebellion. By a semblance of luck other than good fortune, bolstered by those returning home, the scattered landscape of Franks was less affected. Those who had managed to escape the worst had begun to rebuild their lives; many had long ago moved out of harm's way. Those who moved further inland prospered, creating the simile of two separate classes of people within one extended family.

The dissolution of the monasteries by Henry VIII had a profound and permanent effect on North Yorkshire. Thousands of acres of monastic property was divided and sold to former estates and to the scattering of yeomen farmers who had survived and gained status as gentlemen farmers, adding to their landholdings. The main beneficiaries were those yeomen and farmers spread right across from Guisborough Priory to Rievaulx, and Jervaulx to Fountains Abbey and the Dales.

For the most part, the dissolution suited the Cleveland Franks, whose aspirations matched their inland counterparts as determined by wealth, less so concerning status. Indeed, seeing the potential, those still called Franklands became anxious to obtain land adjacent the Franks at Danby, the subsequent purchase of Danby Forest made by the family of Hugh Frankland.

But the process was far from easy with claim and counterclaim rife and always favouring the easily offended militaristic or powerful combatant prepared to vent retribution. And so it was with the Franks, with gains and losses in the end, land-wise, just marginally even, as literate more gentrified farmers having strong links with the Church, their status and preparedness for legal battle well recognised, causing stalemate and good cause for those more powerful to be wary and look elsewhere.

Richard (1484) children:

> **Hugh** born around 1503. Hugh of Nelsing, father of Richard of Nelsing.

Hugh Frankland was briefly of Ness in Rydale, also Lord of Alwick, inherited from his brother Richard a few days prior to Richard's death in March 1587; these included the Rectory and Manor of Alne and Tollerton. His coat of arms was assigned previously in 1556 when living at Ness in Rydale. He later returned to Nelsing, no great distance from his ancestral home in the parish of Linton, close to Grassington, lying five miles north of Skipton.

> William 1504, William of Rye was granted a knighthood and the lordship of Blubberhouses in 1562.

Sir William married Joyce and died 21st Aug 1576. Their son William also died, who having an underage child, revision of the estate passed briefly to William Senior's brother Richard. The lordship and estates of Blubberhouses passing briefly to Richard's son Hugh, named after Richard's brother Hugh, thence to Hugh's brother Ralph in 1607.

> Girl details unknown.

The Extraordinary Franks

Girl details unknown.

Richard 1510, died 1587–1588.

Richard bought one-third of the rectory and manor of Alne and Aldwick in 1585 from John and Katherine Atherton. A few days prior to his death he completed the remaining two-thirds of the purchase, passing the whole of the Blubberhouses estate to his son Hugh. Hugh also having Thirkleby and Roche Abbey died 20th Jan 1606, leaving his estates to his wife Johanne in her lifetime. She, in turn, gave Hugh's brother Ralph the Monasteries of Roche. Meanwhile, the Rectory and Manor of Aldwick and Tollerton, leased for twenty-one years, had passed to Richard's brother Hugh, thence to Hugh's son William. The story of Blubberhouses gifted to Richard's brother William, aka William of Ryes is interesting and a story in itself:

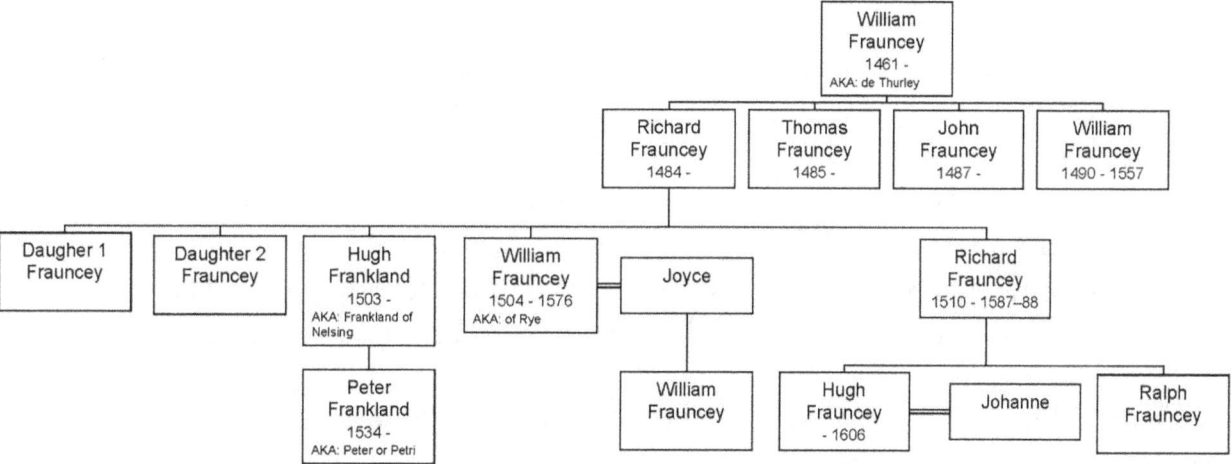

Libera terra; liberque animus

The Frankland motto of 'Frank land Frank mind' translates as 'Free land cum free soul'. Richard Frankland was a Calvinist, and among his many achievements, he was a great preacher. My own grandfather, Thomas Henry Frank, also preached and the Frank Bible, held in safe keeping by my aunt, Ruth Walton née Frank, was verbally gifted to me prior to her death, but the book was never received. It's my understanding she saw me as the last Frank custodian. Ann was also there when visiting her for the last time at Wellington Farm prior to her passing.

There was something about that visit, almost a plea, something anxious, almost conscious of something lost, the Bible a physical link with the past. That feeling has stuck with me. When we left I have never seen anyone before or since so desperately tearful, her entreaty so heart wrenching. Perhaps another reason to get this story right and do it justice.

I know Ruth had visited the Glaisdale seat sometime back and her having relayed details to my mother. But was she more conscious than the rest of the Rubicon between two worlds and her being suspended somewhere between, perhaps as an unknowing messenger and her last words to us akin to a homily. I don't know, but it's all so sad and thoughts of good times and Ruth remain with me.

Blubberhouses was originally part of a great forest. In those times, a forest included areas that may be variously copse, treeless or scrub, but on the whole contained vast areas of valuable woodland. In the reign of King John, William de Stuteville was Lord of Knaresborough and with the King's consent alienated this portion of his charge to Robert le Forester, thence the manor and farm demised to the Priory of Bridlington.

The lands were deforested in 1226 by the then Lord of Knaresborough, Richard Earl of Poicton and Cornwall. Access to the moors being denied, the Prior and Brethren of Bridlington, together with Bolton Priory (situated east of Skipton), made several lawsuits concerning the rights of common pasture across said moors.

In the Register of Archbishop Grey of York, 1216–1255, there is frequent mention of the name Forestarins in connection with grants of land and wardships. The Forestarins seem to have been tenants of the Archbishop's manor of Otley where the manor joined the forest at Little Timble, and where they resided.

The manor and estates of Blubberhouses were dissolved during the reign of Henry VIII, and in the fifth year of Queen Elizabeth's reign in 1562, the Crown granted:

> 'The lordship of Blubberhouses, together with the seite and mansion of the Hall, to Sir William Frankland of Ryes.'

As indicated, William (1504), was the son of farmer, Richard of Nelsing and apart from predecessor Roger, Abbot of Fountains, the Franks were mostly tied to the land or were clerics. William of Ryes was something of a departure for the Franks. Although apparently living in Hertfordshire, and founder of the Guild of Clothworkers in London, he originally settled at Thornton Bishopside, immediately west of Ripon and was an uncle to farmer John Frankland of Glaisdale, Glaisdale being one's immediate family ancestral home.

It is assumed William's interest in weaving emanated from the monastic wool trade, as well as through his nephew John Frankland and his association with the weaving carried out at Hutton-le-Hole and the Rydale surrounds. Incidentally, this is where William's brother Hugh had family adjacent the scatter of great monastic houses of Rydale and their trade in wool with Fountains, which abbey the Franks were already closely associated.

The Extraordinary Franks

As far back as 1224, although situated well inland, many miles from any navigational river or the sea, Fountains Abbey owned their own ship, which was licensed to carry wool. The wonderment of this and the knowledge of a predecessor having traded between London and Cleveland may have wetted William's appetite for business.

Records of Fountains Abbey in 1457 show John Franklyn having a layman connection there as well as links with Lastingham, adjacent to Hutton-le-Hole. The Subsidy Roll for the warpentake of Claro, during the reign of Edward IV in 1475, shows John and Roger Franklyn as of Thornton Bishopside; yet, in relation to Thirkleby, the Frankland already had a foothold. In 1398–1399, the bailiff of the Borough of Thirkleby paid twenty-nine pence and three and a half pence as the rent of free tenements, and by the beginning of the nineteenth century, there were fifty-two burgage tenements of which forty-nine belonged to the Frankland of Thirkleby.

In 1504, Robert Frankland of Linton-in-Craven, in his will, directed his body be buried in the Church of Saint Michael, on the north side. He gave bequests for the fabric of Bolton Abbey and to the Kirk for work at Ripon, also to the Abbot of Cloverham, Middleham, for him to pray for his soul and for prayers for his brother William and his son John, his brother Roger and his sons William and John, appointing his wife as executrix.

William's uncle, also William, born 1490, became Rector of Houghton-le-Spring, County Durham in 1522. He was Chancellor to Bishops Ruthal, Wolsey and Tunstall, becoming Dean of Windsor in 1538, and died in 1557 as Rector of Chalfont, Buckingham. He was said to have been a prominent and remarkable man, surviving the stirring times in which he lived.

Hugh (1503) children:

> William born around 1528, he died 1589, having married with no issue.

> Edward 1529, being known as Edward Franck, recorded in 1583 he had messuages and land at Hovyngham, south of Pickering, near Ness in Rydale.

> Girl details unknown.

> Richard 1530, known as Richard of York.

> **Johes or John** 1532, died 6th Dec 1616 being Johes de Franckland aka Franckland de Glaisdale.

> Peter 1534, Peter or Petri, as denoted in records.

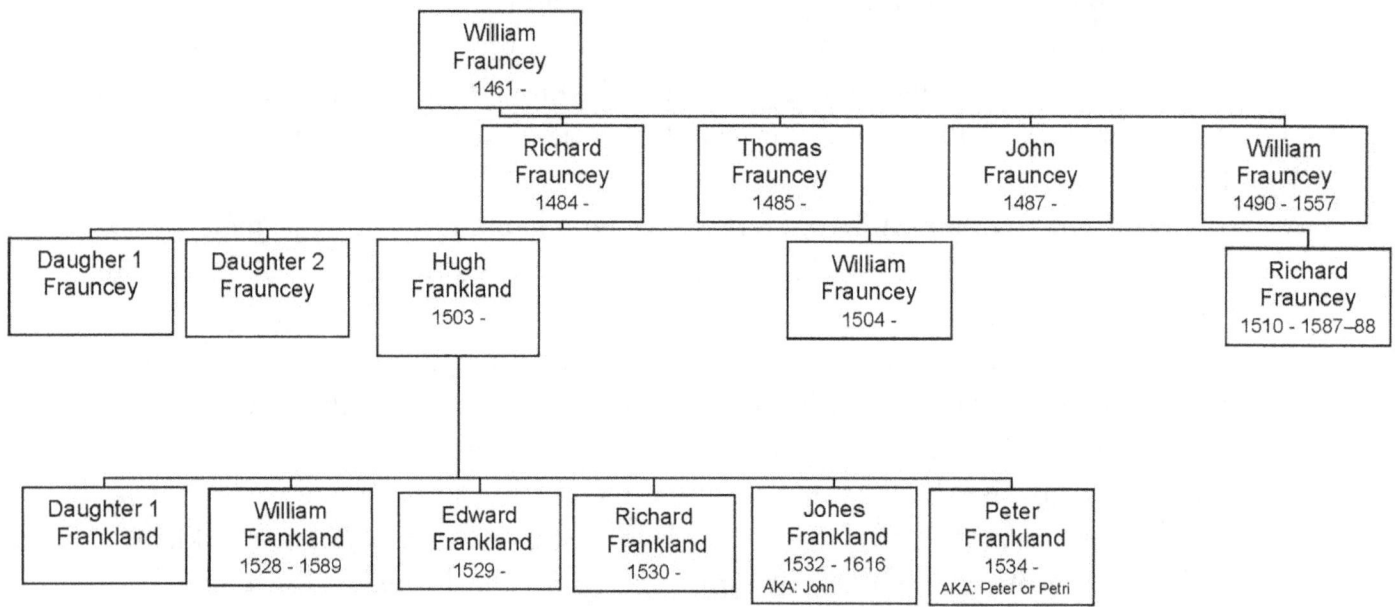

The name Frank and Frankland in relation to Danby, Glaisdale and surrounds

At Whitby, dated 1532, concerning Christanse Franke, the transcript:

> 'Viduse (widow) hoc anno de iiii s de r. red I cot. ib. ibid, ibidum etc. …'

The above roughly translates as:

> 'Widow deprived this yearly produce about … and about to repeat in the same place …'

This poor transcript follows a previous statement regarding a case against Gregory Conyers of Whitby Abbey for oppressing poor widows, and of misleading the Abbot, also to the violation of past engagements. But what of the Conyers and how this fits in? I previously confirmed the Conyers coming from Coigneries France and, like many surnames of the period, the name Conyers is a good example of its French origins. Similar to the Franks and the de Brus, once in Britain the Conyer family graduated north, Sir John and his family settling the other side of the River Tees between Darlington and Durham. All three, the de Brus, Frank and Conyers having common heritage would have had dealings. But being Norman and being hot-headed had its downsides. In terms of wielding power, seen as their right, Conyers was not adverse to being a bully. The above transcript describing Christanse Franke as a widow, its translation shows a member of the Conyers family flaunting his power and authority, the Conyers not so different from others of their kind, always persuasive of wealth and power and the downtrodden viewed as mere fodder.

The Royal Commission survey of St Mary's Abbey, 1539, through the Dissolution, enabled the purchase of land, with the date of around 1557 being fixed for the purchase of Danby Forest.

The name Frankland appeared in Langbaurgh (Cleveland) through the holdings of a Peter Frankland indicated around 1557. Coincidentally, on the 15th July, the plaintiff Agnes Hoggard brought an action against the defendant Robert Frankelande at Danby Whisk, Glaisdale: it appears in relation to maintenance, indications being he had fathered her child.

Born in 1534, Peter Franckland had messuages and land in Danby close to his brother John de Glaisdale shown dated 1558. He had a son, Petri born 1567 and a daughter Jana who married Robtus Featherstone in 1610. Jana had five girls and one boy, Jana dying in 1677. The Frankland purchase of Danby Forest took place in 1557 when Hugh's sons would have been in their mid twenties.

By 1568 Peter Frankland had increased his messuages and land in Glaisdale and Danby Forest, the same land later predecessor Robert Frank held his estate. One hundred years later, a Michael was born in Danby to Petri (Peter) Franke, 15th May 1654, Peter's progeny using the surname Frankland. A decision to drop 'land' from Frankland was taken by some Frankland around 1590, their faith as Catholics a precursor for persecution. For example, formerly Frankland, Petri Franck, was shown as being bereft following the death of his wife Margareta on the 2nd August 1611.

Gradually a growing number Protestant Franklands adopted the shortened version of Frank. As a close-knit farming community with bordering farms, the intervening period saw the rapid escalation of Franks continuing their spill across the Dales and into other areas of employment, whereas the more superlative Franklands kept together as a seemingly transcendent entity anxiously rubbing shoulders with their more confident counterparts.

Exacerbated through lack of male progeny, Frankland numbers continued to decline. Despite their late conversion as absent Catholics it seems the few remaining Franklands stuck together, born of the common need for survival, the Danby Franklands shrinking to a single family. Within 300 years, this offshoot of the Thirkleby dynasty quietly faded, leaving a final determinate legacy in the form of the Franklin Trust.

Joseph Frankland, farmer of Danby, left his estate in favour of his daughter Mary Agar Frankland, who in the period 1838–1885 bequeathed the Trust. It transpires, taxes being due, Joseph's farm, together with the residue of all Frankland land and property was wound up, so ending the Frankland adventure. Yet, why the Franklin

Trust and not Frankland is a question I have been unable to answer. Also the question of why my maternal parentage, the Franks, contrary their Frankland cousins, continued to prosper, seems more than a question of fate.

Having adjoining estates, their interrelationship is unquestioned: their birth, death and marriage records, and common burial plot records intermingle to the extent that Franklands often resorted to Frank as a way of distinguishing between family members, especially for favoured family names such as John. This often caused problems with research suddenly faced with a deluge of Johns: how to distinguish one from the other? A suspicion of awkwardness between the Franks and Franklands seems to have been that of hauteur on the part of the Franklands. Clinging to a latent superiority belonging to the Thirkleby pedigree, its domain and the barony skirting the Dales, Frankland became a secondary and indirect title belonging Sir James Assheton Frankland, the second of two titles coming via James's father's marriage to the sixteenth Baroness Zouche, Mary Cecil Frankland, culminating in both the baronies of Zouche and Frankland.

Whereas the Danby Franklands were doomed, the Franks had deftly switched allegiance to the Protestant faith, later becoming staunch Methodists, the more pragmatic Franklands gradually dropping the latter part of their name, in the end the stronger Glaisdale Franks becoming the inevitable survivors facing the twentieth century.

The period 1557–1597 was awful, Elizabethan England being a dangerous place. Between the years 1557 and 1559 the bubonic plague raged, Queen Elizabeth nearly dying through smallpox in 1562. It was through this period and what people had to endure that brought about suspicion and thoughts of evil doing: the Church and public alike venting their rage mostly on women who were publicly stripped and burnt or hanged, witchcraft being registered after 1563 as a potential form of murder. The following two years, 1564–1565, were followed by extremely harsh winters. Never properly recovering, thirty years later, by 1594–1597, wholesale famine raged across the country.

Catholic subversion and assassination plots were foiled by intensive surveillance, leading to imprisonment, torture and execution. As punishment upon a suspect household, hamlet or community, women were often randomly accused of prostitution, witchcraft or adultery and without proof wrenched from their family as a means of instilling submission through terror. Hapless menfolk were often taken away or publicly executed on a whim, oblivious as to what offence they had caused.

Coming from a Catholic heritage, set against this background, it is amazing that for some recalcitrant souls the apparent normality of everyday business continued unabated. Something inherent correlative to pragmatism must have prevailed within the Franco-Norman mien, to a man the Franks were now staunchly Protestant.

Indefatigable, dogged, resolute, intractable, as if detached from the greater world, their focus a well-ploughed field, as if wrapped in an impenetrable cloak of immunity, the next crop assured in the assuredness and magnificence bestowed the Almighty, the cycle of nature and prayer as one, and faith become 'trust ye in me', one hand upon the Bible.

The manor of Ness, reinstatement of the Frankland arms, and purchase of Danby Forest

In 1086, 500 years prior to the mid 1500s, Richard de Surdeval held Barton and Ness together with fifty-three other manors of the Count of Mortain. At the time, Mortain, in the Manche Department of Normandy, remained the homeland of the Francais and de Brus, who retained lands there. Parentally lords or dukes, they shared a common ancestry, the younger Francais being enfeoffed to the de Brus as knights. In the next reign, just as the Domesday survey was brought to conclusion, the group of manors including Barton and Ness were shown to be in the possession of Ralph Paynell.

The true history of Ness is horrific. Ness lies within Bertona, Barton-in-Hold-elelith, a parish on the southern slope of the fertile valley of Rydale, the area comprising some 3540 acres, of which 1818 acres were then arable farmland and 412 woodland. Today's manor house sits on the site of the former manor. The villages were devastated in the fourteenth century, first by the Scots and afterwards by the Black Death from which all but a couple of residents died. In 1381 the area was once again savaged, being visited by the plague.

An example of the Franks part in the ongoing war between England and Scotland is shown in one such incident summed up in Thomas Tonge's visitation of 1530. As Norray, King of Arms, his visitation staged at the monastery of Durham added to Frankelyng and his existing arms:

> 'Master William Frankelyng, Archdeacon of Durham, given Arms agent, between two saltires engrailed, a pale gules charged with a dolphin hauriant of the field.'

> 'On a chief azure a lion rampant argent between two birds or, collared azure.'

> 'These arms of Master Frankelyng were given to the said Mr Franklin for recovering the Castle of Norham oute of the Scotts liandes by his prowers and pollice.'

The Franks were thinly spread across the north, also present in Durham in juxtaposition to their Scottish Borders, holdings including Ayton on the Scottish coast and their Yorkshire domain. And due to the Scots occupation of the north, Durham was where much of the in-between business of governance and trade was conducted. The Bishop of Durham had the unique title of Bishop by Divine Providence, enjoying extraordinary powers, the city having its own parliament.

In terms of survival, what is amazing is how the Franks managed the trick of seeming passive and at the same time trusted, working between several opposing sides generation upon generation. In a very different way, so far north and vulnerable as a defence against the Scots, Durham Castle was the only Norman keep never to be breached. And the answer for the Frank's survival must lie in the dimidiation between the established Scots bipartite kinship with their southern counterparts. On the surface separate, but in truth maintaining ties with their Yorkshire kin either directly or via the de Brus and their Skelton stronghold. Despite their known allegiances, how the Franks managed the trick of maintaining the middle ground seems to me an enigma.

The stresses and strains on this tenuous bond had worn thin; the present love between known families began to fracture. And having quite separate aims and survival strategies the kinship quickly diminished, their dynasties separately and slowly fading towards obscurity. Yet the Yorkshire contingent of Franks hadn't given up, they were basically landsmen and farming sustained them despite the high mortality rate prevalent at the time. The clan consisted of cousin-related families scattered across the landscape, ranging from the dirt poor to the better off, the wealthier somewhat aloof and obdurate to the idea of an impoverished underclass bearing their name.

Despite shared blood, this was a trait that carried through the Franks, irremovable, deep-rooted, superior, assumptive of one's station and standing within the community, each in their own way stubborn and proud, yet obliged to rub shoulders across field boundaries, necessity finding common cause where politeness and the need to cooperate during harvest time became a necessity. Finding a way through their stalwart Norman pride they acknowledged both their sameness and separate situate *pari-passu*. And much as two estranged brothers might find difficulty in finding commonality, their natural kinship so deeply suppressed as to cause both estrangeship and recognition as if through a looking glass and seeing the pain reflected in each other and themselves, both awkward and ashamed in equal measure.

THE MAIN WILLIELMUS LINE THROUGH HUGH FRANCKLAND AND HIS SON JOHN, PATER DE FAMILIAS FRANKLAND, AND FRANKE AS A SURNAME.

Early on, Petri Franckland, styled himself as coming from around the area of Ness in the Wapentake of Bulraer, Bulraer covering an area north of York across to Malton and Pickering in the north and Helmsley and Easingwold to the west. The Franks I have been able to associate with Ness are Henry Frank and Hugh Franckland who, while resident in 1566, had their 'ancient arms and crest' demised and re-granted. Research has ascertained Hugh Franckland coming of a larger family within the Hambleton Hills, a stone's throw of Ness, bounding Thirkleby.

The status of the Franks was significant, as by 1598 Ness and its surrounds were in the hands of the Queen for payment of debt. Provisionally leased to Sir Richard Martin, in 1600 Hugh Frankland claimed the manor and rectory under lease from Thomas Grey, Thomas Grey being the son of Elizabeth Woodville and John Grey. Following John Grey's death, Elizabeth's second marriage to King Edward IV, made her Queen Consort of England, not a family to be trifled with.

It was during this time of distraction that one of Grey's sons, George, took it upon himself to convey the manor of Ness to one John Darcy, at which point Hugh Frankland lost interest in the whole thing, sensibly cut his losses and looked elsewhere to invest. And through his family, that elsewhere was Danby Forest. Henry had already moved on when in 1583, having obtained property at Worsall near Yarm, he obtained holdings at Middleton Tyas, close to present-day Scotch Corner on the A66 and A1.

Incidental to Hugh's abortive attempt to purchase the Manor of Ness; Ness lying south of Kirkbymoorside adjacent the River Rye, the Rye of Rydale not to be confused with the quite separate Rye in Hertfordshire. The Hertfordshire Rye coincidentally relates to Hugh's uncle, William of Rye, from whom the family derived substantial wealth. The story of how William of Yorkshire became associated with London and be termed William of Rye, Hertfordshire, is found separately within this work.

The coming together of three distinct family groups of different lifestyles, and the trigger for the purchase of the previous de Brus lands of Danby Forest and its surrounds, was in part influenced by land already ceded to the Franks by the Danby family, this and its availability augured considerable value in terms of wood and mining. Estranged but long-established Frank cousins already farmed and raised sheep across the Dales, also their uncle, Sir William, had family links to their Hutton-le-Hole holdings and the weaving carried out there. And it was through the monasteries that William became famous in the wool trade, and it's here in London, having gained the personal friendship of the King, he was granted a knighthood.

For me the apparent absence of arms specifically for the Cleveland Franks had long been a bone of contention; one having assumed such arms as did exist were those of the Franks who ventured north into Scotland. Hence my delight in finding local arms wherein, as for and on behalf of the King, given by William Flower Norray on his heraldic visitation of the northern counties in 1566, his findings read:

> '**Hugh Francklyn,** alias Franckland, of Nessistge in the Countye of York, Gentillman, is dessended of a house of long-time bearing arms and he being uncertayne under what mannor and forme his ancestors beare there crest, he hath required of me to assigne these his old auncient arms a creast. I have demised given and granted upon his helme, on a tors gold and azure, a demy dolfine argent; mantled guls, dubled gold – to have and to hold said creast to the said Hugh Franckland, gentillman and his posteritie. The arms as drawn are a dolphin embowed, on a chief three saltires.'

Henry Frank, gentillman

Hugh and Henry lived at Nessistge, being Ness East Ridge, a village seven miles due south of Helmsley–Kirkbymoorside on the River Rye split between two land-loads, located a stone's throw from my grandfather Thomas Henry Frank's later moorland holdings. In 1530, the following additions were granted to arms already held by Henry Franke, Henry being immediately related to Hugh Franckland of Ness.

For Henry (my grandfather's middle name) there is the addition:

> '**Henry Frank** (Franke) gentillman, vert, a saltue engrailed or, in posteritas.'

Henry Franke held land at Worsall, Yarm, in 1583, also land at Middleton Tyas, close to Scotch Corner, with sixteen miles separating each holding. Significantly, Henry Franke's holdings sat adjacent to Frankland territory; my maternal grandfather being christened Thomas Henry Frank, his name passed down generationally, as with the arms, having direct descent. Granddad had family connections with Worsall linked with those of his immediate family close to nearby Yarm, Barwick and its adjacent farms. The relationship proving more than a passing coincidence, the above arms assume a direct antecedence to Tom Frank's daughter, Dorothy Frank and hence to myself, her firstborn.

The main Willielmus line now reaches a confluence with Hugh Frankland (1503) and his son John, aka Johes de Franckland aka Franckland de Glaisdale (1532), our

The Extraordinary Franks

direct family predecessor, with Hugh Francklyn aka Franckland of Nelsing and of Ness in Rydale and his two brothers having direct links with Blubberhouses and Thirkleby, which line through Hugh is inextricably linked to one's immediate line of succession. This in turn is related through the Cleveland branch via their Scottish cousins having links with de Brus and the Scottish monarchy, thus by descent to the Frankish realm of Richard, first Duke of Normandy.

The following is a short explanation of Hugh's son John and the beginnings of the Franklands of Cleveland and their relation with the Franks already there:

John (1532) children:

> Stephani 1552. This is a terrible time for the family, children die and the records are difficult to unravel.
>
> William born around 1555 (see below).
>
> Edward 1558, Edward Franck was found with messuages and land at Hovyngham, just south of Pickering in 1583.
>
> **John** 1554, initially known as John the Younger, born around Nov 1554, he died September 1625.

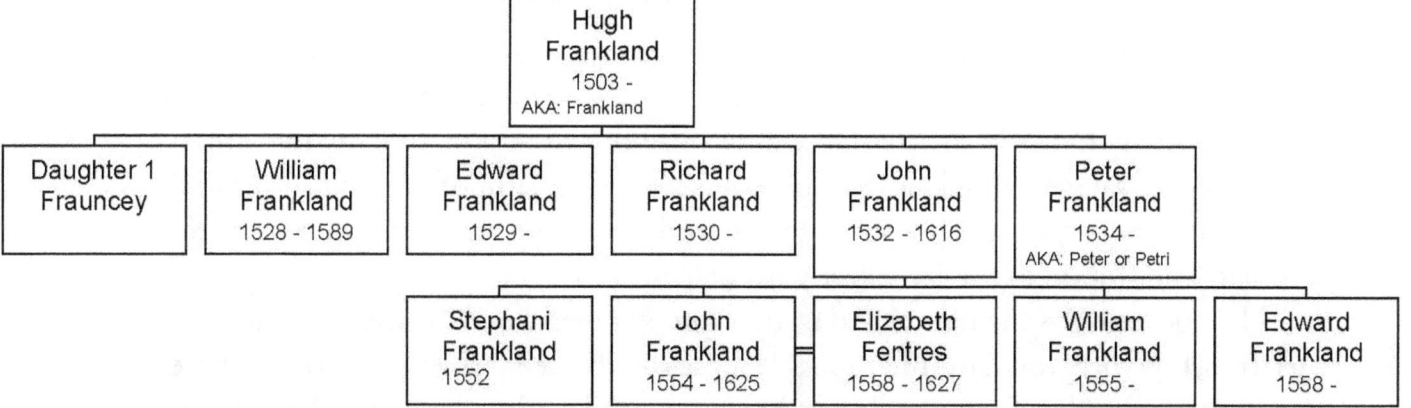

Known as 'Pater de Familias Frankland', John junior was considered to be the originator of the Frankland de Glaisdale meme. Including Danby Forest, in terms of their standing in the community, land ownership was important, having it and working it engendered a sense of pride. Heritage too was important, coming from a well-to-do family, John's status as a spare son presented something of a climb-down faced with the task of deforesting scrubland. Yet the forbearance of fierce determination remained. Imbued with a sense of pride and honour, it had fallen on John's shoulders to uphold the Frankland name and what it represented.

In terms of inheritance, as that of a spare and little in the way of finance, as a gentleman among a strange scattering of Frank cum Frankland yeomen, John had his work cut out. Danby records show the Franklands as a strangely related tight-knit cluster, their later progeny eagerly integrating with the more procreant Franks using the shorten surname Frank or Franke.

At Saltmarsh, Skelton, in the Howden Street Church Warden Accounts, Thomas Frankland arranges for the bell-ringing for his brother John in 1596. The disbursement was approved by William Pearson and paid out by Edward Pearson. Marrying into the Franks, the birth rate of the Pearsons was prolific, its family encroaching disproportionally relating to positions of standing and importance in the community.

Little has been mentioned concerning Hutton-le-Hole. I have already shown the various connections between Hutton, Lastingham and the wool trade relating to the monastery of Fountains Abbey, also something of the Franklands with an explanation of the Franks maintenance of Fountains Abbey and their acquisitions of land around York, and now move on to explain something of Hutton and its early settlement relating to the de Brus of Skelton Castle, and the de Stuteville.

Setting aside the de Brus, the earliest reference to the Franks of Hutton is that of Bernardo Frankeis in 1190. He witnessed a charter of William de Stuteville giving assart, meaning the act of clearing forested land for the use of agriculture, in this case the assart to one John de Ryton 100 years following Domesday. In 1225, Nicholas de Stuteville agreed that the monks of St Mary's Abbey, York, and the men of Hutton could keep as much land as they had cleared in 'Hogtweit'. I hold copies of documentation relating to the clearings and ancient boundaries, the proof of said holdings being found in the charter records of Abbot Robert of York, giving Simon de Riton the same Riding land of fifty-two acres for the sum of 13s 4d per annum. A century and a half later, Bernard Frank paid tax in the amount 10d relating to similar land, found in the lay subsidy list of 1327.

The above shows the nature and stature *Frankas Inexorabilis* as well as their early relationship with York and the monasteries; close to the land yet able to negotiate on behalf of local serfs and landsmen based on family titles. And with their standing close to the King, able to interact with the highest in the land while remaining common to the land they tilled as horn-knuckled workaday farmers, yet at the same time were book educated and possessed of their God-given superior ascent.

Well before the 1400s, surviving male progeny often found themselves having to move on as a means of survival. As a consequence, these interrelated great survivors found themselves spread across the landscape, whose settlement often bounded those of distant cousins.

As has been shown, these families were more mobile than might at first appear. Necessity caused offshoots of the older more static generation to move on, some settling nearby, others further afield. Records show occasional cousin relationships where distance through migration might bring them together again. Evidence of this is shown in the area of Rydale where Willielmus, born around 1276, his son Rogerus, is recorded paying tax in Hutton-le-Hole dated 1327.

Then there is Robert, that old familiar family name. While the historic connection is unclear, an approximate date of birth of 1500 has been set working back from detailed dates relating to his family. For the times he appears to have been someone of stature, a Margaret Frank, possibly his grandmother, widow of Hutton, is recorded granting a messuage and two bovates of land to the monks of St Mary's Abbey in 1446, Robert himself being listed in the Royal Commissioners' survey of the property of St Mary's in 1539 as the third largest tenant in Hoton cum Dowthwayte, being Hutton-le-Hole. In it Robert is shown paying 17s 5d rent on a messuage and eight bovates of land.

Born 1554, John son of John, grandson of Hugh, his line through to the present day continues separate from the following.

The Hutton pedigree

As well as nearby Pickering, the area of Rydale encompassed Hutton, and it is here that John's brothers Thomas and William appear to have settled. Records of this branch of the family appear largely intact relating mostly to the area of Hutton-le-Hole and its surrounds. It is here a Bernard Frankeis appears as a witness to a charter relating to land in Hutton-le-Hole in 1190. And also of that date Bernard 1190, Willielmus 1276, Rogerus 1327, Margaret 1446 and Robert 1500 and 1539 follows with Robert Frank:

Robert (1500) children:

>**John** b. 1530, married Elizabeth Feb 1554. Shown as wife of Johi, Elizabeth b. 1536 d. 25 Dec 1622

>John's burial 28th December 1587 at Lastingham, his will 21st December 1587, Yeoman de Hutton-le-Hole.

>William b. 1532, noted in brother John's will

>Thomas b. 1534, in brother John's will, indicated 21 Dec 1587

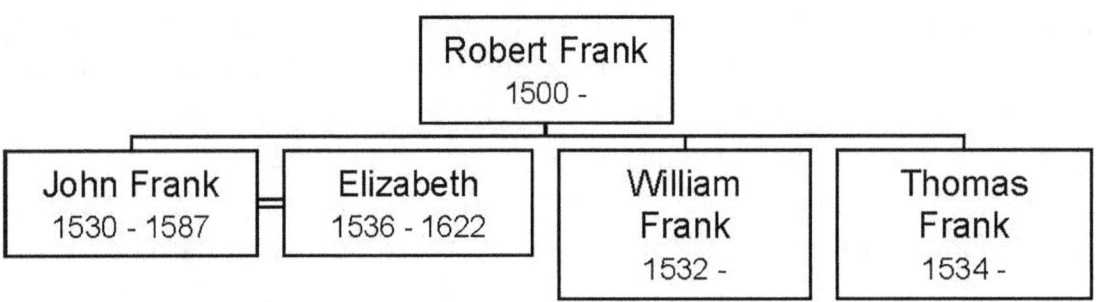

In 1596 there was a legal dispute between Robert and George (below) concerning a messuage with land in Hutton and Spaunton. As ascertained in The Franks: a yeoman family of Hutton-le Hole by Bertram Frank, the area of dispute was probably over Lund House where Hutton-Spaunton's boundary ran through farm buildings.

John (1530) children:

> William b. 1559 (has child)
>
> **Robert** b. 1555, married 2nd wife Christobel Appleby 1595
>
> Nicholas b. 1561
>
> John b. 1557, had a son **Thomas** who died in 1671. Thomas was a Parish Records Plaintiff in 1596
>
> Georgii b. 1563, married Marie Robinson in 1602
>
> Alice b. 1565, had a daughter, Elizabeth

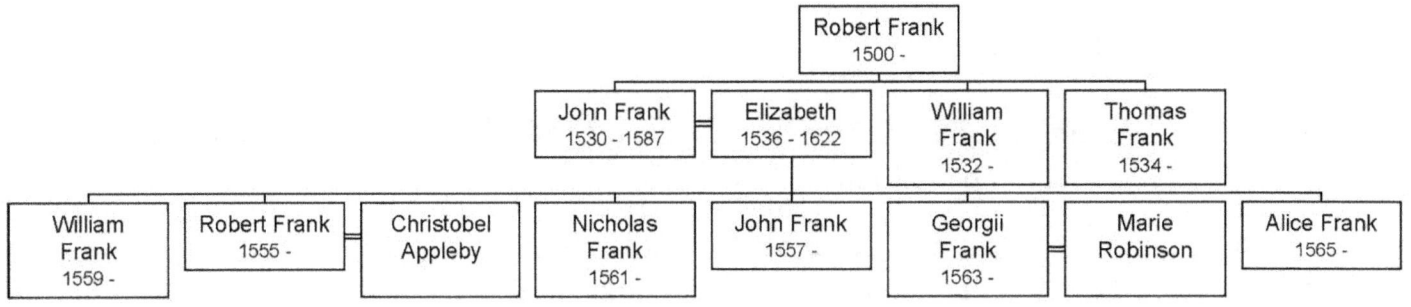

Robert (1555) children:

> Isobella b. 1601
>
> Robert b. 1603
>
> William b. 1605

The Extraordinary Franks

Nicholas b. 1606

Grace b. 1608

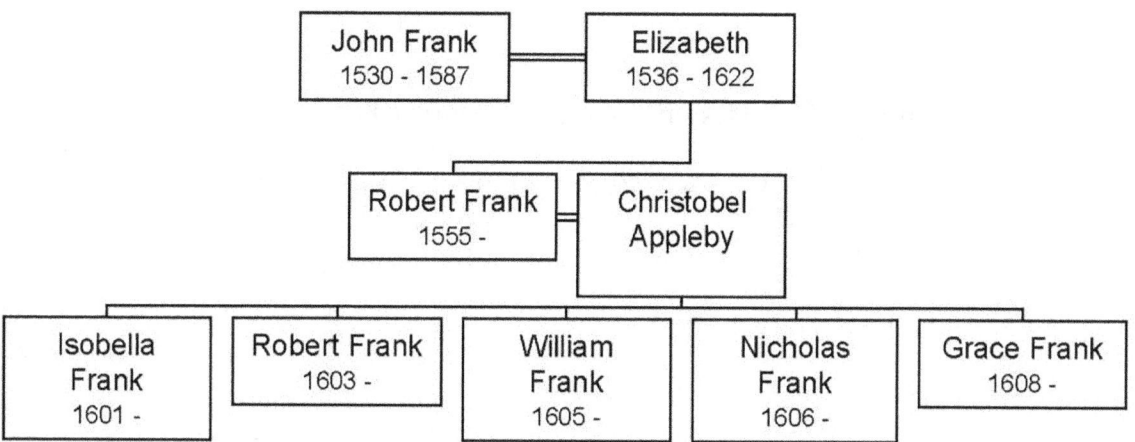

Continuing John's line (1557) through his son Thomas

Thomas (d.1671) children:

    Alicia b. 1639

    Jane d. 1614

    Robert b. 1635

    *Richard b. 1642

    *John b. 1644

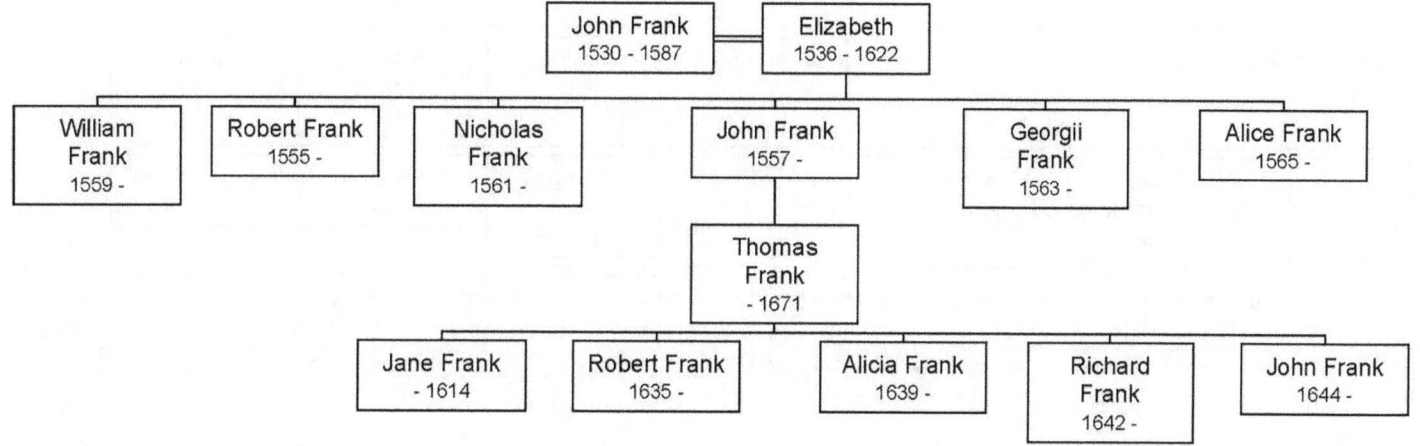

Thomas (father), Richard and John (above*) paid Hearth Tax 1660–1670.

Robert (1635) children:

> Thomas b. 1667
>
> *William b. 1669, assessed tax for war against France
>
> **John** b. 1672, d. 1761. Married Ann Johnson 1702 (b. 1683, d. 1759)
>
> George b. 1674
>
> Alicia b. 1677
>
> Robert b. 1680

John (1672) children:

> Ann b. 1703
>
> **Robert** b. 1710 d. 1757. Married Ellis (Alice) Watson 1730 (d. 1756)
>
> Francis b. unknown, d. 1721
>
> **Thomas** b. 1721, baptised 1722. Farmer of Hutton-le-Hole. Married Catherine Edwards 1759 (1737–1809, aged 73)

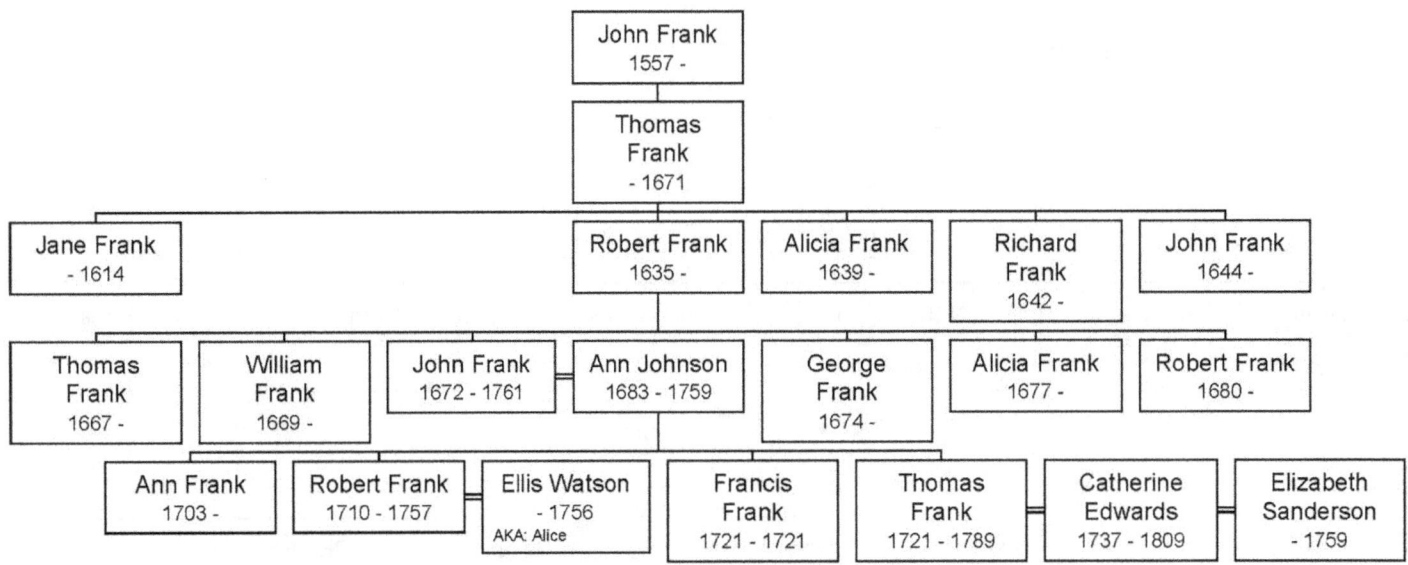

There is record of the above Thomas (1721) having married Elizabeth Sanderson 10th June 1755. Witnessed by Mary Frank, due to Thomas's age, it seems likely this was a first marriage, Elizabeth having subsequently died. Records confirm the

The Extraordinary Franks

Thomas's birth date being correct and a child being born prior to Thomas's second marriage to Catherine. Thomas Frank was recorded as 'Gentleman of Oxclose' who died in 1789 aged 67.

Robert's tree continues here. The other branch relating to Thomas Frank, his tree continues separately.

Robert (1710) children:

> Robert 1733–1736
>
> *Ann b. 1735
>
> Ellis b. 1768
>
> ***Robert** b. 1737, baptised 1738, d. 1811. Married Elizabeth Coulson 1761
>
> (1734–1817)
>
> John b. 1742
>
> Elizabeth b. 1745
>
> Thomas b. 1746
>
> William b. 1751

*The above Robert Frank, weaver, is shown in the Hutton-le-Hole Parish Church register, baptised 1738. The 1739 assessment for Aid to His Majesty Land Tax shows the following payments; Robert Frank 7s 8d, John Frank 11s 8d, Ann Frank 6d.

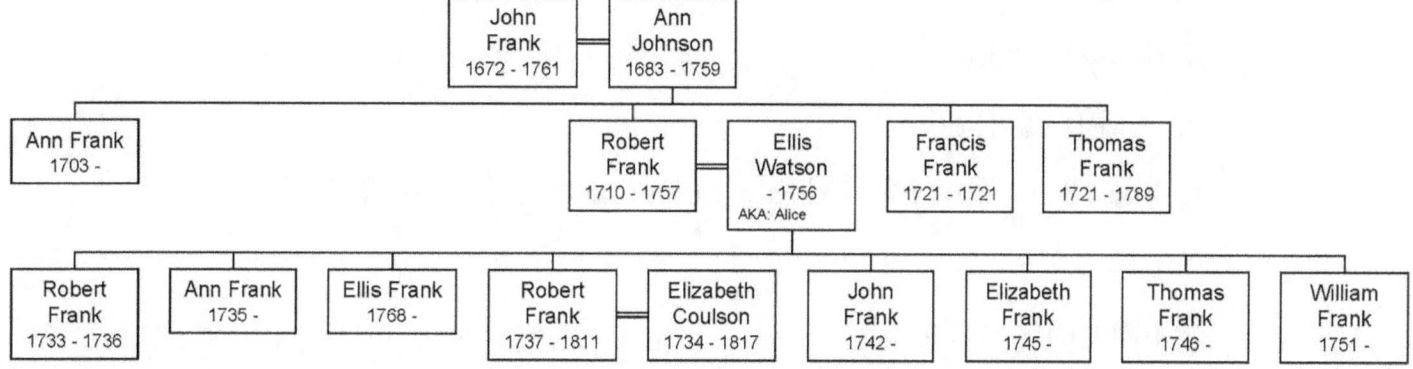

Robert (1737) children:

    Robert 1762–1837

    John 1766–1810

    Anne b. 1768

    Edward 1769–1847. Married Elizabeth Walker (1779–1861)

    Thomas b. 1772

    Sally b. 1774

    Betty b. 1775

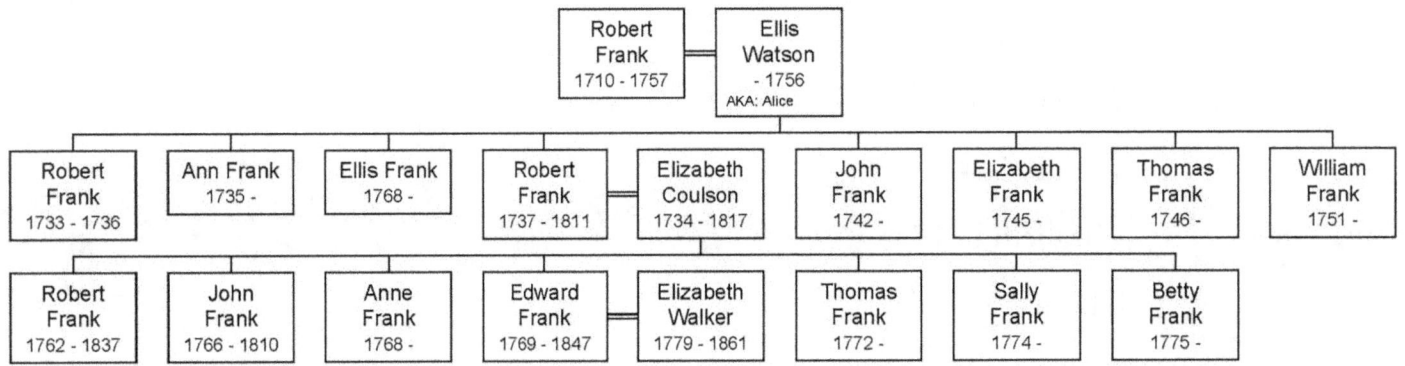

Edward (1769) children:

    Robert 1800–1876

    Thomas 1802–1892

    Anthony b. 1806

    Edward 1808–1866

    Joshua 1811–1898. Married Sally Lumsdon 1843 (1818–1851)

    Anne b. 1814

    William 1817–1893

    Charles b. 1822

The Extraordinary Franks

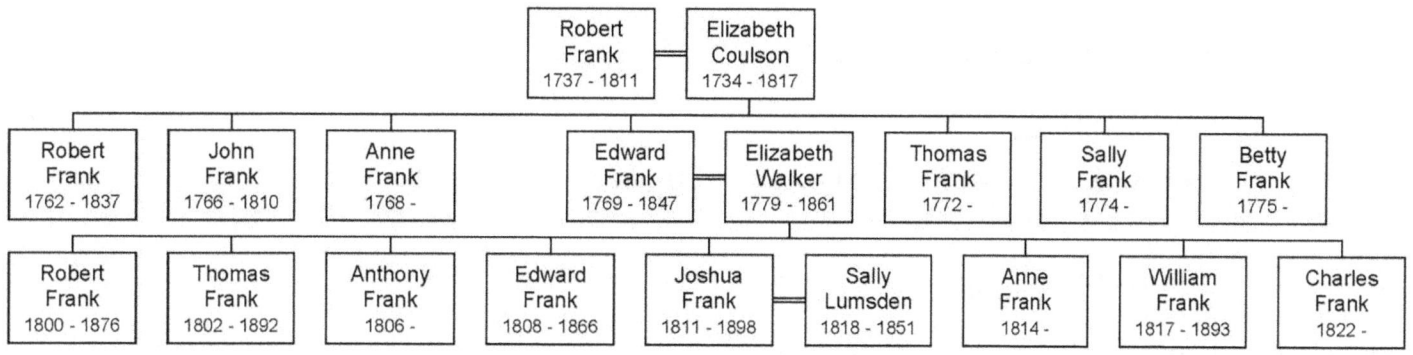

Born 1802, Thomas had a weaving business, exhibiting at the Great Exhibition at Chrystal Palace, London, in 1851, travelling with his brother Joshua by stagecoach; the great family Bible recording his death aged ninety.

As well as weaving, the family had a shop and a knowledge of pharmacy, dispensing remedies for people as well as cures for livestock and poisons for vermin.

Branching out, the brothers went into tanning, paying £20 in 1857 to Lord Faversham for seven tons of larch bark for their tannery at Hutton.

Joshua (1811) children:

Hannah b. 1843

Charles 1848–1931. Married Mary Jane Foster 1874 (1853–1929)

Ruth b. 1845

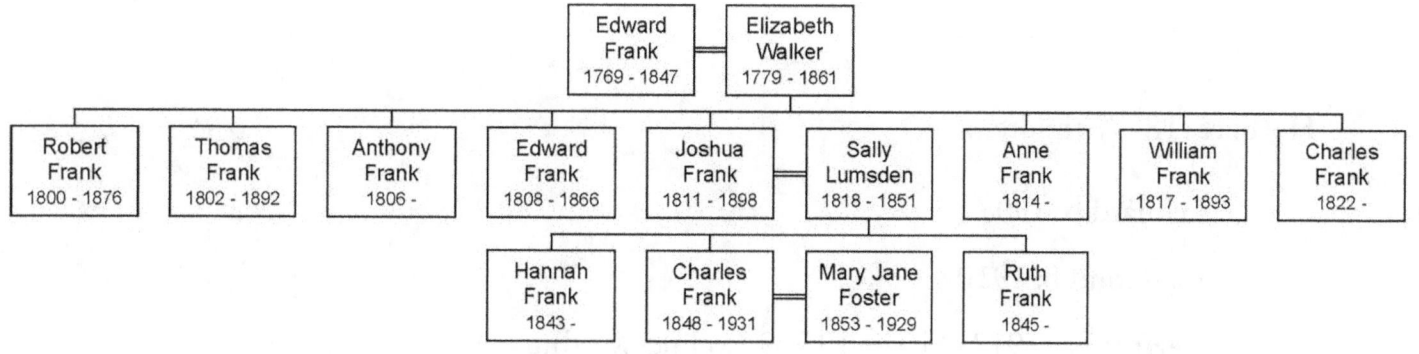

Charles (1848) children:

Wilfred 1875–1956

Hermalinda Jane 1885–1939

Douglas Frank Blackmore

Cyril 1879–1933

Clarice Adelaide 1881–1883

Beatrice 1881–1961

Herbert 1877–1950. Married Margaret Ann Swales 1908 (1885–1973)

Mildred Rosamond 1888–1963

Cordelia Joyce 1891–1976

Olive Myrtle 1894–1929

Annice Evangaline 1895–1900

Ida Leslie b. 1897

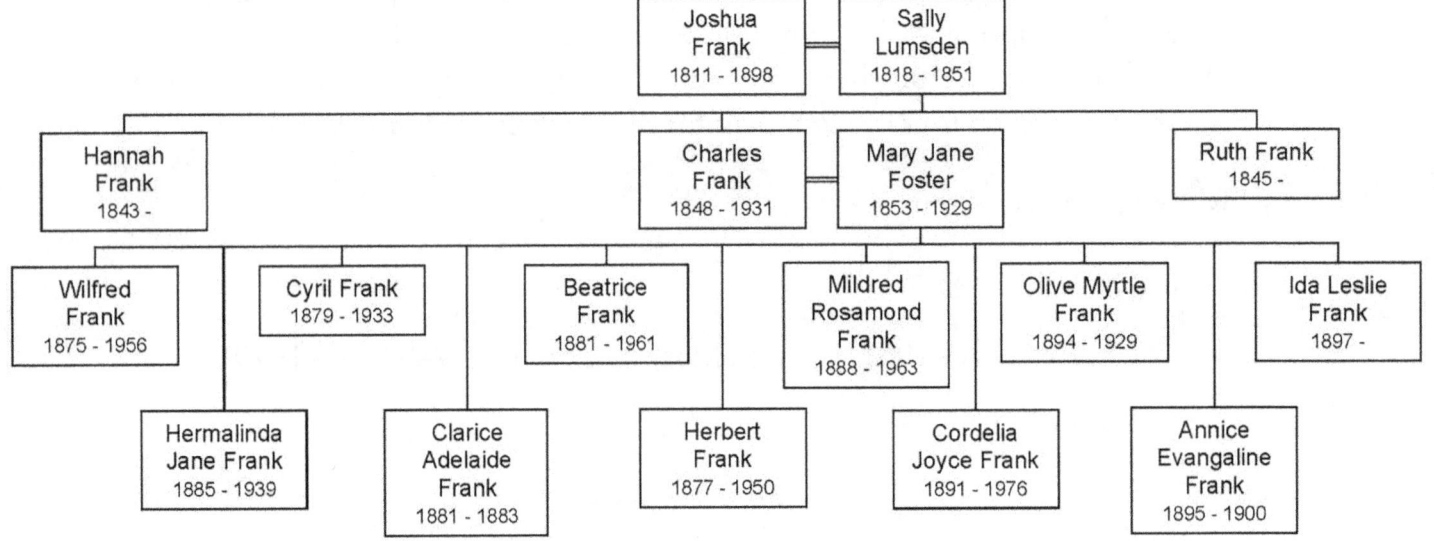

Herbert (1877) children:

Leonard b. 1908

Raymond b. 1910

Bertram b. 1913. Married 1919 Eveline Westbury

Harold b. 1915

Christopher 1918–1943

Annie Doreen b. 1921

The Extraordinary Franks

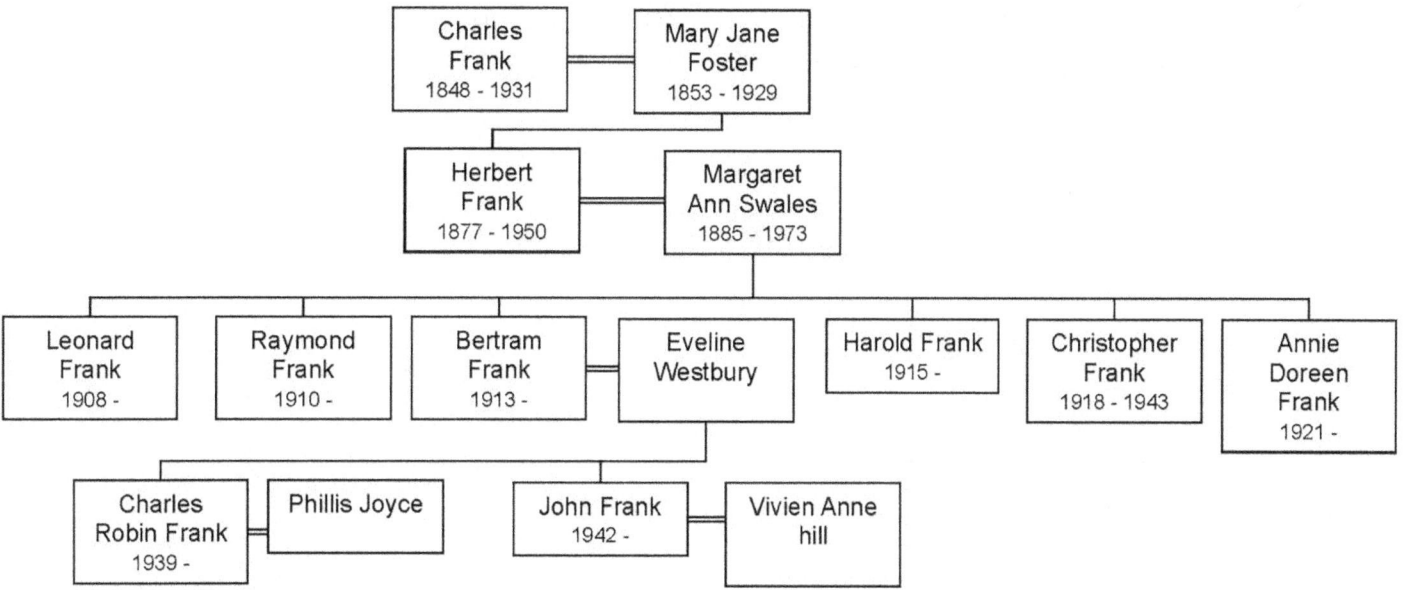

Bertram (1913) children:

    Charles Robin b. 1939. Married Phillis Joyce 1961. Son Gareth Peter b. 1962

    John b. 1942. Married Vivien Anne Hill 1963. Children Martin John (b. 1964) Ann-Marie Julie (b. 1966)

This terminates the Robert branch.

The tree now split at above Robert born 1635. The tree now continues with Thomas Frank, farmer, the William Frank tree to follow after next:

Thomas Frank of Oxclose & Lund Farm's, Hutton-le-Hole, Lastingham

Thomas was born in 1721 to John Frank and Ann Johnson, he married Catherine Edwards (1737–1809) in 1759 who died aged 73.

Thomas (1721) children:

    Thomas 1762–1794

    Nancy 1765–1788

    Betty b. 1767

James (Jemmy) de Lastingham, 1760–1836 aged 77. Married Hannah Dixon (née Hickson 1759–1830) in 1789

Edward 1768–1788

Mary b. 1774

Catherine b. 1776

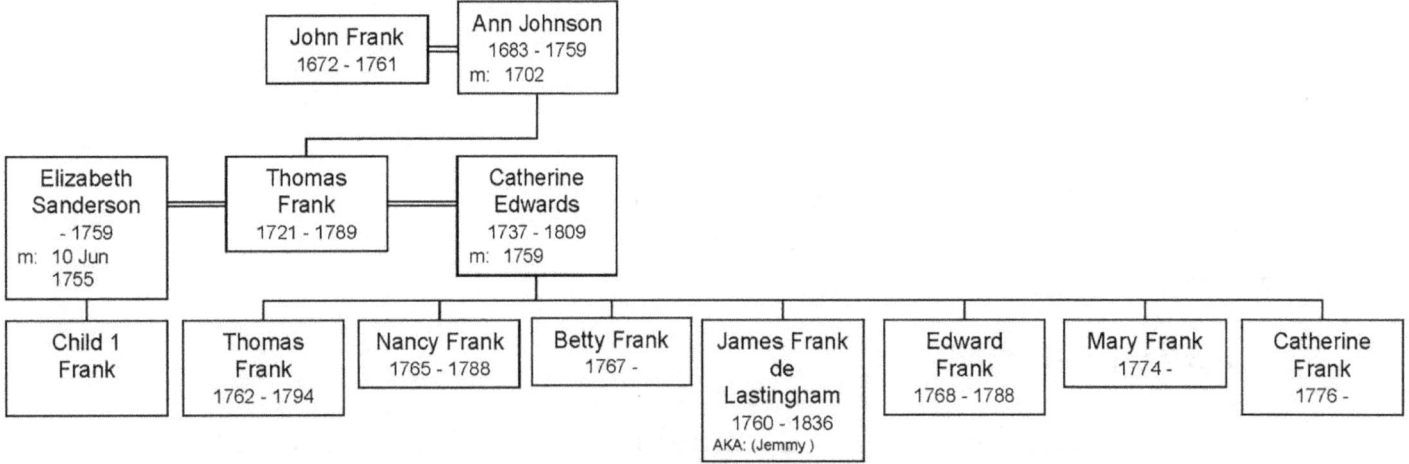

A Rosedale valuation list of 1824 shows James and Edward Frank with eighty-seven-plus acres, James paying £59.00, Edward paying £1.00. Thomas Pierson with twenty-nine acres, Thomas paying £32.00, William paying £1.00. William Shepherd with 252 acres, paying £264.00.

The Piersons and William Shepherd are mentioned due to their subsequent intermarriage with the Franks.

James (1760) children:

    Nancy b. 1790

    Hannah b. 1791

    Polly b. 1793

    Thomas 1795–1873. Marriage 1, 1820 to Jane Strickland (d. 1828),

    marriage 2, 1829 to Mary Fenwick

    James 1796–1883. Married Jane Flintoft 1828 (d. 1875)

    Catherine b. 1798

    Betty 1 1800–1801

    Betty 2 b. 1801

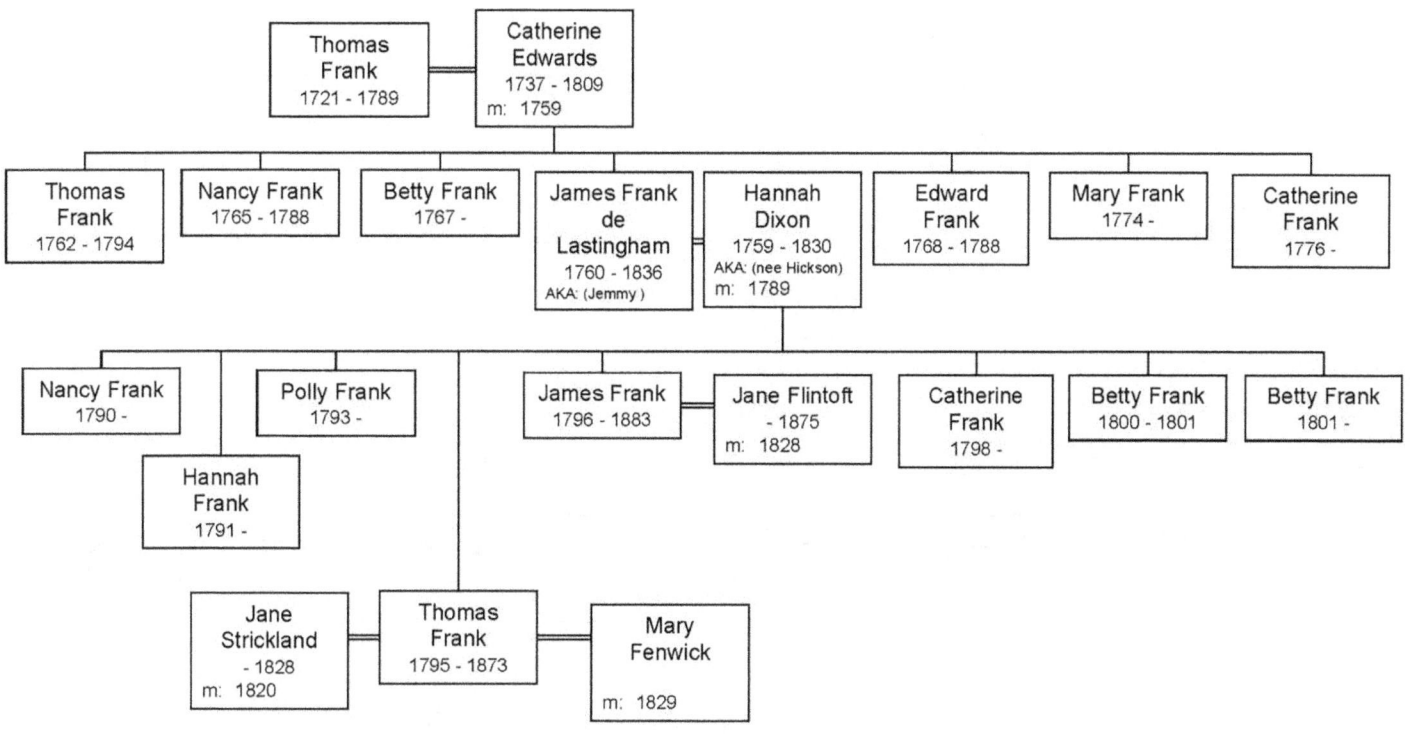

Thomas (1795) children:

To Jane Strickland:

> Manuel b. 1820
>
> Betty b. 1821

To Mary Fenwick:

> Hannah b. 1830
>
> Richard 1833–1919. Married Elizabeth (d. 1901), their son Thomas died in 1906
>
> Jane b. 1835. Married John Farrow 26th Aug 1860. Of Lastingham
>
> James b. 1836
>
> Thomas b. 1839. Married Anne Bulmer 17th June 1875. Daughters Alice
>
> (b. 1876) and Mary (b. 1877)
>
> Edith b. 1842
>
> Sarah b. 1847. Married Wm Bayliff 4th April 1875 aged 28.

Douglas Frank Blackmore

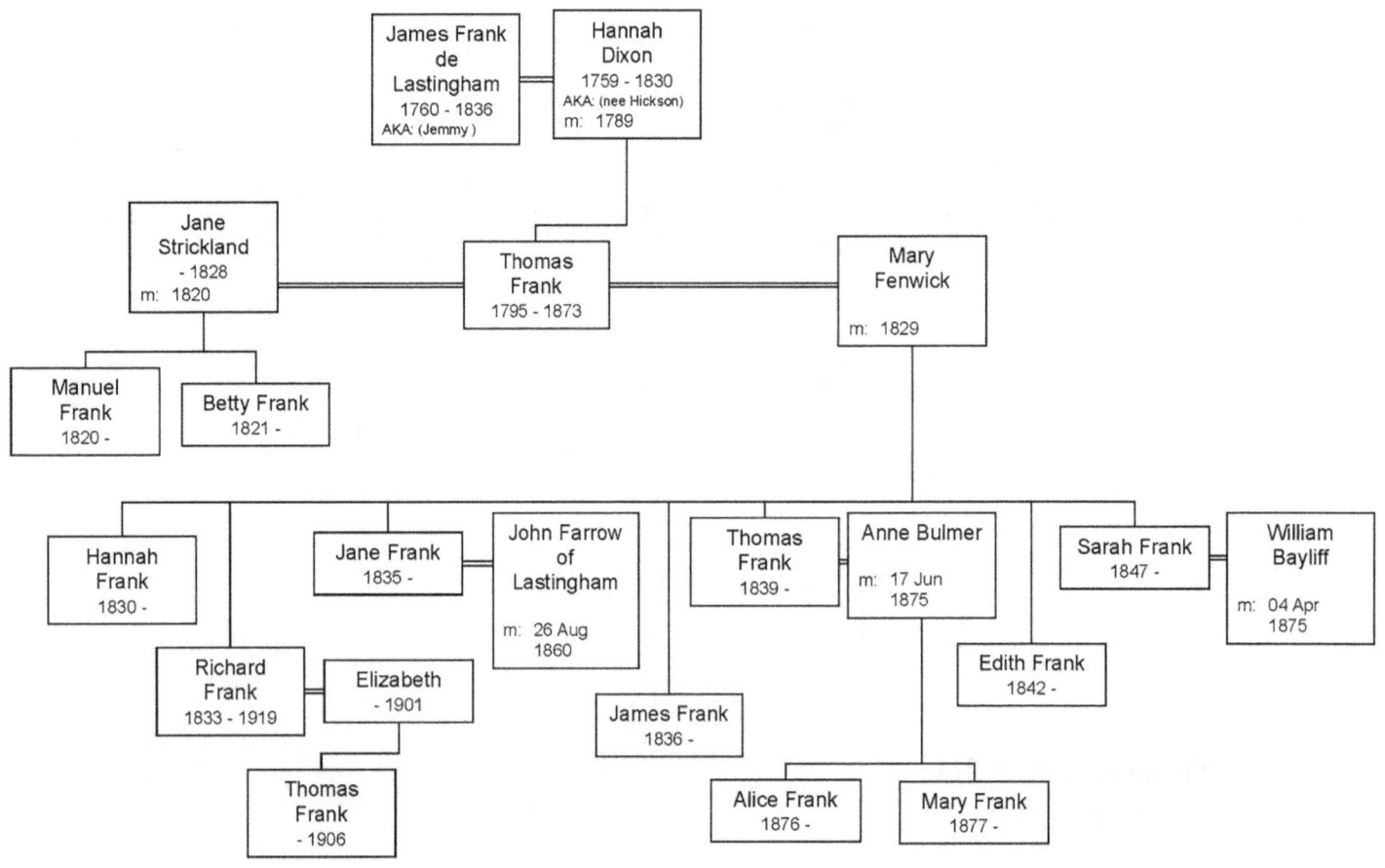

James (1796) children:

    Wilson 1831–1911. Marriage 1 to Tamar Chapman 1853 (d. 1869)

Marriage 2 to Jane Brooke (née Emerson) 1877

    Wilson (1831) children:

To Tamar Chapman:

Mary Jane b. 1854

James 1855–1856 died in infancy, 4th Feb 1856.

James b. 1857

William b. 1862

Ellen b. 1865

Elizabeth b. 1866

Tamar Annie b. 1868

The Extraordinary Franks

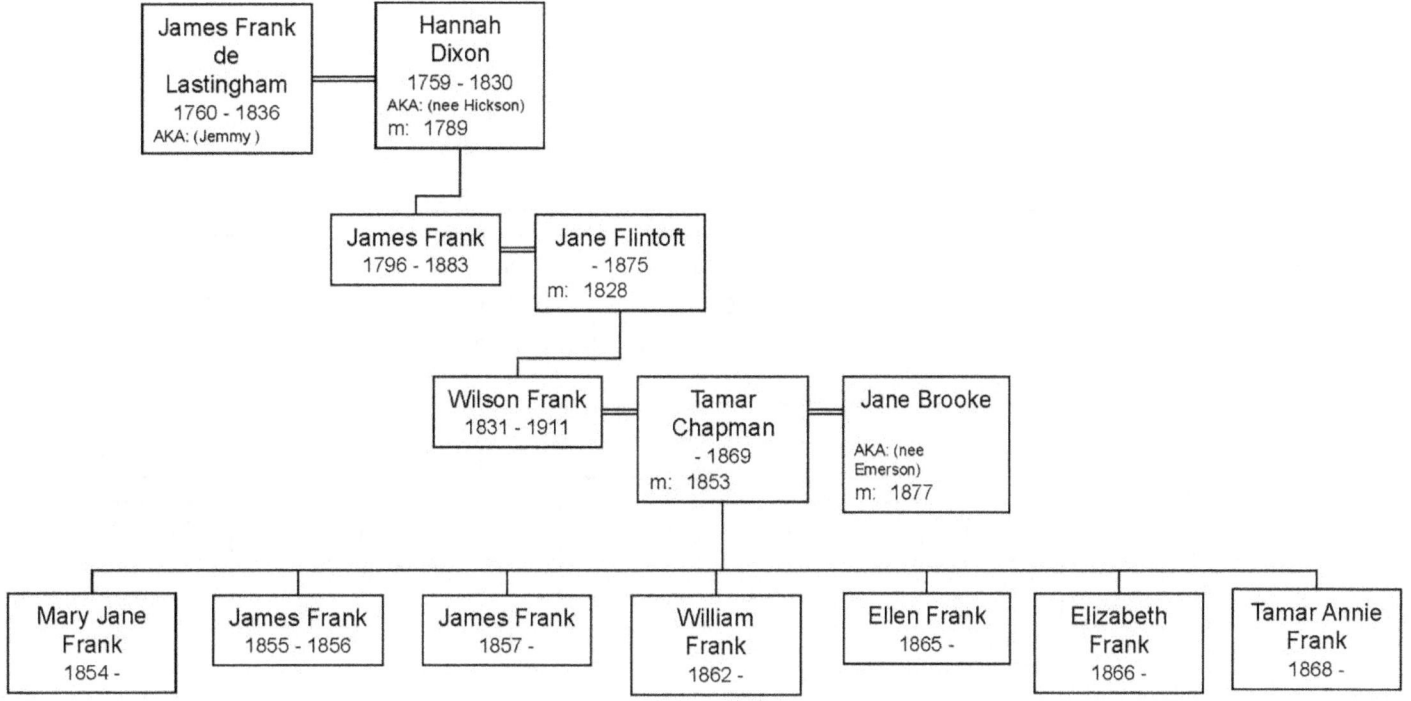

This terminates the Thomas branch.

The William Frankland/Frank tree now continues, William was born around 1555:

William (1555) children:

Catherine

William b. around 1580

Child

Child had a son, Nicholas b. 1620, who had a son, William b. 1645.

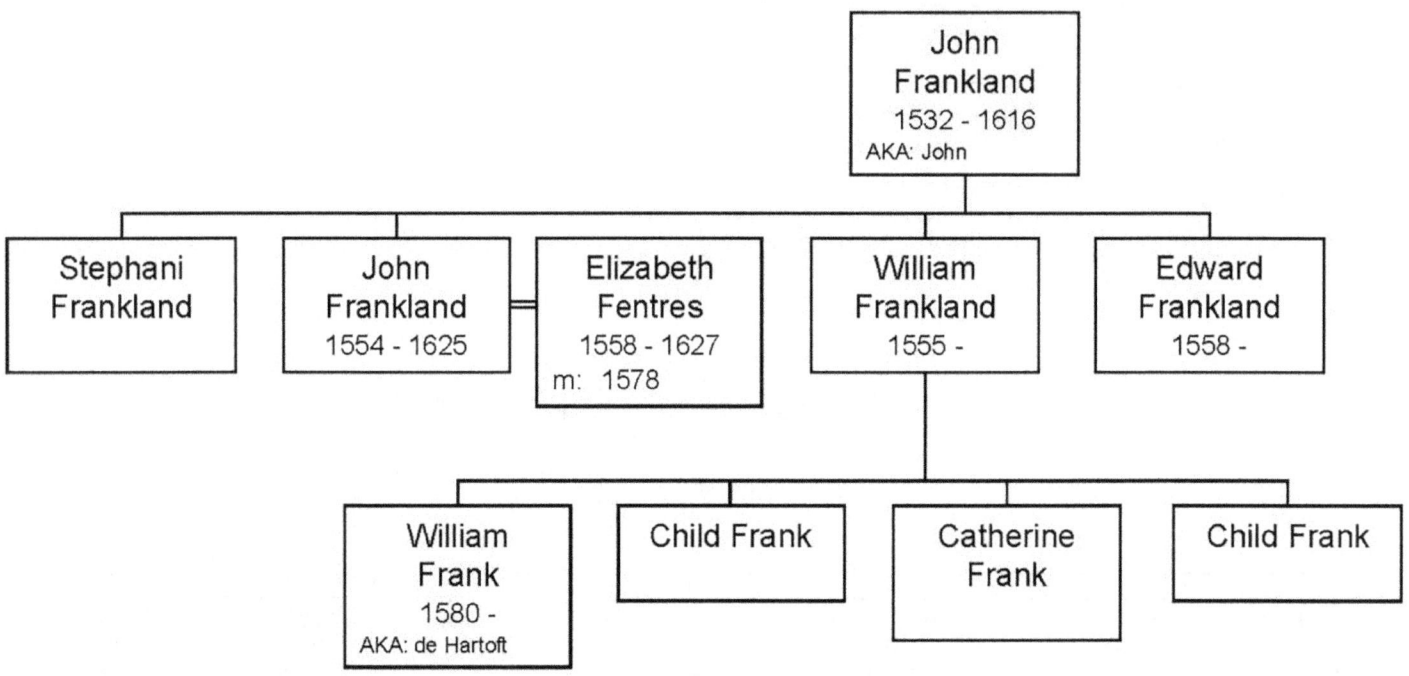

William (1580) children:

    Thomas b. 1610. Married Mary Hobson 1635

    Henry b. around 1615. Had a son, Thomas b. 1640

    William 1615 – 31st May 1685

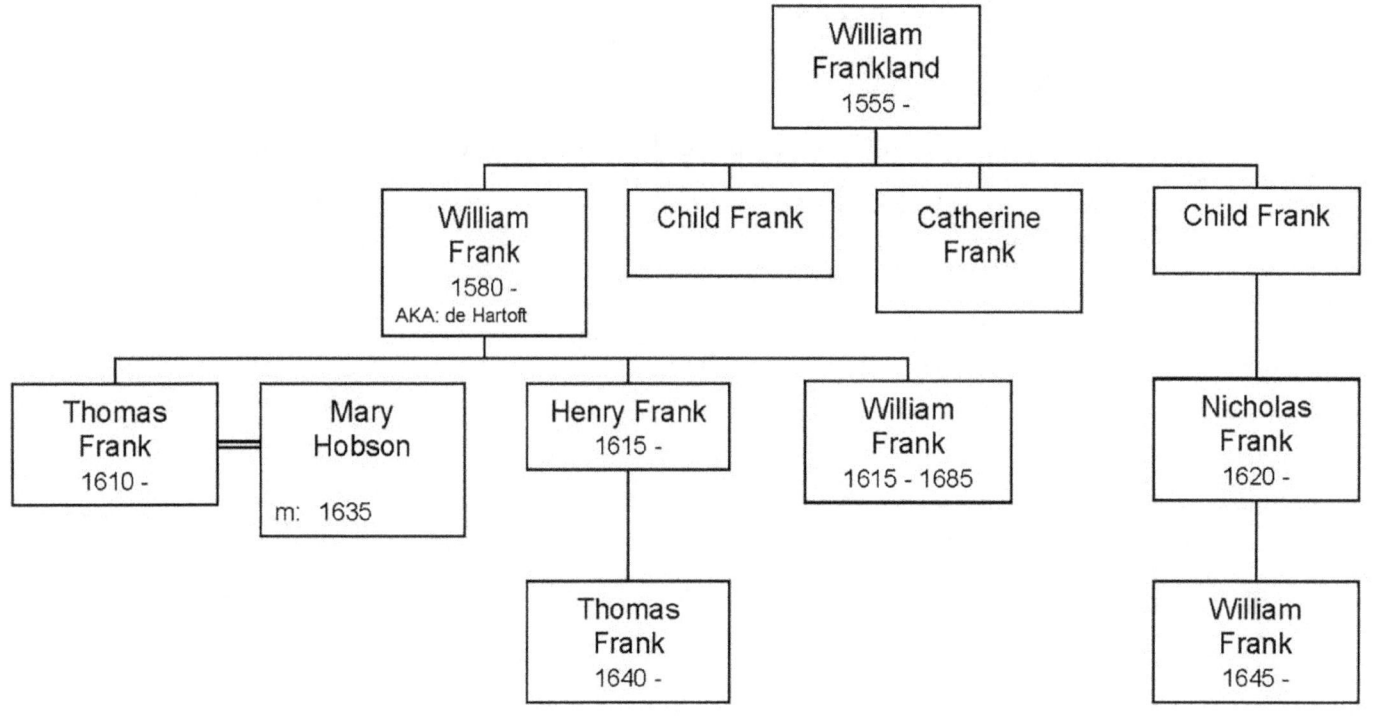

The Extraordinary Franks

Thomas (1610) children:

    Henry b. 1635

    Edward b. 1637. Had a son Robert b 1660

    John b. 1640

Henry (1635) children:

    Robert b. 1660

    John b. 1662

    Henry b. 1679/80

John (1640) children:

    Jane b. 1662

    Robert b. 1664

    George b. 1668

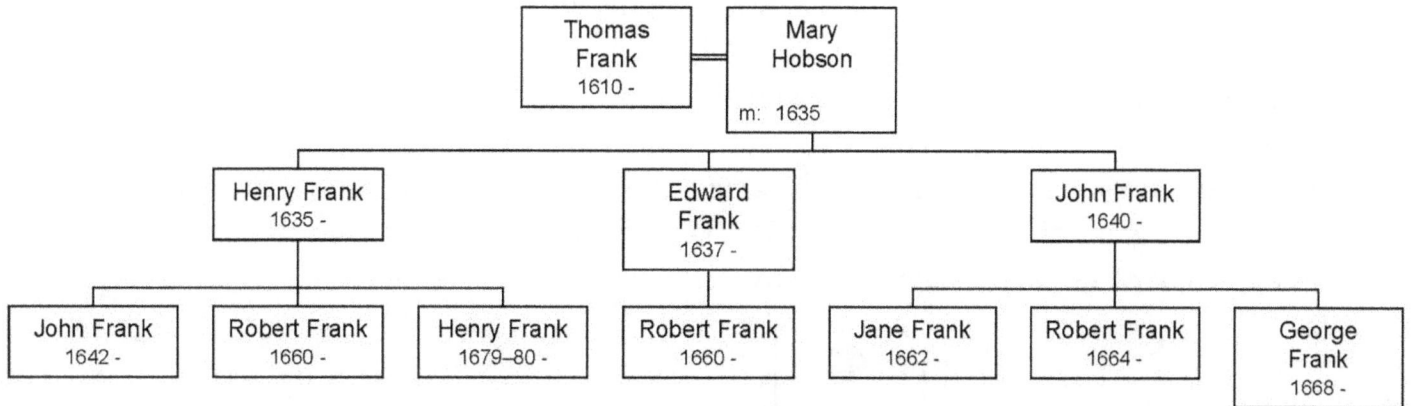

The above represents the Hartoft & Hackness line.

At Whitby, on the 23rd June 1655, the marriage of George Raughton (mariner) aged twenty-five, to Anne Readman, aged twenty-four, was witnessed by Henry Francke of Pickering, probably aged in his early twenties. The other witnesses were from Kirkbymoorside and Whitby. Kirkbymoorside lies west of Pickering in a triangle of Pickering, Lastingham and Kirkbymoorside. Due to his age and proximity to the witnesses coming from Kirkbymoorside, the Henry mentioned is attributed to Henry born 1635.

Also in 1656, John Ripley, joiner, aged twenty-four, marries Ellen Stephenson, aged twenty-seven. The witnesses are all from Whitby and Whitby Abbey, except for Henry Franke of Pickering.

William (1615) children:

Robert baptised 26th August 1637 at Rosedale

John de Rosedale, 1647–1689. Daughers Jane (1665) and Elizabeth (1668)

William b. 1639

Thomas b. 1642

Mary b. 1644

Robert 1655–1722. Married Mary Fletcher/Fletchir 29th July 1680

Dorathy b. 1646. Married Stephen Watson 9th June 1668, Rosedale

Elizabeth b. 1650

Henry b. 1652. Married Elizabeth Raine 4th July 1678, Rosedale

William had an earlier son, Robert, who was baptised 26th August 1637 at Rosedale, and who died sometime prior to his namesake, the second Robert shown below.

Most of the birth dates shown are actually baptism dates indicated at Rosedale. John de Rosedale's baptism was 25th July 1647, his burial 11th December 1689 at Lastingham where he was a Churchwarden indicated in 1674 and 1685. Proved at York, the grant of probate was given 10th January 1690, the papers showing him as a resident of Hutton-le-Hole, East Rydale.

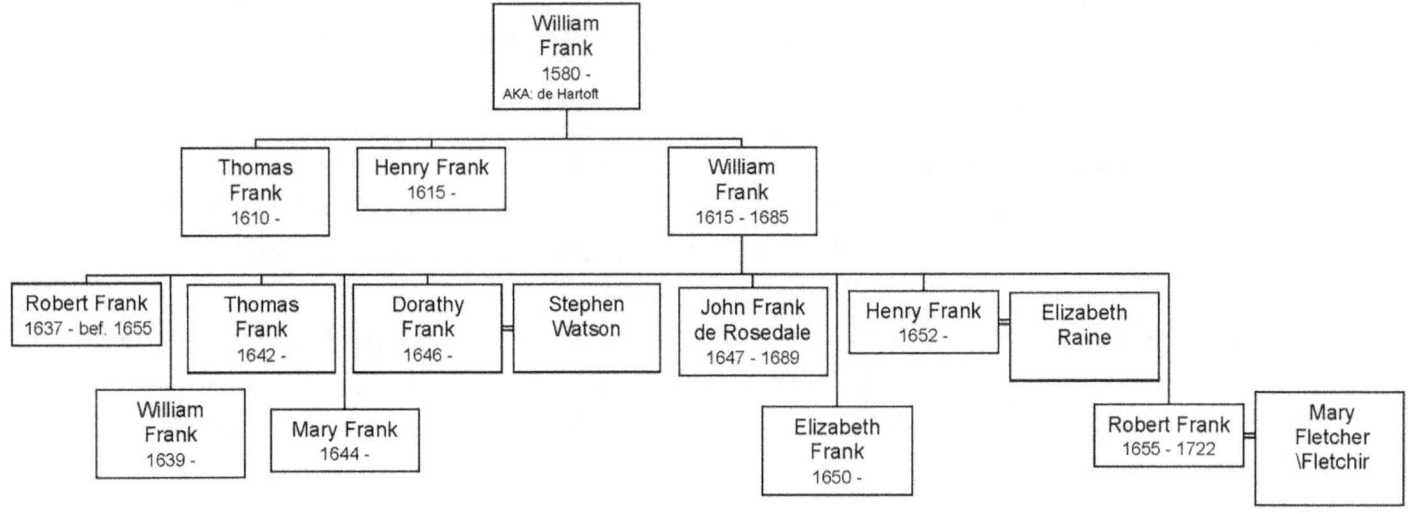

The Extraordinary Franks

Robert (1655) children:

Mary b. 17th Dec 1680

Robert b. 1682. Had a daughter Mary (1702–1777)

Anna b. 13th Nov 1685, died 9th Nov 1688

John b. 23rd Jan 1684

Jane b. 12th Jul 1690

Henry b. 13th May 1688

William b. 1693. Had a son, William b 13 Aug 1710 (although there may be a date problem due to 17 yr gap), who had daughter Mary b 26 Jan 1738)

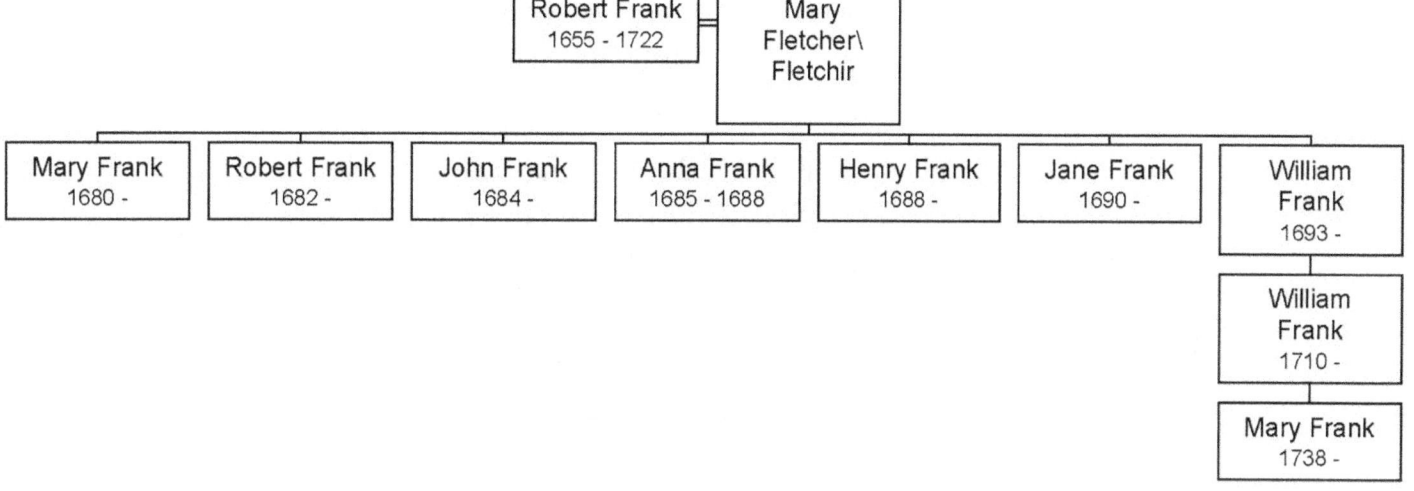

Robert Frank was born around 1655, and although known to have died in Farndale was buried in Lastingham in 1722 with probate 13th March the same year. He married Mary Fletchir on the 29th July 1680 at Rosedale. Further details of the above children of this marriage are as follows:

Mary Frank, baptised 17th December 1680 at Rosedale.

Robert, baptised 30th July 1682 at Rosedale, found resident at Farndale between 12th July 1719 and 11th November 1722.

John, baptised 10th August 1684 at Rosedale.

Anna, baptised 13th November 1685 at Rosedale.

Henry, baptised 13th May 1688 at Rosedale.

Jane, baptised 12th July 1690 at Rosedale, married William Marshall 27th October 1715 at Lastingham, found resident at Farndale 27th October 1715.

William, baptised 18th April 1693 at Rosedale.

The above Robert, baptised July 1682, was himself a son of a Robert. Robert was a popular and much used family name shared with the de Brus and used continually from pre-Norman times. Following marriage, Robert's children appear to be:

Hannah baptised 1st March 1714 at Rosedale; married John Hickson 9th December 1753 at Lastingham, both being shown resident at Appleton le Moors 9th December 1753.

John born around 1718, he married, details unknown and died at Rosedale, details unknown.

Mary baptised 12th July 1719 at Lastingham, she married one William Featherstone 7th November 1745, both being resident at Farndale around the same date.

Robert baptised 11th November 1722 at Lastingham, he married Elizabeth Hill 12th June 1755 at Kirkby Moorside. Elizabeth was born around 1734, and on her death was buried 17th January 1817 aged 82, her husband Robert dying fifty-nine years previous, being buried 30th December 1758 at Lastingham.

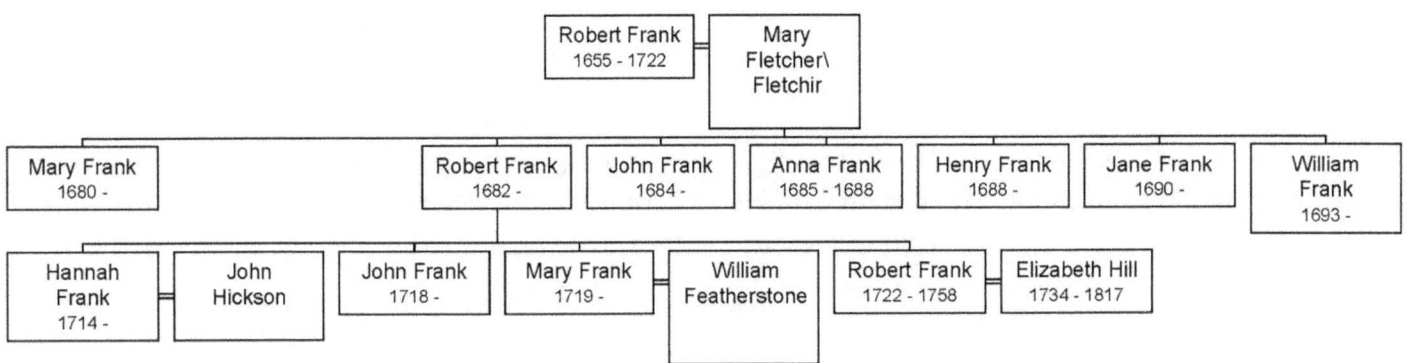

Hutton-le Hole 12th February 1674: Franks assessed quarterly for the purpose of carrying out a vigorous war against France were: 1s each, Alse, William, Merill and Thomas Franke. Additionally, William, Elizabeth and Thomas Franke, also of Hutton-le-Hole.

With firm evidence of migration, Bertram Frank's very knowledge and detailed publication *The Franks: a yeoman family*, confirms my research recognising in Hutton alone three principle branches of the Franks: the first being Lund House, the second, Oxclose, the third the Franks of Hutton. He confirms quote, 'The family tree shows that "other Franks" established themselves in Farndale during the seventeenth century'.

Known coming over from Ness, Farndale adjacent Hutton, Ness belonged to the district of Rydale adjacent neighbouring Danby, Glaisdale and Rosedale. And looking at a map, the cluster of dales well understood, the A170 from Scarborough through the scattering of dales to Thirsk continues along the A61 to the A 59, linking with Fewston and adjacent Blubberhouses, assuaging Sir William and the wool trade.

This terminates the Hutton offshoot.

The Thirsk pedigree

Having shown various connections with one's own line, the importance of the Thirsk related Franks can't be ignored: their story and their links with York and further afield show a family of immense strength of character and resolve, and in its telling, their voice pulls together various strings of disparate groups of Franks showing their interrelation. Live testimony to an amazing yet complex family entity.

As intimated, ancestor Hugh's kin have a story to tell with connections through Thirkleby to yet another branch of the Franks, shown in the guise of Sir John Fraunceys born in Derby in 1422. Also, there is the story of Hugh's brother Sir William Frankland, who founded the Guild of Clothworkers in London.

I have previously shown details of Hugh of Nelsing, his father, Richard of Nelsing, being a relatively wealthy farmer. Richard's will, dated 10th April 1532, is recorded with two daughters and three sons, with the three sons inheriting, shown thus:

> Hugh, at the time also of Nelsing.

> William of Ryes, Hertfordshire, to whom the lordship of Blubberhouses was given in 1562. He died 21st August 1576 aged around seventy-two.

> Thirdly, Richard of Fewston, who upon succeeding his brother William, as well as the purchase of the manor and rectory of Alne and Aldwick, gained Blubberhouses together with William's title, becoming Sir Richard.

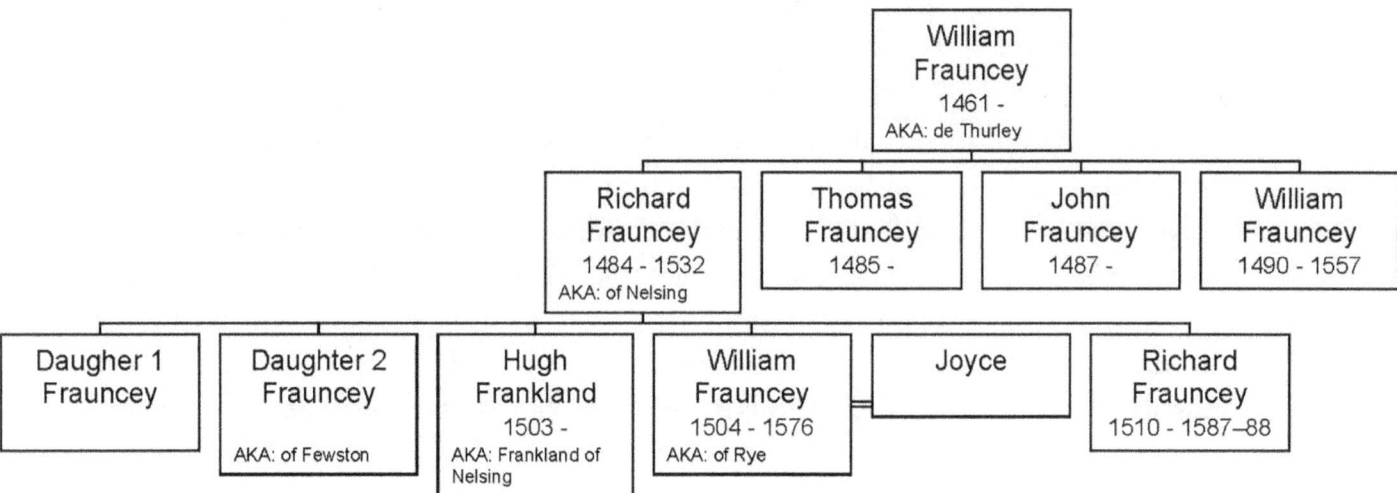

As shown, William died in 1576. Prior to this date, Queen Elizabeth, who at the time held the manor of Thirkleby, passed it to Ambrose, Earl of Warwick. Ambrose returned it to the Queen, but immediately obtained a regrant and at once alienated Thirkleby to William Frankland (1504), who in turn passed it to his nephew Hugh, son of Richard of Fewston (1510). The apparent rush appears to correspond with William's declining health and the need to honour his wishes prior to his impending death. I refer to previous details concerning Queen Elizabeth's ownership of the manor of Ness, Hugh's decision to pull out of negotiations causing the purchase of Danby Forest.

In the fifth year of the reign of Queen Elizabeth, William was granted the lordship of Blubberhouses together with 'the seite and mansion of the Hall'. Although living in Herefordshire, William was the founder of the Guild of Clothworkers in London, yet he originally resided at Thornton Bishopside, immediately west of Ripon, having connections through his brother Hugh to the Yorkshire Dales weaving activity as well as the monasteries: the monasteries having as their industry the purchase and grading of locally produced wool, such activity giving rise to William's interest in cloth production and London as a major centre for that industry.

The heirs apparent relating to William

William's son, also named William, died leaving a grandson. As a minor and heir to a famous grandfather, the grandson was given unto the care of Richard of York, son of Hugh, William's elder brother. Unfortunately, the child died underage, and in the absence of an heir Sir William Frankland, knight of the realm, bequeathed:

1. That his brother Richard and thereafter Richard's son, also named Hugh, be given the Manor of Blubberhouses and all his lands there and at Fuiston.

2. To the Master and Wardens of the Guild and Fraternity of Clothworkers in London, two tenements in Thames Street together with monies received there.

3. Separate provision and monies to the Parish of Skipton.

Referencing the direct line **Roger (1410) children:** Records show Williiam Frauceys (1461) his uncle John Franklyn cum Frauceys having a layman's connection with Fountains Abbey and the religious houses that lay across the Dales, one such being Lastingham, close to Hutton-le-Hole, Hutton being a localised centre of weaving. The Subsidy Roll for the warpentake of Claro, 16th Edward IV, 1475, shows John and Roger Franklyn being of Thornton Bishopside, yet the intermigration of the Franklands and the reduction of Frankland to Frank intermingling with the Franks across the Dales had already taken hold. In 1398, the bailiff of the Borough of Thirkleby paid 29s 3 ½d as the rent of free tenements. And by the beginning of the nineteenth century, there were fifty-two burgage tenements of which, forty-nine belonged the Franklands of Thirkleby.

The Thirsk tree now follows two lines of succession, one through Richard of York, son of Hugh of Nelsing, and the other through Hugh, son of Hugh of Nelsing's brother, Richard of Fewston, this being the Thirkleby line of succession.

Sir Hugh Frankland, his line, Richard, William and John

Dealing with Hugh's line of succession first:

> Richard of York was born around 1530, having four brothers and a sister for whom I have no details.
>
> William, born around 1528, married but had no issue, died in 1589.
>
> *The second brother John, original pater de Frankland aka Franks of Glaisdale, from whom one's own line stems, was born around 1532 died 6th December 1616.*
>
> Petri was born around 1534,
>
> And there was Edward Franck who was recorded having messuages and land at Hovyngham, south of Pickering near Ness in Rydale.

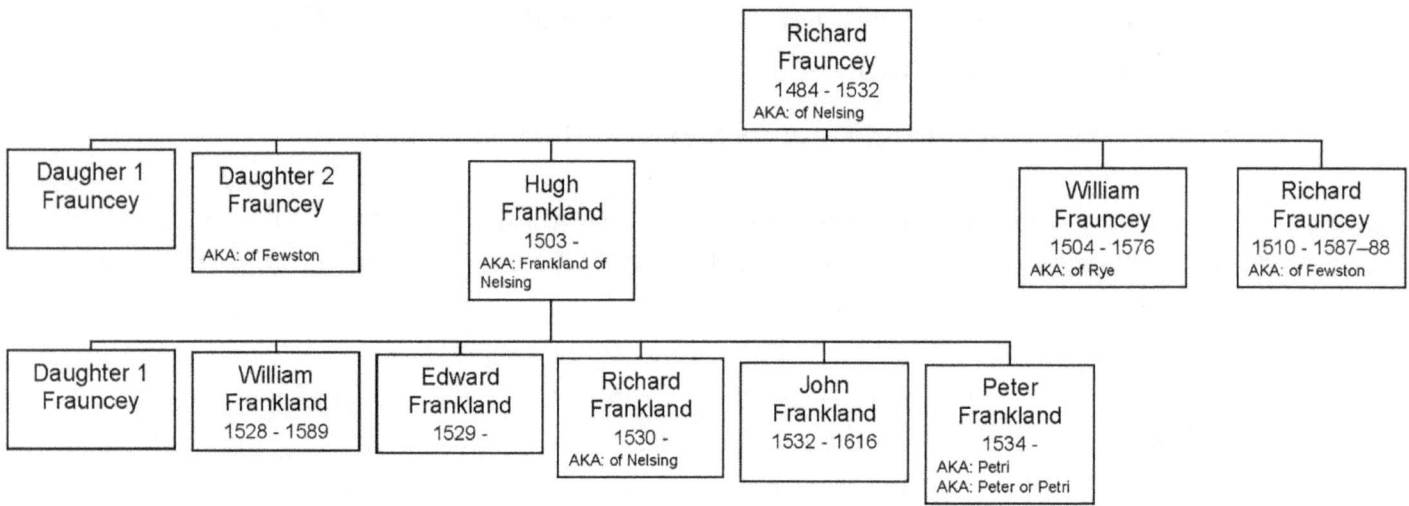

Regarding Richard, possibly prior to his succession and following the Dissolution, at around the age of seventeen or eighteen, he purchased, or had purchased for him, land in Glaisdale and Danby Forest 1545–1550. Following his father's aborted attempts to purchase the Ness estate, Edward was busy acquiring land elsewhere. And from this it appears what money was available had been distributed across several of the children as a means of spreading their influence and wealth. It was Richard's brother John, who was original pater de Frankland of Glaisdale, and as such, became a fulcrum for the rest that followed, the first of one's own line.

Sir Richard of York inherited the title, knight of the realm, and had at least five children:

> Born second, Anthony, around 1556.
> Third was Thomas, born around 1557.
> Fourth one unknown who died 1640.
> William, born 1562, married having a son named Richard, born 1591.

But first born was Henry, born around 1554. Sir Henry Frankland of Aldwick and York succeeded to Alwick in 1591, and married Jane, daughter of Sir Charles Wren. They had at least two children, one of whom was Anthony, and it was Anthony who succeeded to Aldwick. Jane died, possibly in childbirth and Sir Henry remarried producing Thomas and Henry, Sir Henry Frankland dying in 1622.

Anthony decided to dispose of Aldwick selling it to his uncle Thomas in 1636, at which point, Uncle Thomas immediately handed Aldwick to Anthony's half-brother Thomas in 1637. It seems Sir Henry named the second Thomas after his brother Thomas, to whom he was especially close, and in turn, Thomas felt compelled to honour his brother in the purchase of Aldwick for his favourite nephew and namesake Thomas.

Nephew Thomas remained unmarried and died around 1643, at which point, Aldwick passed to his brother Henry in 1644. Henry married Dorothy Holcroft in 1650, and their child Anthony held Aldwick, shown dated 1672. Later, between 1688 and 1735, Aldwick passed to the Thirkleby branch of the family.

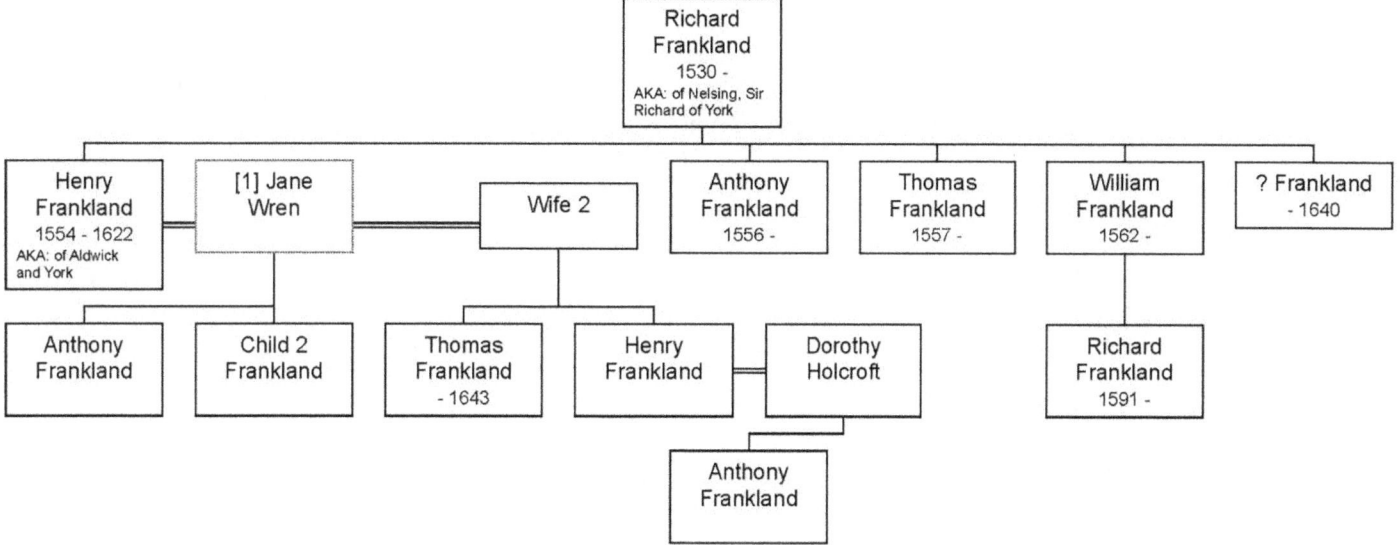

Sir Richard Frankland, his line, Hugh, John and Ralph

Sir Richard purchased the Rectory and Manor of Alne and Aldwick a few days prior to his death in March 1587 aged around seventy-seven. He had at least three sons,

The first son, Hugh of Thirkleby and Roche Abbey, was born around 1540 at Fewston. Hugh married Johanne and on his death in 1606, left her the estate for her lifetime, giving his brothers Ralph and John the Monasteries of Roche, and to Richard, his brother Ralph's son, his properties at Ryes.

Second son John's wife died 11th June 1620, John joining his beloved wife thirty-six years later in August 1656. They had at least five children, and while data is sparse, in reverse order, there are daughters Gill, Maud, and Ann, Ann marrying in 1594, died 1633. Then there was Mary was born 9th September 1618, and John of Fewston born 1599. That leaves Richard. Richard of Thirkleby and Roche, who upon his Aunt Joanne's death succeeded to his uncle Hugh's estate.

Thirdly, Ralph of Fewston, son of Sir Richard, who was born in 1547. He succeeded his brother Hugh in 1607. He married Margaret around 1572, and died 21st February 1630. The line of succession continues:

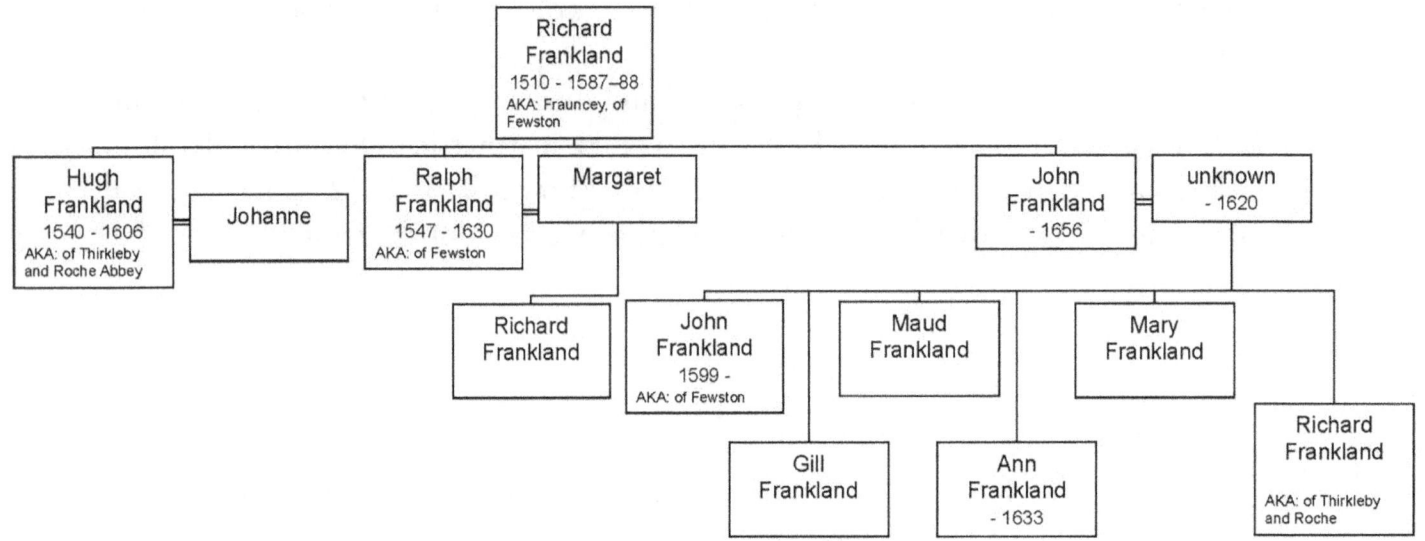

Ralph Frankland

There were four children,

>Daughter Frances, who married Hugh Bethel.

>Ralph, who died 22nd June 1629.

>Richard of Fewston, whose daughter Joan married Thomas Pallister of Newby Wiske in 1638, and whose issue, William Pallister, was born in 1643, becoming Archbishop of Cashel.

>The fourth child, Sir William of Thirkleby, was born in 1573 becoming MP for Thirsk in 1628 and again in 1640, and married Lucy daughter of Sir Henry Botler. Sir William Frankland was knighted in Ireland in 1636, and died in 1640 aged sixty-seven.

Sir Henry

Sir William's son and heir apparent, Henry, was born in 1609. Sir Henry Frankland, knight, married Anne Harris, born 1605. The Court Roll of 7th June 1638 shows William Frankland of Thirkleby, Henry Frankland Knight (Wm's son and heir apparent) and Richard Frankland *de ffuiston gentlemen* surrendering in the forest court at Knaresbrough a messuage of 30 acres of land easily identified as Cragg Hall and the land of which the estate originally consisted. Seemingly part of the Thirkleby estate, the transfer was to the benefit of Henry Fairfax and his heirs. The late Elizabethan cum early Jacobean hall built by William Frankland of Ryes is a fine example still in use today. The tithes arising from the estate appear to have been retained and were dealt with quite separate from those of Cragg Hall.

Sir Henry's issue:

> Sir William, knight and first baron, born in 1640, married Arabella, born 1638, daughter of the Honourable Henry Belayse (Bellasis), eldest son of Lord Fauconberg of Newburgh Priory, situated close to Helmsley. Sir William was created a baronet by Charles II in 1660. Tragically he died in 1665 aged thirty-three, his wife Arabella died twenty years later, in 1687, aged forty-nine, being survived by five children, the eldest Thomas.

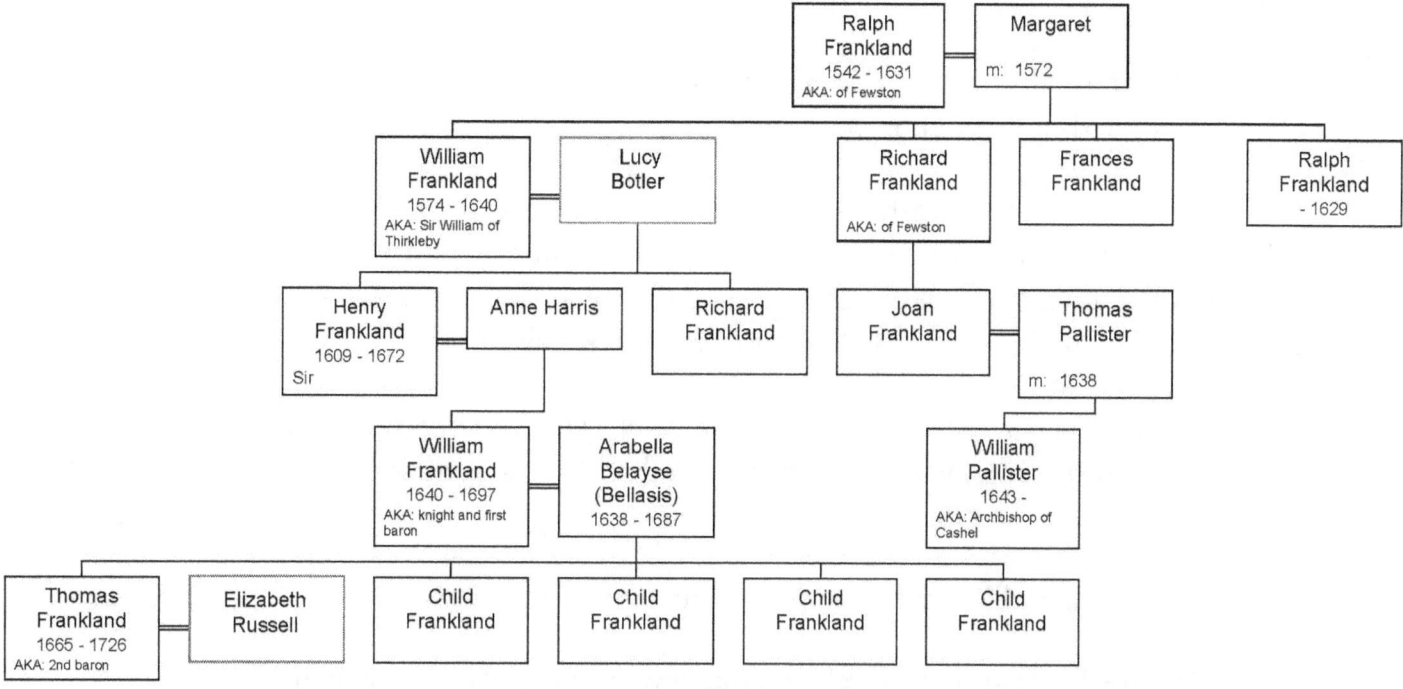

Sir Thomas

Sir Thomas Frankland, born 1665, married Elizabeth Russell, daughter of Sir John Russell and Frances Cromwell, daughter of Oliver Cromwell. Sir Thomas Frankland, second baron, died 28th November 1726, aged sixty-one. He had succeeded the baronetcy in 1697, being also MP for Thirsk.

Thomas Belasyse, the first Earl Faulconberg, 1627–1700, being a strong adherent of Oliver Cromwell, successfully betrothed Cromwell's offspring, marrying his third daughter Mary in 1657. Lord Faulconberg succeeded his father Viscount Henry Belasyse in 1652.

Hawnby is moorland lying between the Cleveland Hill's and the Hambleton Hills to the south-west. The lands were part of the manor of Murton bought by Sir Hugh Cholmeley along with Aisaby in 1632. It was sold to the Belasyse family but was registered among the estates of the recusant Lord Faulconberg in 1717. The subsequent reversion came under his uncle's will to Sir Thomas Frankland of Thirkleby, whose elder son Thomas quitclaimed to his brother Frederick in 1737. The family tree that shortly follows shows Frederick, as too the link with Cromwell. Being unable to find a clear view as to why Thomas quitclaimed to his brother, as well as divorcing his wife, Fredrick served as MP for Thirsk, going on to be Director of the Bank of England.

Records from the North Riding Commissioners Report for Birdforth, York, show that Thomas, First Earl Fauconberg:

> 'Bequeathed unto Sir Thomas Frankland Bart a fee of farm rent lying within the manor of Sigston.'

The above was chargeable with the annual payment of £20 forever. However subsequent land taxes were distributed through the Fauconberg charity to the poor.

It was his relationship with Fauconberg and Cromwell especially that brought Sir Thomas to the attention of King William, who recorded:

> 'He hath very good estate ... a gentleman of a very sweet, easy affable disposition, of good sense, extremely zealous for the constitution of his country, yet does not seem over forward.'

A nearby estate of William Frank is described:

> 'A large forest and moor called Stokesley and Stockdale Moor, consisting of two thousand five hundred acres, which William Frank has freehold land, messuages, farm, closes and grounds adjoining upon the lordship of Westerdale on the east, upon the moors and wastes late belonging Sir Charles Duncomb on the south, and upon the moors of Sir William Fowles Bart, belonging his lordships of Ingleby and Battersby, upon the lordship of Kildale.'

The above is in relation to a lease made to William Fowlis and Thomas Frankland esquire for 1000 years of said manor and estates, dated 1716. This seems to tie in with Sir Thomas, second baron, 1665–1726 and first baron Sir William, for whom I have the dates 1632–1665. With William mentioned first and Thomas later, doubts lie in the absence of titles and the date 1716 which would exclude Sir William. Also, it seems out of place, Sir Thomas taking a lease with another person ten years prior to his death aged forty-five. My contention is both William and Thomas were an untitled branch emanating from the same family having coincidental similar names. The next paragraph supports this theory where no mention of the aforementioned property is disclosed.

Second Baron Sir Thomas Frankland, children

1. Sir Thomas, born 1685, succeeding the third baronetcy, became MP for Thirsk and died in 1747.

2. Richard, 1699–1761.

3. Robert, born 1701 (no date of death).

4. William, who died in 1714.

5. Henry, born 1690 and died in 1728. Married Mary Cross. Following his service as Governor of Bengal was father to Sir Charles Frankland, fourth baron and Admiral Sir Thomas Frankland (1718–1784), who became the fifth baronet.

6. Frederick Meinhardt Frankland, 1694–1768, MP for Thirsk.

7. Mary, abt 1690–1722, married Thomas Worsley a man prone to ill health who was briefly MP for Malton, Yorks, but spent much of his life in warmer climes prior to his death in 1751

After the dissolution, the manor of Murton was granted with the lands of Byland Abbey to the Belasyse family of Lord Faulconberg. A few years later, the whole of the estate passed to the Franklands of Thirkleby.

Due to the aberration of female inheritance, Thomas quitclaimed the estates to his brother Frederick, where through the lack of issue and male protégée, the estate passed to Frederick's daughter Anne, through her marriage to Thomas, the Lord Pelham, her husband was recorded holding the manor in 1778. Following that descent, the estate fell into the possession of the trustees of the late Mrs Hamer, all Frankland interest in the estate having been waved a sad farewell.

Douglas Frank Blackmore

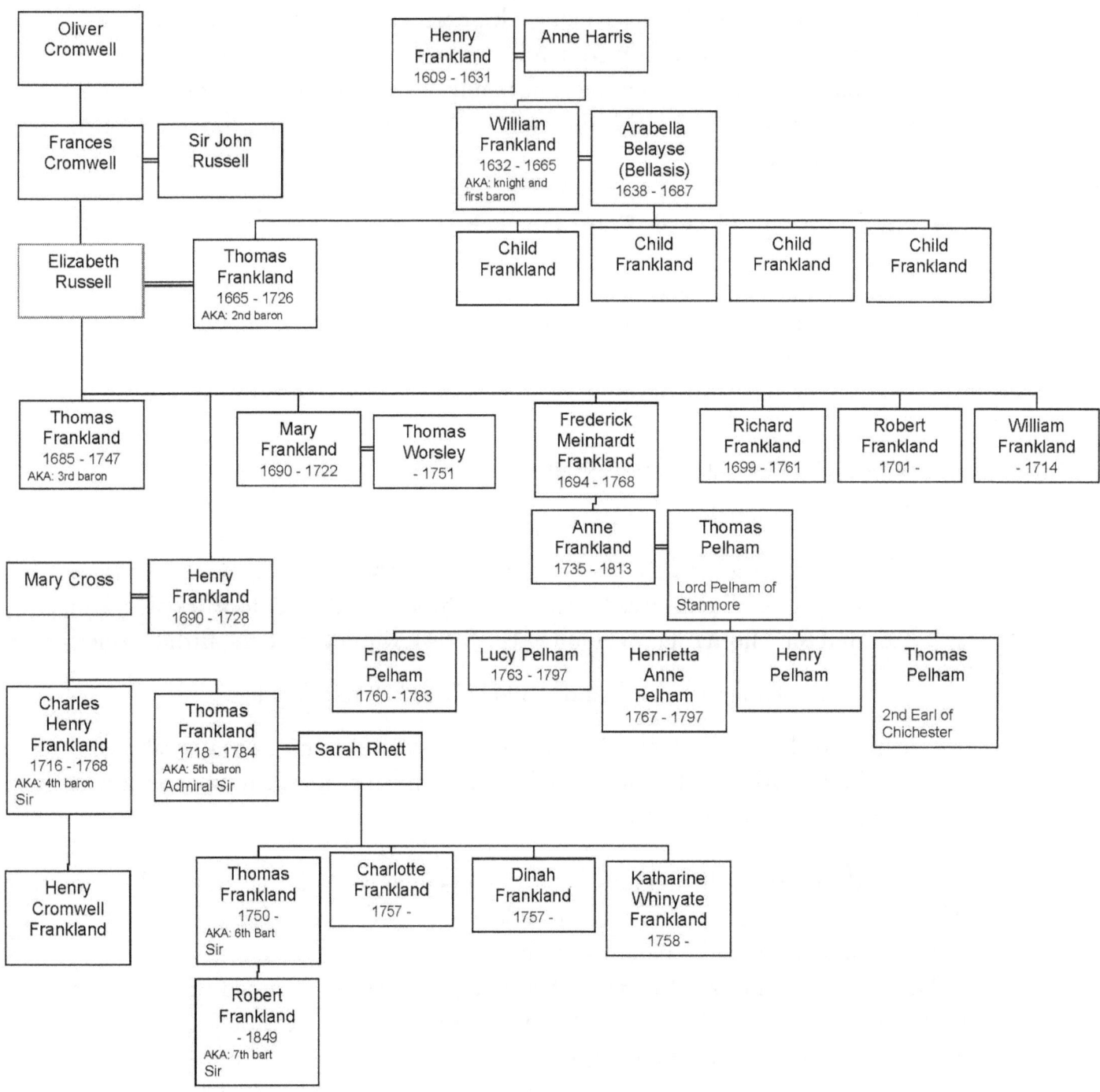

The family line continued:

To Anne Frankland (1735–1813), three girls, Frances 1760–1783, Lucy 1763–1797 and Henrietta Anne 1767–1797, also Henry and his brother Thomas Pelham, 2nd Earl of Chichester.

Third baron, Sir Thomas Frankland 1685–1747

Prior to the Thirkleby quitclaim to Frederick by Sir Thomas, several times MP for Thirsk, Thomas was appointed Lord of the Admiralty 1730–1741. Still residing at Thirkleby Hall, he first married Dinah Topham, daughter of Francis Topham of Oglethorpe, the couple having two daughters: the two girls direct descendants of Oliver Cromwell. Sir Thomas's wife Dinah died in 1740. Their children were:

1. Lady Dinah Frankland of Berkeley Square, Westminster. Born in 1719, she died 8th January 1779.

2. Elizabeth, for whom I have no details.

Marriage two was to Sarah Moseley, 1725–1783. Due to the lack of male issue, this was effectively the end of the line, Sir Thomas passing succession to his nephew Sir Charles Henry Frankland 1716–1768.

Lady Dinah Frankland

Daughter Dinah, descendant of Cromwell, married Viscount Quarendon, George Henry Lee and third Earl of Lichfield, descendant of Charles I.

The Lichfield title was created for his grandfather, Edward Henry Lee, given in anticipation of Edward's marriage to King Charles II's illegitimate daughter, Charlotte Fitzroy, whose mother was Barbara Villiers. The marriage took place in 1677, thus assuring the title and honours that followed.

The titles passed through the father, also George, to George along with the Viscountcy of Quarendon, gained on his birth at Windsor Castle 21st May 1718. Thus George Henry Lee assumed the title Third Earl of Lichfield, Privy Councillor, Captain of the Gentlemen at Arms dated 1762. He was educated at St John's Oxford, gaining an MA and DCL in 1743, becoming High Steward in 1760, and Lord of the Bedchamber to King George III in 1762.

Dinah Frankland's husband became Chancellor of Oxford University, also in 1762, and was created Deputy Lieutenant for Oxfordshire in 1763. As the marriage was barren, the estate reverted to the second earl's eldest surviving sister, Lady Charlotte Lee, which estate upon marriage to the eleventh Viscount Dillon, passed to that line. The titles later passed to George's uncle, who also childless, the whole of the titles became defunct.

Snuffling around for some sort of honour or means of distinction for lay-persons requiring status, the handy title of Earl of Lichfield was to be resurrected several times, the most celebrated holder being that of Patrick Anson, the fifth Earl Lichfield, photographer, born 25th April 1939 dying 11th November 2005.

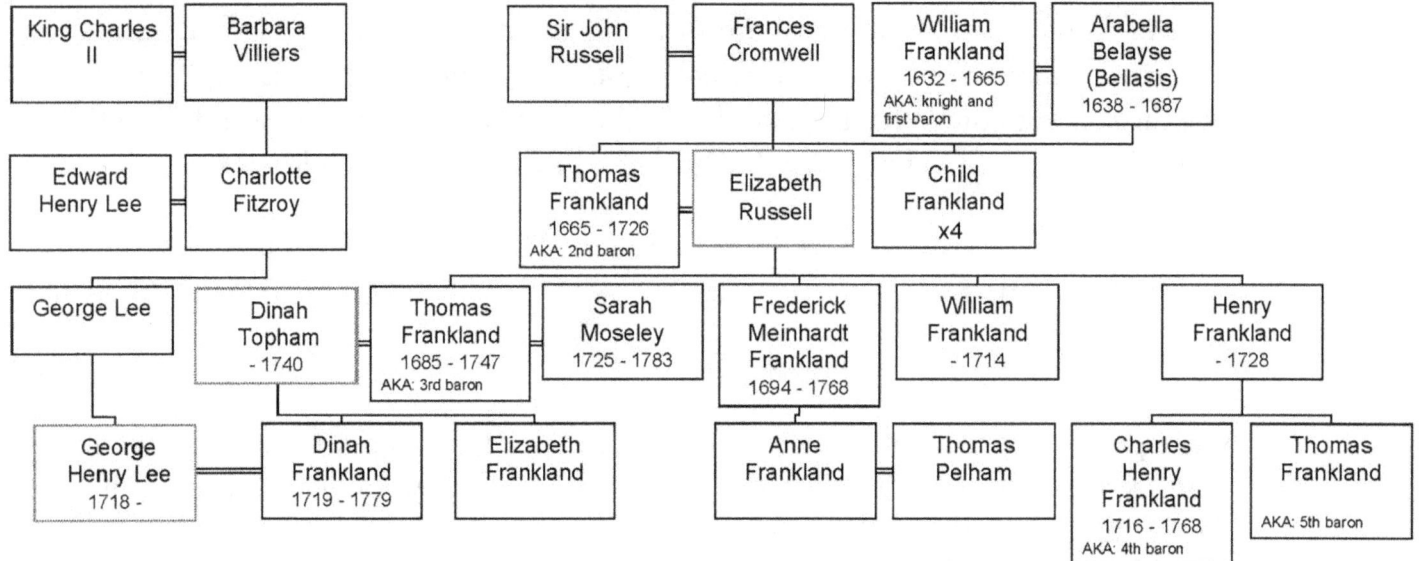

Sir Charles Henry Frankland, fourth baronet

Sir Charles was born in 1716, and as fourth baron became Consul General in Lisbon, previously holding the position of Collector of Taxes in Boston, America. His brother and successor to the title was Thomas.

Speaking of Boston USA, for any American readers I must mention another Frank: born in Boston in 1706, Benjamin Franklin was revered as a patriot and American founding father. He was responsible for bringing France into the War of Independence and in that arena is considered second only to George Washington. For all that, Franklin spent much of his life in England. Being the sixteenth child of an English migrant, his ancestry in England goes back six generations, details petering out with the birth of Pater Francklyne in 1495.

Fifth baron, Sir Thomas

The fifth baron was Sir Thomas Frankland of Thirkleby. Born 26th June 1718, he married his American sweetheart, Sarah, in May 1743, and died 21st November 1784 in Bath, aged sixty-six. Their children were:

1. Thomas, born 1750.

2. Charlotte, born 1757.

3. Dinah, born 1757.

4. Katharine Whinyate Frankland of Bond Street, London, born 17th October 1758.

As captain of the frigate H.M. *Rose*, Thomas visited his brother in Boston in 1742. It was while he was there that Thomas fell in love and married Sarah, daughter of Judge Rhett of South Carolina. But this was the 28th April 1742, coincidentally the date of the very first meeting of American Freemasonry, conducted in the newly formed Boston Lodge. Yet things looked bleak, poverty in Boston had assumed an unsettling presence and was increasing. This was especially so among the widows and orphans of soldiers who had died in the intercolonial wars with the French.

Where Thomas Frankland's frigate lay anchored there were markedly less ships than usual and trade was depressed, caused by increased competition from Philadelphia and New York. In 1742, 8.2% of the population of Boston were slaves; the people felt unsettled, harbouring escalating feelings of disquiet dragged down by thoughts of impending gloom, feeling that however bad things were there was worse to come.

And they were right. Thomas Frankland's ship had long since sailed, the couple having been married for nearly thirty years Sarah was looking forward to their anniversary. It was 1773 and the Boston Tea Party marked the way towards independence from Britain; by 1776 the American Revolutionary War had broken out. Thirty years previous, Thomas's brother, Sir Charles Henry Frankland had also married his American sweetheart, Agnes Surriage of Massachusetts. In stark contrast to the troubled times, theirs was a much-publicised tale of romance, recorded by the pen of Elias Nason of Albany in 1865, forming the subject of 'The Ballad of Agnes Frankland' by Wendell Holmes.

Agnes

Born one of seven in Massachusetts in 1726, Agnes was an American tavern maid, her father a fisherman, too poor to support the whole family. Becoming a waiting girl, aged sixteen, she caught the eye of Harry, Charles Henry Frankland, descendant of Oliver Cromwell, one of the richest and most upstanding families in Northern England. True to form, and with her parents' permission, Harry became Agnes's benefactor arranging for her education in Boston where four years later she became his mistress; all too much for straight-laced Boston society. And it was in this restrained province the tittle-tattle started, where articles appeared and poems were composed.

Having succeeded the barony of Thirsk, Harry and Agnes moved back to Massachusetts, thence to England there being issues over property there. Business matters settled, the couple travelled Europe unaware that nature in its most terrible form was brewing. The terrible event of 1755 was the Great Lisbon Earthquake that buried Sir

Henry along with his coach and horses, the animals being instantly killed, coachman and passenger alike were believed dead and there was nothing to be done. It was Harry's beloved Agnes who went searching and along with several men insisted in heaving and clawing at the rubble, moving boulders with bare and bleeding hands to find him barely alive: she had saved him.

Home in Thirkleby, once the tale had been told to Harry's mother, she gave her blessing to what she previously thought an unlikely marriage. Lady Agnes Frankland and her husband returned to Boston in 1756 living in a purpose-built twenty-six-roomed mansion, the building being a replacement for Frankland House, which property in Garden Court, Boston, still stands. Moving accounts of Agnes's bravery had preceded their arrival in America giving the storytelling another dimension, whereupon Agnes's arrival give her popular approval as a heroine.

After an interval, setting sail yet again across the Atlantic, the wind in her face, gazing west over spew-topped waves, her eyes glistened with dewdrop tears at the fast receding coastline. The horizon hazy and more distant, Agnes must have thought she would never see America again, her life as it had been bringing fond memories and sadness. Once in Lisbon, Sir Harry took up his appointment as consul general, thence to his retirement in Bath where he died in 1768. But alone in her grief, Agnes took stock and looked once more to America.

Totally bereft and with no children of her own, Lady Agnes moved back to America where the outbreak of the American Revolution prompted an early return to England with her husband's son Henry Cromwell, from a previous marriage. Now resigned to living in England, Agnes lived with the Frankland family in Thirkleby until settling for marriage to banker John Drew, drawing her last breath two years later in 1783.

The story of Sir Harry Frankland and Agnes Surriage is told in Sir Arthur Quiller-Couch's *Lady Good-For-Nothing* and various other publications including Oliver Wendell Holmes's ballad, 'Agnes'. The ballad is extremely long, too long when it can easily be found online. However I include a taster or two from it:

First Part, The Knight:

> The tale I tell is gospel true,
> As all the bookmen know,
> And pilgrims who have strayed to view
> The wrecks still left to show.
>
> The old, old story, fair, and young,
> And fond, and not too wise,

The Extraordinary Franks

> That matrons tell, with sharpened tongue,
> To maids with downcast eyes.
>
> Ah! Maidens err and matrons warn
> Beneath the coldest sky;
> Love lurks amid the tasselled corn
> As in the bearded rye!

There are seventeen other verses to part one. Moving to the first three of thirty-eight verses of part two, The Maiden:

> Why seek the knight that rocky cape
> Beyond the Bay of Lynn?
> What chance his wayward course may shape
> To reach its village inn?
>
> No story tells: whate'er we guess,
> The past lies deaf and still,
> But Fate, who rules to blight or bless,
> Can lead us where she will.
>
> Make way! Sir Harry's coach and four,
> And liveried grooms that ride,
> They cross the ferry, touch the shore
> On Winnisimmet's side.

The story continues leading to the tavern, still part two, verse eighteen:

> Poor Agnes! With her work half done
> They caught her unaware;
> As, humbly, like a praying nun,
> She knelt upon the stair;
>
> Bent o'er the steps, with lowliest mien
> She knelt, but not to pray,
> Her little hands must keep them clean,

And wash their stains away.

A foot, an ankle, bare and white,
Her girlish shapes betrayed,
'Ha Nymphs and Graces!' spoke the knight;
'Look up, my beauteous Maid!'

She turned, a reddening rose in bud,
Its calyx half withdrawn,
Her cheek on fire with demasked blood
Of girlhood's glowing dawn!

The first verse of part three, The Conquest, seventeen verses:

'Who saw this hussy, when she came?
What is the wench, and who?'
They whisper. 'Agnes is her name?
Pray what has she to do?'

Part four, consisting of twenty-four verses, is entitled The Rescue. Part five, The Reward, eighth verse:

The vow is spoke, the prayer is said,
And with a gentle pride
The Lady Agnes lifts her head,
Sir Harry Frankland's bride.

Part six is the conclusion consisting of twenty-four verses of which I recount verses one and seven:

The tale is done; it little needs
To track their after ways,
And string again the golden beads
Of love's uncounted days.

The Lady Agnes raised the stone
That marks his honoured grave,

And there Sir Harry sleeps alone
By Wiltshire Avon's wave.

As was the custom, upon their marriage, Lord Pelham inherited Anne Frankland's not unsubstantial wealth. Coincidentally, he was a one-time MP for Rye. As Lord Chichester he married Anne Frankland in 1754, having three sons and three daughters; all three daughters and one son predeceasing him. His third son was aged seventy-six in January 1805, his wife, Anne Frankland, true heir, aka Lady Chichester, died in 1813.

Aldwick

Regarding the Manor of Aldwick and its baronetcy, the arms were Azure a dolphin or and a chief or with two saltires gules therein. As previously shown, sometime between 1688 and 1735 ownership had passed to the Thirkleby seat where it followed descent until 1849, when on the death of Sir Robert Frankland Bart, grandson of Admiral Sir Thomas Frankland MP 1718–1784, it passed to his eldest daughter Augusta Louisa Frankland. Following a common thread, the tale continues through the female line with the marriage of Augusta to Thomas, the fifth Lord Walsingham and it was Augusta's son Thomas, who as lord of the manor, became the sixth Lord Walsingham, the Frank name no longer relevant. An oft-repeated story, a well-documented tale of rising fortune and of a family fading into mediocrity.

A note on Admiral Sir Thomas Frankland (1718–1784): we need to occasionally remind how power and influence can corrupt and, while in many ways a remarkable family, it must be remembered they were often ruthless in pursuit of their own ends and status, Thomas Frankland being a good example of this. A British naval officer and slave trader, he had a difficult temper and in the mid 1700s actively profited when fighting Spanish privateers. It is one thing to compile data and maybe put a spin on one's family tree as wonderful, but as the records show, so often it is the workaday people who come through.

Immediate ancestry, Cleveland Franks

There is an historic association of Franks with Ingleby Barwick and Worsall near Yarm, the original Franks being enfeoffed to the de Brus. Records show a Henry Franke of the Manor of Kneton and Middleton Tyas in 1583 consisting of forty messuages and land in Richmond, Applegarth, Worsall and Yarm. Family links with Langbaurgh show clear ties between Richmond and Cleveland through Yarm's association with the Franks, and Yarm as the River Tees crossing to the north as well as an inland port for shallow sailing ships, hence an important and busy place. As regards Worsall, I visited Frank relatives there as a boy, at the time oblivious that the visit was indicative of a long-standing interrelation.

The family moving from Glaisdale, my grandfather as a child helped work the recently acquired lands lying along the River Tees towards Yarm. The properties consisted of three large farms and a quarry together with some cottages, the largest farm being Ingleby Barwick. As a younger son with no possibility of an inheritance, following a joinery apprenticeship, being in receipt of funds of a school teacher acquaintance and an inheritance from his grandmother, Tom Frank acquired land first in Linthorpe and later in Acklam, estates that historically formed a small part of the vast de Brus lordship enfeoffed to the Franks, now turned over for much needed house building and the rapid expansion of Middlesbrough.

The expansion of Middlesbrough to the west complete, Tom Frank subsequently purchased land in Stokesley and Great Ayton together with a swathe of farmland stretching along the lower Cleveland Hills. In addition he acquired property in Newby that included farmland and various cottages, and in Middlesbrough a number of houses retained for rental, later purchasing and donating several acres of village green to the people of Newby in perpetuity. Not bad for a son of the soil with little regard for financial reward, and the family having no past experience of large-scale construction he could draw upon.

I previously showed a settlement of Franks northward from the Humber, there being many Franks at Burniston, north of Scarborough, and Rillington and Scampton, close to Malton and Pickering. Their proximity to Lastingham and the Rosedale Franks shows these Franks as interrelated, Rosedale being only a short stride from Glaisdale; Glaisdale in Rydale was my great-grandfather's place of birth prior to the family acquiring the aforementioned Ingleby and Barwick.

Athough King of the Scots, Robert de Brus (1274–1329) retained predecessor lands in Yorkshire where a few small parcels were enfeoffed to the Franks. Today it's amazing to find the names of those same holdings in the possession of recent Franks, a family unaware of their heritage. As for being Norman, or their predecessors having kinship with the de Brus, mostly of farming stock not one would stir a heart's beat, preferring to get on with whatever chore forced their attention.

The same might apply to Tom Frank. And although imbued with the same meme, he was a quiet man, gentle, but single-minded and determined in his endeavour to build homes for people and the parish he served.

FROM PREVIOUS, THE MAIN TREE CONTINUED.

As stated John the Younger and his parents show a direct link via Ness, the purchase of Danby Forest and my great-grandfather's holdings both at Glaisdale and Ingleby Barwick, whose holding and others such as Pickering I know well having visited them regularly with Tom Frank.

The family tree via John the Younger, son of Johes de Franckland de Glaisdale, born of Pater de family Frankland continues:

John (1554) children:

> Marriage 1.
>
> **Petri** born around 1574, of the wapentake of Bulraer.
>
> Marriage 2. Elizabeth Fentres, 1578, born around 1558, died 26th May 1627.
>
> Georgius b. 10 Jun 1587.
>
> Francisca b. 15 Dec 1589.
>
> Agnes b. 10 July 1591.
>
> Thomas b. 25 Mar 1592, died 167) (see Hutton line).
>
> Robertus b. 5 Aug 1593.
>
> Petrus b. 21 Jun 1594.

The reason for two Peters is not clear, records often show two children with a similar first name, possibly emanating from adoption or a child from a previous marriage.

The name Frankland is sometimes spelt Franke. Bulraer today is Bulmer in Rydale, lying slightly south of Ness, midway between York and Kirkymoorside. The manor of Ness is where John's grandfather, Hugh, resided.

The first **Peter Frankland aka Petri de Glaisdale,** of the warpentake of Bulraer, was born around 1574, and died 13th June 1661, around the same time as both of his brothers Robert and Thomas Frankland.

Peter (1574) children:

> Marriage 1. Ana Calverte, 27th July 1592. Born around 1575, Ana died 20th January 1607.
>
> **Robertus** b. 25 May 1606, later known as Robertus de Glaisdale.

> Marriage 2. Margareta Eshe, 30th January 1610. Born about 1582, she died 2nd August 1611.
>
> No issue recorded.
>
> Marriage 3. Margareta Sowerbye de Thirsk, 20th June 1620, born 1591, died 6th Sept 1670.

Peter senior's third marriage to Margareta Sowerbye de Thirsk is indicative of an ongoing connection with the Franklands of Thirkleby, Sowerby itself lying close by.

> Petrus b. 20 Apr 1622, Peter and his sister were named after their parents (see details of Peter below).
>
> Margareta b. 25 Nov 1625.

Something of Petrus Franckland Junior:

> Peter was born 20th April 1622 and died 19th Dec 1674.
>
> Married Margareta Wilson 24th Jun 1647. She was born 7th Oct 1623, died 29th Dec 1664.

Margareta's father was Thome Wylson, cleric.

Peter's children:

> Thomas born 8th June 1648, died 16th Mar 1669, aged twenty.
>
> Robertus born 6th June/July 1650, named after Peter's brother Robertus.
>
> Anna born 10th Mar 1653, died 18th May 1668, aged fifteen.
>
> Rebecka born 4th Oct 1658, also died, aged nine, 3rd June 1660.
>
> Mary born 4th March 1660, died two month old, 24th Jun 1660.
>
> Willyam born 27th April 1661, survived, changing his surname to Lacy.
>
> Elizabeth born Dec 1662, is indicated 'filia Petri de Glaisdale'.
>
> Peter born 7th Sep 1663, died aged four months, 11th Jan 1664.

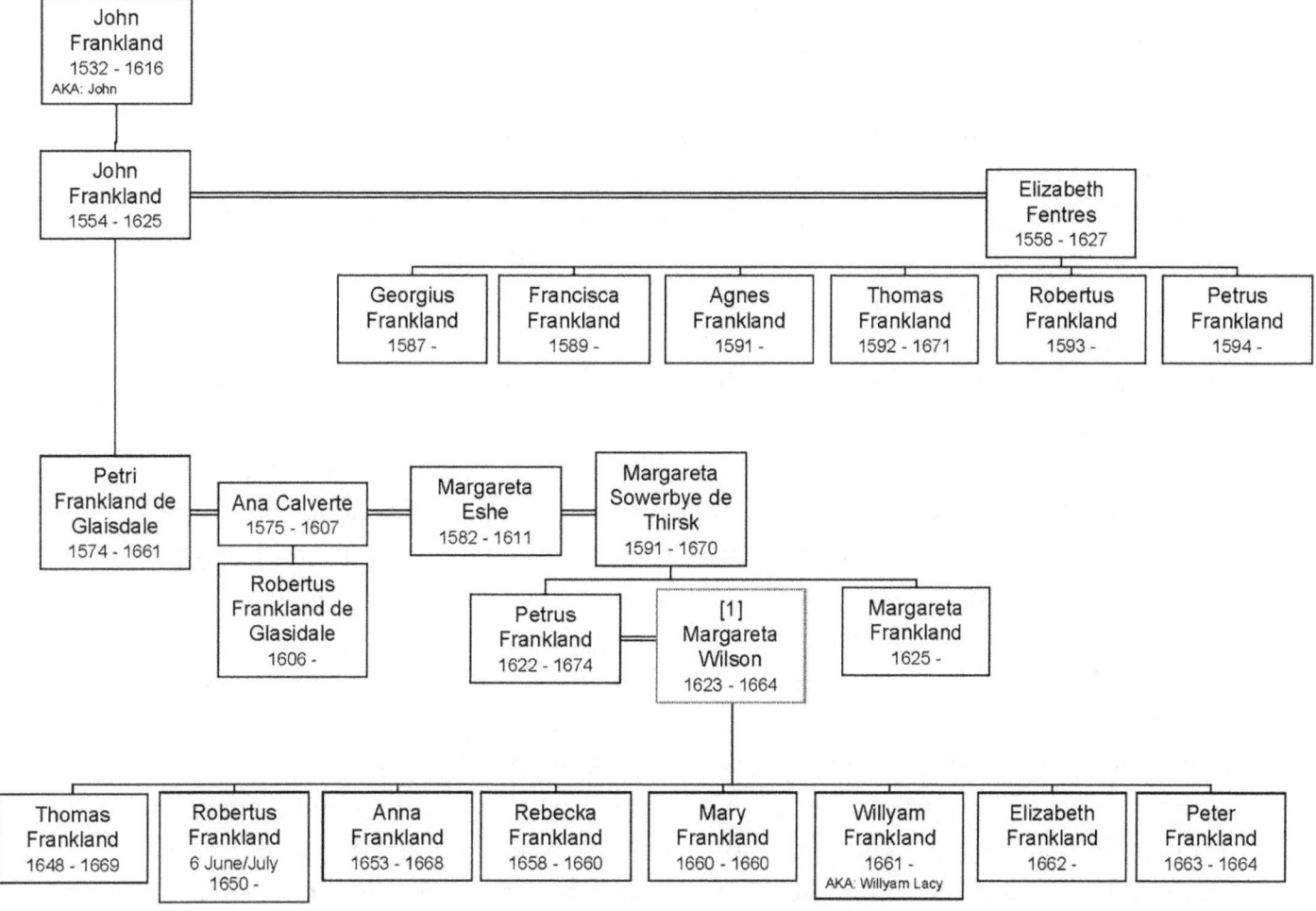

The Reformation

In Saxony 1517 Martin Luther had posted his thesis on Protestant Reformation, and in 1534 King Henry VIII issued the Act of Supremacy. Many people of the time didn't like the route the Catholic Church was taking and by 1549 Thomas Cranmer had put together the *English Book of Prayer*. By 1571 the thirty-nine Articles had become the standard for liturgy and the Franks become fully immersed in the doctrine.

The Recusancy Act of 1593, under the reign of Elizabeth I, targeted and persecuted Catholics who refused to attend Anglican worship. It has to be remembered, the majority of continental European invaders coming from Normandy, including the Franks, were originally devoutly Catholic, the Pope being divine head. It is not surprising therefore, that while many of the Frank's Catholic contemporaries had been registered and listed as recusants and therefore ripe for persecution, of the many lists and surnames of people who would later intermarry with the Franks, throughout North Yorkshire I have been unable to unearth a single Frank listed as Catholic. Yet the local Egton list of 1604, Egton being a hot bed for recusants, notes many Catholic surnames later linked to the Franks in marriage. In line with much of the rural community a majority of later Franks became devout Methodists.

To put this in context, whereas France and Spain was Catholic, the Huguenots in France were staunchly Protestant peaking at two million by 1562, and over the next 100 years as Protestantism gained influence so Catholic hostility grew. A high point was reached around 1685, under Louis XIV, when an escalation in persecution started which spilled over to the beginning of the eighteenth century. By now three-quarters of Catholics had been either slaughtered or converted – hundreds of thousands fled, many of them to Britain where the then stance on religion ensured a modicum of safety.

The point being, the great shifts taking place relating to religion in Europe were so oppositely entrenched, it is difficult today to get one's head around its vicissitude and the fear it induced. Many of those arriving in Britain were craftsmen and artisans bringing with them the very skills and tools necessary for the emergence a more sophisticated society idee; an idee previously foreign to the more earthy Anglo-Saxon.

Then there was the later influx of Jew, Jamaican, Chinese, Indian, Pakistani and Eastern European. Most of these were benign beings with no axe to grind, appreciative, hard-working, with the necessary skills and ability to forge a modern outcome, themselves part architects in the formation of a recognised multi-nuanced yet coherent new society. Today a majority in Britain have no idea that twenty-first century Huguenots alone represent an amazing one in six of British population descent, so absorbed into current society you wouldn't know they exist. Compare this to today's unease that stirs so much resentment, bewilderment and fear within an otherwise largely thoughtful and welcoming society.

In terms of upset versus absorption, something Britain's diverse culture desires is nothing more than the visual affirmation of full integration: an attestation ensuring stability acceding to the basic norms of the Western idee in the assertion of liberal values and traditions, not the imposition of a culture hostile to civilisation and peace across the world.

In her report on integration and extremism Dame Louise Casey says; 'There are certain things we need to draw a line, there are rules of being part of a liberal democracy, that is why people want to come here and live here.' Those who seek to impose an idiom other than our own do so with hate as its everlasting and central core and would be best trying their luck elsewhere. In ignoring civil servant apprehension, and in line with the implications found in a name, Dame Louise's report of the summer 2016 is as the name Frank implies, much as always, to the point, *frank and fearless.*

The Extraordinary Franks

Population movement around the early 1600s found an unusual increase in the Frank population in North Yorkshire, suggestive of an increase in birth rate survival and, in terms of adult population, a possible trickle returning from Scotland adding to localised inward migration from the Yorkshire surrounds. This has to be put in context with employment and the pureness of the iron ore mined locally, some Franks subsisting through farming, mining and work at the nearby thriving port of Whitby. Added to this was the abnormal scattering of abbeys, sheep farming, weaving, glass production, forestry and so on, all abutting the great powerhouse cathedral city of York, and Yorkshire as an extremely productive entity with continuous streams of traffic stopping and passing through, with the tiny settlement of Yarm as its fulcrum north and to the south.

A quick look at the Admissions to the Freedom of York records provides illumination as to names. I start off with Elizabeth I 1558, and finish around 1714 at the time of Queen Anne:

1558–1603 Joh Frankerewe

Roberti Frankerewe

Ricardus Frankland

Milo Frankland

Willelmus Frank previously Frankland

Guido Frankland

Willelmi Frankland

Johannis Frankland

1603–1625 Willelmus Francis

Will Franck

Georgius Franck

Robert Franke

George Franke

Robert Frank

1625–1649 Richard Franckland

Joh Franckland

Guidonis Franckland

Willelmus Franckland

Roberti Franke

Richard Franke

Georgii Franke

Gracia Franck, widow

1649–1660 Lancelot Franckland

Mathew Francis, son of

William Francis

William Francke, son of George

Joseph Francke, son of George

George Francke

Henricus Franke

1660–1672 Thomas Franckland

Thomae Franckland

Willelmus Francis

George Franck

1672–1685 The period, Charles II.

Richard Franke

Thomas Franke

Henricus Franke, coincidentally my grandfather was Thomas Henry Frank.

1685–1688 Among many names, no Franks recorded.

1689–1694 The period, William and Mary.

Abrahamus France

Thomas Frank

Henrici Frank

1694–1702 No record.

1702–1714 The period, Queen Anne.

Adam Franke, a free denizen.

Robertus Frank, mariner.

Changes to the more Catholic name of Frankland for Frank and the family tree from 1606

Whereas earlier date variations of Franckland appear most prevalent, where William and Robert feature strongly the spelling of Franckland quickly diminished. And just as the name evolved from derivatives of Francaise these were replaced with versions such as Francke. The Christian names of Thomas and Henry now come to the fore; these are seen attached to the simpler surnames of Frank or Franke. Shown by local headstones, the birth, death and marriage records for Danby confirm the Frankland and Franks as one interrelated family.

The idea of shortened or modernised surnames had become widespread, certainly across North Yorks and it is a wonder the Danby Franklands managed to hold on to the longer name for so long. Even so, the spelling of surnames altered as a convenient way of distinguishing between breakaway brothers and cousins, and the practice of repeating a father's first name son-on-son generationally.

Around this period the Franks north of York simplified the spelling of their name whereas the Thirkleby Franklands, in retaining their more Catholic stance, had reason to feel somehow superior having resisted the rush to become staunch Protestants. But this was nothing new for the North Yorkshire Franks and their Scottish kin, supremely deft in their conciliatory role, acting as arbitrators between warring factions where the middle ground was the safest, pragmatic in the simplification of a name, and as regards their religion, remaining staunch Christian with the use of lay preachers under the soft-shoe Protestant banner of Methodism.

As superior numbers of Franks spread across the Dales, many Franklands changed their name to Frank through intermarriage and integration. Old mapping shows the scattering of land ownership from the coast across the Dales to York and beyond marking a determination by the Franks to make the territory their own, whereas Frankland holdings sadly diminished practically fading from memory.

Robertus Frankland de Glaisdale, was born 25th May 1606, and died 19th June 1654 aged forty-eight.

Robertus (1606) children:

> Marriage, Jana Boyes, 7th June 1628, born about 1608, Jana died 26th March 1689.
>
> Robertus b. 23 Jan 1629.
>
> Jana b. 30 Oct 1631.
>
> Georgius b. 6 April 1633.
>
> Johis b. 1635.
>
> Agnes b. 10 May 1636.
>
> Elizabeth b. 5 May 1637.
>
> **Thomas** b. 13 May 1638. Thomas Frankland de Glaisdale, was born 13th May 1638, and died 15th January 1706 aged sixty-nine.
>
> Margaria b. 26 Feb 1639.
>
> Willielmus b. 20 Jun 1640. Willielmus Lacy Frankes
>
> Anna b. 16 Oct 1641.
>
> Maria b. 12 Jan 1646.
>
> Margareta b. 26 Sep 1650.

Robertus senior appears to have been hurt early on, between 1638 and 1644, during the war between the Royalists and Parliamentarians when 3000 men were killed between 1642 and 1651, these being the official dates of the war. Whatever the injury, it didn't prevent him continuing to father children nor Jana to produce, although there seems to have been a gap of five years or more likely unrecorded births between October 1641 and January 1646.

The main line now continues with **Thomas Frank,** son of Robertus Frankland de Glaisdale:

Thomas (1638) children:

> Marriage Ellis Suggitt, 6th June 1654, born around 1637, she died 14th February 1715. Ellis was pregnant when they both married aged seventeen.
>
> Barbara b. 18 Jan 1655.

Jane b. 14 Dec 1656.

Robertus b. 29 Jan 1661.

Elizabeth b. 19 Aug 1663.

Thome b. 8 Mar 1665. 10th October 1738, the date Thomas Frank is buried.

Janeta b. 10 Sep 1666.

Ellicia b. 23 Apr 1668.

Maria b. 26 July 1669.

Jana b. 18 July 1670.

Douglas Frank Blackmore

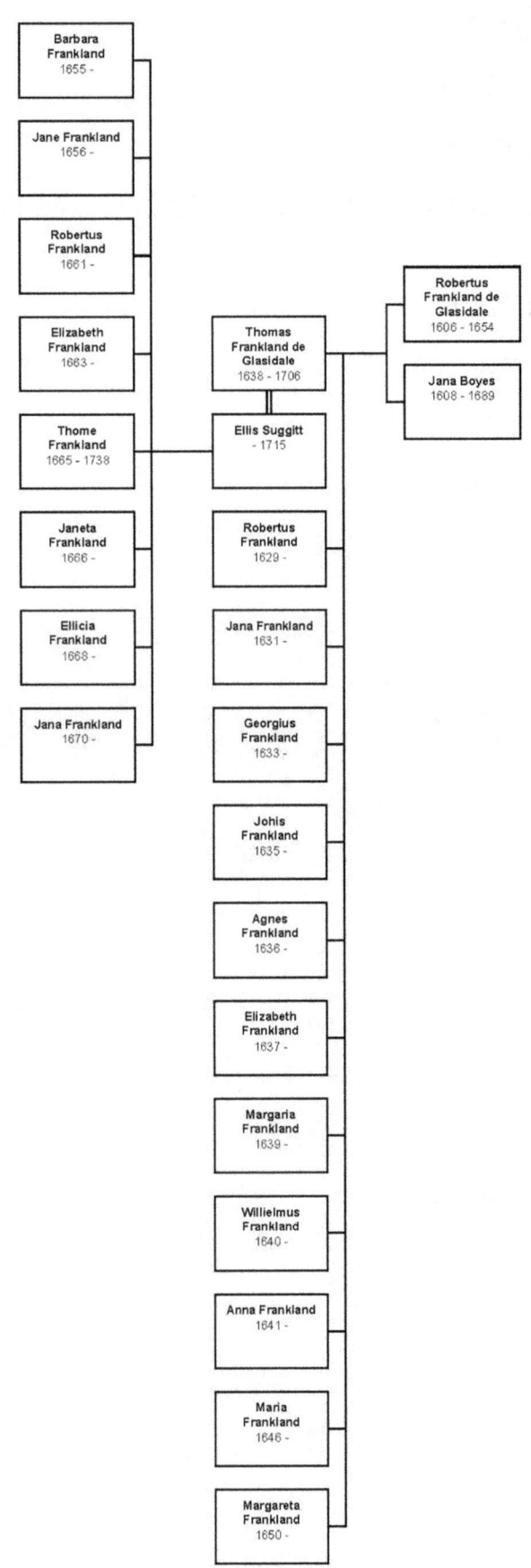

The Extraordinary Franks

Robertus Frankland aka Robert Frank, was born 29th January 1661, and died, buried in wool, 2nd July 1696. Named Robert Frank de Fryup, aged thirty-five, apparently educated, Robert's will appears learned and illustrates a remarkably recognisable modern format and use of words not out of place today.

Robert (1661) children:

> Marriage 1. Ann, thought to be Lacy, around 1677. Ann, born 4th May 1654, died 29th March 1679, her epitaph reading *'Lanea see actum'* meaning 'see and spend time'.
>
> Ann or Anna b. 7 June 1678, her mother died nearly ten months later in childbirth, the baby dying with her. Anna herself died aged four, 19th December 1682. The father is shown as Roberti de Glaisdale.
>
> Marriage 2. Mary Garbutt, 10th February 1680/1 at Danby while expecting Robert's child.
>
> Mary born 13th May 1658, died 23rd February 1682 at Danby, following the birth of Dorothea in the December. Mary's father was Richard Garbutt.
>
> Sarah b. 2 Feb 1681, died eleven months later, 9th January 1682, at Danby, being buried in wool.
>
> Dorothea b. 22 Dec 1681, died 23rd June 1682 and was also buried in wool, shortly after the death of her mother Mary.

A note on Dorothea: the introduction of Dorothea the daughter, or Robert's third marriage to Dorothy Lacy, prompted a female name that carried through the line to my mother Dorothy Frank. Incidentally Mum's sister was Mary, (see Robert, marriage two). It seems the names chosen by Tom Frank for his two girls and John for his son (see Johannes below) were maybe more than coincidental.

> Marriage 3. Dorothy Lacy, 5th February 1683/4, sister of Ann, at Danby. Born around 1661, Dorothy died 27th October 1734. Dorothy and Ann's parents were Richard de Lacy and Margaret Johnson cum Lacy.
>
> Maria b. 27 Dec 1684. Maria was known as Mary, perhaps in recognition of Robert's second wife Mary. Maria was less than two months old when she died 10th February 1685.

Robertus b. 9 Dec 1686, at Danby.

Gulielmus b. 26 Sep 1687, Glaisdale.

Jana b. 13 Jun 1689, died 7th February 1704/5.

Georgius b. 26 Apr 1692, died 27th May 1693, aged one month, being buried in wool.

Johannes b. 12 Apr 1694, the Frank line continuum.

Note: born 1650 (grandson of Petri de Glaisdale 1574) Robertus Frank was indicated in the Hearth Tax for 1673. In his will, he bequeathed that his brother William Lacy be made tutor and guardian:

> 'For this my son Robert, and for William Lacy act as his trustee, to put in trust to look at all things be done to this intent and purpose and true meaning of this my last Will and Testament, Robert Frank.'

The issue of being buried in wool, except through death by plague or destitution, was initiated through an Act of Parliament in order to support an increase in the homeland usage of wool and hence the value of English wool as a commodity. This was the Burying of Wool Acts 1666–1680, where being buried in a pure English woollen shroud became law. Relatives of the deceased were obliged to swear such burials by affidavit. The legislation was in force until 1814, but mostly ignored after 1770, the records of those too poor to afford such burial were marked naked.

To give a sense of the time, Charles I was executed in 1649 at the climax of the English Civil War. Charles II was on the throne when the aforesaid Act of Parliament came into force in 1666, the same year as the Great Fire of London that saved many of its people from a gruesome death through the Great Plague, a swathe that had previously ravished the continent and after crossing the Channel was spreading rapidly across the country.

Readers might have heard of the expression 'on your tod'. A tod was twenty-eight pounds or two stone (English) being a common weight for wool. The usage of wool for burial shrouds led to the word tod becoming 'on his or her tod' for the cessation of life, hence a person left on their own, the slang derivative being 'on your tod' or 'you're on your tod mate' for someone left to get on with it on their own especially in the face of danger, their more fearful companions holding back.

Woodwark Frank

Robertus Frankes born 1629, shown earlier as first son of Robertus born 1606, being senior successor and his name appearing in the 1673 Hearth Tax for Danby, the list of names not appearing to be mainstream they must therefore be cousin related and therefore the probable children of Robertus. That being the case it follows the names Walter, Margaret, Robert, Thomas, Peter, Joseph and Ann being the children of Robertus, them being born between, say, 1650 and 1670. Although confusing with the overlap and plethora of Johns in particular, and Robert, the best I can come up with for a couple of the spare Johns floating about is one of the aforesaid male offspring of Robertus siring a boy, say John, himself siring a John in 1715, this event likely accounts for a miscellaneous Robert being born of a John around 1744.

The scenario is indicative of a scattering of Franks living in close proximity finding a need to branch out. With a profusion of Johns, archivist Ian Hall's proposition of a Robert born of John occurring around 1744 seems at face value as good an outcome as any, likewise with the name Robert. Yet certainty as to progeny, deciding in which generation a family might originate, it is difficult to speculate with reasonable accuracy. That said, irrespective of any misinterpretation, each of the pedigrees feed into earlier common ancestry anyway; my hunch the aforesaid being supportive of my own analysis backed by family documentation of the period.

In one's more recent history the name Woodwark appears in two original, recently found, beneficiary wills, one of the two quite lengthy in the number of beneficiaries and very detailed wherein a William Woodwark was located born of Mary Woodwark Frank who married William 13th March 1880. In searching for parentage, I happened on an article of Judith K Werner of Hayward, California 'Franks of North Yorkshire'. Dated July 1999, the article has been really useful. Incidentally the wills I mentioned were found in a box of old papers passed on by my grandfather. T H Frank later executor to his aunt, Mary (1) Burgoine, (2) Crake, née Frank, both marriages being to a vicar she left much of her estate to the Methodist Church.

In an effort to spread the word to Franks whether they reside the UK, Scotland, America, Australia or wherever, it seems important to share the story of this incredible Dales family. And here are Judith's findings:

'My Franks are English, from North Yorkshire, where Franks are thick on the ground.' These are:

Robert (farmer) b. 1779, m. Elizabeth Woodwark, Danby 1802.

Glaisdale births:

Mary 1804

Hannah 1805

Robert* 1808

Danby births:

George 1812

Joseph 1815

Jane Ann 1817

William Woodwark 1819

John 1823

Robert de Fryup born 1808 m Hannah Elizabeth Rigg, Danby 1834

Notes on both couples: Hannah died in 1847 at Egton aged thirty-seven. Robert married again, living at Brough near Catterick.

Danby births to Hannah:

John Rigg 1835, d. 1859 Brough aged twenty-three
William Woodwark 1837, d. 1914 Buckhurst, Essex (see below)

Joseph 1838, became a grocer in Hampstead, London

Robert 1840, he and family operated a hotel in the Brandon and Byshottles area of Durham

Egton births to Hannah:

George 1842, became an ironmonger and builder in Marylebone, London

Ann Elizabeth 1844, apparently never married

Richard Rigg 1847, became a grocer at Buckhurst Hill, Essex. He died at his son's home in Gosforth, Northumberland 1891

Notes of Judith

'William Woodwark Frank went to London and in 1866 married Octavie Carme, a Parisian born dressmaker, at St Marylebone, London.'

Marylebone births:

Alfred William 1868, d. 1920 Newark, New Jersey, USA

Eugenie Octavie 1871, d. unmarried 1946, Buckhurst Hill, Essex

Notes of Judith 2

'A bookkeeper, my great-grandfather Alfred William Frank emigrated from Essex in 1895. In New York City he married and raised two daughters, moving to Newark after 1915. He was the only one of my Frank line known to have immigrated, so I expect having English cousins who I'd love to meet.'

So there we have it, a Dales family so fixed to their beloved land having the courage to advance into the wider world. Whereas to many these folk might appear an offshoot, for those who yearn to know something of their heritage it is hoped the wider insight involving one's own family story brings perspective and a sense of reality. The complexity in compiling the data, while mammoth, I'm hopeful someone might take on the cudgel and maybe add to the knowledge of this remarkable family in the same way Judith's research has added useful insight.

Knowing the quiet rural backwaters of Danby, Egton and Glaisdale, life being lived much in the same vein, the thing that strikes me are the hundreds of years of continuation and the courage necessary to break free. The mid 1850s are recorded as a time when mechanisation changed everything, and later between the two world wars it took a lonesome, bereaved teenage girl such as Dorothy, having lost her mother, having the courage to strike off alone to Canada and thence to Africa, and by so doing changed everything forever. And for that, dear Mum, I'm immensely proud.

But here I must return to the Normans and the bedrock of a family interrelationship.

The Franks cum de Lacy ties

It seems my mother's name came into use seen in the birth of a Dorothy in Yorkshire in 1531, the name being found in a marriage to Thomas de Lacy in 1560, and later in 1624 and 1661 in Danby with the birth of Dorothy de Lacy, third wife of Robert Frankland cum Robert Frank. The earlier Dorothy's father was John born 1507, her grandfather Thomas, being born in 1440. And with the coming together and later infusion of the two prominent Norman bloodlines, it is important to take a look at the de Lacy, the family having an exact history recording.

The de Lacy were an old noble Norman family of Lascy, Normandy, the name being first recorded around 1005 with Hugh Lord de Lasi whose wife was Emma de Bois-l'Eveque. Born around 992, Hugh was the father of Ilbert and Walter, Hugh being recorded again 1020–1085, Walterus in Normandy in 1043, and Ilbert de Laci also in Normandy in 1045. Additionally there was Hawise de Lacy, daughter of Hugh, wife of Robert d'Evreux, Hawise dying in Rosmar Normandy in 1050.

Like the Franks, the family had strong connections with Bayeux: Hugh's two sons, as Lords of Lasi, were recorded as chevalier knights, Ilbert fighting alongside William at Hastings and during the Harrying of the North in 1069–1070, him receiving vast grants in West Yorkshire, whereas his counterpart Robert de Brus's initial awards were spread across the north-east. Next generation Lacys had associations with the north, a Henry being found in both Lancashire and Yorkshire, and Ilbert, son of Robert, having fought in the Battle of the Standard at Northallerton in 1138. Incidentally the lordship of Lasi is situated in triangulation with Bayeux and Falaise, Normandy.

In 1399 a northern branch of the Lacys held the great lordship of Bowland, of which later holdings passed to the Duchy of Lancaster. I previously mentioned land settlement actions between the Danbys and the Franks and the Franklands who later purchased the land around Danby itself. Thomas Lacy was located there in 1540, his grandson William was buried in Danby in 1597. Later, William who died in 1597, his son Thomas died in 1647, so terribly common, his wife Dorothy having died nearly thirty years earlier (in 1618) in childbirth, an earlier surviving son, John, being baptised in Danby 18th July 1585.

Appalling for women, as too their loved ones, the incidence of death through childbirth ran on and on, century upon century, right through to recent times, my mother, also Dorothy loosing her mother to childbirth when Dorothy herself was a child. When I talk of justice for women, their rights versus subjugation and so on, there is still a long way to go, our longevity today so often taken for granted where we become lazy in the pursuit of fair society for those left trapped or not so privileged.

The Lacy coming from an unbroken line of noble descent, the more recent injection of Norman blood reaffirms successive Frank DNA blood ties with Normandy found in the marriage of Dorothy Lacy to the aforementioned Robert Frank in Danby dated 1683/4, their future blood lines infused by fifteen successive Frank marriages interlaced with the Lacy; for a time the two Norman entities entwined.

The name Dorothy repeated through the Lacy line in combination with the Franks seems as compelling as the families they represent. After a period of the two families having found such warm familiarity, the Franks were alone again, the relationship of the Lacys and Franks petering out in 1865 with a single Lacy male birth and no male issue. The passing of the historic de Lacy name was marked by the brief re-emergence of the Lacy's female Christian name of Dorothy, found in Dorothy Frank and that domain whose heritage this work is dedicated.

I earlier mentioned Hawise de Lacy who married Robert d'Evreux. What I omitted was that Robert was the Archbishop of Rouen, whose father shared the Frank's ancestry in Richard I, Duke of Normandy, his mother being Gunnora, Richard's second wife. The reason for mentioning this is to demonstrate the complexity of this work and how interwoven the various families are, often sharing a common antecedence. But by now the Yorkshire Franks had long since cemented new allegiances having the business of rural life and a firm grip upon the Bible to carry them forward.

Methodists

In 1690, the 'Society of Friends' established a meeting house in Whitby, and prior to Wesley, had many members who were forbidden to serve on ships that carried guns. Methodism was formed in 1747 in King St Chapel, parallel to New Road, Whitby, where the Dales founders and Glaisdale Franks became staunch Methodists and lay preachers, laying the ground that others might follow.

Harland

1st May 1737, to Francis Harland, farmer of Hawsker, a son, Christopher. The Harlands of Glaisdale later become connected to the Franks by both name and marriage.

MAIN TREE CONTINUED

Johannes aka John Frank; I have a copy of John's will which is well-versed and remarkably detailed. He was born 12th April 1694 at Danby, and died 16th January 1772, also at Danby.

John (1694) children:

> Marriage, Jane, 15th Sept 1715. Jane is shown as a main beneficiary in John's will, but being unable to locate their actual marriage records, I am unable to ascertain Jane's maiden name and parentage. Jane died 19th Nov 1769
>
> **Robert** b. 2 Jan 1716, died 31st August 1808.
>
> John b. 15 Apr 1718, d 8 May 1768 (see next for corrections).
>
> Mary b. 11 Sep 1719, Egton, married John Allin 7th June 1753, died 29th March 1801.
>
> Jane b. 3 Mar 1722, of Egton, married James Blackburn.

Sarah b. 12 Apr 1723, married a John Frank, their blood ties unknown.

Ann b. 31 Oct 1727, of Danby, married Danvers Allen 8th May 1750, died 16th March 1784 at Fryup.

Dorothy b 1725 d 1798

Barbara b. not available, married Robert Petch.

Hannah b. not available, married Thomas Porter.

Rachel b. not available, married William Petch.

There is a conflict of data where I have John, born 1729/30, died 15th December 1807 and a birth or baptism date of 23rd February 1719. The latter date seems to be correct, and should be viewed as the date of baptism, with its birth date of April 1718 correct. This would fit in with Mary's birth 11th September 1719. Archivist Ian Hall of Bedford Park has a similar date of birth of around 1718 with a baptism date of 15th April 1718 at Rosedale. He has John's burial as 8th May 1768 at Lastingham. Both John and Robert were educated having the grant of tuition bonds shown in a will of May 1735.

The Extraordinary Franks

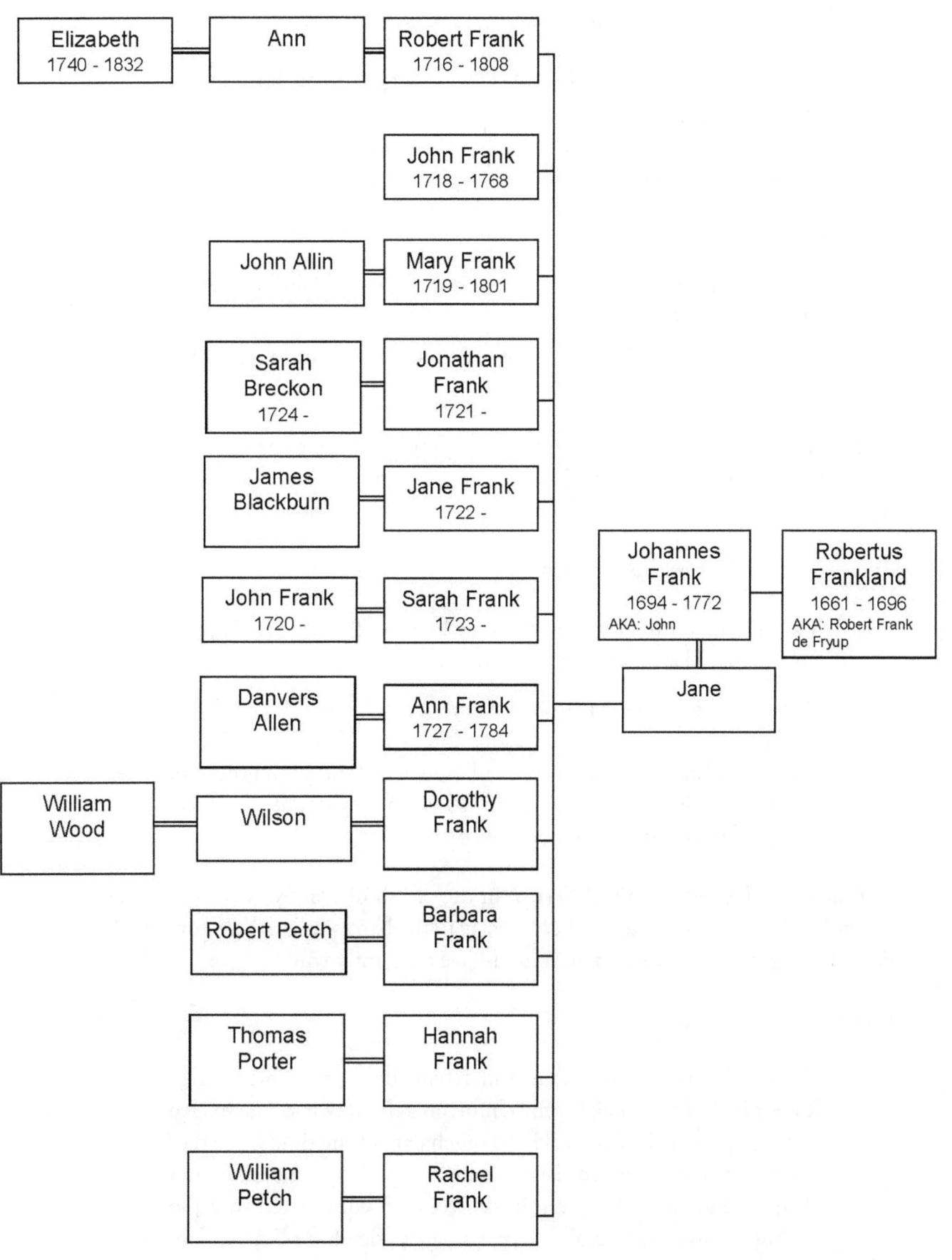

Further details concerning John senior and his will:

> There are three other births, two boys and a girl, who don't appear in the will.
>
> There is a Mary 2, born 6th March 1731, who married John Agar of Egton, 3rd February 1756.
>
> The will seems to show the correct Mary as the one born September 1719.
>
> Two boys, Jonathan, born 20th March 1721, Goathland, married a Mary, born 1718, in 1747
>
> Richard, born 11th January 1718, fits in date wise, but is recorded at nearby Goathland.

Having no other data, as Johannes Frank's will specifically mentions and lists his eight daughters and two sons John and Robert. The two boys found later as executors to their father's will are shown as independent farmers in their own right.

John, brother of Robert, his children are:

> Mary Frank, born around 1742 and who died 29th April 1753, was baptised 20th February 1742 at Rosedale.
>
> One line of thinking has Robert Frank, born 1744, who died 13th February 1838 at Glaisdale, as a son of John, another having Robert as a son of Robert. Either way the family tree follows the route of Johannes aka John Frank born April 1694, and is most likely correct going forward from Robert born 1744.

Born in 1716, **Robert Frank of Fryup**, in the parish of Danby, was baptised 19th November 1730, aged fourteen where a delay in the baptism remains a mystery. He died 31st August 1808, aged ninety-one. I have his family will.

Robert (1716) children:

> The best I can come up with is Ann, having been pregnant, married Robert in 1744 aged eighteen. Unfortunately only badly damaged scraps of paper exist which akin to much data of the time was either not recorded or became mislaid. During this period the huge amount of upset and violence raging in the country culminated in rapid Catholic conversion. As all I have is a date of death for 'Ann wife of

a Frank' immediately following a birth date for Elizabeth of 1749, I'm of the view Robert's wife was indeed Ann.

Robert b. 27 Dec 1744, baptised 9th January 1745, died 13th February 1838 aged ninety-four.

John No real details available.

Joseph b. 1746.

Hannah born around 1748, married Garbutt.

Elizabeth 1749. Elizabeth Frank was born in 1749 at Murkside, Goathland, near Egton. She died in Egton in 1782, aged thirty-three.

His wife Ann having died around 1749, Robert aged forty-six married for a second time in 1762 – his daughter's namesake, Elizabeth. An executrix held by me shows Robert's widow, Elizabeth, having died 24th January 1832; her likely birth date appears to have been around 1740.

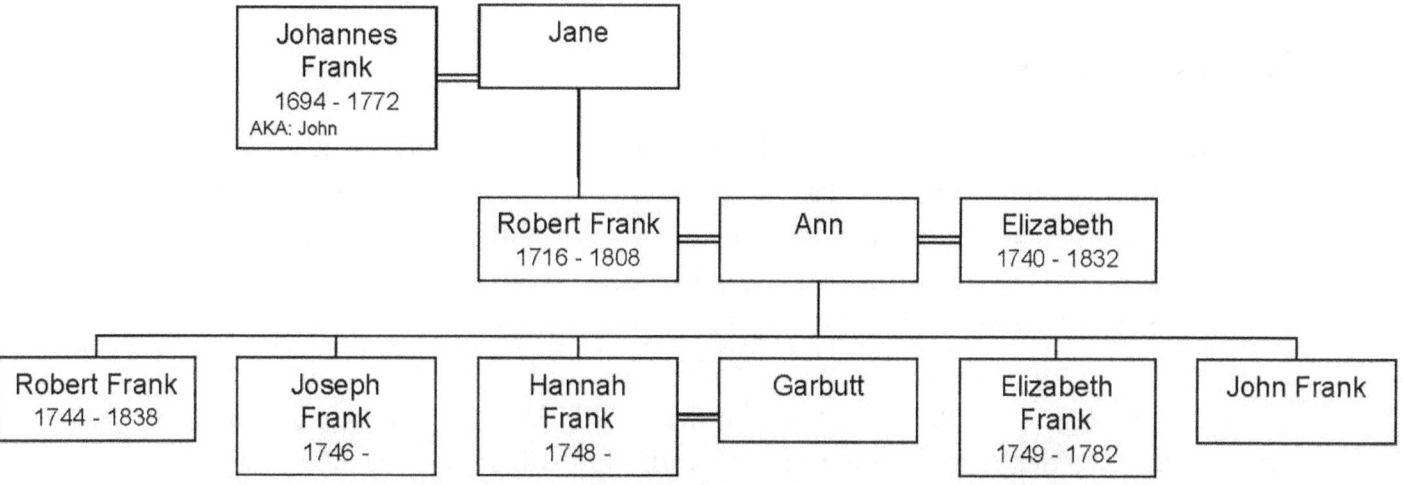

Around the time of Robert senior's birth and the years following, it is possible church records might have been purposely destroyed. Although particularly affecting papists, the brutality of the physical purge may also have affected those who had already declared for Methodism. Whether the destruction of records such as marriages was viewed as punishment for not aspiring wholeheartedly to the Church of England doctrine, or a slap on the wrist for surreptitiously maintaining relations with associates who retained the Roman faith, is seen as two fold: the first being a purposeful act intended to drive, come what may, the whole population to the Anglican faith; the second to expunge all records pertaining the Roman doctrine even though it contained data specific to those already converted.

Not particularly happy times, a number of Frank/Frankland contemporaries, notably Thomas and Francis Harland, Richard Harland senior, and Richard junior of Egton, Francis Peirson senior and junior, also of Egton, and Henry Pearson, yeoman, were all convicted. Convicted recusants were obliged to receive Anglican communion once per annum on pain of a severe fine. These names were all Frank family related and immediate neighbours.

From the outset, the Franks were founding staunch Methodists, remaining so through to the twentieth century. John Wesley was born in 1703, Charles in 1707 and by 1739 both constantly preached around Yorkshire, particularly the Dales where the Franks were known to have given them hospitality and a bed for the night, their first conference being conducted in 1744.

I am satisfied Robert was born of Ann, records, such as they were, showing his sister in relation to her mother Ann, and there being no earlier marriage due to Robert's father being only aged eighteen when Ann became pregnant. Due to the baptism, it appears Robert's parents had married prior to his birth, thus causing the event to be legitimised. But of Robert Frank, what a life, what a man, and surviving to the ripe age of ninety-four; great stuff.

Robert Frank senior

In his will, Robert senior had amassed several freeholds together with lease-held property, among them Woodhead Farm, Hawk Carr, Glaisdale and Mill Lane Farm. Joseph appears to have received Mill Lane Farm, the bulk of the estate going to Robert, having the care of his stepmother Elizabeth. Joseph was still on the census for Fryup in 1839, or probably his son, also Joseph, who married Mary in 1811/12.

To add to the confusion, there was a previous Joseph Frankland appearing in the Quarter Sessions of 5th March 1723, relating to Cold Oak farm, and the West End farm of Aikeley Side, let to Cornelius Frankland. I know from cursory investigation that this part of the family had property and many estates scattered across the Dales and further afield, the whole emerging from a scattering of existing holdings bolstered by the division of a much larger inheritance of land and property. Whether the above two farms were let within the family domain as per Frank lettings to sons-in-law, or of a separate fealty, is difficult to ascertain.

Regardless, the extent of the whole estate I have barely skirted, except to say it was extensive. The details I do have, it seems each successive generation divided chunks of their inheritance, the most successful, such as Robert Frank adding to their holdings as they went along, Robert Frank, Joseph and Cornelius but three of a conflation of Franks spread across the terrain.

Jacobite Rising of 1745, Charles Edward Stuart and the Egton Recusants, 1745

Lt General Sir John Cope, commander of the British Army in Scotland, was in pursuit of Charles Stuart, when Charles, at the head of his ragtail army and having received good information, presented his sword and set off to meet Cope on Falside Hill. Cope was routed in a battle lasting less than fifteen minutes. News of the Jacobite victory sent shock waves and complete disbelief across England that Charles, landing almost alone in a remote corner of Scotland, could accomplish such a feat.

The defeat led to a huge outbreak of anti-Catholic violence in England:

> 'The brave ship carpenters of Whitby, being informed that the papists of Egton in the moors made great rejoicings for the defeat of the Kings forces, took their axes and cleavers to hack and hew the said papists in pieces, and were with extreme difficulty brought back to Whitby after they had marched two miles towards their enemies.'

Records clearly show Franks involved in the timber trade at Whitby around this date. With the Franks also farming in Egton, it seems incongruous they would have been involved in any attack against their immediate friends and neighbours. Exactly the hows and whys of the situation is impossible to unscramble, but many-recorded papist's names are later shown to have converted and married into the Franks.

It seems as founder members of Methodism, through the gospel, the Franks brought to pass the rapid conversion as many of the Catholic population they were able, even into marriage: one, as a means of saving their lives, and two, bringing them into the safe conduct and immediacy of a god they knew and understood through the bosom of everyday existence, quite different from the Catholic inquisitor mindset and paraphernalia of paste idols, incense and the intolerant dictates and canticles of a foreign meme.

Little did people know of the shadow to come with the parade and savagery of raped and abused women and children orchestrated and run by nuns, the distortion of a Christian idee warehousing tens of thousands of children indoctrined within a maelstrom of evil and wholesale priestly abuse? No, what the chapel folk preached was a god envisaged close to nature and the everyday cycle of life, simple, easily understood, no chanting go-betweens adorned with vestments of gold.

Having witnessed it for myself, just as a carpenter may take pride in planning a plank of wood, the same man might become a lay preacher tramping from one unadorned chapel to another, or yokels parlour, his waning strength sustained solely by a true sense of love and compassion, a sup or two and prayer. I've spoken about the Frank Bible, have seen it and although myself more agnostic than atheist, with a little luck hope someday to bring it into safekeeping.

Robert Frank (1744) children:

> Marriage 1. Isabel around 1762. Isabel died, probably in childbirth, around 1767.
>
> Margaret b. 29 Sep 1762, died 16th January 1763, aged three months.
>
> Robert b. 13 Dec 1764.
>
> George b. 14 Nov 1765.

It appears Isabel's death led Robert to foster his earlier children or arrange care for them in some other way as following his second marriage, Mary Peirson's children were sole beneficiaries to his later will. In his will written 17th March 1832, he describes John as his only son, mentioning his three daughters together with their respective husbands.

A mystery appears indicative his first marriage had never occurred, yet records show otherwise, one can only presume the former children had been taken care of in some way separate from his second marriage. As previously shown, as well as farming, these Franks were in the business of salvation where a subsequent marriage might resolve a number of problems in one go.

> Marriage 2. Mary Peirson b 13 Oct 1745, d 31 Jan 1834 at Glaisdale aged 89. Robert Frank married Mary Peirson 14 Jun 1768/9 (unclear) witnessed by Mary's sister Jane Peirson and Robert's brother John Frank.
>
> Robert Frank died 13th February 1838 aged 93. His baptism was 27th December 1744 at Rosedale, and his burial in Glaisdale 17th February 1838.

The Peirsons (variously spelt) were intimately associated with the Franks, my several times great-grandfather Robert Frank married Mary Peirson as seen on the 14th June 1768. Born of a farming family, Robert Frank, in later life acquired considerable landholdings, farms and property, dying a wealthy and prosperous man. Records for the Danby parish June 1768 show the Pearsons recorded as Pierson.

Robert held Whitby Customs House Peace Bonds, a number of farms, messuages, many hundreds of acres of moorland, closes, tenements, hereditaments and appurtenances, situated in Glaisdale and Fryup, Loggerheads Yard and Baxtergate, Whitby,

Wrelton and Middleton abounding Ness, situated between Kirkbymoorside and Pickering. Among his many tenants were Robert Featherstone and George Harland.

The Peirsons had done well for themselves having acquired considerable property and land along the way, distinguishing themselves in many charters and papers of the time. To the Charity for Seamen and Widows 1722, William Pearson gave two houses in Loggerheads Yard, Baxtergate, let at 5s a week, and in 1770 gave two tenements in Newgate Ghaut. Robert Frank knew and had business connections with the Peirsons.

In Robert Frank's will of 1838, among other effects in Whitby coinciding with William Pearson, was included Loggerheads Yard. Having dealings in Whitby early on in his life, he was astute, obviously worked hard and enjoyed good health, and unlike so many during those times did well for himself.

Shown above, an apparent mystery relating to several times great-grandfather Robert Frank appears to have been solved. When trying to get information on Mary Peirson, wife of Robert, despite some old family records showing Mary Peirson as Robert's second wife, I kept discarding references to a Robert relating to Isabel. The persistence of an Isabel, however, left me wondering. The other problem was how a Dales farmer's son could have continued to amass property, farms and shares, together with business interests in Whitby. Part answer to the mystery lies in eighteen-year-old Robert meeting Isabel and her becoming pregnant. Seemingly attracted to Isabel, living only a mile or two from the Frank's farm, made the tryst inevitable.

The problem for young Robert seems to have been his father's strict religious stance, and being obliged to marry pregnant local girl Isabel. It may have been for his own good that Robert had been told to get on with it and support his new wife and child. Whitby being only a stone's throw away, for a strong youth well-used to felling trees and sawing wood, it appears that young Robert may have seized the moment. Robert Frank, sawyer, would be aged eighteen on the birth of his daughter in late 1762. This was followed by the birth of two sons, the later George born 14th November 1765 followed possibly by two subsequent female births. It is not certain what happened to his beloved Isabel, it is assumed she may have died in childbirth, data suggestive of around November 1767.

Old records held by me confirm Robert's marriage to his definite 'second wife' Mary Peirson on the 14th June 1768/9. The histrionics relating to his occupation of sawyer, together with the dates, all fit. Robert seems to have reconciled matters with his father, as he becomes the main beneficiary to Robert senior's will and substantial estates on his father's death during August 1808. With Robert's marriage to Mary Peirson 1768/9, he was able to take advantage of the two families' long association; a subsequent Peirson inheritance furthering a useful addition to an already substantial estate.

Continued acquisitions are exampled by the following: *Extracts of The North Yorkshire Deeds Registry* show Issac Porritt selling several acres of land together with holdings in Moorsholm, close to Glaisdale. The same brief, BT/59/96, 1st April 1781, and BW/127/200, 15th July 1783, shows the release of land to 'Robert Frank, sawyer, having messuages in Baxtergate, Whitby'. Such data combined with the incumbents stated occupation of sawyer cum farmer and landowner, has proven decisive as to Robert's rapid change of status.

Robert Frank (second marriage to Mary Peirson, continued)

> Anne b. 1768/69 born Lastingham, Pickering or Roxby. Died 18 Oct 1849 aged 80. Married Gawan **Peirson** 8 Sep 1799, b. 1 Feb 1769 d 18 Oct 1851, died Goathland aged 82.
>
> Hannah b. 13 Jan 1773, Danby, d. 1844/45. Hannah married William Thompson 21 April 1794 at Danby.
>
> Molly Frank b. 19 May 1782, Glaisdale. Married Joseph Frank 14 Aug 1812, Joseph's father also a Robert Frank, plus Joseph a possible 2nd marriage to Mary. Joseph was mentioned in his own father Robert Franks will.
>
> Jane b. 1785 d 1850. Married Thomas Breckon 18 Sept 1818
>
> **John Frank Yeoman farmer.** b. 16 Sept 1778, d. 30 Nov 1853. Married Jane Harland 12 Apr 1803 Danby witnessed by John Frank. Note: John Frank's wife Jane born 1780, died 30 Dec 1847.

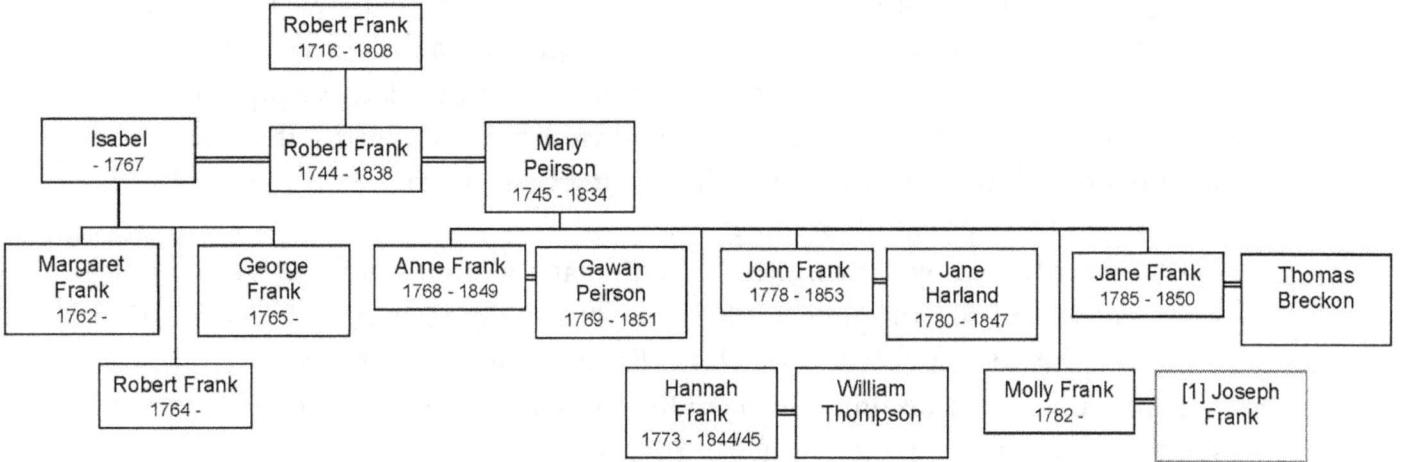

Baptised 8th December 1775, the Kirkby Moorside Census for 1841 shows Anne Frank, sometimes spelt Ann, aged 70, living with her husband at the family farm given as Thorn Hill House, Goathland, Yorks. What is unclear is whether the farm came from the Peirsons, the Franks or a combination of the two close families. I favour the latter. In 1807, John Frank is indicated as a contributor to education via the Fryup Free School.

White's directory of 1831 shows James Frank, yeoman farmer (shown below) and Robert Thomson, farmer. Through marriage the Thomson and Frank families were also strongly interrelated. John was a witness to his sister Molly's wedding on the 14th August 1812. He was sole executor for his father's will, having been bequeathed messuages, farms and substantial grazing in Glaisdale. These were subject to a nominal peppercorn annuity of £25 to his mother, Mary, for life.

The railway built from Pickering to Whitby in 1833 later extended to connect with Middlesbrough. I say this as history shows much earlier Frank associations with that town, and having a railway link to such a growth area, given the steel industry, associated mining and the River Tees, would have brought huge benefits and opportunities for investment.

In 1892, relative William Stonehouse willed £1,561.00 of railway stock and £160.00 annually split between his two daughters, these being Eleanor Pearson, given India Stock and for her sister Emily an annual income commencing in 1903.

Family tree continued:

> Anne (1768) children:
>
> John b. 1796
>
> William b. 1802
>
> James b. 1804
>
> John Tramaine b. 1808
>
> Hannah (1773) children:
>
> Married William Thompson, a Glaisdale farmer (b. 1770, d. 5 Jun 1845)
>
> Mary b. 1804, d. 1847 aged 43

John (1778) children:

> Married Jane Harland. Her parents were Frances Harland, 1737–Jun 1808, and Sarah Stonehouse, 1752–Apr 1832.

Sarah b. 1805, d. 6 Oct 1888. Married George Raw (b. 1805, d .25 Feb 1885 Danby East End aged 80). Had a son Rev John Frank Raw, b. Fryup 2 Nov 1837, d. Danby 29 Jun 1921. Married Hannah Mary (1839–6 Apr 1901)

Harland b. 1808, d, 27 Nov 1872. Married Margaret Mead (b. 1807, d. 23 Mar 1841 aged 33 Egton)

Robert Frank b. 1 Nov 1806, d. 4 Dec 1892. Farmer Glaisdale Head Farm.

Married first Ann Rigg prior to 1842

Second marriage to Mary Hart of Hart Hall, Habton, NYKS 27 May 1846 in Danby (28 Dec 1814–27 Sept 1887), daughter of Robert Hart and Mary Pickering. Mary inherits 50% of lands and house willed by Nicholas Hart 1763. The other 50% went to Thomas Hart who died aged 7. Sister Jane died aged 5, 6 April 1827. Sister Ann died aged 20, 4 Mar 1835, ending the Hart dynasty.

Mary b. 1803 m Thomas Bird of Pickering 25 Sep 1833

A note on Robert Hart, brother to Nicholas Hart of Hart Hall, Glaisdale: both of them farmers, Robert was born in 1786 and died November 1862 having married Mary Pickering in December 1813.

The Extraordinary Franks

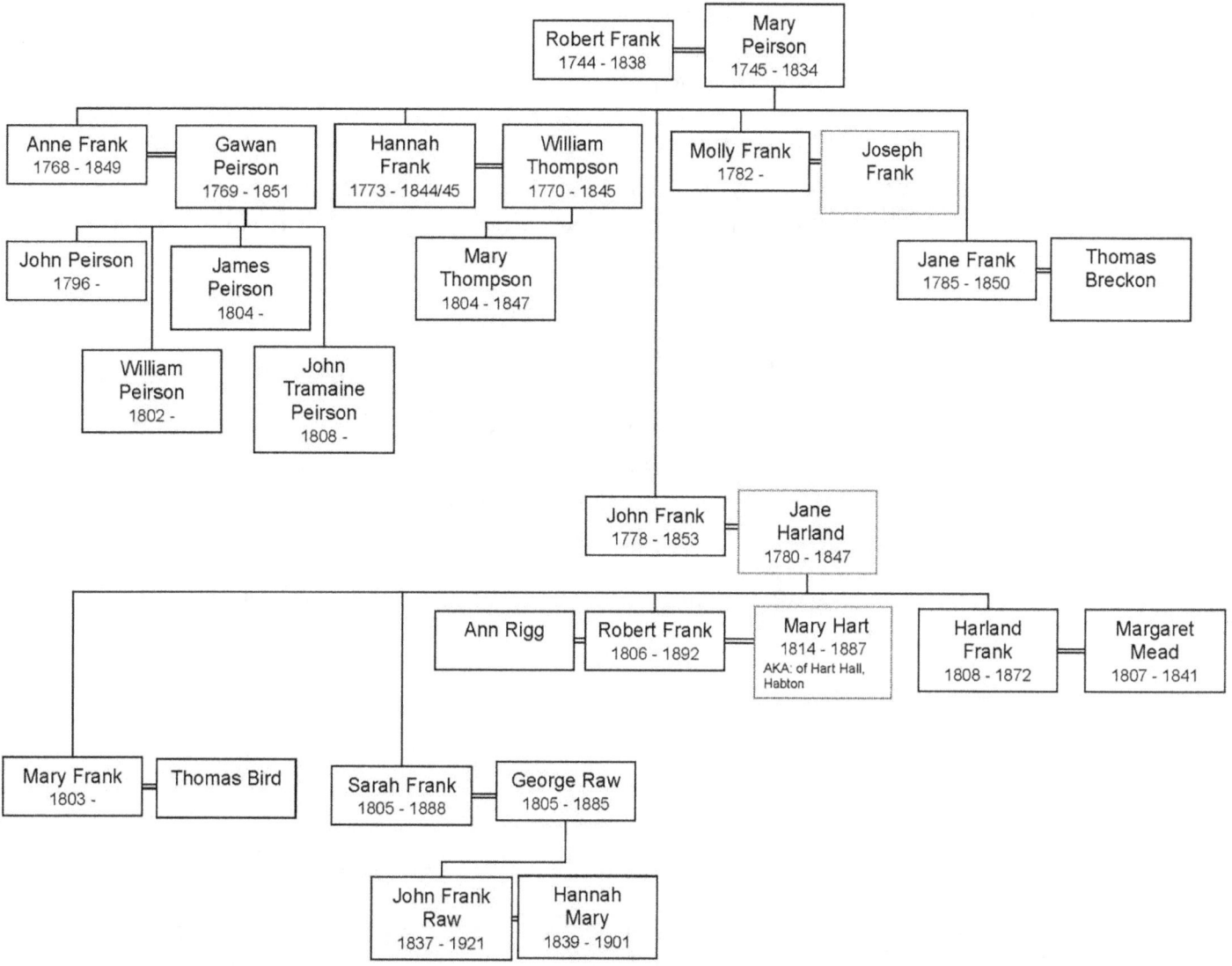

Robert Frank obtained Hart Hall through marriage giving his eldest son the name Hart-Frank. Around 1851 the home farm of Glaisdale Head alone was registered as 90 acres. Although having sole responsibility for Glaisdale Head, Robert Hart-Frank lived adjoining the more substantive family estate. As well as labourers, home farm employed a general farm servant, two house servants and a nurse, still intent on extending their holdings, Robert acquired property in and around Whitby.

Robert Frank (1806) children:

> Jane (Aunt Shanie) b. 8 Jan 1848, d. 13 Jul 1932 *See storyline for Shanie

John b. 26 May 1851, d. 1913 Whitby. Married Rachel Amelia (d. 16 Jun 1823) John, Pharmaceutical Chemist had three children Kathleen, Arthur Stanley and Anne.

Robert Hart-Frank b. 6 May 1849, d. 18 Aug 1917, married Jane Breckon- Featherstone (18 Nov 1851–16 April 1907). Jane, ninth of ten children, eight die in infancy. Her sister, Hannah Frank of Furness Farm married Joseph Thomson of Glaisdale Head

Mary b. 17 Sept 1854. Marriage 1 to Rev H Burgoine (d. 12 Dec 1893), marriage 2 to Rev. J W Crake (1841–1919).

William b. 31 Jul 1856, d. 29 Dec 1936. Married Mary Woodwark 13 March 1880, children Kathleen, Peter Harland and William Woodwark (married Viola, their son William Haslett Frank b.1912, married Kathleen, their only child a daughter).

George b. 6 Mar 1860 married Lydia Robb, children Muriel and George.

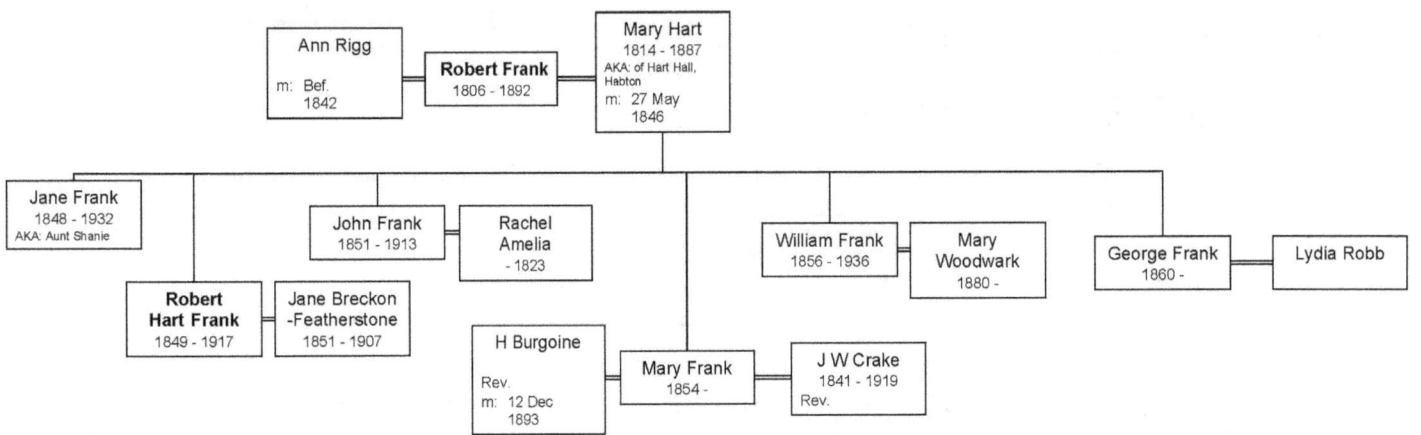

Jane Breckon-Featherstone died in Glaisdale. Her parents were Thomas Featherstone and Margaret Thompson. The census for 1851 shows my great-grandfather Robert Hart-Frank, aged 1, living with his parents at Glaisdale Head Farm.

The Extraordinary Franks

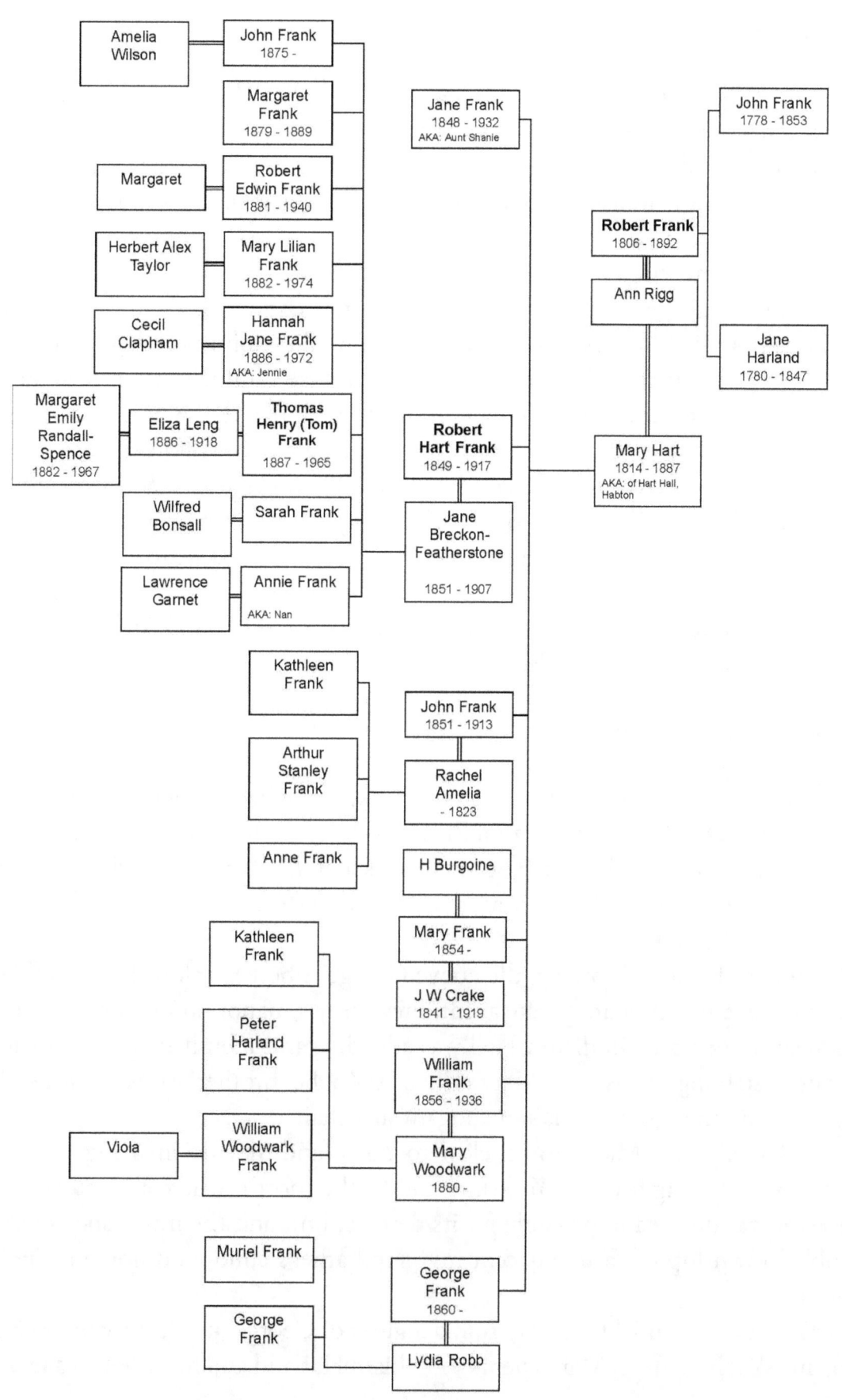

Interlude

Born in 1912, William Haslett Frank, son of William Woodwark and Viola Elizabeth Frank of nearby Knaresborough, was a Second World War pilot. Recorded killed 20th August 1942 and aged just thirty, he lies buried at Stonefall Cemetery, Harrogate. Close on twenty years ago my daughter Jill and her husband John Blundell moved to Harrogate, their two son's being born there.

Coming from Ince in Lancashire, John's ancestors, the Blondel of Normandy, arrived in England with William the Conqueror, becoming Lords of Ince in 1066, the first in Britain of John's namesake, the name-spelling John Blundell was recorded in 1140. By the eighteenth century the manor of Ince Blundell held fifteen manors and three knight's fees. Coincidentally Ann and I happen to live adjacent Ince, and know full well John's pedigree and the historic influence of the Blundell family locally.

The purpose of recording my son-in-law John and the aforementioned William Frank is to illustrate how commonplace we really are, and yet in times of peril how extraordinary such people as the aforesaid William and his winged brigade were, their sacrifice much in the vein of a combative medieval knight, William Frank's a very different kind of war to that of horse and sword, lonely and frightening in the sky, but equally terrifying in death.

Robert Frank continued

The above Mary's nephew, Arthur Stanley Frank, son of her brother John, was known as Stanley of Oak Tree House, Egton Bridge, Whitby: in Mary's will Stanley received the business known as the Thrift Stores in Kirkstall, Leeds together with the residue of her will. Incidentally, I have Mary's will showing she died a very wealthy woman having many bequests.

Another of Mary's brothers, the above George Albert Frank of Low Middleton Hall was an auctioneer and estate agent. Previously a manor house, the main building relating to Low Middleton Hall was added to and rebuilt in 1721, providing extensive stabling. In his sister Mary's will of 1946, her brother was bequeathed their great-grandfather, John Frank's, mahogany armchair.

Incidentally Low Middleton is close to Yarm (and the ancient King's Highway main river-crossing between Yorkshire and further north, where an historic Frank ancestor was deemed responsible for its destruction), and the much spoken about cobbled township of Yarm adjacent my grandfather's childhood home of Ingleby Barwick.

Mary's niece, Muriel Frank of Hull, daughter of George, in Mary's will received a leopard-skin hearthrug. Mary's nephew William Harland and his wife Viola received

£300 in equal share, and Viola, known as Vi, a mahogany wood blanket box with large preserving pan and copper tea-kettle and gold brooch.

In 1824, excluding sheep grazing, the estate's total land under cultivation amounted to 1000 acres, the acreage surprisingly equal to the terrains ancient Domesday survey recorded 700 years before. The above needs to be seen in relation to individual smallholdings and farms ranging from just a few acres to something just short of 100 acres or so. The combination of Frank holdings and lettings, although substantial compared to the average farmer, was now shared across a spread of successive generations.

Nonetheless, previously de Brus terrain fought over by medieval knights, the subsequent piece-by-piece accumulation of comparative small acreage had become quite large. Given the shaky start belonging that of humble sawyer, Robert's was a proud success, whereby in 1890 Robert Frank was shown to be the principal landowner of Whitby and its surrounds.

(Robert Hart-Frank continues second after next)

The following compressed list demonstrates how interwoven the Franks were in relation to their contemporaries. Note the duplication of favoured first names.

1756 Notification of the ownership and occupation of pews relating to:

1. William Frank,

2. Mr Chomley's gallery.

3. Pews for Robert Stonehouse and family.

4. Payment for the new replacement of silver vessels for church communion made by William Franke, 25th December 1759.

10th July 1756 lays, Henry Frank, farmer, deceased, of High Straggleton Farm, Sandsend Road, Whitby, lying at peace near Raithwaite, north of Whitby along the coast road.

8th February 1757, Henry Frank, yeoman farmer, married Ann Sanderson, witnessed by Thomas Frank.

8th April 1759, to William Harland, contemporary of the Franks and farmer of Hawsker, a son, John.

27th May 1759, to Thomas Frank, carpenter of East Row, a daughter, Isabel.

1st July 1759, to Henry Frank, house-wright of Stragleton, a daughter, Elizabeth.

11th May and the 24th August 1760, William Frank, witness to a wedding.

14th September 1760, to William Harland, farmer of Hawsker, a son Francis, named after their Frank landlords (see 1759 above).

7th June 1761, to Henry Frank, yeoman farmer of Stragleton, a son, Henry.

14th January 1761, to William Franklin, Master Mariner, a son, Abraham.

22nd November 1761, Elizabeth Franck witness to a wedding.

13th May 1762, to Thomas Frank, carpenter of East Row, a daughter, Barbara.

To several times great-grandfather Robert Frank, sawyer and timber merchant, a daughter Margaret, born 29th September 1762, christened 31st October 1762, died 16th January 1763.

29th May 1763, to Henry Frank, yeoman farmer of Straggleton, a son, George.

22nd June 1763, to George Frank, Master Mariner, a son, Phillip.

24th September 1763, William Frank is witness to a wedding.

31st May 1765, to Thomas Frank house-wright of East Row, a son, John.

13th October 1765, Bridget Frank, widow of Whitby, deceased.

22nd December 1765, to Henry Frank, Farmer of Straggleton, a son, Thomas.

The Shanie story, see Aunt Shanie, Jane Frank above, family tree

When a girl, my mother, Dorothy Frank, recalled occasional visits to the Reverend's house, Shanie being his wife. She was by all accounts somewhat eccentric, never getting up until late morning, my mother remembering her aunt as something of a character, her sudden changes of demeanour quaintly old-fashioned as if lifted from the pages of an old book and like her sister this her second marriage, each to vicars. But Aunt Shanie took a shine to Dorothy, and whereas Dorothy's younger sister Mary was quieter and less interesting, Dorothy was lively and able to speak up for herself, being singled out to read to Shanie from a book while her aunt closed her eyes and listened.

Although extremely straight-laced, Aunt Shanie would have sudden urges to do something. Inviting the girls for the weekend she took it upon herself to take the girls and their two cousins shopping for new dresses; the dresses they were wearing were really not up to it and something had to be done. So two sensible girls and the other two dizzy, excitable and gregarious and what should have been a wonderful experience. Shanie was shocked to the core at such ostentatious fashion now the vogue; much too provocative. Having gone shopping and now at the point of decision, she wouldn't purchase after all, not wanting her girls to flaunt themselves, and for the first time coming home empty-handed. Loved and adored as much for her quirkiness as her innate kindliness, Mary was dismayed when in Aunt Shanie's will, among a number of items and her best tea service for her favourite niece Dorothy, Mary was left four silver teaspoons. Straight to the point, no messing, blunt Yorkshire through and through.

Talking of teaspoons, among other items of silver and china, I seem to have inherited a set of initial-engraved teaspoons belonging Mary Hart upon her marriage to Robert Frank in May 1846, their son being Robert Hart-Frank. Whether these were passed down through Mary Crake née Frank and formed part of her will to Dorothy or were passed down via Aunt Shanie, whatever the case such pieces give insight into the past and how show interwoven is the legacy belonging the de Brus, the Hart, the Franks and the maze of all that dynastic heritage.

Incidentally my daughter Jill has a lady's gold watch and a couple of other items passed onto her by Dorothy, belonging her mother Eliza, Jill's great grandmother who died 100 years ago in 1918.

Robert Hart-Frank

With the generational carve up and distribution of the original estate, Robert Hart-Frank; namesake of the original Sir Robertus Francaise, Great-Granddad received Yew Grange Farm, Glaisdale. With eight children to consider, Robert decided to acquire the previous de Brus holdings of Ingleby and Barwick together with adjoining Quarry Bank, his niece Ruth, daughter of John Frank, and her husband Stanley, already having adjacent White House Farm, the whole comprising a continuous swathe abounding the upper Tees.

Incidentally Quarry Bank has on it the remains of a Roman Villa built in 140 CE; an important and extensive archaeological site. Recently discovered artefacts are Roman jewellery and Bronze Age pottery, furthermore, hunting tools dating back to 4000 BC.

Upon Robert Hart-Frank's death, elder son, Robert Edwin Frank, subsequently took on the running of the estate, with his brothers George Albert, William, Alfred and Ernest initially still resident. That left Thomas Henry, who as Robert Hart-Frank's youngest son didn't have a look-in as far as a share of the estate was concerned, his father securing for him a joinery apprenticeship. Alfred farmed at nearby Sober Hall Farm, later moving further south. William's son Christopher is assumed still around, but his other son Richard and his daughter Jennifer apparently farm elsewhere. Indicated recently in a press article Christopher apparently farms near Stokesley.

I am immensely in awe of my grandfather a man having the barest mention in his father's will, seeing an opportunity and grasping it with great courage and fortitude, building a business practically out of thin air. Following his early marriage to Eliza, Tom Frank lived at White House, Maltby, assuming the additional role of farm manager for his father-in-law. His young wife suddenly struck down dead together with their fourth child, his second eldest was Dorothy, as a teenager going to Great Ormond Street hospital, London, to train, later located in the Middle East heavily pregnant caught up in the middle of a raging war.

On Dorothy's receipt of a small legacy from an aunt, there is a letter, with tidy writing, from Tom Frank (writing with sight in only one eye he is found apologising); the extra houses he had built, investing some of Dorothy's money – he had to sadly reduce the number of properties he had set aside for her by two. There was a problem over Building Societies not releasing monies for a number of completed houses already under occupation, thus for a while he would have to return to farming and pray for better times. As for Dorothy, Mum had me her newborn to think of, and her capture in North Africa amid a confusion of stillbirths and wounded with only a single grossly over-worked German doctor to guide anyone with a modicum of nursing experience. She too unwell and beset by who was friend or foe wasn't what she had planned for her child.

In terms of doctrine, of all of Tom Frank's holdings, including that of farming, were let on the principle of a fair rent, indeed to my knowledge much more than that. During a time of high inflation, I vividly remember the family's reluctance to face tenants with even a token increase; the Frank's kindness the cause of later problems. The issue came with a Labour government fixing rents at their existing level whereupon the family's rental income failed to cover the cost of maintenance, them having no option but to subsidise their tenants, without exception all of them living high to the determent of the Frank family, my mother and Tom Frank paying out of their own savings for maintenance and repairs.

And come a double whammy, the financial necessity to sell off property to sitting tenants at a heavily prescribed knock-down price legislated by the labour government. So much for Tom Frank's retirement plan, paying out left and right and his largesse blind to a looming tax bill, his dwindling money just enough to see him out, God bless him. Unbeknown to us, we assumed Tom had the best business advice, unaware his chalming solicitor was fleecing his clients. The family had no option but to put up for sale cottages and a couple of houses in Newby, including Tom's own house, orchard, gardens and land and a farm, where due to a colossal 60% tax bill was lost all but the bare bones of a lifetime's endeavour. As for the duplicitous solicitor, time served in prison did nothing in terms of redress, the assumption being his ill-gotten gains remained available to him upon his release.

So the Frank name clings on, different and diluted. The expression 'Last Frank standing' has more to do with the recognition of the passage of time where I feel a comma has to be placed somewhere, and why not here at the interlude between lives as they were and what they became, and what the future holds.

I am not alone in having glimpsed and physically lived the tail end of hundreds of years of unchanged methods of rural existence; assuaged with farming terminology such as band cutting, stooking and shuffling, its work indispersed with a ready vocabulary of words and exasperated terms such as 'fond bugger' when wrestling with the cussedness of an obdurate animal. All hard labour, with fond bugger an utterance akin to swearing when a particularly dank and nauseous tail might swipe across your face, a sharply lifted leg might cause a nasty bruise, a horse might stamp your foot, or horn graze your brow: the everyday stuff of farming.

Ingleby Barwick passed through Robert Edwin (Uncle Eddie) to his son William (Willy). Second son Ernest got adjoining Quarry Farm, each of the farms substantially larger than that of White House. But it was Ruth Frank and her husband Stan Walton's beautiful White House farm I loved to visit, as much for the immense pleasure found in their company as the rolling fields and a particularly favoured old tree; a place I found magical, the whole swathe of rich farmland and individual holdings later purchased by speculators for the construction of a new town.

An oil painting of mine of White House Farm, done for Ruth and Stan, should still be held by Margaret Dickens née Walton, adoptive daughter of Ruth and Stan Walton. Now a grandmother herself, the image I retain of White House Farm is encapsulated in the springtime colour photograph of Margaret Walton as a young girl, her beautiful cheeks aglow. Sat on a mat upon the doorstep, she is in a bright yellow dress playing with a teddy and her favourite doll, an image caught in bright sunlight framed by her sitting timelessly within the frame of an open farmhouse door.

Margaret and her husband Stephen farm at Wellington Farm, Ingleby Arncliffe. Incidentally, Dorothy was godmother to Margaret, Margaret and her husband having recently attended my mother's funeral aged 100. The buffet was held at Mum's beloved Newby Hall accompanied a few surviving attendees, one's impression that of closing the final chapter of a faded novel, the pages turning brown with age. It doesn't matter the title, it would be illegible anyway, that era and its characters now confined to history in an attempt to make sense of its passing, a diminished hazy world existence so far removed from today as to be a paradox, a time so devoid of colour as to be recorded in sepia; old-fashioned photos held loose within musty boxes, a past capsuled in an accumulation of junk, spiders' webs and the all purveying finality of decades' layers of dust.

Robert Edwin's son Alfred, known as Alfie or Alf Frank, farmed at Thormanby Hall close to the previous Thirkleby Franks and nearby Bylands Abbey, the White Horse of Kilburn chalked high upon the hills, and Northallerton Priory where Dorothy passed away. I visited Thormanby on two occasions. Albert's son, as well as Alf later moving to Aberdeen in Scotland, Ann and I meeting him and his wife at my Aunt Doreen Frank's funeral in Edinburgh September 2006. Doreen Frank was the wife of my uncle, Surgeon Colonel John Frank, Alf being a cousin and close friend. After Jack's death Alf continued to keep in touch with Doreen until she too died aged ninety-four. I have mentioned elsewhere John Frank's residence being adjacent to what was the ancient Scottish seat of Frankisland, also of his passing while playing golf.

It's strange linking the events of Frankisland Scotland, the Franks of Thirkleby and the Yorkshire Dales Franks. And as I write, my thoughts drift to Scotland and my waking before dawn, when still half awake I found myself climbing the nearby mountain of Le Pen, fighting my way through a particularly dismal wet and clammy shroud of cloud with thoughts of never reaching the pinnacle, now suddenly arriving at the foreboding summit and the shock of blindness at the very moment of sunrise, jolted by its wondrous beauty in a single heart beats change of mood from that of gloom to one of absolute joy, an astounding visual feast too vast for one person to absorb its entirety.

And what a glorious sight, as part-blinded by the unbelievable light, the sun blazed across the tops of white billowing cloud, a vista of mountain peaks poking through, a spectacular and wonderful spectacle made more perfect by the prospect of a cooked breakfast awaiting one's descent. Despite one's lack of religion, it's at those rare moments of absolute joy one's heart swells to bursting, offering thanks for the experience of something impossible to comprehend, a single joyous moment of infinite perfection and boundless benefaction.

Knowing those hills as part of one's Scottish ancestry and able today to walk the hills of North Yorkshire with my family brings a double dose of happiness. Memory too takes me back, sufficient to look down with a sense of pity for the once horny hands and aching bones of a boy, a lonely fifteen-year-old slavishly tied to the soil with what kind of future in store? Seeing him there those many years ago with his horse, standing high upon a plateau looking across the patchwork landscape where his great-grandfather Robert Hart-Frank's son Tom had recently added White Post Farm to his ever-growing slice of England, and as Granddad's apprentice, the expectations placed upon young shoulders already feeling the aches and pains of physical toil, yet not wanting to disappoint weighing heavy, lonely and alone, with decisions to be made.

Robert Hart-Frank (his children) continued:

John b. 22 Nov 1875. Married Amelia Wilson, had children Ruth (married Stan Walton), Hazel (who was a horse breeder) and Margery Kitson. Margaret, daughter of Ruth, married Stephen Dickens, Wellington Farm.

Margaret 1879–1889

Robert (Edwin) 1881–June 1940. Married Margaret, had issue William, George Albert, Alfred and Ernest (Ernie).

Tom (Thomas Henry) Married Eliza Leng 10 May 1909, died 1918. Eliza Frank, the author's true maternal grandmother (see later following).

Mary Lilian 5 Dec 1882–March 1974. Married Herbert Alex Taylor

Hannah Jane (Jennie) 23 Jan 1886–9 March 1972. Married Cecil Clapham 1905, issue Lillian and Harland.

Sarah Married Wilfred Bonsall. Had issue.

Annie (Nan) Married Lawrence Garnet. Had issue.

Douglas Frank Blackmore

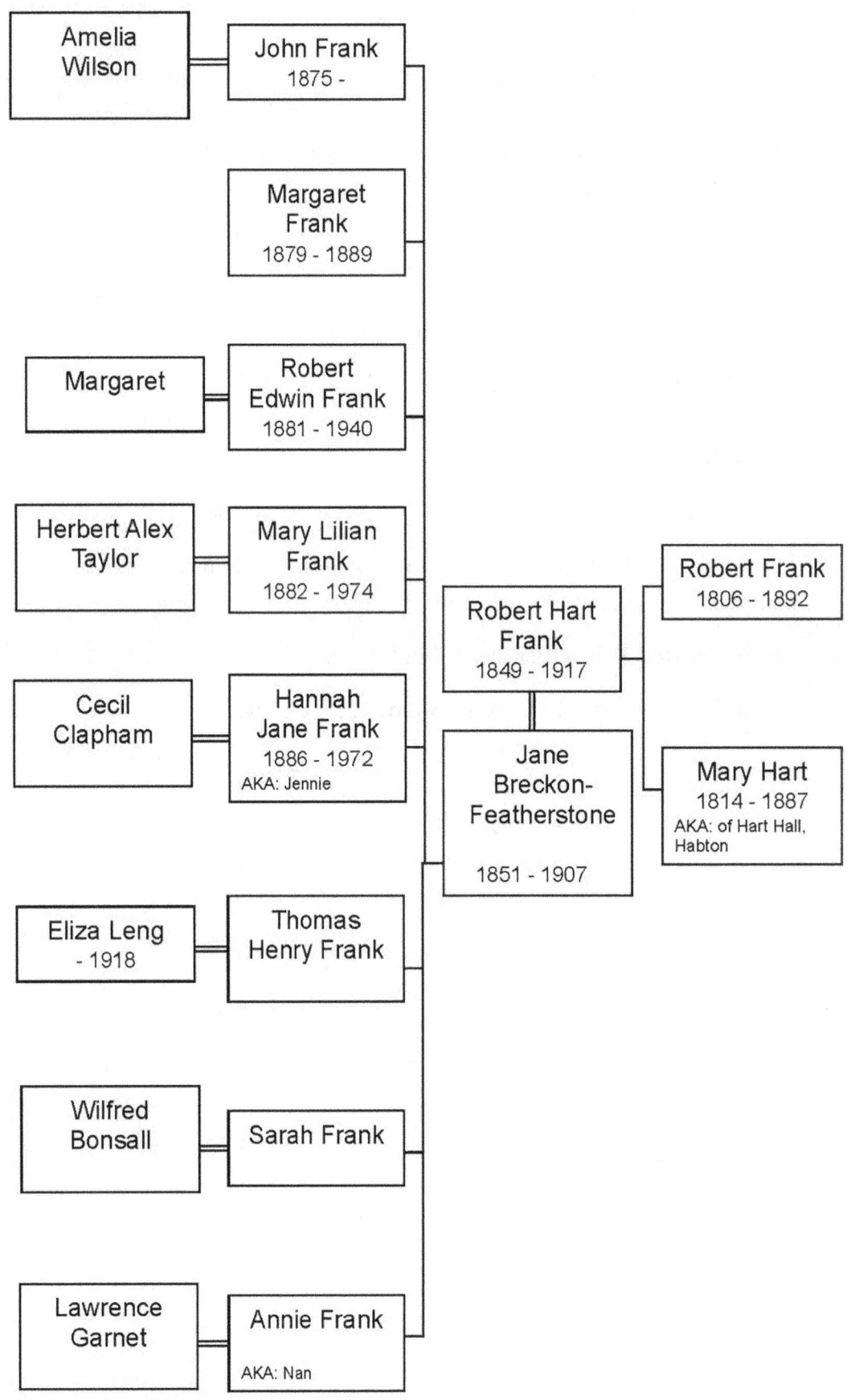

The aforesaid Ruth was a beneficiary to Mary Crake's will of 1946, receiving all of Mary's Midland Bank shares as well as a half of the household linen, which items were shared with her sister Margery Kitson née Frank.

As main executor to his aunty Mary Crake née Frank, my grandfather Tom Frank received a beneficiary of a grandfather clock that was subsequently passed to his son, my uncle, John Frank.

Mary Crake's late nephew Edwin's wife Margaret, received silverware in her will; Edwin's son William, more recent owner of Ingleby Barwick, received furniture; his brother Ernie a clock and two vases; George too was a beneficiary. Ernest and his wife Barbara who farmed at Quarry Bank had two children, Geoffrey and Ann, Geoffrey receiving £100 from Mary Crake's estate, as too Deryck and Clive Frank, also a Helena and Diana Mary Rudd. Indicated in Mary's will of 1946, these latter four folk I'm sadly unable to place.

From the above Mary's estate, Hannah Jane's children, Hazel and Lillian received furniture, Harland some silver items.

Of Tom Frank, in reverse order, his first wife Eliza's parents belonging White House Farm, Maltby:

John Leng	wife, Sarah Craggs

Their parents:

William Leng b. Aiskew 1821 d. 1882 wife, Isabella b. Scrutton 1817	John Craggs b. Kirklevington 1829 d. 1900, wife, Eliza Appleton b Hilton 1829 d Crathorne 1875.
	Married Stokesley 1855.

Tom Frank and Sarah, my true grandmother.

Born in Maltby in 1886, Eliza married Tom Frank 10th May 1909. Tom was born in 1887 and died in 1965, aged seventy-eight, being laid to rest in Saint Martin's Church, Seamer. Eliza Frank, née Leng, was the daughter of John Leng and his second wife Sarah Craggs. Sarah was born 6th April 1856, her marriage to John taking place around 1882 following the death of John's first wife Ann Appleton in 1880. Ann Appleton was born in 1848, John's first marriage producing his first child Sarah in 1869, Sarah being an elder half sister to Eliza.

To complete the picture, my maternal great-grandfather, John Leng's father, was William Leng, all I know is John's mother's name being Isabella. John farmed at

White House Farm, Maltby, near Stainton, both villages being a couple of miles distance from Newby and the town of Stokesley. Coming from Newby, it was as a Stokesley town councillor that Tom Frank was principally responsible for the town's expansion, building the majority of houses. Following retirement and a stroke he set up in business once more, this time building a large housing estate, specifically rental property for those of modest means, indeed a lasting legacy, especially following another stroke and his demise aged seventy-eight.

Beloved Eliza Leng was the maternal grandmother I never knew but instinctively know I would have adored. She was quite striking and said to have had a lovely nature. She died of childbed fever following the death of her fourth child. Named after her, her earlier daughter Eliza was baptised 16th October 1920.

Torn by grief, my heartbroken grandfather had a heart-shaped gold pendant especially crafted. In it he had placed a sample of woven hair taken from each of his deceased wife and short-lived baby. Sealed in perpetuity and everlasting love, I have the privilege of keeping the mourning pendant and photographs. My daughter Jill has Eliza's gold watch locket and chain, a gold brooch and silver thimble together with a silver tea set on which is inscribed 'Presented to Eliza Frank on the occasion of her marriage'. The tea set is shown as coming from High Leven Primitive Methodist Church where she taught Sunday school. Those wishing to know more of my maternal grandmother should know she is buried at Stainton Churchyard, St Peters & St Paul Church. Incidentally I have in my keeping some early photographs of Eliza, also some of the larger family.

On the matter of childbed fever, it was endemic as an infection of the womb leading to septicaemia. To use its proper name, puerperal sepsis, it was for the most part eradicated between 1982 and 1984, yet has since been on the increase, rising today to around 14% of maternal deaths; a shocking statistic and one that with funding and proper attention could see it once again brought under control. Unfortunately, due to the particular effect on my mother Dorothy, her mother's death became the trigger for her to leave home and explore the world. Dorothy died around 10pm 28th June 2015 aged 100 and six months.

Of Tom Frank's brother Edwin; his son William continued to farm Barwick, brother Ernie, Quarry Farm, Alfred, Sober Hall and Thormanby. It was Alf, my uncle, who kept in touch with John Frank who lived in Innerleithen, Scotland, it being much later that Alfred's son eventually moved to Scotland, farming around Aberdeen. John Frank remained a Professor of Medicine at Edinburgh and Peel Hospital until retirement and an early death playing golf.

George Albert Frank's son, John Howard Frank, has been in touch from Florida where he retired as Professor of Entomology. He has been so kind as to confirm his father, who having decided to forego farming, moved to Newcastle on Tyne. Sadly

George died in 1985 aged seventy. Howard graduated in 1966, and having moved to Canada married a Canadian, the couple moving to Jamaica, where in 1972 and three girls later, the family moved to Florida. Incidentally, prior to emmigrating to Canada, as a youngster, John remembers his father taking him to Glaisdale by car and seeing for himself the early Frank holdings so graphically explained in this work.

THOMAS HENRY FRANK
Born 9th April 1887 died 16th Nov 1965 aged 78

Granddad Tom's second, but barren, marriage was to Margaret Emily Randall-Spence born 1882 and who died 24th Sept 1967. In her way she was kindly but a throwback to a long bygone era, unworldly, unknowing and unable to comprehend and adjust to a world outside the safe confines of prayer and religion.

Tom's children were to his first wife Elisa. Sorely missed, his second marriage to Emily was more a marriage of convenience and a case of having someone to look after the children. Emily, as she was known, was consumed by religion and spinsterish, and if the marriage was consummated I'm pretty certain it wouldn't have been a happy experience for her: she frowned on anything that didn't fit her idée fixe. As family we took over the main house following Tom's second stroke, Dorothy's father and stepmother living in a separate wing.

Despite the size of the grounds, when hidden away topping and tailing gooseberries one Sunday, the family did so with trepidation fearing step-mum, or Granddad's foreman Len's prowling wife Doris, would nose out what was going on and unleash the wrath of God. For Emily and Doris, the Sabbath was strictly for worship, no work, no play, observance and giving tea to visiting clergy being step-grandma's one delight. As the wife of Granddad's employee, apart from nosing in other people's business, what was Doris's delight I'm not sure, as like Emily, the two of them like thieves in the night, neither of them having given birth nor seeming inclined in that direction, it seems sex too might have been a forbidden intromission.

Obviously out of sight, the family carried on as normally as possible, where for an all too short interval, Sid and I caused mayhem tearing around the countryside on our motorbikes, and despite his stroke Tom Frank quietly paid for any damage caused by his two headstrong grandsons. Landing up in hospital one time, having skin grafts to a smashed foot, Sid's Norton 600 considered a total write-off, he painstakingly rebuilt it to its original perfection, taking it beyond its original maximum speed only to never ride it again.

Whereas I ran my bike full up the steps, through the door skidding to a stop in the apple store, I remember the undulating countryside, the rise and fall of noise coming near, the roar and Sid blasting to a halt for the last time just a millimetre from my feet down the gravel drive, the too-hot-to-touch metal tapping away, the bike's engine rapidly cooling from its intense heat: two boys yielding to the demands of male testosterone and the sense of freedom so much frowned upon, their libido at times causing more than a little consternation among the fairer sex, and for that infinitesimally short space of time, a heady mixture of freedom, wondrous discovery and sheer joy, that millisecond challenge between life and death we both knew so well.

Incidentally the Cleveland Hills, taking the steep road up from White Post Farm to the hamlet of Chop Gate, brought fantastic biking: bends and undulating hills all the way to Helmsley and beyond. Turn left towards the high cliffs and ever onward to the roaring North Sea, or straight on to Malton and York. Or one might turn right arriving at the Frankland seat of Thirsk, where Mum took residence prior to her death. When farming, local terminology came to play with Chop Gate, as then pronounced *Tjop Yaet* or *Chop Yat*, coming from Old Norse meaning route or gateway beyond. Whether it was something of that name, but when farming, I felt trapped within a burning ambition to escape and venture far and wide.

In a sense the salient thing for me was the biding need to break free, absent of the kind of obligation that might bind me to the past. Chop Gate, no actual gate but within one's mind the sound of rusty hinges rasping harsh upon the ear, an enclave while not yet padlocked might soon be firmly closed forever and the world outside left undiscovered. Yet this was no ordinary boundary, on the one side was the past and the ritual of rural continuity, siding the other, the frightening aspect of an uncertain destiny, where for me the trick was to simply accelerate full-pelt through its imaginary confines and find the distal horizon.

Tom Frank, farmer, landowner, builder of numerous housing estates, Linthorpe, Acklam, Stokesley, Ayton. I have letters of Granddad's referring to visits to relatives at Rosedale, Pickering and Whitby, a maze of first-hand evidence confirming a myriad of ancient associations spread across the northern reaches of Yorkshire. Further afield, Tom's uncle, George Frank, born 6th March 1860, in marrying Lydia Robb, lived around Hull and the Humber estuary, ironically taking us back to the origins of the Franks post-1066, its incursion taking them north mapped by details taken from Domesday.

Thomas Henry Frank part two

At the turn of the twentieth century, grandfather Thomas Henry Frank was indentured as a joiner cum carpenter to Thompson Bros, Tom's father Robert Hart-Frank signing the National Federation of Building Trades indenture 23rd April 1904. Immediately following his apprenticeship Tom Frank set up the construction firm that became so widely acclaimed. As well as his original indenture documents I hold original press documents expounding the firm's virtues and craftsmanship exampled by the following:

> 'Here is to be found the best example of the sound work contributing to modern building by a really experienced company, imbued with the traditions of the past.'
>
> 'He is indeed one of the most experienced builders in the country.'
>
> 'Thomas Frank is the finest designer and constructor of really first class wide scale residential property found anywhere in the country.'

As a twelve-year-old schoolboy, when not on a farm, I often knocked around with Granddad Tom learning how to fell trees, mix concrete, lay drives and dig foundations. By then his fingers and knuckles were so gnarled and thickened I assumed the task of doing much of his paperwork, often sat at his roll-top desk writing cheques or, later, drawing plans adapted from previously approved drawings and drainage for the construction of a large part of Acklam, the completed project consisting several hundred fine-quality houses.

Passing through Acklam not so long ago I was struck by how hugely multicultural it had become; yet a feeling of pride, how the area had stood the test of time, neat and respectable, the roads tree-lined, plenty of space, a multitude of kids of all shades spilling out of school kitted out in their smart uniforms, interspersed with a multitude of darkskinned faces, smiling, laughing, smart, intelligent, well-behaved, the future of Britain in safe hands. An area originally made up of a white middle class, now an unwitting legacy to a proud multicultural meme, a situation of which Tom Frank would instantly be bewildered, I can see it, a dawning delight would come upon his cheeks, and he'd smile and be justly proud.

It's the few areas like these that are the salvation of Middlesbrough, where elsewhere migrants spill upon once respectable inner-city streets, blocking pavements with the purposeful intention of intimidating long-standing residents. And then there are the sink estates, areas of which I have previously written; a sorry blight where for years, Stockton in particular, girls as young as thirteen openly served as prostitutes. Newspaper reports show even younger victims being ferried by Kurdish migrants to hidden rooms, shown by the media as car washes in Hartlepool, always on the move, akin the Rochdale, their young victims passed from place to place, their bodies sold for sex. My previous mention of Hart as a family name, its mention now only bringing me acute disgust and shame how such blight could manifest or enter one's consciousness.

How all this squares with history is difficult to judge or for that matter comment. Though the story does show that over hundreds of years of humanisation, how in just one single generation scattered pockets of respectable and stable society has been infiltrated. The causation an uncontrolled policy on unfettered immigration with no understanding of the mindset belonging to a foreign mien. Such policies have allowed those with absolutely no conscience to vent their putrid idee. Justified by prayers to Allah, shadowy figures prey and prey and prey upon vulnerable teenage girls, their young white victims viewed as degenerate trash to do with as they wish, become a fateful stab to the heart of humanity and its fateful underclass, and a two-fingered snub to all that shines bright and one's hopes for their newborn.

This horrendous aspect come true, throughout this work I have tried to strike a balance with regard to women, in particular relating to religion and the mess successive politicians have made of a once great legacy foist generationally. And while myself lacking in faith, I sense and pray whatever their guiding star, the insight of bright young minds may see a way through the mire.

Returning to the formation of the township of Middlesbrough and its group of early benefactors: each bent on bestowing a town to be proud of, there is a photograph of Tom stood upon the steps of Middlesbrough town hall with a group of fellow councillors, all of them dressed in their waist-coated suits, gold fob chains gleaming. Seeming plump and proud, most belaying their stock in trade, whether butcher or bank manager, or in Tom's case builder, all of them having something really worthy to be proud of.

Faded photos, stuffy and old-fashioned, barely glanced, today's youth more concerned with messaging, having no concept what brought us to where we are. Layers upon layers of history, each in his and her turn adding to what has gone before, the world now turning so fast there being no time to ponder. But for those who might be interested there is something of the goodness of Tom Frank now seems a good time to share.

As a practical man Tom Frank was hands-on and innovative, seen through the subtle variations brought to bear for each of his houses during construction. Of his colleagues standing waiting to be photographed, their smart appearance was the appropriate dress of the period, often-unshapely heavy material, each of their garb setting them apart as proprietors rather than gents.

Of Tom's enterprise, one has to consider we're talking about wholesale house building, where all the roof sections, windows, doors, flooring and kitchen fittings were hand-produced in his own workshops, his main workshop sited in a corner of the paddock adjacent Croft House where we lived. Often the side double door would be flung wide open to the field where the building sat, open to the sight and sound of grazing, bringing fresh air and respite for the craftsman therein, their ten o'clock break, sandwich in hand, sat upon the wooden step, a hot mug of tea in easy reach, peaceful and calm, a break from all the sawdust and wood shavings. Unlike Mousey Thompson of Kilburn fame, having houses to build they had little time to whittle and carve the likeness of a mouse, backs to the grind, having just enough time to slake their thirst with a second top up of tea.

Then there's the expectation placed on sibling shoulders, shown in the confidence placed upon both us boys to get on with it, with no thoughts of falling short however difficult the job or not knowing the work. I think we fared pretty well, or perhaps we did a good job of not letting our deficiencies show.

Tom was in advance of his time and was what one might describe as a true Christian: someone who lived by the concept of hard work and servitude, tempered by acts of supreme kindness. His ethic was uncompromising in terms of a job well done irrespective the toll upon his health, where his expectation was of a man's word, a token shown by a spit and shake of the hand, a deal or resolution to be honoured and repaid in kind, and God's wrath if anyone tried to deceive him.

The deal I speak about relates to 'something back'. This was an old silver sixpenny piece returned to the payee on receipt of full payment for goods or a job well done. Used together with sotto voce, 'good luck' was a gesture of good faith where a deal had been satisfied, honours equal, a time-honoured way of returning to the payee a token of mutual satisfaction and heartfelt gratitude. Quaint acts, but in many ways much missed.

Watching on as Granddad handled a group of Irish itinerates who tried to con him was a lesson I'll not forget. He'd suffered a second stroke and was really feeling his age, but having given the Irishmen the job of renovating the roof of some particularly tall agricultural buildings, their work supposedly complete, in their absence he'd gone to check how things were going, climbing to the very top and finding only the sides of the curved roof tarred, the bulk of the middle section still rusty and untouched, a botched job.

Things don't change; there are always those ready to take advantage. It was their pleadings: 'But Mr Frank, we done the work', their words wafting as if on a soft breeze. Then sotto voce, his demand for the work to be completely redone, which he would check personally prior to payment. 'But Mr Frank' again, but that was his stamp, something he lived by, as if the loss of man's moral compass was his to hold in check. In a sense, each step pained by old age, that perilous climb was akin to the ascension of Jacob's ladder, as if God's faith in man might be in peril, an old man, close to death, feeding off a sense of duty and a code of moral purpose in an act he must have known would be among his very last.

As a child risen out of Africa, recently come to England, I have vague recollection of a tanned-skin self, blond hair bleached white, a boy out of kilter having surviving the perils of torpedo attack and near-oblivion through bombing, all of a sudden thrust upon a strange man's lap: a man I would come to love, Granddad bouncing me on his knee reciting over and again:

> We are building day by day,
> In our work and in our play,
> Not with hammers blow on blow,
> Not with timber sawing so –
> Building a house not made with hands,
> Following Jesus' perfect plans:
> Little builders all are we
> Building for eternity.

As a child coming from the heat and blaze of South Africa I my sorely missed Martha, my Zulu momma who looked after me, and even now in my dotage I can recall her uncompromising soft and kindly presence as someone I absolutely adored, something found sadly lacking in my own parents. What is true, Mum took many photos and, since her passing, found among a stack of old black and white images is one of Martha and me. I don't know what it was, I've heard it over and again, that generation and those before holding back, stiflingly embarrassed to show how much they cared or really loved.

Coming to wartime England, one can imagine the strangeness felt in such a drastic cultural change. Mine had become a faintly remembered existence, sitting on the ground, propped against the shady side of our house while Martha and I read a newspaper; mine was the freedom of hens clucking around bare feet, playing alongside bare soled friends, of sunshine and the thrill of riding my tricycle. Snakes and wildlife were all around, but we instinctively knew the territory we played and, as we explored, what dangers to avoid.

My Africa, that long-lived yearning. But that then existence so suddenly thrown into chaos, interrupted by a long and dangerous sea voyage heightened by explosions, sinkings and repeated convoy delays limping into port awaiting repair.

Then of course the unbelievable new chilling sensation of snow, very deep, very cold and white, occasioned by grey, and of the childish delight of a freshly built snowman. Also, seared into memory, laughter at his red nose, a vision compressed into momentary hysteria by the hair's breadth miss and ear-shattering sound of a nearby explosion. Yet even now, through a half-remembered drumming between one's ears, its causation a V2 rocket aimed at London having over-run its intended target, tipping and so rapidly smashing into the ground so close as to make us deaf.

The Extraordinary Franks

As if some unseen hand had shielded us from the carnage, trying to make sense of it all it seems Hitler, having failed to kill us first in North Africa, thence on our journey to England from South Africa, something akin to a personal vendetta, was doing his best to destroy us here in Luton.

In Yorkshire, the thing was, sat upon his knee, Granddad's bouncing was strictly in time to his favourite rhyme, a very firm bounce, the grip of rough leathery hands holding mine moving my arms up and down in time with his singing, the words and rhythm all pervading, akin to an anthem. It's my belief he was bent on instilling a lesson for life, something to remember and live by. Influenced by his occupation, each brick laid with care and attention, his belief and certainty of faith a resonate influence.

Today my workshop finds home to an old wooden spirit level lifted from the site of yet another anonymous house, another building within a series of yet more homes where, save for a looked-after favourite saw, Granddad's own collection of tools had become knocked about, rough and ready. His own springtime birth, ominously a time of birth within the farming calendar, was a time of joy abounding to the sight and sounds of reawakening and renewal. And now the vision of what he left behind: stalwart, straight and true.

I am certain Granddad saw life in the sense of climbing a ladder. I have this memory, being surprised to find, even in relative old age and after a second stroke, his considerable bulk standing high upon the roof of Croft House fixing some loose tiles, an old, three-tier wooden ladder open to its fullest extent. Whichever way one reads it; Granddad was a man with his faith intact. And me, so much a lesser person, quite lacking in faith, nervous as he swung his legs over the gutter, the wobbly ladder precariously dipping and bouncing in rhythm with his descent to solid ground.

Tom Frank's children:

> Surgeon Colonel John Frank b. 1913, d. abt 1985. Married Doreen who died aged 94. They had two adopted boys.
>
> **Dorothy Frank** b. 10 Dec 1914. Married Thomas Douglas Blackmore (2 Sept 1903– 2 June 1995). Dorothy died 10pm Northallerton Hospital 28th June 2015, Dorothy and Tom having two boys Douglas Frank and Sidney Derek.

Mary b. 1916, d. 16 April 2008. Married Cecil Sturgess who died 25 April 1991. Had a son who died, Janet who died aged 11 and adopted son Raymond.

Douglas Frank Blackmore

Dorothy Blackmore's children:

Douglas Frank b. 11 Nov 1940 (POW Jerusalem)* Occupation, bank board appointment. Retired early, resuming work as a designer/artist. Married Ann Pennock (teacher, b. 16 Nov 1947) (continued).

Sidney Derek b. 4 March 1945. Marriage 1 to Lynn, children Jonathan and Stephen. Marriage 2 to Janet (no issue).

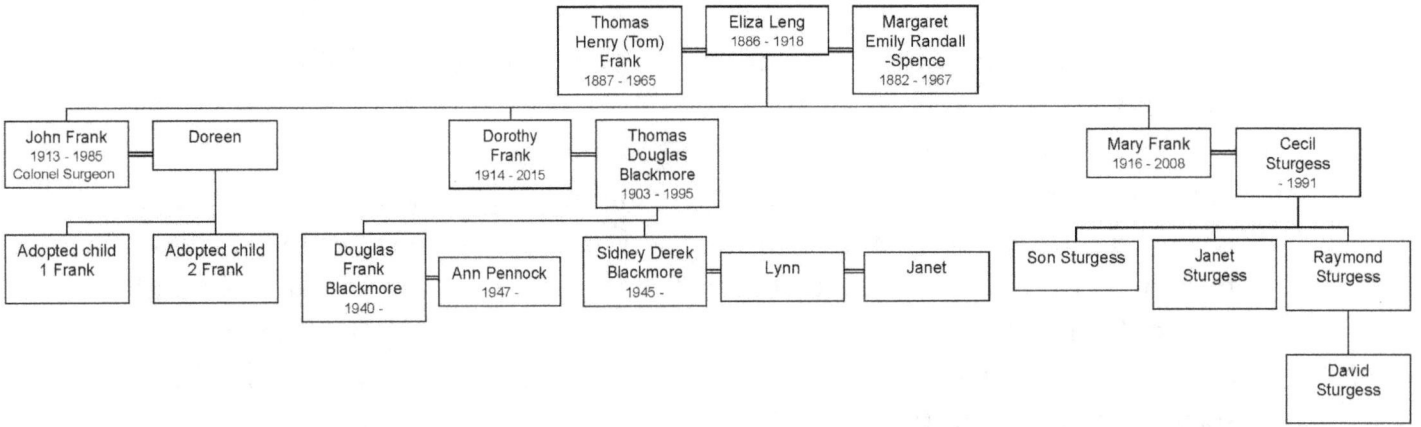

A note on Mary

Mary Frank was named after her great-aunt Mary Crake, Mary Frank becoming a beneficiary in her will of July 1946, her elder sister Dorothy receiving china and silver goods. Mary was in the Wrens during the Second World War, met and married Cecil Sturgess, where they settled in Wiltshire. An earlier boy died of a hole in the heart while their daughter, Janet, surviving to aged eleven, suffering from the same condition, survived an operation to close the hole in her heart only to succumb during recovery. There are photos of Janet, where the subsequent adoption of Ray brought some light and much joy into his parent's lives. Having David from a previous marriage, Ray recently remarried his current wife Fran. Of all my cousins, Ray is by far the closest, he and Fran living on the south coast, in remembrance of good times; we make the effort to meet from time to time.

Dorothy Frank

As a spirited young woman, rather than suffer stifling constraints under the watchful eye of her stepmother, Dorothy left home and trained at Great Ormond Street prior to taking a post with the Governor of Nova Scotia. Returning to England prior to the war, she tossed a coin whether to return to Canada or go south to Africa.

Africa won. En route she stopped off in Egypt and it was here she met her future husband, Tom Blackmore. Tom had been on leave from South Africa where he had been mobilising troops for the forthcoming desert war. The couple married in Cairo enjoying a short interlude of happiness before the world they knew turned on its head. Incidentally a sealed document in recognition of Dorothy's earlier service to the Governor of Nova Scotia was presented to her on her 100th birthday at Thirsk, close to the much earlier Thirkleby countryseat in North Yorkshire.

As a Desert Rat, Tom went off into the sand, remaining there with his contingent until the end of the conflict. Dorothy was captured by the Germans and gave birth under terrible conditions, helped it must be said by a German Doctor. Survival was imperative and she did what she had to do to keep her baby alive, such awful details for my mother as I later found out, remain private. Taking over from their German counterparts, the Italians love of children brought much needed relief. Our plight must have been touching, as they arranged for mum and me, a four-month old baby, and several others to be evacuated to South Africa. Three years later, November 1943, we once more set sail, this time for England, arriving 22nd April 1944. Having suffered a series of sea attacks, including the sinking of the ship immediate to our stern, a trip that would normally take two or three weeks took four and a half months of interrupted passage.

There are many photographs taken in South Africa, as too a number of Dorothy around her earlier time in Canada and aboard ship with friends. There are also several photos around the time of her marriage in Egypt prior to the outbreak of war. Obtained by Dorothy, I have a pair of tiny 5 cm shoes made of bread by some prisoners of war. Coloured red and green, they are among a small number of artefacts, memories and mementoes she managed to bring with her to England.

Continuation of Dorothy's story follows after this:

Wiped out

As if to further demonstrate the darker side and fragility of existence, 100 years ago, even 200 or more, there's the repeated record of a farming family consisting of eight, twelve, even fourteen children. Yet here upon the Dales, within a remote farmhouse, bleak upon a windswept and darkened landscape, are a group of children aged between four and thirty, where a younger child mysteriously dies, then another. One by one each of them gone, all but the eldest son – a family wiped out as if they never existed. But there is more, and having researched it, the story is true.

One dark night as if hell came knocking, viewed through a window from the outside, the yellow flicker of light given by a single candle suddenly flutters and is blown out, only this time for eternity when the son too succumbs, the middle-aged couple's last hope for continuance, all gone in a final heartbeat: all twelve souls.

Standing side-by-side, spade in hand at his burial; distraught beyond human endurance, the parents die a year or so later, John's wife first, unlucky thirteen, and then John their lives a lie to existence itself, all of them Franks, their belief in eternity too, rendered dust.

I have left their details fittingly anonymous, as this is a story repeated throughout history that in some way remains an epitaph to the memory of the many lost souls this book plays testament to.

The Dorothy Frank saga, World War Two, continued

Dorothy's passage from South Africa to England was unfortunate in choosing passage under constant German attack with ships damaged and one sunk, but after four and a half months my mother and I eventually made it to England. The Desert War had been won, and this mysterious man, the father I didn't know, was in charge of Eastern Defences. Luton where we were billeted was a town occasionally hit by flying bombs or doodlebugs, as they were known. Fired from Germany, these were an early version of today's sophisticated unmanned drones.

We had taken the ex mayor of Luton's house, whose garage was also in a bit of a mess. Told to keep away, all I remember was a seemingly endless black void, a pitiless hole devoid of anything but blackness. But for a young boy, given the snow and after the sunshine and bright colours of Africa, everything in this strange world seemed to be black or white, merging into smudgy grey. But of course this was before the introduction of colour into British lives.

It was normal to see flattened houses, piles of rubble and Nissen shelters still upon the streets. Along with rationing, us kids were given thick orange juice, at school our heads thoroughly checked in case of nits. Our smelly wartime gasmasks now discarded, shortages and rationing remained part and parcel, where we were encouraged to save bundles of newspapers for recycling. Worth sixpence, lemonade bottles were bartered for entry into the cinema.

But the war had ended and with my brother Sid a babe-in-arms, it took a momentous decision for my father, a career officer, whether to remain in the army or to follow my mother to Yorkshire. The decision made, we settled in North Yorks, my father buying outright one of my grandfather's earlier houses, around the 200th or so he had built in Linthorpe, a house Granddad had previously lived next door to.

Dad

My father was a man I found it difficult to connect with. In his latter days, sadly and belatedly having failed to break through the veneer, subsequent to his death and in an effort to find some kind of affinity, I settled on holding onto Dad's desert rat insignia and Eastern Command bulldog motif. I know he loved us, but his upbringing was so constrained and correct that demonstrative emotion was considered bad form, where a shake of the hand, even as a child, was as far as it got. But an early glimpse showed something of his emotion, where at around age four a photo shows the two of us, my dad and I observing amphibious army DUKW's crossing to and fro across a park lake, in it Dad has one arm tightly wrapped around his eldest son.

There are other photos too, but from memory the images wore a disguise, masking a parental inability to show unfettered love. Perhaps with parental blame on both sides, what remained was a stalemate devoid of contact, at times bordering on muted hate. What fools we are not to reach out when we have the chance, not once, occasionally or as a remembered afterthought, but always. And isn't it often the case that it is the child who is the more perceptive and adult, and the child who has to reconcile the hurt even into adulthood. Yet despite a succession of smiley family photographs, like my mother before me, the bleak nature of a home devoid of banter, music and laughter, for me made the occasional return home so brief as to search constantly for new horizons.

Granddad Frank and the early expansion of modern Middlesbrough

Following his apprenticeship and clutching his small inheritance, Thomas Henry persuaded a schoolteacher friend to buy a 50% sleeping partnership in his fledgling business. Thus saw the birth of 'T H Frank, Builder', his first build of several hundred houses commencing with the cobbled incline of Rockliff Road, whose offshoot road had a laundry and local shop, with a long garden enabling the cultivation of fresh produce to sell. Behind the garden, backing onto half a dozen houses, lay tennis courts with gated access to the rear garden of Tom's own house.

At the end of the Aysgarth Road cul-de-sac, Tom Frank had preserved a farmhouse and buildings, an orchard, and a couple or more fields converted to use as drying greens attached to a huge laundry with tall chimneys puffing vapour and smoke. Prior to the war, bedsheets were laid out on fields of grass and hedges to dry during the long, hot summer. The practice had long been superseded, but Granddad kept the fields as they were, surrounded by all kinds of fruiting bushes, and most inviting for the local children who safely played, an orchard for scrumping and my favourite, the cherry orchard. The only problem: the old farmhouse itself and its land was private property, but nicking fruit allowed us to become Indians creeping through the undergrowth unobserved.

Tom Frank had moved to Newby, building supersized Croft House for his own use complete with a paddock, huge orchard and surrounding land. Close by was a massive timber workshop consisting of a work area and storage racks for bulk timber where his men produced windows, doors, fitted cupboards, flooring and roofing timbers, hand-built for each and every one of his high-spec houses. The workshop was situated adjacent to where he lived and where he could personally supervise the high standard of work. The motto 'Industry in quiet places' might in its way equally apply to Tom Frank as to Mousey Thompson of Kilburn fame, to whom it belonged.

The Thompson story is the story of a mouse sat washing itself oblivious to a craftsman quietly carving an oak centrepiece in a nearby church. So still was the scene, the craftsman decided to carve a likeness of the mouse, the emblem of the hand-carved mouse becoming obligatory to all Thompson work. But for Tom Frank, his word was his bond, the quality of his work being a trademark unto itself. Standing now and standing for decades to come, roads, streets, avenues, whole towns, silent epitaphs as to the wisdom of their origin.

Prior to Croft House, my brother Sid and I just happened to live in the house next door to where Granddad once lived. Each of the four houses had a gate leading to private tennis courts. In our day the courts had begun to look dilapidated, forlorn and unused, but everything else was just as it had been. At the time we lived in a tiny cul-de-sac with an easy five-foot fence to negotiate at the end, the fields beyond left unbuilt, wild, natural and unkempt; the fruit as fruit should taste, the flowering blossom glorious, the cherries as cherries should taste, for a child, everything wonderful except the regular caning across bleeding knuckles one received at school.

It was a boy's only school, but among my chums the brutal whacks across the head and caning across bruised knuckles felt nothing set beside a growing commonality of optimism and aspiration. There was a new world dawning, we knew it and felt it, it was still the fifties but the sixties were coming, time was racing, all of us ready to flex our muscles and face the world head-on, none of us being inclined to sit around and wait for things to happen. I was spending more time with Granddad Frank either on a construction site or on one of the farms, and by the age of fifteen was chairman of the Young Farmers Club. Blithely thinking I knew everything there was to know about farming, I gave up school as an easy swap for a real man's job. A tenant suffering from heart problems caused Granddad to let me work the farm most single-handed, land I prematurely begun to think of as mine.

But during school we had seen what war had done, evidenced by the local match seller, 'tiny no-legs', perched with his stumps on a low trolley scooting along the pavement propelled by cloth-covered knuckles, a flat tray hung around his neck, fastened with string, upon which was displayed his small stock of matches. A couple of our teachers too seemed half-crazed with limbs and bits missing, disturbed, brutalised and yet having survived sometimes given to great and amazing acts of kindness.

Having learned by example, it was up to us to have the courage to forge a new kind of world against the normality of bombed outbuildings and food shortages. And then there was my individual escape to the nearby military airport bordering Quarry Farm, crawling under barbed wire to the very end of the runway, where at the very point of take off I could witness the scream of Meteor jet after Meteor jet repeating immediately overhead, the world's first fighter jets tipping skyward, roaring into impossible flight, giving inspiration to a unknown entity, a brilliant new dawn where anything was possible. And how right that feeling was, the world today way beyond anything we could then have imagined.

I have previously mentioned the time of my being around aged twelve, Granddad clutching rolls of paper and ink-dip pens, giving me the job of drawing plans for the Rivers Estate, its hundreds of houses and complicated drainage scheme. This was for a huge private estate in Acklam, previously de Brus land, Acklam being a newly formed district of Middlesbrough, the estate's roads named after various rivers. Varying data from earlier plans, each finished drawing was sent for approval and duly stamped.

And, yes, if anyone thinks otherwise, as I write, the houses are still standing, and like so much construction and quality of material then used, the houses were grossly over-engineered by current-day standards. In point of fact, so used to building, Tom Frank's men mostly referred to the plans for the footings, pipework and road layout; the job of bricklaying made more interesting by varying the interior walls of each house, making it up as they went along, purely off the cuff. Later, the quality and open design of these houses were applauded as an example of the very best construction of its kind in the country.

An early environmentalist, Granddad Frank was very much in touch with nature, every house had its rear garden planted with a minimum of two fruit trees, the larger gardens with four trees schemed to cross pollinate across the whole town. Newly married couples were often given their house at production cost as a way of seeing them off right in their new life together. Seen today the whole thing might seem mad and doomed to failure, but not so. Despite being a country held in bankruptcy to America, this was a time of optimism and expansion. Whether misplaced or not, the optimism shown by Tom Frank and others of his kind, shaped and formed the municipal towns most kids grew up in and knew so well. Two world wars, yet against all odds they set to and got on with it, nothing could stand in their way.

There being something quaint in the logic of an Englishman's home as his castle, the thing that remained utmost in Tom Frank's mind was that tiny plot and a front garden separating each house from next door and the road it faced. The simplicity of a garden wall offering a psychological barrier akin to what was known in the Scottish Borders and Northumberland historically as a barmking, a stone wall surrounding a peel tower or bastle house, for the protection of live stock.

The ancient towers were very tall, vertical, thick-walled homesteads with tiny windows and two or three storeys above ground offering protection against marauding reivers bent on stealing cattle. Protected within a stone-walled compound, the most valuable animals were blockaded within the ground floor of the building itself. Quaint in its reasoning, the comparison between an average modern house and an historic peel tower might seem far-fetched, but the idea of one's home having the protection of a garden wall and the relief of bolting the door at the end of a tiring day, assuages a similar psychological buffer of protection against the outside world.

For me there is something about this that seems to echo something about Tom Frank and the ordinariness of him standing in his garden; an extraordinary man thankful for the simple things of life, at the end of the day tired and content in the comfort of his favourite saggy armchair, grateful for a job well done and having witnessed life and nature in all its wonderment. Not for him the loathsome aspect of multi-million pound yachts, their purchase pillaged from the mouths of innocent hard-working families. At night, wrapped in God's grace and blessed by all, Tom could genuinely sleep the gentle sleep of an innocent babe. No knighthood, nonetheless the words give of predecessor Sir Thomas Frankland by King William III might equally apply, 'He hath very good estate, a gentleman of a very sweet, easy affable disposition, of good sense and extremely zealous for the constitution of his country.' Sleep well good knight.

Of life and death.

Something I'd forgotten: the aeroplane that came down. It had missed the runway crashing into Quarry Bank farmhouse during the Second World War. It seems that however remote or removed far from the field of battle, something of the folly of man and conflict will always find you. I remember walking the fields, harvest time, the pure sweet smell of fresh air, drifting clouds, sunsets glorious across the upper reaches of the river, cattle gently grazing and the fall of dusk and wild fowl, duck skimming to land with a splash into the mercurial water of the Tees River, where once shallow draft sailing ships ventured as far inland as Yarm to offload. Unbelievably, now all gone, replaced with the most horrible destructive spoil of overspill construction, a visual terror and a nightmare where once were pasture, summer grazing and gentle rolling landscape. So sad, the passing of something precious, now lost within the fading memory of an old man, a piece of paradise never to return.

It is sad to end this piece on a low when there is so much of life and history to applaud. But it's from history we draw parallels from which to shape the future. I'm no philosopher yet feel the crying need for something of the past, something this fast-moving world can occasionally grab hold and take stock of, else as a species we are in mortal danger, none the least in terms of mental wellbeing and health. We come from nature are part of nature, being neither gods nor machines bent on texting our lives away; a lesson we'd best not forget.

But of life, death, nature and man's invention, comes another story. In 1962, already working for the Americans, I was on short attachment to SHAPE Headquarters in Paris. Having the equivalent rank of second lieutenant, I was living off-base at the Hotel d'Angleterre, 21 Rue Copernic, Paris 16. The date was 22nd August, and it was close to dusk: coming from Versailles and stepping from the military bus at the Etoile, and being a hot day and thinking of a bath, bewilderment struck when among the crush of other pedestrians we were pressed against a wall by armed gendarmes.

It turned out an attempt had been made to assassinate de Gaulle, whereby two motorcycle bodyguards were gunned down and killed and all four tyres of the President's car were punctured. Yet de Gaulle escaped due to the skill and quick thinking of the driver and the superior suspension and mechanics of the Citroen DS19. Known as the Goddess it accelerated out of a front wheel skid and, despite the lack of tyres and with sparks flying, it got safely away.

But my story has less to do with this episode than the hotel itself, its address etched in my mind. What amazed me was its plumbing; its like I'd never seen before nor since. To me quite amazing and obviously of antique vintage, its complex array of bright, shiny, interconnected copper pipes, including that of a shower, was a sight to behold, something to wonder at and puzzle over, and useful to figure out the intricate network of pipes while lying in a handsome depth of hot water soaking away the day's sweat. This was way beyond anything comparable in Yorkshire where unused old tin baths still hung from six-inch nails. And a testament to persistency, as two weeks later, glory; being overjoyed having at last unscrambled the system's complexity, working out how it all operated.

A number of maps accompany this research, and I hope the finished document proves useful in plotting one's Frank heritage where a lost and forgotten historic name can now be seen in its correct light as a hugely historic and important lineage spanning over 2000 years. Truly foremost as both a name and an entity, the Franks were always destined to fade from glory, their presence having been pushed to one side and just as swiftly forgotten as instigators in the forging of a least three nationhoods, common law and language. Truly, for those fortunate to bear the surname Frank, their heritage remains a bloodline to be justly proud.

SUMMARY

So there we have it, a cobble of words, observations, notes and names, put into some semblance of order; I hope it is more than that. Yes there are holes, and someday maybe someone might add, correct or fill in the gaps. I hope the work is sufficiently seminal, reflecting the many ages and the times they speak of, as well as something of the Franks as people. We started in AD428 with Chlodio le Chevelu and, as king, his title of Rex Francorum, and before that the pirates of AD210 and the warlike Salian tribes. Then there's Frank law, exempli gratia, Lex Salica and the birth of the modern-day legal process. Add to that the birth of France and the defeat of Islamic rule over Europe, that and much more.

So these Franks, who were they:

- Germanic tribes people
- Pirates
- Creators of common law
- Christians
- Creators of statehood
- Creators of France
- Kings, rulers, emperors
- Ruler of the Holy Roman Empire
- Thirty-five Charlemagne monarchies
- Generals (defeat of Muslim horde in France)
- Church, state, legislation
- Creators of feudalism
- Inventors of knighthood
- Kings of Jerusalem
- Emperors and patriarchs of Constantinople
- Swordsmen
- Inventors of the Francisca Battleaxe
- Soldiers, knights and horsemen

The Extraordinary Franks

Normandy farmers

Nobles

Peacemakers, war makers

Administrators

Monks

Bishops

Crusaders

Justices of the Peace

Fiefmen

Yeomen

Templars

Archbishop

Lords

Charter witnesses

Scribes

Soldiers

Doctors, surgeons

Commanders

Knights warden and constable

Yorkshire farmers

Sailors

Sawyers

Canons of York

Royal Navy Commanders

Writers

Artists, artisans

Douglas Frank Blackmore

Master Masons, past and present

Builders

Carpenters

Designers

Bankers

Teachers

Councillors

Churchgoers

Lay preachers

Barons, lairds and lords

Lay-people

Poor

Destitute

Rope and sail-makers

Ploughmen, men of the soil, sheep farmers

Wool traders and weavers

Jurymen

Landowners

Judges

Lawyers

The list could go on, but here are some of the Scottish and Yorkshire estates:

Cunynghame

Paxton

Roxburgh

Thornydykes

Jedburgh

Sproustoun

Kelso

Pitcoks

Coldingham

Barony of Polwarth

Frankysland Peebles

Related Yorkshire estates:

The Glaisdale estates of:

Glaisdale Head

Fryup

Danby

Those of:

Wrelton in Middleton

Hutton-le Hole

Lastingham

Rosedale

Yew Grange

Wood Head

Hawk Carr

Mill Lane farm

And Franks of:

Aisaby

Kirkby Moorside

Hutton

Pickering

Helmsley

Brompton on Swale

Great Broughton

Hawes

Whitby

Newsham

Ness

York

Thirsk

The more recent Tees farms of:

Ingleby Barwick

Quarry Bank

White House Farm

Sober Hall

Grandfather Thomas Henry Frank, his estate:

Linthorpe

Acklam

Ayton

Stokesley

Broughton

Newby

Such listing omits the human aspect belonging to the myriad of trials and tribulations, the heartache, triumphs and victories, as too the everyday victims tied to the slavery of toil and existence so quickly extinguished. Yet the complexity of this work cannot be understated nor that concerning its heraldic eminence in piecing together the many intricacies interwoven through history, and how by understanding its craft one might unlock something of its hidden past. Part four in particular brings together the various facets drawing together a conclusive analogy.

But prior to this, the loose strings of part three.

PART THREE

OFFSHOOT CLEVELAND FRANKS

The names John and Robert were so popular as to cause problems sorting one from the other. There is a Sarah Frank and John Frank of Lastingham, probably cousins, who married January 1758. John seemingly related to the Lastingham branch, and Sarah back through Roberti, probably related to the mainstream Franks referred to in this work. In common with the times, many of the following families suffered terrible losses, their womenfolk in particular having only rudimentary medical care, childbirth a lottery for both mother and child, where even as close as more modern times the very presence of death was a shadow to be endured.

The Lacy were an eminent family, their tree easily found online, Roberti Frank marrying Dorothy Lacy in 1683:

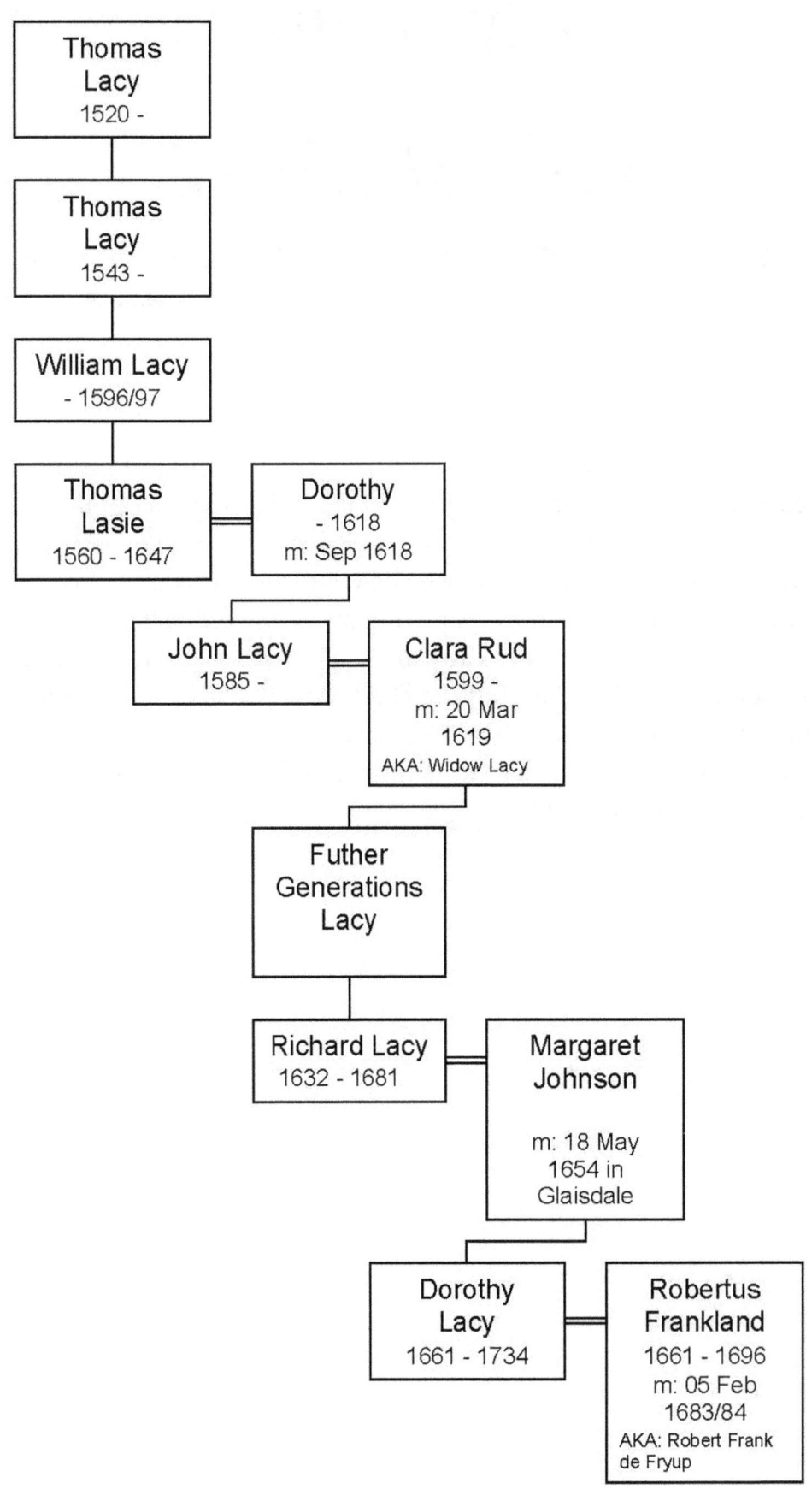

The Extraordinary Franks

Breifly returning to **Johannes aka John Frank.** Born 12th April 1694, I suggest caution concerning referencing John born 15th April 1718, where in his will Johannes appears to mention a son Jonathan born 20th March 1721 who married Mary (1718–1741). Given Mary's early death it seems that Jonathan remarried. His secord marriage to Sarah Breckon, born 8th November 1724, the couple marrying 12th November 1747.

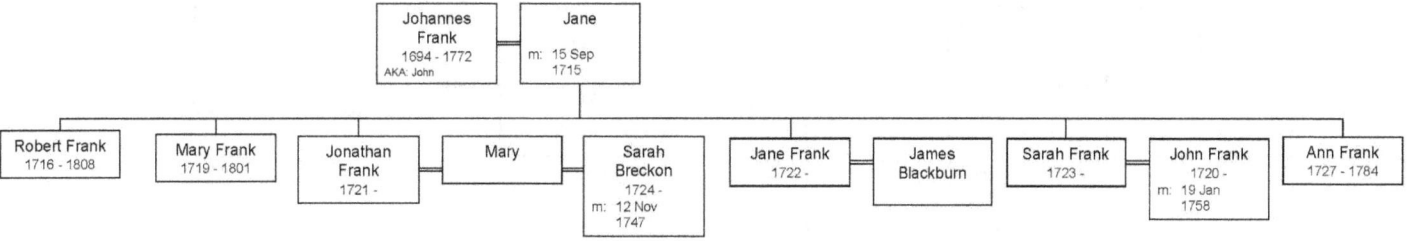

Sarah and John links with John and Jane Frank of Fryup, see next:

Johnathan Frank (1721) children:

> Elizabeth b. de Murkside 1748/9, d. Dec 1822 Egton. Married Thomas Smallwood 23 May 1774 Egton (b. Oct 1750 Beckhole Glaisdale, d. Jun 1831 Egton). Son William Smallwood (1781–1870) Blacksmith and Victualler, Brown Cow Inn and smallholder, Hinderwell.

> Thomas b. 1750/2, d. 1Apr 1821 aged 69. Married Ann (b. 1753, d. 18 Jul 1823 aged 70).

Children:

Dorothy Frank b. 1791, d. 25 Jun 1826. Married Leonard Reah (b. 1777, d. 28 Jun 1849 aged 72) Glazer of Short wait, Leaholm. Their children: Thomas Rhea (d. 12 Oct 1885 aged 71) and William Rhea (d. 1Jul 1895 aged 74).Jonathan Frank d. 31 Jan 1865 aged 82.

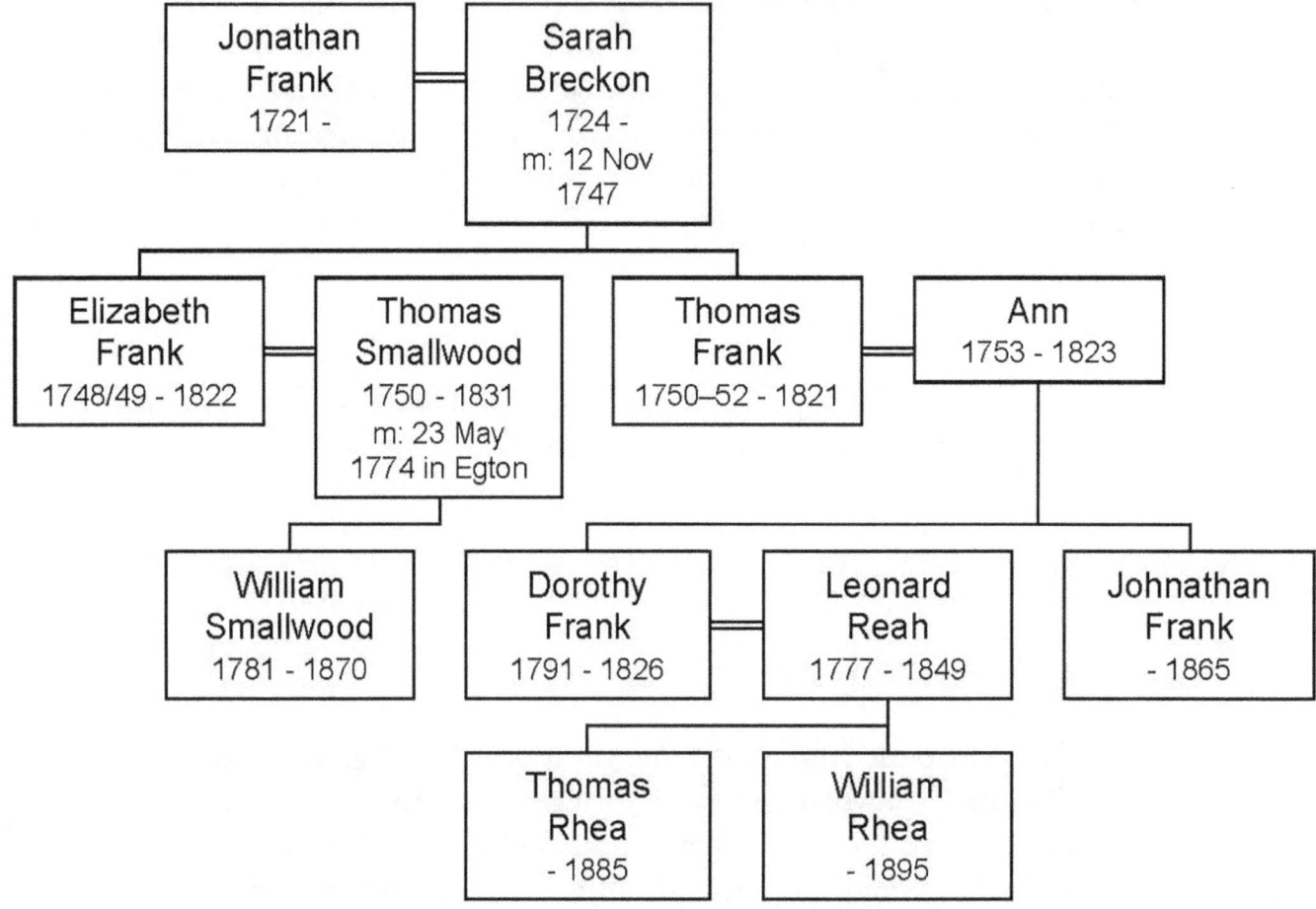

PRIMITIVE METHODISM.

Up to forty-five or so years ago, having taken the pledge, rural Methodist farmers refused to grow barley, barley being principally used for brewing. Except for feeding the animals, no work or noise-some play was allowed on a Sunday, and strictly no hanging out the washing, washing the car, card playing and so on. The Sabbath was strictly for quietude, devotion and prayer. Newby, a supposedly Methodist stronghold, didn't have a pub, yet to my knowledge some supposedly outwardly devout Methodists surreptitiously took a drink or two and relaxed out of sight in some hidden nook away from prying eyes.

MISCELLANEOUS FRANKS.

A mystery – Hannah Frank, wife of George Coverdale, lies between the graves of John and Robert Frank. Hannah was born 1795, died 8th October 1821 in childbirth aged twenty-six, her daughter Rachel having survived. One surmises Hannah was a daughter of one of two men, most likely deceased husbands of Hannah's mother,

The Extraordinary Franks

but the absence in the grave of an older woman suggests Hannah's mother was still alive, and probably looked after baby Rachel.

Mary Duck – Mary, shown below, probable daughter of well-known Danby Methodist Minister Duck whose name appears against many birth, death and marriage records in the area.

Note: Thompson graves close by.

John Frank and Mary Duck's marriage was witnessed by Robert Frank and Manax Duck.

John Tinsdale, husband of Jane Frank (below), was witness to wedding of John Chapman to Ann Frank 16 May 1790.

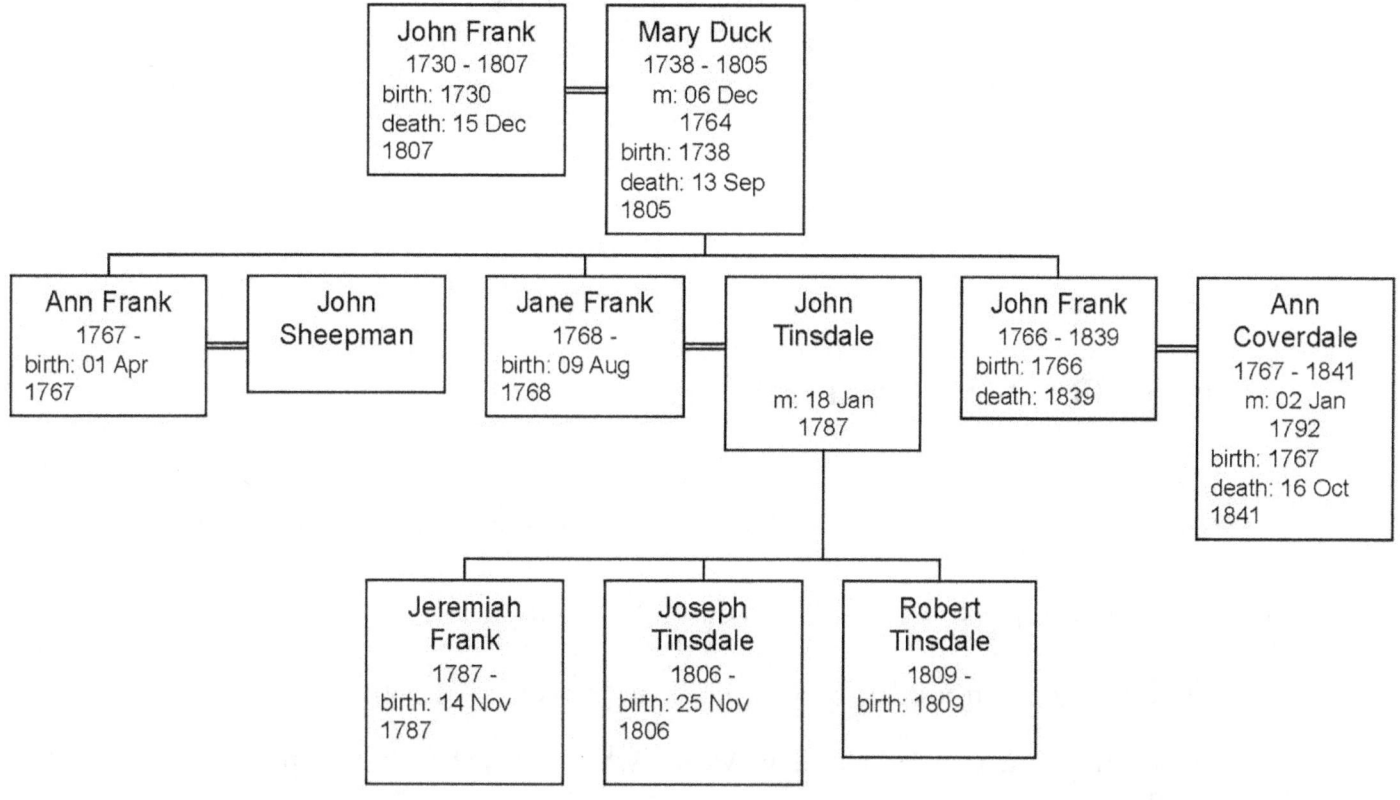

ROBERT FRANK

Yeoman farmer of Hawk Carr farm, Mill Lane farm and Wood Head Farm, Fryup Although not sure, the above Mary could be a daughter or from another tree. Also in the household, a servant, Hannah Jackson aged 12.

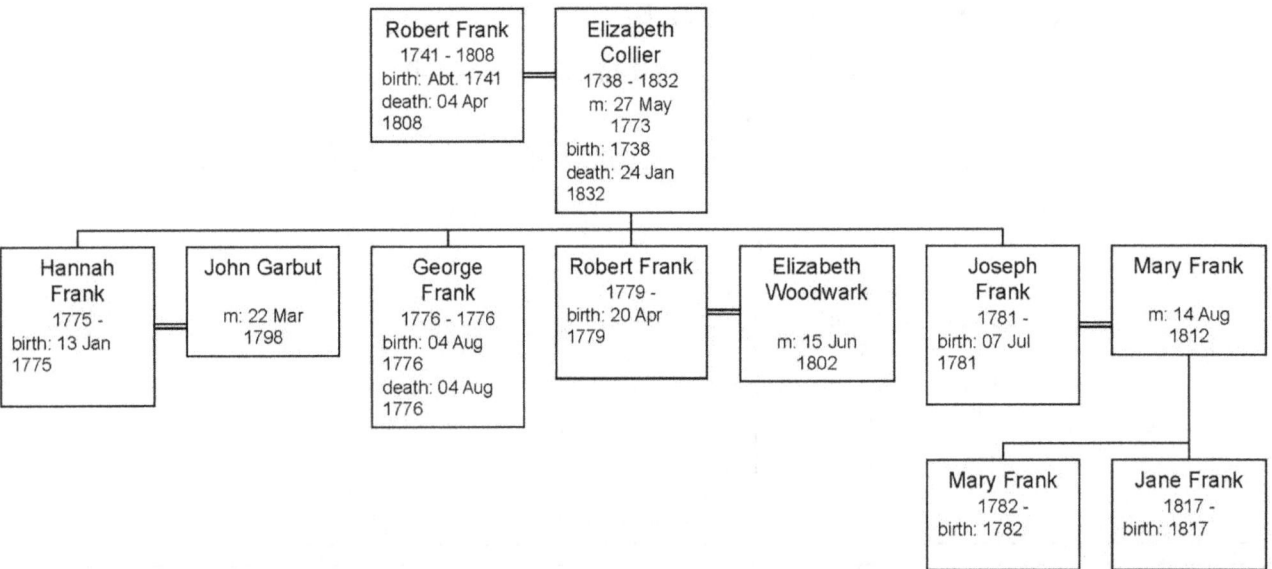

THE MYSTERY OF HANNAH FRANK

Regarding the popular name of Hannah. One assumes this Hannah Frank is not one person, more likely the Christian name Hannah, like Robert, just came to the fore in people's minds as a great name. Here's the list:

Hannah Frank or persons called Hannah married each of:

> Thomas Frank around 1767 (see Thomas Frank tree below).
>
> Anthony Frank married Hannah Watson who became Frank 16 Sep 1780, (see below tree).
>
> William Thompson, 21 Apr 1794.
>
> John Garbut, 22 Mar 1798.
>
> John Unthank, 10 Oct 1807 (John Frank witnesses).
>
> George Frank, around 1820 daughter Hannah Elizabeth b 25 Apr 1832.
>
> (see next tree).

The aforesaid demonstrates just one of a profusion of obstacles relating to identification.

MISCELLANEOUS.

The following seemingly related Franks have been impossible to properly link to the mainstream family:

1.

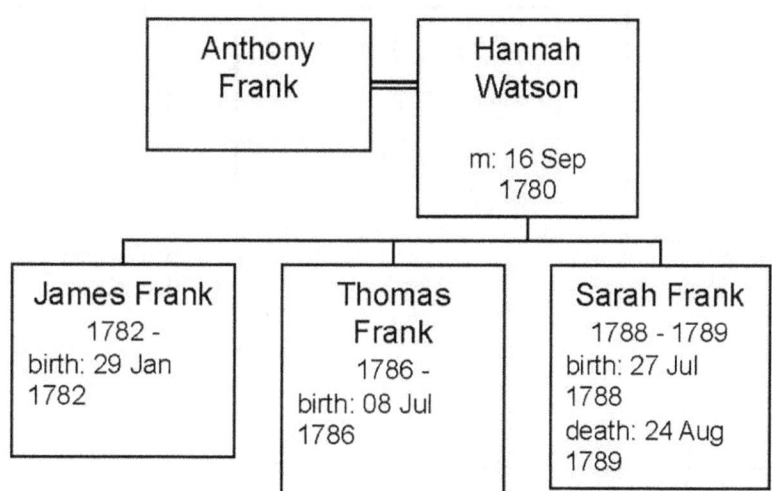

(Tree remains unresolved)

2.

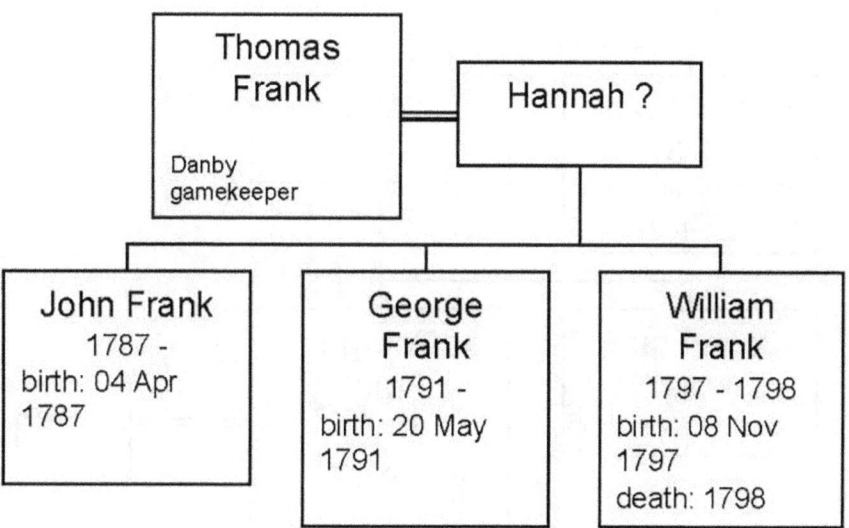

3.

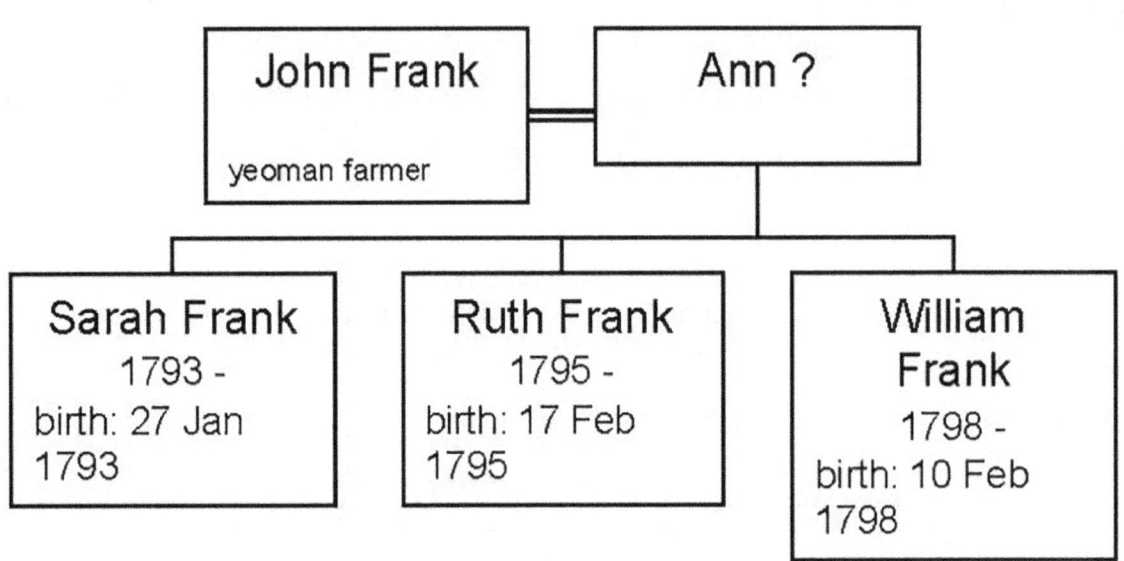

4.

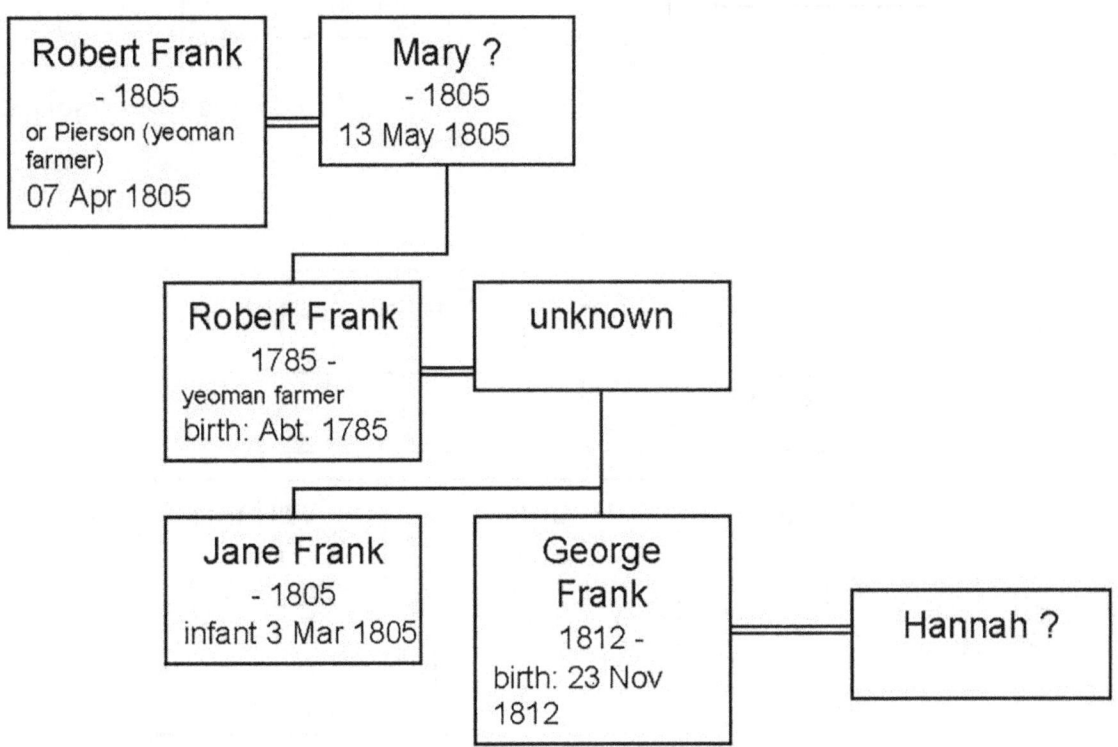

FROM EGTON OLD CHURCHYARD.

5.

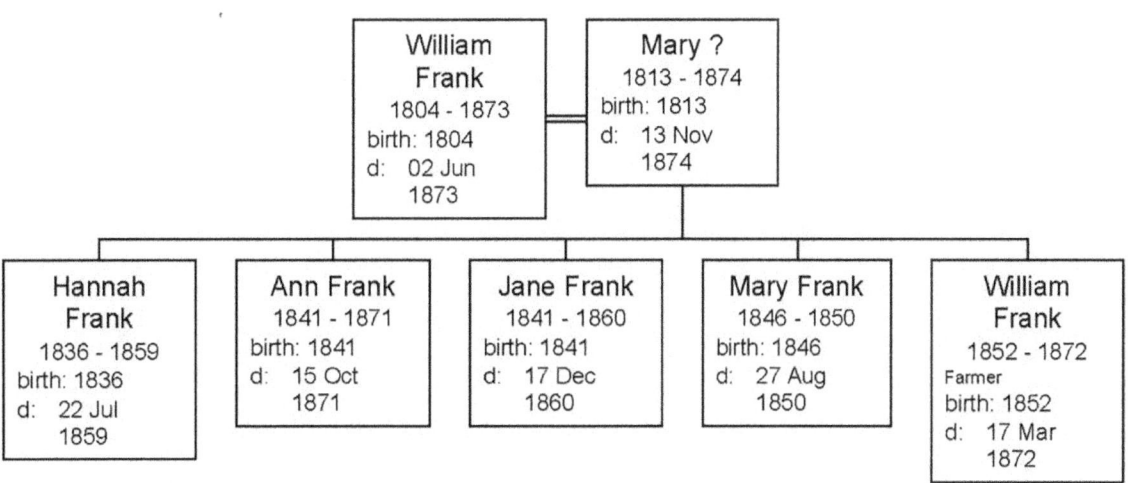

This concludes details relating to unplaced Franks where I concede the possibility of misplaced entries. Yet the case for antecedence is as true as it can be, the surname Frank, its derivative nomenclature as it relates to Frank and Frankland are born of a common entity, emerging through an appellative patronymic lineage found in Sir Robertus de Bayeux le Francais aka Fraunceys, born of a Breton captive in Espriota, a damsel of low degree around 1047–1049, having as his father Roger de Bayeux, his great-grandfather Raoul, king of West France.

I would remind of the origins coming from Frankrike, King Charles the Simple-Frankrike losing in battle to Raoul de Ivry, brother of Rollo Duke of Normandy, on his conversion to Christianity Rollo assuming the name Robertus and the ascension of the name Frankrike, assumed via Sprota in her son Robertus, thus the nuclear evidence determining the family's very origins.

PART FOUR

THE FRANKS ARMORIAL

INTRODUCTION

The Franks Armorial is an addendum reaffirming one's lineage via Dorothy Frank back in time to Sir Robertus Francaise and his descendants indicated in North Yorks and the Annandale. And for thiss section I have occasionally dipped into archives. org, and *Index Armorial* to an emblazoned manuscript.

The Franks were feudally related to the de Brus in Normandy, similarly in Cleveland and through Adam de Brus, across the borders of Scotland. Their affiliation was thereafter perpetuated in the Scottish archives through Williams Francus and his son, Roger Franceis, who continued retention of the feudal holding of the manor of Aclum belonging Robert de Brus previously awarded him by William the Conqueror, details being found in the main entries for 1182, 1218 and 1300.

My deceased grandfather, Thomas Frank's modern-day holdings were located across the same historical land of Linthorpe and Aclum cum Acklam as his predecessors; those predecessors being historically enfeoffed to the de Brus. Tom Frank's father and brothers owned a succession of farms along the River Tees, Robert Hart-Frank senior being the owner of a large part of Glaisdale and its surrounds. The origin of Frank occupancy coincided with the arrival of Robert de Brus in Yorkshire, where coincidently twenty-first century Thomas Henry Frank developed the early mentioned townships, having ownership of scattered land, property and farming adjacent the historic de Brus seat of Skelton Castle and nearby Guisborough.

Thomas Henry Frank served his apprenticeship as a joiner in Middlesbrough, Linthorpe and Acklam, being land he later developed into a thriving metropolis. *Erimus*, Latin for 'we shall be' was appropriated as the motto of the town of Middlesbrough, its motto and coat of arms taken from de Brus who owned the site on which the port of Middlesbrough was built, the arms an azure lion beneath two ships. Of this community little or nothing remains of the de Brus or a single mention of

Tom Frank – people who in their time were so influential yet appear anonymous in the annuls of Teesside today.

You must forgive my acrimony, but for me Middlesbrough's demise might be seen in the thwarted ambitions as a town of real hope. Home of the singer Chris Rea, and summed up in his song 'Windy Town' the words are poignant, the song speaking of him driving past and not stopping. And like the singer my remembering it all and yet in so many ways trying to forget. It seems to be that kind of place where for me one's childhood memories have been all but erased, replaced by an anarchic creeping eyesore of terrible planning, a hideous blight of odious construction and no-go estates bespoiling a once wholesome functioning community, where even the town's motto was unceremoniously derived of de Brus, there seeming to be no clear reference as to the motto's origin or mention of the town's connection with a king of Scotland.

Sincere apologies for this diatribe, but I too remember Middlesbrough. And before he became famous, I remember the sound of Chris Rea playing his guitar above his father's ice cream parlour across from Albert Park, and also the terrible wind as it funnelled ice-cold off the river through the bleakest of shopping areas.

But returning to one's theme, Teesside, the Cleveland Hills and Dorothy Frank, the last surviving issue of a boy and two girls to Thomas Henry Frank and that historic pedigree, now lies asleep. And as I write, Dorothy, having died the 28th June 2015 aged 100, represents a landmark, being the longest-lived Frank in history.

Dorothy was the only child of Tom Frank having issue of her own, these being my brother Sid and myself as the eldest. Honouring Granddad's wish, the surname Frank was incorporated into my name. Apologies to the Blackmores but my affiliation has always been that of a Frank, one's former years being more of a father-son relationship with Tom Frank where he saw me taking on the farming side and we briefly talked about the purchase of land and what to avoid in terms of building. For Tom there must have been an inner sense of loss when as a youth his only son had decided on medicine, expressing no interest at all in his father's businesses.

It must have been heart-wrenching, building something from nothing only later in life wrestling with an obligation to hand it over, but in a sense wonderful of him in later years gifting the business to his original three foremen. But by now my world had become so removed from that of Tom Frank, at a crucial time his last hope of family interest in his business had evaporated. It is only now as I reach a similar age the sadness of it all comes upon me, that unspoken bond, that's how we were, a feeling of guilt and that word love.

Yet unbeknown to Tom I still entertained possibilities regarding the farming side, these being squashed when neither my brother nor I received so much as a mention in Granddad's will. That is until the time came to settle the estate, when much later on a visit to my Uncle Jack in Scotland, and with an apparent sense of guilt, Dr John Frank volunteered the farming side should have passed to me.

Should the reader wonder about my brother and how he fits in; Sid went into engineering rising to director of a top 100 company. It must be said, both of us were happy enough to have been left out of things to get on with our own lives unburdened. Incidentally I'm ever grateful to Sid for taking on much of the load of our mother, her home Aysgarth, and the finalisation of the estate in my absence, and am pleased he and Jan were belatedly and deservedly able to travel the world and get away to their place in northern France.

PREQUEL.

Due to the vagaries of historical data over prolonged periods of history, claims of proof-positive familial connection for 99% of people remains wholly subjective. Historians have their own ideas and often disagree on many areas of research, even in relation to such important and well-recorded families as the de Brus and the aristocracy in general, where under scrutiny their history is often seen as muddy and incomplete. Historians, while continuing to argue areas of disagreement, might agree on the overall weight or balance of historical evidence for a likely scenario for continuance, and it's on the basis of this broader interpretation I have based my argument, portrayed as a story and less an argument for contention.

Areas of difficulty:

> Historical lack of recorded information.
>
> The practice of taking the name of a place or another family name as one's own.
>
> The huge array of different spellings of the name, even with a given family.
>
> For the early Franks, their name being confused with the collective Frenchy for people from France.
>
> Illegitimate usage of names.

In researching the Franks, the huge amount of data to be trawled through, often on lost causes, has caused frustration and delay at every quarter. To allay doubt in proving the case for antecedence, in providing data I have been scrupulous in personally piecing together many thousands of translations and their interpretation, much of it from the original French-Latin. To make it more illustrative, I have used a mix of storyline interspersed with historical events, comments and personal anecdotes drawn together in what I hope is a coherent and compelling argument.

However, as stated, history is littered with half-hidden evidence of illegitimate births, unrecorded child adoption, death through childbirth, the substitution of a male child due to high rates of mortality or female births, a myriad of surname changes, where, for instance, due to the lack of a male heir a man might marry into a family and for the sake of continuance adopt a family name, and so on. The evidence for certitude is non-existent, whereas there is a case for broad-brush continuance in the context of locational or cluster related same-name familial pedigrees, where viewed as possible or likely candidates, even with DNA, family tree absolutes remain non-existent.

In *The Times*, Monday 12th October 2015, Valentine Low reported of pretenders to titles being able for the first time to use genetic evidence to pursue their claim. It concerned Simon from Sussex, due to be awarded the eleventh barony on the death of his father Sir Steuart Pringle, commandant general of the Royal Marines during the Falklands war.

A dispute arose when Sir Steuart's DNA failed to match that of the earlier Pringle line. A rival claim for the title suggested the likelihood of illegitimate succession around the time of the ninth barony, whereby Sir Steuart's previous claim to the title seems to have been less that of bloodline but more that of a modern approach as regards family, where intervention in pregnancy and adoption might skewer the outcome pursuant to legitimate heirs.

Taken up by the judicial committee of the Privy Council, a decision on the case should be quite interesting relating to *fils de bast,* regarding illegitimacy as opposed to adoption and fertilisation. But as for the aristocracy in general, depending how far back one wants to go, were it possible to obtain DNA from centuries old predecessors, the outcome would most certainly prove whole lines of succession invalid, an absolute nightmare for those affected.

CONTEXT.

The first occurrence of the surname Francais in Great Britain was in the County of York in 1097–1101, Robert Francais being one of few recorded knights of the second Robert de Brus. Here the Frank name has been variously spelt, vowel usage changing liberally as if on a whim. Some licence has been used, but on the whole mine are not spelling errors, being mostly used as found so as to report as accurately as possible.

As has been demonstrated, Robertus de Bayeux cum Franceis and Robert de Brus were contemporaneous adjacent the Cotentin, Normandy and each other as brother knights coming to England around 1066, where once settled adjacent the River Tees and Whitby, de Brus, eyeing greater spoils, struck north to Scotland taking with him his knights, William and Sir Robertus Fraunceis, together with an army of Yorkshiremen in their venture for Scotland, de Brus gaining 200,000 acres of estate in the Annandale.

Robert de Brus's friendship with Earl David of Scotland, at the court of King Henry I of England, seems to have culminated soon after David's accession to the Scottish throne in 1124, whereby establishing de Brus in the Annandale, Brus's third son inherited many Scottish possessions.

As early as the late 1100s, we find William Fraunceis and his son Roger, although living in Scotland, still maintaining their Normandy ties, paying dues owed in the Cotentin family seat, William making payment in 1180, and Roger making payment in the same location in 1195.

William Fraunceis was witness to various charters to the monks of Melrose as early as the reign of King William the Lyon. These circumstances, taken in conjunction with later feudatory relations with the de Brus in Annandale, show that William Fraunceis was an early settler with the second Robert de Brus in Scotland.

The Frank contingent that settled inland from Whitby, although knight-related, settled largely as yeomen. Still feudally tied to the de Brus of Guisborough and Skelton, they retained an independent streak shown in their sometimes cruel and haughty Norman mien exacerbated by a superior noblesse.

No disguising the issue, to the Anglo-Saxon, these conquerors were French, arrogant and venal. They would have been recognised as such and singled out as different: different by the clothes they wore, and different by their language, education and capability. They would have been known as knowledgeable and hard-working craftsmen, hugely devout, yet short-tempered and so quick to anger as to draw blood, and without compunction kill.

One and the same, separating the Frank from the Norman is impossible. Even today, the kind of noblesse I've seen in Franks recently buried or sometimes stood over or mumbled a prayer, seems to bring a sense of the ancient, not of clinking armour, but of something time-honoured, arms reaching out with despair whispering entreaties of stories untold. Unaware of their heritage the Franks I knew remained aloof, self-contained and belief-driven, and in their own way instinctively proud of having witnessed existence and to have made their mark, unafraid of mortality.

What these Franks would have been curious of would be stories such as these, stories of their early predecessors pushing ever northward interspersed with tales of conquests and noble acclaim. And today's Franks, perhaps more relaxed and curious about a history littered with brutality, blood-let and death; they might at least understand something of their heritage and of a bloodline that unwittingly spurs them on, as for sure such continuum prevails.

Observed dispassionately and from a distance, their apparent superiority seems to have carried though the centuries, shown in their steadfast demeanour and inclination for hard work, quite consciously having within themselves a persistency of dogged certainty and tenacity of purpose. From my own observation, with no apparent knowledge as to their historical lineage, the very fact of being born a Frank seems to have carried with it an invisible badge of honour, put simply, a tenet to live by regardless the circumstances. The idea of being distantly French or German would be a paradox, where attempts to provide explanation would be an enigma, blinked at with disbelief and dismissed as absurd. It is only with hindsight and being able to view the Franks as if from the sideline one has been able to disseminate, and as a son of the last of that timeline, draw inspiration as to their heritage.

Both directly and aspirationally the Normandy Franks were true kith and kin to those specifically of Cleveland, as those of Yorkshire and Derby, as well as the wider influence of York and the Scottish Borders to the further reaches of Edinburgh and the north. The Franks of Cleveland being the same blood as their Scots counterparts, the same blood as those of Derby, Thirsk, and Normandy from whence Franks the country of France was born and via Rollo the name Frankrike substituted for Franceis and so on.

Paradoxically, while their Scottish cousins fostered hierarchical allegiances, gained honours and fought and died, the bulk of Cleveland Franks became absorbed into a mundane dependency, mostly in agriculture and forestry, whereas sawyers, timber merchants and farmers, their achievements were recognised by few. No accolades, no honours, distant and devoid of shield and shining banners, theirs was a wearisome existence borne of horned and bleeding knuckles, of tired and broken backs in conflict with the concept of heritage.

They might well be fighting a battle to tame the land and build a future, but there were none to record their passing or to praise and reward their achievements. For the Franks in bonny Scotland there might be titles, battles to be won, documents, records and accolades without measure, but not here, here upon the Dales it was grim, wet, grindingly dirty and tiring, but nonetheless work fitting a Frank, a body bent on creating something from nothing.

Exceptions were seen in such as Sir William and Roger, who, while retaining their Cleveland ties, maintained their influence in Scotland, the bulk of their kin continuing to spread across the land. Borne of an inner resilience and strength of character these early pioneers remained largely anonymous and unrecorded for posterity, fortune favouring an endeavour to make their lot much better.

The Extraordinary Franks

There's no fault the yeomen Franks of Cleveland and the Esk became increasingly work-worn and for a time distanced from their Scottish kin. And no fault theirs for not being in a position to seek the acclaim of their peers; yet they remained of the same blood, still Norman, still Franks. Of the rest of England, the Cleveland Franks had no real link or immediate knowledge of their southern cousins, even of the Frenchies who came from Normandy and settled south those many decades before.

Of their larger world their only real connection remained north, north to Scotland and of the stories passed to them by travellers and the caravan of marching armies. What they were mostly focused on was the day-to-day working of the land they toiled and the trickle of family migration inland towards Richmond and of known cousins around York and those scattered to the north and west of York. Yet by no means insular, they became aware of the broader scheme of things and were proud of their steadfast advance.

Constrained by toil the Yorkshire Franks weighed tales of fighting, of wars fought and lost, of death and defeat, also of wars won and of conquest:

> 'A knight travels south; some say a cousin or even closer relative. He is on business, something to do with the lord of the manor, some say on King's business. He's a Frank, here close to Pickering, he's one of our own, a Frank arrived but gone away again, some say back to Scotland, some say the knights men wore armour and held a banner and that he stayed with the de Brus at Skelton Castle and that he is related.'

A fanciful notion based on documentary evidence found in ancient Yorkshire data. The wearing of armour and banners flying are pure conjecture, nonetheless besides adding colour to the argument, the above illustrates a valid point. It would be impossible for news not to travel and for the North Yorkshire Franks not to have insight as to their Scottish kin, after all, at that time, they enjoyed a common domain in an ancient land stretching from the Tweed in the north to the southern reaches of the Kingdom of Bernicia, along the Tees. The southern reaches of the Tees, being Frank fief-land held of the de Brus and the de Brus constant need for heaven-sent stolid Yorkshire soldiery stock.

Taken from *Sweet Civility and Barbarous Rudeness* by William M Aird, Cardiff University:

> 'As it emerged in the eleventh and twelfth centuries, the kingdom of the Scots was a hybrid entity, not really Scots, but composed of

several ethnic groups, only some of whom could justifiably be seen as belonging to the Celtic world of Western Britain.'

Thus at that time, the mainland of Britain didn't contain the separate entity of Scotland. The extract continues:

'The significant ethno cultural frontier was not so much that between Southern Scotland and a Northern England, as that between Lowland and Highland Scotland. The distinction was between the gens maritime, the tame, home loving people of the Lowlands and the gens Montana, wild, proud Highlanders.'

This was most strikingly observed by the Scots historian John of Fordun, writing in the fourteenth century:

'Lothian, Southern Scotland between the Rivers Forth and Tweed, had been settled by the English in the early medieval period and, together with the lands between the Tweed and the River Tees had formed the Anglian Kingdom of Bernicia, one of the two constituent parts of the early medieval kingdom of Northumbria. To that extent, the River Tweed was a political border rather than a cultural frontier between the English and the Scots.'

Countering the accusation of the Highlanders being barbaric, in 1130 the ethnic group known as the Galwegians, were particularly vilified. They were of Gaelic-Norse extraction living around Galloway in south-west Scotland. Not Scots at all, emanating from Northern England, they were depicted as especially savage and godless barbarians accused of atrocities descending into cannibalism. Whether that is true or not, the English, thinking themselves a higher level of civilisation, learned to despise their Celtic neighbours, collectively marking the Scots, especially those towards the west and north of Scotland, as uncultivated crude rapists and butchers of women and children.

It is interesting that within today's SNP there are those having historic links with the IRA, who even today comes across as especially malevolent. Despite the largesse of the English taxpayer through the Barnett Formula paying homage to the Scots, there's a *terra-ferox* emanating largely from Glasgow, who appear to relish rubbing salt into the wounds of the English at every turn and seem to enjoy as much bad behaviour in Westminster as towards those in Scotland who oppose them.

Recent visitors of ours to Scotland from Australia were appalled at the maze of poor housing, the run down towns and boarded up shops reminiscent of desertion and a degenerate leadership with no sense of self-help and moral purpose. Then there is the SNP with a policy seemingly bent on claiming from the EU purse. A far right entity pursuant on handouts and intoxicated by failure becomes increasingly spiteful of their benefactors. Supported by an ever-growing disenfranchised population, as ever its discontent is blamed upon the neighbouring English. The very people with the fortitude and courage to take on the world, the aspirational endeavour, fortitude and Scottish spunk that once helped shape and form the world laden in discontent. Given to jibes and unforgiving diatribe, in contrast to their imagined welcome of shortbread, tartan and good cheer, cold, shamed and embarrassed, our Aussie guests couldn't wait to get away.

This is much to the chagrin of their more enlightened countrymen who see Great Britain as a composite, inextricably interwoven and entwined, English, Scots, Welsh, Northern Irish; a people one and the same spread across the nation, and as a nation Northumberland as much the Borders as the Borders are to Cumberland and so on, its people and successive generations so entwined as to enrich the whole as one entity. How on earth could the English manage without the everyday presence and melodic bur of Scottishness that prevails over every aspect of what each counterpart refers to as Britain, a semblance of Scottish vigour and get-go relentlessly permeating south and to distant shores.

Records show remarkable evidence of the continuous traffic of people travelling to and fro from Scotland in the north, to Whitby and York, where around 1300 relatives like Roger Franceis, having association with the de Brus in Scotland, is shown visiting the Franks of the manor of Aclum and Levingthorp, being recorded making suit to the priors court at nearby Thornaby. Roger's several times great-grandfather William, on a visit from Scotland in 1182, was witness to a charter having confirmation of King Henry II at Gyseburn; Gyseburn being today's Guisborough.

The Frank's more subjugatory role spread northward through Westmorland, Cumberland and Northumberland, penetrated the heart of lowland Scotland at Coldstream and along the Tweed adjacent to Kelso, Jedburgh and Galashiels. These were busy times where in pace with settlement, far-ranging communication accelerated. This was especially focused on the Franks from Danby and the Dales as much as those from Aclum, and Levingthorp. These folk continued their migration inland and north to where many of their number enjoined the family of soldiers and yeomen who formed the invasion force who first entered Scotland. Today, many respectable Dumfriesshire families reveal their origins emanating from Yorkshire.

As the spill of war raged up and down the land, travellers and soldiers necessarily billeting along the way, Yorkshire itself felt the full force of the conflict. Adjacent to Skelton Castle and Guisborough, the Franks and de Brus remained feudally interrelated, whereas in Scotland the Franks, easing themselves from their less stringent feudatory bonds, found new alliances, the de Brus kinship so heartfelt; the Franks were released of their obligation to the Brus as overlords.

Despite family to family spelling variances of their surname, there were those whose status caused them to alter their name so as to distinguish between themselves and the proletariat; the more distinguish altering their name so as to make it sound grandiose. Not shy in flourishing their new-found titles, the Franks were not immune in vaunting pretence, where local demographics, especially in Scotland, continued to dictate strong liaisons in the pursuit of largesse and advancement among the upper class. Yet the status of the Scots comparative to their Yorkshire counterparts was so striking it brought a magnet of opportunity for their brethren south of the border.

Cognitive of their Scottish kin and their titles, despite the Yorkshire Frank's apparent workaday appearance, bolstered their self-belief as a class above, and inspired and encouraged by the notion of a better life, many, especially the young, ventured north. Coinciding with an acute lack of male progeny in Scotland, any increase in the northward traffic of kindred Franks was seized upon and encouraged. Scottish records show affiliated Franks increasingly involved in religious activity, taking up positions within the Church and the courts, which, due to them being of staunch Norman pedigree, was welcomed by the ruling hierarchy.

Continuing their territorial spread, despite their shared antecedence and ongoing connection with Normandy and Scotland, sufficient of the family remained firmly rooted, content to work the same land as their recent forebears, with a mien fully cognitive of carrying a bloodline back to Robertus Francaise and their French royal heritage.

It bears repeating, the Frank's Normandy connection, Mr Dolbet, in his addition to the *Index Armorial* published in 1892, fixes the date of a vital charter of Rannulfus Francus of between 1147 and 1153. The charter observes the Francus family as having sons as well as a daughter of marriageable age, and it's his daughter to whom Rannulfus gives the land of the Abbey-Saint-Sauveur-le-Viscompte. In the charter, Ricardus Francus appears as a witness on behalf of the monks, and the reference to viscompte shows Rannulfus holding the rank of viscount. While having sons to consider, due to such an important dowry being bestowed upon a daughter, Mr Dolbet's investigation assumes Viscount Francus having possessions far in excess of those his abbey fee were overlords, thus consistent with royal antecedence.

In showing that Rannulfus held his possessions directly from King Stephen of England, Dolbet seems to infer that the Frank family's primary status remained in the Cotentin of Normandy, their post-invasion sons sent to Britain holding the lesser rank of knight. Referred to as kin, the Franks in Britain are largely found subservient to an overlord, only occasionally rising to and being referred to as counts or viscounts, most apparent in Scotland. Nonetheless, an esteemed family name, prevalent in Normandy, held great quarter, reflecting personal acclaim and respect for French royal antecedence in Britain.

Chateau d'Adam, castle of the Brus's of Great Britain and Normandy, was located in Brix, being built in the mid twelfth century by Adam de Brix. Adam de Brix founded the church of St Pierre de la Lutumiere, St Jean, at the time of King Henry of England. Also, Adam, son of Robert de Brus, is indicated in the 1119 charter foundations of the Priory of Gyseburne, today's Guisborough, North Yorkshire.

St Martin le Greard, belonging to the Barony of Brix, in 1144, was given by Adam de Brueys aka Bruse, first Baron of Brix to the abbots of the Abbey of St Sauveur-le-Vicompte in the Cotentin. And, the same year, Adam gave the church of Conville to this same abbey, Pierre de Brueys, in 1155, confirming the donation.

Note: for a fuller appreciation of names, donations and charter witnesses of the period above, please refer to items found in the main body of work.

From the authority Abbe Delamare, an earlier period of Normandy shows several people identified with the Cotentin, among them, Ralph, Roger and Richard de Brix, who, as late as 1132, succeeded as Bishops in succession to the famous Geoffrey de Montbray, bishop and builder of the Cathedral of Coutances of the Cotentin.

Drawn from the National Library of Scotland, *Histories of Scottish families Index Armorial (21),* page 17. Delamare continues:

> 'Roger de Brix, who held the see of Coutances for thirteen years, was a widower. William, his son, one brother and three nephews, attachers of Henry, King of England, perished in 1120 off Barfleur, of the Cotentin, the incident become known as 'the shipwreck of Nef Blanche'. Roger Brix, who assisted at the council of Roen in 1118 and at Reims 1119, died in 1126. His successor in the Bishoprick was Richard de Brix.'

> 'King Henry the first confided to Fitz Stephen, Master of the White Ship, that his son Prince William, his natural son Richard and daughter, the Countess of Perche and all their suite, and all on board were lost, save one, a butcher who alone remained to tell the tale.'

INDEX ARMORIAL, CONCLUSIONS ON NAMES.

From the context above, and records of Normandy and Great Britain, conclusions can be made that the earlier Christian names borne by members of the family of Bruce, were Robert, William, Ralph, Roger, Richard, Adam and Pierre. And of these names, Robert, Roger, Richard and Pierre are found in earlier accounts of Normandy before they appear in Great Britain with particular mention of Robert.

The above indicates a desire to perpetuate in the latter country the earlier names particularly associated with prominent families such as the Bruce of Normandy. We have to remember the propensity to use first names was commonly passed down within a family, often in association with a place, as would John of Fox Wood later evolve as John Fox or John Wood as a surname. Despite being a time of change, the concept of surnames per se to Britain was still new; the habitual practice of first name succession remaining indelibly stamped both sides of the Channel.

So we see among these Christian names, Robert, William and Roger were the earliest recorded familial names of those also bearing the surname Franceis, the Franks having proven feudatory relations with the de Bruce's of Great Britain. And in Scotland we find, about the year 1200, Adam Franceis and later most all the Lairds of Thornydykes had Robert as their Christian name. The propensity to perpetuate the original familial and ongoing feudal relations of the Franceis with the Bruce's through given Christian names, is indicative of unbreakable family ties. That their filiation continued generationally confirms the de Brus and Frank's blood relationship in the sense of *fiducia*, being complete in mutual reliance and trust found among the Franks adjacent to Skelton Castle, North Yorks.

Earliest records of the various Franks and Franceis in the Cotentin actually pre-date the few reminiscences of the Bruces and the rolls of the twelfth century of this district. These show only two of the name William and Roger Franceis, the same baptismal names as found in the Annandale after King John of England lost the Duchy of Normandy, and then as feudatories of Robert de Brus as appears in the Scottish records of 1218. There it states that Roger, son of William Franciscus, quitclaims to Sir Robert de Brus, Lord of Annandale, land which the grantee held of him in the territory of Moffat, which William Franciscus, the grantee's father, formally held of Sir Robert de Brus.

The Chateau of Brix was confiscated early in the thirteenth century. This was due to most of the lords who owned the castles of Normandy being far better off in Great Britain, so choosing to retain their more lucrative possessions in England and their most recent acquisitions in Scotland. And under the Bruces, it is in Scotland the Franceis apparently elected to retain their possessions. Those Yorkshire cousins, free of the yoke of the de Brus, having a decision whether to venture inland or to York and its surrounds, there as yeomen to continue farming and hopefully prosper.

Around 1251, William Fraunceis donated one ox-gang of land at Harpham, south of Pickering towards Bridlington, to the Abbey of St Mary's, Whitby. And in a charter of liberation of Thomas de Hastynges in 1256, William de Franceys was witness to the donation of the Mill of Crossby, as well as being witness to a donation to St Mary's. Additionally, located in North Yorkshire, we find Umfridus le Franceis in 1189–1190, Radulfus le Franceis in 1205, and in 1275–1276, Walterus Franceys and Alanus le Franceys.

Around the period of the thirteenth century, whether one was of Norman or Saxon origin, the English language became the mother tongue or lingua franca, as it's more commonly known. This was when the Anglicising of the more modern surname of French, taken from derivatives of Frank, began to take place.

The Earl of Dunbar and March, whose armorial bearings were:

'An argent lion rampant, surrounded by argent roses on a field gules.'

The earl being the earliest recorded overlord of the Frenches, in a charter of Earl George, Robert French of Thornydykes is designated by the earl as:

'Clarissimus consanguineus noster, birthright relation ours.'

In accordance with ancient usage, the Frenches aka Franks, had assumed the arms of an heiress, which was in existence well before the advent of marshalling many coats on one shield, this was:

'Three boars heads in tincture and metal.'

The armorial bearings of their neighbours, the later Gordon arms, were differenced by the addition of a chevron, possibly implying an early marriage with that family. Yet despite an incomplete jigsaw, the information does provide a fair estimation of the overall picture, the Frank's lineage being indicative of them emanating from an older and most ancient and higher ranking order, the lineage showing as **prosapia regius** or ***Francisca regius nos***, meaning family royal or Franks royal us, from whose lineage many eminent names, including the Brus, borrowed details for their own arms.

INDEX ARMORIAL, LINEAGE ADDITIONS.

The following are selected extracts repeated in support of:

> The original Normandy Robertus de Bayeux cum Franceis relationship with the de Brus continuing through North Yorkshire to Scotland.

> Frank continuum for armorial recognition linking the North Yorkshire Franks with the variously spelt Scottish Franks or Frauncys.

Early records of the Bayeux Franks in Normandy pre-date the few reminiscences of the Brus, them being shown as long-established patrons to the monarchy and the first Duchy City of Falaise established in 911.

Mapping of Normandy demonstrates the close proximity of the Bruise and Frank lands.

Following their arrival in England, Robertus Francaise is shown in the published records of York in 1097 and 1101, and as witness to the de Brus who founded Guisborough Priory near Skelton Castle, Cleveland, North Yorkshire in 1119.

Grant of Robert de Brus, his wife Agnes and son Adam in 1120, for the health of King Henry I to the monks of Whitby and Midlesburc, confirmed by Pope Eugenius III, included the church of St Hilda, and was witnessed by *et tres de suis militibus knights*, Robertus Francais being one of the three knights named, Robert's two brothers, one insinuating a local name and the other an historic Norman location used as their own, the later name later used as a place.

Normandy charters of 1147–1153 show Ranalphus and Ricardus Francus feudally related to Robert de Brus in the Cotentin. Supportive of both families' ongoing interrelations betwixt family in the Cotentin and Yorkshire I have previously documented the payment of dues by William Franceis in the Cotentin Normandy in 1180, and by his son Roger in 1195, both of which were recorded around the same time in Yorkshire and the further reaches of Scotland, thus proving the strength of each family union that held them together.

In the Guisborough district, William Franceis, also known as Franc or Francus, was witness to a charter of 1182, which had the confirmation of King Henry II. Walter Ingerram, himself a Frank, made the grant to the church of St Mary of Gyseburne or Guisborough. In it he refers to his overlord Adam de Brus II. The following underlines the close kinship of William Frank to Robert and Adam de Brus. The fact of them appearing familiarly related further underlines that relationship.

In 1182 Walterus Ingerram gives to the church of St Mary, and the church of Erneclive or Arncliffe, two bovates of land and a mansion, the church of Haslintune half an acre of land and a mansion together with the chapel of Haslintune. The donation was made for himself, his wife and sons and for his lord Adam de Brus II, also for the souls of his mother and father and uncle. Significantly, the 1182 donation was also made for the souls of Robertus de Brus and his son Adam and Willelmus Francus aka Franceis.

A charter of Willelmus Forestarius and his wife Gundreda, dated 1230–1250, grant alms for the Church of St Mary Gyseburne and land etc., all jointly testified by Rogero Canonico de Rypum, and Petro Fraunces.

Referring to electricscotland.com/history, *Calendar Records Relating to Scotland 1108–1272* (page 124, item 705), this section observes the Franks or Franceis having feudal relations with the de Brus, appearing in the Annandale. They show William as the father of Roger Franceis, and thereafter the name of William Franceis and Roger perpetuate in the Scottish archives.

In the inquisition of 1261–1262, Willelmus Frauncheys was shown to hold one bovate and one toft in Aslakeby Pickering. This seems to square with William Frank while living in Scotland being shown to have visited Pickering.

In 1262–1280, also around 1300, Roger Franceis aka Franceys, son of Roger, reappears in the records of Levingthorp (shown in the Domesday Book) as belonging to the manor of Aclum, a manor previously belonging to the first Robert de Brus, and given to him by William the Conqueror. The priors of Guisborough became overlords of Levingthorp and Roger Franceis as a freeholder of that place and of Aclum made suit to the court of Ralph the prior at nearby Thornaby.

Here Middlesbrough is mentioned as a settlement distinct from Acklam, Linthorpe and Thornaby, whereas Middlesbrough later enlarged to encompass the former districts of Aclum and Levingthorp with Thornaby part of a larger collective district, namely Teesside. Roger Frauncheis appears in a notice of *assise* in 1275–1276 concerning a novel *disseisin* arranged by Osanna de Leuingethorp against said Roger touching a tenement in Leuingthorp (Linthorpe), and again regarding a tenement in Mildeburg (Middlesbrough).

So while Roger was active in Scotland, he was still embroiled with affairs in Cleveland. The Rent Roll of 1300 relating to Levingthorp shows two entries of Roger le Frauncheys paying for bovates of land. Around the same time on the 14th September 1299, Radulphus Frauncheys made fealty to the Lord Prior of Guisborough for a toft and a croft at the Ville of Levingthorp, also for Lythum, four miles north of Guisborough.

Nearly 250 years followed the arrival of Robertus Frauncheys (domini Roberti Frauncheys militis), Ricardus (b. 1257) and Robert de Brus, the two brothers', Robertus and Ricarus (sons of Gilbertus b. 1225), staus as knights was reaffirmed 20th January 1315 whereby:

> Ricardus Frunce (aka Richard de Vernon) is delivered to Eleanor, wife of the late Henry de Percy, tenant-in-chief, knights fees assigned to her regarding Irton, which he holds.

Irton Manor lies adjacent the North York Moors along from Pickering towards the coast at Scarborough. For the Franks, the position, strategically situated betwixt Whitby and York, was significant. The whole of the area from Middlesbrough on the Tees eastward to Skelton Castle and Guisborough, to Danby and Glaisdale on the Esk, the coast at Whitby, down to Scarborough, Irton and back across to Pickering and the Dales, and north again towards the Tees, encompass the Yorkshire seat of the de Brus, where the scattering of Franks across the region had influence, many becoming farmers and eventual land owners in their own right.

REFERRING TO *'SWEET CIVILITY AND BARBAROUS RUDENESS': A VIEW FROM THE FRONTIER. ABBOT AILRED OF RIEVAULX AND THE SCOTS* HTTP:ORCA.CF.AC.UK/3880/ A D WELD FRENCH, INDEX ARMORIAL: FRENCHES IN SCOTLAND:

In 1113–1114, David King of Scotland sought to gain control of Cumberland and Northumberland, and in doing so, founded English-speaking monasteries at Kelso, Dryburgh, Melrose and Holyrood. Among his tenants-in-chief were a clutch of Anglo-Normans derived from the region of Normandy and Brittany. Most important of all his cohorts were the de Brus, from which military fiefs were created and which the de Brus were credited, although, in relation to feudality and militarism, the idea that the de Bruce were the original architects of this form of rule was not true. Prior to discussing 'A view from the frontier', I offer some thoughts of my own supported by factual information and conclusions drawn from detailed study.

Chief among the de Brus contingent was variously spelt Sir Fraunceis or Francus, knight-militaire. It was from the Franks the feudal system originated, and it is from the system of feudalism the concept of fiefs was originally conceived. In conjunction with the first Robert de Brus, it is my contention the concept most likely evolved in liaison with Robertus Fraunceys and his retinue following the invasion proper. Drawing on information passed to him by Robertus Fraunceys, or most certainly the Frank retinue born of their first-hand knowledge of *feudum* in France, and brought into practice by his own military mind, de Brus transposed the concept of feudalism into the creation of military fiefs.

While I remain adamant on this point, the recognition of the Franks in their quietude shouldn't be understated. While the de Brus gained the limelight and subsequent affirmation, in the rush to heap acknowledgement, the Franks have often been overlooked, and it's here I hope to put the record straight.

Historically, the Frank dynasty reined in France long before the Brus were born, the name de Brus having been an invention taken from the land they lived. And in the Cotentin alone, the Franks pre-date the few reminiscences of de Brus by a huge margin, those Franks who resided and their estates being an offshoot of the ruling class of the time, their origins as likely de Bayeux emanating from Richard I Duke of Normandy.

The Extraordinary Franks

Drawn from history, in terms of warfare and battle knowledge, the Franks were masters. From their Merovingian dynasty, during the fifth to eighth century, the *Francisca,* a weapon conceived by the Franks, was born and used with great effect. This was the battleaxe, a heavy missile cum broad-bladed slicing weapon, initially crafted with a short axe-like handle; it was later adjusted to a much longer shaft. There was nothing that could withstand the weight and force of such a blade slicing through the air. No, the Franks knew all about war and all about strategy, it was in their veins: weapons of war had been named after them.

Drawing inspiration from 'A view from the frontier' and 'Abbot Ailred of Rievaulx and the Scots,' and having already talked about David I of Scotland, I take a look at his great push south:

From his position in Scotland, his eyes already firmly fixed south, incursions had already taken place. David's invasion of Northern England aimed at incorporating the northern counties in a Scoto-Northumbrian realm, hopefully reaching as far south as the Humber. In terms of history, following the events of 1066, the Conqueror's incursion north from the Humber was now turned on its head, the earlier invasion north, perversely culminating in a Scots invasion south.

The Scots possession lasted from 1138–1157. For two decades the dominant political power in Yorkshire was the King of the Scots. Themselves previous conquerors, the Cleveland Franks, had historic allegiances with many of the Scots invaders, also from a militaristic standpoint the significance for the Franks becomes apparent. For the Scots it was important to get onside with those they most easily formed a natural alliance. Coming from Normandy, with great knowledge of war, those Scottish and Yorkshire Franks the Scots already had firm relations with, together with their Brus affiliation, the Franks were natural brothers-in-arms.

The Franks, now fully immersed in the ways of the Scots, their admission is shown in the light-hearted account of Abbot Guibert of Nogent's *Gesta Dei per Francus, The Deeds of God through the Franks*. It was written in the first decade of the twelfth century, where the Franks describe the apparel of the Scots. It brings a smile to the lips and was the first recorded appearance of the sporran. In the following record, it describes the apparent nudity of the common Scot and the lack of cover beneath the skirt.

> 'Quis igitur non rideat, potius quamtimeat, quod adversus tales vilis Scottus seminudis natibus pugnaturus occurrit.'

Translated: 'Anyone therefore, not to laugh at, rather take stock or hold back, because facing his cheap Scots rod, these semi-nude people occur pugnacious (meaning quarrelsome), and are disposed to fight.' For rod read penis or genitalia, personally, I for one wouldn't argue with the above assessment.

I will come to the matter of alms-armorial as they relate to the Franks, but prior to this try to settle the matter of territory and the common ground of Cleveland as it relates to the Scottish Borders, seats occupied by the Franks and their de Brus cousins. For this it is necessary to underline the interpenetration permeated by people of the same gens living north and south of Northumberland, the strange phenomena of the Frank's settlement in each territory formed by cross-border incursion resulting in Scottish and Yorkshire occupation of the other's territory by force of war and natural migration.

Whereas today the existence of North Yorkshire might appear as separate and distinct from the Scottish Borders, in the mid 1100s, that wasn't the situation and the spread of occupancy and settlement, quite opposite from being confined to a limited area, the history of the time shows extensive and continuous travel as far afield as the Holy Lands and for the Franks and de Brus, certainly to Normandy and beyond.

Following 1066, immediate localised settlement quickly spread, accelerated by particular turns in history and events in which people were mutually embroiled. The whole history of the Franks mitigates against the idea of their leaders settling to the quiet life and not wanting to support their liege lords, information placing key players together at crucial and critical times, the Franks of Yorkshire hand in glove with the de Brus in Scotland, cut of the same cloth, both parties feudally related, loyal to their kin either side of an imaginary divide.

Returning to 'A view from the frontier' that by way of introduction I repeat a few previous entries:

In 1107, the second Robert de Brus, together with other Normans, attempted to oblige King Alexander to yield part of the Scottish Kingdom to his brother David. The appeal was in vain causing de Brus and his young son Adam to renounce their allegiance to David throwing the weight of their feudal power against the Scots. By way of feudal power, this would include the de Brus, knights-militaire, hence the involvement of Sir Robert and William Fraunceys.

At a council of all England in 1109, de Brus attests a charter of Henry I confirming to the church of Durham possessions that certain men of Northumberland had claimed.

From 1109 on, de Brus possessed the land of Orm, Turbern, Ulchil and Ravenchil, close to York, together with thegns in Borgescire warpentake, and as Chief Lord, consents to gifts made to the monks of Marmoutier by one of his tenants. Later, he attests King Henry's confirmation of said gift.

1115–1118, de Brus was in possession of manors in Horncastle and Alford, when it is presumed that King Henry had given Robert his Yorkshire fee soon after the Battle of Tinchebrai 28th September 1106.

A grant of Robert de Brus, his wife Agnes and his son Adam, is shown dated 1120, for the health of King Henry I, and to the monks of Whitby and of Midlesburc. This important grant, confirmed by Pope Eugenius III, corroborates the gift made by Robert of lands and his interests south of Middlesbrough and the church of St Hilda.

Significantly, records of the time find the Franks holding the fief of de Brus consisting of Aclum, Leuingethorp and Mildeburg. Also in 1120, Robertus Francais is recorded attesting a confirmation of Alan de Percy to the monks of Whitby.

The above grant was testified by Robertus de Brus *et tre de suis militibus*, knights Rogerus de Rosel, Wydo de Lofthus and Robertus Francais, all three knights being Franks. Apart from demonstrating the largesse of the de Brus:

> The gift granted at his time of life is consistent with the practice of ensuring a place with God.
>
> It also demonstrates the difference in character between various warlords and the de Brus's dominance in the creating a lasting legacy that lives on today.

The document is also important in reaffirming the whereabouts and status of the now elderly Robert Francais as a military man and knight bound by a common bond and affiliation with de Brus.

Following the invasion of Scotland, William Francais and Robertus de Brus are recorded together in Scotland. This time it was in celebration of King David of Scotland's gift of the Annandale to de Brus in 1124.

Adapted from 'A view from the frontier', the following seals the argument for the immediate and close relationship of the two Roberts and William. Even by today's standards, Robertus Francais was elderly, Yorkshire foot soldiers had already accomplished their advance on Scotland, Robert's son William having being found spurring forward alongside de Brus:

> What is not certain is if Robertus Francais was well enough and able to enjoin with his brother knights, and if he accompanied his son William. But we have to look to David the first of Scotland's counter-invasion of Northern England a dozen or so years later.

> King David's invasion aimed at incorporating the northern counties in a Scoto-Northumbrian realm, perhaps reaching as far as the Humber. Scots possession lasted from 1138 until 1157, for two decades the dominant political power in Yorkshire was the King of the Scots …

Drawing from William Aird's 'Sweet Civility and Barbarous Rudeness', adding observations of my own:

The Battle of the Standard was in 1138 near Northallerton. For the purpose of perspective, the territory from the Tweed in the north to a line from Northallerton, approximating west and east towards the North Sea coast, was a geographic and political entity, which I will explain.

David's ruthless push south is said to have caused areas such as Hexham and Durham to suffer huge depredations at the hands of his armies. This observation of the Scots army is in stark contrast to observations concerning the general populace. The relationship of the Lowland Scots to the Northern English counties is said to have been more temperate, as distinct from the gens montana of the wild, proud and barbarous Highlander.

Relating to borders and the meaning of Gens as people sharing the same nomen, common descent or ancestry; Montana meaning mountainous terrain. The ethnic or cultural frontier expected as between southern Scotland and Northern England was further north, the inhabitants' demeanour each side of the imaginary Scottish border being quite distinct. The lowland Scots were seen as tame and home-loving (Gens Maritma, a derivative of coastal), whereas the more northern tribes, including the Western Isles, (Gens Montana) were seen as less civilised, uncouth and warlike.

As well as a cultural frontier, the River Tweed was also a political border. In the early medieval period, the land between the Tweed and the River Tees at Cleveland, seats of the de Brus and Frank, formed the Kingdom of Bernicia. This huge territory itself lay in the greater territory of the then north-of-Humber-land, encompassing a large part of Yorkshire through the Borders up to the Tweed.

Appreciating the non-existence of current-day boundaries is vital in visualising the ergonomics of people living in juxtaposition to the mass of land lying south, yet being attracted to and drawn north, where many of their kin had already migrated. Such a situation existed living just south of the Tees along the lower edge of Bernicia and the Cleveland population having a temperament similar to that of the Lowland Scots.

What must be appreciated is the situation of the time where undoubtedly the land of Bernicia was seen by all its people, both north and south of Bernicia, within the framework and mindset of an established and historic kingdom, one and the same

The Extraordinary Franks

and despite continuous warring its mindful presence provided a natural two-way pathway for movement and settlement graduating northward.

The attraction north for the Norman Franks became apparent following King David's earlier political and cultural education in England. That knowledge made him aware of the advantages to be gained from subscribing to the values of the Norman elite and their entourage of knights. In 1124, as King of the Scots, he modelled his kingship on practices learned at Henry's court, making use of Norman barons in securing Scottish Cumbria.

For lesser nobles such as Robertus or William Franceis, in order to cultivate and secure necessary alliances, David immediately rewarded those he considered most important. Robert de Brus was awarded the most important enfeoffment of all, the Annandale in 1124, consisting of some 200,000 acres. I have been unable to ascertain any initial reward being given to Sir William Franceis, and assume such rewards as were given were left to the largesse of his immediate liege lord de Brus.

In 1139, the composition of David's army reflected his temporary policy of encouraging Franco-French or Norman settlement in southern Scotland. He first focused on those nearest, residing around the southern boundaries of Bernicia, and those with possible relative associations further north. Needful of strengthening his army, top of David's bounty were a core of Anglo-Norman knights.

This policy was precariously balanced on a knife's edge and fraught with danger. Robert de Brus had just about dissuaded the headstrong, malicious and dangerous David from continued aggression against Yorkshire, the source of de Brus's loyal supporters. Not only was the area de Brus's own seat, his family resided there together with loyal followers and related Franks. Loyalty and friendship were everything to the de Brus family, confirming the bond of brothers-in-arms of their military contingent, their families and especially his knights. To add to this, his own possessions in Yorkshire were extensive, not something to be squandered or put on the line for some madman. Balanced against this, the Annandale's 200,000-acre Scottish estate was a prize not to be sneezed at.

De Brus was in a perpetual dilemma being associated with bonds inherent in the barony of Annandale and that of loyalty to his Yorkshire Norman settlers, the Franks and his own lands across Cleveland and beyond. Accused of treason, Robert de Brus decided to withdraw from David's army.

One purpose of this section was a focus on the Frank's armorial identification, adding to previous known information and events, thereby confirming one's lineage. The history of the time and peculiarities of the region of Bernicia have provided insight whereby the Cleveland Franks, by their ties to the de Brus, together with previously data, have put beyond doubt the northward migration of the Franks, their occupancy and settlement in Scotland and subsequent success. What is compelling is:

The call by King David for Norman military knights; the peculiarity of the same Christian names of the Franks and de Brus; the historic and persistent feudal ties of the Franks and de Brus in Britain and the Cotentin.

With the evidence of:

William, Robertus Franceis's son, being close to the de Brus in Scotland following the Annandale; the parties shown repeatedly together either in Scotland or Cleveland; old Robertus Franceis being with Robert de Brus immediately prior to the Annandale.

Together these show convincing evidence for the Cleveland Franks as kin to their Scottish counterparts, reaffirming an armorial connection between the Cleveland and Scots Franks and their relationship to the de Brus.

Some of the Franks were connected to the Church, and around 1139, the influx of Norman influence in Scotland appreciably grew. Gradually and surely, through the arrival and association with reforming monks and their Franco-French baronial allies, Galloway experienced socio-economic and cultural change.

The Franks are recorded repeatedly as being at the forefront of legal and spiritual legislature as the spread of reform and civilisation extended further north and east across Dumfries to the coast along the Tweed, north to Edinburgh and south across the whole of Bernicia to the River Tees. It has been nicely put that democracy moved off the battlefield and into the bedroom as a means of forming alliances and retaining power.

There is little doubt the obeisance and civilisation of an otherwise barbarous 'gens montana', was largely born of wisdom drawn from history-bound sources such as the Franks; a people of intellect, tired of conflict, now imbued with a sense of moral conduct and civic duty. A repeatedly shown name, snippets from records show the Franks widely engaged both in the Church and the judiciary.

It's striking how the experience of civilisation and the lordship of Galloway, Dumfries and for its part, Frankysland, resembled in microcosm that of the Scots Kingdom at large. As if awakening from a darker age, the Lords of Galloway, their counterparts and those beyond became the instrument as well as the recipients of their own civilising process. As the spread took hold, through the Franks and their kin, the lineage that was French in origin led to a political nation, a nation able to look at itself, take hold and successfully resist the imperialist ambitions of their English neighbours.

It is right that the true place of the Cleveland Franks and their Scottish counterparts should be recognised and their armorial identification affirmed. And it's to that end I commend my findings.

FRANK ARMORIAL BEARINGS 1.

For this initial investigation, I have drawn from several sources e.g. The Mitchell Rolls Heraldic Society of Scotland, Slains Armorial, Seton Armorial, Nisbet's Genealogical Collection and MS at the Advocates Library. Chief among the information centres on Lord William le Franceys, aka Franceis or Franciscus, of Thornydykes, also known as William Franke de Pitcohyr.

The private work *Franks in Scotland*, printed on the 19th February 1893 by A D Weld French was presented to the University of California in 1894. In it, he confirms that Willielmus Frank had sasine of Frankysland Peebles, and as their laird had the authority to preside over its people, having jurisdiction and governance over the manor its lands, tenants, property and so on.

Overlord of the Franks or Frenches in Scotland, the Earl of Dunbar and March, his charter of 1275 shows that Robert French or Franke of Thornydykes was designated 'Clarissimus consanguineous noster', confirming a birthright of immediate kinship to that of the Earl of Dunbar.

The Franks and early Frauncey coats of arms

Before the advent of armorial bearings and in accordance with antiquity and ancient usage, prior to the established practice of the marshalling of coats of arms to one shield, there was already in existence a Frauncey's coat of arms born of an heiress, possibly of French or Norman origin. This ancient account is specific as to an heiress belonging the mid tenth century, where fixing a likely candidate seems to have eluded historians. That apparently the case, what I'd like to propose is the following scenario:

Born around 1047–1049, Sir Robert de Bayeux aka Francais, the young Robertus Francais cum Frauncey's who first started this whole investigation, his father also Robert, by degrees through Roger de Bayeux led to an illegitimate liaison with Espriota, her firstborn being Richard the Fearless, born 28th August 933, her child becoming the first Duke of Normandy. Sprota's liaison was with Duke Guillaume de Fresquiennes, son of the Viking Rollo, and due her being shunned by society, any recognition given Sprota whether arms or any other devise would have attracted repudiation.

Guillaume's father Rollo was three times great-grandfather to another Guillaume, known by reputation as William the Conqueror. Also born out of wedlock, this fearful man was termed William the Bastard. William the Bastard and young Robertus Frounceys living in close proximity, our young protagonist having title and family ties with the older William, the de Brus were also shown to be compatriots of that Frank domain. The young Robertus later admitted as one of three knights to the older battle-hardened Robert de Brus; the kinship of all appears assured.

It's here we have to understand Guillaume. His father being Viking and Guillaume known to be consumed by not being wholly Frank, his compatriots taking great pleasure in slighting him and taking the micky, what was he to do? Going back a generation he couldn't undo his birthright, but in salving his wounded pride he could ensure his progeny the status he so much craved. With no other apparent solution, by deft means Guillaume's rank provided the opportunity to surreptitiously purloin his Breton French lover's use of the fleur-de-lys emblem, whereby he could falsely ascribe his firstborn the affirmation and status bestowed the Franks.

The above seems to answer the question of the mysterious heiress, and as the account is specific as to a Frounceys coat of arms, it most certainly would have included the fleur-de-lys. Due to Guillaume's pregnant lover being seen as unworthy, despite his undying great love of her and although he was married to another, Guillaume or William Longsword as he became known, would be obliged to keep under wraps the gift of arms to Sprota, when after a suitable lapse Duke William surreptitiously used his lover's fleur-de-lys under the guise of designing an appropriate device for his son.

I would remind, Espriota, or Sprota as she became known, was a Breton captive and although I first thought her to be French in the way we might see things today, and not a Frank, further research finds the spelling of her name consistent as a Frank. But as things were at the time that would hardly matter one way or the other, where pragmatism was often required and sleights of hand for status regularly practised, and with great skill.

Had the science of blazonry then existed, her son's family arms (see 'Historia de Fresquienne') would have consisted of the golden leopards of Normandy quartering vermandois, check or and asure a chief of the second, three fleur-de-lys of the first and no pursuivant, no pursuivant being consistent with Espriota at long last being accepted as a follower and her firstborn rated a rank below, this due to both mother and son's illegitimate status, such arms as raised being considered absentia inventio.

Once the dust had settled and Sprota's son's affiliation as a Frank settled, the need for subterfuge would have gone, allowing the three fleur-de-lys of the Franks to be incorporated into such blazon as then existed. It must be remembered such depictions were 200–300 years before coats of arms were ascribed to a shield, marshalling commencing around the mid 1100s. Although I have described the bearings as arms, in reality such depictions would have consisted of devices such as the scarlet oriflamme flown above the Abbey of St Denis in northern France, thence becoming the national banner of France, and embroidered alternatives akin to the Roman eagle, and in the case of Sprota, incorporating the royal fleur-de-lys into the Duke of Normandy's banner settled for all time the Fresquiennes families status as Franks.

Not forgetting William Longsword's wife as the heiress indicated, William's crying need for his firstborn to be recognised as a Frank, I form the opinion the early indication of arms most certainly belonged Guillaume's great love Espriota. We have to remember Rollo aka Hrollaugr's conversion to Christianity around 911, whereupon he took the name Robert on his marriage to King Charles's legitimate daughter Gisla, aged five. The diplomatic betrothal viewed as undoubted, from subsequent trials, the assimilation of 'maternal' Frankish-Catholic culture set the ground for the term Norman given to Sprota's child as the first Duke of that province.

Despite her humble birth, due to her lover's status and the Duke Guillaume de Fresquiennes being a son of Rollo, the existence of Sprota could not be ignored forever, especially given the then propensity for births out of wedlock. Whence however reluctant, emanating from the birth of a male heir, ensured Sprota's acceptance among the proletariat and thus the necessity to proclaim her birthright belonging that of a Frank. Guillaume's desire to be seen as a fully fledged Frank saw no alternative but to use Sprota as a subterfuge, thus solving the mystery concerning Frankish arms held of a mysterious heiress.

In terms of Bayeux, Rollo had earlier taken that place by force, the Frankish name of Robert ascribed through his conversion to Christianity. Born of a ruthless antecedence we see Robertus Bayeux de Francais cum Frauceys an emissary of what one might rightly view as a reformed dynasty born out of the love of the son of a Viking king and a delightful Breton captive, the arms borrowed of a Frankish dynasty assuaging the way to glory. Made up it would make a good story, the fact of it being true, all the more amazing.

The whole of this work has been painstakingly researched, where following William's invasion we see a related Norman, a young man heading north upon an unsteady sea, his landing in Britain leading to a succession of descendants spanning centuries, to furrowed fields and a sandy haired group of farming families settled across the Yorkshire Dales and north again to Scotland, the family name of Frank so distinctive one might visualise the youthful Robert burdened with armour carrying the fleur-de-lys from Normandy first brought to York and thence to Scotland, flying high upon their realm.

In questioning Rollo descendants as Franks, commencing with Charles III, subsequent alliances and feminine marital ties vow safe the Frank bloodline, thus young

Robertus was assuredly a Frank both in name and descent. Namesake of Hrollaugr the Viking, Robert Frank and William the Conqueror, three times great-grandson of Rollo, share a common bloodline relating to Henry II of England and the present-day monarchy.

Returning to the earlier analysis of the Earls of Dunbar and the Franks or French's of Thornydykes

These ancient arms are shown to be consistent with:

> 'Three boars heads in tincture and metal.'

Other armorial bearing of the Franks containing the fleur-de-lys, having its roots in antiquity, precedes the boars' heads. Notwithstanding their later usage and acquisition by Duke Guillaume de Fresquiennes, son of Rollo, the fleur-de-lys were conceived by the Franks prior to their rule over France, acquired from their vision of flowers and their piratical beginnings along the Rhine.

In Scotland the Franks of Frankysland, situated close to Moffat, Dumfries, shared a common arms with the Thornydykes of Berwick, these being:

> 'Azure, a chevron between three boars heads erased or, or being gold, azure, bright blue.'

The crest for Frankysland was:

> 'A fox passant.'

Whereas the Thornydyke crest was:

> 'A wolf passant.'

Variations exist where the boars' heads are erased argent or couped argent, silver or white, the motto for each of the above being:

> 'Nee timeo, nee sperno.'

Sometimes shows as 'nee' followed by 'nec', or 'nec timeo, nec sperno' reads:

> 'I neither fear nor despise.'

The Extraordinary Franks

Having confirmed the Cleveland Franks as one and the same family as their Scottish counterparts, I have drawn a mock-up of how the more ancient Cleveland-Scottish Frank Coat of arms may have appeared. Using another pre-marshalling antique arms, which also shows three boars' heads, a helmet and wreath, but wrongly topped with a horses head, I have substituted the incorrect horses head for the correct wolf passant and chevron 'or' engraved. The chevron 'or', or gold engraved is one of several recorded derivatives shown for the Thornydyke Franks. I should reiterate, the ancient arms I have drawn up provide a basic idea of how they might have looked, they merely indicate what the combination of the boars' heads, chevron and wolf may have appeared shown against a background of Azure together with the silver and gold, see Appendix 1

Due to the Cleveland Franks residing adjacent the Scots Franks and Bernicia and being unable to locate a separate arms, I concluded they must have held joint arms under a common banner. By definition, it seemed their honours would embrace all of their congeneric family, including the homeland territory of their overlords the de Brus and fraternal Cleveland Frank. Not so.

Firstly, Thomas Tonge, Norray King of Arms, visitation of the monastery of Durham in 1530, on behalf of the King, was for the award of arms to Master William Frankelyng, Archdeacon of Durham. These were:

> 'Arms agent, between two saltires engrailed, a pale gules charged with a dolphin hauriant of the field; on a chief azure a lion rampant argent between two birds or, collared azure.'

Norray King of Arms confirmed:

> 'These arms of Master Frankelyng were given to the said Mr Franklin for recovering the castle of Norham oute of the Scotts liandes by his prowers and pollice.'

Additions for an existing arms already held by Henry Franke of Ness, also in 1530, these belonging to one's own family pedigree:

> 'Henry Franke gentillman, vert, a saltue engrailed or, in posteritas.'

Also de Ness, Hugh Franckland:

> 'For and behalf of the King, given by William Flower, Norray, on his heraldic visitation of the Northern Counties, 1566.'

I repeat the following:

'Hugh Francklyn, alias Franckland, of Nessistge in the Countye of York, Gentillman, is dessended of a house of long-time bearing arms and he being uncertayn under what mannor and forme his ancestors beare there crest, he hath required of me to assigne these his old auncient arms a creast, I have demised given and granted upon his helme, on a tors gold and azure, a demy dolfine argent; mantled guls, dubled gold- to have and to hold said creast to the said Hugh Franckland, gentillman and his posteritie.'

'The arms as drawn are a dolphin embowed; on a chief three saltires.'

The Frankland motto of 1562 in relation to Blubberhouses:

'Libera terra; Liberque animus.'

Translated as 'Frank lands, Frank mind', or 'Free land; free soul', the motto refers to the Franklands of Blubberhouses and Thirkleby having connections with Ness.

Historically allied in nature and origin, it would be impossible for the Scots Franks not to include and honour their feudal and symbolic forebears and their liege lords the de Brus, as, by so doing, they would confirm both their heritage and the affirmation of kinship. Affirmation was necessary, as the business of affiliation and the juggling for recognition, status and position was a necessary skill, and with good reason, not something to trifle with or cause offence

DE BRUS MOTTO 'FUIMUS' WE HAVE BEEN.

A form of affirmation could also be shown in the adoption or incorporation of a particular name, shown in my great-grandfather's name, Robert Hart-Frank. Robert's father, already wealthy, acquired Hart Hall, Glaisdale together with all its lands and estate through marriage to Mary Hart, daughter of Nicholas Hart, in 1763.

Middlesbrough records show the de Brus influencing the medieval development of both Hart-le-Pool and Guisborough. Hartlepool lay immediately north of the River Tees, but the Hart estates spread both north of Hartlepool and south of the Tees along the River Esk where Hart Hall was built slap-bang in the middle of several holdings of the Franks. It was my great-grandfather Robert Hart-Frank who, in moving from Glaisdale, obtained new holdings along the River Tees to the west of Middlesbrough where they continued to farm, and from where his son, Thomas Henry Frank, in leaving Ingleby Barwick completed an apprenticeship in Middlesbrough prior to setting up his building business developing land north of

Middlesbrough and its surrounds. I have Tom's original indenture papers signed by Robert Hart-Frank.

I find it remarkable that the historic relationship between two family names, the Franks and the de Brus, that started prior to 1066 in Normandy, could continue for hundreds of years and leave such a mark upon northern towns and modern development, while their names appear to have faded from memory. The de Brus motto *Fuimus* seems somewhat apt. Its meaning 'we have been' seeming to reflect the rise to glory and fall from grace of both families.

Affirming their royal status, the North Yorkshire de Brus coat of arms was:

> 'A blue lion standing on top of a crown, with a paw resting on a gold anchor.'

Its arms quite a departure from the arms taken by King Robert de Brus.

The motto *Fuimus* could be interpreted as an epitaph for the de Brus having left their mark. By accepting this, I suspect the de Brus knew their time was drawing to a close, I see no real distinction between the glass half-full, glass half-empty synopsis, other than the de Brus recognising in themselves their own demise. In much the same way, the pragmatism of the Franks might endorse 'we have been' as sufficient testament for having lived their lives worthy of existence.

FRANK AMORIAL BEARINGS 2.

Records show a list of disparate arms depicting boars' heads. And then there are stories such as the Gordon knight, who, saving the life of a Scottish king from a wild boar, explains the existence of the boars' heads appearing on the Gordon arms. Robert de Brus, also, was undoubtedly connected with much of the boars' head depiction.

Following the death of King Robert de Brus, Sir Symon Locard, accompanied by Lord James Douglas and Sir William St Clair, carried the silver casket holding the heart of Robert de Brus on their crusade to Palestine. Unfortunately Sir Douglas was killed in Spain in 1329, their journey impossible to continue, the crusade was abandoned.

Having been entrusted with the key to the casket carrying de Brus's heart, Sir Symon returned to Scotland. In recognition of his successful return, the Lockheart arms were changed to three boars' heads and a heart within a fetter lock sable. Locard became Lockheart later Lockart, the motto now reading *Corda serrata pando*, I open locked hearts. Incidentally the original Locard name was taken from Loc Ard in Scotland.

Prior to taking the throne of Scotland, records show King Robert de Brus, still in retention of his lands in Cleveland. He ruled Scotland as an independent nation from 1306 to 1329, and died June 1329 aged fifty-five. It is well-known Robert was fiercely loyal to his followers, and despite his Scottish escapade, the Cleveland Franks, acting as quasi-judicial, retained the King's largesse and ongoing royal protection.

The Rollo arms, or (gold) a chevron between three boars' heads erased azure, are not too dissimilar to the more ancient Frank arms. A nephew of William the Conqueror, Eric Rollo was kinsman to both the de Brus and the Franks, receiving his first charter of land from Robert de Brus around 1141. This connection with the de Brus and extensive use of the boars' head symbol appears to have been widespread, Abercromby, Baillie, Galbraith, Nairn and Whitelaw being a few of an apparent disparate spread of names. And then there is Rollo; having come full circle we find the Frank arms in direct association with their forebears via de Bayeux and the Rollo dynasty, and as perceived from the beginning, the de Brus, Bayeux and Franks, all of the same antecedence belonging one of the most influential names in history.

It appears to have been an obsession and veritable science of the period to design the most prestigious possible arms, displaying to the world one's allegiance, prestige and influence, the Franks proclaiming their arms and fraternity with the de Brus across the wider territories of Yorkshire and Scotland.

Affiliated to the de Brus, and Scotland's monarchy, Frank nobility within Scotland was to last a mere 500 years and, in due time, the Brus themselves were destined to fade from glory. In 1556, the Franks enjoyed the largesse of Queen Mary who granted the eighth laird lands, a manor and mills. And in 1573, Robert Frank was conferred vicar of Greenlaw by King James. In the early 1600s, John, brother of the ninth laird, became Controller of Horse to King James VI. Another brother, a favourite of the King, was appointed Only Keeper of His Majesty's Outer Door Chamber. The tenth and last laird, Viscount Adam of Frankysland, Peebles, being a minor, became a personal ward of King James himself. This recognition appears to have ceased around 1633.

COURT OF THE LORD LYON, EDINBURGH

This might have been the end of the story for armorial recognition for the Franks but for the fact, in Scottish heraldry, there is no such thing as a family coat of arms.

Bruce Gorie, of the Court of the Lord Lyon in Edinburgh, has confirmed for me that arms are granted to, and identify, specific individuals, the arms descending to the heir in each generation bearing the same surname. Cadet, or junior branches of the family bearing the same surname, may seek to record arms in their own name with appropriate differences added to show their position within the family.

The Extraordinary Franks

This goes some way to explaining the wide range of slightly different arms within a family name.

I previously indicated that the Scottish line appeared to peter out around Viscount Adam of Frankysland, Peebles and being both a minor and an intimate of the monarch, was made a personal ward of King James VI in 1633. Adam, as the only son to Robert the ninth laird, inherited on his father's death in 1603. But Robert himself had younger brothers, James born 1569 and John who became Controller of Horse to the King. Born around 1571, John and a succession of Johns bring us to John Frank, bailee of Peebles, born around 1630.

The Franks and the de Brus being interrelated, bailee John Frank lived at Bughtrig, Coldstream, just north of Kelso, midway between the historic Frank holdings of Thornydykes and Berwick, Berwick lying adjacent the ancient Brus lands of the Annandale, and the Franks of Frankysland, Peebles. In good time, bailee John Frank had a son, John Frank junior's synopsis reading:

> Born around 1654, he became a writer, meaning a solicitor or lawyer.
>
> Was granted his own arms in 1673.
>
> Was registered to the Society of Writers to His Majesty's Signet 2nd January 1682.

I have a copy of John Frank's original matriculation of arms.

By a quirk of fate, with John's much later namesake, my uncle, John Frank (surgeon, of Innerleithen, Thomas Henry Frank's only son) having no issue, ascendancy passed generationally to me as the eldest of two sons to John's sister Dorothy Frank, and incidentally through Dorothy and her father, this work is dedicated.

The Society of Writers was a private society of Scottish solicitors dating back to 1594. Being a senior member of the College of Justice, the earlier John Frank was entitled to supervise the use of the King's Signet. He married Sara, his first wife, 23rd August 1674, Sara Elizabeth being a daughter of Andrew Grier, Burgess of Edinburgh. Sara Elizabeth died 14th April 1689. John then married Agnes, daughter of William Syme, Advocate, 26th July 1690. She died in 1704 or 1720, the records showing different dates.

John Frank, having been granted his own arms, was made Fiscal 1684–1686, Treasurer 1686–1691, additionally in 1692, Treasurer to the Faculty of Advocates in Scotland, and finally Advocate 1691–1699. He died in office, being buried 25th February 1700.

John's personal arms reflect a marked similarity to a number of English and specifically Yorkshire derivative arms pertaining to the Franks. Bruce Gorie, of the Court of Lyon, describes John Frank's Scottish shield of arms as:

'A green shield with a white saltire, having edges similar to a postage stamp; on the saltire, five green fleur-de-lys. The crest showing a leaping or springing two tailed lion in its proper colours.'

The matriculation, dated 1673, reads:

'Master John Frank writer (lawyer) in Edinburgh bears Vert on a saltyre ingrailled argent five flewrs de lis of the first With helmet and mantleing as is usual. Crest a lyon salient with a double or forked taill proper.'

Matriculated the 10th November 1673, John Frank's motto *Non noblis noti* reads:

'Not us, Nation.'

Appendix 2 denotes how the arms may have looked.

To properly understand arms, particularly when dealing with an historic name and a historic past, it is necessary to first examine the past. The de Brus, Bayeux, Frank and others of Norman origin, together with the knights of Norman England, by tradition retained their original title. In Norman French, the title of knight was known as chevalier. Chevalier in heraldry is another name for helm or helmet in a coat of arms. That is not to say that all coats of arms bearing a helmet relate to knights, far from it. Helmet arms ranging from monarch to mere gentleman depend upon a strict set of rules.

The Frank lineage shown through this work betrays its royal heritage. Proof, if it were needed, is determined by an examination of the past together with a look-see of John Frank's Scottish coat of arms:

Before entering Gaul, the Franks lived around the northern reaches of Germany approximately around the Rhine, and for a long time around the River Luts, now the Netherlands. The river, even today, is still bordered with an exceptional colony of the iris flower. The Franks, in looking for a symbolic image reflecting their early roots and to gain inspiration, took to nature, paddling upstream along the Luts. Coming upon an abundance of Iris in full flower their irresistible choice of emblem was duly presented to their lords. Not fully convinced, the Frankish Kings eventually set their minds on a stylised combination of the iris and lily flower.

And so, since before Clovis, the fleur-de-lys became associated with the French monarchy, significantly a simple image born of the Franks had also became a major feature of the Crown Jewels of England. John Frank's prestige and royal heritage ensured his personal arms be adorned with fleur-de-lys; since James I of Scotland, its flower design had became a prominent part of the Scottish royal arms and Royal

Standard. Thus the Franks close association with the monarchy was assured, and I will explain:

John Frank's arms having a historic antecedence, designed and approved for John in his own right, confirms John's Norman heritage with links to the French monarchy and its past. In the granting of his own arms, it appears John took most of the inherited dynastic detail from his father and the family coat of arms, ancient arms that co-existed alongside the Frankysland and Thornydykes arms. It would have been impossible for the arms to be approved without evidence of historic royal assent.

What is evident, John Frank's several times great-grandfather's offshoot of the Frank line would have been unable to use the ancient Viscount Adam arms as these were particular to Adam and that line. Influenced by a familial relationship with the monarchy, Adam's Uncle John, as Controller of Horse to the King, appears to have been awarded the significantly different but distinguished arms held by a connected branch of the Franks. Approval of the personal arms of John Frank in 1673, in retaining all of the historic elements of his forebears *Francisca regius nos*, confirms the family being of direct royal descent.

The historical significance of John's coat of arms is:

*The colour vert or green, conveying hope, loyalty and love.

*The saltyre, the St Andrew's cross, signifying resolution and resolve.

*The metalling of silver, signifying sincerity and peace.

*Not two or four but five fleur-de-lys, conveying historic royal associations with France.

*Regarding the expression 'first', see below.

The expression 'first'; knights were of two classes, the 'first' being all persons admitted into the comprehensive order of chivalry being knights by reason of their common rank:

*The knight's helm or helmet, a steel helmet garnished in gold with an open visor, no grill.

*Also, mantling as usual.

*The above, topped with a lion salient with a double or forked tail borne of its natural form and colour.

*The significance of the lion, meaning great warrior or chief, in this case, is its stance being salient.

Use of a lion salient was extremely rare, emblematic of extraordinary high valour, and indicative of a previous connection with the Scots Royal House and ancient royal heritage, in this case as kings of France. Even for those of royal decent, a lion rampant was used, its forelegs high, one higher than the other. A lion rampant was used for the King, Robert de Brus's descendants, Sire Richard de Breouse shown as:

> 'De ermyne a un lion rampaund de goules, od la couwe forchiec renouwe.'

Later, however, the de Brus lions did bear the forked tail typical of John Frank's arms. French arms bear three fleur-de-lys whereas the Frank arms of *Francisca regius nos* bear five. The use of five fleur-de-lys coupled with the very rare use of a lion salient bearing homage to the Frank lineage based on the ongoing protection of the Scots monarchy vouchsafing its royal heritage. As illustrated, the art of heraldry was a science and a particular art, where reading its language really did tell you who a person was.

Summary

Wondering about that bygone age, thoughts stray to times of huge conflict and uncertainty, where constants such as the Church provided some stability through continuance and the certainty of death, where a pray-full afterlife was seen as essential in the forgiveness of sins, and of a divine and heroic existence bound in the quest for immortality.

Often short-lived, kings might come and kings may go, but there was a still that intangible thing called heritage. Important for the times, physically this might be presented in the form of a banner or standard from which to draw inspiration, rally loyalty and instil pride. For the Anglo-Saxon Norman chiefs that heritage was lingua franca, more than just a common language it formed a common bond, something tangible and constant in a changing world.

Words changed, sounded different, evolved and were spelt differently, but the vocabulary and meaning born of the Franks of yesteryear were increasingly used as a language between those whose origin and native language may have been hugely different, yet subsisted within the spirit of lingua franca and that heritage.

And while separated by distance and culture, akin to recognition there's little doubt the Frank heritage remained steadfast, steering a steady course in times of trouble, a life raft upon which to cling and raise hope, the five fleur-de-lys a family banner confined to history.

In an attempt to validate my assumptions, I conducted a completely separate study into Rollo descendancy, my findings converging with aforesaid heraldic detail its correlation confirms one's determination of royal descent via Rollo to the current monarchy. The mass of detail, although at times on shaky ground, nonetheless provides valuable insights supportive of a unique family mien.

So much emanating from one man's love of a Breton hussy, Rollo's Christian non-de-plume several times great-grandson namesake Robert Frank, with a touch of Viking blood spiced with a soupcon of Frank, becomes a descendancy distinctly Frank, both by name and origin.

FRANCISCA REGIUS NOS; FRANKS ROYAL US.

In Yorkshire we find *a lion salient tail forked,* in Scotland *a lion salient double queued proper,* the salient lion so rare and used equally by the Franks both sides of the Scottish border. Also shared between both families and found in John Frank's pedigree is the motto *Non noblis nati* or *Non-omnibus nati,* ratifying a common entity.

Modern Scots heraldry commenced in 1672 when records and the discipline of arms were systematically codified. John Frank's arms were produced soon after in 1673. However, despite the laws governing Scots arms, 400 years later, versions of John Frank's personal coat of arms seem to have been filched and adopted as universal arms. It now appears commonplace for people to claim the Scots arms in general as their own, apparently happy to use them regardless of pedigree. Personally I consider such action to be thoughtless and an insult to history and heraldry. As a court of law, the Court of the Lord Lyon confirm the usurping of arms, e.g. the use of wrong arms or made-up arms, as a chargeable offence to be tried in court.

In the light of modern times, such consideration might seem trivial. Yet seen through the eyes of one directly involved, whose predecessors designated for me the name Frank, I don't see how it is right that a family arms can be used without permission, trivialised through the dismissal of history and the importance of a noble mien delineated by their inheritors in the maintenance of society standards, values and upkeep.

With this work, I hope to have shown veracity of purpose, however, I am somewhat bemused by the accident of my late uncle, Professor John Frank of Peebles, having the same name as his 400 year predecessor found in the same location. Each man is shown to have had a professional connection with Edinburgh, one medical, the other as an advocate, both having a commonality with Peebles. As I say, pure accident.

I am appreciative of the assistance of the Court of the Lord Lyon of Scotland and their help in the provision of vital information. As Bruce Gorie states, in Scotland the granting of arms are specific to individuals, only descending to the heir in each generation bearing the same surname as does my mother Dorothy Frank via her late father Thomas Henry Frank and his predecessors.

At which point I once again refer to the Scottish arms of John Frank, 1673: John's arms:

> 'Vert on a saltyre ingrailled argent five flewrs-de-lis of the first with helmet a mantleing as usual crest a lyon salient with a double or forked tail proper.'

Observed as of royal descent, the arms bear a likeness to the arms of Henry Franke of Ness, Yorkshire, whereupon Norray, King of Arms in 1530 confirmed quote:

> 'To Henry Franke, gentillman, additions for an existing arms.'

The arms of Henry Franke matching the later arms pertaining John Frank of Scotland in 1673, the Henry Franke additions being:

> 'Vert a saltue engrailed or in posteritas.'

The colour green, the Scottish saltire, its gold engrailing signifying Henry of Yorkshire's ownership of land, endorses the previously held belief of the Scottish borderers Franks having a peerless familial connection with the Yorkshire Franks and their arms in posterity, one and the same. The name Henry was perpetuated through Ness to Hutton become Hutton-le-Hole, with connections with nearby Glaisdale and my grandfather Thomas Henry Frank.

The interconnection between Scotland, Thirkleby, Ness, and Danby is further reaffirmed through the arms of Hugh Francklyn of Nessistge consisting of not one, but three crosses of Saint Andrew bearing the same saltire belonging Henry Franke. Where the arms differ is the existence of dolphin argent the arms signifying high rank shown by a tors of Azure and gold, likewise mantling lined in gold.

Also in 1530, Midway between the Scottish Borders and Yorkshire, William Franke's arms were shown to possess two Saint Andrew crosses and a dolphin huariant. The families' interrelation beyond doubt, it's worth pointing out the significance of the dolphin, its presence signifying the five qualities of swiftness, diligence, salvation, charity and love.

A FITTING EPITAPH.

The affirmation of family descent via Ness to Hutton, Danby, and adjacent Glaisdale together with their interrelated ties with Scotland reaffirms the bona fide nature of

The Extraordinary Franks

the above arms belonging the Franks of Danby cum Glaisdale as positively identifying the late Thomas Henry Frank as bona fide successor. Certainly his life was deserving of the accolade of diligence, salvation, charity and love, attributes those who knew him would happily endorse.

Tom Frank's eldest daughter Dorothy's eyes now closed upon the world, her resting place is simple, viewed through the mists and cloud of distant horizons and undulating hills, now at peace within her beloved Cleveland landscape. Mum's chosen place of rest is marked by an outcrop of rock, her ashes reverently scattered to the winds, the last of her line, a Frank in final repose.

As regards familial armorial bearings, the element of swiftness as applied to Tom Frank and dolphins is not something I especially espouse. Coming from farming stock, his tread was more steadfast and of steady purpose and the idea of dolphins would have been an enigma, cows and sheep more his stock in trade, the rhythm in the laying of house-bricks a litany, in its repetition a solace akin to prayer.

But for Dorothy, unknowing daughter of kings, her latter days having an unrestricted view of Thirsk racecourse; all too soon we can visualize that steady heartbeats gallop towards eternity. If we really listen we might perceive the sound of pounding hooves and the strained sinews of thoroughbred horses, the thunderous pace ringing in their ears; or as if in a dream, the hazy vision of the last hurrah of a cavalry charge, a host of armoured knights, couched lances aimed directly upon the enemy, concentrating on a single point of resistance, the weight and velocity of warhorse and rider, stirrups long, saddle high, galloping downhill, gaining momentum come thick upon their foe, where within a flicker of an eye, vainglorious, sees nothing but the whisper of mortality rent upon the dead and dying. But now the mists have cleared, yesterdays dream, like all the others, becomes just another dream, the banners of triumph and chivalry now all gone, the idea of Robertus Francaise, knight in armour, splendid upon his charger, fanciful or true, just for a crazy moment, deemed possible.

It's impossible to imagine this most wonderful countryside of England as the repeated scene of medieval battle, one after the other across the whole swathe of North Yorkshire. A landscape touching endless landscapes, ever changing, dipping and rising endlessly inland or towards the coast with the ice-sharp sea-salt smell of a North Sea breeze, a coastline rich with coves and smugglers caves. Succession after succession of scattered heaps of war dead long laid to rest in churchyards now quiet and at peace.

Walking among a soldiery of leaning and fallen gravestones, their inscriptions become an illegible litany born of worn and ancient sandstone; its continued corrosion feared by those who lay there, the scattering of broken swords and axes and rusty armour picked over and refashioned as tools, just as much the land they fought over and help reshape, become a world they would strain to understand, all gone, so quick, within the blink of an eye.

NON NOBIS NATI.

Not us, nation, a motto of noble sentiment, and it is fitting this work should end with a soft landing. I started by bringing to attention the Franks as the factual creators of modern-day law, these governed agnatic male successions and statute law. Derived from the Salian Franks, exempli gratia evolved into common law, where the legal expression Lex Salica was born.

As a lawyer, the John Frank of 1654, having been granted his coat of arms in 1673, would be amazed to learn of his forebears' dawn-of-time inventiveness in the creation of laws covering such crime as inheritance and theft, insult and murder, damages and so on; and down through the ages finding the cudgel of ordinance suddenly passed his way. And it is right this book should end as it began in acknowledging the Franks as the leading light in their concern for justice, fairness and truth, since spread across the globe.

Yes they had their moments; at times ruthless, brutal, determined, heartless even, but there was an underlying purpose that drove them relentlessly forward. Yet unaware, really, of what it was that made them who they were, the Franks and others of their ilk who evolved to become special in a difficult and fraught race towards modernity and enlightenment. Looking at the world today I cannot help but read the lessons of history and of man's progress towards high endeavour, the worlds population evolving at different speeds, some like ISIS and the Taliban, light years away from achieving the state of mind of human equality, science and the arts, viewed centuries away from where the west is today, it having evolved largely blind to hate and the differences of race, colour and creed, yet still with a long way to go.

The journey in process sees a long and difficult road, and we must be patient but ever vigilant against those who oppose us and, for me, we should be ever-prepared to smite those who dare an attack on democracy, high endeavour and enlightenment. To that end I virally oppose the idea of Britain scrapping Trident until an alternative more potent deterrent can be found. That small part of the Frank in me would never stand defenceless.

Now in my dotage and as the ink dries upon these words, take note and best beware, there are those whose sole and only understanding remains one of hate, espousing death for the infidel. And for the Russian Bear whose silly game is the kind of cyber attack for which the only answer is to remain resolute, strong and ready to take out and destroy the very tools they employ, for this is a game in the long run they cannot win and will backfire goodtime upon the perpetrators.

The Extraordinary Franks

I can't end without mentioning statehood and the part played by the Franks in the proclamation of nation and insight in the creation of France. Nor can one ignore a family name perpetuated for all time in the everyday words we speak: a family whose very existence helped shape the creation of modern Britain. I have written extensively about the Franks, their story, the parts they played and their influences an indelible legacy.

Granddad Tom Frank, builder extraordinaire, despite his passing decades ago, it's amazing to my eyes to find a son of the soil, born of generations of farming, apprenticed as a lowly joiner, being able to accomplish what he did. I saw a man driven by an unfailing faith, bound by an ethic resolutely tied to the principles of determination, hard work and unflinching honesty; virtues that together with fair play, compassion and humanity, remain the true legacy of the Franks, a legacy worthy of the epitaph 'NOT US, NATION'.

ADDENDUM.

In memory of Dorothy Frank 10th December 1914 – 28th June 2015, aged 100.

Now drawn to a close, it figures succeeding generations may have little or no interest in this work, indeed why should they; also theirs will be a world beyond today's imagination, a superfast digital cosmos where one's poorly written revelations might be seen as conjured figments having no possible significance. But hi there, as I sit here, I am as real as you, comfortably chatting away and maybe these words will never see the light of day, but I hope so, their compilation thereby justified. Also, having struggled with a lifetime's battle with dyslexia, please accept my heartfelt apologies for any literary errors and what might come across as a badly written script.

As Dorothy's son, as an epilogue I crave forgiveness in penning my own last hurrah as if blowing dust from an old battered book, musing over past times. But for me its importance is in its recording. One has to consider me a child of Africa, white yes, but beloved of my Zulu nana and the cluck and fluster of chickens around bare feet, torn from all I knew, thrust into the chaos of war, a stupor of frightened faces, of torpedoes and crashing bombs overlaid by a complexity of shattered bodies and in England the sudden arrived newness of cold, white snow.

And then there was the practised regularity of the gas mask drill; its lingering rubbery smell in unison with the piles of heaped rubble and the bewilderment of first day school among people one had no affinity, a confusion compounded amid the growing realisation the noise of war had ceased.

Then the sudden move to Yorkshire; treated as if one had been born and raised to the relative calming regularity of school, a room where I could draw and paint and later produce architectural drawings for Granddad while visiting the bulldozed upheaval of large tracts of land for house building; the bulldozers an antithesis to the new-found delight of Yorkshire's rolling landscape, of patchwork fields, mucking out and farming.

Initially a class-year ahead for my age, I was no genius: far from it. There was a point at school I decided on a scheme to remain mid-range, not too high as to attract attention, and not so low as to be considered thick, a kind of game thought out and executed aged eleven in cohort with two other boys, a pact carried out with precision with the exception of Barker, who was so clever and despite his best efforts naturally gravitated to the top. A turning point for me came when fed up with him, in the fourth year of high school I worked so hard as to best him by coming top in two subjects.

And it was this that saved me, that and my tutors some months later pestering me to commence a foundation course a year or two earlier than normal. Having left school prematurely they'd located me farming many miles away, and why the three of them, Brown, Cassidy and the deputy head, Marwood, should have gone out of their way to dissuade me from farming remains something of a mystery. I was already acutely aware of having to work twice as hard as my peers and even now find myself having to work everything over and again to the point of exhaustion.

In those early days, dazed as to my mind's confusion, I put it down to a severe form of eclecticism, being able to easily operate across a diverse range of adult disciplines excelling in some things and being exceedingly dull in others. Only with my eldest son's diagnosis did I become cognisant of that forbidden word 'dyslexia'. Our children ensconced at school, the headmaster striding down the corridor, his doctorate gown flapping imperiously about his person, announcing 'I wouldn't know dyslexia if I fell over it', writing Scott off. Initially fighting alone for a diagnosis, results found at Bangor University paved the way for recognition of the condition and specialist help; today a success story, Scott a man of great integrity held in such high regard. And typical also of Stuart and Jill, they shine a beacon others might follow. As for me, many thanks to the inventor of Spellcheck.

But this is not the root of the story. What I wanted to impart is something of the vast timeline that preceded that era's majority of population, the breach between an eternity of servitude and indenture for the many come the sudden impact of war. People had been drawn away from farming for generations to be replaced by mechanisation and a sky mired by soot and clouds of yellow chemicals lying thick among the paving as one struggled and coughed their way to and fro. My own experience has been a midway point between the past and full mechanisation and computers, and where muscle, sinew and sheer brute force continued its battle against nature's worst.

Lack of manpower meant long days and aching bones. And having left school aged fifteen, there was no recourse other than to drive forward, meeting head-on any obstacle assuaging the innate ability of man and might. At the time I had no idea where this disparate and lonely course emerged. But disparaging of religion or the concept of being slave to anyone or anything, while acknowledging my limitations my mindset assumed there were no barriers other than those imagined, and one's instinct was these could be circumvented or ignored anyway.

It was winter, so icy-cold the metal handle of the bucket I was holding had welded within my grip. Taking courage and with the peeling of much skin, I tore the handle from bleeding fingers, ye gods it was cold. Slip-sliding around that icy day, in the middle of what seemed a field of permafrost snagging turnips ready for cattle feed, I had no real concept of the Franks heritage of 1000 years, nor would I have cared.

Yet for the post-war population the period was a fulcrum between what had gone before and the attraction of television, nice clothes and a car. A mini-skirted, knickers-revealing culture balanced precariously against the looming threat of annihilation. The nuclear age had changed everything, the revolution of mechanisation meant the production of thousands upon thousands of tractors, free love and music, the world being thrust relentlessly towards an indulgent mania for pop, fashion, and the thrill of 007 Bond movies, a far cry from the stinging cold of ice permeating through leather soles.

Yet for me something of the essence of time loomed distant yet so familiar, cut off from the teenage world of frustration and the embarrassment of how to buy condoms, and thoughts of touching a naked breast. Consider a fifteen-year-old, his each and everyday 6 a.m. stagger into dung-dried-solid clothes. The lack of electricity bringing the blindfold familiarity of animal husbandry against a cycle of assisted birth, castration and occasional burial.

Consider where vaginal insertion was one's hand struggling against a breach, and sex a young bull's first attempt at insemination missing its target, and laughter as its semen shot through the air, or perhaps a cow shedding its calf bed, a night spent reinserting its bulky uterine and horny tissue through the unyielding neck of a resistant vulva. Mastitis, pigging, mucking out, all familiar come natural and routine, long hours merging into days becoming months, the months becoming two harsh winters, the land ice-solid, the trees decked with snow, the landscape a hazy blizzard of wind borne haw.

The Cleveland Hills, my intended inheritance, the estate consisting of White Post Farm and the lands south of Great Broughton rising both sides of Hasty Bank, climbing higher still, where the land rapidly ascends to the west of Clay Bank and a final impossible climb through gorse and bracken towards the Wainstones. At that time, as a mere kid, thoughts of personal ownership never once intruded upon the magnificence and might of nature, whether animal or the sweet smell of newly turned soil. Seen from the perspective of sixty plus years there's still nothing to compare, the solace and quietude of standing with nothing but nature all around, a tanned blond-haired youth of Africa with an obligation to shape and form the continuance of this little piece of Yorkshire.

Viewed now through hazy memory, the stones stand resolute against the skyline, majestic outcrops of rock jutting invitingly high upon the Cleveland hills, where riding perilously astride a young mare I often looked upon the vista of patchwork fields cognisant of a pre-determined life of expectation, that had been set out for me. Every time, the sight just took my breath away, far below distant fields of unbelievable beauty, a visual myriad of perfection spread before my very eyes, the impression a permanent imprint upon the soul of one's consciousness, the imprint of memory belonging to a long gone era of scything, of binding and stooking sheaves of wheat, and of riding shotgun during harvest in the hope of potting a passing rabbit.

Aged fifteen, I was well into working the land. The larger estate had funded a new tractor and farming implements, those interminably long days extended by ploughing by the light of a full moon, and the vague prospect of agricultural college loomed. But another existence beckoned, the trickle of Frank blood in my veins had become too diluted. My spade heavy from burying another lost animal, thoughts of the schoolmaster intruded, the vision of a scholastic idea, a different world began to open before me.

Sometimes painful, aloneness had become normal to me, something of a companion that later was to stand me in good stead. Now solitary in the unlit cobbled fold-yard, the black void of night wrapped as a blanket, the clatter of horses' hooves resounding against the still dusk of another day, the evening now merging into midnight, the lonely tearful decision to tread a different path entered my consciousness; nobody would inherit, the moment of decision, these were different times, a different world was in the offing.

I seemed to be only part conscious of the sadness placed upon my grandfather, my mother the last of that tenuous branch, that thread and the many hundred years of history, there was no time for remorse, and without anyone to talk it over, I would go my own way and tread a different path.

Familiarity caused me to follow the routine of closing things down for the night, a quiet walk around the farm buildings, the movement of beasts in their stalls, the sudden strange uncertain sounds and squeaks and squeals of animals hunting across the silence of darkened fields and even darker woodland.

It might sound strange, weird by today's thinking, but set in the context of separation from the real world, there was nary a word, no thought of conversation or discussion, the work-ethic dominated my beloved grandfather's existence beyond any notion of dialogue, both of us silent people, neither of us given to nonsensical chit-chat.

In any event, as my mentor, I had only seen him once for less than two minutes in over twelve months. Miles distant, his one good eye leaving me to it, his mind fully focused on the endless pursuit of building yet more houses, the repetitive litany of bricklaying akin to the rotation of a rosary bead become a silent prayer for his time on earth and a job well done. Devoid of talk, no ifs, no buts, in one sense I was free to tread my own path, but not without a prevailing sense of sadness and finality. Something intangible had been lost forever, the spell had been broken and the responsibility was on me, the Franks, the endurable legacy had finally ended.

Three score years and a different life has passed, that half-remembered hazy memory having mellowed into something warm and enduring, memories of a grandfather I loved, grazing cattle, the soft grass under my feet, a newly ploughed field, harvest time, my mare, God bless her, and a gathering storm, surely more than enough for any man.

This concludes my work on the Franks and a period I was concerned to record for my loved ones and future generations while memory and my pen are still capable of capturing the essence of the times. I feel the period we are now living sits astride a vast timeline, awash with an immense history of blood-let, physical endeavour and conflict, but also a time of great learning and wisdom, a time of massive industry created from the furnaces of coal and iron, a time of old empire long faded, but instilled in the memory of Dorothy, now an evolution of bright horizons, technology and ideas.

The advent of India and China rising dominant brings mighty challenges. I have no fears for you with your bright minds, intellect, humour and greatness to grasp the moment. The period I have written about is ancient history, nonetheless, it's about real people, their story, some of it bloody, the Frank half of one's existence, the story about a little bit more than just ordinary people, the extraordinary Franks.

The work now confined to print, there will be folk who have further insights or family data, information they might add. To that end one might conclude the narrative to be a work in progress. Please believe when I say I know the work's limitations, its writing having scope for much more whether in terms of storytelling or information, but I remind, in its making it is nought but a tale. Feel free to contribute or put right errors or omissions and who knows, a revised version may some day arise.

In the meanwhile, I hope such information as the work possesses might be of interest to the many, and in particular our cousins in America where hopefully this work might fill a gap in their understanding as to their British origins and the evolvement of a disparate body such as the Franks and the Norman influence that helped shape Britain and the world.

Take a name, my mother's maiden name, my middle name, look, research and wrap a story around it.

The End.

Appendix 1

Ancient Cleveland-Scots Frank Arms
"I neither fear nor despise"

Appendix 2

John Franks personal Arms of 1673
"Not us, Nation"

Appendix 3

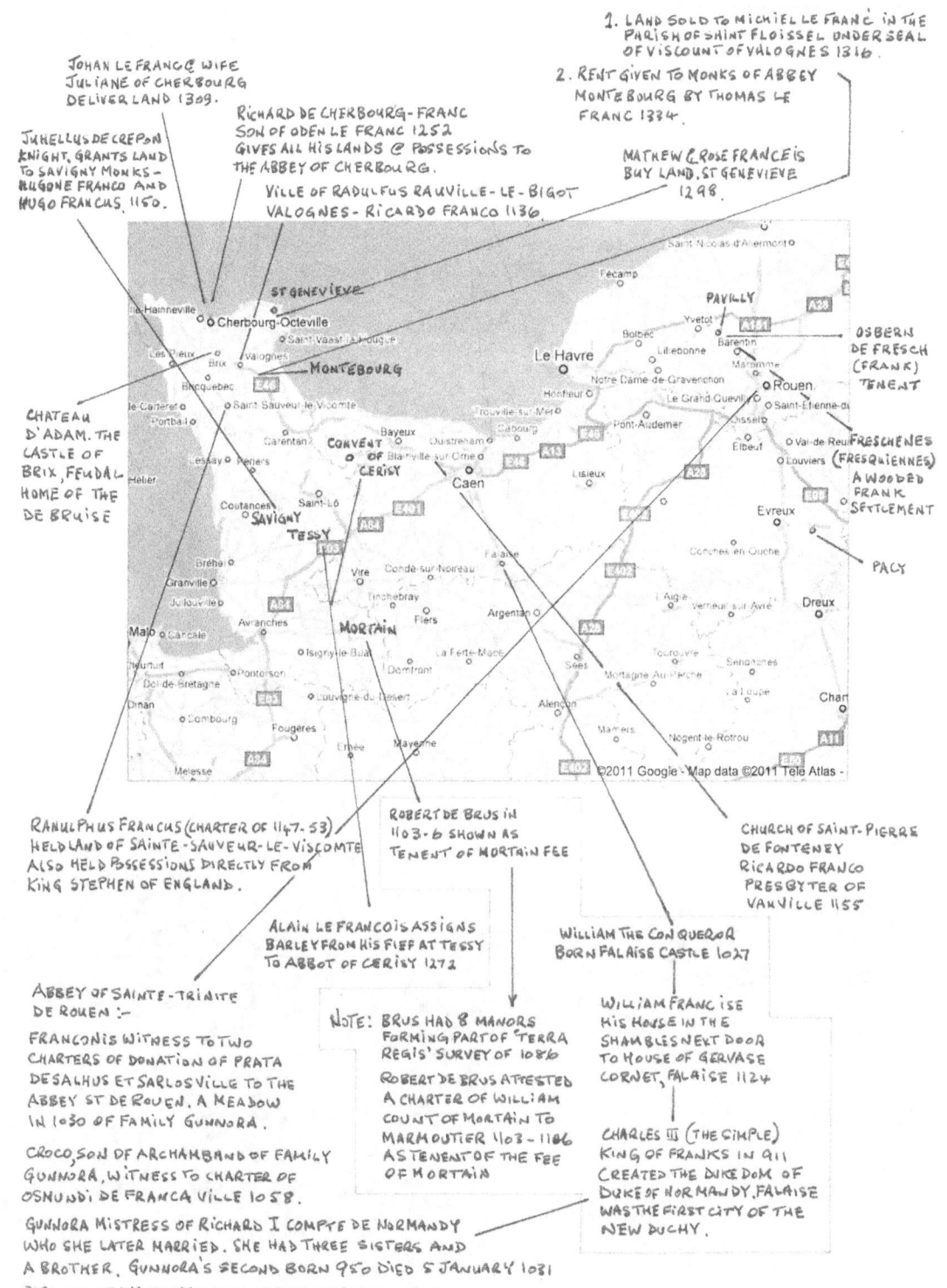

1. LAND SOLD TO MICHIEL LE FRANC IN THE PARISH OF SAINT FLOISSEL UNDER SEAL OF VISCOUNT OF VALOGNES 1316.
2. RENT GIVEN TO MONKS OF ABBEY MONTEBOURG BY THOMAS LE FRANC 1334.

MATHEW & ROSE FRANCE IS BUY LAND, ST GENEVIEVE 1298.

JOHAN LE FRANCQE WIFE JULIANE OF CHERBOURG DELIVER LAND 1309.

RICHARD DE CHERBOURG - FRANC SON OF ODEN LE FRANC 1252 GIVES ALL HIS LANDS & POSSESSIONS TO THE ABBEY OF CHERBOURG.

JUHELLUS DE CREPON KNIGHT, GRANTS LAND TO SAVIGNY MONKS - HUGONE FRANCO AND HUGO FRANCUS 1150.

VILLE OF RADULFUS RAUVILLE - LE - BIGOT VALOGNES - RICARDO FRANCO 1136.

OSBERN DE FRESCH (FRANK) TENENT

FRESCHENES (FRESQUIENNES) A WOODED FRANK SETTLEMENT

CHATEAU D'ADAM. THE CASTLE OF BRIX, FEUDAL HOME OF THE DE BRUISE

PACY

RANULPHUS FRANCUS (CHARTER OF 1147-53) HELD LAND OF SAINTE - SAUVEUR - LE - VISCOMTE ALSO HELD POSSESSIONS DIRECTLY FROM KING STEPHEN OF ENGLAND.

ROBERT DE BRUS IN 1103-6 SHOWN AS TENENT OF MORTAIN FEE

CHURCH OF SAINT - PIERRE DE FONTENEY RICARDO FRANCO PRESBYTER OF VANVILLE 1155

ALAIN LE FRANCOIS ASSIGNS BARLEY FROM HIS FIEF AT TESSY TO ABBOT OF CERISY 1272

WILLIAM THE CONQUEROR BORN FALAISE CASTLE 1027

ABBEY OF SAINTE - TRINITE DE ROUEN :-

FRANCONIS WITNESS TO TWO CHARTERS OF DONATION OF PRATA DE SALHUS ET SARLOSVILLE TO THE ABBEY ST DE ROUEN. A MEADOW IN 1030 OF FAMILY GUNNORA.

CROCO, SON OF ARCHAMBAND OF FAMILY GUNNORA, WITNESS TO CHARTER OF OSMUNDI DE FRANCAVILLE 1058.

GUNNORA MISTRESS OF RICHARD I COMPTE DE NORMANDY WHO SHE LATER MARRIED. SHE HAD THREE SISTERS AND A BROTHER. GUNNORA'S SECOND BORN 950 DIED 5 JANUARY 1031 PARENTS OF DYNESTY UNKNOWN BUT OF VIKING ORIGIN.

NOTE: BRUS HAD 8 MANORS FORMING PART OF 'TERRA REGIS' SURVEY OF 1086

ROBERT DE BRUS ATTESTED A CHARTER OF WILLIAM COUNT OF MORTAIN TO MARMOUTIER 1103-1106 AS TENENT OF THE FEE OF MORTAIN

WILLIAM FRANC IS HIS HOUSE IN THE SHAMBLES NEXT DOOR TO HOUSE OF GERVASE CORNET, FALAISE 1124

CHARLES III (THE SIMPLE) KING OF FRANKS IN 911 CREATED THE DUKEDOM OF DUKE OF NORMANDY. FALAISE WAS THE FIRST CITY OF THE NEW DUCHY.

Appendix 4

FRANK SETTLEMENTS

The areas indicated are only some of the Frank settlement. The Frank locations south of Pickering, immediately north of the Humber, running north and inland towards York and north again from York towards Myton and Norton, feature in the Domesday Book, some twenty years following the 1066 invasion.

I have had to translate into modern day spelling in order to make sense of the various localities, often there were several versions of a particular name.

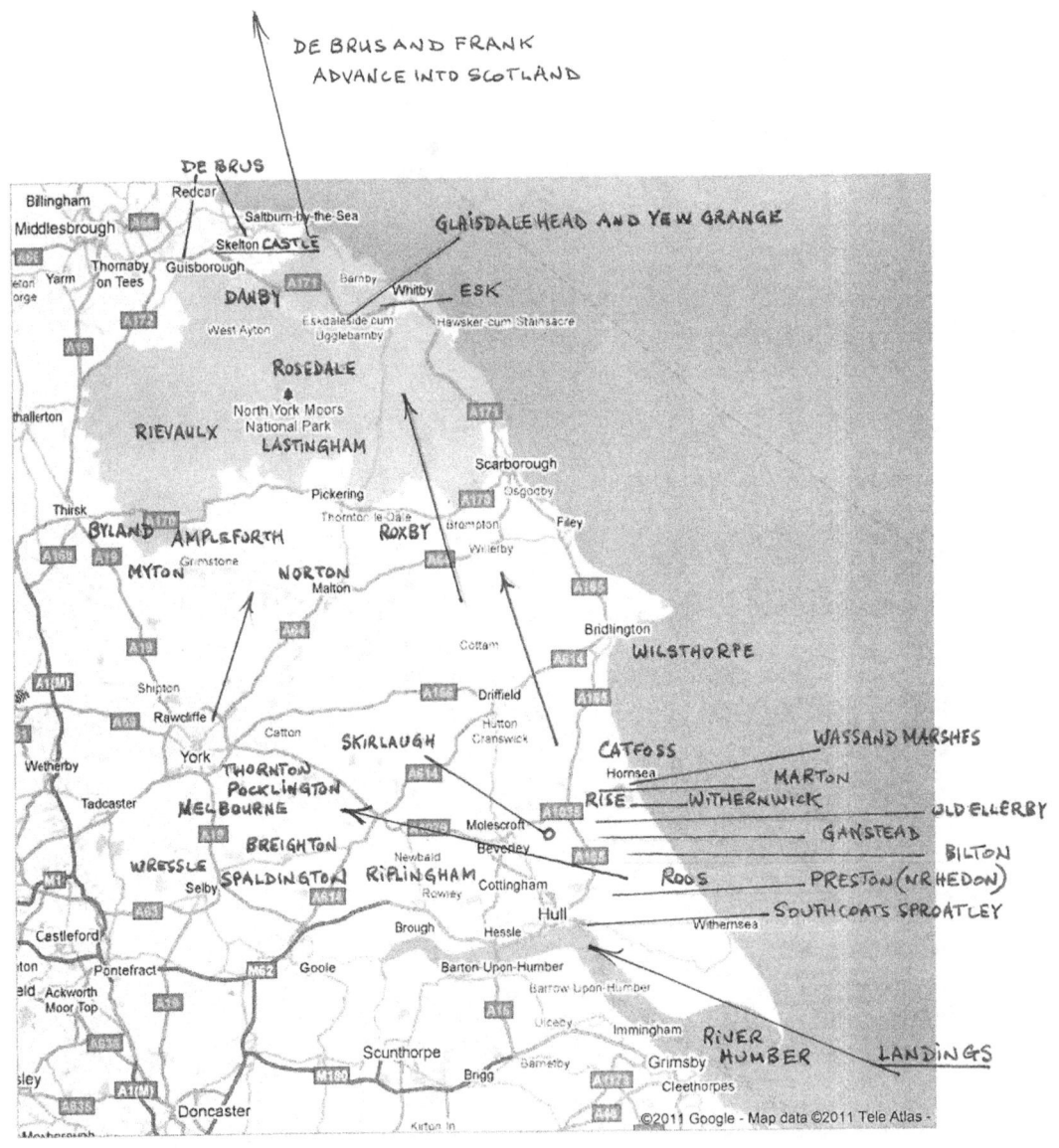

Appendix 5

I have marked just some of the estates held by the various Frank Lairds and Viscounts including that given by Queen Mary, e.g. the Viscountcy of Peebles, Frankislandis Nuncupates.

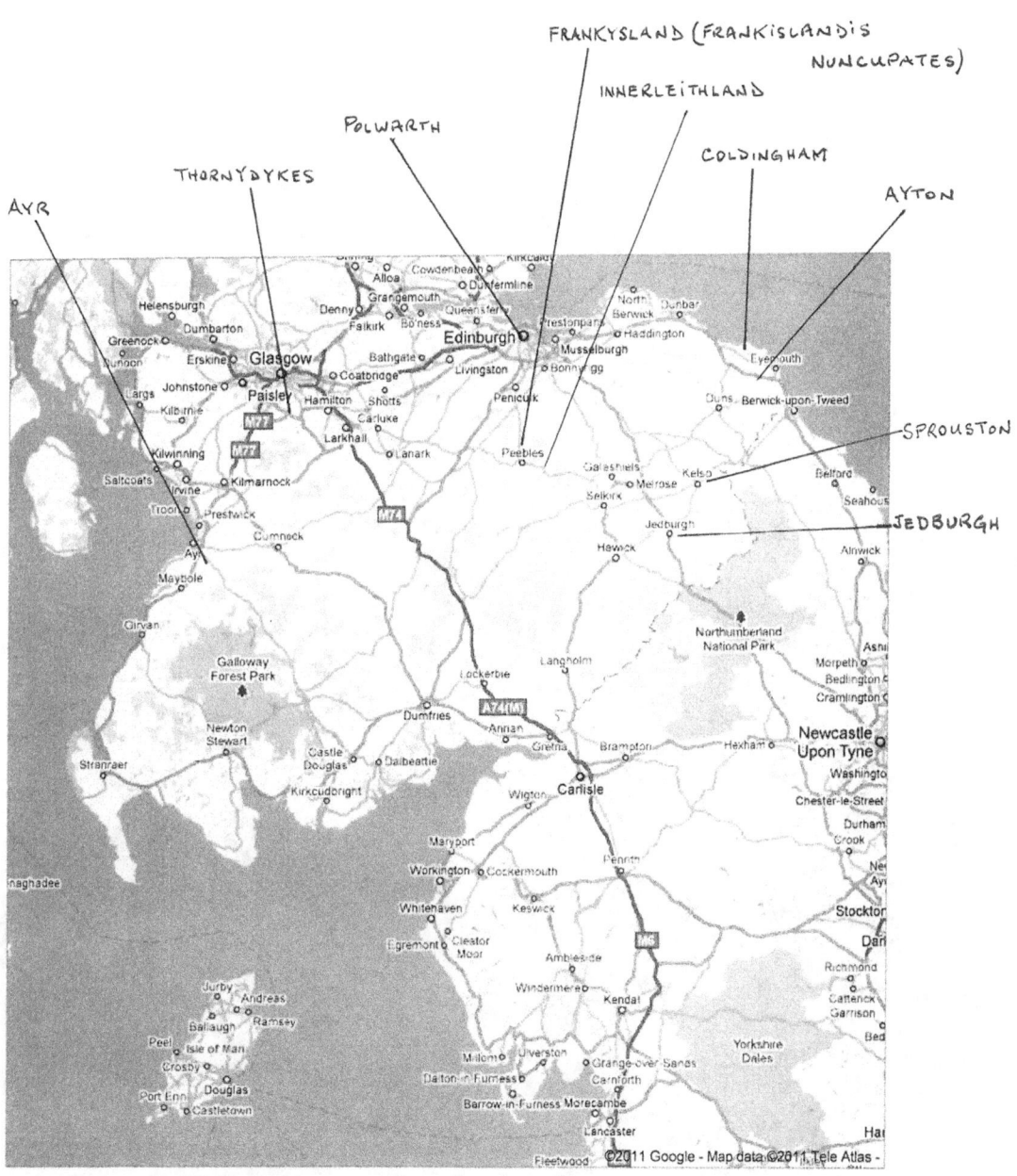

409

Appendix 6